Faces of Nationalism

BOYD C. SHAFER is a historian, a leading authority on nationalism, and professor of history at The University of Arizona. From 1953 to 1963 he was editor of *The American Historical Review* and executive secretary of the American Historical Association. He is now acting president of the International Committee of Historical Sciences. In 1970 he was awarded the Troyer Steele Anderson Prize by the American Historical Association for his outstanding contributions to the development of historical studies in the United States. He is the author of numerous articles and of five books.

Other books by Boyd Shafer

Life, Liberty, and the Pursuit of Bread
    (with Carol Shafer)

Nationalism: Myth and Reality

United States History for High Schools
    (with others)

United States History for High Schools, 1865 to the Present

Historical Study in the West
    (with others)

Faces of Nationalism

New Realities and Old Myths

 BOYD C. SHAFER

A HARVEST BOOK

HARCOURT BRACE JOVANOVICH

NEW YORK AND LONDON

JC
311
S477
1974

Printed in the United States of America

Library of Congress Cataloging in Publication Data

Shafer, Boyd C

    Faces of nationalism; new realities and old myths.

    (A Harvest book HB 296)

    Bibliography: p.

    1. Nationalism—History. I. Title.

[JC311.S477 1974]   320.5'4'09   74-6068

ISBN 0-15-629800-7

First Harvest edition 1974

A B C D E F G H I J

To the children of my children—Kara, Ariel, and those to come—
in the hope that their world will be more peaceful than mine

In any case this business of hatred between nations is a curious thing. You will always find it most powerful and barbarous on the lowest levels of civilization. But there exists a level at which it wholly disappears, and where one stands, so to speak, above the nations, and feels the weal or woe of a neighboring people as though it were one's own.—GOETHE

. . . in modern times, nationalism is the most copious and durable source of mass enthusiasm and . . . nationalist fervor must be tapped if the drastic changes projected and initiated by revolutionary enthusiasm are to be consummated.—ERIC HOFFER

Man—of all ages and cultures—is confronted with the solution of one and the same question: the question of how to overcome separateness, how to achieve union, how to transcend one's own individual life and find at-onement.—ERICH FROMM

Contents

Contents

Preface

This book is a historical study of the faces, the realities and myths of modern nationalism. No one can write a full history of nationalism; the subject is too vast, too complex. As a historian I have tried to study how and why the sentiment has developed. Some attention is given to internationalism, but the book is about nationalism.

I make no secret of my belief that nationalism, especially when carried to extremes, leads to war and destruction. But this is all the more reason for careful study. Realizing my own bias, I have tried to confront my questions and hypotheses with evidence and change them as evidence required.

The approach is basically historical. Beyond this the book is organized around the concepts of "penetration," "participation," and "identification," concepts not unknown to social scientists. A basically historical concept, "conjuncture," conceived and employed by such French historians as Marc Bloch, has also been useful as an organizing principle.

I have attempted to sketch the history of nationalism from about the thirteenth century to the present. It could be worth mention that in study of the "new" nationalisms I gained insights into the "older," just as the previous study of the "older" brought understandings of the "newer."

I am, I repeat, a historian, but I have examined, as the citations reveal, studies in many disciplines and learned much from them. Historical study includes, or should include, all that has been thought and done. I realize that, as Benjamin I. Schwartz wrote somewhere, all general statements about vast expanses of time and millions of men are crude, and I am aware (as I often note) of the existence of views contrary to mine.

I began systematic study of nationalism in 1930–31, planned for years to publish a two-volume work. In 1953 the American Historical Association and the *Review* asked me to become executive secretary and managing editor. I then thought that I would devote myself to the study of history by others and would never write anything more of any length. Hence, I decided to publish the parts of my work that were more or less finished in *Nationalism: Myth and Reality*. This covered (as its preface stated) only western Europe and the United States. In the early 1960's I decided to return to research and teaching, and to do the second volume. But, with the years and the reading that had intervened, I could not do what I had originally contemplated; I had to do another book. This book, then, is no longer volume II, but a new and bigger work than that of 1955 in which I cover some of the same ground (with major revision, amplification, and reinterpretation in the light of new research by others and myself) and go on to consider the nationalisms of eastern Europe and Asia and Africa.

The present book bears the subtitle *New Realities and Old Myths*, because continued study has convinced me that the myths are old, while the realities, because of technology and knowledge, are becoming different. But I should hasten to add that nationalism, whatever its faces, persists because of what it has offered (and now offers) men in security, status, and hope.

As is explained in the text and bibliography, I have studied in and talked with students and scholars in many nations, have, I hope, deepened my understandings, and certainly have arrived at interpretations different from those I held earlier.

Who is this volume for? Well, for students of the most important unifying and dividing sentiment of our time. Specialists will learn little or nothing about their specialties, but, again, it is my hope that they and others might gain an insight or two into the general nature of nationalism. I must note that I rely on specialists, especially in fields and areas about which I have little or no firsthand knowledge—mainland China, for example. But this study is in part a comparative study and must, in any case, be based in part on the writings of specialists.

Every author owes much to his predecessors, his colleagues, his fellow workers. I have indicated some of my debts elsewhere. I also owe much to students who have worked with and on occasion assisted me. These include Suzanne Dockal, Susan (Moxley) Graham, Mark Hansen, James Hudson, Marie (Thourson) Jones, Stanley Keillor, Peter Mickelson, Barbara Phillips, Walter Rundell, Andrew Sarvis, James (Okete) Shiroya, John Stevens, Carol (Mork) Sumerkan, Susan (Gardner) Van Doren, Robert Whalen, and Sam Yamashita.

I owe much to Wiladene Stickel, my secretary and assistant, who is always helpfully and *rightly* correcting me, and to Carol L. Shafer, my wife, companion, and constant critic for forty years, who is, with reason and charity, always saying "yes, but" and "can't you be clearer?"

I do not know, nor does anyone, in spite of learned or breathless predictions, what the world of the future, divided or united, will be. I can only hope that it will provide the same opportunities for learning from others that I have had. But, as is customary and right, I must add that, while I have drawn from the work of many scholars and students, I alone am responsible for what I have drawn.

Faces of Nationalism

I

Problems of Meaning

Ever since scholars began serious study of nationalism they have sought to define it. In history—that is, in human experience—nothing is so certain as flow, change, and variation. Just as the realities of nationalism have reflected human experience, so have the definitions. It is simply not true that when one has studied the nationalism of one time and place one has studied the nationalisms of all times and places.

This chapter briefly describes some of the problems that arise in attempts to define nationalism, the varied meanings that have been given the word (and kindred words), and the realities and myths—the attributes—that are commonly present. Since early modern times there have been common elements in the developing nationalisms and, from the mid-nineteenth century and particularly from about the 1920's when the first scholarly studies were beginning, there have arisen some common understandings about the general nature of the sentiment.[1] Of course, the short, fifty- or hundred-word definitions, which many students (including this writer) have attempted to fashion, are partial and incomplete, and do not and cannot take into account all manifestations of nationalism,[2] but a quick sampling of some of those devised by recent authorities will be helpful.

For Carlton Hayes, the "father" of scholarly American study of nationalism, nationalism was (in 1926 and 1931) "a modern emotional fusion of two very old phenomena—nationality and patriotism," [3] as well as "the paramount devotion of human beings to fairly large [sic] nationalities and the conscious founding of a political 'nation' on linguistic and cultural nationality." [4] To a group of English students of the Royal Institute of International Affairs (in 1939) the word described "a consciousness, on the part of individuals or groups, of membership in a nation, or of a desire to forward the strength, liberty, or prosperity of a nation." [5] For

1. Notes are on pages 379–489.

Hans Kohn, one of the learned as well as most prolific authorities, nationalism was (in 1944) "a state of mind," "an act of consciousness" of a "large majority of a people," which recognized "the nation-state as the ideal form of political organization and the nationality as the source of all creative cultural energy and of economic well-being." For Kohn the nationalist "state of mind," or nationalism, also included the belief that a man should give his "supreme loyalty" to his nationality.[6] A definition of Louis Snyder, another expert, was not strikingly different, though more explicit. He (in 1954) thought it "a condition of mind, feeling, or sentiment of a group of people living in a well-defined geographical area, speaking a common language, possessing a literature in which the aspirations of the nation have been expressed, attached to common traditions and common customs, venerating its own heroes, and, in some cases, having a common religion." [7]

While these definitions show the considerable agreement on the meaning of nationalism, they also reveal the shortcomings inherent in any brief definition. They do not account for the myriad variations, do not adequately cover all the changing realities and myths that nationalism includes, and, partly because of the time of their formulation, do not adequately consider the nationalism of the developing nations in twentieth-century Asia and Africa, where cultural affinities were either at times not strikingly present or, if present, not part of the consciousness of the peoples.

Later short definitions rectify some of the deficiencies. For one of the ablest students of African nationalism, James Coleman, nationalism was (in 1965), "broadly, a consciousness of belonging to a nation (existent or in the realm of aspiration) or a nationality, and a desire, as manifest in sentiment and activity, to secure or maintain its welfare, prosperity, and integrity, and to maximize its political autonomy." [8] Other students of Asian and African nationalism, Rupert Emerson (in 1960) and Richard Cottam (in 1964), thought of nationalism as, in Cottam's words, "a belief on the part of a large group of people that they comprise a political community, a nation, that is entitled to independent statehood, and a willingness of this group to grant their community a primary and terminal loyalty." [9] A German sociologist, Eugen Lemberg, likely reflecting the German experience under the Nazis, characterized (in 1964) nationalism as "in national linguistic usage the vehement and fanatical devotion to a national community (nation, state, *Volk* . . .)" and said that scholars, especially in Anglo-Saxon lands, use the word in this way.[10] A French historian, Raoul Girardet, certainly reflecting the Gaullist sentiment of France, believed (in 1966) that the primary concern of nationalism was to "keep independence, maintain the integrity of sovereignty and to affirm the grandeur of the nation state." [11]

These additional and newer definitions reflect the understandings arising out of recent history, but, as their authors would probably be the first to say, they too scarcely cover all manifestations of the sentiment. It is simply impossible to fit nationalism into a short definition.[12]

There is no denying that even the more informed treatments of nationalism are sometimes less than clear on what should be considered as nationalism. Both Kohn and Snyder in their many works, and other students as well,[13] give considerable attention to the slippery concept of national character and sometimes seem to be more interested in the supposed character of a nation than in what nationalism is. At times, too, even the best and most serious scholars, like Hayes and Kohn, could not (perhaps they should not) avoid bringing in moral evaluation of nationalism, discussing its "curses and blessings" at length, or thinking of western European and English nationalism as relatively "good" or German nationalism as relatively "bad." [14] But these ambiguities and ethical judgments do not greatly impair their works, for the scholarship is solid.

One can also learn much from the authors of recent volumes who, though they treat of nations and nationalism, really focus on what might be desirable policy for the future and hence define nationalism with policy in mind. Thus K. H. Silvert, a political scientist, in the book *Expectant Peoples,* emphasizes the role of the nation-state in modernization and comes, I should say therefore, to the conclusion that "nationalism is the acceptance of the state as the impersonal and final arbiter of human affairs," and to believe nationalism's positive function to be "building of reasonable expectations and security patterns into the greater complexity which is social modernism." [15] Thus Dorothy Dohen, a sociologist, in her book on *Nationalism and American Catholicism,* as she seeks reasons for dilemmas of Catholics in the United States defines nationalism for her purposes as "the ideology which permits the nation [not the universal church?] to be the impersonal and final arbiter of human affairs." [16] To these kinds of definitions important objections are easily stated: they are too present-minded, too *ad hoc,* and omit the cultural and social aspects of nationalism.

A similar objection can be raised to Marxist interpretations, which chiefly stress the economic, the capitalist (and therefore evil) foundations of nationalism. Marx, Lenin, and Stalin thought nationalist thinking reflected bourgeois ideology in the capitalist stage of history, the stage in which the bourgeoisie, wanting to sell its goods at home and abroad, tried to be victorious in the competition with the bourgeoisie of other nations for trade and profit.[17] This interpretation obviously oversimplifies a complex set of beliefs and conditions. Realizing this, contemporary Russian students are seeking for clearer and more accurate understanding.[18]

To define a sentiment in a way that will promote a desired goal is a common practice, not only of "leftists" but of "rightists" as well. The authoritarian nationalism of Nazis of Hitler's Germany and Fascists of Mussolini's Italy was not only more flamboyant and aggressive than that of most western nationalists, but it also stressed the role of the state in developing and co-ordinating the mystical will of the people, the *Volk* of the Germans, or the "organism" the Italians called the *Nazione*. In short, the supreme authority was the state, and the state's duty was to forward its own interest, in peace and in war. These Nazi and Fascist views represent a recent form of nationalism, though no more than one latter-day form. Nationalism has taken other forms, worn the cloak of many ideologies.

Other difficulties face a student trying to encompass the complexities of nationalism. The best sources on nationalism and what it means are, of course, the writings of articulate nationalists. But it is not easy to get behind their heated rhetoric and find out what it is they really have meant. Without humor or perspective, they generally have been deadly earnest partisans, and this was true whether they were politically of the "left" or the "right," whether they were Italian (Mazzini or Mussolini), French (Michelet or Maurras), German (Herder or Treitschke), or whether they were American (Theodore Roosevelt), Arab (Nasser), Ghanian (Nkrumah), or Jewish (Herzl). For their emotional and sometimes deadly earnestness there was good reason. They were involved in struggle for what they considered to be the highest goals: the national independence, the national welfare, the national security, and on occasion the very existence and future of their own nation. To understand and define nationalism one must, of course, read what they have said, no matter how serious or ridiculous it may seem. But their versions of nationalism are not scholarly analyses; they are committed and therefore nothing more than ardent defenses or assertions of the sentiment.

National patriots have sometimes thought of the object of their loyalty, their nation, as an organic being, as an individual, have personified it and regarded it as having birth, life, and death. Here, unconsciously, it is likely, they follow the idealist German philosopher Hegel (1770–1831), who thought "each particular National genius" should be "treated as only one Individual in the process of history." [19] But a nation is not a person, is not conceived and born at a particular time, does not live a certain number of years as an independent sentient being, does not die as does an individual. Hence it cannot be treated as if it were a human individual—a "she," in English colloquial usage—even though mystical patriots may so think. The myth arising from the personification of nation is part of the reality of nationalism, but it remains nonetheless a myth that beclouds rather than clarifies.

In their loyalty to their nation and in their desire to find "the earliest origins," patriots often project the life of their nation backward in time, imagine it to have come into existence, in something like the form they know it, long before it did. Thus it is sometimes believed that France and Britain were becoming nations as the western Roman Empire was declining and that the United States began in 1607 instead of, say, 1776.[20] Those who hold these beliefs are guilty of anachronism. Here again the myth is part of nationalism, though this does not make it true.

The most difficult problem, however, arises out of the changing and varying nature of nationalism. The object of loyalty itself, the nation, changes; those who offer the loyalty, the nationalists, change, and the kinds and intensities of their loyalties vary. This is to say that the sentiment is different at different times, that it is different in different peoples, that it is different for each individual, and that individual views change. The nationalism in France in 1793 was different from that of 1815 or 1939. The nationalism in France in 1815 or 1939 was different from that in the Germanies or Germany of these years. The rocklike nationalism of Charles de Gaulle was different from that of most other Frenchmen of his time and from the staunch nationalism of, say, his contemporaries Jawaharlal Nehru and John F. Kennedy. And the content of the nationalism of even the steadfast De Gaulle himself varied at least slightly during his several careers. Again, a nationalist in France may be a monarchist, a liberal republican, a democratic socialist, or even a communist, and whatever he is, he will probably change.

For a scholar the problem of definition is magnified because even in one language, say, English, word usage is loose. In English (and in its American version) the same general idea may be conveyed by the terms national patriotism, national consciousness, nationalism, and even nationality, and by the adjectives patriotic and nationalist, and each individual uses the words with different connotations. When a student confronts the word nationalism in other languages the problem becomes still more troublesome, for even the cognates—in German *nationalismus,* French *nationalisme,* Polish *nacjonalisme*—do not have quite the same content, while the

words meaning (or translated as) nationalism in nonwestern languages—
qawmiyya (Arabic), *Min-tsu chu-i* (Chinese), *kokka shugi* (Japanese),
and *l'ummiyyut* (Hebrew)—all represent somewhat different ideas that
are rooted deeply in the differing national experiences. Semantic difficulties cannot be completely overcome. For all words, at least all such generic
words as democracy, socialism, or nationalism, not only do meanings
change, but usage also varies. Still, it is possible to seek common historical
meanings for such words—for nationalism, in this case.

The human kinds and degrees of group loyalties depend in large part
on the kind of environment out of which the loyalties arise, the culture of
which they are a part. Nationalism, historically, is one of many group
loyalties, a special and more or less unique form that first began to manifest itself rather late in human history, probably—though the question is
debatable—during the late Middle Ages in western Europe and England.
Not until the seventeenth and eighteenth centuries did it begin to assume
something like its modern form and then again, chiefly, in western Europe
and England. It was not until the nineteenth century that the sentiment
became widespread in the rest of Europe and in North and South America. Only in the twentieth did it spread to the rest of the world.

Members of all human societies of which we have records have given
some kind of loyalty to and felt some kind of unity with a group or groups.
Love of the locality in which one is born is likewise old. Family loyalty
and distrust of other groups no doubt have been universal among men.[21] In
primitive societies, whether nomadic or sedentary, people gave their loyalties to tribe, clan, or like grouping. In ancient Greece they were devoted to
their communities, the city or *polis*, and they often possessed a sense of
"Greekness" and were indifferent, sometimes hostile, to other peoples, the
"barbarians" outside. Some Romans early expressed loyalty to their place
of birth (*patria*), to their city and to the republic, and later to some of
their emperors. In medieval western Europe, though the evidence is not
always clear and full, people professed loyalty to their village and sometimes to their province, customarily to their noble lords, and nearly always
to their religion and church. From the seventh century and the beginning
of Islam, Muslims gave allegiance to their religion, of which their states
were part, and to their fellow people of the faith. Ibn Khaldun (1332–
1406), the great Arab historian and philosopher, thought the foundation of
the state to be *asabiyya*, "the mutual affection and willingness [of a
people] to fight and die for each other." [22]

Direct and specific relationships between loyalties and political and
economic developments of modern history or between nationalism and the

varieties of cultures and environments cannot be firmly established. Nevertheless, nationalism reflects, if it is not determined by, the culture in which it arises—the total political, economic, and social environment.

Whether nationalism existed in any full sense until at least the seventeenth century is debatable. But from the twelfth century powerful dynasties in England (Angevin and Tudor) and in France (Capetian and Bourbon) were building what later came to be called national states, states with central administrative and legal institutions, with shifting and indefinite but nevertheless established territories, and with peoples of recognizable common cultures. In differing but yet similar ways these dynasties commanded the loyalty, or obedience, of their subjects, and they often thought and acted as if they alone were the object of loyalty and unity, they alone were the state. This "dynastic nationalism" might be more accurately called *étatisme*, for the dynastic state (whether that of Elizabeth of England or of Louis XIV of France) acted in its own interests rather than those of its subjects, using the machinery of government to strengthen and enrich the state and promote the power and glory of the dynasty. Still, even in the seventeenth century there was more than just *étatisme*, as Bossuet, Louis XIV's bishop, demonstrated when he described "love of fatherland" (*patrie*). "One sees in it," the Bishop wrote, "all the things which unite citizens together and to their country: the altars, the sacrifices, glory, peace and security, in a word, the society of divine and human things." [23]

During the eighteenth century in France and particularly during the Revolution of 1789 the people, at least the propertied people, were becoming the nation, and the nation itself was becoming the object of supreme loyalty. What those who wanted reform and change now meant by the nation a lawyer of Paris, Lacretelle *aîné*, made clear. "By a nation," he wrote, "can be understood only the sum total of citizens who inhabit its territory, who are attached there by permanent residence, by landed property, or through an industry which makes them necessary to those who cultivate the land, who have adopted its laws, who support its charges, who serve it and obey it each in the manner proper to him. As everything is possessed by them, everything belongs to them. . . ." [24]

Each nation of people, of course, was believed to be both distinct from other nations and to have its own interests, just as each of the older dynastic states was distinct from other like states and had its own interests. Now the word nationalism was coined. In one of the earliest uses (1798) of the term, an abbé Barruel, analyzing a speech of a German *illuminé* named Weishaupt, declared that when men united in nations "they ceased to recognize themselves under a common name—. *Nationalism* or *National Love* took the place of general love. . . . Then it became a virtue to expand at the expense of those who were not under our dominion. Then to obtain this end it became permissible to distrust, deceive, and offend strangers." [25]

Through the nineteenth century governments in the western world generally became more democratic and peoples more widely educated. More and more people, the unpropertied as well as the propertied, came to be included in the nation, participated in the national affairs (through at least the right to vote), and came to believe they owed their allegiance to it and to that for which it stood (or they thought it stood). Between democracy and national feeling the relationship was close, for as people had a voice in their national governments they became more conscious of the national interests—that is, their own. Government of, by, and for the people meant government of, by, and for the people of a nation, and devotion to this nation, their own, became the highest of virtues, while distrust of other peoples, now chiefly grouped in nations, remained universal.

What had begun earlier continued in the twentieth century, especially in the nations that succumbed to nationalist totalitarianism, Italy and Germany. The dictators of those countries ruled in the name of their nations, frequently spoke to the people as if they mattered and even gave them the feeling of participation through managed elections and other devices. Most Italians and Germans, then, either freely gave or were forced to give their loyalty to their nations and nation-states. Very likely, insofar as outward manifestations can be used as a measure, the national sentiment in Italy and Germany became stronger than it had ever been in these countries and perhaps in some respects stronger than in other countries at any time except in time of war. The form of government, or the political ideology, apparently did not matter, though the reality or illusion of participation mattered very much.

Contrary to the hope of internationalists, nationalism became ever more prevalent during the twentieth century. After World War I and particularly after World War II, nationalism spread over the rest of the world to the "expectant peoples." Among them elites wanted to achieve modernization through revolt against imperialist rule and to establish their own independent nation-states.[26] The new nationalisms had their peculiar characteristics, two of which must be mentioned here. (1) Africans especially, but Asians too, made much not only of their color but also of their oppression by European nations. Hence the "racial" overtones of nationalism, which had been a component of western nationalism in the nineteenth century and prominent in German National Socialist ideology in the Hitler period, reappeared in a different context, within the context of oppression by foreign nations. (2) In many of the developing nations the peoples were little conscious of their nation, of common interests, and of a common national culture. In most cases the new nation-states, like the Kenyan, when they were established in the 1950's and 1960's, had to try to create nations within their states, and they are still trying.

This rapid survey of the sentiment called nationalism, which most unites and divides contemporary men, reveals that while nationalism changes with the time, place, and culture, it does have characteristics that can be identified. In 1931 Carlton Hayes, in his *Historical Evolution of Nationalism,* evolved useful historical categories for European nationalism. To identify the varieties, he used the adjectives humanitarian, Jacobin, traditional, liberal, and integral. These varieties appeared in Europe in roughly chronological succession from the French Revolution through the fascist dictatorships of the twentieth century. They still exist, they differ, but they do have common elements. Because Hayes evolved his categories over a generation ago, he did not consider a possible sixth variety, that of the developing peoples of the mid-twentieth century. However, their nationalisms, though they differ from the older nationalisms, have much in common with them. Hence, though the varieties are several, the species is identifiable and describable.

One further problem of interpretation must be mentioned: the degree or intensity of nationalism. Nationalism obviously differs in its intensity among peoples and among individuals. In peacetime, in times of comparative international equilibrium (the 1830's and 1920's), and in times of comparative internal calm (Britain and the United States of the 1880's), individuals may think little about their country—that is, be "casual patriots." [27] In wartime, and especially at the beginning of a war (as in France and Germany in 1914), they tend to be ardently patriotic and demand that every citizen of their nation also be.

In old and new nations alike, nationalism was generally expressed earliest by leaders, the elite—that is, by the officials, the politicians, the educated, the students, the lawyers, the writers, and, in some nations (such as Turkey), the military. It was only later, usually, that it became slowly and widely diffused among the masses, the shopkeepers, the workers, the farmers. Among presently developing peoples, for instance, the Congolese, there is likely as little (or less) national consciousness or feeling as there was among the Balkan peoples of the seventeenth century. Just as the Italian nationalist statesman d'Azeglio remarked when Italy was first unified in the mid-nineteenth century, "We have made Italy, now we have to make Italians," so now most Asian and African nation-states must arouse national consciousness and loyalty among the varied peoples within them. The new nations, as Margery Perham remarked of the African,[28] often lacked all the usual common elements of nationhood (like common history, language, customs) "except a common territory," and even this was "lately and arbitrarily created by an alien power."

It is easy to overestimate the degree of nationalism, for from the eighteenth century the sentiment has been becoming so pervasive and at present is so widely shared. Few people in the world today can avoid consciousness of nation, but certainly not all give their primary loyalty to it. Many, in peacetime at least, are apathetic. Some have used patriotism to cloak other interests, such as their self-interest in prestige or profit; and their nationalism has been, as an American economist, Thorstein Veblen, put it, at least in part a "sense of partisan solidarity in respect of prestige," or a cover, as Karl Marx maintained, for their desire for material or other gain. Some have rebelled against their nation-state, as did southern Americans in 1860–65 and as have revolutionaries in many countries before and since. Some everywhere, like Muslims and Quakers, have given their primary loyalty to a religion or church. And small minorities have long sought new or larger entities, a regional federation or a world state, to which they could be loyal.

For the purpose of description, nationalism can be said to vary in intensity depending upon: [29]

1. The degree to which a national government and national institutions *penetrate,* through taxation or military service, for example, the lives and thought of a people. (Some kinds of national governmental action may arouse protest and resentment, but at the same time arouse national consciousness.)

2. The degree to which members of a people *participate* in common or national affairs, or believe they participate and have a voice in these common affairs. (Though participation can result in overturn of a national government.)

3. The degree to which individuals of a people *identify* themselves with the common or national interests, integrate their own interests with these, and "internalize" national concerns in their own thinking and action. (It is now often quite impossible to distinguish between national and personal interests.)

4. The degree to which individuals are pressured into complying or

forced to *comply* with the national will as expressed by their nation-state. (Coercion may also result in rejection.)

5. The degree of *consensus* among a people—that is, the degree of agreement with the common beliefs and values. (This may be so great, as in nineteenth-century Britain, that it is taken for granted.)

All this is to say that nationalism deepens as individuals among a people become involved in common enterprises, are able to and do communicate with others[30] of like mind, and do act or interact with these others, their fellow citizens, "within a context of shared understandings, mutual expectations, and accepted norms." [31]

Because nationalism has become worldwide, though not universal, it might seem, basically, to arise from what psychologists once called the instinct of gregariousness, to be at root biological. But while all men at all times appear to have been members of some kind of group and to have given some degree of loyalty to it, nationalism is modern, and the sentiment is not now shared by all individuals or expressed with the same intensity by peoples everywhere.

Men are not by nature nationalist, any more than they are monarchist or republican. They become nationalist, within particular cultures and under certain conditions, and more or less nationalist depending upon the particular situation. Nationalism is a learned sentiment. It is molded by the culture and the state that is part of that culture. Except in a legal sense Frenchmen and Italians are not at birth Frenchmen or Italians. They become Frenchmen or Italians (1) because of the influence and power of their political state and its laws, (2) because of their immersion in the culture into which they were born and within which they mature, (3) because of the training and education they receive from parents and schools in the traditions and values of their group, and (4) because their interests and goals, reflecting or flowing out of their culture, seem to be subsumed in those of their nation and nation-state.

The modern English words and phrases stemming from the Latin words *nasci* (to be born) and *natio* (belonging together because of place of birth) are many.[32] They include: nation, national, nationality, national consciousness, national sentiment, national patriotism, nationalism.[33] Three of these require further discussion: nation, nationality, and nationalism.

In any modern sense the noun nation was probably first used in France and England in the early fourteenth century.[34] But until much later the meanings given the word greatly varied. In late medieval times it was used to describe student groups of similar backgrounds at the universities of Paris, Aberdeen, and Prague, and it was applied to groups of representatives of churchmen at great councils of the Roman Catholic church at Lyons (1274) and Constance (1414). In early modern times writers employed it to describe species of animals, and monks, physicians, lawyers, and even young girls. It was not until the seventeenth and eighteenth centuries, as has been pointed out, that nation clearly came to mean the people (at least those owning property) of a country or kingdom, a distinct people who had a common historical background, resided in a particular if still ill-defined territory,[35] and were subject to one state (dynasty). During the era of the French Revolution and later the notions of self-government and self-determination were added to the meaning. More and more all the people of one state and a common culture were thought to constitute a nation, and this people had its own particular heritage and its own separate interests and hopes which separated it from other peoples.

During the nineteenth century, especially the latter part, many politicians, writers, and scholars sought to define what the word nation really did or should stand for, and the great dictionaries gave increasing attention to all the words and terms that were related to it. In general the meaning then given to nation and nationality may be represented by three of these definitions. In 1836 a rising young English novelist and politician, Benjamin Disraeli, thought a nation "a work of art and time . . . gradually created by a variety of [common] influences—the influence of original organization, of climate, soil, religion, laws, customs, manners, extraordinary accidents and incidents in their history, and the individual character of their illustrious citizens." [36] For an Italian professor at Turin in 1851, Pasquale Mancini, a nationality was a "natural society of men, united by territory, origin, custom, language conforming to the community of life and the social conscience." [37] And in 1882 Professor Ernest Renan of the Sorbonne gave what became the best-known definition of a nation when he said, "A nation is a soul, a spiritual principle, two things which are in reality one. . . . One is the common possession [by a people] of a rich heritage of memories, the other is the actual agreement, the desire to live together, the will to continue to make a reality of the heritage they have received in common." [38]

These three definitions gave different reasons for the formation of a nation: that it is natural, formed by history, a matter of desire or will, and that it is something mystical, "a soul, a spiritual principle." Few if any modern scholars would think of a nation in the romantic words "a soul" or "spiritual principle." [39] But Renan's "two things," one in the past and one in the future, a people's common heritage and its common will, have been incorporated in nearly all succeeding definitions, whether these be European or American, Asian or African. In 1957 a Lebanese Muslim, Abd al-Latif Sharara, summed up not only Arabic but much of what is currently meant by the nation and kindred concepts when he wrote:

> The fatherland is the soil and the climate in which live a group of people. The people is that group of men who live in one land, who have the same historical origin, and have the same political order. The state is that political organization which a people sets up in a fatherland. . . . The nation, however, is a wider conception than the state, greater than the people, and more meaningful than the fatherland. It is not necessary for a nation to have one state or one fatherland [this is the Arab view], or to be composed of one people; but it must have its own language, its own history, its own ideals, its own shared aspirations, its own shared memories, and its own particular natural links which bind its members in two respects, the moral and the economic. . . . Nationalism is [the] emotion and common interest combined in one feeling and one idea within the members of the nation. [40]

It must be added, however, that some definitions of nation, especially those of the late nineteenth century and of central Europe, emphasized common race as a major basis for a nation, that sometimes race and nation were used interchangeably, and that the myth of common race as a basis for nationhood has not disappeared—even though old beliefs about racial differences have been shown to be unfounded. [41]

While no two students today will agree in detail on a definition of a nation, at this point, for the purposes of this book, an attempt at a usable description may be risked: the word nation describes a group (of some size) of people united, usually, by (1) residence in a common land (the *patrie* becomes the national land), (2) a common heritage and culture, (3) common interests in the present and common hopes to live together in the future, and (4) a common desire to have and maintain their own state. Individuals become members of the nation by birth and by naturalization, and also by governmental edict when a state, by force or diplomacy, adds them to the nation. In the last case, however, membership may be *de jure* but not *de facto*, for individuals and groups, like the Ukrainians or Biafrans, may not consider themselves to be members of the dominant nation-state. Again, individuals, indeed many individuals in Africa and Asia, may be considered members of a nation without their being conscious of it, and in some cases even if a well-developed nation does not exist. On the other hand, in older contemporary societies members of a nation usually participate somehow in its affairs, though this may only be in opposition, and think of themselves (as do some American blacks) as being members of a distinct and separate group whose interests are different from those of other similar groups within the nation. Finally, members of a nation usually think of their state as being the final, the terminal authority. Nations, however, may not have an autonomous or independent government or state: the Ukrainian, the Basque, the French-Canadian. No definition of a nation is final. For, it must be reiterated, nations are always in process of becoming. It has been so in the past, it is so in the present, and probably will be so in the future.

To this summary at least one serious objection can be raised. If the nation is a human group, how is it different from other groups of men? There is at least one partial, if inconclusive, answer. The nation is not a totally different form of human grouping; it is not totally different from the tribes of primitive peoples or from the city-communities of the ancient Greeks. The nation, nonetheless, is the chief modern form of grouping. It now tends to include all lesser groups, kinship, religious, or other, and to be the most inclusive group. Arising in modern times, the nation has the qualities, economic, political, and social, that modern cultures have given it, and thus it is different from groups that have arisen earlier and in other cultures.

For the term nationality the discussion need not be so detailed.[42] Nationality is usually the term applied to the people—the English, the Chinese—who belong to a particular nation—to England or China.[43] The nationality of an individual depends upon where he is born, his own consciousness of membership, his desire to belong, and the willingness of a nation to admit him. Legally, the right of belonging is usually determined by birth within the nation, but it may also be granted by naturalization or decreed, in the case of conquered people, by the conquering state. In some cases, religion, such as the Islamic in Pakistan or the Jewish in Israel, and race, as in Nazi Germany, have been considered criteria of nationality, but these criteria are no longer as widely employed as they once were. It is also true that a member of one nationality, say the Jewish or Greek, may be a willing or unwilling subject or citizen of a state or a nation not his own, say Turkey, and that a member of a minority group, like the blacks in the United States, may not be admitted fully to membership in the dominant nationality, may be, in a sense, of two nationalities.

The word nationalism was coined later (late eighteenth century) than the words nation and nationality, came into common usage only in the latter half of the nineteenth century and then with considerable imprecision. As the beliefs now labeled nationalist became widespread and strong during and immediately after the world war of 1914–18, serious scholarly study of the sentiment increased—the classic books of René Johannet and Carlton Hayes are evidence of this. Since that time thousands of studies, books and articles, have been devoted to it, and the word (with its equivalents in other languages) has become incorporated in all the world's common languages.

Nationalism is, as Hayes said it was, a sentiment in which patriotism is fused with nationality, or, to put it another way, a belief that an individual should be loyal to his nation, its land, its values, and its state. But this usable shorthand definition tells us too little about the concrete realities, like territory and people, that are tangible elements in the sentiment and the beliefs and myths (realities in another sense) that constitute the sentiment.

The ten statements that follow do not define nationalism but, *taken together,* they describe its basic attributes, both real and mythical.

1. A certain defined, even if vaguely, territory or land, whether this be large or small, inhabited by a people or desired by them. The people believe the land belongs (or should belong) to them, think of it as their own, and in diverse ways love it and oppose any diminution of its size. In older nations, such as France, dynastic rulers largely determined the extent of the territory through war and diplomacy, but the right of possession by the nation has now, usually, been confirmed by long occupation. In most of the new nations, like Kenya, the imperial powers, largely by edict or military force, established administrative boundaries that later became the national boundaries. The boundaries of both old and new states are often declared to be "natural," but they are really those out to which the nation-states have extended their national jurisdiction.

2. A people, called the nation, who share or hope to share, in different and shifting ways, a common culture, and who are able to communicate with each other with some facility. The common culture generally includes language (as in France) or commonly understood languages (as in Switzerland), and common literature, common symbols, common customs, and common manners. When an individual shares this culture, wishes to continue to do so, and is, in some fashion, devoted to it, he is said to be of the nation and to belong to the nationality. In older nations there is now wide sharing, in the newer nation-states of Asia and Africa generally much less. In Africa the ethnic or culture groups are numerous and quite different, and a common culture may be, as in Kenya, only in the process of development, or perhaps may never develop (the Congo?).

But nationalism tends to be stronger when consciousness of common culture is felt.

3. Some dominant social (Muslim or Christian churches, for example) and economic (capitalist or communist) institutions. Again, these institutions are more likely to be present in older than newer nations, though they once had to develop in the old—as in France—just as they now are, apparently, in the new—as in Tanzania. Accompanying or behind these institutions there are common social and economic interests. If there are deep conflicts over these institutions or interests, then the nation is likely to be divided—as was the United States in 1861–65 and Nigeria in 1967–69—and the national unity threatened.

4. A common independent or sovereign state (type does not matter), or, with rare exceptions, the desire for one—as in the case of the Poles in the nineteenth century and the Jews in the first half of the twentieth. Behind the establishment of this state there is the principle of self-determination that arose during the French Revolutionary era, a principle deeply rooted in the idea of dynastic sovereignty in the older nations, and now, particularly for the new nations, a principle of first and major importance. The degrees of loyalty to the governments may and do widely differ. Individuals within nations may be little conscious of their nation-state and some may oppose it while remaining loyal or being disloyal. It is also true that a people who are called a nation, as the Basques are, and who express nationalist opinions, may not press for a completely independent state. Nevertheless, in the contemporary world, a demand for a separate, an independent state is rarely absent.

5. A shared belief in a common history and often in a common ethnic origin, sometimes thought to be religious or racial—as with the Arabs or Jews. The common past and ethnic origin may be real or imagined. In most nations, especially in the new—Nigeria—but also in the old—Great Britain—the people are of several ethnic groups, there is no completely common ethnic origin, and if one the people may not be much aware of it. In any case, to the extent that individuals are nationalist they appear to find shared meaning in common past experience, be this actual or invented, and to feel unified because of it. Consciousness of a common heritage also gives a people a feeling of being distinct from other peoples and enables them to have a sense of identity.

6. Preference and esteem for fellow nationals (Frenchmen for Frenchmen); that is, for those who share the common culture, institutions, interests, and heritage—or at least greater preference and esteem for them than for members of other similar groups (the "foreigners") who do not

share these. The emotional ties usually involve fellow nationals in general, rather than as individuals—an American may dislike another American but like a Frenchman. In the new nations the emotional ties may be as little felt as they once were in the older. In all nations they are likely to be much greater in wartime than peacetime and to be much more in evidence when individuals are in "foreign" lands.

7. A shared, a common pride—like that of the Germans—in past and present achievements, more often the military and economic than the cultural and social, of the group, and a shared, a common sorrow in its tragedies, particularly its military failures. Sometimes it is difficult to find bases for pride, for a nation (as in Africa) may not be established long enough to have accomplished much. Sometimes for an oppressed or conquered people (the Czechs and Poles) shared tragedy may be more significant than achievement. But pride is always there, whether the shared sorrows be few or many. Accompanying and supporting this pride often is a belief —like that of the Jews, of the Germans, of the English and the Americans—that the nation has been "chosen" and is destined to do great things.

8. A shared indifference or hostility to other (not all) peoples similarly organized in nations—before 1945 the French for the Germans—especially if the other nations seem to threaten the national security and hopes, the nation's survival in the present and future. In the new nations the hostility, such as that of the Vietnamese for the French and Americans, is most often directed toward the imperialist nations that once ruled or still do. In the older nations the hostility—that of the Poles to the Germans —is most often against a neighboring nation with which the nation has been at war, though in the contemporary world of jet bombers and missiles and competing ideologies, proximity seems to be losing importance. The French word *nationalisme* has the connotation of predominant devotion to one's own nation as well as an aggressive attitude toward other nations,[44] and while the term in other languages may not have these connotations, the French word seems fairly to fit many nationalisms, particularly those that are expansive. To express these connotations in English the words chauvinism (of French derivation), meaning exaggerated demonstrative patriotism, and jingoism,[45] meaning bellicose, aggressive nationalism, are often employed. That the indifference and hostility may vary from time to time and from people to people is a necessary qualification. Nationalist sentiment divides peoples as it unifies a people.

9. A devotion to the entity (even if little comprehended) called the nation (or *patrie* or fatherland) that embodies or symbolizes the territory, the people, the culture, the institutions, the interests, the heritage, and

whatever else the people have or think they have in common—the "United States, one and indivisible." The nation, for nationalists, is larger than the sum of its parts, becomes a mystical symbol, an organism, a being. Once more, devotion to it develops with time and with consciousness of common experience. Again, some individuals in the old and more in the new nations scarcely feel it. But the nation, representing a vast mass of feelings, "residues," becomes itself a symbol of the heritage and aspiration that unify, a symbol to which subjects owe allegiance.

10. A shared hope that the nation, the nation as a group and the individuals belonging to it, will have a secure and happy future. For the peoples of great nations, of Britain, of Russia, of the United States, this often has meant a "glorious" future in power and expansion on this earth; and in the contemporary world, for Russia and the United States, in outer space, too. At present, however, only a few nations, like Russia and the United States, attempt to expand territorially, though many do economically. For small and new nations the hope has often been little more than hope for survival. Hope, however, there must be, for preservation if not for glory.

These ten attributes are ten generally present. They do not all have to be present at the same time and in the same way or to the same degree. The varieties of combinations and emphases are manifold. Before nationalism can be said to exist, however, most of them must be present, and when all are present at the same time, then nationalism will be strong.

To each of them there are exceptions that force qualification. In modern times Jews did not have a land of their own until recently, nor did most of the black peoples of Africa who are now called developing nations. In old Switzerland four languages are spoken, in relatively new Canada two, and in some of the newer nations, as in Nigeria, many, as well as numerous dialects. The peoples of two or more nations—for example, Portugal and Brazil, or England, the United States, and Australia—may speak the same language. In some new nations, like India, the most commonly understood language, English, the *lingua franca*, is that of the former ruling power. In few if any of the new nations (perhaps Somalia) do most of the people have a common ethnic origin or a common religion. In Lebanon, Muslims and Christians of several sects live side by side, and in India, Hindus, Muslims, Christians, Sikhs, Parsis, and——. Not only Basques but also other nationalities do not have their own government: the Ukrainians, the Palestinians, the Welsh, and some of the Irish. In every nation some individuals are not loyal to their government, or, if loyal, not all the time, though it is unlikely that they would accept a "foreign" government. Some Russians were nationalists under the czar, some are under the present Communist regime; one cannot be certain, but some would likely be if Russia had another revolution and another kind of government. While in older nations the people can be said to have a common heritage, for some of them this heritage may be literally quite short—in the United States a large proportion of the population is descended from immigrants who arrived in the United States after the American Revolution, and only figuratively can George Washington be considered their ancestor. Many of the new nations have little history, little common history to be shared. Indifference and hostility to other nations are marks of nationalism, but individuals of one nation are often friendly with individuals of other nations—international marriages are not uncommon. The feeling of people toward other nations changes rapidly—twenty-five years ago Americans hated Germany and Japan; today they think of them as friends and allies. The kind of secure and happy future national patriots envision for their nation changes with their own shifting versions of utopia, be they democratic or authoritarian. The newer nationalisms of Asia and Africa stress achievement of independence more than they do a common heritage, and the people's hostility to the former imperialist rulers often seems stronger than their esteem for fellow nationals.[46]

These exceptions, these qualifications do not change the realities of nationalism, nor do they prevent identification of its major characteristics. Each nationalism is unique but at the same time there are similarities and common features. Generalizations may hence be cautiously hazarded.

Informed students may raise another substantive objection: that nationalism is, in the main, but a cloak for other interests and hopes of individuals and groups within the nations, that nationalism gathers up all sorts of interests and hopes that can scarcely be called national. This objection surely has validity. Individuals use the sentiment, consciously or unconsciously, to seek profit and status, to obtain excitement and joy, and to gain relief from boredom, frustration, or fear. Business corporations and social and religious organizations may support nationalist values and aspirations in order to win concrete advantages, increases in profits or in membership, and to defend themselves against attack. A people, Ghanian or French-Canadian, for example, may, fundamentally, be seeking modernization and may use nationalism as the instrument to achieve that goal. Nationalism, indeed, does cover a great number of diverse individual and group interests. But, again, this does not deny the reality of nationalism. It is only to say that nationalism, like other sentiments, is a composite of

21

many interests, hopes, fears. Perhaps because it is, it has become at present the strongest sentiment unifying people and dividing them from other peoples.

This writer has no illusions that he has ended scholarly argument about the meaning of nationalism. However simple or complex he has made the problems of definition, he knows that other students will regard his answers as too simple. He nevertheless hopes he has helped clarify what it has meant and means, at least for the purposes of this book.

Nationalism, it must finally be added, may not as yet have reached its final stages of development, or it may be submerged by and transformed into some larger sentiment by the creation of world institutions and enlargement of human consciousness. One thing is certain: it is a complex, dynamic sentiment. And as it changes, so must definitions and descriptions of it.

II

How National Sentiment Developed: Stirrings to 1715 *

Scholars debate the time nationalism began, whether those ideas and practices that may be properly summed up in the term have their origins in ancient civilizations, in European medieval history, or much later in the early modern period of western European history. The debate will continue, for much depends upon definition and interpretation. As the records give evidence, sentiments of loyalty akin to national patriotism—to a kinship group, to a ruler, to a city, or to a religious creed—appear at least as early as the ancient Greeks, Jews, Persians, and Chinese. Earlier peoples, for whom few or no records exist, must have given loyalty to their rulers, their tribes, and their communities or they could not have existed as peoples.[1] Like the early Chinese, most western peoples, too, seem to have had the feeling of being, somehow, distinct and separate and to have been indifferent to, distrustful of other peoples. While ancient Greeks often fought each other, they usually regarded themselves as a single people with some common interests, a people different from the "outsiders" they called "barbarians."

At the supreme crisis of the Persian invasion of Greece, after the Persians had annihilated the thousand Spartans and Thespians under Leonidas at Thermopylae (480 B.C.), the Athenians told the Spartans they would not desert them for an alliance with the Persians, first, because their own temples and images of gods would then be burned and destroyed and, second, because of "our common brotherhood with the Greeks: our common language, our common altars and the sacrifices of which we all partake, and the common character which we bear. . . ."[2] The Greeks, of

---

* History is a continuum. There is no way of exactly dating the end of feudalism or *étatism*, or the beginning of nationalism or internationalism. Dates are used for convenience in the titles of this and later chapters.

course, were more devoted to their own city-communities than to Greece. Indeed, it has been said they exhibited no "patriotism" as we know it and gave their primary loyalties to their friendship groups or clubs (*hetai-reiai*); and a good many of the leaders of their cities, including Alcibiades and Cleisthenes, were, at one time or another, declared "traitors." [3] But the sentiment of loyalty to city must often have been deep. When Socrates, sentenced to death by Athens for corrupting the minds of youth, was urged to escape by his friend Crito, he, as is well known, replied, "Has a philosopher like you failed to discover that our country [city] is more to be valued and higher and holier far than mother or father or any ancestor, and more to be regarded in the eyes of Gods and of men of understanding? to be obeyed, suffered for in silence even when punished, to die for?" [4]

Ancient Romans, like ancient Greeks, were sometimes willing to die for the *res publica Romana* and for all for which this stood.[5] They on occasion expressed deep loyalty to the *patria*. Cicero (106–43 B.C.) told Romans, "Parents are dear, children are dear, as are our relatives and friends; but our fatherland embraces in itself all our love for everyone." [6]

Ancient Jews were intensely loyal to their religion, to the teachings of the Book, the Old Testament of the Bible, which someone once called a "nationalist history." Many of them seemed to believe Moses when he told them they were a "holy people" chosen by God to be a "special people . . . above all people." [7] From the time of the Persian kings Cyrus (600?–529 B.C.) and Darius (558?–486 B.C.) and down to the time of the invasion (334–333 B.C.) of the Macedonian Alexander the Great, Persia was a great power whose various peoples were ruled by strong despots and unified in some degree by their Zoroastrian religion. Out of fear or respect many Persians grouped themselves behind their emperors. Within the great empire, the Persian state resembled the dynastic states of early modern Europe, and the basis of a common, a long-persisting national Persian culture developed.

It can thus be maintained that nationalism appeared much earlier than has usually been believed, or that at least the bases of what was later called nationalism were laid down in ancient Greece, Rome, Palestine, and Persia. Certainly states were established, cultures developed, and loyalties were expressed that are similar in some respects to those of modern nationalism. But the modern nation, in its present form, did not yet exist, nor had it become the supreme object of loyalty. Ancient Greeks gave first loyalty to their own friendship groups and their cities; Greek cities fought against Greek cities; and within Greece centrifugal forces of disruption were nearly always stronger than the centripetal. Some Romans did die *pro patria,* though seldom for the territory they happened to defend, and after the republic became a vast empire the chief unity among the many and diverse peoples was that imposed by emperors and generals. Virgil in his *Georgics* sang the praises of Italy, its land and its people, but as yet there was no Italy and no Italian nation. The Jews were united by their theology and customs but there was no Jewish nation, and after the conquest by the Romans and the destruction of Jerusalem in A.D. 70, the Jews became widely dispersed, a people with a history but no land and no common language. Persia did have potentialities for becoming a nation, but when it was at its height only despotic rule held together the many peoples and far-flung territories. After Persia was attacked and invaded by Macedonian, Roman, and Byzantine armies and then, in the 640's, conquered by the Arabs, and its Zoroastrian religion largely supplanted by the Islamic, it became part of the larger pattern of Islamic civilization. Persian memories were long. Almost a thousand years after Alexander's invasion, Persians fought and lost a battle (Qadisiya, 635) against an Arab-Islamic army; 350 years still later a Persian poet, Firdousi, immortalized this battle in his poetic history of Persia, *Book of Kings;* and until the second decade of the twentieth century Persians commemorated the assassination of an Arab general by a Persian, Abu Lolo Firooz.[8]

In general the loyalties of men in the ancient world were to their kinship groups, their cities, and their religions. It was to these that they chiefly turned for security and for help. It was chiefly these that penetrated their consciousness and with which they identified. And insofar as most people participated in control of their affairs, it was in and through these that they did so.

Given the slow transportation and communication and the many diverse languages and customs of the ancient world, wide and pervasive sentiments of unity and loyalty were not likely to develop. But, it must be remarked at once, a few intellectuals, particularly the Greek and Roman Stoics, did profess a deep regard for all men—at least all they knew about in the western world. The founder of Stoicism, Zeno of Citium (334?–262 B.C.), dreamed of a great city where all men were citizens and were bound together by their obligation to serve and to love one another.[9] And that Roman emperor who was also a philosopher, Marcus Aurelius (121–180), believed his "city and country, so far as I am Antoninus" to be Rome, "but so far as I am a man . . . the world."[10]

However and if ever the debate over the time of the beginning of nationalism is resolved, one thing seems probable: nations in any *modern sense* did not appear until the latter part of the medieval period, and then in western Europe.[11] Loyalties, unities, states, common cultures, group hostilities, yes, but not nations.

To find origins of a modern idea far back in history is easy. So many ideas have been conceived and broached in history, by the Greeks, Persians, Chinese, if not others, that almost no idea is brand new. Moreover, through history men with their common human potentialities and limitations have faced common problems in their living and thinking and have often evolved answers that have much in common. But ideas conceived in the context of one culture or era are not necessarily transmitted to later cultures or eras, and if transmitted may seem to be the same but in the later context may be quite different. In any case, it is a common error of historians to find a direct connection between the early appearance of an idea and what appears to be its direct descendant, to antedate, to see in the past the origins of ideas that, in any proper sense, really take shape much later. When a historian (or anyone else) does this, he may pick out from the past mere anticipations, see things quite out of context, and thus pervert history. And so it is with nations and nationalism.

Some historians, pseudohistorians and propagandists, seriously seeking the earliest evidence for the emergence of nationalism or catering to nationalist "vanity," have been able to divine far longer histories for their nations than the facts permit, to imagine nations long before the rudiments of a national state, a national territory, or a national culture came into existence and certainly long before the people living in the area were aware of much or anything they had in common. Perhaps in Europe these historians inherited this proclivity to stretch out their national histories from the medieval Christian historians who tried to trace the beginning of human history back to the mythical founding of the world in 4004 B.C. Whatever the explanation, they did invest their nations with "fabulous antiquity." [12] The Spanish kings were traced back to Tubal, grandson of Noah. English history was supposed to begin with the giant Albion and Brutus of Troy or with Brut, grandson of Aeneas.[13] The history of Germany was sometimes believed to have begun with the heroic (according to Tacitus) soldier Arminius and his defeat of Roman legions in A.D. 9.[14] Good historians could sometimes even set a specific birth date for their nations. Augustin Thierry (1795–1856), whose letters on the history of France won him fame, put the beginning of France in 888, the year of the dissolution of the Carolingian Empire.[15] J. R. Green (1837–1883), whose texts on English history were long standard works, could perceive the origins of England in the landing of Hengest, the Jute, in 449.[16] Few, if any, serious historians now fall into this kind of anachronistic trap, but myths of "fabulous antiquity" live on and have become part of the new nationalisms of Asia and Africa. Bal Gangadhar Tilak (1856–1920), a traditionalist nationalist of India, attempted to prove that his "Aryan" ancestors "planted the seeds of civilized existence in the world . . . not later than 4000 B.C." [17] Japanese students, with some truth, have found the nucleus of their nation in the eighth-century cultural center of Nara and have mythically traced their emperors back to an emperor, Jimmu Tenno, of about 660 B.C.[18] Recent Ghanian leaders professed to see the forebear of their new nation in the much more northern old empire of Ghana of a thousand years earlier.[19]

During the early medieval period of western European history (roughly to the thirteenth century), nations as we now know them (and hence nationalism) did not exist. The dominant and unifying faith was that of the Christian religion. Though the faith was often rent by dissent, it was or aspired to be a universal faith, to be for all men, at least for all believers regardless of their human differences. Christians owed the first allegiance not to a secular authority but to their God, and to His "one, holy, catholic (universal), and apostolic" church. On earth God's authority was vested in the bishop of Rome, the pope (he was also, of course, a lay ruler), and in his, thus God's, representatives, the priests. All believers belonged to this Catholic church, and it and its doctrines united all Christians, even though they might fight among themselves. Early medieval Christians were supposed to love all men; and while they were, in fact, intolerant of peoples of other faiths and of nonbelievers, they were little conscious of those differences that later would be called national.[20] Of course they had other loyalties, to their families, their tribes, their villages, their cities, to their feudal lords and rulers, or to their emperors, but first of all they were Christians and generally deeply conscious of belonging to the brotherhood of Christians.

Historically, it is possible to find *anticipations* of western European nations, nation-states, and national consciousness from the time of the Carolingian Empire (eighth–ninth centuries), though no definite dates can be established. By the ninth century the inhabitants of much of Italy had become "a relatively homogeneous people," though they were scarcely aware of this.[21] About the same time the lands and people west of the Rhine were becoming clearly Latin and those east clearly Germanic, and the word *teudesca* (Deutsch) was first used to designate the German language, though not a people or land.[22] When in the Oaths of Strasbourg

(842) two of Charlemagne's grandsons swore to support each other in opposition to their emperor brother, Lothair, one, Louis the German, King of the East Franks, used the *lingua romana* (Roman-French) so that his brother's retainers might understand him, and the other, Charles the Bald, King of the West Franks, spoke in the *lingua teudesca* for the same reason. But neither the peoples nor the lands these kings ruled were yet the German or French.

Late in the tenth century (987) Hugh Capet, a feudal lord whose domain was centered in the Ile de France, became King of France (or, more accurately, of the French) and established Capetian rule of the lands and peoples that became the nucleus of France. In the eleventh century (1066) a Norman lord, William, known in history as the Conqueror, defeated the Anglo-Saxon lords of England and began the rule that would establish the English nation-state and greatly shape the English nation. But there were as yet few, if any, expressions of loyalty to France or to England. Nation building was beginning but without conscious foresight or planning. For hundreds of years it would proceed that way, even in France and England.

Just when clearly identifiable national consciousness arose in these two countries it is impossible to say. Possibly for a few men it could have been in the twelfth century. In the great twelfth-century epic poem, the *Chanson de Roland,* the hero of Charlemagne's armies, seeing himself surrounded by Saracens, cried, *"A Dieu ne plaise que la douce France tombe jamais dans le déshonneur."* As his brave companion, Oliver, fell, he cried again, *"O douce France, tu vas donc être veuve de les meilleurs soldats."* Arriving before the body of Roland, Charlemagne in tears moaned, *"Il est mort, celui qui était toujours à notre tête. Ah! douce France, te voilà orpheline."* [23] The words of the poet appear to express deep national patriotism, evidence deep love of *"douce France."* One cannot be certain. Perhaps the poet here is moved by sentiments of feudal honor or dynastic loyalty rather than love of France. It is more likely all three were present, as they were in similar outbursts of emotion much later. Still, until the thirteenth century, expression of such consciousness of nation was rare, and it would continue to be for a long time. When men identified themselves, they were still likely to think of themselves first as Christians, then as subjects of a particular lord, and only third as members of a distinct nation.[24] Loyalties could be strong in the early Middle Ages but, just as nations were then barely more than visible, the sentiment of nationalism was scarcely more than incipient. The development of the sentiment would be slow, would await (1) the building of nation-states that by their actions penetrated the lives of the individuals subject to them and (2) the development of cultures that enabled and fostered common consciousness of heritages and hopes. Indeed, as one of the greatest students of the Middle Ages declared, "The growth of national sentiment was hardly possible [even] among the most educated men. All that survived of culture worthy of the name took refuge till the twelfth century among a fraction of the clergy" whose legacy included "the use of Latin, an international language, with the facilities for intellectual communication which flowed from it, and above all the cult of the great ideals of peace, piety, and unity. . . ." [25]

For the early formation of nations at least three conditions were necessary: (1) not only the growth of the secular state,[26] (2) but also the weakening of the authority of the universal church and faith as well as that of local feudal lords,[27] and (3) development of communication. As the authority of secular and incipient national states increased, that of spiritual religious and feudal lay lords decreased. As communication developed, so did common languages and literatures, consciousness of them, and hence consciousness of common pasts, interests, and hopes.

But how, more specifically, did nation building, as it came later to be called, proceed? The forces that led to the establishment of nations cannot be precisely isolated, enumerated, and evaluated, for they were many, intertwined, and variously effective. It can, however, be said at once that royal families, the dynasties which were, at their beginning, but major feudal families, played a significant if not the greatest role as they sought and obtained territory, wealth, prestige, and power.[28] In France and England early, and later in Germany, Italy, Russia, and nearly all other European countries, they acquired extensive lands and established rule over diverse peoples. Although they were originally hardly more important than other noble families, during centuries of astute aggrandizement they established the monarchical states and governments that gradually became national. If René Johannet, a pioneer French historian of nationalism, exaggerated, he was not basically wrong for much of Europe when he declared, "The cause of the statue is not the marble, but the artist. In the case of nationality, it was primarily the dynasty." [29]

The earlier dynasties and very likely the later as well did not think they were building nations. The feudal lords who became kings in France and Britain sought to enlarge their personal domains, to gain authority over them, to increase their incomes, and hence to augment their own power and glory. With varying but still great success, they acquired land and subjects through war and conquest, diplomacy and duplicity, marriage and purchase, legal and illegal confiscation, and fortuitous circumstance. With extraordinary though varying persistence, they extended and strengthened their authority through royal laws and levying of taxes, through royal military forces and royal bureaucracies—elites of officials and lawyers—and through reduction of the authority of lesser lay and religious lords of feudal society and the Catholic church. In time their kingdoms became national kingdoms and the "crown" the visible symbol of the nation-state, of the nation itself.[30]

The process is most obvious in France from the reign of Philip Augustus (king, 1180–1223) to the final consolidation and apotheosis of monarchical rule of Louis XIV (1643–1715).[31] During this nearly five-hundred-year period, the Capetian kings and their Valois and Bourbon successors, slowly pushing out from the Ile de France, acquired in piecemeal fashion nearly all the provinces that became modern continental France and established direct if not always effective royal control over them. One acquisition led to another, each acquisition increasing the power of the central monarchy compared to that of its rivals. As the monarchy won territory and gained subjects, it obtained greater wealth, more diversified resources, more influence, and greater power to act.[32] The original domain of the Capetian kings, around Paris, was chiefly agricultural. The acquisition of Normandy (1203–04) and other provinces opened the lower Seine Valley and outlets to the channel (Manche) and the Atlantic Ocean, while the acquisition of the southern Midi (1226–71) brought wealthy southern towns and finally an outlet on the Mediterranean.[33] When the dynasty obtained (c. 1286) the rich northeastern province of Champagne, it attained another center of trade, another major trade route, and became richer than most of its rivals. Control of rivers brought increased trade and communication between the peoples. The language and customs of the center of the kingdom spread and tended to become dominant as royal rule extended itself farther and farther and the king's laws made themselves felt through his royal officials.

The process was halting. Territory once gained was often lost again in war or bargaining, given away to a son, a favorite, or as a dowry to a daughter. But while the French kings were sometimes incompetent and weak, they were often either shrewd or had wily advisers. They were so successful, in fact, that some French historians, especially those of royalist persuasion, have seen divine or mystical forces at work.[34] They also had, it is true, almost unbelievable fortune. How else, unless it be their biological potency, can the circumstance that the Capetians had male heirs in the family and hence no serious dispute over succession for three hundred years be explained?

The detailed history of French dynastic expansion need not be retold here. Nevertheless, because it illustrates how an early nation came into being, it is worth some further attention.[35] Toward the end of the twelfth century Philip Augustus decisively began the building of France in ways that were to become typical.[36] Through marriage (Elizabeth of Hainault) and by force of arms, he obtained Artois and the counties of Amiens, Vermandois, Valois, and Montdidier. With the excuse that the English King John, his vassal, would not appear at the French court to answer accusations, Philip confiscated John's fiefs on the continent—Normandy, Anjou, Maine, Touraine, Poitou, and Saintonge.[37] He then also took the county of Alençon on the death of its lord, Robert IV. Thus Philip controlled the valleys (and the trade) of major rivers, the Seine, the Oise, the Somme, covered Paris to the west, opened communication to the sea on the north and west, controlled, nominally at least, provinces running through the west of France to the Loire and beyond to the Garonne.

Subsequent kings through late medieval times, from Philip III (1270–85) through Charles VIII (1483–98), added peaceably or forcibly nearly all the rest of what is now France except scattered lands to the north and northeast.[38] When the Capetian line ran out in 1328, only the Holy Roman Empire provinces of Dauphiné, Franche-Comté, Provence, Alsace, and Lorraine, the feudal provinces of Burgundy, Brittany, Guienne-Gascony, and Flanders, and scattered minor cities and fiefs were partially or wholly outside the jurisdiction of the French monarchy. And Dauphiné was purchased in 1349.

Several times during the Hundred Years' War (1337–1453) the French monarchs, now of the Valois family, seemed about to lose all or much of their domain. But in spite of repeated defeats, they eventually pushed their English rivals almost off the continent, took the last important English possession, Guienne, and remained in control of now much expanded territory. When the Valois Louis XI ascended the throne in 1461, feudalism might have reasserted itself and the kingdom broken up; indeed, one great lord, the Duke of Burgundy, could have become more powerful than the King. But Louis was both shrewd and capable. He crushed less able feudal opponents such as the Duke d'Alençon, the Duke de Nemours, and the Count d'Armagnac. And, fortunately for King Louis, the overly ambitious Duke of Burgundy was killed in a battle against the Duke of Lorraine. Louis then took possession of much of Burgundy through confiscation, diplomacy, and betrothal of his son, later Charles VIII, to a Burgundian princess.

The next Valois territorial objective of importance was Brittany. In the so-called "Foolish War" of 1486–88, the Duke of Brittany, Francis II, was defeated and compelled to promise he would not give his daughter in marriage without the consent of the French king. When the Duke died soon after, Charles VIII saw the opportunity. Whoever married the daughter, Anne, would obtain Brittany. While the future emperor of the Holy Roman Empire, Maximilian, bargained for Anne's hand, Charles secretly negotiated marriage for himself. That Anne was forty and he was only twenty-one made no difference. Land meant more than a woman. The prize was Brittany and the enlargement of the royal territory and power.

For the next half century the French monarchs vainly tried to expand farther, particularly in Italy, while defending what they had already acquired. For another half century weak rulers, internal dissensions, and disputes over the succession to the throne rendered expansion impossible. Even the man who restored order to the kingdom, Henry IV (1589–1610), the first Bourbon, could do little more than validate and consolidate some of the claims of the monarchy. Not until the rule of Richelieu (1624–42) and the reign of Louis XIV did territorial accumulation of consequence begin again. Intervening in the Thirty Years' War, Richelieu increased the royal territory by the Three Bishoprics and Alsace (except Strasbourg). Through four major wars against much of Europe and through not always clever diplomacy, Louis XIV pushed France's frontiers still farther north and east, gaining part of the province of Flanders, Franche-Comté, and a few cities—Strasbourg and Dunkerque being the most important. With the exception of Lorraine, acquired in 1766 on the death of its ruler, the father-in-law of Louis XV, and minor border rectifications, the European territory of the French nation was complete. The "national" frontiers of France—the Alps, the Pyrenees, the Rhine, the Atlantic—could now become "natural," though they had been attained by means other than nature—by force, guile, marriage, inheritance, purchase, and luck. In state building, as in other human affairs, success brought success.

The role of dynasties in building the territorial foundations of other European nations may not have been as decisive as it was in France, but nearly everywhere, in the west and then in central, eastern, and southeastern Europe, dynasties shaped kingdoms (or had kingdoms shaped around them) that became nation-states.[39] St. Stephen (997–1038), greatest ruler of the Arpad dynasty, established foundations in Hungary on which successors would build. In England from 1066 the Norman, Plantagenet, Tudor, and Stuart kings, with the aid of the English Parliament, brought all England under control of the central government and the separate peoples of Ireland, Wales, and Scotland under the royal crown if not under effective control. Later, the Romanov dynasty in Russia, the Hohenzollern in Germany, and the House of Savoy in Italy played differing but vital parts in the shaping of their nations. In general the dynasties were not nationalist in any modern sense: they did not try to create nations, but to enlarge their own state's power. They could and did, however, use national feeling as it arose to consolidate their hold on their subjects and to obtain their subjects' support in wars with other sovereigns and lords.[40] But while the kings were not nationalists, they were building foundations on which nations arose.

As the dynasties extended their domains they created agencies for governing their territory, the personal, executive, legislative, judicial, and administrative staffs of officials (bureaucracies) that would represent the monarch throughout the kingdom, make his will felt, keep records, and thus provide for continuity in government.

It was not, it must be reiterated, nationalism that motivated the kings, but the desire to establish and to strengthen their own sovereign states. If one word can be used to characterize their policies and actions, especially those of the Tudors in England and the Bourbons in France, it would be *étatisme,* the use of the state's power to strengthen the state, in this case the dynastic or monarchical state. When and if kings thought of the nation, they thought of it as existing in them, and what was good for them was good for their subjects. Probably no ruler, not even Louis XIV, said, *"L'état, c'est moi,"* but Louis XIV did say, *"La nation ne fait pas corps en France; elle réside tout entière dans la personne du roy."* [41]

In order to retain and gain power, the kings had to have officials who worked more or less directly for them. They had to obtain monies through taxes and these had to be levied by a king's central government. They had to establish royal armies and navies that were stronger than those of feudal rivals, and they had to make laws and erect court systems that were superior to all others within their realms. In short, they had to establish stable and powerful governments, and this is what they tried to do, and in the long run they were successful.[42]

The royal and later national governments were established in different ways in each country. In early Norman England, but not in France of the same period, all vassals were directly responsible to the king and, except in border lands, did not possess the rights to administer high justice, coin money, or wage private war. Later in England the nobility and upper middle class shared the royal power more than was the case in most countries, while in France the monarchy, with its allies from the middle classes, played a more significant role, the aristocracy usually opposing centralizing tendencies. So far as the nation-state was concerned, the result was much the same. As the royal central government became more extensive and powerful, the governmental bases of the nation were being laid down.

In England the kings from the Norman William the Conqueror (1066–87) to the Stuart James I (1603–25), though they at times were forced to share their power with a parliament representative of the upper classes, used their ancient feudal rights as well as their military might to strengthen the central government.[43] William the Conqueror, treating England as a feudal property, forced all fief holders to swear allegiance directly to him. He collected the facts for the old Danegeld tax in a survey so closely made "that there was not one single hide nor rood of land nor . . . was there an ox, cow or swine that was not set down in the writ." Henry II (1154–89), though no trueborn Englishman, made possible the continued growth of English common law by enlarging the power and scope of the royal courts from the *royal curia* on down, thus reducing those of the local, feudal, and church courts.[44] He began the practices of regularly using juries and of sending down itinerant justices to enforce the royal laws, and their decisions were a significant source of the developing common or universal law of the realm. While his judges were as much interested in collecting royal revenue as in enforcing justice, the royal central government was strengthened in either case. In pressing need of revenue, he succeeded in levying royal taxes upon all personal property and incomes. In 1170 he summarily "removed from office all the sheriffs," reappointed only a few, and subjected all of them to royal inquest, and thus made clear that it was he who governed England.[45] And in his Assize of Arms of 1181 he commanded what weapons all Englishmen should possess for the royal service, thus reducing the power of the nobility and enhancing his own. Henry II thus "left England with a judicial and administrative system and a habit of obedience to government." [46] Henry III (1216–72) continued to send down royal commissioners, the "General Eyre," to examine the financial and judicial business of the shire officials. In order to get taxes for his war with Philip IV of France and expand his own royal power, Edward I (1272–1307) called what was later termed the "Model Parliament," and this parliament was the prototype of the body that much later became the chief organ of the British national government and largely took the place of the monarch in unifying Britain. Under Edward also there were the beginnings of English statute law, which, among other things, restated and more precisely defined the feudal real property laws and made them uniformly applicable to the whole kingdom.[47] Edward III (1327–77) appointed justices of the peace to interpret royal law and justice in every county; these royally appointed officials by Elizabeth's time concerned themselves with nearly all local legal matters from petty offenses to the building of roads and the enforcement of the poor law.

By the close of the medieval period the English monarchy had strengthened the central government, established national institutions, begun English national law, and created a class of governmental lawyers and officials who were always interested in protecting and advancing the interests of the royal nation-state. More important here, it had taught English people to look to the central government rather than to lord or priest for protection and security. If the "King's Peace" was indifferently enforced, it was better than any the lesser feudal lords could offer. Hence, under royal aegis the nation-state in England was on its way to acquiring unlimited sovereignty. Even when opposition to the monarchy's absolute power arose, as in the reigns of John (1199–1216) and Henry II, when English constitutional government may be said to have its beginnings, the result was to stimulate interest on the part of the nobility and burgesses in the central government, a government that was primarily royal but that could become national.

The Tudors in the sixteenth century completed the edifice of royal national government, though the first Stuart king, James I, was to provide the most reasoned argument for royal absolutism by divine right. Henry VII's (1485–1509) "Star Chamber" made the royal power everywhere feared if not respected, and it brought order if not always justice after the anarchic years of the Wars of Roses. Henry VIII (1509–47) founded the Royal Navy, which was to become the chief instrument of England's power throughout the world.[48] What is of even greater importance for the growth of the nation, he broke with the Roman Catholic church and established an English or Anglican church and religion. This break had been long in coming. Popes and kings had disputed their respective powers in England since the twelfth-century reigns of Henry I and II and the struggle over royal jurisdiction of the clergy. The statutes of *Provisors* (1351) and *Praemunire* (1353) in Edward III's reign had stemmed the influx of alien clergy and forbidden appeals to papal courts. During the latter part of the fourteenth century John Wyclif (?–1384) had advocated a national church. And the lands and wealth of the church had long been much coveted by the crown and nobility. In the 1530's, for both personal and political reasons, and with much support from all classes, Henry VIII made himself "Protector and Only Supreme Head of the Church and Clergy of England." Probably the national interests were not uppermost in Henry's mind; nevertheless, his action established a national church. England was now largely independent of foreign control. Another stone had been laid on the foundation of the English nation-state. When James I claimed for the throne absolute dominion over England, he was but rationalizing what the Tudors had done.

Though the details differ, the French monarchy established authority over its lands and peoples in similar ways. From about the twelfth century, if not a little earlier, the kings began to institute royal governmental institutions and controls. They established, at first on a small scale indeed, royal direct and indirect taxes, asked that payments in kind or service from their domains be commuted into much more convenient money payments, and sent collectors to the provinces to gather their revenues.[49] With their now somewhat assured and permanent income, the French kings were able to hire soldiers and eventually to set up a royal standing army. No longer dependent upon the old unreliable and divisive feudal levies, they became not only more independent than they had been but also stronger than other feudal rulers.[50] Hoping to make their laws prevail, they established royal courts such as the *parlements* above those of the feudal lords and the church, and made appeals to these courts possible from anywhere in the kingdom. They employed lawyers to substantiate and extend the royal claims to territory and power.[51] On occasion they convoked (first in 1302) a representative body, the Estates-General, which, while it would lack the power (over finance, especially) of the English Parliament and would not meet at all from 1614 to 1789, would one day, in 1789, become a national body and declare that it represented the nation. With great difficulty the kings forced all vassals to be directly responsible to them and to give up most of their governing functions. At last, in the seventeenth-century civil wars of the Fronde, they, or, rather, their chief ministers, Richelieu and Mazarin, almost completely broke the political power of the nobility, and, through royal agents, the intendants made royal presence felt throughout the kingdom, even in local affairs. As in England, the peace and order the French kings were able to impose on their kingdom were far from complete, but there were order and peace much of the time within their realm.

The royal quest for power extended to the Catholic church and clergy. From the beginning of the fourteenth century French monarchs contested the claims of the pope in France. During the first years of the fourteenth century, Philip IV (the "Fair") and his lawyers (Guillaume de Nogaret, for one) attacked Pope Boniface VIII, because Boniface declared the king could not tax the clergy without the pope's consent and asserted that princes were subject to the pope in temporal as well as religious affairs. The conflict between the French rulers and the papacy lasted centuries. While the French kings did not break with the Catholic church, they gradually established jurisdiction over the clergy and a "Gallican" rather than a "Roman" Catholic church through measures such as the Pragmatic Sanction (1438), the Concordat of 1516, and Louis XIV's "four Gallican articles," all of which reduced or attempted to reduce the power of the papacy in France while giving the French monarchy greater authority in French church affairs. During the first half of the seventeenth century the monarchy suppressed the embryo state within a state that the Protestant Huguenots had been allowed to establish.[52]

Even Louis XIV, the most powerful and glorious of monarchs, was not able to end diversity of interest and establish unity in France, but the French monarchy had brought all Frenchmen more or less under its rule and built the governmental structure of the nation-state.[53] And royal rule, both kings and subjects believed, had the sanction of God. The kings were not only the state incarnate; they were also the "visible image of their invisible creator," and, as both, their subjects owed them obedience and loyalty.[54] They were indeed sovereigns of territory and of people, and this territory and this people were separate from and independent of other territories and peoples.[55]

Monarchical authority never, of course, went unchallenged. In France the monarchy, especially when Louis XIV was king, ruled through its own enormous power as well as reigned by the will of God. But even in the France of Louis XIV the church was not as subject to the royal state as it was in England;[56] vestiges of feudal privilege remained especially in the outlying provinces, and these provinces retained some of their ancient rights of government. In England during the seventeenth century the Stuart kings were forced to share power with the national Parliament that represented the upper classes, were in fact deposed for twelve years by Parliament and the Puritan General Cromwell, and after 1688 the monarchy became increasingly subordinate to Parliament.

As the famous international jurist Grotius (1583–1645) recognized in his book *De jure belli ac pacis* (1625), in western though not always in central and eastern Europe, the monarchical states were becoming sovereign and supreme. At the same time they were becoming national in the support they received from their subjects, in the extent of the power of their states, and in their relations with other states. One of the greatest authorities on the seventeenth century, G. N. Clark, summed up what was happening when he wrote, "Energies which had previously been controlled from a variety of centres—feudal, ecclesiastical, communal, or what not—were becoming polarized about the state. . . ." And the conception of the sovereignty of the national state "had been completed by jurists and political theorists . . . had almost established its domain in international and municipal law." [57]

In most other European countries the royal families established central governments that would become national in the same way, though at a later time. In Brandenburg-Prussia, which became the nucleus for Germany, for example, Elector Frederick William I (1640–88), King Frederick William I (1713–40), and King Frederick II (the "Great," 1740–86) during the seventeenth and eighteenth centuries laid the foundations of universal military service, general liability in taxation, and a compulsory school system. These the nineteenth-century nationalist historian Treitschke would accurately call "the three-fold group of general civic duties by which the people of Prussia have been trained in an active love for the fatherland." [58]

Louis XIV told his grandson the Duke of Burgundy that the nation resided entirely in the person of the king.[59] In a contemporary sense he was right. In his reign as well as during the reigns of many earlier and contemporary monarchs the interests of the people, if considered, were believed to be the same as those of the monarch, and as the sovereign the monarch was synonymous with if not actually the state. But before a nation could come fully into being there had also to be a people who consciously possessed some common customs and ideas, some common history and hopes, and who themselves participated in national affairs.

During the same centuries that the monarchs of France and Britain were establishing what were becoming nation-states, other forces were arising which would both evidence the trend toward the national organization of society and further stimulate national feeling. Certainly among the most significant of these was the gradually developing belief that the inhabitants of a country should pursue a common economic policy. This belief, to be sure, was already incipient in some of the monarchical economic measures, those concerning royal taxes, for instance. It was also true that monarchs such as Philip the Fair and Louis XI in France and Edward III in England had attempted to control shipments of goods out of their kingdoms. But as a conscious and expressed policy it would develop somewhat later than the idea of monarchical supremacy. Only in the seventeenth century would the idea of a common economic policy become generally accepted and fully practiced.

About 1436 an English bishop of Chichester, Adam de Moleyns, outlined a plan for English commerce and a navy to protect it, foreshadowing the future policy that was to contribute to England's commercial greatness. He wished to "cherish merchandise, keep the Admiralties, that we be masters of the Narrow Sea." [60] The idea took hold. The English monarchy and its supporters followed it. About 150 years later Richard Hakluyt published a classic exposition of the view—with not the "Narrow Sea" but the whole world in his purview—the *Principall Navigations Voyages Traffiques and Discoveries of the English Nation*. His purpose was not only to recount but also to foster interest in the commercial development of England. It was, he began the preface to his second edition, "for the benefit and honour of my Countrey" that he had "zealously bestowed so many yeres, so much traveil and cost, to bring Antiquities smothered and buried in darke silence, to light, and to preserve certain memorable exploits of late yeeres by our English nation atchieved, from the greed and devouring jawes of oblivion. . . ." [61]

With De Moleyns and Hakluyt appear the preconceptions of the seventeenth-century state economic policy that came to be called mercantilism. Though mercantilism was primarily conceived as a way of strengthening the state and monarchy, it was also a national policy.[62] The ideas behind the policy promoted the national interests and at the same time they afford us additional evidence of the growing national consciousness. In search of power, western European states, as in the France of Louis XIV and Colbert, attempted to build and control economic life within the country and all trade with other countries. As they molded internal economic life through governmental assistance and regulation, they reduced or destroyed feudal, provincial, guild, and municipal restrictions upon agriculture, commerce, and industry, and thus tended to make national rather than local interest paramount. They assisted national trade by royal or parliamentary edict, by building national systems of communication,[63] and by aiding agriculture and business through bounties. At the same time they tried to so regulate foreign trade, with measures like the English Navigation Acts of the seventeenth century, that the home country had a favorable balance of trade and thus became richer (according to the current theories of wealth), while foreign countries had to ship out their precious metals and thus became poorer. The states, therefore, in the economic as well as the political spheres, now combated the "medieval combination of universalism and particularism." [64] As they did so, they tended to centralize and unify the internal economic activities of each country and, at the same time, to divide and set off the interests of each nation from every other nation. Though the end was state power, the means had to be national. The states had to strengthen their nations economically to be strong, and they had to try to weaken other like nation-states so as to be comparatively stronger. The result was stronger national states, more stress upon common national interests, and great consciousness of nation and the loyalty owed it.

The political and economic trends toward the creation of the nation, of course, reflected or were part of the whole historical development in western, and to a lesser extent in the rest of, Europe. Common group cultures were taking root and these, as people became aware of them and desired their growth, would further accentuate national feeling. In middle and southern Europe, in Germany and Italy in particular, the emergence of national cultures preceded actual political unity to a greater degree than was true in western Europe. But as with the chicken and the egg, it is impossible to tell which came first. Politics, in fact, is as much a part of culture as language and religion. In general the common cultural characteristics took form during the same centuries as political unification proceeded and as the monarchical governments extended their hold upon domains and peoples. As each group developed its common culture, its language, its religion, for example, it usually grew more and more conscious of them and more desirous of a sovereign central government.

The exact time of the emergence of what later became national languages cannot be determined.[65] In their spoken form the western European languages and most of the other European languages were beginning to emerge by Charlemagne's time, though not for centuries were they often to be thought of as national tongues or to be commonly used by some of the peoples within what would become the separate nations.[66]

During the twelfth to fourteenth centuries in western Europe the trend toward national languages became clearer. Then in France and Britain, as well as in the regions that would in the future become Spain, Italy, and Germany, both the spoken and written languages were assuming more definite modern forms and becoming so widely understood and used that they might, somewhat inaccurately, be called national.[67] As the common people spoke, during the long medieval centuries, they established common patterns of speech; these were fairly clear for extended areas in western Europe by about 1200. And as the intellectuals increasingly thought and wrote in the vernaculars from about the same time, they tended to determine and fix the more exact forms of the languages. Dante (1265–

1321), though he did not so intend, made it likely that Tuscan would become Italian when he wrote the *Divine Comedy* in that dialect.[68] As poets and storytellers like Cavalcanti, Petrarch, and Boccaccio wrote in Italian they fixed the language ever more firmly. The fifteenth-century Renaissance humanists might again stress classical Latin. The writings in Italian and the customary speech of the commonalty prevailed.

In France the *langue d'oïl* of the court, Paris, and surrounding regions began to obtain some pre-eminence in the eleventh century.[69] Writing in French began principally in the twelfth and thirteenth centuries when long versified narratives like the *Brut* and the *Rou,* the satire *Roman de la Rose,* Villehardouin's *Conquest of Constantinople,* and Joinville's *Life of Saint Louis* were written. Historians in France, it might be noted, often began to use the vernacular earlier than historians elsewhere.[70] The first official documents in French appeared about the middle of the thirteenth century. In 1539 by the Ordinance of Villers-Cotterets the official administrative language became French instead of Latin.

The story in England parallels that in France, though the literature in the vernacular starts somewhat later. Out of the East Midlands, the dialect spoken in Oxford, Cambridge, and London became the English tongue while the use of French and Latin tended to diminish. In the second half of the fourteenth century Langland's *Piers Plowman,* Chaucer's *Canterbury Tales,* and many of Wyclif's religious pamphlets appeared in the vernacular, and Wyclif with others translated (completed in 1388 after Wyclif's death) the first English Bible.[71] By 1375 William Nassington could note:

> But lerid and lewid [learned and ignorant],
> old and young
> All understanden English tongue.[72]

About the same time English was beginning to be taught in the schools. John of Trevissa noted in 1385 that "in alle the gramere scoles of Engelond, children [now] leveth Frensche and construeth and lerneth in Englische." [73] And in 1362, because French was "much unknown in the said realm" of England, the city of London petitioned for and Parliament passed a statute requiring that all pleadings and judgments in all courts including Parliament itself be in English.[74] By 1450 English instead of Latin or French had become dominant in legal documents and was used by all classes as their customary tongue, though the historical chronicles remained for the most part in Latin until Tudor times.

Thus the foundations of the western national languages were well built just before the use of movable type in printing made possible the wide diffusion of books. Printing made it likely that the already developed languages would find wider and wider acceptance until they actually could be said to have become national.

By the sixteenth and seventeenth centuries the vernacular tongues had won a clear victory. The use of Latin, except in church documents and services and to some extent in the universities, declined rapidly all over western Europe. In France writers like Ronsard (1524–85) and Joachim du Bellay (1525–60) not only wrote in French but praised and defended it, while the translator and publisher Henri Estienne (1531–98) satirized the use of Italian words by Frenchmen and extolled the excellence of French.[75] Across the channel Sir Thomas More, the Christian humanist, wrote his *Utopia* (1516) in Latin, but there also most writing was now being done in the native tongue. At the end of the sixteenth and the beginning of the seventeenth century the "glories of the English language" were being shaped in the comedies, tragedies, and poems of Shakespeare, in the authorized (1611) King James translation of the Bible,[76] and a generation later in the prose and poetry of Milton. The uses of the English tongue led directly to loyalty to it, just as had been the case in France with French. An English antiquary, Richard Carew (1555–1620), was so enamored of his native tongue that he thought it superior to all other languages, "most full of sweetness" because of its "substantialness . . . delightfulness . . . fullness, finesse, seemliness . . . portliness . . . currentness . . . staidness." [77]

In the seventeenth century French became, even more than English, a definite, fixed language when the classic writers Corneille (1606–84), La Fontaine (1621–95), Molière (1622–73), and Racine (1639–99) wrote their plays and fables. In 1694 the French Academy, itself an evidence of growing national feeling, began its monumental dictionary of the French language. Voltaire was right when he wrote, *"C'est dans le siècle de Louis XIV que cette éloquence* [the French] *a eu son plus grand éclat, et que la langue a été fixée."* [78]

To say that the general and basic forms of English and French were fixed and that the languages were generally used is not to assert that French and English were everywhere spoken and understood in the respective countries even by the seventeenth century. Though many circumstances, especially the influence of the royal governments' laws, armies, and taxes, encouraged the use of the common language, widely differing dialects and even different languages were used by sizable minorities in both lands. A Parisian might still need an interpreter at Marseilles, and the poet Racine, traveling in the provinces, could not make himself well enough understood to obtain *"un vase de nuit."* [79] Nevertheless, national languages had evolved and they provided one more basis for national unity and consciousness. [80]

The potential significance of the emergence of national tongues for national consciousness and unity was seldom apparent to contemporaries. Few demanded that all who spoke the same language be within the same political grouping or believed that a common language should be a major social or national tie. But that the significance for the nation-state was coming to be realized is shown by a reported speech of Henry IV of France to deputies of newly acquired provinces: "As you speak the French language by nature, it is reasonable that you should be the subjects of a King of France. I quite agree that the Spanish language should belong to the Spaniard and the German to the German. But the whole region of the French language must be mine." [81] In spite of the absence of much evidence, it probably can be inferred that the already developed language differences served to sharpen the incipient national consciousness while dawning awareness of a common language stimulated some feeling of national unity.

It would be a mistake, nevertheless, to assert that the development of common vernacular languages within groups of people in western Europe before the eighteenth century indicated a high degree of national feeling, just as it is wrong to see in the language differences the sole key to modern nationalism. National languages grew; they did not originate by divine command in a Tower of Babel. They slowly grew out of older languages, out of contact with other contemporary languages, and out of the everyday experiences of the common people, as well as the refinements and uniformities introduced by scholars and writers. They also developed because the monarchs and their governments tended to force a common tongue upon their peoples with their laws, taxes, and armies. They won speakers because the peoples found it convenient in their political, economic, and social lives to have a common tongue. Once a language was well established and came to be used for writing, it grew of itself, became habitual. Usage stimulated more usage. [82] But it was long before patriots realized that language could be used both to unify and to separate peoples.

Language is a chief distinguishing mark of nationality; it is only one element in the emergence of nationalism. In point of fact the sentiment could later develop where a common language was not present, as in Belgium, where two languages have lived side by side for hundreds of years.

And sometimes the sentiment has not evolved among peoples who use the same language, as in Britain and the United States, or Spain and Argentina. Probably language differences help explain why national consciousness arose, but more than a common language was necessary before consciousness of nationality could be widespread.

The growth of national feeling can be measured in part by the emergence of national religions and churches, as has been indicated. Here again the danger of overemphasis arises; the national religions may be as much result as cause. The splintering of the traditional (for western Europe) Christian faith and Catholic church in the sixteenth century was perhaps less an effect of national feeling than a stimulus to more. If, however, the Roman Catholic church had not lost its power and appeal, modern nationalism might have been weaker and less prevalent. Conceivably a world-state based upon religious principles could have arisen. But when the church no longer held the predominant place in men's lives, they sought security and salvation elsewhere—in the monarch, in the nation.[83] Calvinism, with its emphasis on calling and duty, probably reinforced the desire of converts to be good citizens and serve the country. Some Protestants, especially those of the more emotional groups, like the Pietists of Germany, transferred to the nation much of the enthusiasm and loyalty their ancestors gave to the church.[84] But Catholics as well as Protestants would become national patriots.

The medieval Roman church held its doctrines to have universal application. At the same time it had wide territories to administer. For administrative purposes—for government and for the collection of dues and donations—it had to divide these into districts. These were called, for example, Gallia, Germania, Italia, and Anglia. The districts sometimes roughly corresponded to areas that later became those of national states. Within each district the administration tended to centralize and unify.[85] In this way even the universal Roman church contributed to the rise of nations. The ethics and the laws of the church, however, were equally applicable to all who acknowledged the church. The faithful could equally achieve earthly blessing and heavenly salvation regardless of the district in which they happened to live, regardless of their "race" or nationality.[86]

Serious historians debate whether the Protestant revolt against the church was at all based upon national grounds. Dynastic and feudal materialistic interests, intellectual enlightenment, and spiritual dissatisfaction were probably at least as significant. One profound modern scholar, Ernst Troeltsch, failed to see any connection whatsoever between the establishment of national churches and the principle of nationality.[87] Nevertheless, national sentiment in some countries contributed to the establishment of national churches and encouraged the nationalizing of religion. The national churches, once created, encouraged further national consciousness. While Protestantism in itself was not inherently nationalist, most Protestants wanting their own religion to become universal, the revolt denied the established universal creed. It accentuated national habits of thought and speech and, by so doing, it enabled the nation to take the place of the church as the instrument of salvation and as the chief object of earthly loyalty.

Some of the reformers, like Luther (1483–1546), simply preached the supremacy of the prince or state over the church.[88] This was a kind of *étatisme*, not nationalism. While Luther spoke of German interests as opposed to Italian and preferred to speak and write German rather than scholarly Latin, he was scarcely a nationalist.[89] But until his kind of secular supremacy was achieved, the nation-state could not fully command supreme allegiance.[90] A few of the early reformers went further. John Wyclif, far in advance of his times, wanted a national church subordinate to the national state.[91] The Hussite leaders of Bohemia came close to identifying their religious cause with the national interest. Appealing for aid in 1420, they cried that the Emperor "wishes to despoil us [the Bohemian people] of our salvation, foist upon us his heretical creed as proclaimed in Constance and lead us to damnation. Should you, despite it all, wish to take his side, we should be forced to believe that you also favor the extinction of the Bohemian nation and to treat you, with God's help, on a par with the Lord's and our nation's public enemies." [92]

The identification of religion and nation occurred clearly in the seventeenth-century Puritan revolt against royal Catholic absolutism in England.[93] From their study of the Old Testament and their own deep sense of righteousness, the Puritans drew the conviction that Englishmen, like the ancient Hebrews, were a chosen people. To Cromwell (as well as Milton), the English, and of course he meant the Puritan English, were "a people that have had a stamp upon them from God; God having, as it were, summed up all our former honour and glory in the things that are of glory to nations, in an epitomy within these ten or twelve years last past." [94]

Other early reformers who protested might or might not have been so motivated by national loyalties.[95] When in the early 1530's Henry VIII broke with Rome, he was not thinking so much of English as of his own interests. Yet national interest and religious feeling often became identified. This was especially true where the Protestants, such as the Presbyterians, insisted upon individual and local group responsibility for human action and its consequences. No longer for most Protestants was there a priesthood and a central divine representative on earth to intervene for them with God. They had to make their own life, their own future. While they approached God directly for their souls' salvation, they increasingly turned to the state, to the nation, as a source from which all earthly favors could flow. A new way to a kind of mundane immortality was thus opened to them. As the German nationalist Fichte declared much later in his *Addresses to the German Nation* (1807), an individual could now find permanence "promised . . . by the continuous and independent existence of his nation." [96] Men had had in western Europe the guaranty of the authority of the universal church. When this was challenged and shaken, they could gain a sense of belonging and a feeling of security from a new authority, the nation-state.[97]

Of course, the Protestant revolt was not alone accountable for the loss of a universal spiritual authority or for the increasing importance of the nation-state. Probably it was another phase of the trend toward secularization of society. Once successful, however, it tended to accentuate the similarities among the peoples within each of the dynastically formed nations and to sharpen the external differences among them. The various state churches had national heads, national administrations. They usually supported the monarchical governments, which were becoming national governments, and strengthened the hold of these governments upon their peoples. And they were, at the same time, one more cultural force fostering national cultural uniformity and unity.

The national and reformed churches increasingly employed the vernacular in sermon, ritual, and hymn and thus spread the use of the national tongues.[98] The most important book for most Protestants, the Bible, was translated and published and read in these languages rather than in Latin. The German of Luther's Bible became to a large extent the literary as well as the spoken language of the people in north-central Europe. The English of the King James version, the "King's English," fixed still further the language of Wyclif and Shakespeare for Englishmen. In Sweden and Denmark the publication of Bibles in the vernacular helped establish what are now Swedish and Danish.[99]

To assess exactly the influence of these Protestant usages upon national consciousness is impossible. National consciousness was emerging in all western Europe, in Catholic as well as Protestant countries.[100] It was a French Catholic king, Philip the Fair, who, as mentioned, quarreled with Pope Boniface VIII (1294–1303), denied the authority of the papacy in crucial matters of salvation and taxation, dealt the papacy an almost fatal blow when he established at Avignon a French pope "surrounded by a French court," and began a "captivity" of the popes which lasted seventy years. The "Gallican liberties" of the fifteenth and later centuries were national liberties of the French Catholic church only a little less indicative of a desire for independence from Rome than the series of acts that separated the Church of England from the papacy. But whatever the effect of Protestantism, it was not negligible. If nothing more, religion, then as now, supplemented and reinforced other beliefs and prejudices. This was especially true during the wars of the time. The wars of the sixteenth century were usually dynastic and religious in origin. But as they were fought, they became, like the wars of the seventeenth century, increasingly national, with religion contributing to the feeling of national differences on the one hand and national unity on the other. Protestant Englishmen could kill Catholic Spaniards more zestfully because they were both Catholic and Spanish. The Dutch fought for their independence because they were both Dutch and Calvinists opposing Spaniards and Catholics, as well as because they wished to trade without Spanish controls and resented absentee taxation. And much of the Irish national opposition to England resulted from Irish Catholicism's opposition to English Protestantism.

Dynasties were establishing the territorial and governmental bases of the nation; national languages were taking form; national religions were coming into being. Universal church, religion and empire, and atomistic feudalism were alike losing their hold upon the individual and society. All this does not prove, except through tenuous deduction, that national consciousness and loyalty were either widespread or intense. In his play *Saint Joan*, George Bernard Shaw dramatized the Hundred Years' War by having a nobleman declare to a chaplain, "Men cannot serve two masters. If this cant of serving their country once takes hold of them, goodbye to the authority of their feudal lords, and goodbye to the authority of the Church. That is, goodbye to you and me." But if a fifteenth-century nobleman thought this, he was a prophet looking perhaps two hundred years ahead.

Of what the common people were thinking or believing we know little. They were for the most part illiterate, and there were no public-opinion polls. It is chiefly when they committed violent acts, as in the peasant revolts, that we are aware of their ideas at all. On the basis of what little evidence they left we may fairly guess that they were seldom aware of national issues, had little if any interest in them, and possessed little national feeling. The hard facts of their daily lives took all of their attention. When they thought or acted in groups it was only on a local scale, for family, for their village, or perhaps against their lord. If in thought or action they went beyond the confines of the narrow community, it was only because some high authority like the church or monarch compelled.

On the other hand, much isolated evidence can be collected to show that national consciousness was sometimes appearing among the nobles and the bourgeoisie, and among the poets and officials who sprang chiefly from them and may have represented their views. Occasionally individuals exhibited a high degree of national feeling, and the number who did so was growing.

From the twelfth century a persistent historian can pick out expressions of national feeling and distinctiveness in official documents and the growing volume of literature. The royal dynasties and their bureaucracies created more and more documents;[101] these, which sometimes signified the rise of common interests, were later considered to be national and would be stored and ordered in the national archives created in nearly every nation. Literature, not at first thought of as French or English or of any national origin but as universal, later also came to be considered part of the patrimony of national cultures. Indeed, as literature was increasingly written in the vernacular languages (and less and less in Latin), it in itself evidenced growing national consciousness. A careful scholar, however, is aware that expressions of national feeling were sporadic, occasional, and that the great body of literature was not particularly concerned with patriotism but with religion, politics, war, courtly manners, romantic love, and gossip.

Expressions of national feeling in western Europe become more numerous from the sixteenth century, become common during the late eighteenth century. Over the whole six hundred years from 1200 to 1789 they are more frequent during war than peace, but never, even during the French Revolutionary era, do they dominate literature. If these expressions are seen in context and not given undue emphasis, they may be used to demonstrate incipient though not full-grown nationalism. It would be unhistorical and quite wrong to argue that nationalism in its modern form appeared before the late eighteenth century or that continuous evolution of national feeling took place from the late Middle Ages to the eighteenth, or even to the twentieth, century.

In the late medieval period it is often difficult to isolate the national from other sentiments. The various loyalties fade almost imperceptibly into one another. The same individual might feel different loyalties, religious, feudal, and national, at the same time; one might be uppermost at one moment, another at another time. Few gave their loyalty deeply and persistently to the nation. Jeanne d'Arc, long the most sacred symbol of the French nation, was a Christian and royalist rather than a nationalist.[102] The one-hundred-per-cent patriot or integral nationalist was centuries in the future. Still, national feelings were slowly emerging, and the various attitudes that form modern nationalism were appearing, often separately and mildly, it is true, but appearing.

Dislike of foreigners, a feeling that appeared among old and primitive peoples, occurs early and is continuous. In human experience it probably has never been absent.[103] In the middle of the thirteenth century the chronicler Matthew Paris (1200?–59) evinced hatred for foreigners, reporting that the Spaniards were "the scum of mankind, ugly in face, contemptible in behavior, and detestable in their morals," and telling the most hair-raising and bloodthirsty tales of the destructive Tatars who were then overrunning eastern Europe.[104] A participant in the Fourth Crusade (1202–04) wrote the Pope, "It is very important for this business that the Germans should not march with the French; for we cannot find in history that they were at accord in any momentous common enterprise." [105] During the Hundred Years' War (1337–1453) especially, and throughout the numerous wars of the sixteenth and seventeenth centuries, like statements of national antagonisms are not difficult to find. The French and English were often bitter in their denunciation of each other. A French humanist and diplomat, Robert Gaguin (1433?–1501), was possibly as accurate as he was rhetorical when he wrote, "It would be easier to reconcile a wolf and a lamb than an Englishman and a Frenchman." And he could have been right when he said that he had heard of English children being given a bow and a figure of a Frenchman and told, "Go, my child, learn to kill a Frenchman." [106] The antagonisms so often expressed may not have been so much national as personal, and it is certain that they often arose out of the temporary discomfort of battle rather than any deep-rooted permanent prejudice. The fact remains that distrust and dislike on national grounds were taking root. François Villon (1431–146?), poet of the Parisian streets and taverns, was quite modern, though his figures of speech were medieval, when in his "Ballad Against the Enemies of France" he asked that they suffer the most awful torture, encounter monsters belching fire, and have molten coin poured into their bellies.[107]

Love of the state and native country appears equally early. As the state became more secularized, so, paradoxically, it became more and more the subject of a worship akin to the religious. During the late medieval period, possibly as early as the thirteenth century, the political community, for a few men, began to take the place of the church as a "mystical body" for which the individual might make the supreme sacrifice.[108] Henry of Ghent at Paris in the thirteenth century compared the "death of a citizen for his brothers and his community to the supreme sacrifice of Christ for mankind." A French poet of the same age, Richier, "styled the crown of France the most precious of all relics and declared that those who were killed in protection of the crown should be saved in life after death." [109] This high esteem for the state, particularly as it was personified by the monarch, became more intense in succeeding centuries, until by the seventeenth century kings like Louis XIV both demanded and often received worship from individuals of all classes.

Dante's love of Italy is well known. Petrarch's (1304–74) sonnets upon Italy reveal a deep attachment to native land:

> *Is not this my own nest*
> *Where I was nourished and was given life?*
> *Is not this the dear land in which we trust,*
> *Mother loving and kind*
> *Who shelters parents, brothers, sister, wife?*

and great sorrow for Italy's woes:

> *My Italy, though words do not avail*
> *To heal the mortal wounds*
> *That in your lovely body I see so dense*
> *I wish at least to let my sighing sounds*
> *With Arno and Tiber wail*
> *And Po, where now I sit in deep suspense.*[110]

At the beginning of the fourteenth century the chronicler Robert of Gloucester sang of England as a "right merry land, of all earth it is the best. . . ." [111] In 1380, to the French poet Eustache Deschamps, France was a *"pais tres doulz pour demourer."* [112] About the same time another French poet, Alan Chartier, who was also a royal official, revealed deep national patriotism as well as feudal fealty when he wrote, "After the bond of Catholic faith nature binds you above all else to the common welfare of the country (*pays*) of your birth and the defense of that ruler under which God has caused you to be born and to live. . . . And since this is the law that nature has established no work should be grievous for you, no hazardous adventure should be foreign to you if it supports this country and saves this ruler who sustains and nourishes you among the living and receives you in burial among the dead." [113] After the invasions and disorder of fifteenth-century Italy, Machiavelli (1469–1527) pleaded for a princely savior with a patriotic devotion to Italy that seems almost out of place in his hardheaded analysis of contemporary politics. "Italy left as without life, waits for him who shall yet heal her wounds and cleanse those sores that for long have festered . . . she prays to God to send some one who shall deliver her from these wrongs and barbarous insolencies." [114]

In the late sixteenth century Shakespeare occasionally revealed deep pride in England's strength as well as its natural beauties.[115] The bastard Faulconbridge concludes *King John* with the boast

> *This England never did, nor never shall,*
> *Lie at the proud foot of a conqueror. . . .*

And his Faulconbridge was willing to challenge "the three corners of the world in arms." Nothing could harm England if it "to itself do rest but true." To the bard's dying John of Gaunt (*Richard II*) England was "this royal throne of kings," "this other Eden—demi-paradise," "this happy breed of men," "this blessed plot." Shakespeare was not alone in his devotion to England. For the seventeenth-century Trimmer of George Savile (1633–95) the "earth of England" had "divinity in it and he would rather dye, than see a spire of *English* Grass trampled down by a foreign trespasser. . . ." The Trimmer thought there were "a great many of his mind, for all plants are apt to tast of the Soyl in which they grow, and we that grow here, have a Root that produceth in us a stalk of English juice. . . ." [116]

Pride in nationality is more difficult to find until the eighteenth century. It does not early seem to have been as prevalent as dislike of foreigner or love of native land. That such pride was incipient may be deduced from some of the preceding quotations, and in his *Praise of Folly* (1509) Erasmus remarked that such self-love was implanted in the various races.[117] On occasion it was overtly expressed. In Henry VII's time, for instance, one of the keen Venetian envoys declared that Englishmen believed no other men to be like themselves, that whenever they saw "a handsome foreigner" they thought he looked "like an Englishman" and that it was a great pity he was not.[118] About the same time and after Poggio Bracciolini's discovery of the manuscript of Tacitus' *Germania*, some German humanists, like Jacob Wimpheling (1450–1528), Konrad Celtis (1459–1508), and Ulrich von Hutten (1488–1523), began to speak highly of German character, especially its military virtues.[119] Hutten, who was not only a knight and a humanist but also something of a national patriot, wrote a poem entitled "Why the Germans Are Not Degenerate in Comparison with Former Times." [120] During the next century Milton (1608–1674) in his *Areopagitica* eloquently exhorted the Lords and Commons of England with his famous "consider what nation whereof it is ye are, and whereof ye are the governors; a nation, not slow nor dull, but of a quick, ingenious, and piercing spirit; acute to invent, subtile and sinewy to discourse, not beneath the reach of any point the highest that human capacity can soar to." And the great philosopher-mathematician Leibniz (1646–1716), ahead of his time in this as in other ideas, would soon be telling the Germans they were superior in the practical arts and sciences and that God gave them reason above all other peoples. [121]

There are still other ways in which the beginnings of national consciousness before the eighteenth century can be illustrated. The French Academy established by Richelieu and Louis XIV during the seventeenth century was so interested in France and French that it provided for detailed maps of France as well as for that massive dictionary of the French language that is still being compiled. [122] And Louis himself in 1680 established the *Comédie-Française,* still one of the glories of France, and gave it the then large income of 12,000 livres a year.

 Certainly one of the most significant evidences of rising national consciousness was growing interest in the writing of history. [123] It is, of course, quite impossible to determine exactly when the first history of a particular country appeared; so much depends on definitions. From the twelfth century histories or compilations were beginning to appear in the western European vernaculars as well as in Latin. [124] From the fourteenth century histories of dynasties, lands, and peoples appeared with increasing frequency, and more and more of these were in the national languages. The chronicles, annals, and histories written during the late medieval period in England and France are many. In one sense some of them could be called national histories. When they do not treat of the purely local affairs of, say, a monastery, they are often laudatory accounts of the rulers. Often they begin with the then believed myths concerning the origin of the country and come down through the reign of the king with which they are contemporary. Henry of Huntingdon (d. 1155?) wrote, for example, a *Historia Anglorum,* which starts with Caesar's invasions and ends with the reign of Stephen (1135–54). [125] William of Malmesbury, William of Newburgh, Ralph (Abbot of Coggeshall), Geoffrey of Monmouth, [126] Bartholomaeus de Cotton, the St. Albans historiographers Roger of Wendover and Matthew Paris, and many others wrote or compiled chronicles and histories of England and the English monarchs during the late twelfth and the thirteenth centuries. In France from the time of Louis VI (1108–37), of whom his chief minister, the Abbot Suger of St. Denis, wrote a biography, similar eulogistic chronicles and histories were compiled. From about this time and through much of the fourteenth century, the monks of St. Denis acted as semiofficial biographers of the French kings.

How much these histories were read or how great was their influence in creating a national spirit one cannot say. Since they existed only in manuscript and few copies were made, they were not widely known. For this reason and because they devoted most attention to the dynasty and local affairs, and not to the embryo nation, they probably do not evidence widespread national feeling, nor did they serve to create much consciousness of national unity. Yet these histories were often more than accounts of local feudal lords, and later more national-minded historians would draw upon them to create or re-create a common past for each nation. As Voiture, a French court wit and man of letters, surmised in 1636, when those who came later read history they would become enamored of their countries.[127]

Historians who might be called national with more accuracy than these early chroniclers appeared only with the vigorous intellectual life of the Renaissance. Just a few need be briefly mentioned by way of illustration. Paradoxically, an Italian humanist, Polydore Vergil (1470?–1555?), wrote one of the first modern national histories of England. Requested by Henry VII to write a history, he spent twenty-eight years of industrious research upon it. A greater sixteenth-century national history of England was William Camden's (1551–1623) *Remaines concerning Britaine*. Compiled out of "love of country," the book not only narrated the lives of the kings but also described "the country and its inhabitants, languages, names, arms, coins, clothing, high roads, towns and cities, natural scenery, and natural resources." [128] Camden was concerned not just with the customary details about the feudal dynasty but also with the affairs and interests of the whole nation. In the same spirit a group of English historians founded the Elizabethan Society of Antiquaries in 1572 to study and preserve old manuscripts. And five years later a William Harrison (1534–93) published a work with the significant title *An Historicall Description of the Iland of Britaine*.

In France numerous national histories appeared during the latter half of the sixteenth century. Those of Du Haillan, Du Tillet, Hotman, François de Belleforest, and Lancelot Voisin de La Popelinière might be mentioned.[129] The title of the work by La Popelinière is indicative of the trend toward treatment of the secular affairs of the country: *Histoire de France enrichie des plus notables occurrences survenues en Province de l'Europe et pays voisins, soit en paix, soit en guerre, tant pour le fait séculier que ecclésiastique depuis l'an 1550 jusques à ces temps.* While Italy was not unified, nevertheless it acquired a national historian in the sixteenth century when Francesco Guicciardini (1483–1540) followed his *History of Florence* with a *History of Italy.*[130] In long and boring sentences he chiefly treated the diplomatic affairs of the Italian states from the invasion of Charles VII in 1494 to the election of Pope Paul III in 1534. Though Spain was unified territorially but not culturally, it too obtained a patriotic historian in Juan de Mariana (1536–1624), whose *Historiae de rebus Hispaniae* was first written in Latin to acquaint Europe with Spanish history and then translated so that his ignorant compatriots could know Spanish history as well.

A list of "first" (or early) so-called national histories would be as long as a list of the peoples who became nations. In general they appeared earlier in western Europe than in eastern—and in Europe, with some exceptions (China), earlier than elsewhere.[131] In the Germanies during the early sixteenth century Jacob Wimpheling wrote his *Epitome rerum Germanicarum* and Conrad Peutinger his *Sermones conviviales de mirandis Germaniae antiquitatibus,* in which he claimed the "left bank of the Rhine was Germanic before the time of Caesar." [132] In 1555 Olaus Magnus, who has been called "the founder of Swedish historiography," published a large work on the Nordic peoples in order to show the superior accomplishments of the Swedes.[133] The "first" Lithuanian history about Lithuania was written in Latin by a Jesuit, Albertas Vijukas Kojalavicus (1609–72).[134] From about 1700 to 1750 Ludovico Muratori (1672–1750), a great scholar, labored mightily to compile sources on and write the history of medieval Italy in order to reveal the glory of Italy and demonstrate the continuity of its history. His twenty-eight-volume *Rerum italicarum scriptores* was one of the first major scholarly collections of "national" documents and served as a model for others.[135]

Perhaps the early growth of national consciousness is best summed up in the evolution of the word *patrie* or fatherland. For a good medieval Christian the Latin word *patria* meant as much the city of God as any place on earth. In St. Augustine's words, Heaven was the "common fatherland" for all Christians. During most of the Middle Ages in feudal France, for example, the word might denote the local province or town or village, but seldom the whole of France. While the old meanings of *patria* did not disappear, new meanings began to appear in the twelfth and thirteenth centuries. Occasionally men now applied it to the national kingdom and crown, and to these as a "visible symbol of a national territorial community" for which they were increasingly willing to die.[136] By the fifteenth century the French words *patrie* and *patriote* were introduced. Soon French humanists like Etienne Dolet, Guillaume Budé, Joachim du Bellay, and Rabelais were using the first to denote almost what the modern man means by "fatherland";[137] the *pays* (country) was becoming the *patrie*, and the *patrie* was beginning to signify not only the land where one was born and to which one was devoted, but also the people of which one was a member.

In the late sixteenth century, two hundred years before the French Revolution, an obscure Jewish rabbi of Prague, Loewe ben Bezalel, foreshadowed modern conceptions of national self-determination when he asserted "that every people has its own nature and its own character or form [*Gestalt*], that every people has a might of its own and ought not to be subject to any other people, that every people has its natural habitation and a right to live there, and that it must be granted to every people to choose its own God according to its own ideas." [138] In 1688, a century before the French Revolution, La Bruyère, a detached but critical observer of French life under Louis XIV, coined an aphorism that would be often repeated by eighteenth-century reformers who wanted a nation of citizens: "*Il n'y point de patrie dans le despotisme. . . .*" [139] But the foreshadowing of modern ideas by a few learned men did not mean that modern nationalism had arisen. Most people, as late as the eighteenth century, were seldom aware of nation and nationality, though these can be said to have come into being. The national welfare was not yet their paramount interest. Most men still had other loyalties, to church and religion, to kingdom and monarchy, to class, province, and village, which bound them much more strongly than those of nation. National governments did not yet try to regulate and control all life, and men did not yet primarily look to them for the solution of basic problems. Not until the latter part of the eighteenth century would nation and nationality become of supreme importance for most western Europeans. And until they did, nationalism cannot be said to have been more than incipient.[140]

III

The Nation Becoming People, 1715–1789

Nationalists are not born but made—by conditions, circumstances, training.[1] Gregarious by nature, men have formed and been loyal to many kinds of groups. In modern times the nation has become the dominant and highest group in which men live and to which they give their loyalty because ideas and institutions—the total cultural environment—have impelled them to live in and be devoted to a group larger than family, clan, tribe, or city, but have not permitted (or induced) them, with exceptions, to feel themselves part of an international or world society or state. For the past two to three centuries, national states, as they themselves were developing, have increasingly penetrated the consciousness and lives of people; people have increasingly participated, somehow and in some way, in national affairs, or at least, somehow and in some way, have shared national joys, hopes, tragedies, and fears; and people have, generally, come to identify themselves with their nation or have been expected to do so. In short, as governments, national governments, have influenced and controlled the lives of most men, as many men have, directly or vicariously, taken some part in national activities, and as many have identified themselves and their interests with their nation and its interests, many of them have become nationalist.

While anticipations of modern nationalism can be seen as early as the twelfth century, the first full development of modern nationalism occurred in western Europe during the eighteenth-century Enlightenment and the revolutions and wars of 1789–1815, when many Europeans, particularly Frenchmen, expected the coming of a new and happier order—became, in now current terminology, "expectant people." Articulate individuals within elite groups in England, hoping for a just commonwealth, had expressed strong nationalist sentiment in the seventeenth century, especially during the Puritan Revolution. The sentiment, of course, was not absent before the eighteenth century among other western peoples, the Dutch, for instance. During the eighteenth century a few intellectual leaders were beginning to express it in central Europe, in the Germanies and Italies, and even in eastern Europe, as in Russia.[2] It was also nascent in the North American English colonies from the mid-eighteenth century; and when these colonies revolted in 1776 and between 1776 and 1787 formed a nation-state, they constituted the "first new nation" established on the principle, enunciated later, of self-determination, a principle that became a major tenet of nationalism.[3] In general, both the ideas and practices of nationalism spread from western Europe and the United States to central and eastern Europe and South America during the nineteenth century and then, in the twentieth century, to the rest of the world. Usually, while nationalism appeared at varying times, it arose out of similar political, economic, and social conditions and pressures. But the hopes, fears, and hatreds arising out of the Enlightenment and the Revolution (1789–94) in France gave it much of its modern form and content. For this reason the emphasis in this and the next chapter will be on France, though much attention will be given to the nationalism developing in other countries. Indeed, it could be argued, with substantial evidence and reason, that the emphasis should be on England.

Both the events and the writings of the eighteenth century and early nineteenth century (to 1815) offer much evidence on the development of nationalism. In summary these show, especially in France but in degree elsewhere in Europe and the Americas:

1. Rising consciousness of national unity during the same time that other unities and distinctions, such as those of province, class, privilege, and religion, were weakening.

2. Mounting opinion that all propertied inhabitants, though seldom all inhabitants, were part of a nation and should have a voice in (participate in) the sovereign national government—that is, should be stockholders (citizens) with voting rights in the common enterprise, the nation.

3. Growing belief that the sovereign national government of citizens, not the king alone or perhaps at all, should perform the nation-state's functions and engage in nationwide political, economic, and social activities for the benefit of citizens.

4. Increased awareness of or desire for a national culture, that is, a common language, literature, education, and religion.

5. Rising belief not only that all (or all propertied) inhabitants were part of the nation and should share its responsibilities, but also that they

should be devoted to it, its heritage, its present interests, and its future.

6. Increasing emphasis on the right of each people (nation) to be independent and sovereign among nations, the nation taking the place of the sovereign monarch.

From the later Middle Ages, thinking about the nature of society increasingly took a secular turn. Machiavelli usually receives major blame or praise for this, but even in his own time he was one of many writers and actors who thought of the state and politics in terms of temporal and worldly causation and motivation. Secular interpretations multiplied during the next centuries. During the seventeenth century the Englishman Thomas Hobbes (1588–1679) wrote his *Leviathan* (1651), which justified the absolute sovereignty of a national monarch or parliament on the ground that human life was "nasty, brutish, and short," that men above all feared death, and that hence they had to give up, contract away, their natural right of freedom to obtain peace and order. Toward the end of the century John Locke (1632–1704), taking quite a different view of human nature—that it was neutral and could be improved through education—imagined that men created their states by contract among themselves in order to protect their natural rights of liberty and property. Neither Hobbes nor Locke wrote about nations and nationalism as such, but they both wrote within the framework of the English nation, and they and others laid secular theoretical foundations for modern nation-states.

In France, about a half century later, Montesquieu (1689–1755) wrote his famed *L'Esprit des lois,* in which he attempted to show that "men are governed by many things: climate, religion, law, the maxims of government, the example of past things." No more than Hobbes or Locke was Montesquieu an advocate of nationalism, but he directed his thought to what ought to be the nature of national government. Its laws, he declared, "ought to be fitted to the physical conditions of a country, to its climate . . . to the nature of its soil, to its situation [among nations] and extent, and to the way of life of its people." [4] About the same time that Montesquieu was writing, an obscure philosopher in Naples, Giovanni Vico (1668–1744), developed secular explanations of the history of nations in his *Scienza nuova,* a big rambling book little known until the nineteenth century. Each nation, he thought, went through the cycle of childhood, youth, and old age, ages that could be characterized as the priestly and brutish, the heroic, and the civilized.

Belief that God's will determined the origin and nature of nations did not disappear, but major explanations now stressed need, physical nature, natural law and rights, and history rather than religion. In one temporal way or another, through force, by contract, or through long historical development, men had established states, and in the eighteenth century this came to mean nation-states.

This, or so it was believed, also meant that men could create peaceful, rational societies. Belief in this possibility was by no means universal, but, with the encouragement of the new Newtonian science of the physical universe and the new Lockean science of society, leaders of thought in western Europe expected steady progress. Belief in progress became, in fact, an integral part of the climate of opinion not only of the elite but also of followers. Expectancy was high. Progress could be expected, would come through enlightened rule. Life would become less "nasty, brutish, and short," happier and more peaceful, through the efforts of enlightened rulers, through the joint efforts of these rulers and their peoples, who, becoming citizens, would participate in and benefit by wise reforms, or, as it would eventually come to be believed, through the efforts of these citizens governing themselves. Fewer and fewer seem to have thought that a happy earthly future would be achieved through the church or the old feudal order, and most of those western Europeans who expressed themselves thought the instrument would be the nation-state.

Conceptions of the nature of the nation-state did not change overnight. Through much of the eighteenth century the king, or the king and subjects, was thought to constitute the nation. Even in the twentieth century the idea of a monarch as the symbol of the nation was not dead—at least in Britain and a few other countries. Still, from the mid-seventeenth century in Britain and from the time (1715) of the death of Louis XIV in France, conceptions did change and fundamentally.

As early as 1710 a clever archbishop, François Fénelon (1651–1715), who was an enemy of the King's Bishop Bossuet, and concerned about the unfavorable position of France in the then current war, voiced an opinion indicative of the change to come. "The affairs of the King," he wrote, "are violently becoming ours . . . the nation must save itself." [5] Fénelon was ahead of his time but not far ahead. A well-known chancellor of France, Henri d'Aguesseau (1668–1751), a reforming lawyer but no revolutionist, in a panegyric on Louis XIV before the Parlement of Paris (highest law court) in 1715, asked whether "love of country" was not "an exotic plant" in monarchies, a plant that grew happily and produced precious fruit only in popular states, republics. He seemed to answer his question when he said that in the latter "each citizen" regards the well-being of the state as his own, and this makes of all citizens a single family all of whose members are "equally interested in the fortunes and misfortunes of the fatherland." [6] In his *The Spirit of Laws* (1748) Montesquieu likewise noted the close connection of love of fatherland (which he called "virtue" and equated with "love of equality") and the republican form of government.[7] A few years later (1754) the Marquis d'Argenson, a friend of Voltaire, wrote in his journal, "National opinions prevail and could lead far. Never have the words nation and state been so often repeated as today. These two words were never used under Louis XIV; no one even had the ideas. Never have people been so informed as they are today of the rights of the nation and of liberty." [8]

D'Argenson was right in substance but not in detail. The words had been used, but they were now being more and more used and new meaning put into them. While to conservatives the *patrie* still usually meant the king and his subjects, as a journalist in the *Mercure de France* observed in 1765,[9] now the subjects, as part of a family, had an interest in the *patrie*'s, the nation's, affairs and were to be consulted. The nation's laws, argued the aristocratic Parlements (law courts) of Toulouse and Rouen, had to have the "free consent of" or be accepted by the nation.[10]

The transition in meaning in both France and England is well illustrated by the English Tory and friend of Voltaire, Viscount Bolingbroke (1678–1751), in his two essays of the 1730's, *The Idea of a Patriot King* and *On the Spirit of Patriotism*.[11] "The service of our country," Bolingbroke declared, "is no chimerical, but a real duty." Every citizen who was a *real patriot* would bend "all the force of his understanding, and direct all of his thoughts and actions to the good of his country," that is, "to the good of the people," "the ultimate and true end of government." Duty to country, Bolingbroke—who was no democrat—believed, could be best performed in a limited monarchy and by an aristocracy. In England a constitutional king, completely devoted to his "country's interests," together with those who were gifted with a "larger proportion of the ethereal spirit" (the aristocracy, of course), should preserve and guide "human kind." The "true image of a free people," for Bolingbroke, was "the patriarchal family, where the head and other members are united by one common interest, and animated by a common spirit." [12] The patriarch's, the king's, interests were not just his alone. While the king could "most justly esteem" the nation's wealth "to be his wealth, the power his power, the security and the honour, his security and honour," he ought to govern only in the interest of the nation. All Englishmen, on the other hand, were dutybound to give service to their country and would find in it their greatest glory, the fullest use of their lives.[13]

Bolingbroke's "spirit of patriotism" was not, in his mind or in the minds of other aristocratic writers, a spirit to be equally shared by all, and not all the inhabitants of a country were to share equally the duties and privileges of citizenship. To him and to others, nevertheless, the nation was not just a monarch and his subjects, nor was the purpose of national government just the promotion of narrowly dynastic interests. The national interests were becoming increasingly identified with those of at least the people who possessed the "ethereal spirit"—and property.

Nor was Bolingbroke's concern for patriotism just that of an isolated, frustrated statesman turned philosopher. The concern was widespread in England and France and beginning to be expressed in the Germanies and in the American colonies. A student of John Locke and a philosopher in his own right, Lord Shaftesbury (1671–1713), found true morality in a balance between egoism and altruism that men could achieve through their innate moral sense. Of all human affections he thought the "noblest and most becoming" was the "love of one's country." For "a multitude held together by force," he argued, was "not properly united," did not "make a people." It was "the social League, confederacy and mutual consent, founded in some common good or interests," that joined "the members of a community and made a people one." Absolute power killed the public spirit, and when there was no public spirit there was "in reality no mother country or nation." [14]

Shaftesbury wrote as the eighteenth century was beginning. Through the century, and especially from the mid-century, interest in patriotism deepened. In 1755 an enthusiastic clerical, the abbé Coyer, published his *Dissertations pour être lues, la première sur le vieux mot Patrie, la seconde sur la nature du peuple*. Expressing rhetorical surprise and anger that the word *patrie* was no longer used, he contended that everyone—judges, priests, women—owed his first duty to the *patrie* and that soldiers should be taught to die for the public, the fatherland's good.[15] In 1758 an anonymous author published a book in Zurich entitled *Vom Nationalstolze*, in which he caustically discussed the good and bad aspects of national pride.[16] In 1765 one of the few German patriots of the time, Friedrich Karl von Moser, coined the phrase "national spirit" when he published his essay *Von dem deutschen Nationalgeist;* and later he collected expressions of German patriotism in his monthly journal, *Patriotisches Archiv*.[17] In 1762 a French writer, Charles Pierre Colardeau, wrote a poem called "*Le Patriotisme,*" seven years later a lawyer named De Rossel published a *Histoire du patriotisme français* . . . in six volumes, and in 1771 Philip Freneau, then a student at Princeton and later a friend of Jefferson, wrote a "Poem on the Rising Glory of America." During the years 1760–80 the French Academy held competitions for, and there were written elsewhere, eulogies of famous patriots such as Michel de L'Hospital, Bayard, and Colbert.[18] In 1787 the Academy of Châlons-sur-Marne offered a prize for a paper on "the best means of reviving and encouraging patriotism in a monarchy." [19]

So many efforts were made to encourage patriotism that one wonders why it needed encouragement. The plain facts of the matter were that men had differing interests and loyalties, that when they were interested in patriotism their ideas of what constituted patriotism differed, and that hence debate ensued. A pious monarchist, Le Fevre de Beauvray, wrote a paean to his *patrie* in a *Dictionnaire social et patriotique* in 1769, saying he owed to his fatherland his existence, his education, his ideas, and therefore he was responsible (*comptable*) to it.[20] He was not alone in his piety or his monarchism, but the meaning of nation was coming to include all the people who lived in the country, spoke the same language,[21] and therefore should have the right to be consulted on, to participate in the nation's affairs.

Grimm, the German literary critic who corresponded with the best-known writers of western Europe, asked why the abbé Coyer was so surprised that the word *patrie* was not used. He gave his own reply: since orphans could not rightly use the word, it was "necessary to continue to declare we serve the king and the state and not the *patrie*." [22] Actually the family of words stemming from the Latin *patria* was entering more and more into common usage.[23] This was because more and more western European people, those of the articulate elite, at least, were more and more considering themselves members of their nations and coming to believe they should have a voice in national affairs. Again and again writers quoted La Bruyère's aphorism, "There is no *patrie* under despotism." [24] Only in free states, cried the romantic Rousseau (1712–78), where a citizen felt active responsibility for his group, would men be lifted out of their selfishness and inertia, for men acted only in their own interests. When men had freedom, then and then only would they be motivated to act, and then the intoxication of patriotism (*ivresse patriotique*) would be born.[25]

The *Encyclopédie* of Diderot, that massive compilation of eighteenth-century knowledge and opinion, summed up advanced thought on the nature or what ought to be the nature of the *patrie* in its article on the word.[26]

The *patrie* . . . is the land that all the inhabitants are interested in preserving, that no one desires to leave because he does not wish to give up his happiness. . . . It is a nurse who gives milk with as much pleasure as she receives it. It is a mother who loves all her children [and treats them equally, whatever their condition], opens all roads to the highest positions, who does not suffer any misfortune to happen in her family [except those unavoidable, sickness and death], who believes she has done nothing unless she has improved the wellbeing of her children. It [the *patrie*] is a power as old as society, founded on nature and order, a power superior to all others . . . to kings, a power which requires submission to its laws from rulers and ruled. It is a divine being who accepts offerings only to distribute them, who demands more affection than fear. . . .

This is the *patrie*. The love given it leads to high morality and this leads to love of fatherland. This love is love of the laws and of the prosperity of the state, a love particularly strong in democracies. It is a political virtue in which an individual surrenders his own interests, preferring the public interest to his own. It is a sentiment, not a consequence of knowledge. The lowest man of the state as well as the head of the republic may share it.

The *patrie*, ironically, had become the mother of the family. But the family, significantly, included all the children, and, as the *Encyclopédie* also said, they were members of a "free state," the "laws of which assure our liberties and our happiness."

This definition of the *patrie*, when it was written, was an expression of hope rather than actuality. After the revolutions in 1776 in the United States and in 1789 in France it was not quite so visionary, for nations composed of people who were citizens, not subjects, were emerging.

By 1789 opinion in France still favored the monarchy.[27] Nevertheless, the nation—for *patrie* and nation were now given much the same meaning —had come to be identified with people who resided within its borders and shared the same language and views—or at least with the propertied portion of these people.[28] The nation, the people, was thus taking the place of the monarch as the sovereign, the highest legal entity, and as the symbol and reality of unity and power, was itself becoming the object of loyalty.[29] The sovereign "general will" of Rousseau's *Contrat social* (1762) was becoming the national will that he was later so concerned to establish in his *Considérations sur le gouvernement de Pologne* (1771–72). In actuality it was only through the nation-state and its government that reform could be effected, that peace, order, and freedom could be established, or so it was thought. In actuality, and in the long run, too, it was only when, Rousseau asserted, each person put his person and his power in common under the supreme direction of the general (the national, though he did not often use the word) will that the social contract was truly carried out.[30]

The philosophic basis for the revolutionary proposals and acts of 1789–92 was, it is generally agreed, prepared by the enlightened, (both the rational and the romantic) thought of the eighteenth century. It is not so well realized that the instrument for achieving change was to be the nation itself, people protesting and participating in *their*, the nation-state's, affairs. That this was true the pamphlets and cahiers of 1788–89 supply ample evidence.

Perhaps a thousand pamphlets were published in France during 1787, 1788, and early 1789, partly in response to the governmental request for information, partly out of concern for the perilous state of France's affairs, and partly in hope of a new order. They were not written to promote nationalism nor were they directly concerned with theories about the nature of nations. They revealed, nonetheless, strong and growing national sentiment.[31]

Of the many ideas in the pamphlets two are relevant here, the beliefs (1) that the people were the nation and hence it belonged to them, (2) that their will should be the national will and determine national policy. The opinion of the lawyer Lacretelle has already been quoted: "As everything is possessed by them [the sum total of citizens], everything belongs to them." [32] This was, later, the common view of the revolutionists.

The most influential pamphlet of 1789, often cited but seldom read today, was *Qu'est-ce que le tiers état* by the abbé Sieyès. His opinions may be taken as those that were ultimately to prevail in democratic nations.

The Third Estate [the people] embraces everything belonging to the nation, and anything that is not of the Third cannot be regarded as being of the nation.

In every free nation, and every nation should be free, this is only one way of ending differences concerning the constitution. Not by turning to the notables but to the nation itself.

The nation exists before all, it is the origin of everything. Its will is always legal, it is the law itself.

Nations on earth should be conceived as individuals outside the social bond, or, as in a state of nature. The exercise of their will is free and independent of all social forms. Existing only in the natural order, their will needs only to possess the *natural* character of a will. In whatever manner a nation wills, it suffices that it does will. All that it wills is right and its will is always the supreme law.

What is the will of a nation? It is the result of individual wills. . . . It is impossible to conceive of a legitimate association which does not have for its object the common security, the common liberty, in short the public good.³³

Four years later, in 1793, at the height of the Revolution, Robespierre's definition of the *patrie* carried out the full implication of the ideas of Lacretelle and Sieyès. "What," he asked, "is the fatherland if it is not the country where one is a citizen and a member of the sovereign? The word fatherland in aristocratic states . . . means something only for the patricians who have usurped sovereignty. Only in a democracy is the state truly the *patrie* of all the individuals who compose it, and able to count as many interested defenders as it numbers citizens." ³⁴

In 1788–89 there was little or no opinion that France should have a revolution to overthrow its monarch, and general agreement that France was a monarchy. On the other hand, the old formula, "What the happiness of the people demands, the King wills," which the comptroller general Calonne voiced in speaking to the assembled notables of France in 1787, no longer promised enough. A nation of citizens was being born and it was their "will," the national will, that should determine how "happiness" could be achieved.

The over 25,000 cahiers (lists of grievances and proposed reforms) prepared by assemblies all over France in the early months of 1789 at the request of the troubled royal government reflected this national will. These cahiers, prepared on different (preliminary and general) levels and by different kinds of groups, contained quite diverse views and were certainly not unanimous in expressions of national sentiments. Many of them, especially those prepared by local assemblies, were chiefly concerned with practical questions, such as taxes and feudal dues or roads and bridges. Many on every level dealt with class and provincial privileges, and by no means all were opposed. Some of them repeated the high-sounding phrases as well as the demands of the "model" cahiers sent out from Paris.³⁵ But, whether chiefly concerned with national or with local affairs, the cahiers in themselves were a massive outpouring of national sentiment (and protest) for immediate action by the royal, *now* becoming the national, government in Paris. The strength of nationalist views expressed in the general cahiers has been analyzed by Dr. Beatrice Hyslop. She found that only nine per cent (of about four hundred) expressed no nationalism, and classified the nationalism in the others as twenty-one per cent "conservative," thirty-four per cent "intermediate," twenty-three per cent "progressive," and twelve per cent "radical." This kind of analysis, of course, becomes meaningful only in terms of concrete ideas. France was, if the diverse opinions in the cahiers may be summarized, a monarchy, but the representatives of the nation in the Estates-General should have legislative power and its consent was necessary for taxes and loans. All national citizens possessed rights, of liberty, property, and security of person, and the state should guarantee these to them. Sometimes the cahiers, especially those of the Third Estate, advocated specific national legislation that would strengthen national interest; the Third Estate of Toulon, for example, asked that the debt of the state be declared the "national debt." Occasionally, nationalist views were very strong: "It is necessary," declared the Third Estate of Nemours, "that there be no state within a state, no body that can cause trouble or raise money by authority independent of the *patrie*, and without accountability to the people itself." [36]

The monarchical, the dynastic idea died hard. Yet the French nation by 1789 was becoming, in the minds of many who wrote and spoke, a collective but single being, a family above king, clergy, nobility, province, manor, or village. Its instrument, the nation-state, could do anything the nation itself willed. It could wipe out all distinctions lesser than citizen and demand loyalty higher than any to order, to province, or to monarchy.[37]

And more. As the citizens were the sole arbiters of the nation, so the nation was independent of other nations.[38] Just as the king had been sovereign within his domains and he and his domains were independent of outside control, so now the nation was sovereign and independent. Citizens not only constituted the nation; in their collective national activities they were not subject to any control beyond their own will. In 1793 Carnot, the French organizer of victory, put accurately in words what was becoming generally believed and coming into practice as well: "Actually the nations are among themselves in the political order what individuals are among themselves in the social order." [39] Until 1792 and the world wars of the French Revolution and Napoleon began, this did not mean that a nation had a right to do as it pleased, or to force its views on other nations, by war if necessary. Until 1792 the nationalism expressed in France as elsewhere was generally "humanitarian," as Carlton Hayes well described it. National patriotism did not *then*, as a *Dictionary of the Constitution* put it, call for "hatred of men who are not born our compatriots. . . ." It was "not exclusive love for the bit of the earth where we were born," it was "affection for a country ruled by just and humane laws, where it is permissible to love and admire all men who so merit, whatever their country, customs, or religion." [40]

Each citizen possessed rights and privileges within the nation, and each nation had the right to determine its own destinies. If these fundamental assumptions were accepted, groups of men could acquire a common fatherland. They were legitimate children of a distinct family, no longer orphans, as Grimm had declared them, and they could be devoted to it, that is, to their nation, in the way Grimm had implied they should be. During the 1770's the very serious economist-statesman Turgot (1727–81) told Louis XVI that the orders of France were so engrossed by their personal (class) interests that no common interest was apparent, that hence the monarch had to do everything himself.[41] Turgot himself was so concerned about the lack of common interest that he proposed a plan of public education in which the "study of the duties of the citizen would be the basis of all other studies." [42]

But especially from 1776 and 1789, when revolutions occurred in the American colonies and in France, there was increasing awareness of common interests.[43] Citizens then came to possess common interests, the national interest, which was but their own. When they acted patriotically to perform the public duties, they were but serving themselves. National patriotism could now be as deep as the citizen's interest in his own welfare, for his welfare was synonymous with that of his country. As Alexis de Tocqueville later remarked of the United States, patriotism grew by "exercise of civil rights, and in the end, it is confounded with the personal interest of the citizen. A man comprehends the influence which the prosperity of his country has upon his own welfare; he is aware that the laws authorize him to contribute his assistance to that prosperity, and he labors to promote it as a portion of his right. . . ." [44] Even in those countries where kings continued to reign, they now had to do so in the name of the nation. The monarchical interests, as Fénelon had long before remarked of Louis XIV's, were violently becoming the common interests of the people.

The revolution in realization of common interests came first in opinion. Practice followed, first in England, the American colonies, and France, and then later and always in varying fashion in the rest of the world. In England a king was beheaded in 1649 because he thwarted the will of the dominant Puritan group that considered itself the nation, and from 1689 propertied Englishmen constituted the nation. While the monarchy still symbolized the national unity, it was severely and increasingly limited by the will of the propertied, who, realizing they had common interests, acted as if they were the nation. American colonists of property threw off the rule of their legitimate monarch in 1776 and, though some of them were first tempted to establish a monarchy, created a constitutional republic in 1787 that represented the common interests at least of the leaders. From this time onward in the United States the national will, if often shaken, always remained supreme. In France the king was at first, in 1789–91, limited by a national constitution made by the propertied representatives of the nation, then guillotined in 1793 by a National Convention. While one or another type of monarchy was three times restored in France until 1870, nearly all the rulers governed because of not God's or their own but the national will. Even when new rulers attempted to rule absolutely, they felt it practical to consult the nation in a plebiscite or were forced to grant a national charter.

Not only were the kings limited or overthrown. The ancient royal and clerical institutions and functions—the armies, the churches, the educational systems—would become national.[45] In the France of the late eighteenth and early nineteenth centuries, what had been by divine right the king's, the noble's, or the priest's actually became the nation's. In other lands, in the Germanies and Russia, the monarchies continued to play a dominant role. But in these countries as well the rulers could no longer ignore the national will, and in much of Europe the nationalizing of institutions and ideas proceeded during the nineteenth century at almost as swift a pace as in the western lands.

Popular nationalism was thus part of the general movement toward republicanism and democracy, of the revolt against monarchical, aristocratic, and clerical domination. The national idea and the nation-state became the instruments through which men could obtain liberty and pursue happiness. The chancellor D'Aguesseau had asked in 1715 if love of fatherland was to be found only in popular states. The answer of many later intellectuals and political leaders was "yes." They agreed with the seventeenth century's La Bruyère that there was "no fatherland under despotism" and they supported the seventeenth-century epigram of Saint-Evremond that "love of fatherland is truly love of self." When the nation-state could afford protection, rights, and privileges, then it became possible for more men to feel themselves part of it, to become involved in its affairs, to love it and fight for it, to become citizens.[46] And as the national state acquired more and more functions, national feeling deepened and widened. The nation became the being, the entity, even for some numbers of the upper classes, through which the individual obtained what he wanted, a symbol standing for liberty and property, and an institution that could triumph over the arbitrary rule and aristocratic privilege that threatened property and denied liberty. When the *patrie*, the individual's own nation, became something, then he owed it something.[47] Private interest became public; national virtue and the public, the national good became synonymous with the individual welfare of loyal citizens.

Though in western Europe national sentiments and loyalties increasingly prevailed, other group sentiments, loyalties, those of class, for instance, did not disappear. And though national patriotism was becoming more pervasive, highly influential thinkers gave their primary devotion to mankind, were as cosmopolitan in their sympathies and loyalties as any men have ever been.

During the eighteenth century, to 1789 in France, nobles and clergymen (especially the high) possessed much wealth and held positions of power and prestige. They *were* the *first* two orders, and many of them continued to put the interests of their orders first and tenaciously clung to their ancient feudal and clerical privileges.[48] If they seldom won the love and loyalty of lesser men, they did command respect and wield influence. It was, indeed, the legal aristocracy in France who made the demands that led to the calling of the Estates-General.[49] The cahiers of 1789 were full of complaints about privileges, but few of any class advocated abolition of all of them, and some asked that they be confirmed, especially their own. Occasional cahiers, too, often asked that the old and separate privileges of provinces and cities be maintained or, if lost or diminished, be reasserted. It is conceivable, though not probable, that even in the France of 1789 older unities and loyalties, feudal and provincial, might have prevailed (at least a while longer) had the king's, Louis XVI's, government been a little stronger and if leaders of the clergy and nobility had been a little more astute. Outside France the privileged classes generally maintained their power and privileges and their class loyalties much longer, and these loyalties are still not extinct, even in France.

What was true of the aristocracy was also true of dynastic rule and loyalty. In the long run, devotion to the nation superseded loyalty to a monarch. But the monarchical form of government, with reduced powers and prestige, to be sure, persisted, and dynasties still had devoted followers in the twentieth century. In 1792–93 the French overthrew and guillotined their king, but the Bourbon dynasty was restored from 1815 to 1830, and as late as the 1870's almost restored again. There are still monarchists not only in Spain but also in France.

Among western European intellectuals of the eighteenth century the old Graeco-Roman Stoic belief in the common nature, problems, and destiny of man took on new life. Then as now the cosmopolitans who gave their loyalty to man rather than to groups of men were subjected to ridicule. Asserting that there were no longer any Frenchmen, Germans, Spaniards, or Englishmen, Rousseau accused the cosmopolitans of boasting of their love for all the world in order to enjoy the privilege of loving no one.[50] Nonetheless, a few of the best minds of western Europe, philosophers, poets, and playwrights, saw their family as mankind and their country as the world (they meant European civilized society). They were or professed to be not "narrow" patriots, but citizens of the world. While their views differed in detail and arose from different premises, Shaftesbury, Goldsmith, and Hume in England, Montesquieu, Voltaire, Diderot, and Helvétius in France, Lessing, Kant, Goethe, and Schiller in the Germanies, and Franklin and Jefferson in America tried to be above national prejudice, to think in terms of universal goals and values. When they believed in reason, which most of them did, they believed in universal natural law, they advocated rights and duties for man (not national men), and they pleaded for tolerance, friendship, and peace[51] among all peoples. Though some of them saw nations as the way of ascent to a higher international society, others viewed national patriotism as a stupid prejudice leading to hate and war. With Goethe they believed, "Above the nations is humanity," and with Montesquieu (and Marcus Aurelius) they might think any act a "crime" which, though it might benefit their family or their country, would "cause evil to Europe and to mankind in general." [52]

Just how deeply national sentiments penetrated the consciousness of "ordinary" men in France (and western Europe) during the eighteenth century there is no way of knowing—of what they really thought, there is little record. From the scattered bits of information (as in French police records) available, but one generalization seems possible: the "common man"—the peasants, the majority of the people, and the city workers, a small though growing minority—was almost exclusively occupied with the personal and local problems of his daily existence, his bread, his family, and how he could "get by" another day. Rousseau, who had so many opinions on so many subjects, did express concern for the common people. Asking how they could be virtuous, he replied: by making them love their country, by allowing them to enjoy civil security, and by protecting their property, lives, and liberty.[53] But Rousseau's was an isolated voice. When, shortly before the Revolution, the influential Swiss banker Necker, who was then comptroller general of France, feared too great an absorption "in the badly understood virtue" of patriotism,[54] probably he was not even thinking of the "common" people. The word patriot, it is true, was coming to mean everyone "who in a free government cherishes his fatherland, is devoted to his fatherland, or more precisely to the public welfare." [55] But it is clear that those who wrote and had influence thought only propertied people—those who paid taxes—could have a valid interest in national affairs, be true citizens, for only they possessed a stake in the nation. Voltaire, who was no friend of the common man, expressed a dominant view with his usual clarity: "When those who possess like myself, fields and houses, assemble for their common interests, I have a voice in this assembly. I am a part of the community, a part of the fatherland." Only those who owned property, he believed, had a *patrie* and should have a voice in common affairs.[56] Not all the people, then, constituted the nation, but only those who owned its wealth, and it was their representatives who should determine what was to be done, for they represented the sovereign national will.

This will was on its way to becoming omnipotent, even more powerful than the will of the seventeenth-century divine-right absolute monarch. Through a national government it could not only wipe out distinctions of class and province; it could also act to effect the interests and realize the hopes of the citizens, establish and protect their rights, legislate for the general welfare, which was synonymous with the well-being of the individual citizens. In short, it could and should provide for, in Jefferson's eloquent phrase, "life, liberty, and the pursuit of happiness." In most European countries the national governments during the next century and a half would in actuality be much limited in their activities by historical custom and by the opposition of conservative forces and loyalties, some of them deeply rooted in the feudal and religious past. The power of these governments, too, would be limited in other ways, by the slowness of communication and by the inability or unwillingness of their bureaucracies to act. But in spite of the various limitations, the scope and reach of national governments were extending to all phases of life. Especially during internal crises and wars but in peacetime as well, these governments would be able to penetrate the consciousness of their citizens and make them aware of, if not always loyal to, their nation.

In France and England the nation in ideal, not actuality, had become people. When they participated and obtained rights and privileges, the nation's interests became theirs. Generally they did become devoted to their nation and increasingly they identified themselves with it, that is, became nationalists. This was the way to realize their hopes and protect themselves against dangers.

To all the important questions of "why" things happen as they do, history contains few certain answers. To the question of why nationalism developed in the eighteenth century as it did, the answers are several and most of them debatable.

One general and obvious answer is this: the very magnitude of the problems faced by eighteenth-century western societies compelled larger than local, that is, national, solutions. Populations were increasing, and at the same time individuals were being brought closer together by slowly improving means of communication. As trade increasingly flowed beyond provinces, so ideas increasingly circulated beyond courts and capitals. The problems, actions, and ideas of Bordeaux were becoming less and less isolated from those of Paris, those of Manchester less isolated from London, those of Charleston from Philadelphia. Hence national unity and loyalty provided *the* ways of solving the common problems of people brought together by geographic proximity, economic interest, and similarities of culture.

While this general answer might not be seriously challenged, it needs explanation in detail as well as amplification in meaning. When these are attempted much more debate is likely, for firm causal relationships are difficult to establish.

Behind the development of the national idea were the beliefs or myths that God had, as Bossuet thought, created the nations as he had all things, or had chosen nations to carry out his will, as Milton believed of his English nation. These interpretations continued, though eighteenth-century *philosophes* usually substituted nature for God. Nations and national love were products of nature, and the natural rights all men possessed should be re-established and maintained by national governments. Thus, for the *philosophe* Baron d'Holbach (1723–89) in his *Système de la nature,* nature told man "to *love the country which gave him birth,* to serve it faithfully, to blend his interests with it against all those who may attempt to injure it. . . ." [57] Thus, for the economist Adam Smith (1723–90) in his *The Theory of Moral Sentiments,* "the love of our own country" seemed "not to be derived from love of mankind." Rather it was the result of "that wisdom which contrived the system of human affections, as well as every other part of nature" which "judged that the interest of the great society of mankind would be best promoted by directing the principal attention of each individual to that particular portion of it, which was most within the sphere of both his abilities and his understanding." [58]

This kind of rational explanation of nations and national affection did not satisfy romantic contemporaries, who usually followed Rousseau in his vague emotional approach but placed more emphasis on deep historical (or mystical) forces. Johann Gottlieb Herder (1744–1803), who was

72

much responsible for nationalist awakening in the Germanies and eastern Europe but no blind nationalist himself, saw the nation, the *Volk*, as a historically developing unit of humanity, a result of physical environment, especially climate, of education, of relationships with other groups, of traditions, language, and of heredity. Each nation, as an inheritance of time, was a "partnership of the generations," an organic whole, and each had its own soul, its own character, and was worthy of fullest support and deepest love.[59] A little later than Herder and in direct reaction to the French Revolution, the English statesman and orator Edmund Burke developed in ringing rhetoric a similar explanation of the nation. For Burke, as for Herder, the nation was a historical personality embodying the "moral essences," the experience and the wisdom of the ages, an organism above and beyond men and nature.[60]

Both rationalists and romanticists, then, explained and supported nations and national loyalty, though their reasons were different. The rationalists stressed eternal natural laws that they thought governed all mankind, and one of these was "love your fatherland," the romanticists the historical, mystical, and peculiar qualities of the individual nations, and they asked also for love of fatherland.[61] Neither the rationalist nor the romantic explanation will bear hard scrutiny, but both seem to have been persuasive to contemporaries, and they have been often repeated since.

The cultural, economic, and political realities of the eighteenth century afford more substantial hypotheses for the rise of nationalism. History had already brought into existence some national institutions and ideas, and this had determined in some degree those to which eighteenth-century men would turn in hope or in fear. The preceding centuries had seen the creation of national dynastic governments that united territories and peoples, and, through laws, taxes, economic regulations, these governments had extended somewhat uniform and central government over them. Within each of the dynastic kingdoms educated people generally spoke a common language and had become aware of their common culture, their common interests, their common hopes, and hence could and did communicate.

As literacy slowly spread, individuals became more aware of what were becoming their common interests and of the need for common effort that would spring out of common devotion to these interests. If enlightened men could join in common action, they could wipe out injustice and oppression, establish a new order, and everyone could enjoy a freer, happier life. Belief in progress, even in perfectibility, was growing. But the happy future was slow in coming. The rule of enlightened despots, which some *philosophes* had advocated, had been neither enlightened nor very effective. The future would come faster when enlightened citizens could participate, help shape that future. Everything would become possible when men of like mind were able to act together within their nation to improve their condition. Hope ran high, a hope akin to the later hope of nonwestern peoples for modernization, and this hope led to the conviction that it could be fulfilled through national effort when "love of fatherland" became the chief public virtue.

The seventeenth-century English poet Dryden but anticipated the expectancy of the Enlightenment when he predicted a glorious future for his nation.

> *But what so long in vain, and yet unknown,*
> *By poor mankind's benighted wit is sought,*
> *Shall in this age to Britain first be shown,*
> *And hence be to admiring nations taught.*[62]

From the seventeenth century, English and French philosophers (or *philosophes*) taught those who read to hope, and to hope through their nation. Men were not inherently evil, as priests had preached. Men by nature might be neutral, but, as Locke argued, they could be educated to be rational. Men might be depraved because of the conditions under which they lived, but, as Rousseau cried, they would regain their natural goodness once they were freed from restraint. After the catastrophic earthquake of 1755 in Portugal, Voltaire professed pessimism, yet he spent his whole life not only in improving his own circumstances but also in attacking stupidity and injustice, apparently in hope of reducing them. Diderot at times had profound doubts about the rationality of man, but his *Encyclopédie* represented a gigantic rational effort to improve the lot of men.

Still, why was the progress in which so many believed, in spite of the doubts of a few, to come through the nation? Another almost standard explanation has been: the self-interest of the rising bourgeoisie, the middle, the business classes. Popularized by the father of socialism, Karl Marx, but strongly upheld as well by such believers in capitalism as Adam Smith and Alexander Hamilton, the economic interpretation of history throws much light on the origins and development of nationalism. The thesis of Marx and particularly of his followers, Lenin and Stalin, concerning nations and nationalism was briefly this: The bourgeoisie, becoming the dominant class, sought to and did wrest control of nation-states in order to serve their class interests—control of production, acquisition of wealth. To capture the home and foreign markets they had to have a politically united territory with a population speaking the same language and to be victorious in competition with the bourgeoisie of other nationalities. Hence they became nationalists and were responsible for the rise of nationalism throughout the western world.[63]

That the middle classes played *a* prominent role in the rise of nationalism there can be little argument. Many of the most ardent propagators of national ideas in the eighteenth century were of the middle classes. Members of these classes did want national markets for their goods, national protection, and national freedom for their trade. But to this explanation at least three qualifications are necessary: (1) The middle classes were "rising" from the twelfth century, not just in the eighteenth. (2) Some eighteenth-century nobles, like the Marquis de Lafayette, and some clericals, like the abbé Sieyès, who did not evince much interest in markets and profits were nationalists. And (3) the foundations of nations and national sentiment were laid by the dynasties long before the eighteenth century. If these qualifications are kept in mind, it is possible to say that in the eighteenth century members of middle classes, especially lawyers, became nationalists because nationalism did serve their interests, and that they eagerly sought to participate in and control the national governments in their own interests, which they identified with the national.

There is a further economic explanation that, while basically supporting a materialist economic interpretation of nationalism, goes beyond the Marxist explanation. As the middle classes grew in wealth and numbers from the twelfth century, they tended to ally themselves with the national monarchs as both they and the monarchs, for different reasons, opposed the privileged orders, the nobility and the clergy. The kings wished to extend their powers at the expense of the nobility and clergy. The middle classes desired privileges, especially those concerned with property and those having to do with social equality with the nobility. The kings wanted the supplies, wealth, and taxes that the bourgeoisie could provide.[64] The bourgeoisie hoped for security of property and freedom for trade, which the king could provide. Thus both monarch and middle classes often found mutual benefit in the joint extension of their mutual interests, which they also could conceive of as *the* national interests. If ambitious members of the middle class carried trade to far-flung places, if they discovered new lands, this meant increased profits and hence increased royal (national) wealth and taxes. And the royal (national) government provided naval protection for the trade, gave bounties for such colonial products as naval stores, and safeguarded the home market for patriotic members of the bourgeoisie.

The alliance between monarchy and middle class was never complete or solid. It was not born out of mutual affection, but came primarily from the interests of the monarch in power and taxes and the interests of the bourgeoisie in security for property and the opportunity to gain both more wealth and higher social status. When absolute monarchy could not, as in England in the seventeenth century and France in the late eighteenth century, defend the old social order and protect property as well, and could not afford opportunities for gain as the bourgeoisie desired, the bourgeoisie plus some aristocrats limited the monarchical power by constitutional provision and, when this was not enough, removed the king's head (Charles I, Louis XVI). When the kings were limited or dethroned, the propertied citizens became sovereign, and they, the Cromwellians and French revolutionaries, calling themselves the nation, ruled in the name of the nation. Men, propertied men, could now be patriotic. What served the nation served them. What helped them was good for the nation, for they were the nation.[65]

All this, of course, is oversimplification of a complex story. True in substance, the interpretation needs modification in detail. The alliance between the bourgeoisie and monarchs was not an alliance in the strict sense but a marriage of convenience. It was not between two equals, for in the early period the monarchs were the stronger, and in the later the bourgeoisie. The monarchs did not rely completely upon the bourgeoisie but at times allied themselves with priest and noble. These latter were not always at odds with the middle classes: in England the squirearchy and commercial nobility at times jointly fought the royal power, and in France the list of nobles and clergymen who advocated reform is perhaps as impressive as that of the bourgeoisie—the Baron Montesquieu, the Baron d'Holbach, the Marquis de Condorcet, the Bishop Grégoire.

While there is much to be said in support of a class interpretation of nationalism, it is far too simple. But if this is true, what are the alternatives? Again, it must be reiterated, all explanations are debatable and hard evidence that would *prove* any one explanation does not exist. It is clear, however, that people became nationalists for *many* reasons in addition to those already outlined, among them awareness of common cultures and facility of communication, among them growing awareness of differences among peoples.[66] Concretely this meant in the eighteenth century that more Frenchmen and more Englishmen were becoming more and more aware of being French or English, that even Russian intellectuals, who had been so impressed by German and French cultural superiority, were becoming increasingly conscious of being different, that is, Russian.[67]

What was happening is again most clearly seen in France and England, though in other countries similar developments were under way, or, more often, would occur later.

By the eighteenth century high and distinct cultures had developed among the elites of France and Britain. Frenchmen and Englishmen were proud of them, identified themselves with them. Rabelais, La Fontaine, Molière, Racine, and Corneille, Chaucer, Spenser, Shakespeare, Milton, and Dryden had written, and Voltaire and Gibbon were about to write, their great essays, plays, poems, and histories. These writers of genius became symbols of French and British national life. Voltaire, world citizen that he professed to be, was very much a Frenchman, proud of French civilization, and Parisians wildly feted him as the symbol of their hopes and French genius when he returned to Paris just before his death in 1778.

By the eighteenth century the French and English languages had taken on their modern and established forms, and dictionaries, grammars, encyclopedias were appearing to standardize them. Within the two countries the now national languages were widely used, and the ideas they conveyed might circulate among literate Frenchmen and Englishmen. While an educated Parisian might still, like Racine in the seventeenth century when he asked for *un vase de nuit,* have trouble making himself understood in the outlying provinces, he could usually communicate in French with educated men throughout France—just as the educated Londoner could in English with educated men in England, though certainly not in all Britain.

By the eighteenth century, if not earlier, Paris and London had become capitals not only of political and economic life but also of the national cultures, and as their influence, their language, and their values spread, so did national awareness.[68] The *philosophe* Montesquieu looked back with regret to the time "when each village was a capital." In his own time, he said, there was only one: "To conclude a business, to end litigation, to obtain a favor, one must go to Paris." [69] As it was in business, so it was in most aspects of life, in literature and the arts as well as in business and politics. As will be pointed out in some detail later, in France especially, but also in much of Europe, good patriots zealously attempted to inculcate national ideas through national literature and the arts. And they did so chiefly from the great cities. The judgments and values of Paris and London eventually tended to be those of France and England.

Before ideas that were national could circulate among peoples, obviously physical bases of communication had to be established. Modern commentators are likely to think of the mass media, of the telegraph and telephone, of superhighways and jet planes as the ways ideas get around. In the eighteenth century the transmission of ideas was less instantaneous, but ideas did get around.

Most roads were bad—travelers' tales are horrendous—but there were usable roads radiating out from the great capitals, and rivers and canals carried news and ideas as well as freight. The major roads in France, although built primarily for the king's troops, were also used by travelers, and the speed of travel was becoming a little faster. A leisurely traveler in France in the late 1780's, like the English agriculturist Arthur Young, might make by horse only twenty-five to thirty-five miles a day, but the travel time by fast diligence from Paris to Lyons had been cut from ten to five days during the previous hundred years, and speeds of up to fourteen miles an hour were possible on the coach from Liverpool to Manchester. By 1789 France had over 25,000 miles of constructed roads and, though many of them were little more than ruts, the major roads, the royal highways, were thirty to sixty feet wide.[70] In England over a thousand miles of the rivers were open to navigation, and in some stretches they were heavily used.[71] The great age of canal building was to come later, at the beginning of the nineteenth century, but in France Colbert and his predecessors had built them from the seventeenth century, for example the royal canal *"de deux mers,"* from the Aude to the Garonne River, connecting French provinces from the Atlantic to the Mediterranean. In France and England the great roads that most travelers took ran out from Paris and London to the chief towns. The network in France resembled that of French railroads today, Paris-Strasbourg, Paris-Lyons-Marseilles, Paris-Toulouse, Paris-Lille. However slow and difficult the travel, this network did tie French provinces, cities, and Frenchmen together and foster unity. The ideas, the new books, plays, political tracts, of Paris did reach, say, Franche-Comté and its capital, Besançon, two hundred hard miles to the east. An authority on the French language once remarked, "The engineers of bridges and roads without a doubt served the [French] language better than many academicians." [72] His remark could apply as well to French patriotism. In Europe then, as in Africa now, national sentiment grew along the major routes of communication and in and around the great cities.[73] The effects of the swiftness of communication in modern times may be overrated. What is important here is that ideas did circulate in the eighteenth century, and a little farther and faster than they had.[74]

The principal means of communicating ideas were, of course, books, pamphlets, and conversation. There were postal services; they were getting better but carried few letters. There were newspapers but they were few, were subject to censorship, published little news and few new or dangerous ideas. During the early eighteenth century, French authors with dangerous ideas often circulated them clandestinely in manuscript. In the public libraries alone, one recent investigator found 102 manuscripts written and passed about from person to person between 1700 and 1750.[75] After 1750 in France authors were less afraid to publish, though sometimes, because of the censorship, they hid or denied their authorship. In any case, the philosophic works, the *Encyclopédie*, the works of Voltaire and Rousseau, were continually published, read, and commented upon in France and in much of Europe.[76] Educated men *and* women debated and discussed them privately, in the academies and societies, in the socially fashionable salons of the great ladies, and even in the colleges and universities in which religious influences remained dominant.[77] During 1787–89 in France many pamphlets, as has been pointed out, popularized the philosophic ideas, and the cahiers repeated some of them. During the Revolution leaders quoted them and based their proposals upon them. The famous 1789 *Declaration of Rights of Man and Citizen* of the French National Assembly saw those on liberty directly enacted into the highest law of France.

With some optimism Grimm, the literary critic, noted the diffusion of ideas that was forming in much of Europe an "immense republic of cultivated spirits." [78] The republic, however, was not a republic of all mankind, even in Europe. The ideas did not reach the peasants, nor did a great many nobles, clergymen, or bourgeoisie pay much attention to them or approve them. The ideas did circulate, they were communicated, and they did influence the opinions of elite groups within nations. Instead of a republic of mankind, however, there were forming nations of men. And these men in these nations were, in spite of cosmopolitan sentiment, aware of, perhaps becoming increasingly aware of, their diversities.

There is an old saying that travel and knowledge broaden. The saying undoubtedly reflects much experience. It is also true that travel and knowledge lead to perception of differences and to dislike of those who are different. We do not know for a fact whether the proportion of people traveling abroad increased during the eighteenth century, though certainly the number who traveled to other countries mounted, as the growing number of travel books, such as that of Arthur Young, attest. We cannot be sure whether there was much more knowledge of foreign countries, though this seems likely, as the writings of Montesquieu and Voltaire give evidence. Again, there is no proof that mistrust and dislike of foreigners were intensifying—mistrust and dislike of others were old—but mistrust and dislike continued, and at certain times and in some individuals they were intense.

Awareness of diversity, as has been said, was not new. During the eighteenth century this awareness seems to have become keener if not more informed. Each people, it was commonly believed, had its own distinct ways, its own unique character. The French *Encyclopédie* of Diderot in its article on "Nation" repeated the observations of the earlier English *Cyclopedie* (1738) of Ephraim Chambers: "Every nation has its particular character: one can say as a kind of proverb: frivolous as a Frenchman, zealous as an Italian, serious as a Spaniard, wicked as an Englishman, proud as a Scot, drunk as a German, lazy as an Irishman, dishonest as a Greek. . . ." Possibly not many informed writers would have agreed with this rather flippant attribution of national characteristics. But eighteenth-century writers, like those of the twentieth century, not uncommonly indulged in similar easy generalizations, and doubtless they believed them. It was commonly held that "the French are polite, ingenious, generous, but too quick and inconstant, the Germans sincere, industrious but ponderous and given to drinking, the Italians agreeable, refined, gracious in speech but jealous and treacherous, the Spaniards reserved, prudent but blustering and ceremonious, the English courageous to the point of foolhardiness but arrogant, scornful and haughty to the point of cruelty." [79]

However accurate this kind of description of national differences was, diversities of many kinds did exist, if not actually, then in the minds of influential romantics like Herder. Each people was different, the romantics insisted, had its own genius, its own soul, and each should cultivate its own garden, its own ways of thinking and acting. During the later eighteenth century even Russian writers, who until then had been little conscious of nationality, came to resent the dominance of German or any foreign influence in Russia, and demanded emphasis on the Russian language, on Russian manners, on Russian morals. This kind of resentment, sooner or later, arose in all Europe, in the then "unenlightened" Austria-Hungary, for example, when the enlightened Emperor Joseph II tried to force the varied peoples in his empire to use German.

During much of the seventeenth and eighteenth centuries French ways of thought and customs had dominated Europe. The development of the countries of Europe had been quite unequal. France was wealthier and more powerful than any of the other countries, and its culture, by the standards of the time, was regarded as much higher. All through Europe lesser princes tried to emulate the "Sun King" at Versailles, aristocrats to adopt French manners, and poets and playwrights to follow French models.[80] The French language was, or so it was believed, more precise and logical, French customs more civilized. French leaders did not deny this. Rather, they thought French civilization well worthy of imitation. A French lawyer and economist, G. F. Le Trosne, was sure of the civilizing mission of France: "Oh, my country! This is the role which it is your part to play in Europe. . . . From you the light has gone forth which reveals to men their rights and duties, their true interests, the essential principles of justice, the laws and structure of the social order. . . ." [81]

European elites both imitated and envied the French. They tried to be like the French but eventually they resented them, wanted to be different. They became, in short, ever more aware of national differences at the same time as they perceived similarities of interest and culture within nations. This was particularly true in France as Frenchmen compared themselves with Englishmen and fought them over several centuries. French writers often admired English institutions and ways, but some of them expressed dislike of the "turbulent" English character. The four major wars between France and England from 1689 to 1783, especially the Seven Years' War (1756–63) and the war (1778–83) of the American Revolution, aggravated French and English mutual distrust, just as the later wars of the French Revolution would lead to hostility to France on the part of most European governments. War, then as now, unified people within nations; it deepened consciousness of national similarities as it aggravated dislike of other nations. In 1765, just after the Seven Years' War, Parisians emotionally applauded a historical tragedy, *Le Siège de Calais.* In it a king of England (Edward III, king 1327–77) cruelly sentenced six French burghers of Calais to death, then, moved by the heroic willingness of the son of one of them to die in his condemned father's place, did not carry out the sentence. The patriotic author, Pierre Belloy, a minor poet, wanted, by commemorating the virtues of Frenchmen, to convince members of his audience that they too should identify themselves with France. He hoped they would say, "I have just seen a French hero; I too can be such a one." [82]

In 1789 probably few of the elected deputies to the Estates-General, soon to become the National Assembly, thought of themselves as heroes. Some of them, especially those of the Third Estate, did think of themselves as representatives of the French people chosen to regenerate France.

Whatever else the deputies of the Third Estate then did, they "taught the people its power," in the words of a noble deputy, the honest de Ferrières, as they "identified (*lier*) the interests of six hundred deputies with the public interest of twenty million Frenchmen." [83]

As de Ferrières also remarked, the same principle would soon spread to all France, and, it may be added, to all Europe and the entire world. The nation was becoming a people, a people unified by their common interests and distinct from other peoples with other interests.[84]

IV

The Nation Makes Patriots, 1715–1795

Through the eighteenth century in western Europe, particularly in France, the nation and its state were becoming, in the minds of political theorists and moral philosophers, the way to reach the future, to progress toward a good (or better) society, or, to use a newer term, to modernize. This did not happen everywhere or all at once; nor, in the eighteenth century, did the idea penetrate the consciousness of many people—until 1789, not even many Frenchmen. But once the idea took shape among influential writers, it spread, became implanted in the minds of greater and greater numbers of people, became institutionalized, generally accepted. Then it perpetuated itself.

National governments became responsible for the common good and the common defense, the common promotion of common ideals and the common realization of common interests. The actions of these national governments created national institutions and stimulated national consciousness if not always national loyalty. In turn, national consciousness strengthened the national institutions. More and stronger national institutions and consciousness brought still more and stronger national consciousness and institutions. Peoples who were not national-minded were forced in their own interest and defense to become so, and those already so found it expedient and helpful to become still more so. Peoples who did not yet possess national governments and institutions found they had to create them or remain oppressed by their own rulers or by other peoples. Those who were in power in the nation-states wanted more power to accomplish national aims as well as enhance their own status; this further strengthened national governments and intensified national sentiment. As the national governments expanded, obtained and exercised more power, and influenced the lives and livelihoods of increasing numbers of people, increasing numbers looked to the national governments for solution of present difficulties and for resolution of doubts about the future. Eventually much, almost everything in human societies worked to intensify nationalism. Men would be born into national societies; they would, nearly always, be educated in national schools or in schools supposed to train them in national citizenship. Their heaviest taxes and their most onerous and honorific civic duties, including the military, would become mostly national; their highest justice would be obtained, usually, in national courts; their own cultures, their literatures, their arts, and even their churches would condition them to think and dream in national terms; and their leaders, would, with success, persuade or force them to believe in national idols and ideals. The man who under these pressures would not become a national patriot, a nationalist, would be a "rank reactionary," a "hopeless idealist," or perhaps, worst of all, a "traitor."

But this is to look ahead a century and a half, to see nationalism in its full development in the twentieth century. In 1789, or whatever date is used to mark the beginning of modern nationalism, there was no rounded theory about what it was or should become, no conscious plan to develop it into what it did become. No one in the eighteenth century, except possibly Rousseau, consciously thought out a program to "regenerate" societies of men through nationalism (Rousseau did not use the word) or perceived what would happen when the national sentiment did prevail. But those who wanted change and reform and were already nationally minded hoped to increase the number of patriots who gave their first loyalty to their national societies. This they hoped to accomplish by deepening the awareness of national cultures and by establishing governments capable of acting for national ends and of making more patriots devoted to these ends.

The governments, reacting to the pressures of patriots at home and of threats from abroad, became more and more national. Early in France, then in the young United States and in much of Europe, they attempted to make patriots—that is, to nationalize their peoples. That they were not immediately or ever completely successful was the result not of lack of effort but likely either of their own ineptness—they lacked modern techniques of propaganda—or of the stupidity or intelligence, in any case the recalcitrance, of their peoples—their refusal to give up older loyalties or to be satisfied with those of nationalism.

In France by 1789 national sentiment was strong and rising, as we have seen. But France was not yet a country unified by common practices and customs or a nation of people united by common interest in their *patrie.* Old loyalties, distinctions, and differences persisted. As Georges Lefebvre, who knew the France of 1789 better than any modern scholar, wrote:

The development of communication and commerce, the education given in the colleges, the attraction of the Court and of Paris tied Frenchmen together in a thousand ways. But provinces and cities kept their privileges; the South (*Midi*) kept the Roman law, the North its numerous customary laws; weights and measures were not uniform; internal duties and private tolls still existed; the administrative, judicial, financial, religious agencies and districts, encroaching upon each other, remained in general confusion. Finally, and above all, the nobility continued to be a nation within the nation.[1]

To his list of reasons for lack of unity in France Lefebvre might have added others, among them the claims of the clergy to separate status and the little interest in public or national affairs of many Frenchmen at all levels, but especially among the peasants. National feeling ran high in France in 1789 among leaders of opinion who hoped to break down barriers of class and province, to establish a common national government for all Frenchmen, and to unite them through common devotion to the nation. In 1789, however, the hopes of these leaders and writers represented prophecy, not actuality. The prophecy would in part be fulfilled, but only in part and slowly. In 1789–90, when revolutionary fervor was becoming intense in France, peasants forced a Russian traveler, Nikolai Karamzin, to shout, "*Vive la Nation,*" and then asked him, "What is this nation?"[2]

When the French Revolution began in 1789, England, in many ways, was more unified than France.[3] Provincial and class privileges were a little less obvious, less exclusive, and mobility between the upper classes a little more fluid. Among the upper and governing classes there was a kind of assured patriotism that did not, apparently, require much rhetoric until Edmund Burke in 1790, frightened by and reflecting on the French Revolution, superbly eulogized English political traditions.[4] It might, indeed, be argued, as Hans Kohn has done, that national sentiment became strong earlier in England than in France,[5] though such comparisons, resting on insufficient evidence, can scarcely be regarded as more than impressions. In England, unlike the case in France, the power of the crown had been waning since the mid-seventeenth century, and the Parliament in London gave England a national government in which representatives of the upper classes, the landowning classes, did take an interest, did participate, did control the purse and share power, and did have pride. It is also true that in England during the latter part of the eighteenth century, in this case as in France, a reform movement developed that might have led to greater participation by more people in the English government and to greater concern for national goals. But this reform movement died. For many reasons, most of them irrelevant here, England did not have the revolution France did, a revolution that might have further incited national interest and patriotism. England had had a "Glorious Revolution" in 1688, and its upper classes had won or retained political power. During much of the eighteenth century English political leaders were more interested in petty factional politics and in their personal affairs than in doctrines of party or in vast plans for national regeneration. When the reforming zeal was at its height in England, the French Revolution occurred, and in England reform then gave way to reaction, to opposition to any change. England continued to be governed, as it had been, by a confident oligarchy. "In 1752, Henry Fielding [the novelist] defined 'No Body' as 'all the people of Great Britain except about 1200,' and those 1200 saw no reason at all why anything should challenge their unquestioned supremacy." [6] Whether the number was 1200 may be questioned. But at no time during the eighteenth century was the number of "somebodies" large, and, though there were reformers in England, no Sieyès dramatically asserted that the people were "everything," constituted the nation and should govern it. The national patriotism of England was aristocratic, upper-class, and the upper classes (perhaps those with Bolingbroke's "ethereal spirit") governed the nation to serve their interests, which to them were the national interests.

Elsewhere in Europe on the eve of the Revolution in France, national feeling varied but was seldom vigorous. In the phrase of Hans Kohn, there were "stirrings in the old world," but these "stirrings" were isolated, sporadic, and seldom were more than a few individuals involved. In Switzerland national sentiment was, on occasion, ardently expressed, as at the tercentenary of the University of Basle and in the writings of educators such as Professor Johann Heinrich Füssli of Zurich.[7] In the Germanies, where the Prussian state of Frederick II so dominated and the three-hundred-odd small and large states were so diverse, so provincial, and so traditional, only an idealist like the Pietist Friedrich Karl von Moser could dream of German unity, of a united German people with one name and one language, under one head, one law, and imbued with "National Spirit." [8] While in the Italies "seeds of Italian nationalism" had been planted by the economist Antonio Genovesi and were being broadly sown by the writer Vittorio Alfieri, they would not blossom into a *Risorgimento* for two generations.[9] In Russia, in east-central and southeastern Europe, occasional voices were raised against foreign influences or to plead for national languages and literatures. While these voices were harbingers of nationalism to come, they did not represent developed nationalism in any "real" sense, even in the Germanies and Italies, and in central and southeastern Europe even the "stirrings" were faint.[10] In Russia the czarist state was well established, but, except for a few writers, Russians were not nationally conscious or devoted to the Russian nation. Among the Balkan peoples the sense of nationality was incipient, but there were no demands for national independence. In Poland upper-class individuals much resented the recent partitions of their country by Prussia, Russia, and Austria and greatly desired restoration, but as yet there was no general national "awakening."

In the United States, in the New World, where the new nation-state was just being established, national sentiment, first manifested in the years before 1776, was taking root, but the new leaders as well as their followers were still not certain whether they owed their primary allegiance to the nation or to their states. From 1776 some early statesmen and politicians, such as George Washington, John Marshall, and Alexander Hamilton, and educators and journalists, such as Noah Webster and Philip Freneau, valiantly tried to unify the nation and to create a patriotism that was primarily national, but until after the War of 1812 nationalism was incipient rather than well developed or widespread. In South America in 1776 the national uprisings against Spain were three decades in the future; and if one may judge from available evidence, no one in the 1780's could have foretold them, for, while a few writers seemed to realize that they were Spanish-Americans or simply *Americanos*,[11] national sentiments were little expressed. In Asia and Africa, where family, clan, and tribal loyalties prevailed, nationalism of any modern kind had not yet appeared.

In 1789 not many people were nationally conscious, and fewer, certainly, were national patriots.[12] Those who were and the national governments that existed or would be created would have to educate, train, persuade people to take an interest in national affairs and to be patriotic. National patriots would have to be made.

To say that national consciousness and patriotism deepened and spread solely as a result of the exertions of patriots and governments would be, however, to claim too much for these patriots and governments. The individuals, for example, who compiled dictionaries of national languages or who advocated the establishment of national schools did so for many reasons. Perhaps they were chiefly interested in languages and literacy; perhaps they saw opportunities to make money or to win acclaim from their fellows. Much that the governments did, before, during, and after the eighteenth century, was done not with the conscious intention of stimulating national interest or of making patriots, but to promote the government's own interests or the particular interests of groups and individuals within the nation. Behind much that was done by governments and individuals, in fact, one cannot sense any deliberate attempt to foster nationalism at all. Nevertheless, many events and policies that seem quite unrelated to nationalism did, in the context of eighteenth-century culture, accentuate interest in if not devotion to the nation. While governments primarily enacted legislation, established tariffs and banks to favor private interests, they did by this legislation create interest in the nation and its government. While states did not ordinarily go to war to make patriots, their wars did stimulate nationalism, and wars increasingly resulted from conflicts of national interests.

Sometimes, then, nationalism was consciously sponsored; sometimes it arose out of the conjuncture of events and ideas. In either case patriots were in the making. How could they be made? Among the eighteenth-century answers were: by education and appeal to interests.

Much enlightened thought, from Locke to Condorcet, held that men were not evil by nature but that their natures were shaped by their environment and that, if they were rightly educated, they would become good, virtuous men. Good, virtuous men were generally considered or came to be considered the same as good, dutiful citizens. Men could be educated, then, to be good citizens, citizens who loved their fatherland and bent their efforts to improve it, to defend it. Because good citizens, good patriots were not born, they had to be taught to be by their institutions, their societies. Political theorists and, increasingly, political practitioners believed this, and the latter often acted as if they had read the former, as indeed they sometimes had.

Rousseau, the romantic believer in the natural goodness of man, might, it would seem, have thought that men would be good citizens if all the curses of civilization were thrown off and they were again allowed to be "naturally good." And indeed he did so seem to argue in some of his early writings, particularly the *Discours sur l'origine et les fondements de l'inégalité parmi les hommes* (1754). When he was older he was not content with vague moral admonitions or so ready to trust the unaided natural emotions. In his *Considérations sur le gouvernement de Pologne* he gave the ruler of Poland quite practical advice, to form loyal citizens through national institutions. "It is," he instructed the king, "the national institutions which form the genius, the character, the tastes, and the morals of a people, which make them themselves and not another people, which inspire them with that ardent love of fatherland based upon ineradicable habits."[13] Men, he was now convinced, could not be left to their own devices. Institutions had to be established to indoctrinate them.

Like Rousseau, other less emotional leaders of opinion believed that citizens had to be formed. From Locke to Condorcet they formulated many plans to educate men to see their interests. Some of them also thought the governments should appeal directly to these interests. At mid-century in Naples economics professor Antonio Genovesi dreamed, as had Machiavelli over two centuries earlier, of uniting Italy and Italians. The time had come, he argued, to end the brotherly quarrels of Italian states. He appealed directly to their self-interest as he pleaded for economic and other reforms: "If a common and real interest has united enemies, will it not be strong enough to join jealous rivals?"[14] In another context and newer world the authors of *The Federalist* papers (1787), Alexander Hamilton, John Jay, and James Madison, put much the same case in the United States as they persuasively argued for the adoption of the just-written national constitution and for the establishment of a stronger, a national government. The American government, they declared, should be able to address itself "immediately to the hopes and fears of individuals" and attract support from "those passions which have the strongest influence on the human heart."[15]

While views like these were not by 1789 generally held, they were not rare or isolated. They would become more and more prevalent, in France during the Revolution, in western Europe and the United States, and then eventually almost everywhere. And increasingly the governments, themselves becoming more and more national, would enact legislation to establish national institutions to provide for realization of goals increasingly considered to be national goals. What had been responsibilities of king, priest, and noble would become those of the nation-state, and this state would take on more and more responsibility for more people. As it did so, it would act directly on and in response to the "hopes and fears" of individuals, and individuals would look more and more to their nation-states for fulfillment of whatever they hoped for and protection against whatever they feared. Nowhere was this truer than in the France of 1789–94.

To write a history of nationalism during the French Revolution of 1789–94 would be to write a history of the French Revolution, and the converse is also true.[16] But to write a history of the deepening of national consciousness as if it were exclusively a history *only* of ideas and events in France and of *only* these ideas and events *during* this period would be to distort history. France remains the center of most significant nationalist development—France *at this time* did set the example, point the way—but the history must include ideas and events in much of the western world, for thought and action were not then, as they often are not now, confined within the boundaries of any nation.

The Revolution in France came for many reasons, of which one was the desire to "regenerate" the *patrie*. It in turn accentuated national consciousness, deepened national loyalties to France, as well as exacerbated old antagonisms within the country and led to conflict abroad. Expectancy ran high, fear deep, and uncertainty was always present. The first year of the Revolution, '89, was symbolic of the four years to follow, a spring of expectancy tinged with uncertainty, a summer of hope and fear and uncertainty, a fall of hope always mixed with uncertainty and a tinge of fear. And always rumors and rumors of rumors—of brigands, of spies, traitors, and enemies, domestic and foreign, of no one knew quite what or who.[17] And always, until at least July, 1794, and indeed for nearly two decades longer, the almost messianic belief that France was inaugurating a new era not only for Frenchmen but for all mankind. So many believed in '89, as Wordsworth later wrote, that "bliss was it in that dawn to be alive," but so many were uncertain in the years of revolutionary violence and war to follow whether they would be alive. So many found satisfaction and joy in public, in national service. So many suffered and died either in the name of the revolutionary nation or in fighting against it. Whether individuals experienced joy or suffering, they did so for or against the nation. Consciousness of nation was burned into the hearts and minds of Frenchmen.

In the spring of 1789 great hopes of Frenchmen appeared about to be realized through their nation. A cahier glowed with emotion, "Frenchmen will have one fatherland . . . a single family, whose elder members use their superior intelligence and powers only to increase the happiness of the younger, in which the national character will recover its energy, and patriotism will rule every heart, and Frenchmen will show what they can accomplish, once they are at liberty, and can make use of the advantages nature has given them." On the opening day of the Estates-General a noble deputy exulted, "My heart was overwhelmed with love of my country. . . . Here and now I make a solemn resolution. This dear France where I was born . . . the scene of all my experience, the source of all my moral ideas—never will I betray the glorious trust it has placed in my hands: no motive shall rule my mind or will but that of the interest and welfare of my fellow-countrymen." [18] The opening of the Estates-General did indeed open gates for dammed-up hopes of enlightened Frenchmen.

As Georges Lefebvre observed, "So extraordinary an event awakened hope, bright and nebulous at the same time, of national regeneration." [19] The reforms that were expected to follow seemed to promise the return of "an earthly paradise." And in the future, through "national regeneration," a good many men throughout the world would hope to attain this "paradise."

By July, 1789, at the same time, much of France was in the throes of fear, the "Great Fear of '89," as rumors of brigands and plots flew about the country, as peasants rioted and destroyed records of hated feudal (more accurately, manorial) obligations and dues. In Paris, in early July, rumors (based on fact) spread that the royal government was about to use troops to dissolve the National Assembly, restore the old order, and thus end the hope of a new day. One result was the storming of the Bastille on July 14. The fall of this symbol of despotism brought rejoicing, new hope. The people, the nation had triumphed.[20] But rumors continued, fear persisted, the countryside was in an uproar, what would happen? Men of property banded together to keep order, protect property. They would soon organize a National Guard to protect their interests, the national interests. Excitement mounted. What was to be done? After a night (August 4–5) of high emotional enthusiasm and sacrifice, the National Assembly wiped out much of the feudal regime as it abolished privileges and distinctions of class and province and decreed that "all citizens" were to be "admitted without distinction of birth to all ecclesiastical, civil, and military employments and offices." [21] The Decrees of August 4, as the new laws were called, in reality were but legal acceptance of what had already happened. Now all propertied Frenchmen were equally national citizens, subject to the same national laws and taxes, and all were equally eligible to hold national office.[22]

That all propertied Frenchmen could participate as citizens in the affairs of the nation did not, of course, mean the end of fear any more than it meant the full realization of hope. Opposition, bitter opposition to revolutionary ideas and acts led to counterrevolution and counterrevolution to terror, to the revolution *à outrance* of '93–'94. From 1792 revolutionary zeal plus national ambition led to desire for expansion. Frightened by revolution and the threat of French expansion, conservative monarchs and leaders in England and elsewhere in Europe nervously reacted; and, incited by French aristocratic émigrés who detested the Revolution, they threatened France and its Revolution. War came in 1792, war that was to continue intermittently to 1815. High hope, anguished uncertainty, deep fear always. National action for national ends was the answer from 1789 to 1794, as it has usually been ever since. And then as now, nationalism bred nationalism.

When revolutionary Frenchmen from 1789 to 1794 demanded revolutionary change, faced counterrevolution at home and war abroad, they believed they had to unite or die. To achieve the goals of the Revolution, to win the war, to defend the country or enlarge it required unity, the unity that national patriotism would bring. This patriotism could be aroused when citizens were shaped by common education, thought in a common language, shared the common culture, when they identified their self-interests and their fortunes, their tragedies and triumphs with the national interests, fortunes, tragedies and triumphs. And when their patriotism was aroused, or so it was believed, they would understand why they should act together and how their nation's interests were different from those of other nations, and therefore they would perform their civic duties, including military service.

Although, it must be repeated, no systematic comprehensive plan to make patriots was formulated, French revolutionaries and their governments, whether called the National Assembly or Convention, made great efforts to do so through legislation and propaganda, and then by coercion and terror. There was, of course, no divine commandment or natural law that Frenchmen had to have a national revolution, fight international wars, seek their interests through their nation and state. But in the context of the eighteenth century and given the circumstances, they had no alternative. For the nation and its state were becoming, not everywhere or all at once, the ways of meeting present problems and achieving future goals, of securing life and property, of winning liberties and defending against danger.

To this analysis more than one objection can be raised. We do not know, probably cannot know what really motivated individuals, whether they were leaders or followers. Some of the leaders, undoubtedly, were more interested in making reputations, in wielding power, or in making fortunes than in unity or patriotism, and probably the motivations were always mixed. Many of the ordinary people, certainly, were much more interested in obtaining practical reforms, such as the elimination of hunting rights, than in being patriots, and some, very likely, just found satisfaction and even joy in attacking what was then, for many, the despised and envied establishment and in destroying its symbols, the Bastille in Paris, the châteaux in the country. But now, status and power were to be won through the nation, practical reforms through the nation. In fact, all interests could be (though not all were) subsumed in the nation. How could one obtain high status, great power? By being elected to national office. How could hunting rights be abolished? Through a national law administered by the national government.

From 1789 to 1791 the French National Assembly wrote a national constitution and enacted far-reaching national legislation touching almost every aspect of life. The kingdom, the Assembly stated, was one and indivisible, the nation was sovereign, and "all powers" emanated from it and from it only. The law expressed the general will, the nation's will; this will, expressed by national representatives, was supreme.[23] Acting on these general principles, the Assembly provided on a *national* scale for:

A new legislature and an election in which all active citizens could participate

Civil rights or liberties for all citizens

The inviolability of property

Reorganization of governmental administration at all levels

Reorganization of the army and the establishment of the National Guard

Reorganization of the judiciary

A civil constitution for and governmental control of the clergy

Reorganization of the church and limitation of papal power

Confiscation of ecclesiastical property, putting it at "the disposal of the nation"

A new system of taxes under control of the legislature

Abolition of all internal customs and duties, and free trade within France

A single, uniform tariff on all exports and imports

To insure citizen support of the national government and the Revolution, the Assembly further decreed that all active citizens, and especially members of the clergy, had to swear to be faithful to the nation, the law, and the king (the order is significant). And it declared national responsibility, though it did not pass specific legislation, for *public relief* or work for the poor, for free *public instruction* (italics in original) for all citizens, and for national festivals "to maintain fraternity among citizens and bind them to the Constitution, the *Patrie,* and the laws." [24]

Not all the laws were or could be put into effect; not all that were put into effect were effectively administered; nor were all the "good" intentions realized. But what the National Assembly had begun later legislatures would continue, sometimes effectively, sometimes not, though always with a view to unifying France and making patriots. And always the revolutionary events, the governmental decrees stirred interest in the affairs of the nation.

To make France one and indivisible was impossible. Rhetoric generally exceeds possibility. The National Assembly did wipe out the old and confusing administrative arrangements and substitute for them a uniform system. The old, somewhat independent *pays d'élection*, the old royal intendancies, the old *bailliages* and *sénéchaussées*, the vestiges of old provincial and feudal governments, were abolished. In their place the Assembly set up eighty-three departments, each with subordinate districts, and new municipalities. Each administrative unit had the same organization. Because the officers of the new units were elected, they were not at first directly subject to the government in Paris and possessed considerable autonomy, but in 1793 the Convention began to send out representatives on mission to assure their adherence to the national revolutionary policies, and Napoleon later (1800) brought the units under the control of the central government through appointment of their officials. Since that time France has had centralized, uniform, truly national administration. The National Assembly also reorganized the judiciary along somewhat the same lines, establishing a wholly new court system as it abolished the old *parlements* and the old regime's hodgepodge of courts. It only began to compile national codes of law; this would be done by Napoleon and his lawyers fifteen years later.

Complete national uniformity in or control of local and regional administration has never become actuality anywhere, nor has such uniformity and control ever been established for the judiciary and in the law. The national governments, including those of twentieth-century dictatorships, have never been strong enough, efficient enough to establish such uniformity and control, even though they may have so desired. Local customs and practices have persisted, and local loyalties have been tenacious. Everywhere, however, the national governments and courts have become superior and the national law the highest.

The Catholic church in France had already become partly national, the *ecclesia gallicana*, by 1789,[25] and, as has just been pointed out, the French government now declared its property national patrimony, required its priests to become national servants, and severely limited its connection with its universal head, the pope in Rome. This was but the beginning. As Rousseau had earlier advised both the Corsicans and the Poles to do,[26] the revolutionary governments in France tried, not with complete success, to make the church and religion fully national. In 1792 the Legislative Assembly ordered all communes to raise "an altar to the Fatherland" on which "shall be engraved, the citizen is born, lives, and dies for the *Patrie*."[27] In '93 the National Convention abolished the old calendar, which it associated with the Christian religion, and established a new national calendar to commemorate the revolutionary triumphs and destroy the influence of the church. "The French nation," the Convention said in its instructions to citizens, "degraded during many centuries by the most insolent despotism, has finally awakened to a consciousness of its rights and of the power to which its destinies summon it. . . . It [now] wishes its regeneration to be complete."[28] Following Rousseau's advice, Robespierre and the National Convention of 1794 tried to inaugurate a worship of the revolutionary national state in which festivals of reason would inculcate patriotism for the Republic of Virtue. This attempt to substitute "a religion of the virtuous nation for the Roman faith, the *Patrie* for God," was too fanciful to succeed. Religious loyalties were tenacious, as Napoleon, along with other later national leaders, learned. National loyalties, nevertheless, were becoming stronger than the religious. Over two centuries earlier England had established a national church and religion, and it had set a precedent that not all, but most, nations would follow. The eighteenth-century view of a German Pietist leader became general: "Religions are national and modified according to the disposition of the people."[29]

With more success, governments nationalized their armed forces, subordinating them to national authorities, opening their commands to all ranks. The armies, which had been royal, feudal, and mercenary, slowly became armies of citizens whose chief function was to fight for the country's, not the king's, interests. As Barère, the Jacobin orator, advocated, soldiers became citizens and citizens soldiers.[30] To support the regular armies and to keep order within their countries, governments also formed new military forces, called in France from 1789 and in the United States from 1824 the National Guard.[31] The French National Guard carried flags with the inscription "*Le Peuple français. La Liberté ou la mort.*" Particularly in wartime these governments would make it the duty of all young men to serve in the armed forces and of all citizens to serve the needs of these forces. The well-known French *levée en masse* of 1793 called upon all citizens to come to the aid of their *patrie.*

"Let everyone," cried the Jacobin leader Barère as he spoke for the decree, "assume his post in the national and military effort in preparation. The young will fight, the married will forge arms . . . provide subsistence, the women will make soldier's clothing . . . become nurses in hospitals for the wounded, the children will make lint out of old linen, and the old men will . . . be carried to public squares to inflame the courage of young warriors and preach hatred of kings and the unity of the Republic." [32]

Speaking the next year for the founding of an *Ecole de Mars,* the same Barère believed that "love of the *Patrie* . . . will become the dominant passion of the students . . . because it is the *Patrie* that will shape their character." [33] The chief, the highest duty of man would be to bear arms for his nation-state, to fight for the defense of what was "dearest and most sacred," his nation.[34] Once most people, as subjects, had taken little interest in war unless their own city or village was attacked; war had been the king's affair, not theirs. Now, increasingly, national wars became their wars because they were citizens, because they formed the armies, and because the armies defended and extended the national interests, their interests. That their military service in turn intensified their national consciousness seems sure, though certainly not in every case.

What France began, other nations and their governments could ignore at their peril, as the wars of the Revolution and Napoleon proved. When, and apparently only when, German and Spanish armies became in large part armies of patriots, could the French armies be defeated, German and Spanish national soil and interest be defended. Whether this was true or not,[35] it seemed true at the time, and some of the German military leaders, for instance August Gneisenau and Friedrich Jahn, who later led the national uprising against France, drew the obvious conclusion: armies should be armies of men "burning with patriotic spirit." [36] From the 1790's armies became more and more armies of citizen-patriots, the more patriotic the better, it was believed, and, in this belief, governments and armies began what would later be called "indoctrination" programs.

How could patriots for armies or for service of any kind to the nation be educated? The question was asked almost as often in the eighteenth century as it is now. Men were not born with inherent love of country, with "national character" implanted in them, or speaking their "native tongue." Unlike geniuses, patriots had to be made. Nature was credited with much by eighteenth-century thinkers, but they did not trust it to develop the kind of man they wanted. Those who already were patriotic, and eventually the governments that represented them, understood this and acted.

By the eighteenth century cultural similarities had developed among sizable groups of people, and intellectuals had become well aware of these. More were "discovered" and, when they did not exist, leaders hoped to create them. But cultural similarities, it began to be realized, were not enough. Men had to be made loyal to their nation. For this, education to inculcate patriotism was not only desirable but necessary. Through education in free public schools, through national holidays and festivals, through patriotic histories and collections of folklore, national ideals should be implanted, national character molded, and, above all, national loyalties instilled. As Rousseau had advocated, late-eighteenth-century leaders, especially but not only those of France, made great efforts to create loyal national citizens. They may have believed with Herder that men carried the God-given or natural group character within them as did plants and animals.[37] But if they so believed, they also were convinced that their societies, their governments should reinforce God and nature.

Through the century intellectual leaders, particularly in France, encouraged the teaching and use of the national languages. The reasons they gave were varied. People could learn their "native" language and understand it more readily than Latin. They needed a common language in their daily lives, in their businesses, and in their relationships with one another. Very likely lawyers and businessmen saw the various patois as obstacles to commerce and found learning Latin a waste of time and money. But whatever the motive, the belief mounted that each nation should have its own language, which all the nationals should use. Toward the end of the century the arguments became more clearly patriotic. The national language should be uniformly employed throughout the national territory to enable men of the same nation to recognize and understand each other; the spiritual wealth of the nation was stored in its language and could only be tapped by those understanding that language; and the true spirit and character of a nation could only be expressed in the national tongue.[38]

In France, from the time in the early 1700's of the great Jansenist leader of the University of Paris, Rollin (1661–1741), through the Revolution, the demand grew for the teaching of French and the use of French in all instruction in the schools. In 1763 Elie Bertrand in his *Dictionnaire universel des fossiles propres et des fossiles occidentales* expressed a common view: "All our masters teach us Latin and Greek which are never known perfectly and soon entirely forgotten; none teach us to be useful to the fatherland by employing our time, our money, our talents to practical things." [39] After the closing of the Jesuit schools about the same time, French was increasingly taught and used, even in those citadels of conservatism, the colleges and universities.

Almost everywhere in the western world, though usually somewhat later than in France, the same tendencies prevailed. While French dominated in court and diplomatic and Latin in academic circles, Johann Gottsched, Herder, and later Fichte and Schleiermacher in the Germanies pleaded for the use of German,[40] just as Noah Webster desired an American language in the United States and Alfieri demanded Italian for Italians.[41] In southern and eastern Europe as well, movements for the employment of national tongues began. In Greece Adamantios Koraïs was creating modern Greek with his numerous publications of the Greek classics. Josef Jungmann in Bohemia wrote a Czech grammar, a history of Czech literature, and a Czech-German dictionary, proclaiming language the supreme criterion of nationality.[42] A Bishop Mïcu (Samuil Klein) published a Romanian grammar and a cultural program for Romania that included the use of the Latin alphabet.[43] In Hungary John Ribyini asserted the superiority of Magyar as he pleaded for its use, while in Russia M. V. Lomonosov in his, the first, systematic grammar of living Russian, declared it the most expressive of all languages.[44]

With the French Revolution the national languages became a matter of major governmental concern.[45] Again it was France that led. During the Revolutionary years Mirabeau, Grégoire, Rabaut Saint-Etienne, Talleyrand, and Barère, for example, tried in various ways to spread the use of French among the inhabitants of France and thus stimulate patriotic ardor. The National Convention provided that the laws be read to the people in French, and that teachers of French be appointed in all districts, such as the Breton, where French was not customarily spoken.[46]

All Frenchmen were to speak French. This, it was believed, would reflect their unity and perpetuate their liberty. A correspondent of the revolutionary Bishop Grégoire in 1790 wrote, "Unity of language is not only useful for public assemblies; the safety, the public actions, the execution of the laws, the unity of the regime all demand this reform. . . . The great number of dialects could have been useful in the ninth century and during the long reign of feudalism . . . but today we all have the same law as master, and are no longer 'Rouergas' or 'Bourguignons' . . . we are all Frenchmen [and] should have only one language, as we have only one heart." [47] The Jacobin Barère, reporting for the Committee of Public Safety in January, 1794, declared that the dialects and foreign languages spoken in France "perpetuated the reign of fanaticism and superstition, secured the domination of priests and aristocrats . . . and favored the enemies of France." Calling it "treason to the *Patrie* to leave citizens in ignorance of the national language," he demanded that "the language of a free people" be "one and the same." [48]

One of the greatest stimuli to the use of French during the period was the result not of the direct efforts of individual patriots and the national governments but of the change in the nature of government and the enlargement of its functions. As more people participated in government, more had to understand what was being done on a national scale. As radical and new laws were rapidly promulgated, it became advantageous to understand them—for self-protection if for no other reason. As men entered the national services, military and civil, they found it necessary and expedient to understand and use the language of the law, the language of command.[49] In 1812 a prefect of the department Seine-Inférieure summarized these reasons for the increased use of French:

(1) The habit and necessity of reading these numerous laws, the decrees of every kind posted on the walls of all the communes, these public announcements which come daily to excite and feed the curiosity of all citizens. (2) The establishment of municipal duties which oblige so many peasants to write in an intelligible style in order to correspond with superior authorities, especially those of the popular societies, of which all the members must often speak from the rostrum to colleagues as ignorant as they but who are usually disposed to ridicule them if they speak in popular dialect. (3) The military conscription and levy which, taking from home a good part of the youth, places them in position to purify their language through the habit of attempting to speak better or differently. Thus it results that when they return to their homes, they bring with them a way of speaking, which though it deteriorates a little, nevertheless has some effect upon those with whom they associate.[50]

As it was with languages, so it was with all education. More and more the objective came to be the making of national citizens. Here again republicanism and national patriotism were closely tied. In his analysis of government in a republic Montesquieu foresaw clearly the problem that would face later statesmen. If despotism and monarchy were eliminated, they could no longer rely upon the old principles of fear and honor to bind men to the state, but would have to use education to instill love of laws and country and thus preserve the government. "Everything," Montesquieu thought, "depends on establishing this love in a republic, and to inspire it ought to be the principal business of education. . . ."[51] But even in a monarchy some had begun to think of education for patriotism vital. Believing that the first fundamental of public morality was childhood instruction, Turgot in 1775 urged Louis XVI to establish a Council of National Instruction to assure "uniformity of patriotic views."[52]

The great popularizer of patriotic education was, of course, Jean Jacques Rousseau. In his *Considerations on the Government of Poland*

and the *Letter to d'Alembert* on the theater, he proposed a Spartan (Lycurgus) molding of citizens through training in the home and the school and through public celebrations. He pleaded for an education that would place constantly before men, from mother's milk to death, the idea of the nation and thus awaken in them ardent love of their country.[53] To form a patriot (Polish, in this particular case), Rousseau would have the child learn to read by reading about his own country, at ten years know all the products, at twelve all the provinces, roads, and towns, at fifteen all the history, and at sixteen all the laws. There would not be a great action or illustrious man of whom the child did not have "full memory and heart and of whom he could not instantly give an account." His teachers would not be foreigners or priests but patriots, "married if possible, and distinguished by their morals, honesty, good sense, enlightenment. . . ."[54] To arouse patriotism and consciousness of unity, the citizens, in adulthood as well as childhood, would be edified by simple public spectacles, pageants, and folk games.[55] The effect of these would be "to reinforce the national character, augment natural inclinations and to give a new energy to all the emotions."[56]

Whether many of the French revolutionary leaders actually read Rousseau may be questioned. Some, like the orator Barère,[57] did, and many had similar views on patriotic education, which they attempted to put into practice. The Constitution of 1791 provided for a system of free public instruction "in those branches of education which are indispensable to all men."[58] The Convention of 1793–94 decreed the establishment of public primary schools to teach French and train for citizenship. Barère, who so often displayed patriotic zeal, expressed a popular view when he declared that the purpose of schooling was to create "love of country," that each man should prepare himself for service to it. Children, he asserted, belonged to the "general family before the particular families, and when the great family, the nation, calls, all private spirit must disappear."[59]

To issue decrees was easier than to establish schools that would train loyal citizens. Not much was done to establish state primary schools in France until Napoleon acted, though many plans were broached and some initiated. A beginning had been made, however, and during Napoleon's empire many French children and teachers were swearing allegiance to him and to France, just as a century later American school children were pledging allegiance to their "nation one and indivisible."

French revolutionary patriots perhaps were more successful in establishing patriotic commemorative days and festivals to stir enthusiasm for the *patrie* and revolutionary principles. With his usual enthusiasm Rousseau had recommended such festivals "to reinforce the national character, to strengthen natural tendencies, to give new energy to all the emotions." [60] The 1791 Constitution provided for the institution of national festivals "to preserve the memory of the French Revolution, to maintain fraternity among the citizens, and bind them to the Constitution, the *Patrie,* and the laws." [61] From the 1790 festivals of federation to the June, 1794, inauguration of a new religion to honor the "Supreme Being and the Republic of Virtue," many such celebrations were held. There can be little doubt that many Frenchmen experienced intense feelings of national awareness and unity in Brittany, Alsace, Dauphiné, and particularly in Paris during the first half of 1790. On July 14, 1790, perhaps 15 million Frenchmen all over France, and perhaps 300,000 in Paris alone, attended celebrations on the first anniversary of the fall of the Bastille, and many of them took the oath of loyalty to the nation, the law, and the king. This was probably the first national holiday in history.[62] The later *Fête* for Robespierre's Supreme Being on June 8, 1794, to inaugurate a religion of civic virtue, must have been impressive, but whether it made any converts may be doubted, for the Terror was at its height and Robespierre himself was soon to become its victim.[63]

What began in political or patriotic education with the Revolution spread widely in Europe and America. For the most part, the greatest strides were made in the nineteenth century, when every great and small nation moved to make education universal, free, and compulsory in order to create "good citizens," a term that in practice meant citizens more devoted to the nation and more willing to sacrifice themselves for it. Often the first stimulus to these educational reforms arose out of opposition to some real or potential oppressor, as in the German reaction to the Napoleonic conquests after 1806. In many nations, teachers and scholars, as at Berlin in the 1810's, were appointed and paid by the various governments to teach civic duty and devotion to the national welfare.[64] In many countries, as in the young United States with its Jeremy Belknap, Nicholas Pike, and Noah Webster, attempts were being made to shape national character through the teaching of the national language or even, in the United States, national spelling and national arithmetic.[65]

Formal schooling and public festivals constituted but two direct ways of forming national patriots. Much that was written and done, whether or not consciously and directly to inculcate patriotism, stimulated awareness of nation. Over much of Europe, even in lands considered "unenlightened," historians wrote patriotic accounts of the kind that had earlier appeared in England and France. Their histories give evidence not only of their own awakening national consciousness but of their desire to give their peoples deep historical roots and thus awaken in them similar consciousness. A list of the new national histories could be long but need not be here. In Russia Mikhail Lomonosov (1711–65) in his *Ancient Russian History* (1766) traced the Russian people to the "time before the destruction of Troy when the Enety, a Slavic tribe, came from Asia to settle on the shores of the Adriatic." He asked, "If literature can move the hearts of men, should not true history have power to stir us to praiseworthy deeds, especially that history which relates the feats of our ancestors?" [66] A few years later Nikolai Karamzin (1765–1826), as if in answer, wrote an essay (1802) on "Of Love of Fatherland and National Pride," and as official historiographer began a huge twelve-volume and popular *History of the Russian State* which, in the words of a contemporary, "showed us that we do have a fatherland." [67] In Bulgaria, Father Paisi (1722–98) wrote a "first" (1762) history of his people. He told them, "I have written for you that you may love your kin and your Bulgarian fatherland." [68] In Romania George Sinçai (1754–1806) and others called their countrymen the heirs of Rome in their several histories, which had a common theme: "Awaken, Rumanians! You are not sons of slaves, but have illustrious ancestors, ancestors in fact far older and far nobler than these arrogant masters who oppress you!" [69]

Like history, folklore can stimulate national feeling, and the eighteenth century discovered it and its uses. Herder, who believed each people had its own *volk* character, collected and published Norse, Lappish, Finnish, Spanish, Lithuanian, Serbian, English, and other folk songs in his *Alte Volkslieder* and *Volkslieder*. [70] Most of the folklorists, some of them poets, collected chiefly songs and tales in their own languages: Percy and Macpherson for England and Scotland, Tieck and the Grimms for Germany, Bishop Grundtvig for Denmark, A. A. Barsov and N. A. Lvov in Russia. The romantic belief grew that the lore sprang from the people's "innermost uniqueness," and enshrined the wisdom and "the soul of the nation." [71] That each people was unique and had a "soul" was not questioned, and generations of people grew up hearing and reading what were now considered the national folk tales, and thus were inspired to love the past of their own people.

Not everything in life can be nationalized. But much in western Europe—and more slowly in eastern Europe—was becoming national, both by design and by circumstance. French and Spanish academies as well as individuals published dictionaries and grammars of their national languages and—generally later this would be done for each language—set "right" national criteria for speaking and writing. At different times in different nations, but generally in the late eighteenth century and early nineteenth, demands mounted for national theaters with plays in the national languages—the *Comédie-Française,* already established in France —for national societies of the arts and sciences—the French academies— for national museums, for truly national literatures, and for national periodicals and newspapers.[72] Generally and eventually, these demands had results. In 1793, for example, the French National Convention made the Louvre the *Musée de la République,* possibly the first national museum to be established. The National Convention, indeed, used the arts to inculcate republican patriotism whenever it saw the opportunity, calling on poets, historians, painters, and sculptors to teach patriotism through their work, and on occasion it subsidized this work.[73] And other governments would often do likewise. Each nation, too, if it had not already done so, would adopt a national flag and national colors—as France did the tricolor in 1789—and put its soldiers in national uniforms. In revolutionary France during 1793–94, everywhere citizens turned they were confronted with national institutions and propaganda. And this would become increasingly true, particularly in times of crisis, for citizens of other nations.

The influence of institutions and propaganda should not, however, be overestimated. A good many Frenchmen in 1793–94 were not, in the existing revolutionary situation, patriots; in fact, many were bitter opponents of the revolutionary nation and its government. It is also true that some Frenchmen were patriots not so much because they were so conditioned as because the nation afforded them, in theory at least, liberties—to trade or to speak—and opportunities to serve and find satisfaction.

From the vantage point of the twentieth century, it might appear that liberal eighteenth-century views on liberty and property would have been antinational, that if the nation were supreme and national goals paramount, then the nation could control property and restrain individuals as it willed. It is true, on the one hand, that leading philosophers and reformers believed with Adam Smith and the French physiocrats in the inviolability of private property and in *laissez faire* in business and commerce, and that they generally opposed *étatisme* and most governmental economic regulations; it is likewise true that they considered individual liberties, such as those of speech and religion, to be natural and opposed governmental interference with these freedoms as unnatural and harmful. Private ownership of property, *laissez faire,* and individual freedoms seem hardly congruous with strong nationalism. It is true, on the other hand, that those who followed Rousseau believed in the supremacy of the general will, and this belief could lead to the nationalization of property, to the denial of liberties. And in times of crisis and war, especially in the twentieth century, national interests, as they were conceived, of course, led to nationalization of property and authoritarian, national control of thought and action. But in the context of the eighteenth century, at least before the wars beginning in 1792, it was the *national* governments that were expected to protect private property, establish freedom of trade, and guarantee what were coming to be called civil liberties.[74]

If individuals wished to speak or worship freely, it was the national governments, and they only, that were able to guarantee these privileges. If merchants desired to trade without restriction or hindrance, it was only the national state that could establish *laissez faire* and hence promote trade in the wide area enclosed by the national political boundaries.[75] If the freedom to own property or gain profits was threatened anywhere within the country, it would be threatened everywhere within the country; therefore the right to property had to be guaranteed by the only institution capable of exercising nationwide control, the nation-state. Only in a national government that could cut across or ignore local boundaries and that was more powerful than a feudal order or a trade guild was the solution to the problems of economic or any freedom then to be found.

In this significant sense, then, national sentiment was strengthened at the expense of other older religious and feudal loyalties as the drive for liberty intensified and became realized. In the historical pattern of the time, *laissez faire* meant not only freedom from governmental control to seek profit but in practice—as in France in 1789—also freedom from all kinds of hindrances—from tax inequalities based on ancient privileges, from feudal dues, from local and provincial tolls and tariffs, and from craft guild regulations on quality. Individual freedom meant freedom not only from the arbitrary rule of monarchs like Louis XIV and James I but also from religious conformity and from the social inequalities arising out of aristocratic privilege. In these circumstances only a national government, a government with authority above all authorities, could effectively act. While the national governments were not supposed, according to the bills of rights incorporated in most of the new constitutions during the next century and three-quarters, to interfere with the individual's liberties, they were the chosen instruments or policemen through which these liberties were won and preserved.

In 1776 the thirteen united colonies of America ringingly declared their independence from Britain with the statement that all men had "certain inalienable rights," and in 1791 they added to the new federal Constitution ten amendments to prevent infringement of liberties by their federal government.[76] In its Declaration of the Rights of Man and Citizen of 1789 (August), the National Assembly in France proclaimed: "Men are born and remain free and equal in rights" and "the aim of every political association is the preservation of the natural and inalienable rights of man . . . liberty, property, security, and resistance to oppression." The 1791 national Constitution guaranteed these liberties and the "inviolability of property" against infringement by "the legislative power." Thus the national governments and the courts were at the same time the protectors of the rights of citizens and the instruments through which these rights were obtained.

Few, if any, of the political theorists and practitioners, however, thought of the state as just a policeman, a negative restraint on economic privilege. The liberals of the Revolutionary era believed that the nation-state should be a positive force for the defense and promotion of the national interests. The state, for instance, was generally expected to prevent any internal disorder that might harm trade, to establish those uniform conditions (weights and measures) and laws (of contract) that might assist trade, and to protect and subsidize the nation's foreign commerce as well as its domestic manufacture. It is notable that the most influential book on economics of the eighteenth century, that published in 1776 by the archadvocate of *laissez faire*, Adam Smith, was called *The Wealth of Nations*. The economic welfare of nations (England in particular), not individual businessmen, was indeed ever in the forefront of Smith's argument. Did he ask for freedom of trade? This was because freedom increased the wealth of the nation. Did he desire complete freedom for the individual entrepreneur? No. He was quite willing even to limit individual profits in terms of national interest. The severely (in theory) regulatory Navigation Acts of the seventeenth century he called "perhaps the wisest of all the commercial regulations of England" because he believed "defence is of much more importance than opulence." [77]

Smith was willing to restrict freedom of trade in the national interest; others were willing to use the national economy in both old and new ways. The old policies of "provision" established by the monarchs were continued, except that now the king's interests became the national. In the young United States, Alexander Hamilton, the Secretary of the Treasury, pleaded with the national House of Representatives to encourage manufacturing. "Not only," he argued, "the wealth but the independence and security of the country appear to be materially connected with the prosperity of a manufacture. Every nation, with a view to these great objects, ought to endeavor to possess within itself all the essentials of national supply." The defense and security of the nation, especially should war come, thus often took precedence over complete freedom of industry and trade.[78]

With the partial exception of Britain, which later in the nineteenth century saw its national interest in free trade as long as it (Britain) dominated in manufacture and on the seas, European and American national governments followed policies similar to those of Hamilton.[79] They helped national businesses in many ways. They often established national uniformity in weights and measures—as did the French Convention in 1793 and 1795; they often codified a common business law; and if they did not already have them, they provided for national currencies and banks—as did the United States in 1791 and France in 1800.[80] To encourage home manufacture they continued and usually increased tariffs at the national boundaries.[81]

At times, of course, they went much further. National governments in crisis, like the French in 1793 and 1794 during war and counterrevolution, set prices and wages, confiscated land, and in general taxed and regulated and "nationalized" as leaders believed the national interest dictated. The national governments in many cases also took over duties and responsibilities that had formerly been those of noble and priest and of the king. The 1791 French Constitution gave the government responsibility for public relief. And in 1794, after a long report by Barère, who hoped once more "to excite patriotism," the National Convention voted a decree to help the poor, the aged and infirm, the sick, and widows with children.[82]

For increasing numbers of Europeans their nation and their national government were becoming, or would become, their family, their father and mother, and their protector. As the old world of fixed status and values crumbled during the eighteenth century, and especially during the revolutions and wars at its end, the nation became both a refuge and a way to the future. While some people, in quiet times as well as in crises, still turned to old authorities, to lord and priest, many, more and more often, turned to the new national authorities who used the national governments to make patriots. As many became nationally conscious and loyal, they in turn demanded more from their national governments. Again and again this cycle repeated itself. As old loyalties dissolved and societies became fluid, hope and fear sharpened desire for new national authorities who promised fulfillment of hope and assuagement of fear. As the national governments acted, the nation gained significance and meaning. For many it offered (or seemed to offer) much, not only protection but freedom, education, jobs and careers, ways to obtain financial gain and social status.[83] For many it provided satisfaction in service, participation in common affairs, ways to more meaningful lives. National loyalty, nationalism, then, was one logical (and historical) result.

That nationalism provided ways for people to find release from frustration and to express hate is also true. As psychological research beginning with Freud has shown, individuals, especially those who have had psychic traumas in early life, find satisfaction in the discharge of their emotions, their biological drives (the id), in many ways. But here analysis is difficult, for both "normal" and "neurotic" people are involved. That some of the leading and most ardent of the French revolutionary patriots of '93–'94 were not what is called "normal" is certain: Couthon was a paralytic; Saint-Just stole family valuables when he ran away from home in 1786 at the age of nineteen; and Collot d'Herbois, a popular ex-actor, became brutal and Carrier sadistic as they butchered people during the Terror. But it is also true that Lazare Carnot, the firm patriot who organized the French armies, was a sober, serious citizen, as were other revolutionary leaders. Whether, indeed, the new national patriots of the 1790's, leaders or followers, were more or less "normal" than men of other times and places is impossible to determine. The most "ordinary" and "normal" of men, especially in times of stress, find emotional satisfaction if not joy in venting their hatred, in attempting to destroy whatever seems to threaten them or to stand in the way of realization of their hopes, and this seems to have been true during the most violent days of the Revolution when the people marched.[84] The crowds on these days were not chiefly composed of the *canaille* but of workshop masters, craftsmen, wage earners, and petty traders.[85]

The many Frenchmen during the years '89–'94 who were apathetic or opposed to the Revolution were considered by the revolutionaries to be insufficiently patriotic or unpatriotic, were called "enemies of the people," "enemies of the nation." Patriotism and revolutionary zeal had, in fact, become the same. Patriots were those who demanded national action to accomplish the revolutionary ends and insisted that everyone work toward these ends. By 1792 for these patriots persuasion and education were not enough or too slow. All those who were not sufficiently revolutionary or patriotic had to be coerced or eliminated. Members of groups nearly always demand conformity, and so it was then—and with vehemence.

Through the early years of the Revolution, French legislators appealed again and again for support of the nation, as did most of the multiplying number of newspapers and clubs. To "educate" the people the Assemblies sent out their laws and their instructions to the provinces, while considerable numbers of people, especially Parisians but also delegations from the provinces, attended meetings of the Assemblies and also went out to make converts. Club members, the Jacobins, for instance, corresponded, and newspapers from Paris were read in many parts of France.[86] Education in national affairs brought national consciousness and sometimes intensified loyalties. But war and defeat came in '92, and in '93–'94 counterrevolution threatened ever more as rebellion broke out in cities such as Lyons and Nantes and in the region of the Vendée. Those who did not support the national revolutionary government in Paris became "suspect," traitors to the country. As early as 1789 the radical Bishop Grégoire had spoken of the crime of *"les-Majesté Nationale"* and called it the greatest, the worst of crimes.[87] In December, 1792, the National Convention decreed the penalty of death for anyone who attempted to disrupt the unity of the Republic,[88] and Robespierre declared, "The Revolution is the war of liberty against its enemies . . . the revolutionary government owes complete national protection to good citizens; to the enemies of the people it owes only death." [89] In September, 1793, as enemy armies invaded France, the National Convention declared all those "suspect" who in any way opposed the national government, established "Watch Committees" to prepare lists of suspected persons, and ordered all suspects arrested. The Terror was under way as the Convention, its great committees and its Revolutionary Tribunal, along with committees in the provinces, enforced the decree. The Terror, which meant conform or die, reached its height in June, 1794, with the law of the 22nd Prairial that defined "enemies of the people" so vaguely that anyone who disagreed with the representatives of the national republic could be guillotined, and without any legal defense whatever. After July, 1794, the demand for conformity was less imperious and the Terror less ruthless, but for a year and a half before that the edict had been clear—be loyal or die. The words of one representative on mission, Collot d'Herbois, might seem but mad exaggerated rhetoric, yet he did what he said he would do as he set out in late '93 to destroy the counterrevolutionaries at Lyons, the second city of France: "It is not Collot d'Herbois who leaves for Lyons, it is the representative of the people who goes to display the national power to restrain [*contenir*] the rebels. . . . I leave tomorrow and I swear that I shall return to tell you that the South [*Midi*] is purged [*purifié*], that only patriots will remain there, or that I shall die at Lyons." [90] He did not die, but hundreds of the rebels of Lyons did.

The pressure to conform, to be faithful to the nation, did not come from the government and its representatives alone. The pressures from individual rabid revolutionaries and patriots were high as well. The Twelfth Commandment of a pamphlet of 1793 entitled *The Sixteen Commandments of a Patriot* read, "Be not an unjust reformer, but maintain constant vigilance over the enemies of liberty. Fear not to denounce conspirators, for failure to do so will make you as guilty as they are. . . ."[91] People, anonymously or openly, denounced other people, neighbors informed on neighbors, and the concierges and janitors kept track of everyone. Informers informed for many reasons—petty grudges and envy as well as patriotic duty—and they were themselves often, as are informers at any time, quite "devoid of political scruples" or political faith. But they did inform, and they did frighten people into at least lip service to the nation. Coercion, social and political, was likely effective, for a time, in making people at any rate seem to be patriotic.

There is no way of precisely assessing the effectiveness of the political and social attempts to make patriots. There were no public-opinion polls or surveys of the twentieth-century variety, and if there had been, they probably could not have measured (as they cannot now measure) the depth of national sentiment. Nonetheless, the evidence is clear: many Frenchmen were becoming nationally conscious and loyal.

In speech, writing, and thought, the *sujet* had become the *citoyen*, the *état* the *nation*, and the *pays* the *patrie*. These words, *citoyen, nation, patrie*, represented the new actuality, for the nation had become citizens who participated in shaping their, the national, affairs, and the will of the nation had superseded that of the king, become that of the nation-state which acted (or ought to act) for all citizens. Love of fatherland, patriotism, therefore became, as Montesquieu thought proper in a republic, the chief and most praised virtue, and honor and status went to the patriot.[92]

Not only did a patriot receive honor and status. Again and again patriots testified that they found significance and joy in love of country. In August, 1792, a young peasant joined the army. Later, as Sergeant Fricasse, he wrote, "How many times I had heard that our French army had been defeated. . . . I said often to myself, is it possible that I hear only bad news? It seemed to me that had I been present the misfortune would not have been as great. . . ."[93] Another young soldier, the son of a day laborer, wrote to his mother, "When *la Patrie* calls us for her defense, we should rush to her as I would run to a good meal. Our life, our goods, and our talents do not belong to us. It is to the nation, to *la Patrie* that everything belongs . . . as for me . . . who have always been a republican in my soul . . . the principles of love for *la Patrie* . . . are not only engraved on my heart, but absorbed in it . . ." [94]

The testimony of leaders is more rhetorical and high-flown, but there is no reason to doubt its sincerity. A provincial lawyer, Durand-Maillane, who became a deputy of the Third Estate in 1789–91, declared, "Before [1789] no one knew where *la Patrie* was. Frenchmen saw it entirely in their kings. . . . Finally the Revolution came, and for the first time, each of us tasted the delights of all those relationships which, as we learn from Cicero, united citizens to their fatherland as the center of all their affections." [95] Robespierre's paean was more extravagant: "Yes, this delicious land that we inhabit . . . is made to be the domain of liberty and happiness . . . this acute and proud people are truly born for glory and virtue. . . . Oh my fatherland! . . . I am French. . . . Oh sublime people! receive the sacrifice of my being." [96] The most eloquent of the testimonies came from the sober Carnot in 1793: "Oh France! oh my fatherland! Oh great people, truly great people, it is on your soil that I had the happiness to be born. I would cease belonging to you only in ceasing to exist. You hold all the objects of my affection: the work that my hands have contributed to, the upright old man who gave me life, the family without blemish, the friends who know the bottom of my heart. . . . " [97]

As the Revolution became more violent and as France warred with much of Europe from 1792, the philosophic cosmopolitanism of eighteenth-century liberals tended to disappear and national prejudices and national hatreds to be accentuated. [98] More often now Frenchmen exalted their own nation and placed its welfare first, though this might mean injury to other like groups. The Dantonist Robert declared, with the applause of the Convention, in 1793, "I desire that the Legislator of France forget the universe for a moment and occupy itself with its own country. I wish that kind of national egoism without which we betray our duties . . . I love all men, I love particularly all free men, but I love the free men of France more than all the others of the universe." [99] As has been said, in 1798 the abbé Barruel caught clearly part of the meaning of what was happening as he perhaps coined the word *nationalisme* in French. To repeat his words, when men united in nations, "they ceased to recognize themselves under a common name—. *Nationalism* or *National Love* took the place of general love. With the divisions of the globe and with its countries, goodwill contracted within limits which it could no longer surmount. Then it became a virtue to expand at the expense of those who were not under our dominion. Then to obtain this end it became permissible to distrust, deceive and offend strangers." [100]

The sentiment Barruel described as nationalism developed throughout western Europe during the war years 1792–1815. It became widespread in France from 1792, when patriotism became synonymous with the support of the Revolution against internal and external enemies, when patriotic loyalty in defeat and invasion turned into patriotic pride in victory and expansion. Because of the fear and hatred of France, particularly· of Napoleonic France, it grew strong in England, in the Germanies after 1806,[101] in Spain after 1808, and to a lesser extent in the Italies.·And because of the example of France and the oppression of foreign conquerors, national patriotism with distrust of foreigners was also arising in Poland and Greece, and in some degree almost everywhere in Europe and the Americas. How, more particularly, this came about in these years of crisis warrants further attention.

V

Nationalism Spreads and Deepens, 1790–1815

Through the eighteenth century, enlightened thinkers in England and the Germanies as well as France often, like the Roman Stoics, placed the welfare of mankind above that of the separate nations. Some of them took pride in calling themselves "citizens of the world," as did the German playwright Gotthold Lessing and the English poet and playwright Oliver Goldsmith. While they sometimes conceived of the nation as the group through which individuals could make their special contribution to humanity, many of them, with the German dramatist and poet Johann Schiller (1759–1805),[1] thought of nations as but changing "fragments" of mankind and could have subscribed to Goethe's later phrase, "above the nations is humanity."

This kind of idealist cosmopolitanism was perhaps strongest at the hopeful time the Revolution began in France. Cosmopolitanism did not die as the Revolution became more violent and nations went to war. In 1795 the great German philosopher Immanuel Kant (1724–1804) dreamed of perpetual peace as he advocated a federation of free republics, each of which would give up a part of its freedom in a kind of social contract for peace.[2] While Goethe, who lived all through the revolutions and wars and longer, was not indifferent toward his nation, Germany, he continued to think of his fatherland as that place where he was happy and could be of use, and to believe national hatreds were always strongest where the culture was lowest.[3]

Sentiment veered, however, toward not cosmopolitanism but nationalism. At no time during the eighteenth century had the cosmopolitans been numerous, and they never represented dominant opinion. As he advised the king of Poland to train his subjects to be patriots, Rousseau wrote, with obvious indignation, "There are no longer Frenchmen, Germans, Spaniards, or even Englishmen. . . . All have the same tastes, the same passions, the same customs because they have not been [as they should have been] shaped by national institutions." [4] As if echoing Rousseau, Herder ironically exclaimed, with his fellow Germans in mind, "All national characters, thank God, have become extinct! We all love one another or, rather, no one feels the need of loving anyone else. We associate with one another, are all completely equal—cultured, polite, very happy! We have, it is true, no fatherland, no one for whom we live; but we are philanthropists and citizens of the world." [5] Not the cosmopolitans like Schiller but the believers in nationality like Rousseau and Herder pointed to the future.

Before Napoleon's conquest of the Germanies in 1805–06 a young German philosopher, Johann Fichte, was an individualist and a cosmopolitan, indifferent to national patriotism. After Napoleon's conquest he preached a violent nationalism in his *Addresses to the German Nation* (1808) and other writings: the purposes of humanity had to be achieved through the nation; only the German could be a patriot, only a German could "for the sake of his nation encompass the whole of mankind," only a German, the "original German . . . not the institutionalized, withered man," could save mankind.[6] Not many Europeans ever became as violently nationalist as Fichte, but from one end of Europe to the other writers attacked the philosophical cosmopolitanism of the eighteenth century as an impractical dream of superficial philanthropists, or worse. In England the poet and essayist Coleridge believed "the cosmopolitanism which does not spring out of, and blossom upon, the deep-rooted stem of nationality or patriotism . . . a spurious and rotten growth." [7] For the historian Karamzin in Russia, "the true cosmopolitan" was "either a metaphysical conception or a phenomenon so unusual that it is not worth while to mention him. . . . The personality of every man is narrowly bound up with his homeland. We love her because we love ourselves." [8]

From the 1790's to 1815 revolutions and wars stimulated national feeling almost everywhere in Europe, and in the New World as well. Governments, becoming more national, increasingly penetrated the lives of their peoples. In varying ways and degrees, individuals in western, central, and to a lesser extent eastern and southeastern Europe became more aware of and further participated in the activities of their national governments and their more and more national societies. As they did so, they more and more tended to identify with their national governments and cultures, to become opposed to whatever was foreign, hence to become increasingly nationalist in sentiment.

The extent and depth of national feeling at the end of the eighteenth century should not be overestimated, for many individuals, even in western Europe, were scarcely aware of their nationality, and not many were ardently patriotic. Many clung to old loyalties, and likely many were, as Napoleon believed, led by baubles and the hope of excitement and loot rather than inspired by love of country. As nationalism spread among a growing minority, however, it became, for the most ardent patriots, a cult if not a religion. The scene cannot be duplicated elsewhere, but a ceremony at the opening of the French Legislative Assembly in 1791 symbolized the rise of this new cult. "Twelve old men went in procession to seek the Book of the Constitution. They came back, having at their head the archivist Camus, who, holding the Book with his two hands and resting it on his breast, carried with slow and measured tread the new Blessed Sacrament of the French." [9]

The degree and nature of national feeling, it must be reiterated, varied with the peoples, indeed, varied with individuals and with time. Quite likely the extent and intensity of national consciousness during the twenty-five years from 1790 to 1815 were never higher than they were in France during the early Revolution, but in the Germanies and Spain after 1806 and 1808, and among individuals in much of old Europe and in parts of the New World, national feeling was deep and deepening. And if and when people were not patriotic enough to please their leaders and their fellows who *were* patriots, they were cajoled and urged to be loyal, and on occasion forced to give national service. More and more people, as a result, became nationally conscious, though certainly not always loyal or eager to serve.

In France, during the years from 1790 to 1794, the hope of establishing a new era through the nation as well as the threat to the Revolution posed by émigrés and foreign princes intensified national feeling. Early defeats accentuated the danger and inspired defiance; later victories inspired pride, even arrogance, and hope or ambition for further gains. Many Frenchmen identified the Revolution with France, and France and the Revolution with their own personal interests and ideals. As Albert Sorel, a major historian of French foreign policy, observed, they "saw something very practical and real in the Revolution, the abolition of the feudal regime . . . they saw in the armed emigration an attempt to re-establish by force this hateful regime. The Revolution was being accomplished to assure Frenchmen free possession of the soil of France. The foreign invasion [1792] was taking place to destroy the Revolution, dis-member France and subjugate Frenchmen. They quite naturally identified love of France with love of the Revolution. . . ." [10]

The revolutionary demands for liberty, the strategic demands of defense, the national government's need for money and supplies, the vast personal ambitions of leaders, and the constant foreign threat drove France to vast conquests, first to the so-called natural frontiers and then far beyond. As this occurred, other peoples, or, rather, leaders among them, reacted vigorously, either in support of revolutionary France or in opposition to it. At first this took place chiefly on the borders of France, later in much of Europe and parts of the New World. Their reaction most often took a nationalist form. This was especially true when the French Napoleonic armies began to dominate large areas of Europe after 1805.

Of course nationalist feelings existed throughout Europe and in the United States before the French Revolution. Of course the nationalism that developed after 1789 was not solely in reaction to France and its Revolution. In Europe, from Scandinavia to Spain and from the Atlantic to the Volga and the Black Sea, individuals had become or were slowly becoming, especially during the eighteenth century, aware of their nationalities. Englishmen from the thirteenth century onward were as much or as little nationally conscious as were Frenchmen. Irishmen had never loved their British masters and in 1782 rebelled, asking in the name of English liberties for the "rights of Ireland." Some Dutchmen were becoming national patriots in the seventeenth century. Especially after 1763 some colonists in North America had begun to think of themselves as Americans and in 1776, as everyone knows, established a new nation. Poles had resented the "first" partition of their country in 1772 by Prussia, Austria, and Russia. They had disliked Russians for centuries. In 1791 they had tried to protect their independence in a new national constitution, and in 1794 a great Polish leader, Tadeusz Kościuszko, led an unsuccessful national uprising against Russia. But the great swell of nationalist feeling in Europe arose in reaction to France, its Revoluton, and its conquests.

This reaction, whether for or against, was vigorous. When the Revolution came, the "liberal," the enlightened, and the romantic enthusiastically supported it, for they saw in it the fulfillment of eighteenth-century ideals of liberty and happiness. Like the American Jefferson (1743–1826), the Englishman Tom Paine (1737–1809), the German Anacharsis Clootz (1754–94), they often professed to be cosmopolitan, but they were usually, also, national patriots, like the Greeks Adamantios Koraïs (1748–1833) and Constantine Rhigas (1760–98). [11] Though many of these "liberals" would be repelled by the Terror of 1793–94, they believed the revolutionary reforms would benefit all mankind and that the French example would and should be followed by all civilized peoples. On the other hand, monarchists, aristocrats, "conservatives," members of the old establishment detested the Revolution and revolutionary France. Whether they were already nationalists, like the Englishman Edmund Burke (1729–97), the American Alexander Hamilton (1753–1804), and the Italian Vittorio Alfieri (1749–1803),[12] or oblivious to nationalism, like the brothers of Louis XVI, the Comte de Provence and the Comte d'Artois, they still had to meet the French nationalist challenge. Especially after the French conquests engulfed Europe, the opponents of France had either to become nationalist themselves, as did Johann Fichte, or to act as if they were, as did the Baron vom und zum Stein. France, then, was admired, envied, or hated, but, in one way or another, imitated. Nationalism, it may be repeated, bred nationalism.

It is *impossible* to set exact dates for the swell in nationalism, but 1792 and the outbreak of the French Revolutionary and the subsequent Napoleonic wars will do. At the beginning of their Revolution, French leaders again and again announced their good will toward all mankind and renounced all military conquests.[13] But war was inevitable, because the Revolution was dynamic and the threats against it great, because of the deeply rooted French ambition to dominate Europe, and because of the equally deep-rooted fear of France among the powers as well as their own ambitions for expansion. The war that came in April, 1792, led to more war—to twenty-three years of war—to victories and defeats, to threats and counterthreats, and to exaltation and humiliation for all participants. Patriotism provided *élan* for the French people and troops. To prevail, the opponents of France had, eventually, to strengthen their own nation-states, to become more nationalist than they had been.

As everyone knows, hostility to France had existed for centuries. Revolution, as it aroused the fears of conservatives, accentuated and provided further reason for hostility. Still, the great powers, England, Austria, Prussia, and Russia, were at first cautious; they thought revolutionary France was too weak and confused to be dangerous, and they were interested in their own possible territorial acquisitions elsewhere (as in Poland). In 1791 Austria and Prussia rather idly threatened to intervene; then, their fears fanned by the pleas of the French royal family and émigrés, they began more serious preparations. From France enthusiasts for the Revolution propagandized[14] for revolutionary principles, and their supporters in surrounding territories agitated for reforms and revolution *à la française*.

Opinion in France was divided for and against war. But those who wanted to spread the Revolution and those who feared intervention prevailed, as France decided for war, asserting that it was but "the just defense of a free people against the unjust aggression of a king [the Austrian emperor]." Brissot de Warville, a leader of the Girondists who favored war, made an argument that became one prototype for the later arguments of belligerent, democratic nationalists: "The force of reason and of facts has persuaded me that a people, which, after a thousand years of slavery, has achieved liberty, needs war. It needs war to consolidate its freedom. It needs war to purge away the vices of despotism. It needs war to banish from its bosom the men who might corrupt its liberty." [15] Within a year after April, 1792, France was at war with Austria, Prussia, England, Spain, and Holland. Within ten years Napoleon was favoring France with a new brand of despotism. But nationalists continued to argue for war to protect liberty. It was simply not true, as Herder once argued, that fatherlands, once people had them, would lie peacefully side by side and aid each other.

Through the summer of 1792, as foreign armies invaded and reached Verdun, the war went badly for the French. In late July the Duke of Brunswick, the commander in chief of the enemy Austrian and Prussian forces, issued a fiery manifesto: France, and in particular Paris, must restore the King or the allies would "exact an exemplary and ever-memorable vengeance . . . by delivering the city of Paris to military punishment and total destruction. . . ." [16]

To revolutionary Frenchmen this threat was not idle. Already in early July the French Legislative Assembly had declared the *patrie* in danger. The revolutionary leader Danton, now at the height of his power and popularity, cried, "To triumph over the enemy . . . we must be bold, still more bold, ever bold, and France is saved." Soon, in September, the Terror began—to make the nation safe for revolution by extirpating enemies within and without. For the French, reverse followed reverse, and from the north the "enemy" marched closer to Paris. But at Valmy, on September 20, the dreaded foreign invasion was turned into an indecisive skirmish—termed a glorious victory by French national patriots. From then until 1812 the French, though they suffered defeats in battles and felt themselves constantly threatened, generally won the wars. This enabled national aggrandizment *and* brought retaliation by other nations.

After Valmy and other victories, the French Convention, still fearful but now daring to hope, declared (November 19, 1792), in what is called the First Propaganda Decree, that in the "name of the French nation" it would "grant fraternity and aid to all peoples" who wished "to recover their liberty." [17] The decree was, or seemed to be, simply an offer of fraternal aid to those of like revolutionary views, and it was accompanied by assurances that the sovereignty of other nations would be respected.[18] Less than a month later (December 15) the Convention issued a Second Propaganda Decree that was much less idealistic. Pressed for money and supplies to support the armies, anxious to make conquered peoples pay for their "liberation," and importuned by its now victorious generals, the Convention declared it would "treat as enemy of the people" anyone who refused liberty and equality, and it promised sovereignty and independence to all peoples who adopted "principles of equality and established a free and popular government." [19] French nationalism, as have the nationalisms of most large and some small nations ever since, was becoming expansive and imperialistic. By the December 15 decree its adherents quite openly announced their intention to force "liberty," that is, the French political system, upon any people and make them pay for the privilege. The full implication of this policy would not be immediately clear, but soon the French were forcing "liberty" upon immediately neighboring territories that could, for one reason or another, be claimed as French, annexing, as they were able, Nice, the Austrian Netherlands, and Rhineland provinces. The peoples were required to pay French taxes and establish French political institutions, and were told they were equally summoned to govern, to serve, and to defend the *patrie*. Certain of their own national rectitude, French leaders now believed the Declaration of Rights was to become the model for the "entire world." [20] By 1795 there could no longer be any doubt about French national policy. It became, quite unhypocritically, that stated by a lawyer and member of the Convention, Merlin de Douai: France should indemnify itself for its expenses of the unjust wars waged against it and, "to prevent new wars," should retain by either title of treaty or conquest whatever country served "its convenience, *without consulting the inhabitants.*" [21]

This doctrine seemed to, and did, contradict two of the arising major principles of nationalism, the beliefs in "natural" national frontiers and in the right of each people to self-determination. Further, it raised a question that has bothered revolutionists ever since. Could a major revolution, whatever its motivation, successfully take place in only one country? The answer (sought by Trotsky and Stalin over a century later) was then "No, no," especially if the revolution was connected with nationalism, for revolutionary ideas, including nationalism, were explosive, hard to contain, and instilled fear in other peoples.

The belief that natural frontiers should determine the boundaries of nations was not new. A Roman principle revived in Italy during the Renaissance, it was held in substance by Cardinal Richelieu in the seventeenth century for the lands he claimed for France, those contained (he used the word *pre-carré*) by the Atlantic, the Rhine, the Alps, the Mediterranean, and the Pyrenees; and in the eighteenth century Rousseau believed that the mountains, seas, and rivers that served as the limits of nations seemed naturally to have decided the size and number of European nations.[22] During the early Revolution, French leaders seemed to accept Richelieu's frontiers as rightfully those of France, but French armies were soon to march far beyond them. The principle seemed to make sense (on the surface it still does), but while it became a fundamental tenet of French foreign policy, it was never more than a principle used, when convenient, to support and to forward policy. The "natural" frontiers did not divide French-speaking people from those of other languages (German, for example), and other powers did not agree to the "natural boundaries" France claimed. Moreover, if French armies occupied all the lands within the natural barriers, did they not have to go beyond them in order to defend them? In fact, the natural barriers were not barriers but, at least in the case of the rivers and seas, carriers of people and trade, and Napoleon found the Alps no great obstacle on his way to Italy. Nevertheless, good French nationalists claimed the boundaries they wanted were "natural."

Self-determination was a logical development of French revolutionary doctrine.[23] Each people, following democratic ideology, should be consulted and decide upon their own government. If, however, a powerful nation wished not only to defend itself but also to bring freedom to other less enlightened nations, then what of self-determination or natural frontiers? The contradictions are easily perceived, yet good nationalists then (and later) did not perceive them. The most logical and persuasive statement of both principles was made by the republican organizer of the French armies and "victory," Lazare Carnot. In his too little known report of February, 1793, to the Diplomatic Committee of the Convention, he laid down a policy that was long to be a fundamental premise in the foreign policy of many nations, though not many would ever allow it to interfere with their national interest when they desired to expand.

Among themselves nations in the political order are like individuals in the social. They have, like individuals, their respective rights. These are independence, external security, internal unity, national honor, in short all those major interests that a people cannot lose except when they are taken by force and that they are always able to regain when the opportunity presents itself.

Now natural law desires that these rights be respected, that everyone assist in defending them as long as by this assistance . . . their own rights are not compromised.

To say that sovereignty resides in humanity is to say that France is only a portion of the sovereign, that hence it does not have the right to establish those laws that suit it. But we have, on the contrary, our principle that every people, however small [he was referring to Monaco] the country they inhabit, is absolutely its own master at home, that it is equal in rights to the greatest, and that no other country can legitimately attack its independence, at least if its own is not threatened.

Let us then follow the law written in the hearts of all men and try not to violate it. May the national honor, may French generosity be for all peoples of the earth the certain guarantee of the justice that you owe them and that you wish to render to them. May these sublime sentiments, breaking the irons of oppressed nations, surpass their hopes and desires.

And now I pass to the practical application of this principle.

The traditional and natural limits of France are the Rhine, the Alps, the Pyrenees—the parts that have been dismembered have been so only by usurpation. There would be, then, . . . no undue ambition in recognizing as brothers those who once were, in reestablishing the bounds which were broken only by greed itself.[24]

Carnot, an honest and sincere patriot, was here asserting what nationalists have claimed ever since: that all people who could be said to be of the same nation (for whatever reason) should be united with and within that nation. He was not dreaming of foreign conquest. But France was "threatened," and because of this and the ambitions of its leaders, it did violate the principles of self-determination, did go beyond its "natural" frontiers—just as other powerful nations have done since. In actuality the "natural" boundaries were usually those to which a nation, at any one time, could expand, and, once having reached them, the nation would often go beyond and seek new boundaries, just as France was soon to do, whether or not the peoples affected were willing.

All the same, the right of national self-determination, or in another guise "popular sovereignty," became one of the most sacred political principles of the nineteenth and twentieth centuries. The example of the thirteen colonies in North America in establishing their own government of the United States was followed throughout Europe and then the rest of the world. People after people, "however small," would claim their independence during the next century and three-quarters. The French themselves immediately encountered their own principle in many parts of Europe, in, for example, Piedmont in 1799 when insurgents protested against "the French violation of the sacred right of 'popular sovereignty.'" [25]

While the patriotic desire to acquire, defend, and spread liberty animated Frenchmen, at least at first, the desire for freedom like, and eventually *from*, French *liberté* stirred much of Europe. French victories and French rule, at first rather passively endured by the vanquished, were finally met by sullen resentment and then patriotic fury. The reaction of the subjected nationalities became, as Byron later sang, "the very poetry of politics." What Carnot feared in 1793, that the war might become nationalized, came to pass. As he surmised, the name of France became not only feared but hated as well. In fear and in hate other European peoples came increasingly to desire national unity, independent national governments, national institutions and cultures—their own citizen armies, their own national literatures, and national education. For many of them, as for the French, national loyalty and action provided answers for their anxieties, and their fatherlands became refuges in troubled times. For them, too, as for the French, nationalism became the way to the future.

This way was not immediately taken. Rather, governments hoped to retain the old order, to prevent the spread of new and radical ideas. During the 1790's the "French scare" in Britain led to resolutions for "Preserving Liberty and Property against Republicans and Levellers" ("radicals"), to proclamations and laws against aliens, seditious writings, and treason, to suspension of habeas corpus, to trials for treason of such "agitators" as Thelwall, Hardy, and Horne Tooke who, favoring the French Revolution, desired constitutional reform, and to the hardening of "Toryism" in all aspects of life. To make what was happening in France less attractive to the poor, the justices of the peace worked out a new system of supplementing low wages (the Speenhamland plan). And to pay for the war, Parliament, with Pitt, enacted a complicated national income tax that would become a major source of English national revenue.[26] The agricultural expert Arthur Young, who knew France so well from his extensive travels and who at first favored the Revolution, now became its enemy and in 1792 formed a "Loyal Association" for the "Hundreds of Thredwasty and Thingoe" to unify all those who desired to prove "their content with the Constitution of this Kingdom as Established at Present" and "to secure the Blessings we derive from its influence." As a good many patriots have thought since about their wars, he thought the war of his time, that against France, a "war of humanity against the ravagers and destroyers of the earth." [27]

Hostility to France's Revolution and its English sympathizers gave birth to those classic statements of British patriotism, Edmund Burke's famous *Reflections on the Revolution in France* and the *Letters on a Regicide Peace.* In these he developed his earlier idea that the state, and he meant the British national state in particular, was a historically evolved organism. The liberties of Englishmen he saw as an *"entailed inheritance* derived to us from our forefathers, and to be transmitted to our posterity, as an estate specially belonging to the people of this kingdom, without any reference whatever to any other more general or prior right." A national society he described as a contract, "a partnership in all art; a partnership in every virtue, and in all perfection. As the ends of such a partnership cannot be obtained in many generations, it becomes a partnership not only between those who are living, but between those who are living and those who are to be born." [28] The political institutions, he argued, ought therefore to be the object of "religious reverence." In time of trouble earlier statesmen might have turned to God. Burke, Whig and liberal, turned to a transcendent, organic contract arising out of the English past.

Burke but put more rhetorically and spectacularly the reaction of many British patriots to the French threat. Wordsworth, Coleridge, Sydney Smith, George Canning, Lord Grenville, and the younger Pitt all spoke against France and its destructive uprooting of the past as they defended British institutions. If the British leaders were seldom as vocal as the French about their patriotism, they were as proud of their nation and as desirous of its independence. The British, already territorially unified and not without patriotism when the Revolution hit them, became more nationalist under its impact.

As the war continued, as Napoleon became the ruler of France, first as a Consul of the Republic (1799, 1802) and then as Emperor (1804), and as the French Napoleonic armies swept through much of Europe, more and more of the European peoples became involved, aroused, nationally conscious, and patriotic.

In France itself the patriotism was no longer so ardently revolutionary or so vociferous. While most Frenchmen were not as passionately devoted to Napoleon as was the soldier Nicolas Chauvin, most of them willingly followed their charismatic leader, who stood for their now proud and conquering France. Napoleon was immensely popular, not solely because of his victories, his civil reforms, or his personality, but also because Frenchmen believed he represented them. With his propaganda and his "rigged" plebiscites he established what seems to be a contradiction, an "authoritarian democracy." Though he alone ruled, he gave Frenchmen the feeling that they had a voice in the affairs of their nation. Frenchmen had voted several times in national elections from 1789 to 1799, though the number voting had never been large and though only in 1792 had there been universal manhood suffrage. Thus they, or, rather, some of them, had actually participated in governing France. In each of the three elections or plebiscites of 1799, 1802, and 1805, with universal manhood suffrage, over 3 million voted, and they gave Napoleon overwhelming majorities (however controlled the elections). Napoleon, therefore, could and did claim to represent the French nation, for he had consulted it, and Frenchmen could and did believe him to be the nation's choice. Nowhere else in Europe were the people of a nation so consulted. Even in the new, and in actuality more democratic, American states the suffrage was limited and the people were not so directly involved in national elections.

Still, as the war went on Europeans became increasingly conscious of *their* national interests, as brutal incidents and bloody battles affected their interests and their lives. In late 1805 Napoleon's French armies decisively defeated Austrian and Russian armies at Ulm and at Austerlitz and occupied (temporarily) Vienna. In August, 1806, Napoleon executed a patriotic Nuremberg bookseller, Palm, who had written a pamphlet called *Germany in Her Deepest Humiliation*, and this incident aroused much German indignation. In October his army crushed the Prussians at Jena and took Berlin. By the end of 1806 Napoleon had humiliated the proudest powers in central Europe and made himself master of the Germanies. In 1807 his troops were in Portugal and Spain, and in 1808 he seemed to control Spain, with his brother Joseph on the Spanish throne.

By 1807–08, then, Napoleon had built a "Grand Empire." Directly or indirectly he controlled most of Europe west of Russia, not only the Germanies and Spain but Italy and the Netherlands as well. He had also, without knowing it at the time, become the "midwife" [29] of the nationalism in Europe that was within eight years to contribute to his downfall, for then as now nationalism stimulated nationalism as patriots came to dislike or hate foreigners and the threat or reality of foreign rule.[30] If, it might be argued, Napoleon had stopped in 1807, after his agreement with the Czar of Russia at Tilsit on the ways French and Russian ambitions would bring the "happiness and tranquillity of the globe," his rule and his empire might have lasted longer. But to defend what he and the French had won, he had to go farther.[31] Thus expansion meant more expansion and national uprisings by the peoples threatened or conquered. This was a course of events often to be repeated during the nineteenth and twentieth centuries.

The desire for national expansion was, of course, not peculiarly French. Britain had tried, with amazing success, from the sixteenth century to control the seas and lands bordering the seas.[32] Russia possessed, dominated, or coveted vast territories in central Europe, the Middle East, and Asia; and the United States under Jefferson acquired the vast Louisiana territory (1803) and sent Lewis and Clark to the Pacific (1803–06) to assure the vast West for the United States. Nor was the demand for expansion motivated solely by nationalism. Behind the will for expansion, motives were mixed. Rulers, the czars of Russia, for example, sought dynastic aggrandizement, bourgeois entrepreneurs trade and profits, politicians office and popularity, and some individuals liberty and adventure— or perhaps just relief from the boredom of their daily lives. Nationalism, however, could and did provide an outlet for many interests. Monarchs, businessmen, politicians, generals and admirals, conservatives and liberals, adventurers and seekers of liberty could all pursue their own interests under the cover of national interest as they carried the national blessing to the less fortunate. That this might and did mean denial of other peoples' "right" to self-determination and a *patrie* and likely would bring national uprisings and wars in retaliation did not deter the expanding nations.

This was demonstrated from 1806 in the Germanies and from 1808 in Spain, just as it has been again and again since. German fury against Napoleon and the French was slow in rising and never fully shared by the common people.[33] But the fury did rise among influential leaders—philosophers, preachers, teachers, writers, politicians, and military men—many of whom gathered in Berlin, especially around the new university, wrote and spoke much, and formed or joined patriotic societies that played major roles in the national resistance. Men of both thought and action, they laid the foundations, romantic, philosophical, and practical, for modern German nationalism. Among these leaders were the philosopher Johann Fichte (1762–1814), the preacher Friedrich Schleiermacher (1768–1834), the teacher-athlete Friedrich Jahn (1778–1852), the poet Ernst Arndt (1769–1860), the dramatist Heinrich von Kleist (1777–1811), the statesmen Baron vom und zum Stein (1757–1831) and Prince Karl von Hardenberg (1750–1822), and the soldiers Gerhard Scharnhorst (1755–1813) and August Gneisenau (1760–1831).[34]

The generalizations possible about these leaders are not many. They often had had religious training (Lutheran and Pietist) in their youth; they generally were middle-aged (their average age being around forty-five); their origins were in varied classes; and they were usually well educated according to the German standards of the eighteenth century. Professor Eugene Anderson pointed out a generation ago that several of them were frustrated individuals who had suffered traumatic experiences, and this was true of Fichte, Arndt, and Kleist, just as it had been true of several leaders of the French Revolution, Couthon, for one.[35] Whether or not, however, these leading German nationalists had suffered frustration and trauma more than other Germans of their day, indeed, whether they became fervent nationalists chiefly because of their psychological experiences, cannot be determined without further study.

While they were not of one mind on many matters, they agreed in their opposition to the French and in appealing for, in Arndt's words, a "general love among Germans," for "every Frenchman" was a foe and "every German" a friend. In 1809 Arndt cried—and in this he expressed a common hope— "May a general love grow among us, and an abiding hatred against the crafty foreigners." [36] German leaders, unlike the earlier French, were not united as much by desire for reform as by hatred of the French.[37] Revenge they wanted desperately, and for this a powerful Germany had to be created. In a passionate outburst Arndt shouted, "We'll redden the iron with blood, with hangman's blood, with Frenchman's blood. Oh, sweet day of revenge. That sounds good to all Germans; that is the great cause." And Jahn, who taught gymnastics to German youth to make them strong soldiers and to inculcate patriotism, advised them, "What medicine does not heal, steel heals, what steel does not heal, fire heals." [38]

Unlike some of the French leaders, the German did not advocate actual democratic participation in the political life of the nation; rather, they favored strong and efficient monarchical rule supported by the upper classes, and a trained bureaucracy—in short, "enlightened despotism." This did not mean that they wanted no reforms. To the contrary, they asked that the state effect those reforms they believed necessary to energize the people and drive out the foreign invader. Some of them, Gneisenau, for example, well understood the significance of the American and French revolutions in arousing national spirit. After his experience with British troops in North America and after witnessing the amazing French successes in Europe, that sober professional soldier wrote (1807), "The Revolution [the French] has set in motion the national energy of the entire French people . . . thereby transforming the vital strength of the people and their resources into interest-bearing capital. . . . If the other states wish to reestablish [the] balance of power, they must open and use these resources. They must take over the results of the Revolution and so gain the double advantage of being able to place their entire national energies in opposition to the enemy and of escaping from the dangers of a revolution. . . ." [39]

This kind of thinking, repeated as it was at Berlin, Jena, and Vienna, led to reforms in several of the German states, though always by the state and not by the democratic process. In Prussia the great Stein believed public spirit could "only be vitalized by institutions which kindle religious sentiments and by such political institutions as absorb all the forces of the nation." [40] He, Hardenberg, and others carried through a major reform program that provided for more efficient administration, more economic freedom for the business classes, the emancipation of peasants, and the creation of a national army and militia.[41] The effect was to awaken and to deepen interest in the embryo nation's affairs. Though Germans could not meaningfully participate in the political life of the nation through manhood suffrage or representative bodies, more of them became nationally involved, nationally conscious, and more of the leaders became intense nationalists who preached and tried to inculcate a fervid patriotism. In actuality, all the ingredients of modern nationalism except democratic participation in the national government were now present—common interests, hopes, fears. A German national state did not yet exist, but it was in the making, and it would be established two generations later.

Romantically, the German nationalists of the uprising idealized the national state, could think of it with Schleiermacher as an "organic planetary work of art." [42] They thought, in Fichte's words, that the state had "a higher object than the usual one of maintaining internal peace, property, personal freedom, and the life and well-being of all." [43] Its purpose was "to preserve the consciousness of the unity of the whole people . . . and to express this idea in all forms of life."

The German state represented, stood for, the German *Volk,* an elemental natural force, a "chosen people," a creation of God. It had natural boundaries[44] that included the Rhine; it was inhabited not by "bastardized" alien peoples who were "mongrels" but by an "original" people who by being patriots would be the benefactors of mankind.[45]

These people had a common culture and character, they had a common literature, language, and history, and they had common present and future interests. Hence they should awaken, unite, throw off the "foreign yoke," proudly assert their Germanness, and form a great nation. From Vienna in 1809 Friedrich Schlegel, employed by the Austrian government to arouse patriotism, appealed to his fellow Germans, "How much longer will you be crushed beneath the heels of a proud conqueror? Awaken, Awaken! . . . from the stupor of shame and ignominy! Awaken for the sake of German honor." [46] Schlegel's cry was often repeated in Berlin and other parts of the Germanies. To awaken meant that an individual could not stand alone. He had to stand united with his fellow Germans, participate in and share the common culture, feel his Germanness, and "love the Fatherland" more than "lords and princes, fathers and mothers, wives and children." [47]

No two German nationalists held exactly the same views, but the Germans, it was argued, were linked together by a host of visible and invisible ties rooted in history and culture and blessed by God. From God and their historical experience the Germans had received a wonderful character, a character that was peculiarly theirs. They combined, as Herder had written, "loyalty and simplicity with devotion and fortitude." [48] They should be themselves and cultivate their Germanness.[49]

Their language was a natural, an original, a living language; Latin was a "closed" language and other languages, such as French, were "mongrel" and superficial. German, therefore, more than any other language, provided the means for deep understanding, and in German alone could a man make himself completely understood.[50] German, therefore, should be taught on a mandatory basis in all schools to develop the German spirit. Every true literature had to be national, and the German should exemplify what was most truly German. In 1812 the Grimm brothers published their *Fairy Tales* in the quest for the German spirit. All German education, to be sure, should have the purpose of making German patriots. For Fichte this education should remake the student in such a fashion that he could not do anything except what he was taught, for the German had a calling to be the pioneer and model for all mankind.

National cultural and political awakening around the beginning of the nineteenth century was not, of course, confined to the Germanies. It was occurring in much of Europe, in the United States, and in Latin America, partly and often in imitation of the French or in opposition to them, but also because the similar conjunctures of ideas and events were occurring in much of the western world. It was also true that ideas arising in one part of this western world were, within months, known in others—there was occurring that diffusion (as it was termed later by anthropologists) of ideas that would be characteristic of the whole world in the twentieth century. In Russia, Nikolai Karamzin was writing articles and beginning that big *History of the Russian State* mentioned previously "to inculcate in Russians a consciousness of their own value." [51] In the Balkans, in Hungary, in what later became Czechoslovakia, in Lithuania, in Scandinavia, patriotic writers were using, extolling, and demanding that others use the national languages and were trying to instill national consciousness.[52] Norwegian patriots formed (1809) a patriotic society, the *Selskabet for Norges vel*, and Greek the *Philike Hetairai* (1814) to arouse national feeling.

From 1808, with the French invasion and the *Dos de Mayo* uprising in Madrid, Spain flamed with nationalist passion. In part the Spanish feeling, already stimulated by the eighteenth-century Enlightenment, stemmed from dissatisfaction with the reactionary and corrupt monarchical government and with unhappy social and economic conditions, but it came to be chiefly directed against the hated foreign rule Napoleon had just imposed. In 1808 an official, Juan Pérez Villamil, issued a call to arms much like that of 1793 in France: "The country is in danger. Madrid is perishing, a victim of French perfidy. Spaniards hasten to save her." Though Spaniards did not so hasten, national feeling mounted. In 1809 a journalist predicted that "we will recover our former customs, sing our own songs, dance our own dances, and dress in ancient style" because the "nation is formed, not by the number of individuals, but by the union of the wills, the conformity of the laws, customs, and language, which maintain and keep them together from generation to generation." In substance though not in detail his prediction was not inaccurate. The Cortes, claiming it represented the nation, the union of wills, decreed (1810) conscription on the ground that "all Spaniards" were soldiers. In 1812 it proclaimed a new constitution, declaring that the national state was obligated to protect liberty and property and that love of country was a duty.[53] With the aid of English troops under Wellesley (Wellington) and in fierce guerrilla warfare, the Spanish drove out the French by 1813.

Meanwhile, nationalist ideas had spread to the Spanish possessions in South America, where the thinking of a few leaders had also been stimulated by the eighteenth-century Enlightenment.[54] From 1810 to the 1820's Latin American leaders, from the Argentine to Colombia and Mexico, instigated several successful national revolutions against the "tyranny" of Spain. Once more, the motives were mixed, but could be contained within the nationalism and the reformism of the kind that revolutionary France represented. The most famous leader, Simón Bolívar (1783–1830), had read Rousseau and believed in his romantic doctrines. Another, Antonio Nariño (1765–1823), had translated and secretly published (1795) the *Declaration of the Rights of Man and Citizen*, and a third, Francisco Miranda (1750–1816), had fought in French revolutionary armies.

For the future, though perhaps not at the time, the most significant national awakening might have been that in the new United States. By the

1790's the idea of a separate, independent American nation that deserved the loyalty of its citizens was well developed, though not always evident, and the loyalty was certainly not shared by every inhabitant.[55] A common national loyalty, of course, did not unite everyone in the United States.[56] Some, an increasing number, did give their loyalty primarily to the federal or national government in Philadelphia and then in the new village of Washington; others still gave it to their respective states. Many of the new immigrants, like the German, seem to have felt little loyalty of any kind, were little conscious of any political affiliation, state or national. The war in Europe, as might be expected, further divided Americans, for they feared either foreign intervention in America or the introduction of foreign and radical ideas. Conservatives, like Hamilton, favored England and English institutions and principles; liberals, like Jefferson, favored France and the revolutionary ideals (though not the Terror). To stop the spread of radical ideas *à la française*, conservatives (Federalists) believed in firm national action to control aliens and curb sedition. To prevent involvement in the war and damage to unhampered American development at home, liberals (Republicans) tried by national action to reduce or stop trade with the combatants in Europe (Nonintercourse and Embargo acts). But conservatives and liberals alike thought America different, and they were coming to believe that it had its own national interests and its own God-given or naturally determined destiny.

About 1760 a British economist, Josiah Tucker, expressed the opinion that Americans could never have a "centre of union" and "common interests" because of their mutual antipathies and clashing interests,[57] and twenty-odd years later Hamilton had his doubts.[58] Nevertheless, Washington in his "Farewell Address" expressed an arising common sentiment when he said, "Citizens, by birth or choice, of a common country, that country has a right to concentrate your affections. The name of American, which belongs to you in your national capacity, must always exalt the just pride of patriotism more than any appellation derived from local discrimination. With slight shades of difference you have the same religion, manners, habits, and political principles. You have in a common cause fought and triumphed together. The independence and liberty you possess are the work of joint councils and joint efforts, of common dangers, sufferings, and successes. . . ."[59]

In their Revolution, as John Adams later put it, patriots had tried to make thirteen clocks strike as one, and occasionally they were able to do so. In the 1780's and 1790's some citizens labored hard, in Hamilton's words, to establish "principles more and more national." While they might realize with Gouverneur Morris that "a national spirit is the natural result of national existence" and would take a generation to develop, they could also believe with Noah Webster that "every engine should be employed to render the people of this country *national* . . . , inspire them with the pride of national character." [60]

Americans had had about a generation of existence as a nation when they fought the War of 1812 against Britain. That experience and that war deepened and spread consciousness of "general objects of attachment" and of common "hopes and fears." [61]

For nearly forty years, from 1776 to 1815, Americans had feared foreign intervention or interference, that their "noble experiment" might therefore fail. From 1789 and 1792 Europe was engulfed in revolution and war, and in 1812 the danger that the United States would lose its "second war of independence" was great. Neither Britain nor the United States won the War of 1812, but at its conclusion in 1815 Americans believed the foreign threat over. Fear had been one bond uniting them. Now the possibility of the realization of long-held hopes would unite them even more.

Americans have never been known for their humility. Hope ran high in the new nation. Puritan Americans from Jonathan Edwards on believed themselves a people chosen by God. For patriots this belief was now coming to be transferred to the nation. Providence, and nature as well, had destined the nation to be great.[62] Seldom has nationalist boastfulness reached greater heights (or depths) than in the wilder speculations of patriots of the young nation. Its literature, its arts and sciences would equal or surpass those of other nations; there was no longer any reason for cultural subservience to England.[63] Its freedom, its institutions, and the ingenuity of its people would enable it to expand, to occupy and make a garden of the whole rich continent of North America, even to emancipate all mankind, end barbarism, and bring the millennium.[64] Like Jefferson, American patriots generally preferred "the dreams of the future" to the annals of the past, the "history of the yoke." [65] "The proudest empire in Europe," Gouverneur Morris prophesied, would be "a bauble compared to what America will be, *must* be, in the course of two centuries, perhaps one. . . ." [66] During the next century, in spite of a civil war that almost disrupted the Union, the material and ideal interests and aspirations of Americans were to become increasingly bound up with their nation. Not all, but many of them would have approved of naval officer Stephen Decatur's toast of 1816: "Our Country! In her intercourse with foreign nations may she always be in the right and always successful right or wrong." [67] And domestically the hope that America would be a garden for its inhabitants as well as an example for mankind was constantly and ever more extravagantly expressed.

Out of hope for more freedom and a happier future, out of oppression and fear, out of the yearning for identity through belonging, out of the belief that each group of men could best determine for themselves how they should live, out of the propaganda and coercion of governments, and out of the desire of individuals to satisfy their own interests and achieve their ideals—in summary, out of deep-rooted needs of men—the sentiment of nationalism developed from 1789 to 1815 and began to assume its modern form. Through their nations and nation-states patriots sought and believed they had found ways to meet their dilemmas, to find security, to fulfill their dreams. It may be that men need some authority to which they can turn as they worry and hope. It may be that every human society, if it is to remain a society, must be bound together by some authority imposed by force or accepted more or less voluntarily. In an earlier age men had turned to religion and its priests, to feudal masters, to paternal monarchs. But in the revolutionary era, when old values were disintegrating and old certainties seemed uncertain, the old authorities no longer sufficed and new ones were sought. The nation and its government were becoming the authority, the bulwark and refuge, the means to a promised land. And nationalism was likewise becoming the dominant, though not the sole, faith, a major religion of western peoples and eventually of many peoples throughout the world.

As a religion it propagated itself, grew stronger, more pervasive, ever more widespread. Patriotic faith led to more faith as patriots persuaded or forced others to believe. Calm reason might counsel cosmopolitanism and caution hestitancy; romantic emotion proved the stronger. The nation, for some in peace and for many in time of war, became a deity, a chief object of religious worship.

As the eighteenth-century Enlightenment weakened the hold of the Christian religion and churches and cast doubt on the doctrines of supernatural religion, individuals increasingly sought not heaven but new havens on this earth. The nation proved to be the chief of these.[68] Through it an earthly paradise might be won if men only possessed enough faith and performed the necessary works. A poetic son of the Enlightenment, the French revolutionary Marie-Joseph Chénier, clearly revealed the transition from the old faith to the new in a speech in 1793: "Wrest the sons of the Republic from the yoke of theocracy that still weighs upon them. . . . You will know how to found on the ruins of dethroned superstition, the single universal religion . . . which has neither sects or mysteries [he was wrong] . . . of which our law-makers are the preachers, the magistrates the pontiffs, and in which the human family burns its incense only at the altar of the *Patrie,* common mother and divinity." [69]

Those who steadfastly clung to the old supernatural faith were usually less enthusiastic, but some of them became as patriotic. As early as 1765 Friedrich Karl von Moser told Germans they must believe in their fatherland as they did in the Christian church.[70] Thomas Lindet, a French liberal priest, identified the interests of his religion with those of his country.[71] The German Protestant Schleiermacher in a long series of sermons from 1806 to 1813 repeatedly declared that "Christianity demands attachment to the nation" and that he who did not feel the unity of the nation was an "alien in his house of God." [72] American divines, as has been mentioned, thought Americans were called by God to serve their chosen nation.

The loyalty and devotion once given to the monarch or the royal family also turned to the *patrie;* or the royal family, as in Britain, was thought to be part of and to represent the nation. As subjects became citizens and were the nation, the kings could no longer claim they ruled by divine right, but the nation itself now was given the sanction of religion. "How will you know a republican?" cried Barère, and his answer was: when he speaks of *"la Patrie* with religious sentiment," and of "the majesty of the people with religious devotion." [73] For the most ardent patriots the fatherland became the repository of their hopes and fears, the source of life, the giver of joy, and even, in Fichte's eschatology, the way to achieve "earthly immortality."

In the circumstances of the time, this developing religious attachment to the nation is quite understandable. When heaven and hell were losing their power, when for intellectuals the hope or dread of going to either seemed irrelevant, when monarchs and lords could no longer protect and assure the life and welfare of their people, the nation and its state could offer security and a promising future—freedom from anxiety and the chance of a better life. Through its national executive (whether king, president, or committee), its national courts, its schools and its army, the nation-state could provide order and justice, create opportunity, and offer the promise of happiness and glory, or so many came to believe. The nation was, then, becoming the chief instrument for the satisfaction of age-old desires of men, desires that are likely fundamental in the forming of societies at any time. And peoples, then as now, were "expectant."

As patriots fought and suffered for their nations, they loved and exalted them more. The staid Girondist Roland demonstrated this when in 1792 he spoke of the *patrie* as "a being, to which men are more attached each day because of the cares it brings, that is created by great efforts, that is raised up in the midst of anxiety, and that men love as much for what it costs as for what they hope from it." [74]

While the new faith did not assure supernatural bliss, it possessed many of the distinguishing marks of a religion. It developed a morality with rewards and punishments, virtues and sins, rituals and symbols, and a missionary zeal. Indeed, as Ferdinand Brunot remarked, a great number of religious terms passed into the domain of politics during the French Revolution, and many of these had to do with the fatherland and patriotism. [75]

In the minds of many Frenchmen the great reforms and passionate hopes of 1789 became synonymous with the nation. In other lands the nation became the symbol for relief from oppression both from without and within. So much is this true that to separate the hopes concerning security and liberty from love of nation becomes almost impossible. And since in the minds of contemporaries the distinction was not made, no attempt is made here. The nation may have been only the instrument of obtaining the heavenly city on this earth, but the means was not separated from the end, and in any case the nation was becoming an end in itself.

The precise content of the religion of nation, of course, varied with time and place. In England it might mean devotion to the English past, to Burke's "entailed inheritance" of English law and liberties. In France during the Revolution it involved belief in the principles of liberty, property, and equality before the law. In the Germanies during the wars of liberation it came primarily to signify deliverance from French domination. In the newly independent United States it usually included opposition to the old ruler—England—trust in the doctrine of liberty, and faith in the boundless future of the nation. But convictions common and basic to all were that the nation should be sovereign and independent, that it was a people with distinct characteristics and a common territory, that its present and its destiny were somehow different from and better than those of like groups, and that it was a being above the individuals who composed it, a father or mother giving life, protecting, and promising a better future.

From these basic beliefs flowed the moral code dictating in Rousseauean fashion, that whoever helped his own group, even at the expense of others, was good and worthy of the highest reward, and, on the contrary, that whoever harmed or threatened the sovereignty and unity of his group, whatever the interests of the rest of mankind, deserved punishment

—death if the offense were severe. The commandments might vary; obedience to them was obligatory and brought reward. When the individual was an integral part of the nation, when he helped or harmed his nation, he was helping or harming himself. Patriotism was thus at one and the same time individual necessity and moral duty. By its standards all men could be judged.

Whatever the code and however intangible, every good man, that is, every patriot, was expected to believe and to prove his belief by his conduct, by works. If he was faithless and acted contrary to the national interests (whatever the rulers conceived these to be), he made himself subject to prosecution by his government and persecution by his fellows. If he did conform, if he was willing to sacrifice even his life, then he was virtuous, of the elect, and would attain the ultimate joy found in service to the fatherland. Perhaps he might attain the rank of national hero, be "sainted" by his compatriots and have his remains placed in a pantheon, as did many French patriots, or have a monument later erected in his memory, as did Admiral Nelson and the Duke of Wellington in England and George Washington and Simón Bolívar in the New World.

To enforce patriotism the British might use their courts, as they did during the reform agitation of the 1790's, and the French the Terror, as they did in 1793–94. In both cases, they were repeating what many of their "enlightened" philosophers had loathed in the Roman Catholic church. They were re-establishing the Inquisition, excommunicating and sometimes sentencing to death men whose chief crime was heresy, this time to the fatherland. To be traitorous had long been a crime; to be a national traitor now became the most heinous of crimes. Frenchmen regarded Dumouriez and Americans Benedict Arnold not only as despicably disloyal but also as hellishly impious, and would have executed them had they not found protection in "perfidious Albion." Once a major crime had been *lèse-majesté;* now this became *lèse-nation.*[76] Henceforward the nation-state apparently had the moral and legal right to enforce a code of conduct that signified not only love of nation but conformity and uniformity in loyalty to it.[77] The French Convention on December 16, 1792, had decreed death for anyone attempting to harm the unity of the French Republic,[78] and other national governments were sooner or later to act likewise.

Public sentiment voiced by the faithful probably played a more effective role in enforcing national loyalties than did the governments. Social pressures to become patriotic and to conform to the national will mounted steadily. A French newspaper in 1791 noted a patriotism akin to the religion of earlier times in its exaltation and ardor. And it pointed out similarities, even to the mysticism and fanaticism with which those of contrary opinions were persecuted in the name of the new "divinities"—liberty and fatherland.[79]

Few western Europeans or Americans became permanently so fanatical. Indeed, some remained devoted to the older ideals and institutions of church, monarchy, and feudalism, and a few, like Goethe, retained their eighteenth-century cosmopolitanism. What is true is that one belief came to be dominant: that all men were born for, should live for, and should be willing to make the supreme sacrifice for the *patrie*.[80] As Barère, the Jacobin, put it, now many believed that "all moral and physical faculties, all political and industrial talents belong to *la patrie*." [81] Hence, all men could be called to serve their country, and as they served they often worshiped it the more. With the festivals of federation in 1790 Frenchmen began to erect altars to the *patrie*,[82] and in the future men of many nations would worship at *their* national shrines.

At the same time nationalism began to assume the outward forms of religion. To be a patriot was to be a member of the faithful, and the faithful were to be known not only by works but also by signs. One striking illustration of this is the amazing growth in France, already noted, of words based upon *le patriote* and *la patrie*.[83] In the coining of words French revolutionaries may only have shown they were more enthusiastic patriots than other peoples. For the outward signs, songs (hymns), and symbols of nationalism manifested themselves in much of the western world. "Rule, Britannia" appeared in 1740 with its verse

> *The nations not so blest as thee,*
> *Must in their turns to tyrants fall,*
> *Whilst thou shalt flourish great and free,*
> *The dread and envy of them all.*

And "God Save the King" was sung at Drury Lane in 1745.[84] Joseph Haydn (1732–1809) in Austria wrote patriotic songs, including the music for what later became "Deutschland, Deutschland, über Alles." The story of the "Marseillaise" and Roget de Lisle in 1792 is familiar to everyone, as is that of Francis Scott Key and "The Star-Spangled Banner" in 1814. These inspirational hymns with their appeals to the free and the brave to defend their nation aroused deep reverence. A fiery Girondist, Barbaroux, recounted an incident at a fraternal banquet in his home in June, 1792: "My house was surrounded and filled with citizens. A group of musicians came. They sang Provençal songs written in my honor and the hymn of the *Marseillaise*. . . . I always remembered with emotion that at the last verse where the words *Amour sacré de la patrie* are sung, all the citizens in the house and street bent and kneeled." [85]

Similar outward manifestations (and stimuli) to patriotic feeling are evidenced by the adoption of new flags, such as the tricolor of France and the Stars and Stripes of the United States, by the beginning of national holidays, such as the Fourth of July in the United States and the Fourteenth of July in France,[86] by the idealization of national heroes in the paintings of, for example, Jacques-Louis David in France and Charles Willson Peale in the United States, and by the creation of symbolic figures such as John Bull and Uncle Sam.[87] Patriots in France showed their faith by civic oaths, by erecting altars of the *patrie*, by planting trees of liberty, and by holding civic baptisms.[88] The scene of the archivist Camus carrying "the new Blessed Sacrament of the French," described at the beginning of this chapter, may not have been imitated elsewhere, but in the western lands men came or were coming to regard their national histories, their customs, their ways of life as sacred, and in some countries, as in France and the United States, their declarations of rights, their constitutions as sacred books.

The nation had not yet become, for many men, an absolute guide or bearer of certainty. Nonetheless, it was becoming a kind of common mother as well as father to whom men could go in trouble and find blessedness, just as Christians had to the Virgin Mary and to God. No statistical calculations are available to determine how effective the patriotic rituals were in making nationalists. That contemporary patriots used them to win converts indicates they believed in their efficacy. And patriots did want converts.

By 1815 peoples in the West had formed or were forming nations. This did not at all mean that everyone was or was becoming a nationalist. Far from it. Bits of evidence, such as occasional acts of self-sacrifice and expressions of devotion, indicate that common men sometimes were deeply patriotic, but the records do not permit a generalization on how widespread nationalism was among the common people. It hardly seems likely that many poor, ignorant, and illiterate peasants were much concerned with national questions or that they were devoted to the new deity, the nation. Among the upper classes many looked back with nostalgia to the "good old days." Among the intellectuals a few, like Goethe, steadfastly remained cosmopolitan. Still, foundations for the developing strong nationalisms of the nineteenth and twentieth centuries had been laid. Conscious of cultural similarities, patriots possessed or hoped to obtain their own sovereign nation-states, while governments that were becoming national tried to unify their respective peoples, exacting from them devotion and service unto death. Carnot's appeal in 1814 for a "strong noble passion," for "love of country," would be heard and heeded often in the future.[89] Patriots, and they were not few, agreed with Carnot that a national spirit, if it did not exist, had to be created, and it eventually would be—in most lands and among most peoples.

VI

Political Bases of Modern Nationalism, 1815–1921

In 1815 the guiding principles of high statesmanship were restoration and legitimacy: return to the dynastic, religious, and class arrangements and to the territorial divisions of the old regime. For thirty-three years Metternich from the old seat of empire in Vienna, the Bourbons and their followers from France, the Romanovs, their officials, and their churchmen from Russia, and, to a lesser extent, the Tory landowners and their allies in Britain struggled to preserve the world as it had been. In the short run they had successes. In the long run, of course, they failed. They failed because an industrial, urban world was taking the place of the rural, agrarian one that had produced them, because new elites, living under new conditions and backed by increasing numbers of people, demanded different political, economic, and social arrangements, and because the old doctrines and practices no longer suited their desires or fulfilled people's needs. The new and then revolutionary doctrines were liberalism and nationalism. Of these two, nationalism proved the stronger, the more universal, and the more permanent.

Two political powers, both nation-states and nations, England and France, had been in the vanguard: England because of its industry, commerce, and wealth and because of its parliamentary government; and France because of its impressive power and culture and because of the appeal of its Revolution. Though the old regime was temporarily restored, these two nations were still models for those who wanted change. No other peoples could or did follow them exactly, but what they had done others would often try to do. When London parliamentary leaders spoke and the British bankers acted, all Europe reacted. When Paris, as the old saying goes, sneezed with revolutionary colds, so indeed did all Europe. In the New World a people had declared their independence and formed a new nation, the United States; it set another example, an example that seemed to promise life, liberty, and happiness, a lamentable malady to conservatives but a desirable state of health for liberals. In the Italies, Poland, and Hungary—and throughout Europe—young men, enthusiastic, energetic, idealistic, would look at British political and economic life, at French rights of man and citizen, at American frontier democracy, and be inspired. The dreams of the eighteenth-century Enlightenment could be realized—in their own nations—or so the young Count Széchenyi of Hungary, the young Mazzini of Italy, and the young as well as the older men of the revolutions of 1830, 1848, and 1870 in much of Europe dreamed. And the agent of change was *their* nation. The term modernization had not yet been invented, but, if it had, then in a real sense nationalism was the instrument with which European peoples could, in the nineteenth-century sense, become modern. At the same time, nationalism could be and often was an instrument of protest against domestic governments held to be oppressive and against foreign rule that was detested if it existed and feared if it might be established. In short, nationalism seemed to provide relief from oppression and fear as it offered hope of a better social order and more individual happiness.

The forces and circumstances that had led to nationalism in Britain and France were beginning to influence all of Europe and the New World, not all at once but gradually and unevenly. Industrialization and urbanization lessened the power and prestige of old authorities, eroded old ties of loyalty. Inventions and improvements in communication made it possible for larger numbers of people to become aware of and to develop common interests and for governments to exercise closer control over wide areas. Belief in the possibility (even necessity) of progress became widely diffused and, for many, an article of faith,[1] and the nation and its state were considered the vehicles of progress. Memories of old dynastic rivalries and conflicts persisted, and developed into rivalries involving nations of people. The resultant conflicts of national interests brought threats of war, and war deepened consciousness of national differences as it sharpened national fears.

The forces and circumstances of the century after 1815, whether old or new, called for national state action, for increased popular participation in national governments, for individual identification not with the ruling families or churches but with nation-states and fellow nationals—with nations. The arising new nationalisms differed just as had and did the older nationalisms of Britain and France. As each people, German, Polish, or Irish, differed, so did the content, style, and development of their nationalisms. As the economic conditions, the religious beliefs, the cultures of Italians and Russians differed, so did their consciousness of and devotion to their nations. And as political ideologies not only differed but also changed, so did the content of the nationalisms. Conservatives who really wanted to return to the traditional ways of pre-1789, paradoxically, came to want the national state to preserve them, or if lost to restore them. Liberals who at the beginning opposed state interference came to believe that only the nation-state could protect the property they prized and establish the liberties they wanted.[2] When new "radicals"—socialists, for example—began to appear, say in 1848 or 1870, they wanted class action on an international basis, but eventually they too turned to nation-states to accomplish their revolutions.

Everywhere in the western world after 1815 states were making nations and nations were creating states, and both fostered nationalism, which, in turn, nourished the nations and their states. The world of the old regime could not be restored, was forever lost. The coming "legitimate" guiding principles were nationalism and liberalism, then nationalism and welfarism, then nationalism and socialism; and usually, as it turned out, the first noun in each combination dominated.

In France, just as the revolutionary passions of '89–'93 were spent by 1815, so were those of intense patriotism. France was still a great nation unified by its past and its culture. Most of its citizens, apparently, still regarded it as their *patrie* and were not unloyal. But after twenty-six years of revolution and war their enthusiasm for liberty and glory dwindled. Where, within France, there was not inertia, divisive rather than unifying sentiments dominated. While old institutions, the monarchy and the church, were restored, revolutionary ideals, the "rights of man," were not forgotten, nor were the victories and conquests of Napoleon. The feeling of devotion and the desire for unity, so basic in nationalism, did not then dominate French emotions. In 1814 the sturdy Carnot, who had so well served the Republic and the Empire, again pleaded for love of country in which each man sacrificed his "own interests to the general interest" and forgot himself "for the safety and glory of the country" because he believed his own "private fortunes linked to the public fortune." But Carnot's plea was isolated, and he himself believed that Frenchmen then so lacked a national spirit as almost to prevent thought about it.[3]

If Frenchmen were devoted to France, they had different conceptions of what the country was or ought to be. The Vicomte de Castelbajac in 1815 meant by *patrie* "the land of my fathers, with its legitimate government, a government which accords me protection by reason of my obedi-

ence to the laws and which I am obliged to serve with fidelity and honor
. . . the fatherland is France with the King; and King and France are
inseparable in my eyes for constituting the Fatherland.[4] The several varieties of liberals, momentarily silenced, looked back with nostalgia to the
constitutionally limited monarchy of '89, to the Jacobin republic of '93–'94,
or to an idealized Napoleonic Empire which had not only won glory but
also brought a semblance of equality in law and in fact for those who
served the Emperor. For most of the liberals, the propertied and professional classes were the nation or best represented it; and the nation, they
thought, ought to act chiefly in their interests and not those of the old
nobility and clergy or of the unpropertied and unlettered. Members of the
lower economic classes, usually illiterate, had never vocally evinced as
much nationalism as "their betters," though by their actions they had on
occasion showed their patriotism. In 1815 they did not evidence much
patriotism in either word or deed; they obeyed insofar as it was necessary
and tried to make a living.

As it was in France so it was in much of the western world. Almost
everywhere national feeling had been born, but within the various nationalities there was neither agreement on national interests and purposes nor
vigorous expression of national loyalty. England, though not Great Britain, was a unified nation, and the several peoples of the British islands
(except some Irishmen) had generally given their loyalty to Britain during the long wars against France. But after 1815 it was not primarily questions of national loyalty and unity that interested the people of the islands.
While Englishmen apparently continued to agree that England "should
ever be," they disagreed over the kind of England it should be, as conservative Tories sought, in the midst of severe economic depression, to preserve their old England and fought reformers, liberal and radical, with
troops at Peterloo and with parliamentary legislation (the Six Acts of
1819) to repress agitation for change. Moreover, one dissident group in
Britain, the Catholics, still remained loyal to the Roman rather than the
Anglican church and could not by law hold public office. Among minority
groups that were themselves nascent nations, the Irish, Scots, and Welsh,
many individuals had little or no love for the dominant English. More and
more Catholic Irishmen hated or were coming to hate England. Oppressed by absentee landlords, subjected to English Protestant rule, and
led by the "King of the Beggars," Daniel O'Connell, they were beginning
to develop their own nationalism.[5]

In the United States national consciousness had been developing
since at least the 1750's, but not even during their Revolution had nation-

alism become the dominant loyalty for many Americans. During the Revolution patriotic leaders like George Washington had been willing to lay down their lives and fortunes for the independence of their country *and* their own states, and after the Revolution zealous statesmen like Alexander Hamilton and Thomas Jefferson were building the government in Washington and expanding the nation's boundaries. But many Americans, to the extent that they were patriotic, were primarily loyal to "county, province or section," [6] to their states, and from the 1790's perhaps to their parties as well. Neither the states nor the inhabitants were as yet tightly knit. Each state customarily regarded its own interests as or before it embarked on common national ventures. Among the people were many immigrants, such as the Scotch-Irish and Germans, with little or no attachment to their adopted nation except to the opportunity it offered, especially in cheap land. The beckoning frontiers drew thousands of old and new inhabitants from the compact settlements of the East where they might more quickly have sensed the need for national rather than local institutions. In the expanding West (then the Middle West), settlers were chiefly interested in clearing the forests, in making a living, or, sometimes, in land speculations to make a fortune.[7] As they pursued their own interests, they had little occasion to look to the new village of Washington and the government just established there. Except for the infrequent assistance the federal or national government afforded against the Indians, the British in Canada, and the French and Spaniards in Louisiana and Florida, western Americans were scarcely aware of it. The War of 1812 against Britain, it has been often noted, awakened new loyalties to the nation. In 1816 the ex-secretary of the treasury, Albert Gallatin, a keen observer, noted that the people "are more American; they feel and act more like a nation. . . ." [8] But whether states or sections were to command more loyalty than the nation was still to be determined, and would not be until 1865, if then.

Elsewhere in Europe the national emotions aroused by the French conquest and example subsided, and the clamor for reform was momentarily stilled. Individuals expressed national feeling, but it was never then the ruling sentiment anywhere. German intellectuals were not so ardent for unity once Napoleon's insolent rule had been thrown off, nor were they quite so devoted to their dream of a unique great German culture, and for leading German conservatives German unity now consisted "in the fact that each part, even the smallest part of the German fatherland, has its own pulse beat and that all these pulse beats together provide nourishment for the heart." [9] Austria, Prussia, Bavaria, Saxony, and the thirty-odd other, smaller German states claimed what loyalties the people manifested beyond their personal, local, and class interests and relationships. The longing for a Germany did not disappear. In 1817 patriotic student societies, the *Burschenchaften,* held a congress at Wartburg, burned reactionary books and emblems (as had Luther the Papal Bull three centuries earlier), and demanded liberty and a German fatherland. But the Carlsbad Decrees (1819) of the reactionary governments effectively repressed nationalism and liberalism for a generation. In Italy, which was still only a "geographic expression," nine reactionary governments, including that of the papacy, suppressed new ideas whenever they could, and they usually were successful. Though patriots formed secret societies, the *Carbonari,* for example, to throw off the tyrannies of their own governments and of Austria, they were ineffective and won, as yet, little popular support.[10] Among individuals in all of the Italies the national spirit flickered, but the monarchies and the papacy kept it under control, and in southern Italy most of the people were too poor and too ignorant to care. The dominant force and material reality in the Germanies, in the Italies, and, in fact, in much of Europe was the crafty reactionary in Vienna, Metternich, and he believed in the old Empire and—with the other dominating ruler in eastern Europe, Czar Alexander I of Russia—in monarchy and in the nobility and clergy so far as they aided in the maintenance of order and the status quo ante 1789.[11] For this reason, as well as others, independent nation-states could not be established among such peoples as the Poles, who had evinced nationalism.

In the minds of adherents of the old order, that order was not yet dead; they did not know it was dying; and, in fact, in the memories of a few of their descendants it is still not buried. The age of nationalism had not yet arrived, though it was soon to do so. In Europe monarchy, church, feudal class, province, and village still usually commanded more loyalty than did the nation. King, priest, and noble were not about to relinquish their authority or share it with citizens of nation-states.

The nation as institution and idea had not yet attracted most people, offered them the means to gain their wants and a father object to which they turned in time of crisis. Most peasants and urban workers, mired in poverty and ignorance, did not lift their sights to national horizons, did not become nationally conscious; generally they gave their traditional obeisance to the traditional and established authorities. In Europe individuals in all classes still placed king above country and found in the royal service recognition and satisfaction. Some, like the Vicomte Chateaubriand (1768–1848) in his *Génie du Christianisme,* published in 1802, still turned to the age-old solace of the universal church, and believed the pope and the church fathers the supreme authority in matters of faith and much else. A very few, like the English utilitarian philosopher Jeremy Bentham (1748–1832), still dreamed, as had *philosophes* of the Enlightenment, of a cosmopolitanism where in universal brotherhood individual men were able to think out their own solutions to life's problems. As yet, the nation did not "integrate" all thought and action, nor had the nation-state become the master, lawgiver, and father to which most men turned and which, in turn, controlled their lives.

Nonetheless, foundations of modern popular nationalism had been laid in western Europe and in the New World, and the structural materials existed in all of Europe as the sentiment of nationalism swept eastward.[12] Upon these foundations and with these materials patriots of the next century and a half built the institutional and ideological structures of modern nationalism. While individuals and classes would seek and receive different things from their nation, and while their loyalties to it would vary in nature and intensity, the nation would become the most consuming end of their endeavors and its state the institutional instrument that most effectively provided for their needs and hopes. To their nation and state, then, most men would give their supreme loyalty. The French and American declarations of the late eighteenth century proclaimed the "rights of man."[13] The abortive 1848 Frankfurt Constitution spoke of the "rights of Germans." Until the Universal Declaration of Human Rights in 1947 there would be much talk about rights, but nearly always it would be about the rights and duties of particular men, national men. After 1947, in spite of the rhetoric, the same was still true, for nationalism was a reality of life and cosmopolitanism a vision of dreamers.

In the West, in France, Britain, and the United States, citizens demanded, acquired, and were given more rights and duties, and the nation-states demanded, acquired, and were given more power and loyalty. In the Germanies and Italies, in central Europe and the Balkans, patriots clamored for both national unification and civil rights. They usually achieved the first, though their newly established states would more often stress duties than they would rights. Even in Russia, where the czars— Nicholas I, for one—thought first of the duties of subjects to "orthodoxy and autocracy," a growing number of Slavophiles began to put their nation, Russia, first. By the first decades of the twentieth century in Europe and the Americas the national idea had nearly everywhere integrated almost all human interests and values within it, and the national state tended to swallow almost all lesser jurisdictions. In sum, societies and cultures and political and legal authorities became not universal or local but national.

From 1815 the process of creating independent nation-states that had already occurred in England and France was repeated again and again, with significant differences of detail, in Europe, in the Americas, and later over the vast continents of Asia and Africa and on islands of the oceans. The table[14] on pp. 146–47 indicates the dates of independence of western nations down to 1921, though because states changed and because interpretations of "independent" differ, many of the dates can only be arbitrary.

This table, obviously, does not reveal the shifting intensity of emotion that was behind the several nationalisms, or their differing content. Inspired by romanticism and liberalism and motivated by public and personal interest, more and more people, and especially the leaders, hoped to win dignity and happiness, peace and prosperity, and power and glory through their nations and the states built upon them. The more they became nationally conscious, the more many of them saw their nation, once it was unified, independent, and sovereign, as a way to a kind of paradise of good free men, or a leviathan of authority protecting life and property against violence from within and aggression from without. Their dreams as well as their interests led them to nationalism.

Especially when coupled with liberalism[15] but also when joined with conservativism and authoritarianism, nationalism first of all and most strongly appealed to men of business and property, although eventually and strongly to men of every class and persuasion, even to those of the proletariat who were socialists. Nowhere did nationalism grow steadily, nowhere was it without enemies and obstacles, nowhere, it must be repeated, were the nationalist ideas and actions exactly the same. In some cases, as in much of mid-twentieth-century Africa, states were established when nations hardly existed, and in other cases nations or potential nations, like the European Basque and Catalan, obtained no states of their own. But everywhere the institution and the idea became dominating forces in the minds and lives of some, of many men, in times of peace and especially in times of revolution and war. During the nineteenth century this was true in nations with a long history of unity and independence (France and Britain); in new nation-states (Belgium, Italy, and Germany); among historic peoples (the Greeks and Serbs) who achieved independence, or (the Poles) would in 1918; among peoples almost forgot-

WHEN PRESENT WESTERN NATION-STATES
BECAME INDEPENDENT
To 1921

Independent Before 1783
(Alphabetical Listing)

Country
Austria (separate state 1919)
Denmark
France
Netherlands (United Provinces 1648)
Portugal
Russia (later part of U.S.S.R.)
Spain
Sweden
Switzerland (confederation, 1648)
United Kingdom (England, Great Britain)
United States (1776 or 1783)

Europe, Including British Islands
Independent to 1921
(Chronological Listing)

Country	Time of Independence	
Greece	1829–32	
Belgium	1830–31	
Italy	1861	(1870)
Germany	1867	(1870)
Luxembourg	1867	(1890)
Romania	1878	
Norway	1905	
Bulgaria	1908	
Union of South Africa (if western)	1910	(part of British Commonwealth to 1961)
Albania	1912	
Czechoslovakia	1918	(Bohemia more or less independent to 1526)
Finland	1919	
Hungary	1919	(1867)
Poland	1919	(independent before 1795)
Yugoslavia (Serbia)	1919	(Serbia 1878)
Ireland	1921	

North America and Atlantic and Pacific Oceans

Country	Time of Independence	
Canada	1867	(still part of British Commonwealth)
Australia New Zealand } (if western)	1901	(still part of British Commonwealth)
Iceland	1908	
(See Mexico below)		

Latin and South America
(Dates may vary as interpretations of independence do.)

Paraguay	1811	
Guatemala	1813	
Argentina	1816	
Chile	1819	
Colombia	1819	
Mexico	1820	
Peru	1821	
Brazil	1822	
Bolivia	1825	
Uruguay	1828	
Venezuela	1830	
Costa Rica	1838	
El Salvador	1838	
Honduras	1838	
Nicaragua	1838	
Haiti	1840	
Dominican Republic	1844	
Cuba	1901	(if independent)
Panama	1903	

ten by Europeans (the Bulgars); and for individuals among peoples who were just beginning to develop a sense of nationhood (the Catalan and Ukrainian).

In Europe during the nineteenth century one people after another "found" (if they had not already done so) that they had a common historical culture and common aspirations, worked—and sometimes revolted and on occasion warred (as in 1830, 1848, and 1870)—to establish a united territory and sovereign state, and then often attempted to expand their boundaries[16] to include all the people and land that could by one criterion or another be called theirs. From 1821 to 1832 Greeks, remembering with Byron their history and stirred by the teachings of the patriots Rhigas and Koraïs, rebelled against their Turkish rulers. By the latter date they were able, with assistance from Britain, France, and Russia, to establish an independent state with an autocratic and later constitutional monarchy and to begin trying to enlarge their territory.[17]

During the nineteenth century, the Greek, Italian, Czech, Serb, Irish, and other peoples that were subject to foreign rule came to blame all their woes on this rule, feeling themselves oppressed and envisioning a national utopia once they had a unified, sovereign nation-state. Hence, again and again there were calls for revolutionary action and unity. The oath of the Greeks of the early 1800's who formed a secret patriotic society, *Hetairia Philikè,* to drive the Turks out of Hellas became the prototype of other similar oaths, down to that of Kenyans in the 1950's: "I will nourish in my heart irreconcilable hatred against the tyrants of my country. . . . I swear by the future liberty of my countrymen, that I shall consecrate myself to [my country]; that henceforth [it] shalt [*sic*] be the scope of my thoughts, [its] name the guide of my actions, [its] happiness the recompense of my labours." [18] A famous Garibaldian song of the 1850's drives home the same ideas of suffered oppression and hope in unity: "We are spurned and scorned by the centuries because we are not a real people but divided. Let us form a united band, on a common hope." [19]

From 1830 onward national feeling spread, boiling into action again and again.[20] When in that year the French dethroned an "aristocratic" Bourbon and enthroned a "bourgeois" Orleanist king, the spirit of revolt spread. The several uprisings, in Poland, the Germanies, the Italies, and elsewhere, both liberal and nationalist in aim, were generally abortive. But that of the Belgians against the Dutch resulted, with British assistance, in the creation of the liberal kingdom of Belgium.[21]

Initial failures did not slow the trend toward nationalism. Three widely different phenomena, all discussed in greater detail in chapter VII, demonstrate this. Within the then nascent nations patriots organized societies, among which Guiseppe Mazzini's Young Italy (1831) is best known, to agitate for national unity and independence and against the "yoke" of foreign oppressors. In the Germanies most of the states (but not Austria) organized a *Zollverein,* or customs union (1833), which, in fostering trade, tied them together economically. And scholars and political leaders in several developing and to some degree developed nations more or less officially started to collect and publish source documents concerning the origins and history of their nations, such as the *Monumenta Germaniae Historica,* begun in 1824.[22]

The nationalist and liberal revolutions of 1848–49 burst the bounds of Metternich's Europe. Metternich's flight to London, in which he disguised himself as an "elderly Englishman," symbolized the end of an era and the beginning of a new, just as did the return of many patriotic exiles, for instance Mazzini, to their homelands. After the French Revolution of February, 1848, and the overthrow of the monarchy, revolts broke out all over central and southern Europe, in Austria, Hungary, Bohemia, Poland, in what later became Romania and Yugoslavia, in Prussia and several of the lesser German states, and up and down the long Italian peninsula from Naples to Venice. These revolts, like those of 1830, generally failed to achieve their immediate objectives, independent, liberal national states. But while the chances of liberalism were more or less permanently ended in central and southeastern Europe, those of nationalism improved almost everywhere.

If at the Frankfurt Assembly of 1848–49 German "idealists" talked themselves into inaction, and if nowhere else independent national states were immediately established, during the next two decades men of action in Italy and Germany—Cavour and Bismarck—united their respective nations and established national governments, and within seventy-five years nearly all the "subject" nationalities of Europe achieved, temporarily at least, nationhood and independence. For a brief time federalism, which could have united several nationalities in one state, seemed possible.[23] But this was not to be; the forces of nationalism and the ambitions of statesmen were too strong. Cavour was not a strong Italian and Bismarck was not a fervent German nationalist; both of them wanted to strengthen their own small states, Sardinia (Piedmont) and Prussia. To accomplish their ends, however, both led, had to lead national crusades that ended in the creation of modern Italy and Germany. Their success effectively ended attempts to set up federations of central European and Italian states.

With that firm but vague believer in the "principle of nationality," Napoleon III, as his ally, Cavour instigated a war against Austria in 1859. On the verge of defeat, he utilized the ardently patriotic Garibaldi's daring deeds in southern Italy, and with skillful diplomacy united Sardinia, Lombardy, Parma, Modena, Tuscany, the Papal States (except Rome), and the Kingdom of the Two Sicilies. In 1861 Victor Emmanuel II (Cavour's king in Sardinia) became king of an Italy united except for Rome and Venetia (both to be acquired within a decade) and scattered border regions (*irredenta*) in the north and east.[24]

In much the same fashion Bismarck succeeded in unifying Germany.[25] At the helm of a militarized Prussia he provoked wars with

Denmark (1864), with Austria (1866), and with France (1870). His purpose was to create a German state in which Prussia and his own Junker class were dominant. In the Danish war Prussia won the right to administer Holstein and obtained the tiny duchy of Lauenburg. Through astute diplomatic maneuvering and the effective force of the Prussian army, Bismarck then isolated and militarily defeated Austria to gain Hanover, Hesse-Cassel, Nassau, and Frankfurt for Prussia, and was able to create a North German Confederation, composed of all the German states north of the Main River, in which Prussia controlled the military forces and was therefore paramount. Through equally astute diplomacy and again the superb Prussian army, he then isolated and defeated France to unite all the Germanies except Austria into the German Empire proclaimed at Versailles in 1871.[26] Immediately it must be added that neither the Italian nor German peoples were fully united and all of them devoted to Italy and Germany. While Italian and German leaders had established political and territorial unity, while Italian and German were the common languages, and while there were cultures that could rightly be called Italian and German, older loyalties, provincial and class, still existed. To make fully developed and unified nations of the varied peoples in Italy and Germany took another half century or more, and was perhaps not yet realized when Italy and Germany became authoritarian states under Mussolini and Hitler.[27]

In widely different ways the process of nation-state making continued during the same and ensuing years, in the Balkans, in central Europe, and in the United States.[28] Arising out of many circumstances, including the diplomacy and wars of the established powers, the process of nation-state building continued. Individuals of the caliber of Cavour and Bismarck seldom played leading parts as some had earlier. The stress, especially after 1918, was on the right of each people to determine their own present and future, and the new nationalism was usually democratic and republican in language if not always in fact. But the trend was the same, though the circumstances and the arguments changed. Generally, it was believed that a common culture and a real or imagined common past or race gave a people the right to have their own nation-state, and that all the people of a nationality and the territories they occupied should be unified and incorporated in that state. Actually, the creation of new states was sometimes as much the result of the actions of the great states—Britain, France, and Russia—to gain advantage in the competitive international struggle for power as it was of the inhabitants' desire for self-determination; without this power struggle there might have been no Romania, Bulgaria, or

Czechoslovakia, at least at the time and in the form these states were created. Again, in one case, that of the United States, an issue scarcely relevant to nationalism—slavery—was one cause of a civil war (1861–65) that settled the question of whether the federal (national) government or the state governments were supreme, and hence whether the United States would continue, as it did, as one unified, independent nation-state. But whatever the variations in thought and action, independent nation-states were created. In the Balkans, Serbia, Romania, and Bulgaria became independent during the thirty years from 1878 to 1908 after a long struggle in which they were assisted by the great European powers (chiefly Russia) against their Turkish rulers.[29] While the Czech, Slovak, and Polish peoples continued to struggle in vain, the Magyars in Hungary won semi-independence in the compromise (*Ausgleich*) of 1867 with the Austrian Germans. In 1907 Norway peacefully gained its independence from Sweden. As a result of World War I and the several treaties of 1919–20, Hungary, Poland, Czechoslovakia, and Finland became independent nation-states; the Serbs, Slovenes, and Croats were united in an independent Yugoslavia; and three other small states were temporarily (until 1941) established on the Baltic Sea, Lithuania, Latvia, and Estonia. Finally, after long bitter years of struggle against Britain, Irishmen were able to establish the Irish Free State (Eire) in 1921.[30]

The long and often violent struggles for nationhood and independence brought sorrow and tragedy, exhilaration and joy, and sharpened awareness of common national bonds. The deep wounds inflicted were not forgotten, while the pleasures of triumph were fondly remembered. Old opponents of national dreams, like Metternich and the Russian Czar Nicholas I, became villians, while the patriotic leaders of national struggles became the new heroes: Cavour and Garibaldi in Italy, Bismarck and General von Moltke in Germany, Kossuth and Deák in Hungary, O'Connell and Parnell in Ireland.[31] And old heroes were resurrected—for example, Milos Obilić, the Serb who at the Battle of Kossovo in 1389 sneaked into the Turkish camp and assassinated the Sultan Murad.[32] The heroes, old and new, some of them, like Mazzini, martyrs in national causes, symbolized the national strivings, unified people, made them conscious of the bonds that patriots believed tied or should tie them together in national brotherhood. If many ordinary people had been little excited by nationalist agitation during the early struggles because they were too busy eking out a miserable existence, if some had cared little about who ruled them because they would be ruled in much the same fashion whatever the government, they now had national pantheons of heroes to inspire them, just as medieval people had stained-glass windows of saints. That appreciable numbers of men of all classes were, for many reasons, so inspired the war of 1914 gives ample proof, for many were then willing to risk death and to die for their nations.

Almost no new or old nation-state believed it included all the people or territory that rightfully should belong to it. Patriots in almost every nation felt their nation wronged because it did not possess territory once allegedly part of it in an actual or mythical past, or because its boundaries did not embrace people who spoke the nation's language or who were thought to be of the nation's race.[33] By 1919–20 the principle of self-determination had won general acceptance and had become a major justification for nations and nationalism. Each nationality, it was believed, had a right to be united in a land of its own and to have its own sovereign nation-state. And in fact, with few exceptions, by 1921 each of the nationalities in Europe and in the New World did possess a territory and its own independent state.

It made little difference that the lofty and popular principle of self-determination could hardly be fully put into practice because in border areas nationalities were much mixed and because every established state included people of "other" nationalities.[34] When, in June, 1914, the young Serbian Princip shot the Austrian Archduke Francis Ferdinand and ignited the fire of World War I, no one thought it strange that he was motivated by the nationalist desire to end Austrian "oppression" and unite Serbs, Croats, and Slovenes into what later became independent Yugoslavia.[35] He and his accomplices acted upon generally accepted doctrine and ideals, and in Serbia they became martyrs and heroes. During the war, major Allied leaders again and again declared they favored self-determination. For European peoples, though not for colonial subjects overseas, it was proclaimed a major goal of the war. Sometimes the declarations were obviously propaganda to gain the support of subject peoples, but it cannot be doubted that they often were based on deep conviction. The scholarly Lord Bryce well represented an ideal of western thought when he described the English ideal for the future as "a world in which every people should have within its borders a free national government, resting on and conforming to the general will of its citizens." [36] The greatest idealist among the victorious statesmen, Woodrow Wilson, proudly announced that his nation was "fighting for the oppressed nationalities who submerged or standing alone could never have secured their freedom." [37]

The Treaty of Versailles and the several associated treaties made by nation-states at the end of the war created six new nation-states in Europe, bringing the total number to twenty-seven. The principle of national self-determination now appeared to be an axiom for action. The national organization of peoples was certainly now the general and accepted way men did organize, at least in Europe and the Americas. Even the international organization that was established, the League of Nations, was no more than a league of sovereign nations, each with its own people and territory, each limited in its actions not by any international power but only by its own capabilities and will as it confronted other equally "independent" nations. But while the Allied statesmen who made the treaties evidently believed in the principle of self-determination, they did not, in fact could not, completely follow it. National strategic reasons, arising particularly out of French fear of Germany and the general western fear of newly Communist Russia, partly determined which new nation-states would be established and where new borders would be. In central and southeastern Europe, especially, it was simply not possible to include all the people of one nationality (or claimed to be of one nationality) within the same nation-state.[38] From 2 million to 3 million Germans lived within Czechoslovakia, and peoples of several nationalities were within the borders of Poland. Nevertheless, the principle of self-determination was still a major tenet of political doctrine and faith. It continued to haunt Europe. Hitler was to use it (with a racial twist) to justify the Nazi aggressions from 1938 on and Allied statesmen to justify their opposition to these aggressions.

It was also true that in 1919 the principle was not applied to colonial peoples, though the League of Nations provision for "mandates" implied that these peoples were to become, at some distant date and when "prepared," independent nations. In the future, however, Asians and Africans would also demand the right of self-determination, as Jews and Hindus were already doing through leaders such as Theodor Herzl and Mohandas Gandhi. Even the established dominions of the British Empire were dissatisfied with the considerable self-government they had, and the Statute of Westminster (1931) recognized them as "autonomous communities . . . equal in status, in no way subordinate one to another in any respect of their domestic or external affairs."

The right of each people to be self-determining and independent seemed logically to flow from and be an end result of the democratic process, and it was so argued again and again. Essentially a political argument, it was just one of several employed in the nineteenth century to explain and to justify why peoples organized or should be grouped by nations. Other arguments ranged from the biological to the metaphysical. That these, by hindsight, were at best intelligent guesses and at worst but rationalizations or nonsensical myths makes little difference. Leaders of thought believed them and stated them with utmost conviction.

From the mid-nineteenth century, racial interpretations of all aspects of human behavior multiplied and became a standard explanation for the establishment of nations and for the kind of nation racialists thought ought to be established. The nation was or should be, so the racialists claimed, really a family held together by ties of blood, and each nation therefore had its own peculiar character and destiny.[39]

In the 1840's and 1850's, for differing reasons, an Englishman, Robert Knox, a Frenchman, the Comte de Gobineau, and two Americans, Josiah Nott and G. R. Glidden, published influential books that, placing great stress on the racial interpretation of history and civilization, purported to prove the white races superior and others, particularly the black, inferior.[40] Gobineau declared "the negroid variety" to be "the lowest," of animal character and limited intellect though it had well-developed senses and energy; it could never, he stated, found a civilization. The white races, on the other hand, according to Gobineau, were "gifted" with "reflective" and "energetic intelligence," and, though inferior in ability to feel, were honorable, vigorous and courageous; they, and they only, could create a civilization, and all civilization derived from them.[41]

Though the propagators of these racial myths did not themselves always directly promote or even favor nationalism (Gobineau did not), their myths became political arguments for the division of peoples into nations and for the supremacy of certain nations. This was particularly the case in England, the United States, and Germany, where Walter Bagehot, Houston Stewart Chamberlain (1855–1927), Senator Albert J. Beveridge, and many others strongly upheld the supremacy of the Anglo-Saxon, the Teutonic, or the Nordic race and claimed for it (or them) the standard of civilization and the right to carry its salutary benefits to benighted other races.[42] In France, where racial mixtures were more obvious, the argument that one race should be the core of the nation was made much less often; instead, as the historian Michelet believed, it was sometimes held that a desirable and healthy fusion of races made the nation. Whether one or several races made the nation, however, race and the ethnic differences that arose out of supposed differences in blood became major ingredients in nationalist thinking. Sometimes the words nation and race were used interchangeably. In any case, it was argued, differences of race (or race mixture) determined how people (or *Volk*) should be grouped in nations, and ties of blood should be the basis of unity while race should determine which nations were destined to be dominant. For Beveridge—and his was not an isolated voice—God had been preparing the English-speaking and Teutonic peoples "for a thousand years," had made them "the master organizers of the work to establish system where chaos reigns," and had "marked the American people" to lead "in the regeneration of the world." That nations might no longer exist if one race or nation organized the world nationalists apparently never perceived. And racial myths did become at least rationalizations for political action, for national imperial ventures like those of Rhodes in Africa, and for limitations, especially in the United States, on immigration of peoples of "inferior" races in order to keep the nation "pure," and they became as well grounds for violent national animosities.

Americans like Beveridge were not unique, of course, in their belief that God or nature or mystic forces had created and marked their nation for a supreme world role, either as a missionary nation to reform the world or as an ideal model for other nations to emulate.[43] For true believers in many nations, their nation's destiny was also "manifest." During modern times, and particularly from the mid-nineteenth century, proponents of nearly every people have glowingly portrayed their own people as chosen by God, who had assigned them a particular mission.[44] "Every people" declared the fervent Italian believer in nationality, Mazzini, had its "own special mission" just as did his Italy.[45] And in almost every nation or nation-to-be, some patriotic writers claimed their nation did. God, then, or some force, had ordained the division of men into nations, and, since this was divine will, men should be devoted to their nations.

The interpretations of the national missions varied with the prophets.[46] The mission of England, so empire builder Cecil Rhodes (1853–1902) proclaimed (and his was not an isolated voice in England), was to be the "chosen instrument" to bring a society based on "peace, liberty, and justice [or English values, business, and government?]." [47] Michelet the historian, Victor Hugo (1802–85) the poet and novelist, and Clemenceau (1841–1929) the politician, thought of France as the "motivator of progress"—the "pilot of humanity"—in the civilizing of the world. A good many Germans, Kaiser William II and the poet Emanuel Geibel, for instance, thought Germany the "block of granite" on which the Almighty "would finish his work of civilizing the world," that is, bring German *Kultur* to the lesser peoples of the world.[48] And such Russian prophets as Nikolai Danilevsky (1822–85), the philosopher of Pan-Slavism, and Feodor Dostoyevsky, the great novelist, believed the Russians and Slavs would purge evil and bring a new dispensation for mankind.[49] Not only the prophets of the ancient Hebrews but also those of modern western nations thought of their people as "holy," "special," "above all people on the face of the earth." [50]

Racial arguments for nationalism assumed competition among peoples for supremacy. About the same time as racial interpretations of history were becoming popular, during the last half of the nineteenth century, Darwinian doctrines about the struggle for survival were winning wide acceptance, and they too were used to justify and strengthen nationalism. Darwin himself little applied his theories[51] to nations, but others did as they evolved what has been called "the natural theology of nationalism," Social Darwinism.[52] There was no standard version of this theology, and it was more popular in Britain and the United States than elsewhere. As preached by Herbert Spencer (1820–1903), Walter Bagehot (1826–77), Benjamin Kidd (1858–1916), and Karl Pearson (1857–1936) in England and by Admiral Alfred Thayer Mahan (1840–1914), John Fiske (1842–1901),[53] and Homer Lea (1876–1912) in the United States, Social Darwinism held that life was competitive struggle and that the race went to the strong. Applied to nations, this meant that closely knit, bold nations would triumph and that therefore citizens should patriotically strive to strengthen their nation and fight for it, for it was the law of life that the strong (which was equated with the best) nations would triumph while the weak fell and would be conquered or simply disappear.[54] As Walter Bagehot, British banker and popularizer of Darwinistic social sciences, put it, "Those nations which are strongest tend to prevail over others; and . . . the strongest tend to be the best." [55] Hence, logically or illogically, the conclusion was drawn that every good man should be intensely loyal to his natural group, the nation, and that national patriotism, decreed by the laws of nature, was admirable and should be encouraged in every possible way. That laws of nature so dictated could hardly be substantiated by evidence, though much rhetoric flowed. But individuals and nations, it is obvious, did compete, and fear of other nations did stimulate nationalism. War, rumors of war, prophecies of war, and profound fear of conquest by foreigners deepened national loyalty and aggravated hatred of foreigners.[56]

Again, around the mid-nineteenth century, another theory was put forward to explain though not to justify nationalism: that based on economic determination and class interest and most vigorously and fully developed by the founder of modern communism, Karl Marx (1818–83), his collaborators, and his successors. This theory, too, was based upon struggle, in this case the struggle between classes. The national state, and therefore nationalism, resulted from the national bourgeoisie's efforts to wrest power from feudalistic aristocrats and each other, to capture the home market, and thus to obtain economic profit. In short, the national organization of political and economic life was a stage of the historical evolution toward international communism, the stage of capitalism, and nationalism was simply the loyalty demanded by the bourgeoisie of each nation to accomplish its ends. The government of the national state, so Marx maintained, was "nothing more than a committee for the administration of the consolidated affairs of the bourgeois class as a whole." [57] Joseph Stalin, once *the* Communist authority on nationalism, bluntly declared in 1913,

The chief problem of the young bourgeoisie is [was] the problem of the market . . . to sell its goods and to emerge victorious from the competition with the bourgeoisie of another nationality. . . . The market is the first school in which the bourgeoisie learns its nationalism. A nation is not merely a historical category but a historical category belonging to a definite epoch, the epoch of rising capitalism.[58]

This Marxist, class explanation, based as it was on the complicated structure of dialectical materialism and the inevitability of revolution, was neither widely understood nor widely accepted during the nineteenth century. But that nationalism had (and has) a class basis was (and is) held by many later students of various political points of view. A common interpretation is that of Louis Snyder, well-known non-Marxist author of a recent survey, *The New Nationalism*: "Modern nationalism was initially a bourgeois phenomenon, created of, by, and primarily for the middle class, which was very much aware of its politico-economic aims and strongly determined to achieve them." [59]

There is, it must immediately be stated, considerable substance to this interpretation. A chief purpose of many of the revolutionary nation-states of the late eighteenth and nineteenth centuries—as the American and French revolutionary leaders Alexander Hamilton and the abbé Sieyès and not a few later political theorists and activists agreed—was to protect liberty and property, and these *were* prime interests of the middle classes. It is also true that in western countries individuals of these classes, often men not only of property but also of ambition and energy, did lead and govern. As they conceived the nation-state to be something like a modern business corporation controlled by the common (active) stockholders (property owners) in hope of dividends (profits), the shape of the nation-state they helped establish did indeed reflect their economic interests. Finally, it was often members of the middle classes who, as they in their self-interest became nationalist, fostered nationalism, demanded that all men ought to be national patriots (though they thought some were not intelligent enough to be) and that governments should seek, by every means, to instill patriotism in the governed.

To explain the phenomenon of nationalism in terms of class interest, however, oversimplifies a complex process. Individuals of all classes became (and are now) nationalists.[60] Without doubt *one* major reason for the establishment of national states and the demand for loyalty to them was the desire of the middle classes to protect the interests and values of those who held property and wanted more, or who had or hoped to win more power and status in their societies—that is, for people like themselves.[61] In rough proportion as the nation-states responded to these interests and desires, they probably did win the loyalty of propertied and ambitious people and thus stimulated nationalism. Yet neither self-interest nor national feeling was limited to members of the middle classes. In fear and in hope, individuals, rich and poor, and of the upper, middle, and lower classes, became nationalists, and for many reasons, some self-serving and some idealistic, but also because they were so taught or influenced by their societies and knew no alternatives.

Other theories, rationalizations, myths to explain and justify the rise of nations and nationalism were many. But they are touched on elsewhere.[62] In actuality, the national governments, both the established and the new, increasingly penetrated the lives of the peoples, and as they did so made them nationally conscious and patriotic. In actuality, the people themselves increasingly participated (directly or vicariously) in the affairs of their nations and increasingly identified their interests with those of their nation. As a result of the penetration, participation, and identification as well as the dawning realization of common cultures (always in process of creation), nationalism spread and deepened.

What established nation-states like France and Britain had begun in promoting national sentiment and unity, they continued and amplified. The new nation-states, when they were created, likewise intervened in all aspects of their citizens' lives from birth to death and for similar purposes. The nation-states, or more precisely the national governments, became the chief instruments for achieving security for life and property, for establishing and safeguarding whatever liberties were won, for protection against foreigners, and increasingly for the fulfillment of the hopes of citizens. If the citizens were not sufficiently receptive and loyal, then the governments, through their laws and courts, by control of information, or by force (police or military), demanded or commanded their loyalty. The more energetic and public-spirited, perhaps the more honest and intelligent the governmental officials were, the more they tried to make national patriots and, likely, the more they succeeded. It did not, apparently, matter whether the officials were democratic or authoritarian, liberal or conservative, for governments and leaders, whatever their political ideology, won support and believers as they constructed political bases for nationalism. National governments, at different times and in different places, became bulwarks for the status quo and reaction, or agents for change and modernization. Nationalism could marry almost any ideology, and it did.[63]

National governments in the nineteenth century generally acted as if their leaders had read and believed the 1787 American plea in *The Federalist* papers (number 16) for a strong national government that would address itself "immediately to the hopes and fears of individuals" and attract support from "those passions which have the strongest influence upon the human heart." But European governments scarcely needed this counsel, for European political traditions (though not some of the English) generally favored strong governments and European political leaders well knew how to appeal to passions.

What the various governments did in fact do varied widely. In Russia the czars were chiefly concerned with order and stability, docility and obedience, hence with a strong army and an effective police.[64] In Austria as well as in other countries it sometimes appeared that the government existed for the officials. In Latin American countries, more often than not political leaders were chiefly interested in gaining office, staying in power, and lining their pockets, and this kind of official was not unknown anywhere. But everywhere, in response to hopes and fears of people and out of the desire to enhance their own power, political leaders generally strengthened their nation-states, and generally they found their peoples, different segments at different times and for different reasons, quite willing and even insistent that they do so.

The number of officials filling the national bureaucracies steadily mounted as the states augmented their services and as the bureaucracies themselves promoted their own growth. From 1870 especially, the size of national armies and navies grew steadily as in fear and ambition nation-states sought security and power, introducing, or continuing, military conscription, and, as in France and Germany, drafting young men for two to three years of military service. When World War I came, even Britain and the United States, which had had but small volunteer armies, introduced mass conscription. Both the bureaucracies and the military forces required larger and larger national expenditures, the latter from the 1880's especially, as weapons became heavier, more complicated, and more costly.

Throughout the western world from the 1830's,[65] and after the 1860's in Japan as well, national governments greatly expanded their activities. In spite of the professed *laissez faire* doctrines of a good many politicians, particularly those of the United States and Britain, this expansion took place in every nation. The national governments, not always but usually, aided business by protective tariffs, by money subsidies, by protecting and fostering, both diplomatically and militarily, foreign trade, and by supporting elementary education (as did Germany) to supply workers literate enough to become productive in industry. Nearly always (as in France in the 1880's) they made at least elementary education free, public, and universal with the aim of making good patriots. They established (or continued) national banks, national currencies, national systems of weights and measures. They subsidized, or favored in some manner, the building of canals (as in England), railroads (as in the United States), and roads (as in France), and they established and maintained postal services (everywhere). From the 1880's (as in Germany) they usually began to provide national accident and old-age insurance, and they often made (as in Britain) investigations into working conditions and passed national restrictive laws on the employment of women and children and the length of the working day. As the national activities and laws proliferated, so did demands for enforcement. Generally, the superior court systems became national and so did interpretations of justice, and in some nations the police. Maintenance of "law and order" became a major responsibility of the nation-states, just as it had been of the dynastic states, and they accepted this responsibility—though only within their national boundaries—and used troops and police as well as the courts to keep order, that is, protect property and life and the national values.

As the national services multiplied, so also, naturally, did the costs of government. This meant higher national taxes, and it brought directly levied and felt national income and inheritance taxes (as in England in 1911) that made even the rich conscious of the nation-state's power.[66] During the world war of 1914–18 national military efforts, as well as governmental intervention in every vital aspect of life, necessitated colossal expenditures, hence brought steep increases in national taxes and mammoth national debts. As the debts mounted, so did the number of bondholders and thus the number of citizens who had a direct financial stake in their nation's stability and survival. In peace or war few citizens, in fact, could have avoided becoming nationally conscious. Apparently most continued to be or became loyal, though always some were apathetic and some alienated and disloyal. In 1914 not even the majority of socialists—believers in the world brotherhood of the proletariat—could resist the appeal of national patriotism. And when, as in 1919–20, some peoples in hope, anger, and despair did rebel, they nearly always protested within the national frameworks and against a particular government (the Kaiser's or the Czar's), not against their nation. In 1918 the shrewd conservative General Wilhelm Groener and officers of the German army in defeat believed themselves released from oaths of fealty to their Kaiser, but they affirmed their loyalty to the German fatherland.[67] When, during 1917–21, radical revolutions against the existing governments occurred in central and eastern Europe, they were chiefly revolutions for new national governments or for new national states, and hardly ever against the idea of nationhood.

Throughout much of the nineteenth century, in western "democratic" countries like England and the United States, old liberal doctrines, inherited from the eighteenth century and professed by many leaders, ran contrary to what was actually happening as governments became leviathans. In practice democratic statesmen, as in the United States, often voiced one view—the less government the better—and did something else—expanded their government's activities. In states with more authoritarian traditions (Germany after 1870) the governments could and did act without this contradiction. In every case, during the latter half of the nineteenth century (the time differs for each country) governments did act and expand.

It is too often overlooked that the democratic national governments—and in much lesser degree even the authoritarian—established and protected whatever liberties and rights peoples enjoyed, whether these concerned freedom of religion and speech or the right to own property and to accumulate more. During the nineteenth century even conservative rulers had to grant (however much they regretted it) national constitutions, and every liberal and democratic nation had a national constitution (usually written) with some kind of statement and guaranty of rights.[68] It is true that constitutions were often ignored or violated and the rights they proclaimed denied, especially in the authoritarian countries but also, on occasion, in the democratic, and that constitutions and bills of rights meant little in any country in wartime. Nonetheless, the constitutions and the rights were national, and in democratic countries it was in national courts that they were upheld, modified, or denied. When individuals had rights, then, they obtained them not from God or nature but from their nations, and the civil liberties that so many came to prize were not local or universal but national.

If, through their activities and whatever rights they granted and protected, the national governments did not win the loyalty of their citizens in the degree they desired, they could encourage it through control of opinion. While, after 1848, direct censorship of information was possibly less employed, except in wartime, than it had been, it was still practiced, and not only in dictator-ridden Latin American countries and in reactionary Russia but also in liberal France. There were, of course, subtler and less offensive ways of controlling opinion for nationalist ends. Though before the twentieth century national governments seldom had organized "public relations" offices as such, each government tried, with some success, to see that citizens learned the "facts" most favorable to the nation, its rulers, and whatever were believed to be the national purposes. From World War I governmental attempts to control and sometimes to manufacture the news became better organized and more astute. At the outbreak of World War I most of the warring nations issued "color books" to present their versions of why the war came, and each one portrayed the high-minded, peaceful intentions of the issuing nation and the evil deeds and ambitions of the enemy nations. During the war and ever since, national governments (virtually without exception) have constantly and systematically attempted to influence opinion, in authoritarian states by direct censorship as well as by propaganda, in democratic states more often by offices of public information or public relations, which issue press handouts and hold official press conferences. Often it has been difficult if not impossible to determine whether the releases and conferences were designed for the nation's welfare or to keep the particular government and its officeholders in power. But in no case did a governmental official or agency promulgate antinational news, and in all cases governmental policy and practice were equated with what was good for the nation. Few citizens were certain enough of their own rectitude and knowledge to disbelieve, and most easily believed in the rectitude of their own nation and the perfidy of other nations.

It is hard to imagine how people could have thought or acted differently, for political life had become or was becoming predominantly national. The major effective means of political action, the emerging political parties, were organized on a national scale with the purpose of capturing national power—the Whig (Liberal) and the Tory (Conservative) parties in Britain, the Democratic and the Republican in the United States, the National Liberal and the Free Conservative in Germany. The parties, with exceptions such as the largely Prussian Conservative party in Germany and the Socialist parties in several nations, promoted nationalist goals, and even the exceptions (like the Socialist) became nationalist in wartime. After 1848 most of the successful political leaders, the Palmerstons, the Gambettas, the Poincarés, the Lloyd Georges, the Theodore Roosevelts, the William II's, were ardent nationalists. They were nationalists either out of conviction or because they had to be in order to win support— probably both. But whatever the reason, they were nationalist, did lead, and did influence people in nationalist directions.

There is no precise way of determining just how effective the national governments were in making patriots.[69] Sometimes it was in protest against these governments that individuals became nationally conscious and began to act nationally. During the Mexican Revolution from 1910 to 1917, workers, women, Indians who had never taken part in national affairs began to do so.[70] During other revolutions in other countries in Europe and Latin America, segments of the populations, urban and rural, industrial workers and farmers, and members of racial and religious minorities, demanded rights that could only be obtained from national governments, hence became interested in and engaged in activities that were national, in short, became active national citizens. But, in general the governments themselves were, as judged by crucial tests in time of war, quite successful in their efforts to promote national unity and loyalty. This does not seem strange in light of what the governments did.[71] Usually, and not only in the ways already described, they took over the political and social work traditionally performed by monarchical, feudal, and local governments and by the churches. These older governing bodies gradually lost many of their functions, and loyalty to them declined. The monarch, the feudal lord, the country squire, the village priest were gradually superseded by public officials, the most important of them national officials. More and more it was national agencies, bureaucracies, and courts that registered a man's birth and death and certified his marriage, settled his quarrels with others, sentenced him to punishment if he broke a law, and in sum provided, however little or much, for his welfare, his duties, and his liberties. By the beginning of the twentieth century, in much of the western world, everywhere a man turned he encountered his nation's political being, the national state. A man was born in, matured in, and died within the political matrix of his nation-state. He had little choice. But always, it was true, some individuals were molded more than others and always some escaped the matrix. Totalitarian nationalism had not yet arrived, and even it, when that time came, was not quite total.

As national governments influenced the lives and thinking of citizens, these citizens increasingly participated in national affairs and, in diverse ways and degrees, influenced the policies and actions of their governments. State action made people become nationally conscious, and people, it is likely, became more patriotic when they became involved. Actually, of course, substantial numbers of people in every country were little interested in national questions, evinced little or no patriotism, and seldom participated, except when forced, in any national activity. But more did participate and more did become more involved and loyal.

There were, it is clear, immense differences in kinds and degrees of participation in different nations. During years of peace, participation was more direct and tangible in the liberal and democratic countries than in the conservative and authoritarian. In the latter, involvement was more likely to be vicarious, in emotion and feeling rather than in concrete political activity. In wartime, from 1914 to 1918 especially, all nations became nations in arms, and between liberal and conservative nations there was little difference, for citizens served alike in armies, factories, and fields for the defense and in the interests of the fatherland. But even in peacetime the most authoritarian governments encouraged some kind of participation (if only in public service and in public ceremonies and celebrations) as long as it did not mean the granting of much power. It is also true that after the 1848 revolutions most states, even the most conservative, did give or were forced to concede rights to their peoples—at least to appear to allow them some semblance of power—in order to maintain and promote national loyalty and unity.[72] Further, it was in the totalitarian states established after World War I that nationalism became the most intense as their governments really involved people, without granting power, in the performance of national duties.

Democracy meant that people should have rights. Now these rights were becoming national, and if they were to be significant they had also to be exercised on a national basis. Among them was the right to vote, to determine who should govern and how; in the nineteenth century this became the right, on the highest level, to choose national representatives and to have a voice in the determination of national policies. The right to vote, it is no secret, might or might not mean much. On the one hand, the voting could be and was sometimes manipulated in various ways in order to control the result; on the other, individuals might have the franchise and not exercise it. But, in general, people demanded it, and the trend, especially in western nations and haltingly even in conservative nations, was toward giving more and more adult men (and later women) a voice in national affairs, toward making them active national citizens.

The French Jacobin Constitution of 1793 provided for universal manhood suffrage but was not put into effect. Even in the most politically democratic nations the suffrage was severely limited by property and religious qualifications until well into the nineteenth century. In the United States such restrictions, established by the states, existed until the 1830's; not until after 1865 was the Negro given the right, and then only in hollow theory. In Britain, so proud of its representative parliamentary institutions, property and other limitations were only gradually removed, principally by the reform bills of 1832, 1867, and 1884. In France from 1848 adult Frenchmen could vote (if elections were held), but not until after the overthrow of the Second Empire (1870–71) did voting imply a real voice in government.[73] In Germany, where conservatism was stronger, there was universal manhood suffrage from the time of unification (1867–70), but the three-class system of voting in Prussia, which dominated the Empire, severely modified it in practice.[74] Yet even the authoritarian Napoleon III held plebiscites (three) in France, ostensibly to ascertain the national will, though actually to strengthen his regime. And after World War I the right of people in disputed border areas to choose their own national affiliations in plebiscites was recognized. As the French scholar and patriot Ernest Renan once remarked, the choice of a nation was becoming a continuous plebiscite. With the choice, national loyalty was more likely.

However slowly peoples obtained the right to an effective vote, by the early twentieth century nearly everywhere in Europe and the Americas (except Hungary, Romania, Spain, and Russia) most adult males did possess the legal right, and the extension of the right to women was beginning. By that time, insofar as available statistics permit generalization, from one-fifth to one-fourth of the total population in most western countries had the right,[75] though by no means all of those who had the right actually voted. Sizable proportions of the adults in democratic countries, then, did share in the making of national decisions. And when an individual made the effort to vote, marked a ballot on national candidates and issues, he was committing himself to his nation, becoming an active part of it. With a vote, to paraphrase the American poet James Russell Lowell (who was alluding to the familiar statement attributed to Louis XIV), every man could say, "I am the state." [76]

Steadily increasing numbers of citizens directly participated in the activities of the national governments as employees and officials. By the early 1920's more than one of twenty Frenchmen was in the civil services and armed forces,[77] and France was not untypical. In every nation, too, appreciable numbers of people joined national organizations outside the government, patriotic societies, such as the Royal Empire Society (1869), the Daughters of the American Revolution (1890), and the French League of Patriots (1882), or the numerous scholarly and professional associations founded during the last third of the nineteenth century, such as the Royal Historical Society (1868) and the American Historical Association (1884). And citizens, some glowing with pride, went in ever larger crowds to the growing number of patriotic celebrations, like those of July 4 in the United States and July 14 in France.[78] Again, it must be repeated, everyone did not become nationally conscious and certainly not everyone patriotic. The poor, the illiterate—the "underprivileged," in contemporary terminology—ordinarily did not, could not. And, indeed, individuals in all classes remained apathetic and, if interested in civic activities at all, gave their time and energy to local affairs.

Clashing national fears and hopes sharpened national animosities and brought violent conflicts. All through the nineteenth century peoples subjected to foreign rulers feared and hated them, rebelled and fought against them, and if they were able to throw off the foreign "yoke" feared it might be reimposed. When a people had an established independent state, they feared other nations because these threatened the values and interests of their nation and might attack, subjugate it and end its existence (as did happen during the eighteenth century to Poland). But it was not only fear that led to national conflicts. The nation had become the vehicle of hope. For patriots endeavoring to establish independent nations, the achievement of independence was the threshold of a happier, freer life. For patriots of established nations, the continued existence of their nation and often its expansion were believed essential for a happier and more prosperous life. When a nation was unified, independent, and expansive, however, its interests conflicted with those of other nations— over claims to people and territory in border areas and, in the case of large nations, over power and imperial ambitions as well. Whatever the nature of their interests and ambitions, the nation-states believed they had to defend and forward them, for not only was the nation's future well-being at stake but its very survival. If in the competitive race a nation faltered, it would fall behind, might itself be subjugated. Yet when any nation attempted to expand or did expand, it threatened the interests, perhaps the very existence, of other nations.

Because the nations were unequal in wealth and power, each felt insecure. "Other" nations were always believed to be stronger; "other" nations' motivations were always suspect; and hence the "other" nations were always dangerous. Each nation, therefore, had to do whatever it could to keep the "balance of power" (it was forever becoming unbalanced). Each nation had to be strong, powerful, had to prepare for any eventuality, strengthen itself economically, acquire colonies, increase its armies and armaments, make alliances, while it did everything it could to ensure the loyalty of its own citizens. Each effort of each nation meant that other nations had to not only make similar exertions but exceed them.

The rivalry was ruthless, and it led to conflict. Probably it is true that most people at most times cared little about what happened internationally, but their leaders and influential groups of their fellow citizens did. Probably most of the leaders and members of these groups did not want the race with other nations, did not want to prepare for any eventuality, including war. But if the national survival, interests, and honor were at stake, what other choice did they have in the international anarchy that characterized nineteenth-century international politics? The rivalry was ruthless and the race without end—unless one nation conquered the others. Yet no nation, not even Napoleonic France, was strong enough. Under the circumstances, the closer the race, the stronger the spirit of partisanship became.

For over thirty years after Napoleon's downfall in 1815 rulers in the dominant states of Europe chiefly feared their subjects' rebelling for liberal and national causes. For over forty years after 1870 the great nation-states as well as the small chiefly feared each other. During the intervening period, 1848–70, the peoples of Germany and Italy struggled and fought to become and did become unified, independent nations; and from 1848 especially, the several other European peoples who (like the Serbs) could be called nationalities but did not have their national independence clamored for and sometimes obtained it. If history had stopped in 1900, the nineteenth century could be called *the* age of nationalism.

Never, except perhaps in time of war, were all or even almost all the people of any nation fully agreed on national goals or activities. Rather, in each nation individuals and groups with like interests tried to make their interests the national interests, and if they had the power they were successful. Enough politicians in search of popularity and power and enough intellectuals in search of acceptance and fame generally supported the strongest interest groups (and sometimes led them) that their interests became the national interests.[79]

To describe fully how international rivalries and conflicts accentuated nationalism during the nineteenth and early twentieth centuries would be to show the spread and deepening of nationalism. Examples will suffice.

All through Europe and in the Americas, too, nation-states disputed over border areas and over peoples. The long controversies between

France and the Germanies over territories lying between them were not unique; scarcely a frontier was firmly fixed or agreed upon—not even the Scandinavian—and claims and counterclaims followed each other in confusing profusion. In eastern and central Europe the existing states—Russia and, when it was established, Germany—included dissatisfied minority groups that were claimed by other nations or that, like the Polish, sooner or later would demand their independence. In central and southeastern Europe nationalities subject to Austria-Hungary (in some cases nominally also to Turkey)—Serbians, Croatians, Slovenes, Czechs, Slovaks, Romanians, Bulgarians—sought more self-government and then their own nation-states. If they gained independence, as did Serbia, Romania, and Bulgaria, they then claimed people and territory outside their borders as rightfully theirs and thus aroused national feeling both within their own country and in the country of the current possessors. After independence (and on occasion before), they were always backed by or allied to one or another of the great powers, who were themselves seeking competitive national advantage in the race for security and power and who themselves, like Austria-Hungary or Russia, were not above taking people and territory if they could get them. And always the nationalisms of the great and small nations were thereby further aggravated. In the New World, Cubans, in their struggle for independence from Spain, gained the support of the United States, which was then beginning its far-flung expansion. The result was a short war between the United States and Spain that excited nationalists in both countries.[80] The cause of peoples oppressed by foreign rulers became indeed, to quote Byron once more, "the very poetry of politics" as minority nationalities, inflamed by nationalism, struggled for nationhood and clashed once they attained it, and as large nations, similarly inflamed, competed and clashed in their search for the security and hegemony they could never quite attain. The fiercer the struggle became, the higher the pitch of national rhetoric rose.

The impact of the competition is nowhere better demonstrated than in the bitter quarrel between France and Germany over Alsace and Lorraine from 1870 to 1918 (and later). France, long in possession of the provinces and preferred by Lorrainers and most Alsatians, believed the provinces to be French.[81] Germany, because the provinces were considered vital to German security and because many Alsatians spoke German, believed they should belong to Germany. Germany took them when it decisively defeated France in 1870.[82] From that time the anguish of French patriots was intense. The recovery of the "lost provinces" became the single most important goal of French foreign policy, the cause of

French patriotic intellectuals and politicians, *the* cause that most aroused many Frenchmen to devotion and fury.[83] Politics scarcely mattered. Leaders of many views and many interests were deeply convinced that France had been grievously humiliated by defeat and terribly wronged by the German conquest. These were men of influence, such as Maurice Barrès (1862–1923), the ex-Lorrainer novelist who wrote so movingly and artistically of the earth and the dead and their union with the living in the *patrie;* Raymond Poincaré (1860–1934), the proud and stubborn ex-Lorrainer who was Prime Minister and President of France during the crucial years from 1912 to 1920; Ernest Lavisse (1842–1922), specialist in German history who wrote and edited moving patriotic histories read by children and adults; and Ernest Renan (1823–90), distinguished historian of the Christians and Jews who so superbly and with patriotic emotion answered his own question in his often reprinted lecture, *Qu'est-ce qu'une Nation?* [84] For over forty years French leaders spoke of the "open wound," of bleeding France, and waved the tricolor to stimulate devotion to France and hatred of Germany. The "wound" may have stirred the emotions of conservative more than of moderate and radical patriots, but men of all parties fervently hoped for the day when—Alsace-Lorraine returned —France would be "healed" again.

The conflicts over national frontiers and nationalities in Europe were, of course, both a product of nationalism and a stimulus to more. Of as great import were the conflicts that arose out of imperialism, that proclivity of nation-states to acquire, by one means or another, foreign territories and peoples, and hence to achieve greater security and power.

It seemed that once any nation attained independence and unity, it wished to expand.[85] Particularly from the 1870's the great nations—Britain, France, Germany, Russia, and to a lesser extent Italy, Japan, and the United States—raced for empire.[86] As they did so they provoked each other's ambitions and fears, aroused each other's nationalism. "Patriotism, conventionally defined as love of country," turned out also to be "love of more country," [87] more people, more trade, more investments and profits, more security, more prestige, more power. And so Britain and Germany competed for these ends in East Africa, the Middle East, and around the world; Britain and France in Egypt; Britain and Russia in the Middle East and central Asia; France and Germany in Morocco; France and Italy in Tunisia; the United States and Spain in Cuba and the Philippines; Russia and Japan and other powers in eastern Asia; Germany, Austria-Hungary, Russia, France, and Britain in the Balkans; and——.

It was once generally believed that imperialism and the resulting conflicts were almost exclusively the result of economic drives, of the capitalist search for profit.[88] The economic stakes were high. British investments abroad more than tripled from 1880 to 1913, amounting to nearly £4 billion (about $19 billion) at the latter date. While the foreign investments of other great nations were much less, they too rapidly mounted, as bankers and businessmen, in Germany and France in particular, sought the highest rates of return on their capital. Between 1871 and 1900, the period of the most rapid imperial expansion, Britain acquired around 4,250,000 square miles of territory and 66 million people, France 3,500,000 square miles and 26 million people, Germany 1 million square miles and 13 million people, and Russia 500,000 square miles and over 6 million people. These territories (not all, but most) produced raw materials and offered opportunities for employment and for investment. These people bought English, French, German, and Russian goods and paid the interest on loans.

The national imperial governments acted in many ways, from offering their good offices and diplomatic assistance to military protection and political annexation, in order to encourage and assist their own merchants and investors. Thus the economic interests of individual citizens became the nations', and national governments were obligated to defend and promote them. When they did so, they collided with other national governments equally obligated.

Nevertheless, imperial expansion and the resulting conflicts cannot be explained so simply; the motivations of imperialist leaders were several and complex. It is true that some of them were chiefly interested in economic gain, if not for themselves, at least for their fellow nationals. But of more concern to many of them were the vital interests of their nation as it competed with other nations—basic issues of national survival and well-being, of national power, prestige, and honor. For Leroy-Beaulieu (1842–1912), the educator and publicist who influenced so many French leaders with his books and as director of the famed *Ecole des Sciences Politiques,* colonization was a "matter of life or death" for France,[89] and leaders in other nations held similar views. Some imperialists were also convinced (ridiculous as this may seem to later critics) that the very future of civilization depended upon the spread of *their* nation's way of life (the "civilizing of lesser breeds") to all mankind. Many individuals in the major nations sincerely if pretentiously did indeed believe their civilization to be "the greatest instrument for good" [90] and its dominance over the world the prerequisite for justice and peace. Economic, political, and humanitarian motivations were thus all present and intertwined, but all could be subsumed within the national interest. Indeed, it was usually the national political leaders in pursuit of national interest who took the lead in imperial ventures as much as and probably more than private businessmen.[91] No one can determine with certainty which motivations were uppermost in the minds of the statesmen in every case of expansion, but in general they and their governments were concerned with the present and future national safety and hence wanted not only economic but also strategic and military advantages—"defensive outposts" and soldiers for their armies. Leaders of Britain, already the greatest imperial power, wanted to protect the "life line" to India and the East, and were proud of the vast dominion on which the "sun never set." British statesmen from Palmerston to Disraeli and Salisbury, convinced that Britain's strength depended upon its Empire and governed by the prevailing concepts of international strategy, steadily consolidated and extended that Empire.[92] When and as they did so they were supported, indeed pushed, by fellow citizens of great influence, like the financier-politician and greatest of imperialists, Cecil Rhodes, for whom personal interest, Anglo-Saxon superiority, and British dominance were synonymous,[93] and the popular imperialist poet Rudyard Kipling, who believed it Britain's duty "to carry light and civilization into the dark places of the world." [94] German leaders wanted their nation to have a "place in the sun," to be a (if not the) great world power, and to carry its *Kultur* to the world. As German expansion was beginning in the late 1870's, the influential historian Treitschke (1834–96) asserted, "All great nations [meaning his Germany] in the fulness of their strength have desired to set their work upon barbarian lands and those who fail to participate in the great rivalry will play a pitiable role in time to come." [95] Thirty-five years later, as a result of the "great rivalry," Germany was at war, and then a well-known nonpolitical writer, Richard Dehmel, justified the war and his own participation in it in an "Open Letter" to Germans: Germany was fighting, he wrote, for the physical and moral world position appropriate to it, for "we Germans *are* more humane than other nations; we *do* have better blood and breeding, more soul, more heart, and more imagination." [96] French leaders wanted France again (after 1870) to become a great power and to bring a French peace to the world. Patriotic professional politicians, like Jules Ferry (1832–93) and Théophile Delcassé (1852–1923), and professional patriotic propagandists, like Charles Maurras (1868–1952), believed France should have ambitions greater than those of little Belgium and Switzerland, build its Empire ever greater, and carry its "customs and values [*moeurs*], language, arms, flag, genius" everywhere.[97]

As the great nations sought safety and power, they encountered other nations seeking the same ends. Ambition sharpened fear and fear ambition, and both deepened nationalism. In the atmosphere of intense nationalism that was developing before 1914 no statesman could avoid the aggressive assertion of national interest in expansion, and none could risk the humiliation of suffering diplomatic defeat by allowing another nation to get ahead in the imperial rivalry. Thus each nation's security and its future position in the world became anchored to its present prestige and honor. And for these exalted ends, if for no other, patriots felt so deeply that they would fight, as both the British Prime Minister Lloyd George and the German Kaiser William II declared Britain and Germany would do during the international crises of the early twentieth century.[98]

Imperial conflicts were between nations, not individuals and not classes. They arose out of nationalism and led to more. The cumulative momentum in national love and hate meant spiraling nationalism throughout the western world.

As national leaders sought national security, prestige, and power in a world of competing nation-states, they used the normal and traditional channels of diplomacy; they made alliances with other nations; insofar as they were able, they prepared their own nations militarily and economically for any eventuality—including war; they promoted patriotism and unity at home; and, when all else failed, they led their nations to war. Now, most national leaders desired peace. The difficulty was that the leaders of the different nations had similar *national* objectives—security, prestige, and power—but each for his nation, and no nation could realize its objectives without jeopardizing those of other nations.

About the middle of the nineteenth century the impulsive and energetic foreign minister of Britain, Viscount Palmerston (1784–1865), set forth the policy that national statesmen generally followed in foreign affairs:

The principle on which I have thought the foreign affairs of this country ought to be conducted, is the principle of maintaining peace and friendly understanding with all nations, so long as it was possible to do so consistently with due regard to the interests, the honour, and the dignity of this country. . . . If I might be allowed to express in one sentence the principle which I think ought to guide an English Minister, I would . . . say that with every British Minister the interests of England ought to be the shibboleth of his policy.[99]

Presidents and prime ministers, foreign ministers and diplomats in all western lands sought to serve their nation, to protect and foster its and its citizens' interests in dealings with all other nations and nationals. This was indeed the shibboleth of their policies. They were usually intelligent, rational men who, from their nationalist backgrounds, did what they could to maintain friendly relations with other nations, *but* at the same time they did put their own nation's interests first.[100] While, generally, they could and did act honestly and with good will, they had on occasion, naturally, to be enigmatic and secretive, and to dissemble and to lie—this was part of the game. They did, on solid grounds, suspect other diplomats of being less than candid and were themselves suspect. The roots of international distrust, however, went deeper. Each minister, each responsible official had to protect his nation and to get as much for it as he could. Each, whether he was English, French, German, or Russian, whether his name was Lord Salisbury, Théophile Delcassé, Bernhard von Bülow, or Sergei Sazonov, tried to do just that. He had to—to be true to his own nationalist convictions, to hold office, and to represent his nation. Nor did it make much difference in this respect whether he was a high-minded liberal like Sir Edward Grey (Grey of Fallodon), who wanted to preserve England's world,[101] or a chauvinistic reactionary like Aleksander Izvolski, who fanatically wanted Russian dominance in the Balkans and the Middle East. Whatever his personal quirks or his ideological limitations, he had to do what he did, or at least so he thought. He acted as he believed a patriot should: used persuasion, gave out information and misinformation, remained mysteriously silent, or threatened—reluctantly, of course—the "application of force." Always he was obsessed with the desirability, the "art," of balancing the national powers. But always this really meant tilting the balance in his nation's favor, and hence always the balance was precarious, moving, becoming unbalanced, as each nation sought and won temporary weight on the international scale, lost it, gained it again, and——. The "art" was doomed to perpetual juggling and, if peace was the objective, to ultimate failure. Always one result was more nationalism.

No national statesman could admit failure unless he resigned. There were ways of succeeding, or so it was believed. If a nation could not be strong (powerful) enough alone, it could find allies, just as had monarchical states in the past. In fact, no nation ever believed it could "go it alone," and alliances were always in process of being made and breaking up. After Napoleon the Quadruple Alliance (Austria, Britain, Prussia, and Russia) and then Metternichian Austria in concert with other like-minded conservative powers dominated Europe until 1848. All through the century the nations—France, for one—seeking security or dominance, or both, formed other alliances. From the 1880's France, Britain, and Russia (and Italy eventually) came to agreements that enabled them to have a

Triple Entente on foreign policy in order to provide a counterweight to the Triple Alliance (Germany, Austria-Hungary, and Italy), which was also formed to ensure an "equilibrium" in Europe.[102] These alliances, called "leagues of defense" to maintain the "balance of power," were believed to be the "only check on the abuse of political predominance." [103] But the "abuse" could never be checked for long, because national capabilities and ambitions changed and the international balance of power constantly shifted. No statesman could be certain an alliance would hold, how long an ally would be an ally or an enemy an enemy, nor could he be sure of the terms of opposing alliances, for they were secret. Hence new agreements, new deals and counterdeals, embodying ever more promising promises, had to be made again and again. Hence the national interests were always threatened and national fears were constantly aroused. It was not really true, as a German ambassador told the British in 1914, that the war "all came from this d--d system of alliances." [104] The alliances resulted from the fear and ambition of competing nations, but they did manifest, at the same time as they aggravated, the prevailing nationalism.

Each nation, ultimately, relied on its own strength, most directly upon its military manpower and its armaments.[105] Here, too, the nations raced, and again the race provoked fear and the fear nationalism. Other nations were always getting ahead or about to do so, and any nation's arms were always becoming obsolete. If Germany fielded a superb large army (as it did), then France had to have one as good or better and as large or larger.[106] If voluntary enlistment did not produce enough manpower for a nation, then compulsory service was necessary, and if one nation had it, others felt compelled to. If Germany conscripted young men (as it did), then France and other nations had to; if Germany (as it did) conscripted for two years' service, then France, because of its smaller population, had to require three years (as it did). If Britain had (as it did) the biggest and strongest navy, then Germany swiftly had to build one big enough to challenge it, and Britain, to stay ahead, swiftly had to build still more and still bigger battleships in order, in the words of three of its admirals, to "place the British navy beyond comparison with that of any two powers." [107] If the United States wanted to play a world role, then, in the opinion of some of its patriots, it had to have a "navy second to none," and by the early twentieth century, as a matter of "national policy," it had built its navy to third rank in the world.[108]

If any of the major nations was to defend itself and play the leading world role its leaders thought it should, then it had constantly to increase its military forces so that they would be, at least combined with allied forces, more than equal to those of any potential enemy. This required each nation to devote larger and larger proportions of its governmental revenue to military purposes, and before 1914 the proportion had generally risen to half or more.

This table[109] dramatically illustrates what happened in the cases of six major nations from 1870 to 1914.

THE NATIONS ARMING, 1870–1914

		Standing Army (*in thousands*)	*Naval Tonnage* (*in thousands*)	*Per Capita Cost*
Germany	1870	403	42	$1.33
	1914	812	1,305	8.52
Austria-Hungary	1870	247	73	1.16
	1914	424	372	3.48
British Empire	1870	302	633	3.74
	1914	381	2,714	8.53
France	1870	380	457	3.03
	1914	846	900	7.33
Russia	1870	700	363	1.34
	1914	1,300	679	2.58
United States	1870	37	175	1.98
	1914	98	895	3.20

Each national government built and spent, of course, in the name of "national defense." But, as Grey of England finally understood and stated, each regarded similar building on the part of other governments as "preparation to attack," and "each measure taken" was noted and led to countermeasures and a "sense of fear," and fear begat "suspicion and distrust and evil imaginings of all sorts, till each government" felt "it would be criminal and a betrayal of its own country not to take every precaution." [110]

A few statesmen, like Grey, had misgivings about the international race in arms. But the more usual mood was expressed by an English song of 1877 (during a "scare" of war with Russia):

We don't want to fight, but, by jingo, if we do,
We've got the ships, we've got the men, we've got the money, too.

And "jingoism" led to "jingoism."

There is no way of determining with any exactitude how aware most nineteenth-century people were of foreign threats and dangers. There is no way of knowing, for that matter, just how many people in any nation, at any one time, could be termed patriots, or in the case of those who were patriots how intense were their loyalties and their fears. The facts that men had to be conscripted for military service in peace and war and that the wealthy resisted high national taxes even in wartime probably indicate that many, rich and poor, were casual patriots and that an appreciable number cared little. But it is certain that many were deeply loyal to their country and mortally feared other nations, and that in times of crisis the devotion and the fear were widely shared.

The vast number of books and pamphlets, speeches of leaders, governmental documents, newspaper stories, discussions in private diaries and letters devoted to national issues, all attest to the wide and serious concern for national loyalty, unity, security, and expansion, and to the grave apprehension of foreign attack. The concern varied, of course, with the state of the nation and the international situation. But there were always rumors of wars,[111] and, indeed, few were the years in the nineteenth century that one or more European powers were not at war somewhere.

Bismarck boasted in an 1886 speech to the Reichstag concerning a Russian threat, "We Germans fear God, and nothing else in the world." This was not true of his Germans, or of the people of any nation. Whether some of them feared God may be questioned, but they did fear other nations and with some reason.

International crises occurred almost every year, and they generally produced alarming "war scares." In 1875, when France decided to strengthen its army to overcome the German superiority, the *Berlin Post* grimly headlined a story, "Is War in Sight?" In 1877 Britain almost went to war against Russia when the latter, at war with Turkey, threatened British interests in the eastern Mediterranean, that is, along Britain's "life line." In 1895 the United States and Britain could have fought what would have been an absurd war over a Venezuelan-British boundary dispute. In 1896 Germany aroused Britain's ire and its own emotion when the Kaiser sent a congratulatory telegram to President Kruger on the Boer victory over the Jameson (English) raiders in the Transvaal. In 1898 Britain and France were at the point of war over control of the upper Nile when British forces under Kitchener confronted French troops under Marchand at Fashoda. In 1899 there were rumors of Franco-German-Russian intervention against Britain in the Boer War. In 1904 Britain and Russia narrowly avoided war when a Russian fleet, on its way to the Far East during the Russo-Japanese War, fired on British trawlers at Dogger Bank and sunk one. In 1905 France and Germany were on the verge of war when the Kaiser visited

Tangier as France was moving into Morocco. In 1908 general European war threatened when Austria annexed Bosnia and Herzegovina and Russia did not get "compensation." From 1908 to 1914 the crises arose almost monthly or even daily as the great European powers disputed over who should get or control what in the Balkans, in Turkey, in Asia and Africa, and as small nations in the Balkans bitterly fought among themselves. There had always been "war scares," true enough, but now they frightened *not just* monarchs and their officials *but* whole nations. And they came frequently enough to keep national feeling at high pitch.

The actual "scares" were scary enough to arouse fear in any people. Those imaginatively concocted, chiefly after 1870,[112] by popular writers and journalists were designed to frighten people into patriotic action, to prepare them for any eventuality that might endanger their nation.[113] Soon after the German triumph in 1870–71, an English military officer (Royal Engineers), George Tomkyns Chesney, published in *Blackwood's Magazine* a horrendous and heart-rending tale, "The Battle of Dorking," in which he described "a successful invasion [by the Germans] of England, and the collapse of our power and commerce." The tragedy happened because the English were unprepared, incompetent, and weak, while the Germans were prepared, disciplined, and possessed secret weapons. Chesney could write, and he knew how to tell a tale that obsessed readers with fear. His immensely popular story was widely read and commented upon—even by the powerful Liberal leader Gladstone, who attacked it in an important speech. As a book *The Battle* had many printings in the Empire, in the United States, France, Germany, and elsewhere. It became the prototype of many like tales of science-war-fiction that would appear during the next one hundred years in the western world, for the peoples of nations were becoming so patriotically conditioned that they were eager readers of tales of terror describing their national fears and shocking them with ominous predictions of possible national catastrophe.[114] In France from 1889 to 1893 a Capitaine Danrit (Emile Driant) wrote a series of books on the "next" war with Germany with one constant theme: "On every side the nations are arming and preparing for war . . . I have tried to inspire my French readers with confidence." In 1890, when American agitation for a big navy was becoming vigorous, an anonymous author wrote *The Stricken Nation* to show how the British fleet, aided by an army of prying spies and paid traitors, destroyed most of the eastern coastal cities of the United States—because the United States was innocent and unprepared. In 1900, when the German Reichstag was debating the size of the German navy, a patriotic author, Gustav Erdman, told Germans why their sons would rest "with their ships at the bottom of the sea": it was because Germany was *Wehrlos zur See* (*Defenseless on the Sea*). In 1906 a William Le Queux,[115] commissioned by the ultrapatriotic, pound-seeking editor of the *Daily Mail*, Alfred Harmsworth, wrote an immensely appealing and much promoted serial called "The Invasion of 1910" in which "cliché by cliché" he depicted the nightmare of the early German successes because of English unpreparedness: "distressing news—complete bewilderment—hopeless defense, scowling Uhlans—desperate fight—our own dear London—shot without mercy—literally a shambles—sad page of history." [116] In book form *The Invasion* was translated into twenty-seven languages and sold over a million copies, and the German edition, much revised and with a different conclusion, was designed to arouse German patriotism.

No one can be certain about the motives of the men who wrote of the "wars-to-come." It cannot be doubted that they were greatly interested in money and fame, and a few of them gained much of both. But they were, in their own minds, above all serving their nations—they were nationalists trying to excite national patriotism. Frequently their stories, after the initial frightening portrayal of defeats owing to their own nation's unpreparedness and the enemy's perfidiousness, "turned into a species of nationalist utopia in which the superior virtues, intelligence, and vigor of the fatherland" defeated "an enemy without honour, without honesty, and without intelligence." Mercenary as the scaremongers were, there is no reason to think that they disbelieved their own nationalist visions.

The same can be said for the "yellow" journalists who manufactured news in all the great nations, Alfred Harmsworth (Viscount Northcliffe, 1865–1922) of England, William Randolph Hearst (1863–1951) and Joseph Pulitzer (1847–1911) of the United States, and even, perhaps— though it is hard to believe—some of the more venal journalists of France and Russia who were both cajoled and bribed to support their national governments and their nations' allies.[117] Harmsworth feverishly sought circulation and advertising for his newspapers and magazines with his principle that "war not only created a supply of news but a demand for it," and he succeeded in building the largest publishing combine the world had ever known, as well as amassing a huge fortune. But that he combined profit with patriotism does not deny his patriotism. Harmsworth (like Hearst and Pulitzer) thought of himself as a good and useful national citizen, and so did his government, which made him a viscount in 1917. The very fact that he and men like him, patriots all, were so successful attests to the depth of national feeling in western nations, especially when there were threats of war and when war actually came.

It is commonly believed that the hundred years from 1815 to 1914 were comparatively peaceful. Perhaps this is true if the comparison is with the years since 1914. But from 1848 wars occurred about as frequently as in the earlier modern centuries, though with two major differences. They often involved more people in each nation and they became more dangerous, both because peoples were becoming nations in arms and because the weapons—the rifles, field guns, and machine guns (Maxim gun, 1884)—were becoming more deadly.

Herder, Heine, and Mazzini had prophesied that once peoples had formed their own nations, their fatherlands would lie peacefully together. Their prophesies were wrong. All through the hundred years the king's affairs were becoming the people's, and hence the king's wars were becoming the people's, that is, wars in which peoples were arrayed against peoples, and the peoples—not mainly the nobility as in medieval times—crusaded and died for their fatherland, *pro patria mori*.

The great war of 1914–18 was the culmination of the threats of war, rumors of war, lesser wars between nations, and wars to establish nations from 1848 on. It was true that during the years from 1815 to 1848, the years of Metternich's repressive dominance, the nations and the kingdoms seldom fought, though national revolutions constantly threatened and occasionally, as in 1830, broke out. But from 1848 international war came frequently. Unsuccessful wars for Italian (and other nationalities') independence occurred in that year, the Crimean War involving Britain, France, Russia, and Piedmont in 1854, the war of France, Piedmont, and Austria in 1859, the Austro-Prussian War in 1866, the Franco-Prussian War in 1870, the Russo-Turkish War involving the awakening Balkan nationalities in 1877, the Spanish-American War in 1898, the Russo-Japanese War in 1904, and the two Balkan wars in 1912–13. And these are only the major wars, and do not include minor clashes or the numerous colonial wars fought in Asia and Africa.

The "causes" of the wars were many. The wars cannot be attributed solely to national ambitions, fears, and hatreds. Nationalism, however, was always one basic cause, and it probably was the important cause of most of them, especially the world war of 1914. To paraphrase in reverse the famed German military expert, Clausewitz, war was the continuation of national policy and diplomacy by other means, just as policy and diplomacy were a continuation of war by other means. It is undeniable that the wars tested the nationalism of western peoples, found it not wanting, and at the same time greatly accentuated it.

Every war from 1848 through 1870 to 1914–18 multiplied the demands of the nation-states for manpower, taxes, and production, and thus magnified the powers of the national governments. In every war the national states called upon their citizens for service and sacrifice unto death. In 1914 the calls were answered, if reluctantly by a few, enthusiastically by many.[118] Perhaps, as people became more and more sedentary and urbanized, war attracted them the more, especially when, from their schooling and from the "yellow" press, they knew only its romantic "do and daring." [119] But if war became an ultimate test of national feeling, then the test proved that nationalism had become strong indeed.

Again and again, especially after Darwin, leading publicists and politicians glorified war. It was, they cried, a heroic endeavor that purified a people and fired them to the height of their physical, mental, and moral energy. Belligerent patriots in Europe and America agreed with the German General Friedrich von Bernhardi (1849–1930) that "war aroused national life" and "expanded national power." They agreed with him, too, that war evoked "the noblest activities of human nature," rejuvenated ailing nations, and eliminated the biologically inferior.[120] For an energetic young aspiring politician of the United States, Albert J. Beveridge (1862–1927), war was "the divine instrument of progress" as it renewed "men's conscience" and as in its fires men found the "hidden gold" of their "souls." [121] For a tubercular English poet, William Ernest Henley, whose "Invictus" and "England, My England" were so much read and quoted, a people in war

> *Sheds its old peddling aims,*
> *Approves its virtue, puts behind itself*
> *The comfortable dream, and goes*
> *Armoured and militant,*
> *New-pithed, new-souled, new-visioned up the steps*
> *To those great altitudes, whereat the weak*
> *Live not. But only the strong*
> *Have leave to live, to strive, and suffer, and achieve.*

Neither Henley's nor Beveridge's views were representative, but they were not unique. War, in the minds of the most ardent nationalists, apparently was "the father of all things," as Heraclitus of Ephesus (535?–475? B.C.) had said. And, indeed, it was one father of what the twentieth-century

Polish-English historian, Lewis Namier, called "pathological nationalism," if not of all nationalism.[122]

Near the end of the great war of 1914–18, fought largely because of national fears and ambitions, President Woodrow Wilson (1856–1924) stated what he believed ought to be the object of the war: to make the world "safe" for "every peace-loving nation" that wished "to live its own life [and] determine its own institutions." He advocated a "peace without victory" and a "general association of nations" to guarantee "political independence and territorial integrity to great and small states alike." But his dream, which was itself in a sense fundamentally nationalist, and his program for co-operation among nations foundered on the rock of nationalism. The hate and fear engendered by the war propaganda and by the war's awful bloodletting had made western peoples more nationalist than ever. The Peace of Versailles was a peace of vengeance by which the defeated nations were sorely punished and the winning nations, France and Britain in particular, took what they could in spite of the protests of a few of their own leaders and the admonitions of the American Woodrow Wilson.

Nation-states were created or re-created, as Poland and Czechoslovakia were, to allow peoples to live "their own life" and to "determine their own institutions." There were attempts to set frontiers along "clearly recognizable lines of nationality." And a League of Nations to keep the peace was established. But the newly created nations were carved out of old nations and empires, and thus reasons for international conflicts multiplied. Frontiers of nationality that every nation clearly recognized could not, of course, be set, and instead of fewer, there were more disputes over them. The League of Nations turned out to be a league of sovereign nations; it lacked power to enforce the decisions it did make; and it became, in considerable part, an instrument the victorious nations employed to maintain the status quo and their own dominance.

In the elections, the "khaki" elections, held in the victorious nations immediately after the war, the forces of extreme nationalism won.[123] In these nations major political parties as well as the numerous newly formed veterans' associations preached national loyalty, national preparedness, and fear and distrust of other nations. In defeated Germany nationalism appeared to decline for a brief time, only to become ever more intense and bitter later, as Germany sought revenge and again to become a dominant nation. In the new Soviet Union the Communist leaders advocated the creation of an international proletarian world order, but within twenty or fewer years Russian nationalism reasserted itself, communism became more national than international, and the U.S.S.R.'s objectives in foreign policy hardly differed from those of the old czarist regime.

Instead, then, of an orderly world of nations living side by side in peace, the western world remained an anarchical world of competing nations, each pursuing its ambitions and living in fear of other nations.

In the western world there was resurgence rather than diminution in nationalism, and this occurred as nationalism took new root and began to grow in Asia and Africa. Though a headquarters for Wilson's league to keep the peace was established in neutral Geneva, the sovereign states did not acknowledge an authority above their own capitals,[124] and each continued to act in its own interests with but occasional attention to international action that *would* keep the peace. The twentieth century became not an era of peace and good will among peoples but, as Julien Benda, a French critic, predicted, "the century of the intellectual organization of political hates." [125] And the nationalist hates were not only the most intellectually organized; they were also the most viscerally felt. It almost seemed, to paraphrase the British imperialist Lord Cromer, that the more closely peoples came into contact with one another, the more they tended "to dislike one another." [126]

VII

The Nation Nationalizes: Economic, Social, and Cultural Pressures, 1815–1921

Through the nineteenth and twentieth centuries economic and social developments, pushing people in the same direction as the political, intensified consciousness of nation and promoted loyalty to it. As technological and other improvements facilitated communication, people within actual or potential national groups became increasingly conscious of common interests and of cultural affinities, and they, or, rather, their leaders, sought to enlarge and deepen these interests and affinities. But the strengthening of nationalism was only in part a result of deliberate effort. Although the inventors of the steam locomotive and the telegraph did not set out to create nations or foster nationalism, their inventions strengthened forces that did. It is closer to actuality to say that the conjuncture of particular economic and social forces with the particular political forces of the nineteenth century was conducive to a national organization of life and hence to nationalism.

The development of improved and new means of transportation and communication during the nineteenth century[1] undermined old provincial and feudal ways of life. The construction of new roads (and the hard surfacing of old) throughout the century, of new canals (especially to about 1840) and improved riverways, of new railways from 1830, and of the new telegraph from 1844—and later the new telephone lines from 1876—tied together peoples of somewhat similar cultures but different regions, just as had the military-road systems of Louis XIV the peoples of the provinces of France. Thus communication and transportation made possible the realization of common interests and the adoption of common ways of life on the part of larger and larger numbers of people. The modernizing Hungarian Count Széchenyi observed in 1830 that steamboats could "not stand the smell of feudalism." [2] Nor could feudal provincialism withstand the smell of coal-burning locomotives. As Goethe, prescient as usual, foresaw in 1828, the Germanies could "become one, for our good roads and our future railroads will play their part." [3]

An exact correlation cannot be shown, but it is undeniable that the national organization of life developed as means of transportation and communication did, and that as the means improved so national feeling grew stronger.[4] It has been argued, of course, that the improvements could have led to other and to larger forms of organization, and indeed they did and still do. Even in the world of the nineteenth century the highways, the railroad tracks, and the telegraph lines did not stop at established or projected national boundaries, and on occasion businesses did develop interests beyond and above these boundaries. But for political and financial reasons the transportation and communication systems were usually built within the nations and regarded as national assets. More important, perhaps, most of their traffic, in freight, in passengers, and in messages, was national, and so were most of the relationships they encouraged. The nations, incidentally, increasingly prided themselves on their technological progress as well as on the growth of their populations, and compiled statistics to display it. The collection of statistics became, in fact, a major preoccupation of every national government as it tried to impress its own citizens and other governments, and this remains true to the present.

It is not necessary to trace the growth of all the national means of communication; a brief note on the expansion of railroads will suffice.[5] From about the 1840's in the United States and western Europe, and somewhat later in most of the rest of the western world, this expansion was rapid. In the United States, where distances were great, rail expansion was greatest: the railroad mileage in 1840 totaled less than 3,000; in 1860 nearly 31,000; in 1890 nearly 167,000. In Britain, a much smaller geographic area, there were less than 2,000 miles in operation in the early 1840's, by 1890 about 20,000. Elsewhere the growth was usually slower and later, but the kilometers in operation in France increased from a little over 400 in 1840 to around 17,000 in 1870, and in Germany from about 17,000 in 1870 to about 64,000 in 1914.

The railroads, as well as the roads, the telegraph, and the telephone, enabled national governments to control their peoples more closely and, at the same time, enabled peoples of different parts of each country to become better acquainted, to become more aware of national events and news, and to acquire ever more common habits of speech, styles of clothing, and social customs. Moreover, various national territorial groups, west and east or south and north, tended to become economic counterparts of each other.

In the United States the tremendous railroad construction from 1840 brought the diverse economic sections of the East, Midwest, and Northwest together and thus strengthened the forces of nationalism. It may not be too much to assert that the railroad enabled the North to triumph over the South in 1865 and to establish firm national government from Washington, if not a completely unified nation. And after 1869 the transcontinental railroads tied the mountain areas and the Far West to the nation. In Canada the transcontinental Canadian Pacific, completed in 1885, brought new unity as it asserted "Canada's national existence in the face of the expansive dynamism" of the United States.[6] In France and Britain, when the tracks crawled out of Paris and London into the provinces, they brought together widely differing interests and peoples, gave them common economic interests as they made them dependent on one another for primary materials and outlets for local production. This was also the case later in the Italies, where the railroads, in the economist Giusti's phrase, "stitched the Italian boot," thereby making possible a national economic base (chiefly in the north) upon which nationalist politicians and idealists could erect a more unified political and cultural superstructure.

Just as the railroad and the telegraph fostered national consciousness, so did improvement of national postal services and the availability of inexpensive newspapers. The English and some other western public postal services began as early as the seventeenth century. Sooner or later every national government established such services. When a new nation came into being, say the United States, one of its government's first creations was always a national post office. The English introduced the "penny" post in 1840, and in all other nations the cost of mail likewise became low—in France, for example, from about 1848 and in the Germanies from about 1868—and the rates were standardized as well. Postage stamps were "first" used in the United States in 1847, and national postage stamps became national symbols in every country. With the railroads, delivery became faster, the English beginning to use the rails in 1838 and the United States on a systematic national basis in 1862.[7] The volume of mail mounted enormously; the number of letters in France in 1830 totaled 64 million, and forty years later around 358 million.

The publication and circulation of newspapers mounted rapidly as well.[8] The steam press, introduced in England about 1814, brought swifter and cheaper printing. In 1816 the social reformer William Cobbett (1763–1835) cut the price of his weekly *Political Register* from a shilling to two pence and won many new readers. Cobbett had a host of imitators in England; and in other countries, as the cost of newspapers fell, circulation increased. Newspapers were considerably more unrestrained in the United States and western Europe than in eastern Europe, where the censorship was severe, and everywhere their number, character, and quality widely varied, but everywhere they became major instruments of national and nationalist indoctrination. From the early nineteenth century journalists organized agencies to collect and sell news to papers. While the biggest of these agencies—Havas, France, 1835; Reuters, England, 1851; Wolff, Germany, 1849; and Associated Press, United States, 1882—collected international as well as national news, they were primarily national agencies and sold primarily to papers in their own nations. As they, to some degree, standardized the news within each nation, they contributed to national consciousness, for the people of each nation tended to get the same national news. From the 1860's national agencies were organized in many European countries, and some of them were little more than agents of their national governments. One mark of a new nationalist movement anywhere was the publication of newspapers by patriots hoping to spread the gospel. Established nation-states often used the press to inculcate loyalty.

Technological changes were part of, as they contributed to, those vast changes in ways of life and in attitudes commonly described under the general headings industrialization and urbanization. Statistics on urbanization, which appears to be closely related to nationalism, are easily available. Here again, only illustrative examples are needed. In Germany, by 1910 three of five inhabitants lived in towns of 2,000 or more, and about one of three in cities of 20,000 or more. In England, where industrial and urban growth came earlier, half the population lived in towns by 1850, and in 1900 one-tenth of the population of England and Wales lived in London. In 1820 the United States contained only 61 cities of 2,500 or more; in 1910 there were 2,262, and about one-third of the population then lived in manufacturing centers. By 1900, throughout the world, fourteen cities had populations of 1 million or more, and the larger cities generally were growing fastest.[9] What all this meant in the lives of people has been the subject of many studies, though as yet the implications for nationalism have been little explored.

As industrialization and urbanization developed, from England and western nations to other countries, as more and more people lived in cities, engaged in business, and worked in factories, the old ties of feudal, rural, and handicraft society were further loosened, and old values and authorities further weakened. People needed new authorities, new objects of belief, new havens of security. Their nation-states and their nations in part supplied these.

It is probably an exaggeration to assert, as did the English critic of imperialism J. A. Hobson, that extreme nationalism was the result of the "neurotic temperament generated by town life." [10] But in the rural and feudal Europe of the old regime, ordinary people did have the security and ties of family and village life, and the nobles and clergy those of their class and of the church. Most people then did not really need the nation or deeply sense the desirability of loyalty to it. In the cities and factories to which people flocked in increasing numbers, they had fewer traditions, shallower roots, fewer intimate relationships, and hence were less secure. In short, they suffered from somewhat the same tensions contemporary Asians and Africans do as they move into the modern world. Gathered together in the cities, however, they could more easily communicate with others and over wider areas, and were more easily accessible to national influences, whether these were public or private. Thus more and more of them slowly came to identify themselves with their nation and with the values and the interests for which they thought it stood. Whatever the exact correlation or the precise causal relationships, national consciousness, and likely loyalty, too, deepened and spread with urbanization. [11]

The old village and family life afforded a comparatively quiet and settled existence, communities where each man possessed some status, low or high, based upon age-old ties and customs, or at least was accepted for what he was and knew his place. If he had to make decisions, the possible answers were few and authoritative, and could be expected from traditional masters, the lord or the priest. But as the old, relatively fixed society disintegrated, so did old loyalties and traditions. The men who moved into the faster tempo and uncertainties of urban, industrial life were deprived of the certainties and status their ancestors had had. They lacked respected authority and lost comforting myths at the time they were moving between worlds, and hence were maladjusted and felt oppressed and insecure. They sought, therefore, some nucleus, something to which they could belong. At the same time, the new science and the new liberal and democratic doctrines seemed to promise, at any rate for literate men, a more secure, a freer, happier life. How could this be achieved? For many, the nation and nationalism offered ways to the future. By belonging and participating, they could achieve some status and find some certainty. And they could hope. No wonder many of them, then, became loyal and some of them worshiped national deities.

Actually, most people, whether in cities or in rural areas, were not constantly occupied with or motivated by idealistic nationalist dreams. Few were patriotic dreamers like the mid-century Italian patriot Mazzini, and only a few were professional patriots like the members of the numerous patriotic societies formed during the last quarter of the century. But people, as individuals and as groups, did have concrete economic desires that could be and were satisfied through the nation and its government. If businessmen wanted higher profits and favorable conditions at home or abroad for their enterprises, if workers wanted better working conditions, higher wages, and insurance against hazards, if farmers wanted higher prices and roads and bridges to get their crops to market, it was to their national governments that they increasingly turned, and as they did they could not help becoming nationally conscious.

While class interests continued to divide people—though not as much as Marx predicted—members of each class usually believed their interests could best be served through the nation. This might reflect the hope of members of a class that their interests would dominate or the belief that the nation could represent all classes—that the interests of all classes could be subsumed in the national. In the United States in the 1820's an ambitious and influential statesman, Henry Clay (1777–1852), projected an American System in which the various sections and economic interests would complement each other, and though his system was never systematically tried, other American statesmen of similar views followed him in attempts to bring economic unity. In other countries as well, statesmen continued to try to build self-sufficient economies in which regions and classes worked together in the national interest. Nearly always in western Europe and the United States the various business class*es* were able to use their national governments for their varying business purposes; and when members of other classes, workers or farmers, later had enough power, they did likewise—though less effectively.

From the eighteenth century, economists hoping to promote national economic growth and unity argued for the abolition of internal customs barriers. The American Constitution of 1787 specifically prohibited the laying of internal "imposts and duties"; indeed, this was one chief reason for the making of the new Constitution, the first purpose of which was to "form a more perfect union." During the early days of the French Revolution, for somewhat the same reason, all internal customs duties were eliminated in France. By the 1820's such duties were abolished in Great Britain, as they had been earlier in England. In 1833 seventeen German states, with 26 million people, formed a *Zollverein* that leveled customs barriers and established free trade within the boundaries of these states, and this customs union was enlarged until it included all the German states (except Austria) when the German Empire was created in 1870. Though the *Zollverein* of 1833 was established largely on the demand of agricultural interests, it became a major foundation of German unity. As a British observer, J. Bowring, noted, "The *Zollverein* . . . brought the sentiment of German nationality out of the regions of hope and fancy into those of positive material interests." [12] When internal customs barriers were leveled within nations or among peoples becoming nations, then economic interests joined those of sentiment in promoting national development and unity.[13]

How business and in some cases agricultural interests were able to use the protection and assistance of the national governments is clearly revealed by the exterior tariff policies of the great nations from the 1860's. As economists and politicians—for example, Friedrich List (Germany), Mathew Carey and his son, Henry Charles Carey (United States), and later Joseph Chamberlain (England)—proposed, the national governments, eventually even free-trade Britain's, protected their domestic producers by limiting and taxing foreign imports. In the United States during and after the Civil War, the federal government raised duties on foreign manufactures in order to encourage "infant industry" as well as to protect "not-so-infant" American industries against foreign competition. One by one other nations followed the same policy, each, naturally, to protect its national businesses and its farmers against the actions of others: Italy in 1878, Germany in 1879, France in 1881, and, finally and hesitatingly, Britain after World War I, when it became apparent that free trade did not benefit the dominant national economic interests in Britain.[14]

Among the welter of arguments about protective tariffs, one is incontrovertible: some national businesses, like the textile and iron industries in the United States, did profit from them, and some agricultural interests did benefit, like the Junkers in Germany. That profit gained in this way served the economic interests of all a nation's people is debatable. If classical economic theory has validity, peoples *economically* may have lost more than they gained by such national restrictions on trade, but *psychologically* they did obtain income, "psychic income," from the pride in national economic development.[15] But whatever the gains and losses, it was believed everywhere that the interests of business and of the nation were identical. The national tariffs were, then, both evidence of growing nationalism and a cause of more.

It was not, however, just business interests that were considered the same as those of the nation, but the interests of all classes. Economic theorists generally held that the promotion of the national interest was of first importance for all classes, conservatives and liberals alike agreeing with the dictum of Adam Smith that national defense was "of more importance than opulence." [16] And some theorists, including the influential German sociologist Max Weber (1864–1920), argued for a strong national state on the ground that it was necessary for economic development, and economic development and national well-being went hand in hand. [17] From this high, abstract point of view, the national interests transcended those of class.

Actually, members of all classes became interested in obtaining protection and benefits in much the same way as did businessmen. From the 1870's agricultural groups in various nations, as in Germany, hoping to preempt national markets for themselves, demanded and often received protection against foreign competition. From about the same time labor groups, as in the United States, began to demand and sometimes obtained measures to protect wages and employment against "cheap foreign competition." On occasion members of various classes joined, as in Britain, in support of national imperial ventures, in the belief that colonies were essential to maintenance of their homeland's standard of living. Just as for Germans the *Zollverein* brought "nationality out of the regions of hope and fancy into those of positive material interests," so for many groups in many nations real or prospective economic benefits deepened interest in the nation. For within each nation the immediate and future economic welfare of people of all classes appeared (or was thought) to depend upon markets open to national but closed to foreign producers.

The nationalizing that took place in customs and tariffs occurred in many spheres of economic life. For purposes of business and trade, national standards of weights and measures were desirable. Many nations introduced the metric system, France requiring it from 1840, while others, like the United States, standardized their own different systems. Businessmen, especially if they were creditors, desired national "sound" money and national "safe" banking systems. The British, French, and American governments (as long as certain creditor groups dominated) provided for the "gold standard" and, with varying success, for privately owned but nationally controlled banking systems. Both of these, it was fondly (vainly,

in light of later experience) hoped, would stabilize money and investments so that a dollar (or pound or franc) would always be "worth a
dollar" and invested dollars would bring an assured return. But when in
the United States heavily indebted farmers from the 1870's through the
1890's became vocal in the Granger and Populist movements, they wanted
"cheaper" national money in order to get higher prices for their crops and
be better able to pay off their debts. They then demanded national action,
the printing of "greenbacks" and the introduction of bimetallism. The
growth of national governmental debts likewise stimulated increased interest in national governments, as Alexander Hamilton, the American financial genius of the 1790's, had prophesied. For military reasons especially, national debts mounted in all major countries. For long it was the
propertied who chiefly invested in national securities, but ownership of
national governmental bonds spread widely among workers and farmers
during World War I (as it did later in World War II), and the investors,
now of all classes except the poorest, had financial reasons to wish and
work for the continued prosperity of their nation.

Because, as has already been discussed, Marx and many later able
scholars attributed the rise of the nation-state and nationalism to the middle class, to the bourgeoisie, further examination of the economic class
nature of nationalism is desirable. When Marx began his grand analysis of
society in the England of the 1840's, his view that the nation-state arose
out of the bourgeoisie's attempts to gain the home market seemed to reflect the actualities, though even then it was much too simple an explanation. His interpretation retained much, though decreasing, validity
through the next century, and it still provides a partial explanation. When
in 1917 the erratic but keen American economist Thorstein Veblen (1857–
1929) observed, "The American national establishment . . . is a government of businessmen for business ends," he came closer to the truth than
some of his contemporary flag-waving politicians would have admitted.[18]
Through the years after the resurgence of conservatism during the early
nineteenth century, the national governments of Britain and France
chiefly represented the interests of the middle and propertied classes, and
this was likely true of the government of the United States from its beginning. This was true in Britain under the Liberal party with leaders like
Macaulay and Gladstone and, with a difference, under the Conservative
party with leaders such as Disraeli and Lord Salisbury. This was true in
France during the monarchical rule of Louis Philippe (1830–48), the
"bourgeois king," and the empire of Napoleon III (1852–70), as well as
during the Third Republic with leaders from Thiers to Gambetta to Poin-

caré. This was true in the United States especially with the Hamiltonian Federalists but also less clearly with the Jeffersonian Republicans, and with the later Republicans and Democrats, and of major American political leaders, with few exceptions, down to the present.

But, as has been noted, workers and farmers also became nationalist, and not even class-conscious socialists were immune. The nation-state could be used as a vehicle for winning benefits, as it was in western countries, or for winning class victory, as in Russia in 1917. As a later expert on Marxist communism, Franz Borkenau, pointed out, a worker could not be disinterested, "even in the purely material sense, in the fate of the nation-state which gave him protection." And, he continued, "the protection of the working classes through social legislation partly depended upon the position of an industry vis-à-vis its competitors abroad," while the standard of living and wage rates were "directly dependent upon the international market, not only of labour, but of commodities." [19]

That nationalism could overcome class differences was well recognized. During the 1880's the astute Bismarck deliberately tried to win over German workers with national social insurance against sickness, accidents, old age, and incapacity. Obviously his efforts, and others like them in other countries, met with some success. In the great crisis of 1914 German workers remained loyal not to the socialist ideals of the Second International but to their nation.[20] In general in 1914 the workers in other countries, whatever their political views, were loyal to their nations just as were the German. In 1914 workingmen and capitalists, regardless of political party, patriotically united in defense of their nations.[21] There were no general strikes against the war and very little opposition to it—indeed, on the contrary, much enthusiasm. With some exceptions members of the working classes had, by 1914, become "nationalized" as they had acquired a stake in their nation, just as had propertied people earlier.

Instead of dividing the workers from the capitalist bourgeoisie, national economic interests tended to unite them within nations against the workers and bourgeoisie of other nations. "Modern industrial labor" certainly did not, as Marx and Engels had predicted, strip the workers "of every trace of national character." [22] Realizing this, governments on occasion sought to use national patriotism to overcome the always potential and the frequently feared struggle between classes.[23] When Charles Maurras, a violent French nationalist, advocated the formulation of a "strong and well-organized national doctrine" to be employed to promote "social understanding," he was suggesting no more than politicians were already doing.[24] Though radical critics thought labor was thus duped, both labor and capital in the capitalist nations, and later labor and the state in communist, found in the "necessities of fatherland" motives for collaboration and agreement.

Workers became nationally conscious, if not always loyal, not only because paternalistic governments threw them crumbs but also because they came to expect and did receive tangible benefits from their national governments. That they might have received greater help from an international government if, as socialists advocated, the workers of the world had united is hardly relevant here. The workers were no more farsighted than were the middle classes. The fact is that workers did become nationally minded as they received concrete benefits in the present, not in some remote future. To paraphrase and reverse a slogan of American members of the International Workers of the World, when they got a cut (whatever its size) of the national pie in the here and now, they did not concern themselves as much about the international "pie in the sky."

National governments, however reluctantly, did increasingly through the nineteenth century, and especially toward the end of it, enact legislation regulating and limiting hours of work and the labor of children and women; they did provide for inspection of factories and mines;[25] and, eventually, they generally did legalize national labor unions. As earlier monarchical governments had done, the national governments also provided minimum care for the needy and dependent. From the last quarter of the nineteenth century, and in some cases earlier, they usually provided, as mentioned earlier, free, public, and universal education through which the worker and his children might "better" themselves.[26] If, as later radicals argued, a main purpose of this education was to provide workers who had elementary skills and could read and write—that is, cheap labor —for capitalist businesses, it makes little difference insofar as nationalism is concerned. Workers did demand education, and most national governments, at first those in western Europe but eventually those in eastern Europe and other areas as well, provided it, and expected and received a *quid pro quo*. As Francis Delaisi, a keen French political commentator, once remarked, the nation provided a worker "with the means of education and the possibility of rising in the social scale"; hence it was "incumbent upon him to join the others [the other citizens] in defending . . . the great principles, the ideals, and that culture, superior to any other, which" came "to him from his ancestors." This, Delaisi continued, produced a "mystic feeling, impelling the individual to make supreme sacrifices for superior ends" that "acted more potently on the masses than considerations of purely material interests." [27]

National legislation was but one reason for growing national consciousness among workers. More and more they worked for big businesses like those associated with the names of Krupp in Germany, Wendel in France, and Carnegie in the United States, businesses that drew on the raw materials and capital of the nation, had national markets, and became national combines, corporations, and trusts. By the last quarter of the nineteenth century in western countries, and even more so in the twentieth century, these enterprises became, though privately owned, in a real sense national enterprises. In proportion as they did, workers felt they had to organize national unions to defend their interests. By the early twentieth century, total union membership had risen to 4 million in England, 3 million in Germany, and 1 to 2 million in France and the United States. And in the first three nations, unions had begun to support national political parties that demanded national action in support of labor. Perhaps symptomatic of what was happening was the formation in the United States in 1886 of the *American* Federation of Labor, which was opposed from 1895 by the *National* Association of Manufacturers. Increasingly, both labor and capital used national symbols to identify themselves—the United States Steel Company was formed in 1901. But individuals in all classes were participating in national affairs and more and more identifying their interests with those of their nation. For more and more people the way to economic reform, to modernization, and to a better life was the national.

There were, it is clear, several reasons this was true, among them the social and cultural pressures to which, increasingly, people were subjected from birth to death.[28] Family, schools, historical writing and teaching, literature, customs, patriotic societies, all exercised pressure in the direction of nationalism.

During and after World War II, American anthropologists and psychologists[29] attributed considerable importance to childhood training in the formulation of national traits or character. While there was and still is much dispute over national character and over what might be termed the anal-oral interpretation of personality, one older psychological generalization seems fairly obvious: a "child forms most of his ideas about the world of humanity from his impressions of his parents. . . ." [30] When parents are nationally minded, it is likely that a child will imitate and follow. It is also likely that when a child is loved in his home, he will be more tolerant of others and less disposed to nationalist prejudices, and that an unloved child will be more inclined to dislike other people. About the exact effect of parent-child relationships on nationalism, however, we know very little.

There is no evidence that children are born with an inherent notion, let alone love, of nation. Until about the age of eight or nine they apparently little understand what the "homeland" is, and the concept develops clearly only when they are a little older. A famed Swiss psychologist, J. Piaget, in a study of two hundred Swiss children, was "struck by the fact, that . . . children in the initial stages of their development, did not appear to display any marked inclination toward nationalism." "A slow and laborious process was necessary," he found, before children attained an "awareness of their own homeland and that of others." [31]

From their families, nevertheless, many children at an early age learned respect for the law, awe for policemen, and love of national heroes. Often, too, in their early family life they were conditioned to respond favorably to words and symbols representing their homeland, to enjoy the flags, parades, music, the excitement of national holidays, and quite certainly to dislike foreigners. A great many parents in western lands came to feel as Clemenceau, the French republican leader, felt about France: if there was a country that had a right to the love of its children and to obtain their first smile, it was theirs,[32] and this feeling they transferred to the children. As parents became more aware of and loyal to their nations, their children, born into the parents' culture, could not help absorbing patriotic attitudes that would remain with them through their adult lives.[33] As members of the human race, they had gregarious tendencies; the home environments in which they began to mature shaped these tendencies toward national patriotism.[34]

The shaping that parents began in the homes the schools continued and carried further.[35] One distinctive quality of man, compared with other species, is his "teachability." While the schools and the kinds of education varied from nation to nation, governments and patriots everywhere used the schools to teach national patriotism. By the twentieth century, western European nations and the United States generally had free, universal, and compulsory education on the elementary level (only occasionally on the secondary level as well), and eastern European and Latin American nations were beginning to do so. Everywhere one major purpose of education, at all levels, came to be the making of "good citizens," and that meant, in popular thinking, the making of national patriots.

From the time of the French Revolution (in a few cases earlier), rulers, whether monarchical or republican, realized the value of formal training of all children for the inculcation of loyalty. From about the same time some universities and colleges became centers of nationalist feeling. As early as 1827 the American states of Massachusetts and Vermont required the teaching of American history in the schools, and since then all states have set up some kind of similar requirement. In times of war especially, university professors, like those at Berlin during the Napoleonic wars, in Paris in 1870–71, and at American universities during World War I, pleaded and propagandized for their nations, and in peace and war students on occasion agitated for nationalist causes.[36] From the 1870's, with the continued rise of universal public education,[37] efforts intensified to make all educational institutions centers of patriotic inspiration. In France in 1879 Jules Ferry, an ardent advocate of secular education as well as imperial expansion, made clear the primary purpose of the major French laic education laws that were to be enacted in the 1880's. "The State," he said, "is certainly not at all an instructor in physiology or in chemistry. If it suits it in the public interest to pay chemists and physiologists . . . it is not in order to create scientific truths. This is not its concern in fostering education. Its concern is to maintain a certain state morale, certain state doctrines that are important for its conservation." [38]

Ferry was more explicit than most national leaders, but many of otherwise differing views emphasized the national purposes of education. In Denmark Bishop Grundtvig (1783–1872), whose major interest was religious morality, spent much of his life establishing folk schools, one purpose of which was to free Scandinavians from foreign influence so that they could rediscover their own national character (soul?).[39] In Germany Kaiser William II (kaiser, 1888–1918), "occupied with the idea of making the school useful in combatting socialistic and communistic ideas," declared the school should "lay the foundation for a healthy conception of political and social relations, through the cultivation of fear of God and love of country." [40] In the United States, Albert J. Beveridge, a prominent Republican senator from Indiana and an aggressive imperialist, in 1903 concluded an address to the students of a small midwestern college, "So the American school must be the great nourisher of the nation. The nation, the nation, always the nation! The school for the nation! All education for the nation! Everything for the nation!" [41] And in 1909 in Argentina an influential professor of literature, Ricardo Rojas (1882–1957), declared his national government had to control education to "restore the national spirit . . . and save the Argentine school from the foreign clergy, from foreign gold, and from foreign books." [42]

The schools, the teachers, the textbooks generally did, more or less directly, what they were expected to do, taught love of country and distrust of foreigners. Regardless of whether the state directly controlled ed-

ucation, as was usually the case, there was great stress on "civic education," and by civic was meant patriotic education, for officials and fervent
nationalists demanded it.[43] If in England Lord Cromer thought it not necessary "to instil nationalist sentiment in the great private [public] schools"
which trained so many leaders, it was because he believed these schools to
be, "as a result alike of inherited traditions, social connections, and home
associations . . . natural nurseries of a very perfervid patriotism." [44]

In the United States, as the American historian Henry Steele Commager pointed out, the readers (like the McGuffey), spellers, and histories
in the American schools inculcated patriotism on almost every page
through the repetition of "a common body of stories, hero tales, legends
and maxims." [45] From a study of over eight hundred American textbooks
of the period 1776–1885, a careful student concluded that the elementary
schools "operated as a primary instrument for the inculcation of nationalism in the United States," a nationalism that "not only taught the child
hatred and contempt for other nations but exalted a conservative brand of
nationalism for domestic use." The remarks of an American authority,
Bessie Pierce, about American texts of the first quarter of the twentieth
century generally fit those of most, if not all, western nations: "Textbooks
are permeated with a national or patriotic spirit. . . . On the other hand
the attitudes engendered toward other peoples . . . must, in many cases,
redound to their ignominy, in contrast to the glory of America." [46]

No nation's textbooks are typical, but illustrative are two of France. A
highly popular (five hundred editions) children's book, *Tour de France
par deux enfants* (1877), described the early history of France:

France was then called Gaul. Our ancestors, the Gauls, were big and
strong. They prized courage and liberty above everything; they laughed at
death. . . . The armies of Caesar, composed of the best soldiers in the world,
had to take seven years to subdue our fatherland [*patrie*]. A young Gaul [Ver-
cingetorix], born in Auvergne, resolved then to drive them out of the country.[47]

A widely used civics book, *Les Enfants de Marcel,* told a story of a sergeant and his fourteen-year-old son fleeing from the Germans to Switzerland in 1870 as they fought a rear-guard action to enable the French army
to escape. The father lost an arm, but the two got to Switzerland, listened
to an old (!) member of the Swiss Guard of Louis XVI tell a good republican story about the French Revolution, and then went back to France,
where the family prospered by practicing the solid bourgeois virtues of
industry and honesty.[48] In textbooks everywhere in the West a child was

197

told, "The Fatherland is the nation which you should love, honor and serve with all the strength of your body, with all the energy and all the devotion of your soul." [49]

With few exceptions, texts and teachers alike taught the student that his country had had an inspiring history and that, though it might have suffered tragedies, it would have a happy future. He was told much about his nation's high ideals and virtues—its devotion to justice, its courage— and heard little that was admirable about the ideals and character of other nations. England was the "mother" country of Americans but even it, so the American child was sometimes told, was "perfidious." [50] When his nation went to war, it was for defense; the foe was the aggressor. When his nation won a war, that was because his countrymen were braver and God was on their side. If his nation was defeated, that was owing to the enemy's treachery and overwhelmingly superior forces or to traitors at home. If his nation lost territory, as France lost Alsace-Lorraine in 1870, that was a crime, but whatever the nation gained, as in colonies, was its rightful due and benefited humanity.

Again and again the student was taught the lesson expressed in the American aphorism "My country, right or wrong, but always my country." Often he was instructed that he should be "prepared to endure hunger, thirst and cold for the sake of the Fatherland," and "be ready to die rather than abandon" his post.[51] In the United States from the 1890's more and more school children were forced by law or social pressure to salute and to "pledge allegiance" to their "Flag and the Republic for which it stands: one Nation indivisible, with Liberty and Justice for all." [52] This particular kind of school oath may be unique, though governments sometimes exacted similar oaths of their youth as well as older people. Schools in western nations tried hard to "kindle the fires of patriotism and feed them constantly," and this was one kind of indoctrination that nearly always went unchallenged and was nearly always praised.

There are no well-developed tests that reveal how effective the schools were in making people nationally conscious and patriotic. But more and more children were attending school, until by the twentieth century nearly every child in western Europe, the United States, and a few other nations (such as Canada and Japan) had some schooling by the age of eleven or twelve,[53] and in eastern Europe and Latin America, though even the most elementary education was far from universal, increasing numbers of children were going to school. With schooling came an increase in literacy. A higher percentage of children, and adults, too, was thus exposed to national ideas and pressures through the printed word. In the United States, a prosperous nation that much prized education, the public-school enrollment rose from about 7 million in 1870 to over 19 million in 1920, and during the same years the illiteracy rate fell from twenty per cent to less than eight per cent.[54] In poor, so-called backward nations, attendance naturally was much lower and illiteracy much higher, but even in poverty-stricken Ireland schooling was becoming available, and from 1842 to 1872 illiteracy dropped from seventy-two per cent to fifty-two per cent, and these years, though cause and effect cannot be disentangled, were when the Irish were becoming steadily more nationalist.[55]

Mass education and mass literacy institutionalized national languages, literatures, attitudes, and traditions, brought consciousness of common cultures and interests, and probably more. When in 1897 in France examiners asked candidates for the baccalaureate, "What purpose does the teaching of history serve?" eighty per cent answered, "To promote patriotism." [56] When in the late 1920's Bessie Pierce questioned 1,125 students in the public schools of Pennsylvania and Iowa, she found that the great majority regarded defense of country as the highest form of patriotism, and only four admitted that the United States "has carried on some enterprises which we can't be proud of." [57]

One of the ways to make patriots was to use history, and many a patriot was born of Clio. Historians have studied, written, and taught history for many reasons: to reveal the will of God, to support (or attack) a ruler or a cause, and to satisfy genuine curiosity. These purposes did not disappear, but after the French Revolution more and more historians desired to describe how their nation began and developed *and* to foster love of and loyalty to their nation by depicting its common sufferings, fears, joys, achievements, and triumphs, and by showing how their own nation was different. Historical study thus became centered upon the nations while nationalist interpretation predominated.

To find roots for their nation, historians searched for its origins far back in time and, whether mythical or actual, of course found them. And they were able, as well, to find (or divine) a common history for the people long before their so-called ancestors could have been or actually were aware that they had much or anything in common.[58] Thus they could show a long development during which the nation grew and prospered even though attacked by enemies; or how, if it were oppressed by foreign rule, it won its independence; or how, if it were still subject to foreign rule, its people had a common language, culture, and interests, and should be independent.

French revolutionaries, as is the nature of revolutionaries, and their followers in other countries at the end of the eighteenth century disliked tradition (though they appealed to the Roman), and they protested against the dead hand of a past they despised. For justification of their ideas and acts they appealed not to the past but to natural law and reason (common sense), not to what was (except perhaps in some mythical golden age) but to what ought to be. On the other hand, after the Revolution reactionaries wanted to revive tradition, and romantics revolted against universal laws of nature and cold reason.

During and after the Revolution the revolutionaries wrote tracts, memoirs, and histories to praise, justify, or defend what they had done, while their opponents, using historical precedent, attacked them because they had fractured the "organic unity" of society or of the state and the nation. Both the revolutionaries and the reactionaries, then, appealed to history, but to different histories, the first to the immediate past (with a bow to Rome), the second to the Middle Ages and *ancien régime*. Both increasingly stressed what they thought was best for their nation, however they defined it, or, in the case of some conservatives at least, what they thought was good for the national dynasty.

A massive outpouring of history of the nationalist variety resulted. Augustin Thierry, a well-known French historian, was not wrong when he predicted, in 1834, that history would become a mark of the nineteenth century, just as philosophy had been for the eighteenth.[59] And it did come "to pass," as Lord Acton, a profound English historian, remarked of the "German Schools of History," that historians almost everywhere in Europe, "having abolished the law of nature which was the motive of 1789, instituted the law of nationality, which became the motive of [the revolutions of] 1848." [60] And, it may be added, of the next century or more.

Among nearly all western nations historians began to look back on their own nation with pride and to its future with hope, and as they did so they began—the English, French, and German historians in particular[61] —monumental collections of their own national historical sources. G. H. Pertz began to edit the great *Monumenta Germaniae Historica* in 1824 (first volume 1826), François Guizot commenced the publication of *Documents inédits sur l'histoire de France* in 1833, and the British Parliament in 1834 authorized the publication of documents concerning the early history of Great Britain and Ireland, which began under the title Rolls Series in 1838. These early collections were followed by many others during the ensuing century, some in hundreds of volumes, until there were few "undocumented" periods in the history of any nation—though it must be added that the quantity and quality of the documentation much varied. In the United States similar national historical publication did not begin until the 1930's (or later in actuality), but in 1908 a distinguished committee of American historians recommended publication of "Documentary Historical Publications" for a purpose that was common to all such projects: "Like all other enlightened governments, that of the United States has felt the obligation to publish historical materials as among the surest means of maintaining [or creating?] an intelligent patriotism." [62]

While the national historical documents were being collected and published, national libraries and archival institutions were being either enlarged or newly created. Nation after nation established or strengthened its *Bibliothèque Nationale* (the French dates from the sixteenth century) or its Library of Congress (established in the United States in 1800), its Public Record Office (the British) or its National Archives (not until the 1930's in the United States).

To these libraries and archives historians, if they were serious historians, increasingly went to find source materials for their works. A minority of them were always students of the history of other peoples, but most of them were chiefly or solely interested in the past as the prologue and experience of their own nations. This was understandable for several reasons: they were good national citizens themselves, the national records were the most easily available, were written in the languages they could read, and their cultures and governments *were* increasingly national.[63] The records a people keep and organize tell us much not only about how they organize their lives but also about their values. From the eighteenth century, and increasingly, national governments have given prideful attention to "the record," especially the national record.[64]

Though serious historians tried, following the "father" of modern historical scholarship, Leopold von Ranke, to be objective and tell what really happened (*wie es eigentlich gewesen*), they nevertheless chiefly selected national topics and wrote about their own nations from a nationalist point of view, as indeed did Ranke himself. Many of the popular historians, like John Clark Ridpath (1840–90) in the United States, deliberately and with "glowing fervor" wrote eulogies of their own nations to encourage patriotism.[65] Few historians, serious or popular, were critical of their own nations' acts or ideals and many deprecated those of other nations, especially if those nations had once ruled them or had been or might be their enemies in war. The advice Jules Michelet (1798–1874), the popular and patriotic historian of France, gave his countrymen was not untypical of the views of patriotic historians in all western nations: "Frenchmen of every station, of every class and party, remember well one thing. You have on this earth, only one sure friend, France."

In France, among many patriotic historians, François Guizot, Augustin Thierry, Henri Martin, and Michelet portrayed with pride the triumphs and tragedies of their nation and its glorious civilization, as did the later Ernest Lavisse and Alphonse Aulard and the still later royalist historian Jacques Bainville.[66] In the United States George Bancroft,[67] Henry Adams, John Fiske, James Schouler, John Bach McMaster, Frederick Jackson Turner, and many others fondly depicted the rise and character of the American people.[68] One well-known school of American historians, in which Herbert Baxter Adams, James K. Hosmer, and Moses Coit Tyler were notable, proudly discovered the roots of American (and English) political institutions in the tribal organization of the Teutonic forests, and thus attributed to these institutions and to their own nation an ancient genealogy that was somehow superior. In this they were not unique, for historians in other nations were able somehow to find genealogies that were also superior.

During the nineteenth century English, German, and Italian historians (as well as those of every nation) likewise gave their nations histories of which they could be proud. Among them in England were not only the popular and brilliant Whig historian, Thomas Babington Macaulay, but also the more prosaic (and perhaps better) historians J. R. Green, Edward Freeman, Bishop Stubbs, and Sir Henry Maine. Among those in Germany (especially Prussia) were more ardently nationalist historians, such as Friedrich Savigny, Friedrich Dahlmann, Johann Droysen, and Heinrich von Sybel, and the most belligerently nationalistic of them all, Heinrich von Treitschke.[69] And among the Italian historians of their nation's national awakening (*Risorgimento*) were the novelist Alessandro Manzoni, Carlo Troya, Cesare Balbo, Michele Amari, and later Pasquale Villari, who had an "overmastering desire to see his country united and free from foreign domination." [70]

Many times historians in the developing nations, like the Germans and Italians just mentioned, helped create and arouse national consciousness and were leaders in the struggle for national unity, or for independence if it had not been attained. Czechs learned from František Palacky (1789–1876) and Serbians from Sima Milutinovich, as the Bulgarians had a little earlier from Father Paisi, of their common past and right to nationhood, and as did Danes and Norwegians from Bishop Grundtvig and Peter Munch.[71]

All through the nineteenth century, particularly from the 1830's, patriots and historians formed associations and societies to encourage the study of history.[72] Though most of these were local and provincial in character,[73] the largest and most important from the 1880's on became national. And though their purpose, like that of the American Historical Association (founded 1884), might be to promote the study of all of history, they primarily, like the *Société de l'Histoire de France* (1834) and the Royal [British] Historical Society (1868), devoted their efforts, in their meetings and publications, to the professional study of their own national history, and their memberships were almost exclusively national. The formation of these professional societies was accompanied by the establishment of scholarly national historical journals, for example the *Historische Zeitschrift* (1859), the *English Historical Review* (1866), the *Revue Historique* (1876), the *Revista Storica Italiana* (1884), and the *American Historical Review* (1895). These journals, while not limited to national history, chiefly published articles and reviews of books on national subjects, and most of them, like the *Mississippi Valley Historical Review* (1914)—now the *Journal of American History*—were exclusively concerned with the history of their own nation. The purpose of each of them slightly differed, but their founders would not have fundamentally disagreed with the views of the solid scholar and first editor of the *Revue Historique*, Gabriel Monod, who announced a purpose of the *Revue* to be "to awaken in the soul of the nation consciousness of itself through deep knowledge of its history, for it is thus that all will feel themselves products of the same soil, children of the same race, not disowning any part of the paternal heritage and at the same time all citizens by the same right of modern France." [74]

Thus the collections of documents and sources, the repositories of historical materials, the very study of history, and historians themselves, all came to be organized along national lines and for national purposes. Scholarly historical study, of course, was not as blatantly nationalist as was much popular history. Nonetheless, it both represented the awakening national consciousness and deepened it wherever it existed.

Precisely how much influence scholarly historical studies had in making nationalists it is not possible to gauge, for most people did not read them. But, as Augustin Thierry believed for Frenchmen, patriotism was enhanced by knowledge of history, especially by history that included the people, involved them, and "stirred their hearts." [75] Further, it cannot be doubted that when a fervent, dogmatic, nationalist university professor like Heinrich von Treitschke spoke, he had a wide hearing and exercised great influence.[76] When the national history was taught in the schools and universities as it came to be in all the nations, students learned of the real or imagined history of their own nation, of its heroic achievements and awful agonies, and thus came to possess common "sacred and memorable traditions," [77] which they could revere, as well as common hopes, about which they could dream. When Irishmen began to go to school during the mid-nineteenth century and "their Repeal Association libraries were stocked with Irish histories and nationalist periodicals," they learned about the glories of the Irish past and how awful their oppression by the English had been. If nothing more, history offered them a "substitute for whiskey," [78] and thus hope for the nation could take the place of escape in inebriation.

Few historians, if they were scholars, were as nationalistic as Treitschke, and not many deliberately set out to make national patriots.[79] Nevertheless, their stress on the study of national history gave at least those who went to school and those who listened or read a feeling of belonging to their nation, a sense of national continuity, and a desire for national unity.[80] At the same time it gave students and readers belief in the mission, the purpose, the promise of their nation, *and* a sense of its uniqueness, its peculiar and distinct character, its difference from other nations; *and,* therefore, it tended to arouse distrust and dislike of other nations. It was believed, seriously if superficially, that the study taught lessons, the lessons that a good citizen, an upright patriot, ought to know and ought to follow.

What serious nineteenth-century historians began, twentieth-century historians generally continued. Not many, perhaps, would have gone as far as the famous French historian Ernest Lavisse, who once cried, "If I did not give to the flag a pagan's cult for his idol, I do not know what I would do in this world." [81] But few dared, like the American Charles Beard,[82] to be genuinely critical of fundamental values and policies of their nations. Twentieth-century popular historians and writers of school textbooks were so nearly unanimous in propagating nationalist views that children in their schools and adults in their homes and libraries could easily believe that only their own nation was great or virtuous, or both, that only their own nation was brave, that only their own nation was inventive; in short, that only their own nation had much history worth knowing. In 1898 a New England teachers' group wrote a description of American history textbooks that could have applied (with changes of detail) to the history textbooks of many modern nations:

. . . extol the virtues of the noble Indian; dwell on the brilliant intellect, the
undaunted courage, and the magnificent faith of Columbus, the hardship of
the Pilgrims, the simplicity of the Quakers . . . show how the Revolution
was due solely to the brutal tyranny of the British, and how Washington and
Franklin had, in supreme degree all the virtues . . . and not a single fault;
characterize the Constitution as "the greatest product of the human mind";
. . . dwell on the enormities of the British after . . . 1783, and the glorious
victories of the War of 1812; . . . show . . . how the South went all wrong;
. . . and enliven the whole by a profusion of fancy pictures.[83]

Out of nationalist interpretations of history such as this rose the symbolic heroes upon whose lives the young were taught to model their own:
Vercingetorix, Chevalier Bayard, Jeanne d'Arc, Robin Hood, Francis
Drake, Admiral Nelson, Arminius, Frederick the Great, Gneisenau,
George Washington, Patrick Henry, and John Paul Jones,[84] or for Albania
the old hero Skenderberg and for Ireland the contemporary hero Parnell.
Out of them came inspirational phrases, "Give me liberty or give me
death" and "Don't give up the ship," and out of them likewise came hatred
for the domestic traitors, the Benedict Arnolds, and for the foreign enemies, the "Huns," the barbarians who threatened, attacked, and oppressed
the nation. Paul Valéry, a French critic and poet, was not entirely wrong
when he wrote, "History turns races [nations] into day-dreamers and
drunkards . . . national glory or national persecution-mania drives them
into collective unconsciousness." [85]

Occasionally an isolated voice would protest against nationalist indoctrination through the study of history. A prominent Scottish-American
professor, H. Morse Stephens (1857–1919), in 1916, during the horror of
World War I, would plead with his colleagues, "Woe unto us! professional
historians, professional students, professional teachers of history, if we
cannot see written in blood, in the dying civilization of Europe, the dread-
ful result of exaggerated nationalism as set forth in the patriotic histories
of some of the most eloquent historians of the nineteenth century." [86] But
his, indeed, was an isolated voice.

The traditions embodying the loyalties and the hostilities of people
are carried not only by their history but also by their language, literature,
folklore, and arts. Through modern times language became—if not the
most distinguishing—one of the most distinguishing marks of nationality,
and this was true even where people of the same nation (as in Switzerland) used more than one language and the people of two or more nations
(the United States and Great Britain) used substantially the same lan-

guage. To speak one national language rather than another became a "ritual act" of great significance, for it was a statement not only about personal status and identity but also about solidarity with or distance from other individuals.[87] A man belonged if he spoke the language; he was an "outsider," a foreigner, if he did not. The language of a nation, in brief, was the "set of habits by which the members of the nation" communicated with one another,[88] and thus acquired feelings of common interest; and of all habits those of language were the ones that most clearly separated the people of one nation from those of other nations and hence potentially became the basis of hostility.[89] This was true at least in part because a man felt comfortable when speaking or hearing his own national language and was tense and uncomfortable when foreign languages were used.

The increasing predominance of national languages was evidence of growing national consciousness. These languages were also used as instruments to deepen this consciousness. Among each of those peoples who were becoming nations, great efforts were made to develop a common national language. In already united and independent nations, great efforts were made to widen the use of and to refine the national language. Ideally and logically, if the views of many nationalists had been followed, each people who had a common language ought to have become a nation, and "linguistic nationality" ought to have become *the* basis of nationhood. In practice and without reference to logic, what happened was that the language of the dominant group within an actual or potential nation-state became the national language, and nonusers of the language within the state were persuaded or pressured into using *the* national language.[90] It came to be believed that the national language somehow expressed the character, the distinct character of a people, that it was necessary and desirable for everyone in the nation to speak, read, and write this language, and that this would supply an indispensable bond of unity.

In his attempt to awaken Hungarian nationalism, Count Széchenyi in 1834 wrote *Hunnia nyelve* (*The Language of Hungary*) to plead for the use of Magyar as Hungary's official language. "The greatest treasure of Hungarians," he said, "is their national idiom; this is the only safeguard of their entity as a nation, for no nation can exist without a national language. Hungarian progress depends on loyalty to the dynasty and on the promotion of national characteristics predetermined . . . by the free development of the language." [91] Though the circumstances varied, all over Europe and eventually all over the world patriots like Széchenyi pleaded for the development and use of their national languages. And their pleas were answered. In Hungary Magyar did officially replace Latin in the

1840's, and wherever national languages were not used their use was demanded. The trend toward national languages that began in the late Middle Ages was culminating and their employment became general, with only rare exceptions, wherever a people were or claimed to be a nation.

Both among those peoples already united in nation-states and among those who wished to form them, patriotic scholars produced philological studies, grammars, dictionaries, and encyclopedias in profusion, not only to further knowledge but also to develop and "purify" the national language and thus encourage unity. When in the new American states Noah Webster published his famed *Speller* (1783), he wished "to promote the honour and prosperity of the confederated republics of America" and therefore, as he wrote, he "chearfully" threw "his mite into the common treasure of patriotic executions . . . to promote virtue and patriotism. . . ." [92]

Not all the scholars of the languages were so consciously and deliberately patriotic as Webster, but everywhere they fondly studied and fostered the use of their national tongues. In 1823 Webster himself published his two-volume *American Dictionary of the English Language,* a work that became the prototype of later, much used American "standard" dictionaries. From 1814 the Serbian Vuk Karadžić (1787–1864), who has been called "the father of his country" and certainly was a father of its literature, published a Serbian grammar and a dictionary as well as a collection of Serbian folk songs.[93] During the 1830's Josef Jungmann (1773–1847) produced his five-volume Czech-German dictionary, *Slovnik českoněmecký.*[94] From 1819 the Grimm brothers, Jakob and Wilhelm, in the Germanies produced not only their well-known collections of German folk tales but also a grammar, a history, and dictionaries of the German language, and in 1854 planned and inaugurated the great German dictionary in sixteen volumes that was only completed a century later. In Norway, where as in other countries patriots were demanding the establishment of a national tongue, Ivar Aasen (1813–96) compiled a dictionary, *The Language of the Common People* (1846), and a grammar, *The Language of the Norwegian People* (1848), which standardized the dialects and made the speech of the people, the *Landsmaal,* the national language.[95] In France and England, where dictionaries—those of the French Academy and Samuel Johnson, for example—had, of course, been produced earlier, the work of classifying and giving precision to the languages continued, often on a monumental scale. From 1863 to 1872 Maximilien Littré, a professor of history and geography, published his superb and detailed *Dictionary of the French Language* in five large volumes, and in 1905

Ferdinand Brunot, inspired by his love of *patrie*, began to publish his learned multivolumed *Histoire de la langue française*, a work at which he lovingly labored for over forty years. In England from 1879 the erudite Sir James Murray (1837–1915), with the collaboration of many scholars, edited the giant *New English Dictionary* (*Oxford English Dictionary*, completed in 1928) to reveal all the possible historical meanings and usages of words in the English language. During the century or more in which the great dictionaries were being produced, national encyclopedias that were to become "standard" were also being produced or begun. The first edition of the *Encyclopaedia Britannica* appeared in three volumes in 1771, the monumental German Brockhaus' *Konversations-Lexikon* from 1796 to 1808, and the *Encyclopaedia Americana*, edited by the German-American Francis Lieber, in thirteen volumes, from 1829 to 1833. All the great nations and some of the small ones were to have similar encyclopedias.

By the twentieth century everywhere in Europe and the Americas nearly all people were using or demanding the right to use the national languages. The latter was, as might be expected, especially true among the nationalities striving to gain (or regain) their independence—the Irish, the Welsh, the Finnish, the Lithuanian, and the Albanian, for example.[96] No sharp lines demarcated linguistic frontiers. Particularly in eastern Europe and the Balkans, peoples and languages were much mixed, and all through Europe there were still within many states significant minorities who spoke languages other than that of the state—the Lorrainers who after 1870 were subject to Germany, and the Poles, Czechs, and Slovaks who were governed by Russia, Austria, or Germany.[97] Local languages, like the Provençal in France, did not completely disappear. In Roman Catholic churches the ritual was still (until the 1960's) in the Latin tongue that had once been "universal" in much of Europe. But everywhere the national languages were stressed and did dominate.

Language was a matter of state concern; the state had to make sure of the loyalty and unity of its citizens and that its will would be both understood and followed.[98] The governments conducted their business in the national language—it was official. To get a government position or favor —or avoid disfavor—an individual had to use the language. The language of command in the armies, increasingly filled with young conscripts, was the national, and if conscripts did not know it they were forced to learn it. The schools taught the national language, the newspapers were in the national language, the literature (the novels, the poems, the histories) was in the national language. Patriotic societies, like the Gaelic League in Ireland at the beginning of the twentieth century,[99] demanded the preservation of the language and extension of its use. Whenever a nation did win its independence, as the Irish did in 1921, it promptly made the teaching of the language compulsory.

If a man wished to take a full part in social life, he had to use the national language. Increasingly most men did, and they identified themselves and others by their languages. Few individuals (except some intellectuals and clergymen) protested against the decline of Latin and few against the swiftening disappearance of local dialects (except for occasional romantics and conservatives). Many citizens in many nations, and not only in France but in Lithuania,[100] came to believe their national language the clearest, the most expressive, or the most beautiful. For them the national language became a sacred treasure to be cherished, guarded, and preserved. A Lithuanian short-story writer quite seriously recounted *A Sad Incident* (1911) about a "Polonized Lithuanian who, having died," discovered "all the souls in heaven" were "grouped by language" and therefore could join neither the Poles nor the Lithuanians. "Man's mission being the glorification of God," he was condemned for his renunciation of "your father, your mother, love of your country, and the dearest gift of the Holy Ghost to every honorable man—your native language." [101]

In much of western Europe, in Britain, France, Italy, and Spain, national literatures were old as the nineteenth century opened and, being deeply steeped in tradition, they were guarded and treasured as they were further developed. In much of the rest of Europe, in Scandinavia, in central, southeastern, and eastern Europe, they were being created or were soon to be born, and when they came into existence they too were treasured and further developed. Poets, novelists, folklorists, scholars of many varieties all over Europe, themselves in part motivated by national feeling, helped create and develop national consciousness, and sometimes labored hard to promote national loyalty and unity. In Germany, as one of Bismarck's English biographers observed, "Poetry, philology, comparative mythology and folklore, the comparative study of institutions, palaeography and the archives, the philosophy of law—history in its widest streams, explored and mapped by the severest science—were exhibited to enforce a single moral—the greatness of the German contribution to the civilization of the past, a greatness in proportion to its fidelity to its racial and national character, and the certainty that a similar fidelity in the future would produce no less momentous results for Germany and humanity." [102]

It cannot be argued, for it would not be true, that all writers and scholars consciously and deliberately promoted nationalism, though some did; nor can it be asserted that many of them set out to prove their nation's contribution to civilization was greater or finer than that of other nations, though some did. Nevertheless, scholars did attempt to give their nations a "pure" language, did explore the origins and try to show the continuity of what they believed to be the national laws (as did the historian Friedrich Savigny [1779–1861] in the Germanies), and did seek out and publish (as did the brothers Grimm in Germany) what came to be considered the national folklore. And writers, novelists, poets, and essayists did increasingly use national settings, describe national scenes, depict national characters, and, on, occasion, attempt to inspire their countrymen with patriotic emotion. Whatever their motivations, those writers, who wrote not in the old universal western language, Latin, or in the old eastern Slavonic, but exclusively in their national tongues, and who wrote about national subjects almost exclusively, expressed and deepened national feeling and gave voice to national hopes.

During the eighteenth century in western Europe, particularly in France, literature had tended to express cosmopolitan ideals, and writers who might be quite French, like Voltaire, or, later, quite German, like Goethe, appealed to an international audience. With the rise of romanticism and from the time of the French Revolutionary and Napoleonic wars, writers more and more stressed their own people's experience as they appealed for national literatures, customs, and hopes. In the Italies Giacomo Leopardi (1798–1837), perhaps the greatest Italian poet of his era, poured forth patriotic songs (*Canti*) as he tried to fulfill his own hope for an Italian culture. "Italy," he wrote in 1819, "has nothing to hope for unless she has books read and understood from one end to the other of the country. The recent example of other nations shows us clearly all that can be done, in our century, by truly national books, to arouse the sleeping spirit of the country." [103] In what later became Czechoslovakia Jan Kollár (1793–1852) romantically exalted Czech and Slavic culture as he blamed Germany for suffocating it in a famous poem, *The Daughter of Slava* (1821–24). In Poland and later in exile in France, the great poet and teacher Adam Mickiewicz (1788–1855) powerfully pleaded for Polish culture and independence in many works, such as *The Books of the Polish Nation and of Polish Pilgrimage* (1832) and his epic *Pan Tadeusz* (1834). In Norway about the same time (1833) Henrik Wergeland (1808–45), much influenced by French revolutionary ideals, ardently espoused Norwegian culture. "We wish to be," he wrote, "Norwegian in everything, in our ways of life, in our language, in our conduct, in our habits." [104]

From parts of the New World came similar calls for national literatures and cultures. In Latin America after the wars of independence scholars wanted to create them; in Chile, for example, a Victorino Lastarria, at the time of the organization of the first Literary Society, wanted Chilean writers to study the Castilian and French languages but to base their work "on an independent spirit and application to the national reality." [105] Perhaps the strongest demand for a national culture and literature came from the new nation in North America, the United States. Pleading for less dependence on foreign literature and the cultivation of American, William Ellery Channing (1780–1842), a Unitarian minister who greatly influenced American authors (Ralph Waldo Emerson, for one), asked in 1830, "Shall America be only an echo of what is thought and written beyond the ocean?" [106] Channing was only one of many who wanted a "truly American" literature. Again and again through the nineteenth century and on into the twentieth the cry was repeated, at times boastfully, in the belief that America was or would become "the Athens and Rome of the New World." [107] In his *Democratic Vistas* Walt Whitman (1819–92) sought "to make patent the appalling vacuum . . . of any school of great imaginative Literature and Art, fit for a Republican, Religious, and Healthy people—and to suggest and prophesy such a Literature as the only vital means of sustaining and perpetuating such a people. I would project . . . an entirely new breed of authors, poets American. . . ." [108] For Whitman as well as for his contemporary, Emerson, and for many of the writers who came later, America was, in Emerson's words, "the country of the Future . . . a country of beginnings, of projects, of designs, of expectations."

Such "platitudinarian optimism" was not shared everywhere. But the belief that each nation should have its own literature, or should create it, was manifest everywhere in the western world. In the early twentieth century the young Yeats (1865–1939), Ireland's marvelous poet, dreamed of "a national literature that made Ireland beautiful in memory and yet had been freed from provincialism. . . ." [109] Along with other Irish nationalists, one of the founders of the Gaelic League, Father Michael O' Hickey, wanted to "cultivate everything that is most racial, most Gaelic, most Irish," and asked for (in the words of Thomas Davis), "a literature made by Irishmen, and coloured by our scenery, manners and character." [110] In Lithuania, Vincas Krėvė-Michevicius, a great literary figure, had his bard, Dundys, declaim, "Let the warriors use their swords. We, brothers [bards] will go forth into the wide world on narrow paths, on broad boulevards, we will go from border to border, wherever Lithuanians live, and we will proclaim: one sun in the sky, one fatherland on earth, one ruler for all the land in which the holy language of our fathers is heard." [111]

Just how deeply national literatures penetrated the consciousness of ordinary people cannot be ascertained, for most of them read little if at all. But that the literatures influenced those who could and did read can scarcely be doubted, and very likely the ideas expressed did filter down, even to children, in the inexpensive simple little magazines and storybooks that were being written for them.[112] In any case, not only was much patriotic literature written but much was also read and quoted. Alfred Tennyson (1809–92) advised his fellow Englishmen to "Love Thou Thy Land"; William Ernest Henley (1849–1903) reverently wrote of "England, My England"; and Rudyard Kipling (1856–1936) told his fellow Englishmen to bear "The White Man's Burden" and to be courageous, conscientious, and self-reliant patriots as well. John Greenleaf Whittier (1807–92) exalted the United States in his "Our Country" and his contemporary, Oliver Wendell Holmes (1809–94), asked his countrymen to be for "Union and Liberty." The ultrapatriotic Paul Déroulède (1846–1914) sang glowingly of French soldier heroes in his *Chants du soldat* and other poems, and Maurice Barrès in his *Le Roman de l'énergie nationale* and many other writings exhorted Frenchmen to reawaken the dead and unite with them for France.[113]

So much did literature become national that the nationality of a writer and his subject matter sometimes came to mean more than the quality of his writing. Though great writers perceived universals and in their humanity appealed to readers and theatergoers everywhere, novelists, poets, and dramatists came to be known and often to be judged by national criteria rather than their literary or artistic ability. And their readers or viewers read or saw chiefly and probably only their national writings and productions in the national languages and on national themes. It is a wonder that more of them did not become ardent national patriots.

Almost every artistic activity came to represent or express what was believed to be the national culture, and much of it directly tried to arouse national feeling. Writers, as was usual in modern times, primarily concerned themselves with the experiences and problems of individuals— especially their relationships as male and female—and some were more interested in questions of religion and class, or region and village, than in those of nation. Rarely, a great writer (Alexis Tolstoy or Romain Rolland) was able to surmount national prejudices and become an internationalist and pacifist. Nonetheless, literatures had become national, and writers— French, German, or American—were regarded as representatives of their nationality and so regarded themselves.

As it was in literature, so it was in all the arts and even, to some degree, in the sciences. All over Europe and in some of the nations of the New World national museums, national theaters and opera houses, national academies, and national literary and scientific journals were established.[114] In the land that later became Czechoslovakia, patriotic Czechs during the mid-nineteenth century built a National Theater for national plays in the national language. The statement of the committee in charge in its first (1851) public appeal for funds read in part, "The Czech patriot can now view with inspiration and hope the progress which our fresh national spirit has already made in education and culture."[115] When the theater, over a quarter of a century in the building, burned three months after it was opened in 1881, new subscriptions were immediately collected from Czech patriots, and it was rebuilt and reopened in two years.[116]

Painting, sculpture, and architecture came to be called Italian, French, German, English, Russian, American, as if nationality were the basis of artistry. Painting was not "impressionist" but "French impressionist"; a sculptor was an "Italian" sculptor; a building was designed not by an architect but by a "German" architect.

Among the arts, nationalist tendencies were probably strongest in music, in part, it is likely, because of the romantic interest in folk music. Bach, Beethoven,[117] and Haydn became "German" composers, though the first wrote for the aristocracy, the second was often inspired by the French Revolution and Napoleon, and the third borrowed from Italian composers. Verdi, an ardent patriot, became the great Italian composer of opera and hence "the very soul of Italy." His name became a nationalist acrostic for Vittorio Emmanuele Re d'Italia, and the first performance of *I Lombardi* (1843) the occasion for patriotic demonstrations. Karl Maria von Weber's *Der Freischütz* became a classic "German opera," and the heroic operas of Richard Wagner, a man of many violent opinions, came to symbolize "Germanism."[118] "Hungarian" music (like that of Liszt) was "Hungarian," perhaps because it so often used the melodies and rhythms of gypsies who lived in Hungary. Chopin was a "Polish" composer, pianist, and patriot, and Smetana and Dvořák "Czech" composers and patriots. Musorgski (*Boris Godunov*) and Tchaikovsky were passionately devoted to Russia, the latter writing, "I am a Russian through and through."[119] Debussy and Ravel, though not violent nationalists, wanted "good French music."[120] That there did develop national styles in music is obvious; that music was consciously used to arouse national consciousness and loyalty may be less obvious but is no less certain. That national boundaries could not and did not confine melodies and that the counterpoint, harmony, and notation of music were international did not matter. Music was national, or so it was believed.[121]

It was, of course, in the national songs, increasingly called anthems, that the intensifying nationalism was most obviously demonstrated.[122] From the eighteenth century onward, as new national and sometimes revolutionary governments were established, composers (as had Rouget de Lisle in 1792) wrote popular lyrics to inspire love of and loyalty to the nation, and some of them, unofficially or officially, became national songs known and sung by many patriots. Though these songs, naturally, varied with the composer and from nation to nation, they were strikingly similar in sentiment. Often they asked God's blessing on the nation and, whether they did or not, they hailed the nation unreservedly. They sang of union, the unbreakable union of brothers. They proclaimed the beauty of the land and asked that all true patriots love it. When set to martial music, as many lyrics were, they called on patriots to march on, awaken to glory, be heroes, live, die, and be victorious for their nation, and they glorified the flag, the "star-spangled banner," and exulted that the banner was there though "bombs burst in air." Many rejoiced in freedom from bondage or simply freedom, and many joyfully prophesied a wonderful future, a great destiny for the nation.[123]

These national anthems, whether unofficial or official, many people knew and sang, especially on important occasions such as the national holidays that every nation, following France (July 14) and the United States (July 4), began to celebrate.[124] Indeed, children were taught to memorize the songs and usually they did. National holidays were established chiefly to mark the date of national independence (as in several Latin American nations),[125] or the establishment of a radically new government (France), or sometimes the birth date of a national hero (George Washington). They were days for rejoicing, with parades, waving of flags, martial music, displays of military might, and long speeches describing the triumph of the nation through or in spite of dire tribulations.[126] If at no other time, people of each nation did feel patriotic, sense feelings of group loyalty and solidarity. A well-known Minnesota professor (1913) recalled the "first lessons I ever received in patriotism," at a Memorial Day (May 30) ceremony (commemorating the dead in wars) in a little Wisconsin town. Schoolchildren, of which he was one, gathered, joined the parade. "I remember with what pride we did this. We circled the little square and stood and listened while the speeches were made and then went to the little cemetery . . . dropped our tribute of flowers . . . it was a scene I never think of without being deeply moved . . . and the effect of that Memorial Day on my mind and, I suppose, my character was tremendous." [127]

Everywhere western men turned, their evolving cultures influenced if they did not condition them to become nationalists, became a sort of cultural envelope that clothed them. Food and drink came to be known not primarily by their regions or their qualities but by whether they were French, English, German, or American. French cuisine, with its sauces that enhanced flavor, was supposed to excel, English cooking, with its watery vegetables, to be bad; while German foods, the pork sausages and the sauerkraut, were thought to be fattening; and the American diet, its steak and potatoes with gravy, to be hearty, a "man's food." The French "national" drink was wine, the British tea (or gin), the Russian vodka (or tea), the German beer, the American in the United States bourbon whiskey (or later Coca-Cola), the Swedish akvavit, and the Serbian plum brandy. Of course, the people in each nation ate and drank whatever was at hand that they could afford, but they were supposed to prefer whatever was "national," and generally they did.

While eventually dress was to become somewhat similar around Europe and the world—for men trousers, shirt, and maybe a jacket—many (if not most) peoples were said to have a "national" dress. Quite often these were in origin local or regional peasant costumes—though in Scotland the "national" dress became the aristocratic kilt[128]—and to please patriots they were adopted as the "national" (in some cases it was also to please the foreign tourist trade). Dress apparently reflected the national character, whatever that was, despite the fact that what people wore was simply whatever they were accustomed to wearing in their village, or could afford, or what the current fashion dictated.[129]

Sports likewise tended to become national. Cricket became the sport of English gentlemen and hence of England—it was supposed to teach "fair play"—and horse racing the sport of Hungarian aristocrats and hence of Hungary. Baseball, during the last quarter of the nineteenth century, became the American "national pastime." Sometimes, as in France during the late nineteenth century, organized sports were planned to develop not only physical fitness in young men, so that they would make good soldiers, but also patriotism, so that they would be good citizens.[130] The so-called international Olympic games, revived in 1896 (fully developed from 1908), became competitions between national teams, competitions that engendered at least as much nationalism as they did international amity.

Each nation began to have its own symbolic flag, animal, flower, or tree, and its own half-human national character that somehow was supposed to personify it. Just as John Bull and Uncle Sam were coming to represent Britain and the United States, so Marianne and Ivan were coming to mean France and Russia. For the people of each nation these mythical characters or stereotypes represented their finest qualities, their virtues—doggedness, humanness, rugged strength, or honesty. For peoples of other nations, especially when they were enemies, the stereotypes had quite opposed connotations—boorishness, flightiness, uncouthness, crudeness.[131] A shamrock stood for Ireland, a lion for England, a bear for Russia, and an eagle for the United States. These symbolic objects took on mystical qualities, qualities that were good, heroic, beautiful, true, unique, worthy of protection, never to be desecrated, always to be reverenced.[132] Most basic customs and ceremonies, in fact, that had once been basically religious, even those of marriage and death, now took on "national" characteristics, though in some respects they were no less sacred than before.

Why should this have been true? Part of the answer has already been given. But there were other reasons as well that lay deep in the development of modern national cultures. As the philosopher-historian David Hume (1711–76) observed in the eighteenth century, "The human mind is of a very imitative nature; nor is it possible for any set of men to converse often together, without acquiring a similitude of manners and communicating to each other their vices and virtues. . . ." [133] Once some men in any nation became nationalists and acquired the so-called national characteristics, others in their nation consciously and unconsciously acquired their virtues and vices.

Once nationalism had become a dominant and moving force, individuals caught the spirit as if it were a virus. From birth to death their governments persuaded and forced them to be national in their interests, and at the same time their national cultures fashioned them to hold national values and to have national hopes. The pressures on each individual to be nationalist were inescapable and pervasive. Whatever their initial impulses or biological urges, they were, in the nineteenth and twentieth centuries, conditioned or at least directed toward national loyalties and goals until it almost might be said western men acquired patriotic reflexes. If the language of Freudian psychoanalysis might be applied, their unconscious (superego) controls and their conscious (ego) thinking were both shaped by patriotic pressures, and these enabled their biological drives (id) to find satisfaction in striving for national unity, security, and power and in being loyal to their nation and to that for which they thought it stood.

Indeed, if they did not choose this way, they could lose the respect of their fellows, their chance for economic advancement, or even their livelihood. But if they did choose this way, they might win fame and status, or at least the respect of their fellows, and they could look forward, or so they thought, to a happier life than they had otherwise, or at least find an escape from worry and frustration. "Job, family, friends, and comfortable existence" were "all hostages insuring loyalty," [134] and, it might be added, much in their whole human environment pushed them toward nationalism. Again, the wonder is that national feeling did not become more intense than it did.

The pressures on individuals to imitate others, to conform with others, and to excel in patriotism became ever more insistent and incessant during the nineteenth century. In every country patriots formed societies or groups to exhort people and government to adopt and promote the national, the "right," views and ideals. From early in the nineteenth century these societies, like the *Hetairia Philikè* in Greece, the *Carbonari* and Young Italy in the Italies, the *Burschenschaften* in the Germanies, the *Selspabet for Norges vel* in Norway, the Philomathians in Poland, and *La Joven Argentina* in Argentina, attempted with varying success to instill national consciousness and desire for unity and to push toward national independence. Sometimes, as with the *Burschenschaften* and Young Italy, they were composed primarily of youth. Rarely did they have large memberships, though the *Carbonari* in Italy in 1820 may have had as many as 300,000 to 600,000 members and Young Italy in the 1830's 60,000 members.[135] Occasionally, as was true of Young Ireland,[136] they were movements rather than societies. Often, if they were agitating for independence and hence were regarded by the ruling authorities as subversive, they had to be and were secret societies. Some of them, such as the *Carbonari*,[137] had elaborate initiation ceremonies, and sometimes initiates had to take fiery oaths to drive out the hated foreign ruler and to strive to establish an independent nation. As has been said, to join the *Hetairia Philikè* a Greek had to swear to "consecrate myself to [my country]; and that henceforth [it] shall be the scope of my thoughts, [its] name the guide of my actions, [its] happiness the recompense of my labours." [138] The oath of Mazzini's Young Italy was as emotionally charged: "In the name of God and of Italy . . . of all the martyrs of the holy Italian cause. . . . By the love I bear to the country that gave my mother birth, and will be the home of my children. . . . By the blush that rises to my brow when I stand before the citizens of other lands, to know that I have no rights of citizenship, no country, and no national flag. . . . I swear to dedicate myself wholly and forever to strive to constitute Italy one free, independent, republican nation." [139]

If a nation was independent, patriotic organizations were formed to propagate and inculcate nationalism—or, more likely, particular, customarily conservative varieties of the sentiment. From the 1880's in both old and new nations these became numerous, and now they were more often public or at least less conspiratorial societies.[140] They preached loyalty and they demanded defense and expansion of the national interests, power, and territory. Composed, most often, of respectable, middle-class, conservative citizens, their membership included war veterans, military officers, and in some cases intellectuals and aristocrats.[141] The members had a stake in the established order in the nation as it was, asked and expected that all citizens give one-hundred-per-cent devotion to it, and wanted to make sure that "superior" people, like themselves, controlled the national destinies. They prodded governments and schools not only to indoctrinate all children and adults with a perfervid patriotism but also to nationalize (or eliminate) aliens, minorities, and "hyphenates" who, they thought, threatened the "purity" or the security of the nation.

By the twentieth century in the western world patriotic societies of one kind or another numbered in the hundreds. In Germany alone in 1914, on the eve of the First World War, there were at least 84. In a brief search of the American records the present writer was able to identify over 50 patriotic and military societies in the United States when that country entered the war in 1917, and another American scholar found that some 106 patriotic, veterans', and hereditary societies had been established in the United States by 1900.[142] No such counts are available for other nations, but (in proportion to population) the numbers were similar. Among the best-known societies of the several varieties were the Royal Empire Society and the Primrose League of Britain, the Daughters of the American Revolution and the Grand Army of the Republic in the United States, the League of Patriots, the National Alliance for the Increase of French Population, and the *Action Française* in France, and the Pan-German League and the Navy League in Germany.

These groups and many like them held meetings to hear inspirational patriotic talks. They published magazines and occasionally newspapers, and handed out propaganda in pamphlets and news stories. They brought pressure upon their governments to increase military appropriations and adopt aggressive, "strong" foreign policies. They demanded the teaching of patriotism and tried to weed out unpatriotic teachers and teachings.

They exhibited the national flags and relics and publicly celebrated national holidays. They attempted to "Americanize" or "Germanize" the foreigners within their gates, and to "purify" the national languages. They were vociferously for any and all policies that in their view enhanced the prestige of their nation. They were just as vociferously against anything they thought foreign or international.

Their memberships, like those of earlier patriotic organizations, were usually not large, the better-known organizations numbering 40,000 to 300,000 and only occasionally, like the American G.A.R. and the British Primrose League, exceeding a million. But they spoke loudly and with self-assurance. While a few, like the Pan-German League, would be unpopular with their governments, while (perhaps because) most of them were filled with old gentlemen and ladies, they served to make national patriotism respectable. Not infrequently, as in the case of the various navy and security leagues, they influenced political leaders who wished to be re-elected and thereby were successful in increasing the size of the military establishments. If they were not effective in any other way, they spread fear of other nations, caused many of their compatriots to "view with alarm," and hence accentuated distrust of foreigners and sharpened feelings of national exclusiveness.

Though there was no society that might be termed "typical" among them, the early activities of one, the Daughters of the American Revolution, are not unrepresentative.[143] The Daughters held patriotic assemblies to inspire themselves and their communities. They presented copies of national songs and documents to schools, convinced boards of education and legislatures that the American flag should be flown on every school, decried any "misuse" of the flag, and asked that men (not women) doff their hats when it passed. They reviewed the national history, especially its glorious moments, made pilgrimages to historic places, gave entertainments in historical costumes, and erected national monuments. They gave prizes to children for patriotic essays and made certain that the "right" books were in the libraries. "In every way" the Daughters desired to "cherish, maintain and extend the institutions of American freedom, to foster true patriotism and love of country,"[144] which, of course, meant they wanted other Americans to be loyal to their kind of nation. While, like most of the patriotic societies, they shunned politics (on paper), they were always on the side of the national authorities, particularly the conservative ones. They were always fearful of the "foreigner"; they were always against any "radical" doctrines like socialism; and they were always for "adequate" defense, which in practice meant the biggest army and navy the country could afford without heavy taxes upon the well-to-do.

The establishment and growth of patriotic societies were in themselves evidence of mounting national feeling. Just how effective they were in making nationalists cannot be known. Individuals everywhere in the West were subject to so many pressures that would make them nationalists, from their governments and from their parents and their schools as well as from organized patriotic groups, that it is impossible to disentangle and weigh the effectiveness of any one.

Individuals also became nationalists because they internalized (and could not avoid doing so) the values and goals set by their governments and their cultures; in short, because of internal pressures or, perhaps more accurately, inner compulsions. For nationalism, by affording a sense of belonging to a group, afforded them ways to identify themselves, to achieve status, prestige, and even profit, to realize hopes, and to escape from frustration and fear.

To repeat, as individuals in western countries moved from rural, agricultural to urban, industrial societies, they tended to lose their old identities, their sense of belonging to a village, parish, or regional group and of being distinct from people who lived in other villages, parishes, and regions. Gradually, though always more and more, they and their sons and daughters began to think of themselves as members of nations, of nationality groups, and to identify themselves by what came to be, increasingly, *their* national cultures, their language, their customs, their symbols, their leaders. To an ever-growing extent they came to think of themselves as, to call themselves Poles, Germans, Italians. And, as important, other people tended to call them by these names.

As the traditional societies deteriorated, so did their structures and the values and goals these structures supported.[145] In the traditional societies each man had a niche, belonged to a community, and knew who he was. He was a laborer or a landowner in a village in, say, Vaucluse, and this was his village. He held land from or worked for a larger landowner, perhaps a count, and owed him a fixed sum or so much work and produce as well as respect. He was, say, a member of his village Catholic parish and he usually recognized the curé as a guide and moral authority. Now, when he and his sons and daughters moved to Paris or to a large market town, they had no niche as sure, no authority as certain, no community that was as much their own. They were not as sure then who they were. Where could they turn? To what could they belong? To their *patrie?* [146] Not everyone did, of course. But those who did could find a niche in and play a role in the larger community, their nation, and thus know who they were—Frenchmen. This meant that they were men who were different from Englishmen and Germans, men who had their own language, their own customs, their own common past, their own symbols, their own heroes, their own leaders, and therefore their own interests and hopes that differed from those of Englishmen and Germans. Somehow they, Frenchmen, were like other Frenchmen and unlike other peoples—or at least so they believed. And so an individual could answer the questions "To whom do I belong?" and "From whom do I differ?" [147] Without really knowing what national character was, he believed in it and that he somehow partook of it.

In their homes and in times of peace, individuals probably felt no overwhelming need for national identity. If and when they encountered foreigners, however, many did perceive differences and "feel" their nationality. This perception, this feeling, particularly manifested itself in times of national rebellion against "foreign" rulers and in times of threats of war and war itself. But in peace or war a great many individuals wanted to have not only the security of knowing who they were and how admirable their group was but also the satisfaction of making invidious comparisons. Thus individuals of one nation generally applied "good" characteristics to the people of their own nation, their "in-group," and "bad" characteristics to other peoples, who were outsiders and therefore suspect. So much was this true that people of one nationality seldom made complimentary remarks about people of another but were quite ready with slurs ("ethnophaulisms").[148]

Modern western individuals did not always, even by 1914, identify themselves with their fatherland, and a few hated it. On the other hand, an articulate few at times became as mystical about their union with it as had the romantic German patriot Ernst Arndt during the Napoleonic wars. "When," Arndt glowed, "a great crowd moves before me, when a band of warriors passes by with flowing banners and sounding trumpets and drums . . . in my exaltation I am freed at once from my sins, I am no longer a single suffering man, I am at one with the *Volk* and God. In such moments doubts about my life and work disappear." [149] A century later ardent French patriots, like Maurice Barrès and Charles Péguy, and patriots in much of Europe felt similarly as their nations went to war and they identified themselves with the living and the dead, the vital present and the hallowed past of their nations. By losing themselves in their nations, patriots could, it appears, find themselves.

Not only could individuals find themselves through and in their nation, but through it they could seek and acquire personal status, prestige, power, and profit. And since these were major goals of western men, individuals felt pressures to obtain them.

Few individuals, as individuals, ever acquire high status and prestige. But they could do so vicariously through their nation because they shared in their nation's achievements and in its praiseworthy qualities, or, as the English critic Matthew Arnold once put it, "in the sense of self-esteem, generated by knowing the figure which his [the patriot's] nation makes in history; by considering the achievements of his nation in war, government, arts, literature, or industry." [150] God, so many patriots thought, was on their side. He had chosen their nation, given it a special mission.[151] Thus, when they had faith in their nation and did its good works, they were but carrying out God's "manifest" will. But whatever God's will, patriots could find personal significance, purpose, and guidance for their lives in *their* nation's triumphs in war and in *their* nation's real or imagined contributions to civilization. Frenchmen took pride in the magnificence of Louis XIV's reign, in the revolutionary achievement of liberties of 1789, in the great triumphs of Napoleon, or in the rationality and the mission of French civilization; Englishmen in the model for government that their parliamentary system provided, in their Empire on which "the sun never set," in their belief in "fair play," in their "white man's burden," or in the size and invincibility of their navy; Germans in the German addiction to hard work, in the German philosophical profundity, in the victories of Frederick II and Bismarck, or in the efficiency of the German army; Americans in their liberties, in the size and material progress of their United States, or in the belief that their nation "never lost a war"; Russians in the vastness of their country, the mystical nature of the people, the rugged strength of the peasantry; and Italians in the brilliance of Italy's Roman and Renaissance past. Even individuals of small nations found personal significance through their nation—the pride of the Swiss, for example, in Switzerland's freedom from war (after 1648), in Switzerland's cosmopolitanism, and in its federative form of government. The personal status and pride, of course, did not need to be acquired through high and mighty deeds. They could be and often were attained in mundane ways—the quality of the wine (France), of the beer (Germany), of the milk and cheese (Switzerland), of the ballet (Russia), of the opera (Italy); the "common sense" of the people (England) or the victories of athletes (United States).

Patriotism likewise enabled individuals to hope for and to obtain concrete personal gains and thereby to identify their personal fortunes with the national. To gain and to hold office, liberal and conservative politicians alike, the Gladstones and Disraelis, the Clemenceaus and Poincarés, the Theodore Roosevelts and McKinleys, had to be patriotic and to preach patriotism. And as it was for those who held the highest offices, so it was for the lesser politicians, like Senator Beveridge in the United States, and even for minor officials. Statesmen and officials, great and small, became spokesmen of nations, not, as were Colbert and Metternich, of dynasties and empires. This was especially the case in the more democratic nations, where eager office seekers vied with each other in rhetorical expressions of their patriotism and had to prove themselves to be even "purer" in their patriotism than were their opponents and their constituents.

What was true of politicians was true of businessmen, bankers, merchants, industrialists, and their lawyers. To be successful, that is, to make money, they too had to think and speak in national terms and identify their own interests with the national. Symbolic of this were the national names they increasingly gave their businesses and corporations—the American Telephone and Telegraph Company, for example.

Individuals identify themselves not only through the experiences they share with other individuals but also through the hopes they have in common with them. More and more individuals more and more identified their hopes, and their hopes of many varieties, with the future of their nation. During the years from the Napoleonic wars through the First World War and later, Europeans and Americans were *expectant* peoples engaged in what later was called modernization. Individuals increasingly believed in progress, and they expected this progress to come in and through their nations. If they wanted—and many did—independent, free constitutional governments, if they wanted civil liberties, it was through their nation that they expected to get them.[152] If they wanted roads and bridges built and harbors dredged, they more and more turned not to local but to national authorities. Thus their desires and hopes attached them as individuals to the larger cause of the nation, and this attachment in turn gave purpose and direction to their lives.

As a contemporary Jewish scholar, J. L. Talmon, has remarked, nationalism gave an "outlet to the dynamic quality of modern man. It supplied at the same time in the nation a centre of loyalty and a framework of a more concrete and tangible nature than the airy heavenly cities of the world proletariat or liberated Humanity." [153] Nationalism, indeed, seemed to promise "a Mazzinian paradise of moral dignity," "a Cobdenian paradise of commercial prosperity," [154] the end of oppression and servitude and the advent of a utopian future.[155]

By working for, by having faith in his nation, an individual could open the way to a happier, freer, more secure life for himself and his brothers.[156] Nationalism more and more offered what religion once had, a vision of a heaven, though this time an earthly heaven (see pages 131–35). Through their nation, their community, individuals could eventually hope to achieve personally meaningful and creative lives. All through the nineteenth century and on into the twentieth, nationalists—the liberal Mazzini and the conservative Paul Déroulède alike—found personal meaning in striving for the future well-being of their nation. Mazzini in his inspired humanitarian nationalism was, of course, unusual and outstanding.[157] More than almost any other man he devoted his whole life, much of it in unhappy exile, to work for the unity and happiness of his beloved country. Other men, by comparison, seem less inspired, less involved, less exciting. Yet the whole history of the last century is filled with individuals who identified their personal goals with the national aims. A cynic might rightly ask: were not these individuals motivated by self-interest? And the answer is "yes," but their personal ambitions were subsumed in the national, and at the same time they made the national dreams their own. The ends of self-interest and of national, of individual careers and of the national welfare, became for them the same. And the ends, the dreams could be realized in and through the combined efforts of the people of the nation.

In 1830 Count Széchenyi in his book *Hitel* (*Credit*) told Hungarians, "The *Past* has slipped from our grasp forever but we are masters of the *Future*. Let us not bother then with futile reminiscences but let us awaken our dear fatherland through purposeful patriotism and loyal unity to a brighter dawn. Many think: Hungary *has been;* I like to believe that she *will be.*" [158] A generation later, in 1860, the Russian novelist Dostoyevsky declared that Russians had at last "come to understand" that they too were "a nation with a clearly defined and highly original character" and that their task was "to create a new form of life, developed from our own earth, drawing its resources from our own soil and our own popular tradition." [159]

In all western nations patriots indulged in similar affirmations of nationalist faith, and they made them frequently and enthusiastically. But nowhere was nationalist hope expressed more fervently and often than in the United States.[160] The United States was then, in the nineteenth century, *the* expectant nation. Americans were, so believers announced, the advance guard of the world, the "pioneers" (Whitman) who were breaking the path to the future. Unspoiled by the Old World's decay, with untold resources at their command, and with the precious liberties they had won, they could and would become the people of plenty,[161] of happiness, of justice, the envy of the world, a great nation beyond any historical comparison. In the United States the "sciences and the arts of civilized life" were to reach their highest development.[162] For Americans, asserted a popular American writer in 1844, a "career of improvement and glory" was "the near and certain prospect," and they should find "ennobling inspiration in the cheery anticipations of a happy future." [163] In the American nation, at last, so American patriots believed, the messianic, the Edenic myth was to be realized, as "moral regeneration," coupled with material progress, "became the collective mission of the American people." [164] Not all Americans were taken in by the bombastic rhetoric of superpatriots, though some undoubtedly were. But many, identifying themselves with the nation and with its interests and its dreams, gained thereby a sense of security and hope that in America utopia would at long last be realized.[165]

As people moved into the faster tempo and deeper uncertainties of urban, industrial life and lost the respected authorities and comforting myths to which they and their ancestors had been accustomed, many were troubled, felt rootless and lonely, and hence experienced unusual tension and anxiety.[166] Many of them therefore sought a community to which they could belong, be accepted, feel secure. In modern times the nation became that community and the dominant community. But it is likely, if not obvious, that some individuals—most probably those with the greatest anxieties—needed acceptance and security more than others, and thus might become more ardently nationalist than others.[167]

One self-evident hypothesis is that groups and individuals who have suffered from direct oppression by foreigners will, in modern times, become strongly nationalist. The evidence is so ample that substantiation of the hypothesis seems hardly necessary. Members of "oppressed nationalities"—Czechs, Poles, Serbs—often became intensely nationalist as they struggled for independence; and Irishmen, who were sorely oppressed by the English, and eventually the Jews, who were everywhere persecuted, have become as nationalist as any people in modern times.[168] It is also possible to say that the sons and daughters of immigrants—"the second generation" in the United States—have been eager to prove their loyalty and have often become strongly nationalist because they have not been fully accepted in their new nation.[169] And that defeated peoples—the French after 1870 and the Germans after 1918—did become more nationalist after than they had been before the trauma of defeat.

Other hypotheses are less obvious and less capable of proof, though they warrant serious examination. Lord Acton once remarked that "exile was the nursery of nationality." [170] While their countries were struggling for independence, many nationalists of central and southern Europe escaped into exile or voluntarily emigrated. Among the many were Mazzini and Gioberti of Italy, Rhigas and Koraïs of Greece, Mickiewicz of Poland, and Drahomaniv of the Ukraine. A good many Jews, like Theodor Herzl and Leo Pinsker, must have usually felt themselves to be in exile, even when they resided in the country where they were born. And a good many Irishmen when they emigrated to America became more patriotically Irish than they had been in Ireland.[171] But whether nationalists went into exile or emigrated because they were nationalists or became nationalists after they were exiles and emigrants is not always clear. Mazzini, because he was maladjusted and alienated, might have been an exile at any time anywhere; he said himself he still felt in exile when in 1848 he returned to Italy.[172] Perhaps, then, he became a nationalist because in his time that was one way to overcome his alienation. Probably all that can be said is that residence abroad, whether forced or voluntary, often intensified the national feeling of men who were already national patriots, as was the case with the many Poles in exile who lived and agitated so long in Paris for Polish independence. Again, a good many nationalist leaders—those of Ireland, for instance—were imprisoned by "foreign" governments as they agitated for independence. But imprisonment did not make them nationalist, though undoubtedly it made some of them more so than they had been.

Among the possible hypotheses is another that on first examination appears plausible: that individuals become intense nationalists because they suffer from some stigma such as physical disability[173] or have had shocking traumatic experiences. Charles Maurras, one of the most zealous French nationalists, became deaf at the age of fourteen and could not enter the naval academy as he had planned. Heinrich von Treitschke, the dogmatic German nationalist historian, would have followed a military career had he not been deaf. The extreme nearsightedness of Rudyard Kipling, England's imperialist poet, prevented him from entering the army, and his loneliness and his concern over the gossip about his dark coloring contributed to his extreme insecurity and alienation.[174] The belligerent German Kaiser William II and Paul Déroulède, the French nationalist poet, each had a shortened arm. Both the Italian idealist patriot Mazzini and the aggressive American President Theodore Roosevelt were sickly children. William Ernest Henley, the sentimental English patriotic poet, suffered from tuberculosis of the bone, and the editor of the Lithuanian nationalist newspaper *Varpas* (*Bell*), Vincas Kudirka, a man of "gigantic will and burning eyes," had tuberculosis.[175] Dostoyevsky was troubled by epilepsy, and Kita Ikki (1883–1937), an influential totalitarian Japanese patriot and socialist, was forced to leave school three times because of an eye ailment. Perhaps Count Széchenyi tried so hard to create a nation in Hungary because he was disappointed both in his army career and in his love affairs, and had a "guilt complex"; always a high-strung individual with many frustrations, as he grew older his mind did deteriorate, and finally he committed suicide.[176] The German composer Richard Wagner, whom German nationalists including Hitler so admired, neurotically blamed others for his failures and always felt his work did not get its due, and his frustrations seemed only to be equaled by his enthusiasms.[177] Léon Daudet, a French conservative nationalist writer, rejected everything his more famous father, Alphonse, stood for.[178] Jews like Theodor Herzl were subjected to agonizing insults as *Saujud* (dirty Jew), and Jews in Russia (from the 1880's), living in constant fear of pogroms, suffered intensely. The three young Serbian nationalists who went to Sarajevo in June, 1914, to assassinate the Archduke Francis Ferdinand all had trouble in school and all suffered from ill health.[179] The list could be greatly extended, and certainly among later nationalists the ne'er-do-well and psychotically ill Hitler would be a case in point.

It is altogether likely that many individuals who have a "stigma" of some kind, or have had a violently disturbing experience, do suffer more than "normal" individuals, do try harder, do sometimes become emotionally violent, and do in some cases, therefore, become leaders in any movement or ideology. But there is not sufficient evidence to verify the hypothesis that individuals become intense nationalists or nationalist leaders because of such "stigmas" or experiences as those just described,[180] or, more precisely, that they become so more than "normal" individuals. The vogue of Freudian psychoanalytic interpretation during recent years has made psychological maladjustment and frustration seem the motivation for much human thought and action, and they have become catchall explanations, just as divine reason explained much to medieval theologians and natural law to eighteenth-century *philosophes*. But, in fact, the evidence does not permit correlation of personal insecurity with nationalism except in a general way. Insecure individuals have taken many other escapes from freedom, both in our and earlier times: dogmatic religion, authoritarian communism, drugs, suicide. Further, secure and insecure men have become nationalists, and insecurity may be either a cause or a result of nationalism. The hypothesis seems insufficiently supported by evidence and may be based upon a fallacious, *post hoc, ergo propter hoc* argument.

Leaders in any belief or activity are probably more highly strung and more imaginative, more sensitive and aggressive than are "normal" individuals. This writer's own studies of over one hundred nationalist leaders of the past show that they were, in general, better educated than the "average"; that a considerable proportion of them were lawyers; that they came from all classes, though more often from middle-class professional groups; that a significant number of them were, at least once, unusually psychologically disturbed; that many of them did go into exile or were imprisoned; that a good many of them were "marginal" members of their societies and probably, more than seems usual, felt insecure;[181] and that a number of them probably possessed the qualities of leadership summed up in what the sociologist Max Weber called "charisma." [182] But on the basis of evidence few other generalizations seem possible. As a Princeton historian, Martin Duberman, has remarked, "A connection between inner problems and outer convictions probably always exists to some degree. But an individual's public involvement is never completely explained by discussing his private pathology." [183]

Albert Camus once observed that all men carry within themselves their "places of exile," their "crimes," their "ravages." [184] All individuals carry within themselves frustrations, tensions, uncertainties, guilt feelings, and a sense of deprivation. Nationalism is one way for them to overcome their frustrations, to purge themselves of guilt, to be fulfilled. "All forms of nationalist sentiment" may derive "their force [in part] from repressed emotions and . . . unconscious (because repressed) psychic disturbances." [185] But the nationalist sentiment, nationalism itself, derives, as this book reveals, from a multitude of forces, pressures, motivations, *and* from the aspirations as well as the frustrations of people as individuals and of people in groups. No monolithic, no single explanation is satisfactory.

VIII

Nationalism in the West After World War I: Persistence and Doubt

By the early twentieth century in the West the nation had become the chief way men formed in groups, the nation-state their dominant political institution, and loyalty to the nation and its state their supreme unifying and dividing sentiment. In Europe, in the United States, and in differing ways in the rest of the Americas, nearly all peoples had formed into separate nations and obtained their own independent national states. True, there were, to repeat, peoples (or groupings of individuals within them) who aspired to be but were not yet separate nations with independent states: the Catalans in Spain, the Basques in Spain and France, the Ukrainians in the Soviet Union, the Quebecois in Canada, in lesser degree perhaps the Scots and Welsh in the United Kingdom, and in a different way, especially in the late 1960's, some of the blacks in the United States. But, in the main, western peoples did feel that they each constituted a nation, had their national state, and, usually but not universally, gave their chief loyalty to their own nation and state. In short, they had become nationally conscious, and most of the time—especially in times of war—they were nationalist. What had begun in nation building and nationalism down to 1921 continued unabated. While certain ideological and technological forces worked against nationalism and critics predicted its decline, nationalism did not abate. With variations and with ups and downs, it became in fact stronger and more pervasive.

The nation-states, both in pursuit of their own objectives and in response to pressures of many kinds from their peoples, constantly expanded and strengthened their powers. They shaped their nations and in turn were molded by their nations.[1] Scholars have long argued whether it was the states or the national cultures that were the most powerful force in creating nationalism. But the contemporary political, the national, state is one aspect of a people's culture, just as are their economic and social arrangements. Hence all that can be said is that the political, economic, and social myths and realities interacted and that nationalism is a manifestation of the total culture of a people at a particular time.

The economic and social desires, needs, and problems of peoples became so vast and so complex that only a national state, armed with great power and prestige, seemed to be able to cope with them. In meeting these desires, needs, and problems, the nation-state became the "organized expression" of the nation,[2] and in turn determined, in no inconsiderable degree, the form and content of the nation's economic interests and cultural aspirations. Certainly by the last third of the twentieth century the nation-state had generally come to have the power the German sociologist Max Weber had thought it ought to have—"the monopoly of legitimate physical force." [3] Functioning in government, it had become, in the words of the seventeenth-century political theorist Hobbes, a kind of "Mortall God," a leviathan, and it promoted its own power and expansion and directed the energies of peoples grouped in nations. Indeed, the nation-state, which romantics and Hegelians of the nineteenth century had sometimes regarded as an object of poetry if not adoration, had become the hard, pervasive political reality of the twentieth century. But what the governments of these states actually did always reflected what the peoples of their nations wanted and demanded. In being loyal to their state and their nation, then, individuals were being loyal to themselves, or to what at least their leaders *thought* were *their* interests, *their* aspirations. The nation and its state became the means of attaining and defending these interests, these aspirations, and, as so often happens, the means became an end in itself.

Of course, there were differences in the nature of the national states and in their use of power. Of course, some national governments were stronger and penetrated the lives of their citizens more than others; and, of course, some were more totalitarian and authoritarian than others. Naturally, the effectiveness and influence of the various national governments waxed and waned depending on conditions—in war all tried to do more and became *de facto* if not *de jure* totalitarian, monolithic leviathans. Naturally, the loyalties of citizens to their states and nations fluctuated and were more or less intense depending on the circumstances—their hopes and fears in times of peace, in times of crisis. It was true that "rightist" groups were usually, but *not* always, more aggressively nationalist than were "leftist." And certainly the nationalism of the various peoples and of individuals differed at any one time and varied with time.

The differences and variations were many. Still, for most western men most of the time, nationalism continued to be the most powerful political emotion. During the twenty years between the two great twentieth-century wars, articulate intellectuals, dreaming of universal peace, denounced nationalism, and some of them, like some of the American expatriates in Paris during the 1920's, apparently felt little loyalty to any country. Everywhere during the 1920's and the 1930's many ordinary people gave little attention to national affairs and expressed national loyalty, if at all, chiefly on special occasions, as during the celebrations of national holidays. But the cosmopolitans and internationalists never constituted more than a small and ineffective minority; and in wartime ordinary people, their emotions aroused, generally became ardent patriots.

National feeling ran high and was widespread in France and England at the end of World War I. During the 1930's the socialism and pacificism of many Frenchmen appeared to be stronger than their nationalism, and some young Englishmen were taking an oath (the Oxford Pledge) never to fight for king and country. By 1940, nonetheless, some of these young Englishmen were risking and losing their lives for England, and from 1942–43 some valiant Frenchmen were resisting German domination to the point of torture and death. Just after the war of 1914–18 nationalism appeared to be weak in Germany; stung by defeat and unsure about their future, Germans were divided and confused. But German nationalism, aggravated by racialism, reached feverish intensity under the National Socialists, in power from 1933 on. In Italy at the end of the war, Italians, like the Germans of the time, often despaired and were confused, and only a small minority remained militantly nationalist; but from 1922 on through the long years of Mussolini's Fascist rule, nationalist rhetoric (however much or little it reflected the opinions of Italians) rose to high pitch. In Russia after 1917 the Communist leaders preached proletarian internationalism, but by the 1930's, under Stalin, they were trying to instill love of motherland, and from 1941 Russians and other nationalities in the Soviet Union fought heroically against Hitler's invading armies. In the Spain of the 1920's the regime of Miguel Primo de Rivera, a pale replica of Italian fascism, commanded little loyalty; a few years later the semimilitary Falangists led by Primo de Rivera's son, José Antonio, were belligerently nationalist, as were many of the adherents of Franco's successful rebellion (1936–38) against the republican government.[4] American nationalism continued to be as vigorous as ever during the whole period from 1919 to 1939. While it was more conservative in the 1920's than in the 1930's, it was belligerently anticommunist and dominantly isolationist (or, more accurately, noninterventionist) during the whole twenty years.

During World War II the threats, the fears, the suffering, and the hope for security accentuated nationalist feeling in Europe and the Americas. At the end of the war, however, and just after, internationalism became more widespread and popular than it had ever been, as nations, eager for peace, established the United Nations and as some leaders spoke of the universal rights of mankind. For a few years the awfulness of war and the dream of universal peace, as well as swift technological and economic change, made internationalism appear to be the way of the future. But then rivalry between the two great powers, the U.S.S.R. and the U.S.A., aggravated nationalism in both superstates until their leaders, in fear of each other and in ambition for dominance, brought their peoples to the brink of war, not once but several times. For a brief time the invention of a final, an absolute weapon, the nuclear bomb, made nationalism seem obsolete—that is, if men were to survive. Both states (and Britain, France, and China as well) made the bomb national, however, and nations continued to threaten each other until only continual miracles or a first strike could save any nation. Nationalism, not internationalism, was the path chosen not only by leaders, like De Gaulle, but also by their peoples. In every country at least an influential and vocal minority was strongly nationalist, continuing to look to the nation for assistance at home and protection against threats from abroad. And in general national patriots made their views prevail.

Immediately after their agonizing experiences during World War II, Frenchmen seemed as divided and as little interested in national loyalty and unity as they had been before the war. But when their General de Gaulle became President in 1959, he revivified French national feeling as he vigorously tried, with the solid backing of French patriots, to reassert France's civilizing mission and again make France a world power. Britain, like France, had declined as a world power and was losing its vast Empire. Even while in the United Kingdom itself Irishmen, Welshmen, and Scotsmen were manifesting national consciousness of their own, however, British national feeling remained tenacious and, in spite of the disclaimers and disbelief of some intellectuals, faith and hope in Britain were widespread and profound. In central Europe the Germans, beaten and divided, were much less aggressively nationalist than they had been. Yet remnants of the Nazis still clung to belief in Germany's, in the Nordic race's destiny, and there were signs of a new and emerging nationalism that would attempt once more to make Germany one of the powerful nations of the world.[5] Farther east in Europe and in southeastern Europe, in countries that the Soviet Union had conquered or controlled—Poland, Czechoslovakia, Bulgaria, and Romania—the appeal of nationalism proved stronger than communism, and the Soviet Union again and again had to use economic pressure and political force to keep the conquered peoples in line, that is, within the Soviet orbit if not faithful to Marxist communism. With one nation, Yugoslavia, the Soviet Union failed, and there the regime of Tito was national—national communist. The socialization or communization of a nation apparently meant the nationalization of socialism or communism.[6] "Now socialism, like the Mass," could be "chanted" in the native tongue.[7]

The so-called capitalist countries of the Americas were as nationalist. In the United States from World War II both liberal and conservative leaders—in different fashion, to be sure, but similarly—put national interests at home and abroad first. Spokesmen for the two major political parties, the Democratic and the Republican, vied with each other in patriotic exhortation, in what Tocqueville a century earlier had called Americans' "garrulous patriotism." The government of the United States assumed more and more responsibilities within the nation and energetically defended and expanded the interests of the nation outside, generally with the solid backing not only of professional patriots but also of the majority of the people. And from the 1940's in Latin America—in Argentina, for example—nationalism mounted steadily, partly in opposition to the Yankee "colossus" of the north and partly for indigenous reasons.[8]

Nationalism, then, did not decline as internationalists hoped or as had, seemingly on the basis of evidence, been predicted.[9] It remained the dominant political emotion in the western world. Everywhere in that world the national governments penetrated the lives of their citizens ever more persistently and pervasively. Few individuals could escape their influence or evade their power, and few tried. The nation-state had become the way through which men sought to provide for their present and their future. And the means, again, was becoming the end.

History, human experience, is a seamless fabric. Only for the purpose of clarity is the role of the state in nationalism being treated separately and first. By the twentieth century, it must be reiterated, everywhere in the West the nation-state had become the sovereign authority; it did not acknowledge an executive, a legislative, or a judicial authority above it, and it was superior to and generally master of all authorities within it. It had become the source and the wielder of legitimate and decisive power;

and through the national governments this power was used, manipulated, and constantly expanded to forward the interests of the nation as these were conceived by leaders who believed, rightly or wrongly, that they represented the will of the nation and could act in its name. This was true regardless of political ideology, whether, indeed, the governments were democratic, socialist, communist, fascist, or any combination thereof. As General de Gaulle asserted in 1950, the nation-states became the "only entities" that had "the right to give orders and the power to act." [10]

The national governments acted in response to demands of their citizens as these were interpreted (and formed) by leaders, or in reaction to protests of these citizens against governmental policies and actions. Both the demands and the protests were generally made within the framework of the nation; the appeal was nearly always to the national governments to do or to cease doing something in order that the "interests of the nation" might be best served.

During the nineteenth and the early part of the twentieth century, when liberalism was at its height in western Europe and the United States, it was liberal doctrine that government should be limited to protecting life, liberty, and property, that the policy of *laissez faire* should otherwise be followed on the theory of "the less government the better." Logically, then, the national governments would have had few responsibilities, being simply policemen who kept order, and would have had little power. In practice the doctrine was seldom if ever followed, except perhaps for brief periods in a few countries, like Britain and the United States; and even in Britain and the United States in the heyday of liberalism governments were always more than passive policemen as they aided business at home and forwarded national interests abroad.

Importuned by individuals and pressured by economic, political, and social groups seeking assistance and protection, the national governments steadily expanded their activities. Officials, high and low, continued well into the twentieth century to give lip service to the tenets of *laissez faire*. Actually, their governments not only assisted business in dozens of ways—by tariffs, subsidies, and the like—but, as described in chapters VI and VII, assumed a multitude of responsibilities, including provision for the social welfare of all citizens. In wartime, putting the national ahead of all other interests, they governed their people in every way thought necessary for victory. During the American Civil War the federal government, while still far from totalitarian, had conscripted men, levied heavy taxes, regulated trade and finance, controlled opinion, and freed slaves—thus confiscating slaveholders' property. During World Wars I and II all governments actively and directly controlled their citizens, intervened in all their activities, decided what they should know, in effect became almost totalitarian.

Laissez faire liberalism was short-lived, if indeed it was ever really tried, and certainly little slowed the growing power of national governments. On the contrary, the democratic tendencies of nineteenth- and twentieth-century liberalism contributed to the continued growth of nationalism. It was not through a church or an international organization that individuals obtained freedoms and the right to vote, but through their national governments.[11] As more and more people obtained freedoms and the vote, they could and did express opinions and make demands that their governments, their leaders and their bureaucracies, could not, did not ignore. As people participated they became ever more expectant, asked their governments to do more and more for them. The governments did do more and more, not only what citizens demanded but also what the governments themselves thought "good" for their peoples.

For most of the nineteenth century, even in the most liberal nations, only the upper and middle classes participated in national affairs, and it was chiefly members of the latter that were strongly nationalist. But, as has been pointed out, when members of all classes obtained the vote, became more literate, and voiced their demands, then they too became national-minded. This was true, as 1914 proves, even of socialist workers and their supporting intellectuals who had preached proletarian and class rather than national solidarity. Thus the interests of more and more individuals and groups came to be identified with the national interests[12] and, as might be expected, the national governments that represented and attempted to forward these interests became ever more omnipresent and omnipotent.

From the 1920's in Italy and the 1930's in Germany, authoritarian governments denied their citizens liberty and an effective voice in national affairs. But as the dictators Mussolini and Hitler built their totalitarian states, they did *not* deprive Italians and Germans of their sense of belonging. Rather, quite the opposite. Through shrewd use of symbols and propaganda, through threats and use of force, through what seemed to be appealing solicitude for their peoples, they aroused and intensified national feeling and thereby strengthened their states.[13] During World War II when, for purposes of war, the western democracies became authoritarian and totalitarian—"coordinated" activities and thinking and suspended liberties—they too constantly encouraged the feeling of belonging—"our country," "our enemies," "our war effort," "our boys," "our whole future."

Stressing hopes and fears, they too aroused national emotion as they called for complete involvement, a "total effort," by all citizens in all national endeavors. When the war was over, the national governments were expected to provide in some way for almost everyone. The national governments in consequence grew ever larger and more powerful. They had obtained the power the influential authors of *The Federalist* had advocated for the American Union of 1787–88: "to address" themselves immediately to the hopes and fears of individuals; and to attract to "their" support those passions that have "the strongest influence upon the human heart." And twentieth-century American leaders, as well as those of other nations, were never reluctant both to "address" and to "attract." [14]

When Louis XIV acted as if he were the state, he gave little heed to the people. When Mussolini and Hitler spoke at their huge rallies, they shouted in the name of the nation to the nation. In the democratic nations the leaders (with fewer absurdities) likewise spoke to the nation in the name of the nation. Democratic leaders and authoritarian dictators alike were leaders of peoples united by national loyalty in national states that these peoples believed to be theirs. The nation-states, then, became *the* means of realizing the present interests and fulfilling the ambitions and dreams of all citizens, for when the state and the nation were identified, the national governments were called upon to govern for all general and special interests.[15]

The German historian and political theorist Heinrich von Treitschke has been rightly judged an extreme, conservative nationalist. He believed the state to be a "moral community," whose ultimate purpose was "to help a nation develop a distinct character in and through it" by taking positive action to promote "the entire spiritual and material life of its people." [16] Not many nationalists of his or any time were as extreme or conservative as Treitschke, but he could be said to be a prophet, for the national governments did steadily expand their activities to promote the entire life of their nations.

As early as 1820 the great Chief Justice of the United States Supreme Court John Marshall (1755–1835) set down for his own nation a national doctrine that was to be followed everywhere in the West during the next century and a half. "The United States," he announced in the case of *Cohens* v. *Virginia,*

form, for many, and for most important purposes, a single nation. . . . In war, we are one people. In making peace, we are one people. In all commercial regulations, we are one and the same people . . . and the government which is alone capable of controlling and managing their interests in all these respects, is the government of the union. It is their government and in that character they have no other. America has chosen to be, in many respects, and to many purposes, a nation; and for all these purposes, her government is complete. . . . It can, then, in effecting these objects, legitimately control all individuals or governments within the American territory.[17]

Twentieth-century national governments moved far beyond Justice Marshall's still limited nineteenth-century conception of their responsibility and power. Whether democratic or authoritarian, they became supreme within their borders, more or less masters of their people and territory. In peacetime the power of democratic governments was limited by due process of law and by constitutional liberties that protected "rights" of dissenters and minorities. In wartime, however, these governments became as much masters of their citizens as were the authoritarian governments of their subjects in peace and in war. The German Nazi belief that the national welfare should take precedence over the individual (*Gemeinnutz geht vor Eigennutz*) was a belief shared by people in all nations, and Adolf Hitler but stated bluntly in *Mein Kampf* what became more or less the reality everywhere when he wrote, "It is clear that everything must be subordinated to the nation's interests; and in particular, we cannot permit any single State within the nation and the *Reich* (which represents the nation). . . ." [18]

The authoritarian governments, whether national socialist (fascist) or national communist, could not, of course, ever become as completely totalitarian as they tried to be.[19] But the German Nazi government came close to being as totalitarian as a government can be when it attempted to carry out Hitler's further pronouncement: "The German *Reich* as a state must embrace all Germans not only for the purpose of uniting and maintaining the most valuable racial elements of this nation but also for the purpose of raising the German nation gradually and safely to a dominating position." [20] Mussolini, with his usual ringing rhetoric, stated the most all-embracing conception of the state: "Outside it no human or spiritual values may exist, much less have any value. Thus understood, Fascism is totalitarian and the Fascist State, as a synthesis and a unit which includes all values, interprets, develops, and lends additional power to the whole life of a people." [21] Mussolini's Fascist state was never able to obtain the power (or be as powerful as) he and his henchmen so vociferously demanded. But the fascist states of Italy and Germany were national states perpetually organized for war, and as such they exercised, in the name of the nation, as great a power in peace and war as any states ever have. As one keen student observed of Mussolini's dictatorship, "All was geared to one goal: a strong state in the hands of a strong man, giving unity and purpose to the nation." [22]

While national governments exerted their authority in diverse ways, little in the life of their citizens escaped their attention. Through burgeoning police and military forces, through ever more pervasive security agencies, through expanding bureaucracies and court systems, and through all the multitude of regulatory departments, agencies, and commissions known to the twentieth century, they controlled their peoples more than even the most absolute of monarchs had ever done. Always, whether in peace or war, the purpose was to promote the national interests as the national officials conceived them.

To accomplish this end, the expenditures of the governments constantly mounted, to sums that would have seemed incredible to the rulers and ruled of any other time, and took an ever larger proportion of the gross national product (GNP) of their people. In 1959, a year of relative peace, the expenditures of the national government of the United Kingdom were about thirty per cent of the GNP, the expenditures of the governments of France and the United States were over twenty per cent, of Italy over eighteen per cent,[23] and through the 1960's these percentages generally increased.[24] The largest governmental expenditure was that of the United States, the richest nation, which in 1968 totaled nearly $200 billion out of a GNP of about $654 billion, and the United States that year spent nearly $80 billion on current national defense alone. But the expenditures of the American national government were higher only in amount, not in percentage, than those of most developed nations.

Through much of the nineteenth century and certainly through all of the twentieth so far, economists and reformers called for strong national governments to promote the national economies. Before 1914, at first George Friedrich List in Germany, and Paul Louis Cauwès in France, and later many others, like the American Herbert Croly in his *The Promise of American Life* (1909),[25] advocated vigorous governmental action to protect and develop the national economic life. After 1914, few reformers took a contrary view, and most thought such action both desirable and necessary. From a democratic point of view the more radical theorists, such as the Americans Henry George and Edward Bellamy and the Fabian socialists in Britain, and later from a fascist view Alfredo Rocco of Italy and Alfred Rosenberg of Germany, argued for national control of all economic activity and sometimes for nationalization (government ownership) of some or all economic enterprise. Radical socialists from Marx to Lenin (those who came to be called communist), though they in theory called for a world economic order, in practice demanded first the nationalization of all means of production through revolutions of the national proletariats against the national capitalistic bourgeoisies.

While the specific economic proposals of twentieth-century reformers and radicals and the political doctrines that accompanied them were often vehemently opposed, the nationalist aspect of their thinking found ready acceptance. In capitalist countries the national governments—that of the United States, for one—generally conceived assistance to and protection of economic enterprise to be a primary if not their major function. In the more or less socialist countries, like Sweden, the national governments took over large segments of the economies, and in the communist—like Russia —owned and operated all the major means of production. All the governments, whatever their ideology, stressed national economic production, for increased production meant increased wealth, and increased wealth brought not only higher levels of living for citizens but also greater national power both for defense and for further expansion.[26] From their origins national governments have sought to make their nations self-sufficient, believing that this would make them more independent and stronger if war came. Though no nations could be entirely self-sufficient, they continued to try to be, and in the twentieth century this required rigid control of many parts of the economy. Nazi Germany went far toward becoming an autarky with the prime purpose of preparedness for war.

Through much of the nineteenth century, governments first of all assisted and protected private business at home and abroad. But when, as pointed out, all individuals became part of the nation, the governments acted for all the groups that could bring pressure on them, including farmers and workingmen. In the twentieth century they continued, on a larger and larger scale, what they had begun to do from the 1880's: to provide (often, to be sure, in niggardly fashion) for the economic welfare of even the lower classes. During the worldwide depression beginning in 1929, even the most conservative governments not only subsidized business but "made" jobs and provided relief to the dependent.

The enlarging economic housekeeping functions of national governments required more funds, more surveillance, more controls. Assistance to and protection for national commerce, industry, labor, and agriculture meant higher tariffs and stricter trade quotas, more generous provision for corporations and banks and for currency and credit, more comprehensive regulation of wages, hours, and working conditions, greater control of farm production, and larger subsidies for many kinds of economic activities. Aid for the dependent—the unemployed, the old, the disabled, and the sick—meant expansion of the kind of social security Bismarck had initiated for German workers in the 1880's, until the national governments were expected to assure all citizens of minimum subsistence from the "cradle to the grave"—the national "welfare states." In communist states the governments naturally took full responsibility to provide for all "loyal" adherents, and by the 1930's no national government of any political variety could avoid (even if it had so desired) the provision of some kind of minimum care for most of its citizens. In assuming this responsibility, the national state took the place of the church of medieval and the monarchies of early modern times. Even if, in the minds of some of its citizens, it lacked divine sanction, it ruled in the name of the nation's omnipotent general will.

Always hard pressed for funds, the new national governments were more ingenious than the old monarchies had been as they taxed property, income, inheritances, and transactions (such as purchases) of many kinds. While citizens usually disliked the taxes, they wanted the services the taxes provided. They could not help, then, but become more and more nationally conscious, both when they were served and when they paid the taxes. The taxes mounted constantly, reached ever deeper into the pocketbooks of members of all classes, at times even those of the very rich whose ancestors may have escaped taxation and those of the very poor whose ancestors may not have had enough to pay taxes.

The only other acceptable way for governments to finance their activities was through borrowing—selling bonds and bills chiefly to their own people. These people, naturally, took deep interest in the stability of *their* government and had to be loyal to it. The national debts, mostly held by banks, trusts, insurance companies in which substantial citizens were much interested, and by citizens as individuals, became larger and larger until, by comparison with earlier times, they reached astronomical heights. By 1971 the national debt of the United States totaled nearly $400 billion and was still mounting.

In good times and bad the national governments assumed more responsibility for the well-being of their people. They provided for it in many ways, and thus bound the people to them and demanded their loyalty in return. It even became a duty of the governments to predict the weather so that citizens could take adequate precautions. More important, in all nations it became a responsibility of the governments to inquire into all the material aspects of life. All governments now took periodic censuses. When in April, 1970, the United States Census Bureau sent its forms to all "residents," it asked them to answer because "our progress as a nation depends today, as it has in the past, on meeting our national challenges. . . . Every question asked in the 1970 census has a national purpose. The Federal Government, our States, cities, schools, businesses, and citizen groups all use census figures to plan their work and to measure our country's problems and progress. The census is deeply rooted [from 1790] in America's heritage." The same purposes were behind all twentieth-century censuses of all nations.

The citizens most directly controlled by the national governments were those they directly employed in their civil and military services. In wartime in all nations and at all times in communist nations, most citizens were, in some sense, government employees.[27] But in all nations the number and percentage fully in the national civil service and in the armed forces substantially mounted over the years. Around 1960 western governments employed from two per cent (the United States) to eleven per cent (Sweden) of the working-age (15 to 64) populations, with France and Britain employing six to seven per cent. With exceptions, such as West Germany,[28] they had usually from one to three per cent of the same age group in their armies, navies, and air forces.[29] In 1969 the United States government had over 3 million civilian employees and nearly 3.3 million in its military forces.[30] Every nation-state, in addition, indirectly employed many more people in defense industries and through various kinds of subsidies, like those to local governments and to schools. No available statistics show just what percentage of the people in each noncommunist nation were dependent for their employment upon their national governments, and the percentage varied in peace and war and with the nation, but even in peacetime fifteen per cent would be a conservative estimate and twenty per cent in some cases certainly not too high.[31]

The national governments wielded, it is obvious, great influence over the ideas and the lives of their employees. They controlled the jobs—hired, promoted, and fired—and hence the economic livelihood of the employees, and generally they demanded their political loyalty as well. Few of the employees were antinational, and many were patriots who sincerely desired to serve. The present and future of all of them depended in large part upon the stability and expansion of their governments. The employees themselves, it is likely, as representatives of their governments and as individuals who were better educated than many of their fellow citizens, wielded influence disproportionate to their numbers in promoting loyalty to and increasing the power of the governments. In any case, the better they did their work the more effective the national governments were.

Even in the most democratic countries the governments with their numerous employees exercised considerable and at times major influence over public opinion; indeed, on decisive issues they often "created" it. Governmental agencies, particularly those having to do with foreign and military affairs, were chief sources of information (press handouts, background conferences) for newspapers, the radio, and television. When important officials—the presidents, prime ministers, and legislative leaders—spoke, their messages, whatever the media, immediately went out to the people. Because the agencies and officials were national, internationalist or antinationalist views were seldom voiced. In wartime in all nations and always in authoritarian nations, what the people read and heard was heavily censored and always, on the ground of national security, weighted to promote national loyalty and unity. By "good" public relations, governmental officials meant relations that not only buttressed their positions but also strengthened the government in power, and in their minds achievement of these goals was synonymous with the national interest. And the national interest, however interpreted, was always the end, and everything a government did was supposed to accomplish this end.

It was not only in twentieth-century Asia and Africa that the national governments were expected to be the agents of modernization; in the major western nations as well, they were called upon to lead the way to the technological wonders of the year 2001. The governments were supposed to support and did provide the chief support for much scientific research—in atomic energy, in orbiting satellites, in shots to the moon. They were asked to plan and promote and they did promote the many kinds of economic and social activities that represented progress—superhighways, schools, hospitals, and sewage systems.[32] Western peoples, likely more skilled and more ambitious than any people in history, expected their governments to provide leadership, funds, and the "know-how" that would make them ever more prosperous, ever more bountifully supplied with material goods, ever more fully protected against the hazards of life. Indeed, some western men came to expect, as their birthright, the eventual creation of a material utopia, a secular heaven. And some, especially the young, thought this utopia, this heaven could be attained as instantaneously as television provided its selective camera view of happenings in the global world. The national governments were not manned by gods or supermen, but their officials were expected to be, and sometimes they acted as if they were.

It was not only hope that drove the national governments but also fear, for the nations continued to be unequal, and in the international anarchy that still prevailed every nation seemed, at one time or another, to threaten another nation or nations. The stronger any one nation became, the more it was a potential or real threat to others. For its own security each nation believed it had to be as strong as possible, be as united as possible against every other nation that might possibly war against it. Each nation, then, had to make maximum use of its manpower and resources, build its military forces, seek alliances, and attempt through diplomacy to gain whatever advantages it could. And large nations—the United States, Russia, Britain, and France—which had the capability and the ambition to dominate, believed they had to have military bases abroad and, for reasons of defense, as far from the borders of their nation as possible.

Until the arising nationalisms of the mid-twentieth century in Asia and Africa prevented, France and Britain possessed huge colonial empires to serve their national interests and bolster their national power, and they still maintain far-flung outposts throughout the world. After World War II, the Soviet Union pushed westward in Europe, kept and incorporated Lithuania, Latvia, and Estonia, made Poland, Czechoslovakia, Hungary, Romania, and Bulgaria satellite nations, and strengthened its Siberian bases in eastern Asia with the object not only of national defense but also of national power. And the United States, with similar objectives, ringed the world from Japan to Spain with air and naval bases and became in the 1960's deeply involved in war in Indochina. Each and every effort for defense or expansion meant that the national states had to strengthen themselves and demand ever more loyalty and unity. But always the gauge of national power was relative as each nation took readings, fearing that others would get ahead, become dominant. The race for power was endless, and collisions almost inevitable.

No nation that valued its independence or coveted power could stop strengthening itself unless others did. The others never did. All the large nations and most of the small believed they had to build, build, build, especially in military might. When that committee of three British admirals in 1888 (see page 174) gave it as their view that the British navy should be larger than those "of any two powers," they were leading the way to an accelerating naval race that other great powers felt compelled to enter, a race that was one reason for the world war of 1914. Germans led by Admiral Tirpitz and their Navy League and Americans influenced by Admiral Mahan, President Theodore Roosevelt, and their patriotic societies and steel manufacturers responded and built great navies—indulging in the fantasy that in order *to be safe and to expand* the national interests they had to have a navy capable of meeting and defeating possible opponents wherever these interests might be challenged. As it was with navies, so it was with armies, the race being joined by Germany, France, Russia, and lesser nations. And so it was with the air forces from the 1930's and eventually, from 1945, with nuclear bombs and missiles. As leaders rattled nationalist swords and the race intensified, military expenditures steadily mounted, going up, for example, about nine per cent during the years 1965–68.[33] A cause was fear and a result accentuation of nationalism.

Every national diplomat and military officer felt bound to forward his nation's might, to pursue a firm foreign policy, be prepared for "any eventuality." If he did not, he was considered a traitor who had betrayed his country. Just as Palmerston, the astute nineteenth-century British Foreign Minister, thought every British minister ought to "consult the interests of the country in preference to every other consideration," [34] so the twentieth-century diplomats and officials of every nation thought the interests of their own country paramount. Most of their constituents would have had it no other way, for they too believed their welfare and safety depended upon their nation's power.

Fear of war and its possible consequences forced the nation-states to become ever more powerful, their citizens to favor or to acquiesce in every effort to increase their nation-states' strength. For modern war demanded utmost national effort if defeat was to be avoided and victory to be won.[35] The obvious result was a vicious spiral. As each nation confronted other nations, national loyalty and unity in each became imperative. But under the prevailing anarchic conditions of international politics each national effort compelled greater national efforts on the part of every possible opponent. These efforts eventually necessitated the total involvement and service of all good citizens. And this in turn——.

To obtain this involvement and service, the governments believed they had to "educate" their citizens to act willingly for their nations and, if this did not occur, to compel them to do so: to support their government, to pay taxes, to serve in the armed forces. Always there was fear, real or imagined. In modern times the British government used national fear of France and later of Germany, the French government fear of Britain and later of Germany, the German government fear of France and Britain and later of Russia, the American government fear of Germany and still later of the Soviet Union, and all for the same purpose: to build national unity and power. Because people believed defeat meant oppression, perhaps death, they generally did not object; in fact, they often urged their national governments to act ever more forcefully. And when wars occurred, these people usually became more nationally conscious, gave greater loyalty, became ever more nationalist as they increasingly feared, distrusted, and hated the people of other nations. Thus they not only acquiesced in but demanded the creation of omnipotent national governments. These governments in turn eagerly fostered national sentiment. But this only created greater fear on the part of the opponents, and on all sides nationalism intensified. When war brought frustration, disaster, or actual defeat for some nations, as for Italy and Germany in World War I, the nationalism reached a point that justifies the use of the word pathological.[36]

Established as a going institution, the national state possessed an accumulative momentum of its own, was self-perpetuating, self-aggrandizing. One activity led to another, one success to the likelihood of more, one failure to renewed effort. Power fed desire for power and more nationalism. A modern Catholic critic of nationalism, Don Luigi Sturzo, was not wrong when he observed, "Once a country or a people has succeeded in developing a consciousness of its own personality and affirming it in the struggles with which history has confronted it, there is no stopping."[37] And there was no stopping the growth of power of the nation-state. It could and did act and command, deal with and supersede other institutions.

Individuals, of course, continued to use their own means to achieve their own ends, just as had (see page 173) the democratic liberal leaders of the nineteenth and early twentieth centuries. Winston Churchill, Franklin Delano Roosevelt, Charles de Gaulle, and lesser leaders sought and won personal status and fame. Fascist *führers* and *duces,* Hitler and Mussolini and their henchmen, shouted and fought to achieve personal ambitions. But they were all at the same time, though in differing ways, staunch patriots. The ends of self-interest and national interest, of individual career and the national welfare, became for them much the same. And as it was for leaders, so it was for their followers.

The nationalizing of a people, Adolf Hitler wrote in his *Mein Kampf* (1923), was "first and foremost one of creating the social conditions as a foundation for . . . educating the individual. For only when a man has learned through education and schooling to know the cultural, economic, and above all the political greatness of his own Fatherland can he and will he gain that inner pride in being permitted to be a member of such a nation."[38] The western states, democratic and authoritarian, largely succeeded in educating their citizens not only through their schools but also through calls to service and penetration of their people's lives and thinking on many levels.[39] But the states could not have been so successful if, as has been demonstrated, the peoples had not themselves been forming nations and ready for nationalism.

While no adequate quantitative studies are available to prove that people *increasingly* identified themselves with their nation,[40] the evidence nevertheless is clear. Unlike medieval men, who tended to think of themselves as Christians, subjects of a king or lord, and members of a village community (see page 28), twentieth-century western men, with few exceptions, thought of themselves as citizens of a nation, as Englishmen, Germans, Frenchmen, Americans, Poles, or Swedes.[41] They spoke often of "my country" or "our country." They felt pride (on occasion humiliation) in their country's experiences. The nation's language was "their" language, the nation's leaders were "their" leaders, the nation's possessions were "their" possessions, the nation's enemies were "their" enemies, the nation's victories (or defeats) were "their" victories (or defeats), the nation's fortunes were "their" fortunes, the nation's way of life was "their" way. And they generally shared this sense of ownership regardless of their political party or views.

Not only did people identify with their nation; they also increasingly participated, or believed they did, in its affairs. Their participation, of course, contributed to their feeling of identification. Nearly everywhere in the western world after World War I there was universal suffrage (however meaningless in some cases), and women as well as men obtained the vote. No longer did individuals need to possess property in order to be "active citizens." Citizenship was bestowed, with rare exceptions, on all adults who were born in the nation or who became naturalized. Some, it is obvious, were more active and "more equal" than others, and only a few wielded much influence. But all, in theory, had the same right to belong and to participate.

The percentage of potential voters in proportion to the total population more than doubled in most nations during the first fifty years of the twentieth century, in the United States from sixteen per cent in 1909 to nearly forty per cent in 1950, in France from about thirty per cent to sixty-two per cent, in the United Kingdom from seventeen per cent to about sixty-eight per cent, in West Germany from about twenty-two per cent to sixty-eight per cent. And around 1960 in these major democratic countries the percentage of those of voting age who did vote was sixty-four per cent in the United States, ninety per cent in France, seventy-eight per cent in the United Kingdom, and about eighty-seven per cent in West Germany.[42]

Individuals could scarcely avoid becoming involved in their nation even had they so desired. Most of them had to pay taxes, and all except the very poor (and sometimes the very rich, who could afford the best legal advice) were subject to the national income tax—the one tax that made people directly aware of their national governments, at least on the days the tax was due. All of them had to fill out census and social security forms periodically, and some of them, to get government grants or to conform to various laws, several other reports as well. Many of them, as previously mentioned, worked directly or indirectly for their national governments and often had to swear oaths of loyalty to obtain and to keep jobs. Many of the young men were obliged to serve in the armed forces. A good many adults contributed to or belonged to national political parties. Many adults and children participated in and enjoyed celebrations on national holidays, and on patriotic occasions (as on June 14, Flag Day, in the United States) or at times of international crisis householders flew their country's flag.[43] Those citizens who traveled abroad had to carry national passports, and in many countries all inhabitants had to possess national identity cards.

Though democracy and nationalism are not necessarily connected, they did develop together. Participation in national affairs brought a sense of belonging. When people had a place (however inconsequential) in the national family, they were conscious of their nation and usually loyal to it.

Occasionally, an individual gave up his citizenship. Always, for one reason or another, there was a continuing stream of emigrants from one nation to another—from the 1920's particularly in and from Europe because of the persecution of minorities and the comparative lack of economic opportunity. But during the twentieth (as during the nineteenth) century, a western man was always born within a national culture, and that culture, while it did not form his inner character, did tend to determine some of his characteristics. He learned his "native tongue" and rarely, and then with difficulty, another. If an individual read, he read his national literature and newspapers, and both tended to become more and more national. Much of the time he was subjected to commercial advertising that had a patriotic slant consciously designed to enhance buying.[44] From the 1940's he and his children spent much time watching television programs produced by national companies. In some countries, such as France, these companies were owned by the national states, and their programs were devised to tell citizens what they ought to know and think. With occasional exceptions, neither private nor public stations produced programs that any patriot could think antinational. Certainly a citizen had

247

access to more national information, though whether as a result he was a better-informed citizen than his father had been was not so certain.[45]

When he went to school he was taught primarily the national language, the national literature, the national history,[46] that to be a good citizen was to be a loyal citizen ready to do his duty and die if need be for his country. Generally, he knew best (if he knew any) the music and the arts of his own country. Generally, he participated in or viewed (especially after the development of TV) national sports—in the United States baseball, football, and basketball—and these sports were professionally organized—in the United States into, say, the National and American baseball leagues. If he bought corporation stocks he might, in the United States, buy United States Steel, American Telephone and Telegraph, or National Cash Register.[47] In every nation, as he grew up, he acquired customs that were called national—gum chewing (American)—and even his fashions in marrying and dying became increasingly national.[48] Likewise, his churches, though less well attended, became more national in organization, in doctrine, and in ceremonial observances. While the Roman Catholic church and its pontiffs continued to maintain supranational principles "above national diversities," [49] the churches in Nazi Germany became direct instruments of the state. If, occasionally, members of such sects as the Quakers put conscience before country, priests, pastors, and their flocks everywhere usually supported country, and Christian churches flew national flags. Generally, the heroes—the Russian and American astronauts—were those of the nation, and the scapegoats were foreigners—depending upon the nation, Hitler, Stalin, Mao. Each people tended to see other peoples in invidious stereotypes. These shifted as the other people became friends or enemies, but at times during the twentieth century John Bull for Germans became "a caddish, insolent ogre-like figure"; Uncle Sam for Europeans "a desiccated, heartless Shylock"; and the German Michel for Frenchmen "a sly, double-crossing fool. . . ." [50] Even food came to be judged, not by its excellence, but by where and by whom the cooking was done. Every good patriot liked his own "steak and potatoes," his own "fish and chips" best.

After Hitler's racial madness,[51] race no longer seemed to hold as conspicuous a place in western nationalist doctrine as it had. But individuals still believed in the racial basis of nationality, though the racial myths were denounced because of their inhumanity and because scientific research had destroyed their credibility. Some Americans, like Governor George Wallace of Alabama, believed white, Anglo-Saxon Protestants (WASPS) the only true Americans. From the 1960's especially, a minority of black Americans, believing "black is beautiful," advocated black nationalism.[52] In tolerant Mexico, where the world's most expensive and finest anthropological museum is being built, the ideal type was a mestizo— "some kind of brown girl or guy."[53] And in the Britain of the 1960's, where racialism seemed surprising, the resentment against Asian and African immigrants of color was so strong that the government was forced to limit immigration severely.

Sometimes the beliefs about race were transferred to those about national character. In any case, individuals firmly continued to believe that (1) each nation had a unique character, (2) members of each nation were born with or acquired national characteristics stemming from the national character, and (3) every citizen of a nation should have these characteristics. In these beliefs they had considerable support from scholars (social psychologists, sociologists, anthropologists, historians) who, without being able to agree on what they meant by national character, were certain it existed.[54]

To possess the national characteristics was to be virtuous. To be virtuous, obviously, was to be both good and politic. Patriots everywhere brought pressure upon those who did not, at least outwardly, conform, insisting that their fellows be cast in national molds. Those who did not had "strange," "queer," "foreign" ways, were perverse, that is, "un" American or "un" German. They were subjected to admonition and then to vituperation and insult. While no authority could, as yet, completely control the inner life of every man, most individuals willingly or unwillingly did conform, and on those who did not the social pressures were heavy.

In light of the recent revolt of the young in much of the western world, it might easily be concluded that the old (those over thirty) were more susceptible to nationalist pressures than the young. But from the time of Young Italy up to the 1960's the young, as evidenced by the numerous "young" societies, leagues, groups, like the Falange in Spain, were as much nationalist as their elders—perhaps more so.[55] It may well be that they were much more enthusiastic (or dogmatic) in their desire to conform and to make others conform and, if the past is precedent, that some of the presently rebellious individuals will become more and more nationalist as their idealism is frustrated and they demand action.

All men, young, middle-aged, and old, had loyalties other than national. Some were troubled by conflicts in their loyalties,[56] and some seemed to have little loyalty of any variety. Nationalism could and did contain many other loyalties; only for a few men did it become all-inclusive or the unique and only loyalty, and for a few it had little or no appeal at all. In western societies the nationalism of individuals ranged along the entire spectrum from passionate one-hundred-percentism to an unemotional zero, and the generation gap did not seem to be significant—unless it has become so quite recently.

Within western nations individuals lived in and gave affection to their families. While the family was changing and marriage vows were not considered as sacred as they once had been, men and women continued to be devoted to each other and to their children. Much of the time this devotion was stronger than that given to the nation, though most families—often willingly but often, too, reluctantly—gave their sons when the nation called.

Nor did western men give up loyalty to their local communities, their villages, their regions. This loyalty was often of a different level, if not kind, than nationalism. Certainly it did not preclude and, in fact, it often enhanced men's nationalism. Still, a man could most easily comprehend and be fond of what he could see, feel, smell, what he was familiar with. The loyalty of a Mexican to his hacienda could not perhaps be duplicated elsewhere, but it was not unique, and everywhere when men went "home" they returned to the region of their birth and childhood. Nor was the old pride in cities gone as cities became more and more impersonal megalopolises. A Londoner, a Parisian, a Berliner, a New Yorker away from "home" soon let every stranger know where he was from.

There were, indeed, as many kinds and degrees of loyalty as there were men. These might at times, as did the loyalties of ethnic and language groups, contribute to nationalism, but often they were separate, and within nations they did, as was true in New York City, unite and divide peoples.[57] The ethnic and language loyalties could, as was the case of some minorities in the old Hapsburg Empire, run contrary to the prevailing and dominant loyalty in a country, and they often pointed to an embryo or developing nationalism, like that of the Welsh in the United Kingdom, the Catalans in Spain, and the blacks in the United States. Men gave their loyalty to their schools (none more so than Oxfordians and Harvardians), to their lodges (the Masonic), their social or service clubs (Rotarians), their occupational groups (printers), and their employers (even in 1970 when, in capitalist countries, these might be giant, impersonal multinational corporations).

Some workers and intellectuals, in peacetime if not in wartime, believed firmly in international class unity and, depending upon whether they were socialists or communists, advocated peaceful or violent revolution against their national governments. Over the world true believers often put their church and their religion first. While, say, most Roman Catholics or Muslims were able to reconcile the claims of their universal faith with the particular aspirations of their nation, a few members of all faiths continued to put their religion above the demands of their nation. Within every nation, too, there were always what sociologists call "substructure groups"—the *clochards* of Paris, the hippies epitomized by the American Woodstock Festival. Members of these groups paid little attention to nation.

Some individuals everywhere were either too stubborn or too weak, too ignorant or too wise, too self-interested or too involved in making a living, to give much more than lip service to their nation. A few, as an old adage had it, could be said to "hate the hand that fed them," and a good many were "casual patriots" who were national patriots only in time of crisis, if then.[58] That a good many thought of their own material or spiritual well-being before their love of country is evidenced by the fact that many emigrated. During the hundred years from 1812 to 1914, over 20 million people left the British islands, and of these nearly seventy per cent went to countries outside the British Empire.[59]

During the world wars of the twentieth century, most western men gave themselves to their nations more or less willingly. But during these great crises some businessmen, workers, and farmers were more interested in personal financial gain, in class solidarity and status, or in the claims of their religious faith than in national affairs; and a few individuals—conscientious objectors or members of messianic religious sects—were willing to stand against their national states for what they considered higher ideals.

In peacetime the "ordinary" citizen (whoever that unknown creature was) paid much less attention to his nation and to the shibboleths of nationalism. He probably did profess patriotism. He generally did, with some grumbling, pay national taxes. And many of his sons, willingly or unwillingly, gave two years of their lives to military training. But most of his time an "ordinary" man gave to the concerns of his personal life. Except on occasion, he ate, went to bed, worked, thought, dreamed without paying much heed to flags, oaths, the rhetoric of professional politicians and patriots, or, for that matter, to many, if any, of the most serious national problems. As child and as adult he was generally too absorbed by daily concerns to be intensively interested in the national affairs, unless major disaster threatened. As a child he had his play (if poor, his hunger), his little personal joys and tragedies within his family and his neighborhood. As an adult he had his job (or worry about getting or keeping one), his hobbies, his local social organizations, his family, his sex drives. These interests, usually though not always, seemed little related to his nation and its faraway government in the great capital. Set against the emotions and compulsions of nationalism, the folkways and mores established by the difficulties of individual survival and by family and neighborhood custom proved tenacious and oftentimes stronger.

Moreover, provincial particularism persisted within every nation. Even during the second half of the twentieth century in the United States, where jet transport was so swift, the people so mobile, and the mass media so pervasive, a Texan remained a special breed and a southerner was proud to assert he was a southerner. In Britain a Yorkshire man was different, in France a Breton retained customs that set him apart, in Germany a Bavarian knew he was not a Prussian and a Prussian not a Bavarian, and in the Soviet Union Ukrainians believed themselves to constitute a distinct nationality. Even in small nations, in Switzerland, the Netherlands, Sweden, provincial outlooks and customs persisted. Nowhere in the western world did provincialism disappear—in spite of all the forces working against it.

From the eighteenth-century Enlightenment and through the next two centuries, scattered intellectuals were attracted by and preached internationalism—economic and political co-operation among nations—and occasionally cosmopolitanism—world co-operation of people free from national limitations. During the same centuries adherents of old religions still believed in the universality and the primacy of their faiths.

From Kant onward, internationalists, many of whom were strong nationalists as well, pleaded for internationalism because it would bring peace, facilitate economic exchange and thus increase wealth, and enhance cultural exchange and thus enrich life. They therefore hoped the national state would be but a station on humanity's way from feudal to world organization of society.[60] The ardently patriotic Mazzini dreamed of this ultimate goal for mankind, telling the Italians, in his *Duties of Man*, that they were men before they were citizens.[61]

After World War I and the horrors of four years of slaughter, and even more after World War II with the rising fear of the awful destructiveness of the atomic bomb, some kind of international organization to keep the peace seemed to be imperative. Internationalists renewed their attacks on nationalism and their appeals for international collaboration. Though few of them thought it realistic to establish world order immediately, most of them advocated limitations on national sovereignty and national ambitions. Catholic leaders continued to see "exaggerated nationalism" as "idolatrous worship" outside the "order of things created and commanded by God." It brought, they stated, fear, disorder, and war. One of Pope John XXIII's (pope 1958–63) most powerful encyclicals, *Pacem in Terris* (April 10, 1963), called for "mutual collaboration" among peoples based on "the sentiment of universal fatherhood which the Lord has placed in our heart." [62]

If there were few world citizens of the twentieth-century world, that world did not lack international organizations, both governmental and private. In varying ways these all had goals and functions transcending national boundaries. Among their strongest supporters were "idealists" like Robert Schuman, who conceived of a Europe united by economic and then political ties, and Dag Hammarskjöld, who strove for international co-operation as he dreamed of universal peace. The great governmental international organizations, as is well known, all fundamentally represented not the world's people but sovereign nations. The League of Nations, the United Nations, the International Court of Justice (World Court), the United Nations Educational, Scientific and Cultural Organization, and the World Health Organization were all international but dependent upon the will and actions of the nations, which retained decisive control of their own affairs and took only such international action as seemed consistent with their interests. But these organizations gave evidence of long and sincere effort on the part of individuals for international co-operation. This was true as well of the numerous voluntary international organizations: for example, the Red Cross, which acted to alleviate human suffering in major world disasters, and the World Federalists, who, in well-meaning fashion but without much practical planning, proposed "world order under law." In almost every field of knowledge and endeavor, members of international organizations met periodically to discuss and carry on international collaboration in the scholarly disciplines, as in physics and history, in business, in labor, in religion.

Examples of the beneficent results of international co-operation were easy to find. The common electric light was a product of the Scotsman Watt, the Italian Volta, the Frenchman Ampère, the German Ohm, and the American Edison. As it was in science and technology, so it was in many fields. In medicine most of the major advances, in preventive measures against typhus and yellow fever, for example, were the result of informal and formal international collaboration. And so was the virtual elimination of both slavery and the "white" slave trade.

Ideas flowed across national lines even faster than organizations did, or for that matter faster than travelers, who in the millions in the 1960's visited abroad. But travel did not necessarily "broaden" those who traveled, nor did the international flow of ideas prevent national hostility. International co-operation in science and technology in, say, the development of atomic energy did not stop the use of the results in wars and threats of wars between nations. Nor did all the individual and organizational work and effort bring a diminution—not yet, at least—of nationalism. In general, western men and their leaders had little faith in international organizations, and these organizations little affected them in ways they found meaningful—were indeed "never visible on the map [and] scarcely real in men's awareness." [63]

Men were organized in, by, and for nations, and those who professed internationalism or cosmopolitanism continued to be castigated as men without "color, race, or sex." [64] Some kind of international organization and policing of men's affairs appeared to be essential if mankind were to survive, but most men placed their faith in their own nation. In 1969 American astronauts placed a plaque on the moon with the words "We came in peace for all mankind." But they carried the American flag.

As nationalism was reaching a peak during the last third of the twentieth century, it was possible that the classic movement of Hegelian dialectic was taking place, that an antithesis—international or world patriotism—was arising. If this was true, it could be partly because the homeland, the planet earth, and the human species itself, the family of mankind, were both threatened by the proliferation of the bomb, of people, and of pollution. [65] But, with exceptions and variations, nationalism had become for western men as dominant a religion as it had been for some Frenchmen during their eighteenth-century Revolution, [66] and the nations (the churches) even more organized and exclusive bodies of believers.

Analogies are never perfect and may mislead, but they can be useful. Nationalism does, as pointed out earlier, have many of the characteristics of religion, and these have become even more striking as the sentiment or faith has developed. It continues to demand devotion and sacrifice, to reward believers and punish unbelievers and disbelievers. It has, from the eighteenth century, further developed its particular rituals, ceremonies, and symbols. And within the nations more believers have generally accepted and performed their national (sacred) duties of citizenship.

When the faith of modern western men in the gods and miracles of ancient paganism and medieval Christianity declined, they likely had to have something else to believe in, some institutionalized authority and seemingly certain dogma to which they could turn, some community to which they could belong and in which they could find significance, and some bases for hope that the future would be better. But this is, at best, conjecture. They need not *necessarily* have turned to their nation and to nationalism. What is not conjecture is that they did so turn.

To his nation, his fatherland (*la patrie*), the twentieth-century nationalist (just like his nineteenth-century counterpart) gave devotion and love, and usually to its authorities or their offices honor and respect. God, nature, or historical circumstance, or all three, had, he could believe, given his nation a mission, a destiny that all good patriots should see fulfilled. His nation had a lay priesthood—the high national secular officials, the Churchills, De Gaulles, Franklin D. Roosevelts—who cared for and preached to citizens to inform them of their duties. His nation also had its regular (the *regula*) defenders of the faith—the soldiers, the Rommels, Montgomerys, MacArthurs, and their men who went out to battle against the forces of evil, the devilish enemy nations.

For its doctrine his nation had its constitution (holy book) and its laws (its moral commandments), which all citizens were obliged to obey.[67] His nation, further, had a body of approved beliefs and customs, ill-defined, it is true, but still to be venerated and protected because they were "American," "British," "French" and marks of membership in the nation. To violate the laws, to have other beliefs, to adopt other customs was to be "un," that is, a sinner or a heretic, and those guilty might be imprisoned, exiled, ostracized, or even executed.

In the practice of his faith the nationalist did the good and proper works of citizenship, took part in the accepted rituals and ceremonies, acted as a good member of the national community should. He paid his taxes (higher than medieval tithes) and served when called upon. He flew his country's flag, saluted it, hung it and folded it properly, and, like the Christian with the cross, never let it be defiled. He sang—with head bared —his national anthem. From childhood he took oaths (sacraments) saying he would be a good and faithful citizen (servant). He made pilgrimages to his capital and its famed buildings—its Westminster Abbey, its White House, its Kremlin—and to its historic spots and monuments—its Verdun, its Red Square, its Lincoln Memorial. His heroes (saints and martyrs) were buried in solemn national cemeteries (Arlington) as well as in impressive pantheons (Paris). He honored and gave a kind of immortality to these heroes by giving their names to cities, streets, parks, libraries, theaters, and airports.

If he were an ordinary soldier, his own name might be commemorated on a bronze plaque in a public place, and if he should die unknown, he would be honored by a tomb to unknown soldiers in which a perpetual flame burned. If he killed a fellow citizen at any time he was a criminal, but the more enemies of his nation he killed during war, the greater was his renown. If he performed heroic service far beyond the call of duty, he might receive the "highest honor" the nation could bestow, the Croix de Guerre, the Victoria Cross, the Iron Cross, the Congressional Medal of Honor.

Within any nation those who radically differed—the unbelievers or disbelievers—were considered, just as they had been during the French Revolution, disloyal and subversive. If they, like a Quisling of Norway in World War II, betrayed (or seemed to patriots to betray) their country by treacherously dealing with an enemy, they were traitors. Once the word heretic was perhaps the most opprobrious epithet that could be applied to a man, but now a traitor was the lowest and most despicable of criminals. And treason was punishable by death or, even worse, universal condemnation.

But perhaps an even sadder if not more awful fate could befall a man: to be "a man without a country." An influential clergyman and chaplain of the United States Senate, Edward Everett Hale (1822–1909), stirred Americans during their Civil War and later with his fictional tale of Philip Nolan, who, being such a man, had never wished to hear the name "the United States" again. After terrible suffering, Nolan lived to tell an American boy, with the words rattling in his throat, "for your country, boy, and for that flag, never dream a dream but of serving her as she bids you, though the service carry you through a thousand hells." [68] The moral of Nolan's story was generally known to twentieth-century patriots, and generally they agreed with it.

To serve one's nation, to cherish and love it became, for many, the greatest virtues. During the twentieth century no church, religion, or community of any kind could demand more. And by and large the demand was met.

For the most ardent patriots the nation had become the beginning and the end—the alpha and omega—of life as well as a way of life. In the rhetoric of the nineteenth-century American orator Daniel Webster, in his famous debate (1830) against Hayne, the nation provided "safety at home," "consideration and dignity abroad," "a copious fountain of national, social, personal happiness," and "high, exciting and gratifying prospects." Patriotism to the nation became, in Hegel's philosophical prose, "the sentiment of regarding the weal of the community as the substantial basis and final end." [69]

Because staunch twentieth-century patriots believed this, they could easily subordinate themselves to their nation. Their interests, economic, political, social, could be contained and usually were within the national. They could, as Theodore Roosevelt told Americans and Maurice Barrès the French, apply the national solution to every problem, resolve every question by reference to the national interest.[70] For them truth became not universal but national. The nation, and that for which it stood, was a fit object of worship. The slogans they generally used to guide and justify their actions were no longer the Christian Trinity or the French revolutionary "Liberty, Equality, Fraternity," but "My country, right or wrong," "America First," "Deutschland über Alles."

In the nineteenth century a liberal patriot, the poetic historian Michelet, held his country "above everything, as dogma and principle." [71] Before World War I the most enthusiastic nationalists—the Frenchman Charles Maurras, the Englishman L. J. Maxse, the German Heinrich Class, the leaders of patriotic societies and the professional patriots everywhere—had come to believe that everything should be integrated into the nation and made to serve its interests.[72] After World War II, though the language was at times more sophisticated, the appeals were not less passionate. "Ask not," a young and determined President of the United States, John F. Kennedy, told his fellow Americans in 1961, "what your country can do for you; ask what you can do for your country." [73]

Everywhere in the western world nationalists asked and demanded that all efforts of all citizens be directed toward the welfare, the defense, the power and the glory of their nation. They agreed with that previously quoted French schoolbook: "The Fatherland is the nation which you should love, honor and serve with all the energy and all the devotion of your soul." [74] "The true nationalist," as a French royalist newspaper, *Action Française,* declared, still placed "the fatherland above everything." [75]

Nationalism, like religion, then, gave individuals a feeling of exaltation through service and a promise of immortality through sacrifice. For the very young (age twenty) Daniel Webster, patriotism produced "an elevation of soul" that lifted a man "above the rank of ordinary men. . . . Above fear, above danger, he [the true patriot] feels that the last end which can happen to any man never comes too soon if he falls in defense of the laws and liberties of his country." [76] Although Webster's eloquence might have been unique in the young America, his views were not in western nations, young or old. "Yes," cried Gambetta of France to a friend after the defeat of 1870, "yes, everything for the country, we must love it absolutely and be ready to sacrifice everything for it. . . . I prize nothing more than that beautiful title: *Patriot before all else.*" [77] When men died in the name of country, asserted the ultranationalist Maurice Barrès during World War I, they could feel "a magnificent sweetness." [78] They could even, promised the Belgian Cardinal Mercier of World War I fame, by such an act of perfect love, "wipe out a whole life of sin." [79]

By commitment to their nation patriots could become part of a power that was felt to be "unshakably strong, external, glamorous" and participate "in its strength and glory." [80] For them the future of their nation, the earthly city, could become what the heavenly city was for the medieval Christian.[81]

Nations and nationalism in some respects thus gave modern men answers similar to those the medieval church and religion gave medieval Christians and that totem and totemism gave some primitive men. If nationalism did not demand belief in a supernatural God or inscrutable magic, it offered faith, hope, morality, and myths as well as "an organized and cooperative system . . . designed to secure for members of the community . . . the commodities of which they" had "need and . . . immunity from the perils and dangers to which man is exposed in his struggle with nature," [82] and with other men.

Within western nationalism major human emotions and attitudes were gathered and expressed: love and hate, hope and fear, aspiration and ambition. If it contained a Faustian arrogance and a "near-mystical sense of destiny," [83] nevertheless it was modern western man's way of organizing his communal life. And during the twentieth century it was becoming the way most men, those in Africa and Asia as well as those in Europe and the Americas, were organizing their communal lives.

Certainly not all western men were firm and constant believers. A growing number in western nations were apparently becoming "dis" or "un" believers. Nationalism had indeed become a secular religion and the contemporary faith that had greatest appeal for most people. Still, from the late 1960's, especially among the young, there was growing disregard for the nation-state, and among small radical minorities a burning hatred for its authority and a revolutionary hope to destroy the state itself. While the fervent believers were dominant and through persuasion or exercise of power attempted to re-educate or repress the "heretics," the heretics often could not be re-educated or always be repressed, and they continued to appear in increasing numbers and to protest with augmenting vehemence.

Nor, to repeat, did nationalism as a secular religion supersede or eliminate loyalties to other groups and ideals, to family, village, and region. And throughout the world there were individuals who believed in and worked for federations of nations, or, more rarely, a world state.

Nationalism was, then, neither a sentiment universally held nor necessarily the sentiment that would most unite and divide men in the future.

In spite of the breathless predictions about the world of the future of prophets who called themselves social scientists, one could not be certain what loyalty would be dominant in, say, the year 1984 or the year 2001. At the beginning of the last third of the twentieth century, the nation was the chief object of loyalty for more people than before. More people identified themselves with their nation and participated in its affairs. The nation-states, with their pervasive bureaucracies, had more power and more effectively penetrated the lives of their citizens and, with the mass media and a knowledge of psychological devices, could condition the thoughts of their citizens more than ever. Finally, the peoples themselves, with their constantly rising hopes and fears, expected their national governments to do more and more for them. The immediate outlook, therefore, was for more nationalism, or "nationalism as usual." [84] Though in human history the unpredictable is almost as likely as the predictable, it seemed probable, if not certain, that western peoples and especially the developing peoples of Asia and Africa would be national patriots.

IX

Developing Nationalism Among Developing Peoples: General Nature and Variations

The twentieth has been a century of war and revolution, of bright dream and shattering hate, of heroic valor and wretched squalor. The wars were in part produced by nationalism and they in turn accentuated it. The revolutions, principally, were for socialism and nationalism, and of the two "isms" the second proved the stronger. Regardless of political ideology, nationalism continued to be the principal sentiment of unity and division among peoples, and socialism where attempted was less international than national. Jawaharlal Nehru's remarks in 1950 about Asia could apply to Africa and, for that matter, the rest of the world in the twentieth century: "Any other force [such as communism], any other activity that may seek to function, must define itself in terms of . . . nationalism. No argument in any country of Asia is going to have weight if it goes counter to the nationalist spirit of the country. . . ." [1]

The invention of an ultimate weapon, the nuclear bomb, might have been and was expected to reduce nationalism and reduce or eliminate national conflicts by making international organization or a world state imperative. But the two superpowers, the United States and the U.S.S.R., that emerged from World War II and possessed the power to destroy the world were both supernations; and a third power, China, that arose to challenge them was a rejuvenated nation with a long, proud history and a fourth of the world's population. Fear of the bomb deterred the supernations from warring, though for how long no one could guess. The bomb did not deter nationalism or reduce its intensity and spread, despite the fact that if the great powers should conflict they might eliminate nations and produce one world—a cemetery. The world is one planet, but there has not been—not in the minds of men—one humanity. By the 1970's the planet and its humanity had been divided into nations as they had never been before. Instead of "one world" of people, there were around 140 nations, most of them with their own "independent" nation-states, and a good chance that still more would come into being.[2]

It was true that the old concept of the balance of power among nations had become obsolete as the scales now registered the terror of nations. It was true as well that the character, the places, and the actors of the conflicts had changed as the peoples of Asia and Africa forcibly entered the modern world created by Europeans and Americans, and as those who had been among the "wretched of the earth" aspired to and valiantly struggled for independent nationhood.

Perhaps the most striking political events of the twentieth-century world have been the emergence of new nations, like Indonesia and Nigeria, and the rejuvenation of old peoples, like the Chinese, who in revolution against European colonial powers became new nations.[3] Few "expectant" peoples in the so-called third world did not experience revolution of one kind or another. Whether democratic or authoritarian, populist, socialist, or communist, these revolutions, like those of Europe earlier, were primarily revolutions of leaders and peoples to throw off alien rule and influence in the brave hope of attaining freer, richer, happier lives. These leaders, these peoples wanted more than all else the right to govern —or it could be to misgovern—themselves, to constitute independent nations and states.

While old rulers were overthrown and new governments established, the revolutions often failed to achieve the better life the revolutionaries sought. To choose the national way of becoming "modern" was to choose the way that was old in Europe and that could, in contemporary times, be obsolete. Nevertheless, when a people wanted action to right old wrongs and realize their hopes, they protested, they demanded *their* own national governments, and they wanted these national governments to act in *their* interests and fulfill *their* ideals. Though their leaders, on occasion, spoke of the well-being of mankind, though the new nations if in trouble appealed to the United Nations, though the very existence of these nations was often in jeopardy, and though the loyalty of most inhabitants in many nations to the current national governments was often doubtful, no people gave up its nation-state once it was created, and no nation disappeared. On the contrary, as the new national governments established themselves and penetrated the lives of their peoples, as these peoples increasingly became conscious of their nations and developed more common ways of life than most of them had had, and as these peoples increasingly participated in national affairs, the more it appeared that most of the nations and their states would achieve some degree of permanence and that nationalism would become even more prevalent. To the question "What is the future of nationalism in Asia and Africa?" the likely answer is "more nationalism" —just as the answers in nineteenth- and twentieth-century Europe turned out to be "more nationalism" or, at a minimum, "nationalism as usual."

Was the nationalism of developing peoples in Asia and Africa different from that of the West? Much evidence is in, but it is too soon for firm answers.[4] In basic ways the nationalism seemed quite similar. Through it individuals obtained a sense of belonging and significance, a means of meeting personal wants and of group protection against enemies, and a vision of a hopeful future. Yet the new nationalisms arose in cultural contexts different from those of the West and usually came into being and evolved much later in time—much later, that is, in the developing cultures of the world. Further, Asia and Africa are such vast continents with so many different peoples that many varieties of groupings and loyalties have existed and do now exist, and still others, perhaps of different nature, will arise.

During the twentieth century in Asia and Africa, as during the nineteenth in Europe and the Americas, two aims were common and universal. Leaders of the peoples and many, though certainly not all, peoples—or even in many cases the majority of any people—aspired (1) to regeneration (or new societies) through their nations, and therefore (2) to self-determination, self-government, independence, and the establishment of nation-states. With exceptions they had, by throwing off imperial rule, achieved the second aim by the 1970's. Whether or not the regeneration will take place as leaders hope, and if it does the forms it will take, remains to be seen.

The general nature and variations of the growing nationalism among Asian and African peoples is the central theme of this chapter. As the theme is developed, similarities to and differences from western nationalism will appear, as will some of the differences among the nationalisms of the various peoples. The reader probably need not be warned that all interpretations and judgments on recent Asian and African phenomena, especially by western students, should be regarded as tentative if not suspect. The admonition of an African, "From experts on African questions, Deliver us, oh Lord," might well be applied to "experts" on Asian as well.[5]

The content of nationalism varies with the locale, with the people, and with time. Though the genus nationalism is easily identifiable in Asia and Africa, there are several different species, some with a broader nature than others and some with a more unique character. Loyalty to Africa and Africans is called African nationalism, but in addition an African, say a Kenyan, may be loyal to his particular state, Kenya, and be called a Kenyan nationalist, and may also be loyal to his tribe, the Kikuyu, in a way ("tribalism") that is scarcely if at all distinguishable from nationalism.[6] In North Africa, Arabs may be loyal to a unique nation—Egypt—and be called Egyptian nationalists; to the more comprehensive if less definite idea of Arabism and their fellow Arabs, and be called Arab nationalists; and also to a still larger but more tenuous concept of Islamic unity to which non-Arab Muslim people in Pakistan and Indonesia may also be loyal, and be called Muslim (or Islamic) nationalists. If there has been African, Arab, and Islamic nationalism, on the other hand there has been little or no comparable devotion to Asia as a whole. Perhaps this is true because particular Asian peoples, more often than African, have old and deep cultural traditions, because China and likewise India are so large, and because Japan, modernizing comparatively early, itself became a dominating imperialist nation in eastern Asia from about 1915. But, in any case, there has been little Pan-Asian sentiment and little sentiment for Asian unity.

There have been, however, dozens of variations of nationalism in both Asia and Africa. To mention only some of the most obvious, not all Africans are black, but nationalists within the new African states and in Africa as a whole south of the Sahara (except for the Afrikaners)[7] have had a common bond in their blackness and in their opposition to white alien rule. In Asia color as such, be it brown or yellow, does not seem to have played as large a role, though antagonism toward white rule and racial dominance has been no less vigorous. In eastern Asia, particularly in Korea, nationalism arose in part out of resentment against the Japanese, who were of the same color as the peoples they attempted to dominate.[8]

For an ardent Arab nationalist—to repeat a portion of Abd al-Latif Sharara's statement of 1957—it was "not necessary for a nation to have one state or fatherland or [even] to be composed of one people," but it had to have "its own language, its own history, its own ideals, its own shared aspirations. . . ."[9] Until 1917 (or later) the Jews, who were "long on history and short in geography," had no land or state they could call their own. Like the Arabs, however, they did share a religion with well-defined and deep traditions, and they were, in common with many Arabs in modern times, victims of western religious and racial prejudices. And so, from the 1890's, Zionist Jews, in the European tradition, demanded their own particular national land and state.[10] In most cases, so, increasingly, did leaders and to an extent the peoples of Asia and Africa everywhere. In Africa and in certain instances in Asia, though, the "land" was the colonial territory, the boundaries of which had been set more or less arbitrarily by the European imperial powers, and it usually contained the *patries* (or native places) of several different tribes or ethnic groups.[11]

Likely the most special cases of new nationalism were those of China and Japan. China's history was long; in many senses it was not a new nation but an old one, or, rather, a "universal empire" and culture with a traditional Confucianist pride in Chinese superiority and with persistent hostility to foreign ("barbarian") rule. Roughly from the beginning of the twentieth century, it underwent the transformation (or resurgence) that is symbolized in the May Fourth (1919) Movement[12] for modernizing reforms but that was directed specifically against Japanese aggression. The transformation culminated in a major communist (or Maoist) revolution and the creation of the People's Republic of China in 1949.[13] From a "universal" and weak empire China thus became a huge and powerful, though still unwieldy, nation. However, whether the Maoist government's goal was to return to empire, this time as the center of a communist international state, was not certain. In any case, Chinese nationalism was communist and had, in its own way, international aspirations.

In Japan, with its semireligious Shintoism—reverence (*kokutai*) for the emperor and the land and all that this signified—nationalism had its own peculiar character. An island kingdom, isolated for hundreds of years and never (until 1945) occupied by a foreign power as were most Asian and African countries, it contained a "remarkably homogeneous people." For these and other reasons Japanese nationalism manifested itself early, at least from 1868 and the Meiji restoration. This nationalism became aggressively and progressively right-wing and imperialist from 1895, and culminated not only in swift development at home but also in vast imperialist expansion until Japan's defeat in 1945.[14] Since 1945 the nature of Japanese nationalism, except that it is recovering, has been ambivalent; but with Japan's booming economy and need for markets, some variety (likely right-wing) of resurgence is almost certain.

The differences among the Asian and African nationalisms, however, are not as striking as the similarities. As the fine Africanist Thomas Hodgkin has pointed out, much of the language and many of the ideas of African nationalism, and I should add of Asian as well, are drawn from the "common stock of the western democratic traditions" and can be traced back to the French and American Revolutions and to the later Russian as well: the desire for national union and independence, the anti-imperialism, the stress on freedom as a birthright, the animosity toward religion and tribalism, the beliefs in science, the democratic right to vote, progress, and socialism. Usually, too, there has been romantic idealization of the past and of the popular will in the manner of Rousseau.[15] This does not necessarily mean that Asians and Africans took their ideas directly from Rousseau or from Marx, for it may well be, as Hodgkin has also remarked, "that a certain kind of historical situation, certain fundamental human problems to be resolved, tend to stimulate a particular way of thinking about the situation and the problems," [16] that, in short, Asian and African peoples were reacting in fundamental ways as Europeans had earlier in response to similar situations.

Nearly always present, indeed, were elements common to nationalism everywhere, the elements, for example, stressed in 1902 by Liang Ch'ich'ao, the prominent Chinese publicist who was becoming one of the truly radical leaders of China. "What does nationalism mean?" he asked in an essay entitled "The Renovation of the People." He answered as a European intellectual of his time might have.

It is that in all places people of the same race, the same language, the same religion, and the same customs regard each other as brothers and work for independence and self-government, and organize a more perfect government to work for the public welfare and to oppose the infringement of other races.[17]

Liang's definition did not, to be sure, include all the varied facets of nationalism. To it would certainly have to be added the romantic sentiment of "feeling," which Arab and some African nationalists, like many earlier European and especially German nationalists, have stressed. Only when individuals are conscious of what they have in common and, so a familiar argument has been, *feel* they are members of the group, and in consequence share its goals, does their nationalism really manifest itself. Ndabaningi Sithole, an influential African leader from Rhodesia, defined African nationalism specifically as a special "political feeling [principally] manifesting itself against European rule in favour of African rule." [18] But the feeling of unity inspired by antagonism to foreign rule has been common to nationalism everywhere.

It can be argued that nationalist feeling is old in parts of Asia and to a lesser extent in Africa. It can also be argued that nationalism is new on the two vast continents, a sentiment that arose during the last century and became particularly strong during the last thirty years. Both arguments are valid, or, rather, can be supported with evidence. Much depends, naturally, on what is considered to be the content of nationalism. Certainly sentiments akin to nationalism are to be found much before the last century: love of place of birth, loyalty to a government, dislike of other peoples. Certainly common and peculiar cultures, languages, and customs had developed within groups of people, and these could and would later be called national. But widespread consciousness of membership in a nation, loyalty to a nation and to fellow nationals, distrust of other nations, and *the* desire for self-government and for independent nation-states are (or seem to be) relatively new.

Only during the last hundred years, and especially during the last generation, did leaders of peoples and to an increasing degree individuals among these peoples, particularly those with some education, begin to identify themselves as members of nations and to demand a government that, freed from alien control, would govern in their interests. During the last thirty or even twenty years people have, in addition, increasingly demanded the right to participate in national affairs and have in fact increasingly participated. But at the same time it cannot be denied that roots of nationalist sentiment were deeply imbedded among peoples of the two continents.

China is old, the centralized imperial system having been established by the Chou dynasty during the late third century B.C. Moreover, Chinese culture, though it has undergone many changes, including those recently instigated by the Maoist revolution and government, is the oldest continuous culture in history. Persia (modern Iran) and a Persian sense of identity are old. As early as the tenth century the Persian poet Firdousi declared, "If there is no Iran then let me not be," [19] and Persia as a political entity, a semi-independent or independent state, has at least a thousand years of history—or, if Cyrus, the Emperor, is considered the "founding father," about twenty-five hundred years! Japan is old; for all the swift modernization of Japanese life, the Japanese government and Japanese ways of living and thinking can be traced back—even without myth-making—to eighth-century Nara. Israel is new, but the Jewish faith and ethnic customs are as ancient as the Bible's Old Testament—in their religious beliefs no people have been more constant than the Jews. Arab nationalism is new, but the Arabs' religion, Islam, which so shapes their nationalism, dates from the seventh century, and the Arabic language is even older.

Those western or eastern students, then, who breathlessly tend to think of everything in terms of the specious present and doubtful future only reveal their ignorance. There is always, it is well known, danger in seeking antecedents for ideas, finding them, and describing them as if they were the same as the contemporary ideas. But there is also danger in refusing to see that sentiments such as nationalism have roots in Asian and African experience, that natonalism, for example, is not just a "European invention" [20] imitated by other peoples.

Of course, no exact dates can be set for the beginning of modern nationalism among those Asian and African peoples who now constitute nations or have established nation-states. For each people the time during which nationalism may be said to be beginning and developing is different. Further, it is impossible to determine the precise moments that local and sporadic resistance movements of economic, religious, or whatever nature became general and national protests against alien rule, as well as national affirmations of desire for social reform. In India the nationalist awakening could be said to start with the mutinies and revolts of 1857–58 (the so-called Sepoy) and to reach one climax in 1947 when India gained its independence.[21] But the rebellions of 1857, though they embittered relations between Indians and the British for nearly a century, were of local and religious nature, and it is chiefly in retrospect that they have nationalist significance. On the other hand, the achievement of independence in 1947 did not mean that nationalist struggles were over, that India was truly unified, or that its citizens generally identified their fortunes with those of the national government in New Delhi. And so it was with the nationalisms of other developing countries. In fact, argument over the *exact* time nationalism arose in any country is probably futile and unproductive.

Insofar as it is possible to generalize, it may be said that clearly identifiable stirrings of modern nationalist sentiment occurred in both Asia and Africa around the middle of the nineteenth century. Modern Jewish nationalist feeling possibly manifested itself at the time of the Damascus affair in 1840 when "Israelites of different nations took council and action together for general defense against common peril." [22] But more likely the origins of Zionism were both older—going back to early biblical times—and more recent—appearing after the senseless Russian pogroms of the early 1880's and with the writings of Theodor Herzl (1860–1904) advocating a Jewish homeland and state about the time of the Dreyfus affair (1894) in France.[23] Chinese nationalist opinion could be said to arise during the Opium War (1839–40) when Chinese hostility toward Britain became intense.[24] But modern Chinese nationalism really emerged around the turn of the century, after China's defeat (1895) by Japan, with the leadership of Sun Yat-sen and the revolution of 1911, and with the May Fourth Movement. Quite probably it reached a high point with the establishment of the People's Republic in 1949; still, China's history is so rich and varied that one cannot be sure of its direction—whether indeed it will become a nation or a conglomerate empire. Arab nationalism emerged during the latter part of the nineteenth century and became vigorous during the first decades of the twentieth with the meeting of the first Arab Congress in 1913 and the revolt of 1916, but as "an ideology and as a factor in Middle Eastern politics [it] is a recent development." [25] The nationalisms of most Middle Eastern and North African peoples likewise became significant in the twentieth century, and especially after World War II.[26] The first signs of modern African nationalism south of the Sahara are less easy to identify; from the mid-nineteenth century, however, the West Indian Edward Wilmot Blyden (1832–1912) was in West Africa (Sierra Leone, Lagos, Liberia) and laid foundations on which later African nationalists, chiefly in the twentieth century, attempted to build both African unity and African nations.[27] The nationalism of specific peoples in Africa—the Nigerians, the Kenyans, the Congolese (if any real nationalism exists among them)—arose long after Blyden's valiant efforts, though again unique events, such as a gathering of chiefs in Ghana in 1852, foreshadowed later nationalist activity.[28] In summary, with the exception of the Japanese, most of the modern Asian and African nationalisms of any magnitude manifested themselves chiefly in the twentieth century.

It is neither desirable nor necessary to enter further into the arguments over when nationalism arose. But it is desirable to point out that events in Europe and the Americas, as well as in Asia and Africa, considerably determined what happened. The ideas of the eighteenth-century American and French Revolutions, as is well known, spread throughout the world.[29] Had they not been formulated and had they not become known to educated men everywhere, the course of events and the nature of loyalties everywhere would have been far different. The American Revolution set an example of self-determination, and the first Declaration of Rights of the French spoke the rights of man and citizen. Both the self-determination and the rights came to have almost universal appeal. The vast advances in Europe brought about by the scientific and industrial revolutions gave Europeans the power to dominate the world and impose their rule and ideas on other peoples, and it was in large part in reaction to European imperialism that nationalism arose elsewhere.

The Japanese victory over Russia in 1905 not only stunned Europeans but also revealed that European nations were not omnipotent and led to the belief that European domination might be ended. Lord Curzon, a great British empire builder, remarked, "The reverberations of that victory have gone like a thunderbolt through the whispering galleries of the East." [30] He was right, and the thunder, in this case, was succeeded by lightning.

The First World War further informed leaders and peoples outside Europe about the weaknesses and idiocies of their imperialist rulers, while it enlightened them about the sources of Europe's power—science and technology. The Russian Revolution of 1917 provided yet more hope and goals for the downtrodden of the earth as it apparently proved that the impossible in economic and social action was possible. For young, idealistic nationalists like Nehru in India, that revolution and its promises were "a bright and heartening phenomenon in a dark and dismal world," and sent "forth a message of hope." [31] The League of Nations Covenant of 1919 declared that the development of peoples was a "sacred trust of civilization" and, with its mandate system, seemed to promise them eventual self-government. President Wilson's Fourteen Points had already announced a "principle of justice to all peoples and nationalities, and their right to live on equal terms of liberty and safety with one another whether they be strong or weak," while the British Balfour Declaration had promised "a national home for the Jewish people," a promise that seemed a precedent to other peoples as well.

Through the 1920's and 1930's African and Asian students in Britain, France, and America learned about democracy and nationalism at the Sorbonne, the London School of Economics, and Lincoln and other universities in the United States, where liberal and socialist professors (Harold Laski, among others) also taught them the language of protest and expectancy. World War II, even more than World War I, revealed the strengths and deficiencies, the vices and the vulnerability of white western men; and African and Asian soldiers went home to expect and to advocate social reform and national independence. At the end of the war, the United Nations Charter recognized the principle that the "interests of the inhabitants" of territories "not self-governing" were "paramount," and announced that members of the U.N. controlling these territories would "develop self-government, to take due account of the political aspirations of the peoples, and to assist them in the progressive development of their free political institutions. . . ."

The examples and the pronouncements of the West and the western weaknesses revealed by war, then, influenced Asians and Africans to cast off the "spell" [32] of European domination, to become nationalist, and to demand peaceful or violent action to achieve independent nationhood.

Before 1783, as the following table[33] shows, only ten countries or states in Asia and Africa could be said to be "independent," that is, to have their own political state. From 1783 through 1945 ten more achieved this status. But from 1945 through 1968 fifty-four became, at least officially, independent states, and in other parts of the world nine more. The question rightly could be raised whether all of these states, new and old, can be called nations, but in nearly all cases the people's leaders at least used the language of nationalism.

WHEN PRESENT ASIAN, AFRICAN, AND A FEW OTHER COUNTRIES BECAME INDEPENDENT

Independent Before 1783
(Alphabetical Listing)

East and South Asia
    Bhutan
    China (People's Republic, 1949, and Taiwan, 1949)
    Japan
    Nepal
    Thailand

Middle East and Africa
    Afghanistan
    Ethiopia
    Iran
    Muscat and Oman
    Turkey (as Ottoman Empire, but as Republic of Turkey, 1923)

Independent 1783–1945

East and South Asia		
Korea	1945	(two Koreas, 1950)
Mongolia	1921	(if independent)
Middle East and North Africa		
Egypt	1922, 1953	(United Arab Republic, 1958)
Iraq	1932	
Lebanon	1943	
Saudi Arabia	1925	
Syria	1943	
Yemen	1918	
Tropical and Southern Africa		
Liberia	1847	
South Africa	1910	

Developing Nationalism Among Developing Peoples

Independent 1946–1968

East and South Asia

Burma	1948	Maldive Islands	1965	
Cambodia	1954	Pakistan	1947	
Ceylon	1947	Philippines	1946	
India	1947	Singapore	1965	
Indonesia	1949	Vietnam	1954	(two Vietnams
Laos	1954			from 1954)
Malaysia	1957			

Middle East and North Africa

Algeria	1962	Morocco	1956
Israel	1948	Somalia	1960
Jordan	1946	Southern Yemen	1967
Kuwait	1961	Sudan	1956
Libya	1951	Tunisia	1956
Mauritania	1960		

Tropical and Southern Africa

Botswana	1966	Lesotho	1966	
Burundi	1962	Madagascar	1960	
Cameroon	1960	Malawi	1964	
Central African		Mali	1960	
Republic	1960	Niger	1960	
Chad	1960	Nigeria	1960	
Congo (Brazzaville)	1960	Rhodesia	1965	
Congo (Kinshasa)	1960	Rwanda	1962	
Dahomey	1960	Senegal	1960	
Equatorial Guinea	1968	Sierra Leone	1961	
Gabon	1960	Swaziland	1968	
Gambia	1965	Tanzania	1961	(Tanganyika and Zanzibar)
Ghana	1957	Togo	1960	
Guinea	1958	Uganda	1962	
Ivory Coast	1960	Upper Volta	1960	
Kenya	1963	Zambia	1964	

Other

Mediterranean

Cyprus	1960
Malta	1964

Oceania and Indian Ocean

Mauritius	1968
Nauru	1968
Western Samoa	1962

Other (Cont.)
    Middle and South America
        Barbados   1966
        Guyana   1966
        Jamaica   1962
        Trinidad and
           Tobago   1962

The creation of new nation-states is not over. How many more may be expected cannot be known, but it is possible—indeed, probable—that in Africa, for example, Angola and Mozambique, now Portuguese colonies, will someday be independent nations and that South Africa and Rhodesia will no longer be "white" republics but black African. It is as likely that certain existing Asian and African states, perhaps Jordan and Iraq in the Middle East, Laos and Cambodia in Southeast Asia, and the Congos and Botswana in central and southern Africa, will be merged with other states, broken up, or eliminated as political entities.

Nothing is certain about the future of any nation. Certainly no nation-state will last forever. On the other hand, just as could happen in Europe with the Ukrainians or Scots, it may be that some peoples—the Palestinians in Palestine, the Ibo in Nigeria, the Ashanti in Ghana, and the Luo in Kenya—will someday be self-governing and independent.[34] It is further possible that nations—the Arab and the East African, for instance—will combine through federation and form larger political entities. Or it may be that war will eliminate most or all nations everywhere.

X

How the Developing Nationalisms Developed

Why did Asian and African peoples become nationalist and form the nation-states they have? [1] Some of the larger reasons have been mentioned in the previous chapter. But to understand what happened requires more detailed analysis. Generally the peoples, or more accurately their leaders, found in nationalism the way to protest against their colonial masters and the vehicle of hope for better lives, that is, the way to achieve the modernization they thought would accomplish their goals. Yet no monolithic or simple explanations will do.

In some cases, as pointed out earlier, the roots of a people were deep, as in China, Japan, and Persia, and the people had long shared a common cultural tradition or a religion—Confucianism, Shintoism, Islam. Even a common culture, however, did not ordinarily produce nationalist fruit, in the form of nation-states at least, until after European peoples had formed nations and nation-states, expanded, dominated Asia and Africa, and set up colonial administrations with arbitrary boundaries. Then European nations, comparatively powerful and affluent, became models. For many of those becoming nationalists, Britain or France, and to a lesser extent Germany or the United States, became the model, and for some, such as Liang Ch'i-ch'ao of China, Italy and its *Risorgimento*. [2]

European power and mastery meant inferiority and inequality for the ruled peoples. The latter's grievances accumulated. They learned from European experience and values as well as from, in some cases, their own traditions that their treatment was wrong and unjust, *and* to expect that the future would be happier if and when they were their own masters. That to imitate western nations would not necessarily bring a better life some were aware, and these wanted to keep their own spiritual traditions but at the same time to adopt western technology and win the advantages of western material progress. Nevertheless, the western examples, which the elite came to know through their European-centered education and ordinary people through seeing westerners in Asia and Africa, seemed to hold great promise. Westerners had, or seemed by comparison to have, riches, power, and freedom. Why should not Asians and Africans?

Asian and African leaders, for personal as well as social reasons, slowly came to demand independence. They protested ever more vigorously, through the many newspapers they established and the many varieties of voluntary societies and political parties they organized, and they led local and then national demonstrations and movements. National movements stimulated more nationalist feeling, more movements, more protests. The inevitable violent incidents led to more violent incidents, sharpened hates and hopes. Confused and hurt but hopeful and determined, colonial peoples followed their leaders in protests, revolts, and revolutions (nonviolent and violent), always dreaming of a promised land where, if they might be poor, they were nevertheless independent, where they would not be considered inferior and subjected to daily insults, where they too would have the benefits of science and technology, and the privileges, rights, and dignity of citizens.

This is not the place to recount the history of European imperialism[3] except in relation to the rise of nationalism in the developing world. The "center" of the world, if there was ever a center, was not in Europe until modern times. But from the sixteenth century, and especially from the nineteenth century, the political and economic power of western European nations, in particular of France and Britain, enabled them to dominate in varying degrees much of Asia and Africa and to impose, in one way or another, their values and ways of life upon the peoples who lived there. Asian and African peoples were increasingly drawn into the culture and politics of the western world, but always in subordinate ways, and the peoples and the lands became pawns of European power politics, with their welfare fundamentally and ultimately subject to the demands of the imperial powers in their competitive race for "gold, glory," and the spreading of the gospel.[4]

The reasons for European imperialism are many and much debated. It is true that individual Europeans sought profit, power, status, and sometimes won all three. It is also true that European imperialism was itself a manifestation of nationalism as western nations sought, in their competition for power, strategic bases and defensive outposts, raw materials and trade, cheap manpower and commercial advantages—pursued their national interests. Whatever the reasons, when Europeans went to Asia and

Africa, they believed themselves and their civilization superior and the "natives" to be of lesser breeds and inferior civilizations. In brief, Europeans imposed their rule, and out of greed and ignorance were generally arrogant. The "natives" (the word itself took on a pejorative meaning) were at first, in the main, submissive, acquiescent, and even co-operative. But, with western examples always before them, they began to resent their masters' rule. As they did, their slowly realized need for self-assertion and identity was fed by nagging bitter memories of previous humiliations. The result was "an explosive mixture of frustration and expectancy." [5]

Western imperialists imposed their rule by treaties that the subjected peoples sometimes did not understand, and by force that required little or no understanding. They often deposed traditional rulers, as in India and Africa, or, nearly everywhere, subordinated them to imperial officials. They set up colonial administrations and bureaucracies manned in key positions by these officials. They arbitrarily established boundaries for their colonies or administrative districts and sometimes split up peoples, like the Bakongo, Ewe, Masai, and Yoruba in central, western, and eastern Africa, or Indians in Bengal.[6] They took the "natives'" land, as in Kenya,[7] and exploited a colony's resources—the ivory and rubber of the Congo[8] or the oil of Arabia. They often taxed their colonial subjects not only to make them pay for imperial rule but also to force them into the labor market. The imperialists claimed and obtained special judicial and tax privileges for themselves, such as extraterritorial rights in Egypt and elsewhere,[9] and they maintained their own superior schools and exclusive clubs. They pre-empted the best and highest-paying public and private positions everywhere. They employed "natives" and only "natives" as servants. They generally controlled the press and other means of communication, and prohibited political assemblies if these seemed to threaten their rule. They jailed "agitators" and used their police and military to "keep order."

At the same time most of them believed in and preached the superiority of their own ways of life, their Christian religion, and their western customs. They looked down on the "benighted" native people (and let the "natives" know it), and in ignorance, in vanity, and usually with good intentions tried to make the people over in their image. At times, or so it seems, such arrogant westerners as Sir Eldon Gorst, a British official in early-twentieth-century Egypt, could not have more effectively alienated the ruled people if they had tried.[10] With rare exceptions they treated the "natives" with condescension if not contempt. Macaulay's 1835 self-righteous judgment that "a single shelf of a good European library" was "worth the whole native literature of India and Arabia" is well known. It was not, however, just "native literature" that Europeans looked down on, but all the native ways of life. A 1908 remark of an Englishman about the Egyptians was not untypical: "There is no question in Egypt more important than that of education, except the necessity of the English Occupation. To hear the Egyptian talk, you would imagine that his one desire was to improve his mind. . . . As a matter of fact, the Egyptian has no mind . . . he is not a white man." [11] Europeans made "local people feel second-rate in their own lands." [12] No wonder nationalism arose and national revolts occurred. The wonder is that the revolts took so long to materialize, just as it is a mystery why, in Edmund Burke's words, it took so long for western imperial powers "to know the right time and manner of yielding what it" was "impossible to keep."

But European ignorance and arrogance do not sufficiently explain the rise of nationalism in Asia and Africa. How, why, more specifically, did nationalism arise and develop?

Devastating attacks on modern western imperialism date from at least the time of J. A. Hobson's *Imperialism* in 1902, in which he attributed the evils of European imperialism to the excesses of profit-seeking capitalism. Whether Hobson and all the other critics of imperialism were right (as they often were) or wrong (as they sometimes were), or, rather, in what specific ways their attacks were justified or unjustified, is not relevant here. What is important is how varieties of western attitudes and actions laid foundations for nationalism.

Western nations, particularly Britain and France, were dominant, conquering, and seemingly successful. They became models because they were rich and powerful, because they set the standards and goals in government and economic life, because they "educated" Asian and African leaders, because western ways of life increasingly appealed to local peoples, and, probably, because these peoples had no other viable alternatives.

More concretely, as Europeans (and some Americans) explored and stayed in Asia and Africa, they:

1. Brought and established new or different ways of carrying on and organizing economic life—greater use of money, the introduction of the wage system, of contracts, and of centralized state taxation[13]—as well as new and more efficient means of carrying on trade—the development of railroads, steamships, and later air transport. This meant that the traditional ways of producing and consuming, the old, more or less agricultural and communal bases of life tended to disintegrate or disappear, that

fundamental aspects of life were changed, and that the new models tended to be urban, industrial, and national.

2. Introduced new or different kinds of law and order and brought relative peace to wide regions. That the imperial powers usually acted in self-interest—for purposes of profit—and that they also introduced different kinds of violence is here incidental. They did establish some kind of unity (often very tenuous) among the various peoples within the colonial administrative boundaries, and when they did so, it was on western models.

3. Set boundaries. These were often artificial, established for and at the convenience of the imperial power, or fortuitously; and, as mentioned, they split tribes or combined disparate tribes and peoples. But generally they delimited territories that became those of the new nation-states, just as in early modern Europe monarchical governments established boundaries that became national.

4. Established bureaucratic administrative and judicial systems within these boundaries, thereby reducing the functions of native tribal, clan, or caste systems. In varying degrees they thus created westernlike governmental structures (however weak or oppressive) that later became those of the new national states.

5. Introduced western Christian and secular customs and values. In so doing, they modified and sometimes destroyed the legal and actual tribal, clan, or caste social arrangements and undermined the traditional relationships involved in marriage and the family and in communal property, and hence the traditional moral customs and values. The new relationships, just as had been true in Europe, increased dependency on the colonial (later national) state as laws, judicial decisions, and administrative edicts penetrated the consciousness of subject peoples.

6. Introduced western liberal political ideas and ideals about democracy and freedom and, later, socialist views of equality. This meant, though practice was far from theory, that people, or more accurately their leaders, increasingly expected to be (like westerners) self-determining and to participate in state affairs. This meant, too, that they slowly and haltingly identified their interests with those of other people outside their immediate tribe, clan, or caste.[14]

The impact of western power and ideals was everywhere different. Japan, though greatly influenced, was never a colony, and while it too followed western models, its nationalism developed more independently than did the nationalisms of most African and Asian peoples. Algeria followed the French example and Nigeria the British. Under Belgian control the Congolese were less affected by the views of their imperial rulers than were Ugandans under British. Nevertheless, western imperial governments laid foundations on which Asian and African nationalisms arose. Of course, western imperialism was not the monolithic result of monolithic European policies and did not result in uniform reactions. The clear French doctrine of assimilation and the vague English policy of preparation (tutelage) of the peoples for self-government had different consequences. French Africans, it has been said, were more concerned with culture and wrote poetry, the English more concerned with politics and wrote constitutions.[15] But as the models and impacts of the imperial nations were not greatly dissimilar, so the developing nationalisms had much in common. And in every case, as they confronted their western masters, Asian and African peoples became more aware of themselves and how they were seemingly different.

Western imperial rule might not have been so resented and resisted had not the westerners so often paraded their belief in their own superiority, or if the imperial powers had moved faster in granting equal political rights, equal opportunities, equal pay for equal work, and the social justice (equalities) they talked about and sometimes practiced at home. Indeed, given enlightened rule, Asian and African peoples might have been content to remain longer within the British Commonwealth, the French Empire, or other imperial jurisdiction, or even to be assimilated, as French leaders thought they eventually should be. But the "natives" were too often subjected to daily humiliation, were seldom treated as equals in any way, and suffered injustices of many kinds.

Though the imperial governments were becoming less oppressive and native peoples were at times and hesitatingly given political representation, memories of past treatment, of, say, the horrible atrocities in the Congo during (1876–1908) the Belgian King Leopold's private rule, hung on tenaciously. These memories became no less vivid as some Asians and Africans were educated, in the West and at home, and learned of the professed ideals of western democracies, and as new cases of imperial aggrandizement (in Ethiopia in the 1930's) and new instances of violent repression (in Kenya in the 1950's) occurred.

In fact, and in spite of swifter and more frequent communication between the peoples and their imperial officials, opposition to domination steadily intensified, particularly after World War I and even more so after World War II, when the weakened European powers were both less able and more reluctant to maintain their control. The colonial peoples were far from the seats of power, both literally and figuratively. *Their problems,* as *their leaders* were more and more aware and ever more vigorously asserted, were *different* from those of the metropolises. And they were governed, many of them believed, by foreign rulers, with, as the Arab Edward Atiyah put it, "spiritual arrogance, racial haughtiness, social aloofness and paternal authoritarianism. . . ." [16]

Their resentment grew so strong that anti-imperialism became almost synonymous with nationalism. [17] This was true in much of Asia and Africa, though in the case of China and Korea the resentment was directed against not only western but also Japanese imperialism. Nehru was not inaccurate in his autobiography, *Toward Freedom,* when he described nationalism as "essentially an anti-feeling" that fed and fattened "on hatred and anger against other national groups, and especially against the foreign rulers of a subject country." [18]

Specific reasons for the hatred and anger are not difficult to find. As has always been true, until perhaps recently in rich countries, most people have been almost completely occupied with feeding, clothing, and warming (or cooling) themselves and have given little attention to the great questions of politics and economics. In their daily pursuit of material necessities, Asian and African peoples generally had to give first attention to the acquisition of basic necessities in their immediate surroundings. What went on elsewhere, whatever its philosophic or practical import, seemed irrelevant. But when western economic practices were introduced, different problems arose and on new levels: the village or local economies became part of larger, even international, arrangements. *Now,* who obtained wages and salaries and in what amounts, *now,* who owned the land and businesses and obtained whatever rents and profits they afforded, became vitally important. The imperial powers naturally developed their colonies economically in their own interests, and they, their officials and settlers, took a great, a disproportionate share of the rewards, while the "natives," or most of them, remained poor. One response, in the long run, was rising resentment among the emerging peoples.

The situation in no Asian or African country or colony was typical. Roughly stated, however, the individual Asian and African ceiling in income was the European floor, [19] though all wage comparisons should be viewed skeptically, for differences in prices, standards of living, and indirect incomes varied with group and locality. Still, for example, in Indonesia in 1928–29, most Indonesian workers for western firms received no more than $40 a month, while most Europeans received over $160 and some much more; and in 1925 the average annual income of Javanese workers ranged from $49 to $148 a year, [20] less than a tenth of the income of workers in western Europe. In Southern Rhodesia in 1952 the average earnings of an African worker amounted to a little over £56 annually, those of a European £595, over ten times as much.[21] Again, nearly always in the colonies westerners obtained a disproportionate share of the best and highest-paying positions in the civil service and in business, while even educated natives had to take the lower jobs and sometimes (this was especially exasperating) could not obtain employment at all.[22] European firms in much of Asia and Africa handled the bulk of the lucrative large-scale enterprises,[23] and in much of Africa, for example in Kenya, Asians—foreigners—did the retailing. The sometimes large profits were usually sent out of the country and not used for local development. Further, westerners often took, or obtained for a pittance, the best lands, or had these farmed for them.[24] All this meant that the native levels of living, though they might be higher than they had been, were much lower than they could have been, that most of the Asians and Africans were poor, that many were hungry and destitute, that their huts and hovels were, compared with those of European officials and settlers, small and dirty, that their quarters (*bidonvilles*) in the villages and especially in their growing cities were muddy, dusty, unlighted, unsanitary, and ugly. This meant too that they were ill oftener and died at a younger age than the Europeans in their midst.[25] The "natives" might not by themselves have realized their destitution—the "nasty, brutish, and short" nature of their lives—and therefore might not have rebelled. But they had European examples before their eyes, and increasing numbers did slowly come to perceive the contrast and begin to dream that they too might expect and aspire to better and healthier lives.

It was true that, in general, Africans and Asians were less trained and educated and therefore less qualified than westerners to perform the tasks required by western economies. In Africa it was also true that few people, with such exceptions as the Hausa traders of Nigeria and the "Mammies" of Lagos, entered business, preferring to leave its conduct to foreigners (Indians, Lebanese, Europeans). But Asians and Africans wanted material goods—bicycles if not automobiles; they saw Europeans well fed, well clothed, and well housed, and they envied them. For them nationalism was the way to modernization,[26] and this many of them wanted very much!

Their desire for material goods—for alleviation of their poverty—is well known, as is the belief of some of them that national independence —the elimination of foreign domination—would magically bestow on them the affluence of their masters. What is not so well known is that some of the most intelligent, as Sékou Touré, the Guinean leader, told De Gaulle in 1958, preferred "poverty in freedom to riches in slavery," or, as the Filipino senator, Manuel Quezon, declared earlier (in 1926), "We would prefer a government run like hell by Filipinos to one run like heaven by Americans." [27] In actuality, not a few individuals in Asia and Africa were willing, even anxious, to exchange poverty with humiliation for possibly even greater poverty with national identifications.[28] "Nationalism," as a British correspondent in Southeast Asia, Dennis Bloodworth, observed, "is not rationalism, and its devotees will practice its rites without counting the costs." [29]

There is no quantitative way to measure the intensity of this seemingly irrational feeling. One can possibly understand it, demonstrate it, with further illustrations of humiliations the "natives" suffered. The leading great politician and activist of Ghana, Kwame Nkrumah, once wrote, "We prefer self-government with danger to servitude in tranquillity." [30] One may question the "tranquillity" of life under imperialist rule; one cannot deny that this life brought intense protest against indignity.

Westerners made Asians and Africans feel inferior in every way because of their race and their culture. This was particularly true of black Africans, many of whose ancestors had been captured and enslaved. Slavery left a deep stigma of inferiority, a belief on the part of the white that the black was a primitive child, incapable of individual improvement or group progress, and this legacy begat "suspicion, servility, or hostility" [31] on the part of the blacks. The brown and yellow peoples of Asia were likewise believed to be backward, lacking ability to improve or to govern themselves—good servants or manual laborers, perhaps, but lacking in intelligence, character, and will—and they too became suspicious and eventually hostile. Westerners, naturally, judged Asians and Africans by the arbitrary standards of their own culture. They were, for the most part, quite unaware of this, believed theirs to be the only right and civilized ways and hence those that should be universal. When westerners and Asians and Africans in modern times first encountered each other in numbers, and for many years after, Asians and Africans generally agreed with or submitted to the western judgment and acknowledged their inferiority. Behind the myth of western and white superiority there was always also the will, power, and ability to dominate. Not until recent times was the myth or the reality effectively questioned by westerners or by Asians and Africans.

About seventy years ago an adventurous, perceptive Englishwoman, Mary Kingsley, who traveled much in Africa, recounted an improving fable, that of a she-elephant who inadvertently trod upon a mother partridge and then, seeing its nested babies, dropped a tear, said, "I have the feelings of a mother myself," and sat down upon the brood.[32] A little over a generation later, Kenya's famed leader, Jomo Kenyatta, told another fable. An elephant took possession of the hut of a man who was his friend. A commission of the lords of the jungle appointed by their king, the lion, investigated to settle the dispute, but no man was allowed to sit on the commission, and the dispossessed man had to build another hut. This hut, too, was occupied—by a rhinoceros, a member of the commission. The hut building and evictions went on until all the members of the commission were housed at the expense of the man. In desperation he burned down the last big hut, in which the whole commission had gathered, and returned home saying, "Peace is costly, but it is worth the expense." [33] The moral of the fable was "You can fool the people for a time, but not forever." It correctly foretold what would happen.

It was, however, not only economic exploitation that led finally to revolt but also thousands of little daily humiliations along with massive political domination and social discrimination. Frenchmen addressed as if they were children (*tutoyer*) men who were to become prominent Africans (like Senghor, President and poet of Senegal), and Englishmen called them (as one did Harry Thuku, who became a Kikuyu leader) "natives" or "boys"—just as in Europe Jews were sometimes called "dirty Jews." The manners and dress of "natives" were ridiculed. They had to doff their hats and give way on the sidewalks, and often they were rudely received in white shops. Their cities and their streets were given European names. Always the conveniences they had to use were separate and unequal. An African speaker in Southern Rhodesia had to climb up to his lecture room by the fire escape because Africans could not use the elevator, and a black official in Nigeria was refused a room in a white-owned hotel. Everywhere Africans turned they ran into the westerner's customs and laws. In Egypt a village peasant was tried for washing his clothes in the canal. The judge and the peasant exchanged words:

"You are charged with having washed your clothes in the canal."
"Your honour, may God exalt your station—are you going to fine me just because I washed my clothes?"
"It's for washing them in the canal."
"Well, where else could I wash them?"
The judge hesitated . . . said, "The Legal Officer. Opinion please!"
"The State is not concerned to inquire where this man should wash his clothes. Its only interest is the application of the law."

The judge turned his glance . . . then spoke swiftly like a man rolling a weight off his shoulders: "Fined twenty piastres. Next case." [34]

The little humiliations mounted up to much more than their sum. Black, brown, and yellow men, or for that matter the Caucasian "natives" of North Africa, especially when they were educated in the western fashion, remembered them, as Jews did the insults inflicted on them in the most "civilized" of western nations. In the long run the petty humiliations and insults may have weighed more in the rise of nationalism than the large issues of political domination and social discrimination. They were, indeed, concrete manifestations of domination and discrimination.[35]

Nowhere in the colonies did the peoples have a decisive voice in their government; usually they had no really effective voice at all. In some British colonies—India, for one—the peoples were reluctantly and slowly given (as a result of protest) greater and greater representation, but even then they were always subordinate because the imperial power, on vital matters like those of war and finance, kept the reins. Always a comparative handful of aliens—the imperial representatives, who held the chief offices and power, and the settlers, who possessed the legal rights—enjoyed the same privileges (and more) they would have had at home.[36] Most often the local peoples, as in South Africa, the Congo, and Southeast Asia, had no political rights, or, for that matter, any rights that could not be revoked at will. Generally, their speech was not free, their newspapers were censored, their movements about the country restricted—especially if there was a crisis—and in southern parts of Africa they had to carry passes.[37] *Their* courts were usually separate, *their* "justice" different, and *their* punishments heavier than those for Europeans. Usually they could be arbitrarily arrested and jailed, often without any "due process," and in political cases convicted and imprisoned without a jury or even a trial.[38] Ndabaningi Sithole, the eloquent Rhodesian clergyman and nationalist, asserted, probably correctly, that in his part of Africa no European was ever convicted of the murder of an African and sentenced to death, though many Europeans were convicted of the murder of Europeans and so sentenced.[39]

If a native rebelled or committed a crime (and rebellion was a crime), the superior force was against him: the police, the army, the courts. Even in those countries that were not actually colonies—Iran, Japan, China—western political power was often dominant if not supreme. Britain and Russia quarreled over but controlled much of Iran as if it were a colony during the first half of the twentieth century.[40] Japan was "opened" by American naval forces, and the chief Chinese cities and waterways were controlled by western businesses and gunboats until recently. But it must be remarked that from 1915 the independent and imperalistic Japanese humiliated and tried to dominate the Chinese through the Twenty-one and other demands.[41] Humiliation was the customary lot of most Asians and Africans, whether at the hands of westerners or of other Asians and Africans.

Not all westerners regarded "natives" as Afrikaners customarily did blacks: "Bless you my servant. Curse you my brother." It was rare that the imperial powers, as Senghor once claimed, took "away the crowns of princes" and made them "petty clerks," for actually there were few princes. But Africans and Asians so believed, and with reason. Western customs, habits, values, outlooks were different and, westerners believed, superior. Those of Africans and Asians westerners considered queer, wrong, and ridiculous, and so inferior. Hence westerners tried to change the "natives'" ways, or, failing that, to keep them in their place (separated and segregated), and in both cases subjected them to humiliation.

With the best of intentions, missionaries in Africa, as they endeavored to Christianize (bring the "lamp of life" to) "benighted" peoples, disapproved of African practices of initiation and funeral ceremonies, of nudity, of polygamy, and of witch doctory.[42] Many Asians and Africans did try to adopt Christian and western ways, but most of them, understandably, could never quite adapt. In hope of making as much profit as possible, western businessmen and settlers disapproved of Asians' and Africans' indifference to material progress—their lack of efficiency, their refusal to work more than necessary; in short, their seeming stupidity and laziness. Asians and Africans might try to meet western standards of productivity, but most of them had difficulty and could seldom do so. And in western eyes they were therefore inferior breeds. As the "twin acids" of Christian teachings and the western money economy ate into family, clan, and tribal life,[43] "natives" frequently became uprooted men, with the "pathology of uprooted men," difficult to manage and therefore, to westerners, even more inferior. The changes that destroyed the life of custom indeed raised dreaded questions, led to unruly behavior[44] and seemingly irrational rebellion, and thence to seemingly irrational national revolts.

The realities of the colonial situations are of utmost importance. Of equal or perhaps even greater significance is what "natives," particularly their leaders, believed or said these realities were. In the private routines of daily life, in casual roadside encounters, as well as in the conduct of public affairs, many individuals felt themselves to be rudely treated, and they could not help but be aware of and hurt by many inequalities and injustices. Westerners associated with each other socially and not with the "natives," lived separately, tended to be exclusive, formed their own clubs, and generally and condescendingly thought of the local peoples as servants who were, by nature, fit chiefly for menial tasks, servants who should perhaps be pitied and charitably cared for but "handled" with firmness and, if necessary, by force. "Natives" should live (and did live) in their own separate and segregated shabby quarters, and they knew this. They might work, as "boys," in the western clubs—the Gezira in Cairo, the Army-Navy in Manila, or the various clubs of Shanghai—but they had to enter through the servants' entrance and were expected to be subservient —to take orders and, on occasion, slights and insults quietly, be called "black monkeys" or "slant-eyed," yellow "s.o.b.'s." [45]

Satirically, an observer commented, "We [westerners] have never been called 'natives'; no people from the other end of Asia came to put signs at the entrance of our parks that 'dogs and Europeans are not admitted'; no foreign race ever stepped over our starved bodies to reach its gay night-clubs; we have never been forced to live for centuries with the humiliating knowledge that our colour or birthplace condemned us to be second-class citizens." [46] In Southern Rhodesia an African angrily exploded that white Rhodesians "do not look upon the black man as a person, they just treat them as dogs. The only time they look after them, is when they want money from them. I am a person, not a dog." [47]

Men in the world are of many colors: black, white, yellow, brown, red, and all gradations (including the pink of this author) in between. For reasons that are beyond the scope of this study, whites have for centuries looked down on men of other colors, identified or confused color with race, and considered the "colored races" to be inferior, apparently the darker the more inferior. Nowhere has this prejudice been more deeply held than in Dutch (Boer, Afrikaner) South Africa.[48] But the prejudice was shared in varying intensities by white men everywhere, in the United States, in Europe (less, perhaps, in France), and wherever white men resided.[49] Indeed, it was in the United States that black men sometimes encountered the prejudices that contributed so directly to the rise not only of black nationalism in the United States but also of nationalism in black Africa.

The famed nineteenth-century African from the West Indies, Edward Blyden, a very black man, felt deep hurt when he learned from personal experience in an American city that "no colored person [in 1862] was allowed to ride in the street cars of which the city [Philadelphia] was so full." [50] Blyden labored long and faithfully to establish black nations. In the 1930's Kwame Nkrumah, later first president of Ghana, was refused a drink of water in a Baltimore bus terminal restaurant and told, "The place for you, my man, is the spittoon outside." According to his account, he bowed his head and "walked out in as dignified a manner as I knew." [51] A few years later he was passionately leading the nationalist revolt in Ghana. Increasing numbers of black, brown, red, and yellow men suffered indignities in every part of the world, slowly realized it, were deeply hurt, protested, and endeavored to build nations and erect states in which men of their own color governed. At the ceremony for the independence of the Congo (1960), Patrice Lumumba, soon to become premier, could not hide his still-smoldering resentment at

. . . the mockery, the insults, the blows submitted to morning, noon, and night because we were *"Nègres."* . . . We have known that in the cities there were magnificent homes for the whites and crumbling hovels for the Negroes, that a Negro was not admitted to movie theaters or restaurants, that he was not allowed to enter so-called "European" stores, that when the Negro travelled, it was on the lowest level of a boat, at the feet of the white man in his deluxe cabin. [52]

Asians and especially Africans, reflecting in reverse the white man's biases, became ever more conscious of their race and color. As they did, they, and particularly their leaders, came to believe in the worth of men of their own race, in their past great contributions to humanity, in their own possibilities for "progressive advancement," in the future cultural contributions they would make. In English-speaking Africa Edward Blyden, as early as 1874, pridefully declared, "I would rather be a member of this race than a Greek in the time of Alexander, a Roman in the Augustan period, or an Anglo-Saxon in the nineteenth century." During the early twentieth century a West African nationalist, J. E. K. Aggrey, coined the aphorism that both black and white keys were necessary to play the piano; but he also said that if he went to Heaven and God asked him whether he wanted to return to earth as a black or a white man, he would reply, "Because I have work to do as a black man that no white man can do. [*sic*] Please send me back as black as you can make me." [53] From the French colonies, beginning in the 1930's, such poets and scholars as Léopold Senghor, Aimé Césaire, and Alioune Diop spoke imaginatively of the black "soul" and spirit that would rejuvenate the world—*Négritude.* For Césaire *Négritude* was "neither a tower or a cathedral," but "thrusts into the red flesh of the earth," "into the livid flesh of the sky," and he shouted, "Hurray for joy / hurray for love / hurray for the pain of incarnate tears." [54]

As Africans began to take pride in their blackness, some of them came to dislike white rule the more. The Yoruba word for Europeans meant "peeled" men, and some Africans believed white men exuded a disagreeable "rancid odor." The time was coming when Nigerians and Ghanians and Africans everywhere would find the smell (acts) of "peeled" men beyond endurance.

As it was in Africa, so, with variations, was it in much of Asia. If in eastern and southern Asia brownness and yellowness were less significant than was blackness in south-of-the-Sahara Africa, race was still a major issue. Brown and yellow men in India, China, and especially Japan resented western white claims of superiority, and at least a few of them took pride in the accomplishments of their own peoples and expressed belief not only in their superiority but also in their magnificent destiny. In India a violent nationalist, Vinayak Sāvarkar (1883–?), calling his nation (in 1924) the "richly endowed daughter of God," thought it had the greatest possibilities of all nations except China.[55] In China, "that central country," the belief never disappeared that the Chinese possessed the only "genuine civilization," and the voice of the radical Liang Ch'i-ch'ao did not go unheard in twentieth-century China when he said the destiny of the Chinese was to synthesize and transform western and Chinese civilizations "to make a new civilization" and thereby "benefit the whole human race." [56] In Japan belief in the virtues of the Japanese race and in its destiny to champion the East against western racialism and imperialism was often expressed, especially after the victory of the Japanese over the Russians in 1905. By 1937 Watsuyi Tetsurō, an influential philosopher, was arguing that Japan had a mission to be the beacon for the whole world.[57] Imperialist white dominance became an evil to be eradicated. No longer would men of color tolerate their dependent status—the inferiority that had seemed to result from their having been born the wrong color. In 1959 Sithole summed up reasons for the rise of nationalism in Africa in terms of black reaction to white supremacy:

. . . the basic ingredients . . . may be enumerated as the African's desire to participate fully in the central government of the country; his desire for economic justice that recognizes fully the principle of "equal pay for equal work" regardless of the color of the skin; his desire to have full political rights in his own country; his dislike of being treated as a stranger in the land of his birth;

his dislike of being treated as means for the white man's end; and his dislike of the laws of the country that prescribe for him a permanent position as a human being.[58]

How basic race and color were, however, in determining western attitudes and actions and Asian and African reactions cannot be quantitatively established.[59] As Sithole's summary illustrates, Asians and Africans protested against many kinds of inequalities—political and economic—and many varieties of indignities—social and cultural. But when men of color became aware that pigmentation of skin did not determine the quality of a man or his culture, there was no longer a natural, a biological barrier to national independence, and protests against white dominance grew louder, more persistent, and more effective.

The white rulers, their officials and their missionaries, often professed their intention to prepare the "backward" peoples for good, moral lives and for self-government through education and religion. There can be no doubt that in their colonies they did, at times and with occasional success, make great efforts to put these intentions into practice. They did introduce western medicine and improve sanitation. They did provide elementary education for some (usually a small minority) of the native children and higher education for a very few. Their missionaries did—even at times against the will of their own governments—give moral, that is, Christian, instruction to as many as they could reach. But——.

In Morocco, a fairly advanced French colony, in 1930–31, European primary schools had an enrollment of 22,770, of whom 144 were Moroccans, and in 1931–32 European secondary schools (*lycées*) an enrollment of 5,644, of whom 122 were Moroccans. A few Moroccans were admitted to institutions of higher learning in France, but most were rejected.[60] In Nigeria, a comparatively well governed English colony, in 1939 only about twelve per cent of the children of school age, 350,000 out of 3 million, were in school.[61] In some colonies (Senegal), the proportions were higher, in some (the Congo) much lower. In Japan, however, a highly visible independent Asian nation, nearly all children were in school, and, at least in Asia Japan could be and was on occasion viewed as a model.

Imperial officials, like Lugard of Britain in Africa, argued against educating more people in the colonies on the ground that few jobs were available, but then appointed few "natives" to good positions because they were not educated enough.[62] A few "natives" did obtain advanced education at home or in France, Britain, and the United States, or, in the case of the Chinese, in Japan. Ironically, it was these Asians and Africans who, after they had learned about western technology, ideas, and ideals, often became, like the American-educated J. E. K. Aggrey of the Gold Coast, the most ardent nationalist opponents of western rule. This was especially true of those who did not obtain positions for which they believed themselves qualified.

With their spirit of "Christian soldiers marching as to war," missionaries made converts almost everywhere. But while they, and their fellow Christians who became officials and settlers, influenced many "natives" to be followers and submissive, they also brought hopes and practices that led to nationalism at the same time as they aroused hostility to western ways that pointed in the same direction.

This hostility was sharpened when imperial governments favored or seemed to favor the converts and discriminated against "natives" who, as in India and Morocco, maintained their own old and deep religious faiths and were determined to maintain them undefiled. The French government, following the policy of assimilation, offended Muslims when, for example, it gave (the *dahir* of 1930) special French legal privileges to the Berbers in Morocco in an attempt to win them over and split them from the Muslim Arabs.[63] But all through Asia and Africa the imperial governments were identified as Christian, and hostility to these governments was transferred to their religion.[64] In many cases, as among Hindu and Muslim peoples, the traditional religions became fundamental bases of nationalist feeling, and resentment against the foreign religion a reason for nationalist action. In the Islamic world the *umma* was itself "a solidary entity" with a tremendous drive of its own. The state and the religion were traditionally and actually considered one, and the religion itself was "a measure of identity and a focus of group loyalty." [65]

As missionaries offered education to local peoples, small numbers became literate and more aware of the examples of western national development. Further, missionaries—such as the Protestant Eli Smith in the Middle East and Jacob Spieth in western (Ewe) Africa[66]—prepared dictionaries, manuals, and grammars of native languages that could later become national, and also translated the Bible and other Christian books into the native tongues. Perhaps more important, their Christian religion offered hope of a better future, either on this earth or hereafter, and promised equality, at least before God.

A native minister trained by missionaries, John Chilembwe, who led an early, tragic revolt in Nyasaland in 1915, was inspired by the Old Testament and the example of the Jews (in Egypt), and in turn he inspired his small band of followers to dream of more possibilities than helpless acceptance of whatever Europeans offered or a return to tribal allegiances.[67] As the mission-educated African Rhodesian leader Ndabaningi Sithole argued with reason,

One of the unique teachings of the Bible, especially of the New Testament, is the worth and dignity of the individual in the sight of God, and there is a relation between this teaching and African nationalism. . . . The Bible redeemed the African individual from the power of superstition, individuality-crushing tradition, witchcraft . . . [and] helped the African individual to reassert himself above colonial powers.

A story told by Sithole strikingly illustrates the African awareness of injustice aroused by biblical teaching. Two South Africans were arguing one day. One said,

"You see, the missionary . . . said 'Let us pray' and we closed our eyes, and when we responded, 'Amen' . . . we found the Bible in our hands, but lo! our land had gone!" The other replied, "When Europeans took our country we fought them with our spears, but they defeated us because they had better weapons and so colonial power was set up. . . . But lo! the missionary came . . . and laid explosives under colonialism. The Bible is now doing what we could not do with our spears." [68]

While the Christian teaching of the missionaries offered hope, it also threatened old religious beliefs and ways of life. In response to both the hope and the threat, Africans and Asians reacted in differing ways, all pointing toward nationalism. One reaction was the rise of messianic sects, as in the Congo, which, some scholars believe, were precursors of later nationalist groupings.[69] A much more important reaction was the strengthening of traditional religions through vigorous, inspirational, religio-political reformist movements, such as the Brahma Samaj in late-nineteenth-century India and the Salifiyya in twentieth-century Morocco.[70] These movements and groups aimed at nothing less than the political and cultural rejuvenation of their nations based on religious tradition. In Afghanistan a newspaper editor (from 1911 to 1918), Mahmud Tarzi, found the *raison d'être* of Afghanistan in the teachings of Islam and made an ingenious attempt to link its aspirations with the cause of Pan-Islamism, Pan-Asiatic solidarity, and modernism.[71] In India a father of its nationalism, Swami Vivekananda, who was both saint and patriot, "put nationalism on the high pedestal of spirituality and the past glory of the Hindus." [72] In Islamic countries especially, as in Somaliland and what would become Pakistan, religious history and doctrine added "depth and coherence . . . to [the] common elements of traditional culture," [73] and gave a basis for unity within and opposition to the foreigner without. Hazem Nuseibeh, a recent student of Arab nationalism, exaggerated little when he asserted, "To Islam is due the birth of a nation, the birth of a national history, and the birth of a civilization." [74] In different fashion the differing nationalisms of the Jews and the Boers, as well, were based upon their religious traditions, upon their peculiar interpretations of the Old Testament and God's will for his chosen people. [75]

It was Christianity's identification with white domination, however, that most stimulated hostility and nationalist feeling. Christian egalitarian teaching itself revealed to black Africans the enormous contradiction between humanitarian ideal and imperial practice. Disaffection for white men, judged by their own principles, thus led to the "powerful emotional inspiration of nationalism." [76] Africans and Asians, with the evidence before their eyes, saw that so-called Christians, their masters, drained justice and liberty of political meaning, established two standards, one for themselves and one for those men of color they ruled. "There is," wrote one Charles Domingo in a pamphlet of 1911, "too much failure among all Europeans in Nyasaland. The three combined bodies, Missionaries, Government and Companies or gainers of money, do form the same rule to look upon the native with mockery eyes. . . . If we had power enough to communicate ourselves to Europe, we would advise them not to call themselves Christendom but Europeandom . . . the life of the three combined bodies is altogether too cheaty, too thefty, too mockery." [77]

Many Africans and Asians finally came to understand that under western domination they danced and marched to *foreign* music[78] and lived according to *foreign* ways, and they did not like it. Europeans, some of them believed, came to "Africa [or Asia] with Christ and the gospel. It appears that on their way back they left both there. The gospel must be taken back to Europe. Europe must be re-educated . . . re-civilized. Europe needs African evangelists." [79] And Africans and Asians, too, began to believe they needed *their own* cultural and political nations.

Nationalism, *slowly and then swiftly*, became for increasing numbers of Asians and Africans their new religion, whether based on their old religion or not. This was clearly the fact in Shintoist Japan, where the *Fundamentals of Our National Polity* (*Kokutai no hongi*, 1937) demanded "filial piety . . . [because] our country is a great family nation and the Imperial Household is the head family of the subjects and the nucleus of national life." [80] And it became eventually, though less obviously, the fact in much of Asia and Africa. In India a nationalist prophet, Aurobindo Ghosh (1872–1950), declared, "Nationalism is not a mere political program; Nationalism is a religion that has come from God; Nationalism is a creed which you shall have to live. . . . If you are going to be a nationalist, if you are going to assent to this religion of Nationalism, you must do it in the religious spirit." [81] And in India a member of the Servants of India Society, founded by the nationalist G. K. Gokhale in 1907, swore "that the country will always be the first in his thoughts and he will give to her service the best that is in him."

Adherents of the nationalist faith proposed and took oaths that in their emotional intensity recalled the fervor of Greeks and Italians in the nineteenth century. In the Philippines a leader's (Mabini) decalogue began, "Thou shalt love thy country after God . . . and more than thyself: for she is the only Paradise which God has given thee in this life, the only patrimony of thy race, the only inheritance of thy ancestors, and the only hope of thy posterity; because of her, thou hast life, love, and interests, happiness, honor and God." [82] At the height of the Mau Mau rebellion in Kenya in the 1950's, many oaths were sworn, and now with Kikuyu symbols—the meat of a goat instead of the Bible. A leader described his oath: "I held the blood in a calabash in my right hand and the meat in my left . . . and repeated these words to my people. 'If I become an enemy of my land or my people . . . let this meat and blood kill me straight away. If I am ever bribed to abandon my people, . . . may this oath kill us [sic].' " [83]

Subjected to the acids of western ways, Asians and Africans were long uncertain, confused, and fearful. Westerners undoubtedly misunderstood them, or at least failed to realize that they were men, men who had needs and should have rights as other men, indeed, men who owned the country before westerners came and who would one day declare their title to it again.[84] Believing in their own superiority, westerners seldom comprehended that the many Asian and African peoples were all different from each other, with their own laws and customs, their own languages and faiths, their own rhythms, and that they would someday demand to choose from among the *hors-d'oeuvre variés* the course that suited them.[85] European misunderstanding (or lack of understanding) undoubtedly contributed to both continuing tension and eventual revolt.

Whatever the case, for Asians and Africans the old ways of life were disintegrating, and they were puzzled. Who were they? A Reverend S. R. B. Solomon of West Africa, who changed (about 1897) his name to Attoh Ahuma, expressed a malaise increasingly and ever more deeply felt throughout the colonial world: "The greatest calamity of West Africa that must be combatted tooth and nail . . . is the imminent Loss of Ourselves . . . let them rob our lands . . . , but let us see that they do not rob us of ourselves. They do so when we are taught to despise our own Names, Institutions, Customs and Laws. . . ." [86]

The fear of loss of identity was great and real. It did not necessarily result in nationalism. But even those Africans who, like the famed South African leader Albert Luthuli, were grateful for European tutelage and willingly suffered the gibe of "Black Englishman" came to believe they were African. Luthuli exclaimed, as he pleaded in his *Let My People Go*, "I remain an African, I speak as an African, I act as an African, and as an African I worship the God whose children we all are. I do not see why it should be otherwise." [87] And even Indians who, like Gopal Krishna Gokhale (1866–1915), believed in the "integrity and beneficence of British rule" became Indians first. [88]

Basically, the fear, the confusion over identity reflected the long struggle between traditionalism and modernization, a struggle not unknown in nineteenth-century Italy, Russia, and the Balkans, and earlier in much of western Europe. Asians and Africans, or those who were leaders and were called the elite, wanted to maintain their cherished traditions *and* to acquire westernized political institutions and western economic and scientific techniques. They wanted no less than to keep their historic cultures—especially their spiritual beliefs—and at the same time to harness the future for material progress and affluence. Nationalism became the instrument of mobilization, of retaining identity as well as fulfilling expectation. With this instrument, developing peoples, or so their leaders thought, could look both backward and forward, preserve the threatened roots of their cultures while they molded their desired and desirable future. In India, Bal Gangadhar Tilak (1856–1920), who looked back in pride to ancient institutions and customs, and Gokhale, who looked forward to "the liberation of the Indian mind from the thraldom of old-world ideas," vehemently fought each other. [89] But they were both nationalists. In China the radical early-twentieth-century nationalist Liang Chi'i-ch'ao "cloaked his appeal" to emulate western achievements in the authority of the Chinese classics: "A good Confucianist must long to see railroads through mountains. . . ." [90] The early and only partially successful revolutionary leader, Sun Yat-sen (1866–1925), derived his three principles, nationalism, democracy (people's rights), and socialism (people's livelihood), from western thought and in particular from Marx. [91] But the more radical and successful revolutionist, Mao Tse-tung (1893–), drew on Marx while he resurrected Chinese heroes and peasant traditions. [92] Pre-World War II Japanese leaders combined Shintoism with western material goals and ambitions. They adopted European technology, armaments, and imperialism—"western material civilization"—while they retained their traditional filial piety, and thus believed they were following eastern morality and western arts.[93]

The Arabic peoples wavered between assimilation and rejection. On the one hand, their nationalism was of the conventional European style and therefore modernizing. On the other hand, it was a "thinly disguised movement aiming at a forcible purification of Islam," a return to the *umma*.[94] The issue for Arab peoples is still not settled, for there are those who, especially in recent years amid the antagonism to Israel, demand material advance and disassociate themselves from the religious inheritance, and those who, like the Salafiyya of Morocco, recognize "the *Qur'an* and the *Sunna* of the Prophet as the only acceptable basis of religious and social legislation" [95]—of life. But adherents of both views saw nationalism of their own variety as the solution of Arab dilemmas. In Africa south of the Sahara, the tendency was to neglect or forget the traditional cultures; especially was this true among the so-called achieving peoples, such as the Ibo (of Nigeria) and the Buganda (of Uganda).[96] Nevertheless, black African leaders from Blyden onward tried to revive the traditional cultures as the bases of the new national. Even now, as African leaders in Tanzania, Kenya, and other countries try desperately to industrialize, the issues are not settled, though few are sure what in the past they wish to save.[97] The old-fashioned wife of Okot p'Bitek's contemporary poem, *Song of Lawino*,[98] laments the modernization of her husband, who now despises her, and begs him to allow her, with ankle bells on her legs and to the accompaniment of nanga music, to "dance before you." But if many ordinary people like Lawino held back and disliked "modernism," leaders like Lawino's husband moved (or were moved by forces beyond their control) always to forward it. And as they did, they used nationalism as "a vehicle to carry all the people along to a new world, a structure which [could] house the aspirations of all classes of society." [99]

Increasing numbers of Asians and Africans wanted to be their own men, to have rights, dignity,[100] and the material things western white men appeared to have, and therefore to attain the power to make their own futures. Especially was this true of members of the gradually growing middle classes—minor governmental officials, entrepreneurs, lawyers, physicians, journalists, trade union officers, military men (in some countries, like Turkey), and students[101]—increasing numbers of whom lived in the expanding urban areas where they stimulated each other with ideas as they associated in common enterprises. These rising and hopeful individuals seldom fully comprehended, though they certainly knew, that most white western men did not in fact enjoy many rights or much riches or live in an Eden.[102] But they imagined that they themselves could build a garden of freedom and abundance, and more and more of them so believed and believed more intensely.

While they were often humiliated and much oppressed, their spirit was not crushed, or, if it was, not for long. When old and somewhat conciliatory leaders fell—died, gave up, or gave in—new ones, ever more demanding, arose. Neither the oppression nor the poverty was ever so great that all hope was extinguished or all protest stifled. Rather, as the oppression and poverty became (in some cases) less awful, the protests mounted. Always, intelligent and informed Asians and Africans could witness the comparative western freedom and affluence as well as the madness of westerners fighting and killing each other. Again and again they learned that westerners were no more wise or godlike than other men and that they were just as mortal. But, at the same time, they came to believe (without realizing the irony) that they too, if they had the chance —that is, were freed from imperial domination—could establish governments of, by, and for their own people.[103] And they too came to believe they could create national societies suited to the spirit (though few read Montesquieu) and conditions of their own peoples, and that once these had been created economic and cultural progress would follow.[104]

In diverse ways and at different times, increasing numbers of the various peoples became convinced that the dream of independence would be realized and that then all would be well—or at least much better.[105] Hence they became more and more involved and participated in what became not local but national struggles. As they hoped (indeed, in proportion as they hoped), they became ever more aware of their grievances and that they shared these with others. As they became aware, they became more vocal and their protests multiplied.[106] And as they grieved, hoped, protested, and participated, they became increasingly nationally conscious and in increasing number and degree nationalist.

The nationalist movements did not spring into existence overnight, and they are still in process. During the late nineteenth century, Indian reformers—Rajendralal Mitter, for one—were hoping that "we shall be living as a nation," and Islamic enthusiasts—like al-Afghānī—were saying that surely "the greatest happiness to be desired is the happiness of the *umma* and of the *milla* within which the person has grown." [107] But the sentiment these early nationalists were evincing was becoming more and more shared, and eventually, especially after World War II, it became a phenomenon to be seen all over Asia and Africa.

Asians and Africans were taught by westerners—by Christian missionaries and optimistic intellectuals—to hope. Increasing though still small numbers of them were "educated" in the West and at home to be expectant. From the 1920's especially, their own leaders, through the press and later the radio, through embryo political parties, mutual aid societies, and trade unions, taught them to believe that their future of freedom, justice, and abundance would be achieved through their nations. Asians and Africans, too, heard (if they could not read) of the pronouncements of the United Nations and other international bodies, of "fundamental human rights," "the dignity and worth of the human person," and of "fundamental freedoms for all" regardless of race and religion.[108] They believed these pronouncements, saw no reason they did not apply to themselves. They were, though their understandable ignorance was often profound, ever more expectant and demanding. Blyden, in the middle of the nineteenth century, had pleaded with the young men and women of Liberia to give "their country a moment's thought," to arise from their "lethargy," bestir themselves, bravely and nobly achieve the glory that awaited their country.[109] Chilembwe in 1915, in his last sermon, calling his congregation patriots, asked them "to go and strike the blow and then die" as the "only way to show the whitemen that the treatment they are treating our men and women was most bad. . . ." He believed the "whitemen will then think, after we are dead, that the treatment they are treating our people is almost bad, and they might change." [110]

The white men did change, reluctantly and slowly. But it was too late to maintain their colonial rule, no matter how benevolent, against the thrust of expectant nationalism. By the early twentieth century, nationalism, in the words of Sun Yat-sen, was becoming "a treasure, the possession of which causes a nation to aspire to greater development." [111] And in Indonesia in 1930 an ambitious young nationalist, Sukarno (1901?–69), who was later to become the first president of his country, declared, as he defended himself in a subversion trial, "First we point out to the people that they have a glorious past, secondly we intensify the notion among our people that the present time is dark, and the third way is to show them the promising, pure and luminous future and how to get there." [112] How many Asian and African people actually learned of their "glorious past," or envisioned the "promising, pure and luminous" future of the nations they were forging, cannot be known. The numbers were sufficient to establish at least fifty-four nation-states from 1945 through 1968.

What Asians and Africans expected greatly varied, of course—they numbered hundreds of millions of individuals. Yet generalization is possible. First of all, they hoped for freedom *from*—freedom from colonial domination, from economic exploitation, and from social and intellectual subservience—all of which was a rather negative freedom but nonetheless the requisite for *self*-development. Second (though not necessarily in importance), they wanted opportunity *for* reacquisition of land, for jobs, and for education—all of which could be loosely summed up in self-improvement or perhaps egalitarianism.[113] These generalizations, however, hide a multitude of expectancies.

Some Asians and Africans undoubtedly hoped for a kind of Rousseauean utopia—a return to the age of innocence before men were contaminated by civilization.[114] One primitive people, the Melanesians, developed the "cargo cult"—a belief in the coming of a mysterious ship, brought by ancestors, which would give the people the high living standard of Europeans.[115] Expectancy could also mean, as it did to some inhabitants of the Cameroons, the end of all hated things and the beginning of all that were desired—no one need work any longer, the police force would be disbanded, women would be able to get divorces as they wished, it would be possible to go to a store and take what one pleased without paying.[116]

For ordinary peoples, however, it is likely that the hopes were for far more prosaic reforms, not only for relief from the humiliations described earlier but also for practical improvements in their daily lives. In India the National Social Conference asked for education and housing for the masses, for care of the sick, and for employment of all, as well as for removal of caste restrictions and the ban against remarriage of widows.[117] In Nyasaland the African Congress, in addition to asking for condemnation of color bars and for full citizenship for blacks, "humbly requested the government to permit Africans to enter movie theaters, to purchase goods from European-owned stores without being forced to ask for them through a hatchway, and to wear shoes and hats in the presence of whites." [118] A good many ordinary men wanted little more than jobs at somewhat higher pay, slightly higher prices for what they had to sell, a road to the market town, some elementary education for their children, and an extra pair of trousers (or a second dress), or a cart or a bicycle, for themselves.

Educated men, as in India, the Middle East, and North Africa, naturally wanted much more, and they could speak in larger and more conceptual terms—of liberty and justice, public finance, education, and health service. And they, in Tunisia, in India, and almost everywhere, formulated grand plans for the national governments they hoped to establish.[119] Black intellectuals from the French colonies of West Africa and the West Indies who had lived in Europe (in Paris usually), such as the poet Alioune Diop, rejected Europe and its civilization as a *machine à travailler* destined to produce suffering and death as they dreamed of that black civilization attuned to the rhythms and jobs of the blacks[120]—*Négritude*. Among the Jews, the highly cultured Viennese Theodor Herzl, who was to become the "father" of Israel, dreamed of the "Promised Land" where Jews were free "to live as free men on [their] own soil," of a Zion where they could "have hooked noses, black or red beards and bandy legs, without being despised . . . ," and where (he was not being facetious) "salzstangel, coffee, beer, customary food were not ordinary matters." [121]

Nationalism was thus an envelope for the most exalted dreams, for daily wants, for the joys of the flesh. When national governments were established, there would be great rejoicing[122]—as there had been in France on July 14, 1790, when the triumph of the nation's government over the king's was celebrated. As will be seen, after independence the disagreeable realization dawned that the establishment of a national state did not automatically usher in a utopia and make the dreams of fraternal brotherhood come true. But this was not apparent until new governments were actually established.

As early as 1881, an Indian patriot, Vishnu Krishna Chiplunkar of Maharashtra, told a parable.

"There is," he wrote, "a great difference between the bird who roams at will through sky and forest and the parrot who is put into a large cage of gold or even of jewels! It is a great disaster when a bird whose God-given power is to move wherever he pleases unrestrained on the strength of his beautiful wings must always remain chirping in a confined cage." [123]

His parable had substance, though when his bird, India, was freed nearly seventy years later, its people were not conditioned to freedom and the glowing hope of the parable dimmed. But during the great days of the struggles to break out of the imperialist cages, the chirps steadily grew louder until they became the veritable songs of nationalism.

The emerging national feeling was constantly aggravated by tragic and violent incidents and by traumatic experiences of those who were becoming converts. Who caused the incidents—the arguments still wage—makes little difference here. What is important is that they fed resentment and rebellion, led to more incidents and more resentment and then revolt. The incidents were many and occurred everywhere in the colonial world, from at least the Sepoy rebellion in 1857 in India, through the pogroms in European Russia, and down to the present in those countries (like the Portuguese colonies) that are still under foreign rule.

It is not necessary to give a detailed account of the hundreds of incidents, some of which were chiefly of local, tribal, or religious significance and but indirectly related to the rise of nationalist feeling. Perhaps the Russian pogroms, with their awful, senseless persecution, were the greatest stimulus to modern Jewish feeling. The soul-shaking shock led Jews in Russia to another exodus, to the Zionist movement, and to dream and work for a land of their own.[124] In 1906, in the Dinshaway incident in Egypt, a small party of British officers on a pigeon shoot accidentally shot a peasant woman. There was trouble, a clash. When four villagers were condemned to death and others to imprisonment, nationalist reaction mounted.[125] In 1915, as already recounted, John Chilembwe led his predoomed revolt—"to strike a blow and die." He and his little band of followers were either wiped out in the fighting or later rendered "harmless" by hanging or imprisonment. But his revolt, one of many in Africa earlier and later, marked one beginning of nationalist emotion in that part of the continent.[126] In Tunisia in 1911, when officials tried to take over a Muslim cemetery, a crowd of Tunisians reacted violently, a battle occurred, and Europeans and Tunisians were killed. Thirty-seven Tunisians suffered punishment, seven by death sentences.[127] In 1919, amid a long series of similar affairs in India, a British general, Reginald Dwyer, ordered fire on a crowd of Indians; 379 were killed, 1,200 wounded.[128] The action severely shocked a young man named Nehru, and in later nationalist demonstrations both he and his mother were badly beaten.[129] In China, in another long series of incidents, British-led Shanghai police in May and June, 1925, fired on a crowd of students, and in 1926 a Chinese war lord killed more than two hundred demonstrators. One result was that students "flocked" to the cities to "save" China by revolution.[130]

All through the 1920's, '30's, and '40's, violent encounters continued. After World War II and during the '50's, the provocative incidents multiplied. By this time most of them could be properly called national revolts, as they were in Kenya, in Algeria, in Vietnam—in fact, in many parts of Asia and Africa.[131] Europeans killed and imprisoned thousands of people and themselves suffered heavy casualties. Inflamed national feeling now led directly, not just to riots and rebellions, but—where it had not already done so, as in India—to national revolutions. By the late '50's, especially in Africa, and elsewhere as well, "natives" were willing, as Kenneth Kaunda of Northern Rhodesia asserted, "to pay the price of freedom" whatever the consequences.[132] A wonder could be why there was not more violence, even more than that of the Israelis and the Arabs, or of the Vietnamese and the French and Americans.

The motivations of the leaders of the nationalist movements, of course, were as varied as their peoples and their own individual personalities.[133] They hoped and they feared and they were ambitious for themselves as well as for their peoples. Some of them (Sukarno of Indonesia comes to mind) undoubtedly much coveted personal power and the emoluments that at times accompany high office—fine houses, big cars, beautiful women. Some of them (Nehru of India, Nyerere of Tanzania, and Senghor of Senegal), though not immune to private ambition, were high-minded idealists who put country above private gain. As they are for all men, motivations were mixed and changing. But it is also true that many of them had painful experiences that drove them further and further along their nationalist roads. When many of them began their political lives, they were mild reformers, willing, if only reforms were granted and evolution toward self-government seemed likely, to work within the colonial systems. But as they advocated and worked for reform, they suffered threats against their livelihoods and their lives, they were forced into exile, they were imprisoned or sent to detention camps, and on occasion they were beaten and tortured beyond endurance. Some were executed, as was the Filipino poet and patriot José Rizal (1861–96),[134] and, as martyrs, became powerful symbols for their nation. Those who lived protested ever more, and the more they protested the more they suffered. A list of those who were at one time or another imprisoned (or had for their personal safety to leave their countries) would read like a *Who's Who* of African and Asian nationalism. To choose at random, Gandhi, Nehru, and Tilak were jailed in India, and Banda, Bourguiba, Kaunda, Kenyatta, and Sithole in various parts of Africa. All of them were more nationalist after their imprisonment than before, and they became heroes to increasing numbers of their countrymen. No amount of punishment, no imperial repression actually blunted national feeling; rather, it exacerbated it.[135] And it may be added that the more a people—the Jews, for instance—suffered persecution, the more they became nationalists—in the case of the Jews, the more Jewish.[136]

At varying times, chiefly after World War II, leaders of the various peoples realized, if they had not already done so, that they must establish independent states. And more and more they came to believe that if their protests were loud enough, their demands firm enough, and their actions sufficiently threatening, they could establish these states. The protests grew not only louder but more insistent as well, and they were supported by more and more people, people who became ever more aware of their oppression and of the need for and desirability of concerted action. As the colonial powers reluctantly gave ground, the nationalists took it eagerly. As Lord Lugard once remarked of Africans, the people's "very discontent" was "a measure of their success." [137] And success was no longer to be measured by reforms within colonialism, but by independence.

By persistent protest (everywhere),[138] by "passive resistance" (India),[139] by revolution (Algeria), through civil war (China) and colonial war (Vietnam), over fifty African and Asian peoples, led in most cases by charismatic individuals, did win their independence after 1945 (see table, p. 270). In many cases they won this independence even though most of them did not, by European standards, constitute nations or have the resources (economic or human) to maintain viable states. Independence they could achieve for many reasons: because the imperialist powers were weakened by war; because European and American liberals and radicals believed imperialism wrong and favored, inside and out of their own countries, the right of peoples to national independence; and because the "native" peoples themselves, imitating western peoples and becoming aware of their own traditions *and* their own oppression, finally realized their own power. Not only "could" they achieve independence but they *did* have the power to achieve it.

As the great African nationalist Sithole observed for Africans, so it was for many peoples around the world as they finally found the myth of "white supremacy" to be myth: "As soon as the African knew how to read and write, how to drive and repair an automobile, how to build a modern house and install modern plumbing, how to operate properly on a human body, how to run a business, how to do countless other things that his white god did, why the myth fell asunder, never to come together again." [140] If Sithole exaggerated the progress of Asians and Africans, he did not overestimate their perception of the myth. And when the myth of white superiority was destroyed, the establishment of independent national states was not only likely but inevitable.

Nationalism was not the sole reason for the revolutions that brought self-determining, independent nation-states, for the revolutions were usually not only political—to throw off foreign rule—but also economic and social—to establish new and ideal societies. A declaration of the United Nations General Assembly in 1960 only recognized what in fact had occurred or was occurring: "All peoples have the right to self-determination; by virtue of that right they freely determine their political status and freely pursue their economic and social development." [141] As nationalists strove for states, they nearly always promised westernlike democratic institutions—constitutions—to provide for universal suffrage and civil liberties. Increasingly, they were also influenced not only by western social welfarism but also by Russian Marxism-Leninism,[142] and in some cases by Chinese Marxism-Maoism. Hence, especially after World War II, they emphasized egalitarianism. For more and more of them the way to modernize was through nationalism *and* socialism.

The stress on egalitarianism differed in each new state. In Japan before 1945 the dominant right-wing nationalists "knew next to nothing about the happy marriage of nationalism and bourgeois democracy [or] popular sovereignty as seen in classic western nationalism." [143] Nor were these Japanese nationalists, with rare exceptions,[144] egalitarians except in the mythical sense that all Japanese were equal (no matter how unequal in reality) within national polity (*kokutai*), that is, before the symbolic emperor. But usually elsewhere in the twentieth century, among many peoples—North Africans, Middle Easterners, South Asians, East Asians—socialism in one or another of its varieties became a guiding ideology of nationalist leaders, and after World War II the socialism became both more radical and more pervasive. From Russia, for reasons of doctrine and power politics, there came support for those developing peoples who, like the Chinese from the 1920's, wanted to fight capitalist imperialism.[145] From China after the Maoist 1949 revolution came support for leaders and groups that favored the peasants in, for example, Vietnam and Tanzania. In Paris from the 1930's Marxist-Leninist communists tried hard to convert black African students, and some, in Senghor's phrase, "succumbed to [their] seduction." [146] To gain power in China, Mao used nationalist appeals, and as early as 1939 he was arguing that "Chinese communists must . . . combine patriotism with internationalism. . . . For only by fighting in the defence of the motherland can we . . . achieve national liberation" and thus by victory help peoples of other countries.[147]

Both Marxist-Leninists and Marxist-Maoists won over leaders in some countries, as in Vietnam and Algeria, but their success was scarcely commensurate with their efforts. Black leaders like Aimé Césaire rejected communism because they wanted Marxism placed at the service of blacks and not blacks "at service of Marxism and Communism." [148] Muslim and

Indian leaders often opposed communism because it conflicted with their religions. And, of course, after 1945 American military power and financial aid blocked the spread of communism as the United States pursued its own national interests. Nonetheless, the new nationalisms of Asia and Africa tended to be socialist (or, as some preferred to call them, populist), and at the same time their socialism was nationalist. This was true in India and Indonesia, in Morocco and Egypt, in Ghana and Uganda, and to a greater or lesser extent in much of sub-Sahara Africa and the Middle East.[149]

Beyond their nationalist and generally socialist goals, some Arab (Islamic, too) and African leaders had another dream: federation or union of all the Arab or Islamic peoples, federation or union of all black Africans. These dreams, with their high idealistic appeal, may have originated in nineteenth-century Africa with Blyden[150] and in the Arab world with the Pan-Islamic preaching of Sayyid Jamāl al-Dīn, or "al-Afghānī" (1838?–97), though Arab nationalism in the sense of union of all Arab peoples was a twentieth-century phenomenon.[151] Based largely on color and opposition to white domination, Pan-Africanism attracted ardent followers from about 1900 when the first black congress, with delegates from the United States, the West Indies, and a few claiming to be from Africa, met in London.[152] After World War I three congresses were held. In 1945, at the end of World War II, an enthusiastic group of blacks in which Africans (Nkrumah and Kenyatta) first played an important role laid grand plans at a congress in Manchester, England.[153] From 1958 and the first conference of independent African states, chiefly African leaders held several conferences (or congresses) at which federation or at least common action was debated and planned.[154] Promoters of the ideal dreamed of a united black Africa, united *against* white imperialism and *for* the flowering of an African civilization. They also, in more practical ways, tried to organize specific federations—in West Africa of, for example, Senegal and Mali, and in East Africa of Kenya, Uganda, Tanzania, and perhaps Zambia. With Julius Nyerere, who was to become president of Tanzania, they seemed to agree that "Africans, all over the continent, without a word being spoken . . . looked at the European, looked at one another, and knew that in relation to the European they were one." [155] And they believed in the slogan "Africa for Africans," and, it must be added, most of them did share a continent, a color, and a hated colonial experience.

In 1944–45 several Arab states, inspired by a common "Arab spirit" and Muslim religion as well as united by common opposition to western dominance, formed the Arab League. They hoped thus to strengthen the ties among themselves and to co-ordinate their political activities in order to promote Arab interests[156]—particularly at that crucial time vis-à-vis Israel. From the mid-1950's Gamal Nasser of Egypt led the movement for Arabism, and in 1958, by uniting Syria with Egypt, he established the United Arab Republic. This republic, which he and other Arab leaders hoped would be the base of further Arab union, lasted in fact but three years. Nasser himself saw his Egypt "in a group of circles." [157] It was in Africa, its peoples were Arabic, its religion Islamic. Were Egyptians first of all Arabic, Islamic, or African, or were they simply Egyptians? Egyptians and other Arab peoples were never sure where their chief interests lay. They still apparently are not, though plans for federation persist.

Pan movements in the Middle East, though enthusiastically proclaimed, generally, like the United Arab Republic, have failed. They were abortive because the peoples were not any readier to unite on the basis of Arab culture or the Islamic religion than were Europeans on the bases of their culture and religion. And the same was true in black Africa, where tribal, ethnic, and language differences were almost insurmountable. Actually, both the Middle Eastern peoples and the diverse and many African peoples had great difficulty in forming nations, let alone federations, and the nation-states they did establish were usually within old colonial boundaries. Both Arabs and Africans were scattered over vast areas; neither in the Middle East nor in Africa was communication easy or quick; few Arabs or Africans, faced with the daily tasks of living, could envision grand dreams of unity.[158]

The nationalism that produced nation-states could not be effectively enlarged, at least by 1970, to Arabism or Africanism. In the Middle East the peoples of Syria, Lebanon, Iraq, Saudi Arabia, and other states each had different traditions and interests. In Africa the peoples within the nation-states had widely different cultures and few common interests. Finally, after the various states were established, each had ambitious leaders and officials who were eager to keep their status and power and so the national independence. Few idealists and ideologists among the Arab and African leaders thought in terms of still wider groupings of humanity, perhaps all humanity, and could not subscribe to federation or union of only the peoples of their own "spirit" or color.[159] But unions of people beyond nations just did not occur. "Pan-ism," like "one worldism," broke on the rocks of nationalism.

On winning independence, the new national governments tried, with undeterminable success, to arouse national feeling and loyalty in much the same manner that European governments had done. In dozens of ways they aroused the consciousness and penetrated the lives of their citizens. In turn, these citizens participated in national affairs and learned to identify their interests with the national. In the past, people's protests against foreign rulers had made them more and more aware of common bonds. When new national governments were established, their protests were against their own governments. If the protests, past and present, did not result in loyalty, they did heighten consciousness of common aspirations that could be fulfilled through the nation-states.

In one way the task of the new governments in creating national feeling was harder than that of the preindependence nationalist movements. As Immanuel Wallerstein remarked, "the existence of an external enemy—the major motivation for unity in the nationalist movement" had largely disappeared.[160] But what the independence movements had begun, the new national governments continued. Striving not only to arouse national feeling but also to instill loyalty, they fostered and promoted these sentiments whenever and however they could just as from the 1880's the Japanese government had so successfully done, and in the 1920's the Turkish government under Mustapha Kemal had so strenuously tried to do. The Japanese Ministry of Education's directive of 1937, *Fundamentals of Our National Polity,* which summed up the Japanese way of loyalty, revealed how effective the government had been in creating the "great family nation"—over 2 million copies were sold.[161] During the Turkish revolution of the years after World War I, Mustapha Kemal created "all the paraphernalia of a nation-state," the institutions as well as the symbols, as he carried through, one by one, secular reforms affecting the lives of all Turks.[162]

The newer governments in Asia and Africa were established by national constitutions that in fact they themselves had usually framed. These constitutions provided for national institutions (civil and military), and for whatever rights and duties the citizens of each nation were supposed to possess. As the new governments carried on the old colonial administrative arrangements, they modeled themselves on European national governments, basically attempted to do what the latter had done. So much is this true that much that follows will, except in detail, repeat what has been said earlier about governments and nationalism in the West.

Asian and African governments set up foreign offices and diplomatic services with all the officials—ambassadors, consuls, and delegations to the United Nations—they could afford, and more. They established national court systems, taxes, treasuries, and currencies. They organized national military services (with national uniforms and conscription), national post offices, regional administrative offices of the national government, national universities and school systems, and national social security and public-relations agencies. They regulated, more rather than less, foreign trade and domestic prices and wages. They controlled, often severely, the means of communication and expression of opinion. They passed laws prohibiting employment of foreign workers. They built roads, railroads, and harbors (nearly always with foreign capital and technicians). They built impressive governmental buildings in the centers of their new and occasionally impressive capitals. Frequently they nationalized what had been foreign-owned banks and businesses—the trading companies, the oil wells, the mines—and they usually made it impossible for foreigners to own land. When, in November, 1969, this writer stood in a street of Kampala to watch the British half of a bank name being obliterated by sand-blasting, he was witnessing but a single minor example of the nationalizing process that went on all over the two vast continents.

To do all these things and more, the governments employed more and more people and made them dependent on the nation-states, created burgeoning bureaucracies that perpetuated themselves. And they accumulated filing cabinets by the thousand and began national archives to keep account of what happened,[163] essential record keeping in all nation building. The new national governments appreciated the value of national record keeping.

The governments and their followers went further. They fostered study of "national" histories and of the "national" language, the adoption of national dress and customs, the initiation of national holidays, and the creation of national heroes and symbols. Of course, each new national government attempted these things in differing fashion, but they all did them.

In Turkey during the 1920's, Mustapha Kemal, interested in modernism, directed his fellow countrymen to wear western clothing—hats for men, no veils for women. In Egypt in 1955 a minister of social affairs appointed a committee to regularize "the national dress," which recommended the abolition of "robes and turbans and also the long nightshirt-like *gellabiya.*" In Kenya in 1970, when aspiring individuals tended to wear western clothing (including, for young women, the miniskirt), a minister of co-operation and social services launched a drive "to design a national dress." [164] In the days of mass production, unique national dress might be hard to promote, but promotion there was.

Since most of the new nations were indeed new, they, with rare exceptions, had little history that could be called national. Long before independence, however, national-minded Asian and African historians, as well as historians from Europe, began studies that inspired national feeling.[165] The value of historical study for national purpose came to be well understood. In 1938 an Arab leader, Costi Zurayq, in a book entitled *National Consciousness,* expressing the belief that national consciousness drew inspiration from the past, concluded that a people like the Arabs "must sense the spirit of its history and comprehend the elements which have gone into its making." [166] A noted Indian historian, K. M. Pannikar, wrote in 1947, "Ever since India became conscious of her nation-hood . . . there was a growing demand for a history of India which . . . reconstruct[s] the past in a way that would give us an idea of our heritage. . . . I do not think it is an exaggeration to say that it was a spiritual adventure for most of us. . . ." [167] In 1953 an equally noted Nigerian historian, K. O. Dike, averred, "For young and emergent nations there is no study as important as that of history. . . . Our past is very much a part of our present. . . . Most great and far-reaching movements have begun with a romantic appeal to the past." [168] An African nationalist journal in 1956 declared that every culture had "need of ancestors to assure the legitimacy of its acts and thoughts." [169] And so it was.

Japan did have a long and recorded history, and from the 1880's Japanese studied it assiduously. The Jews had a long and much studied history, though the conscious movement for a Zion developed only from the 1880's. Educated Persians and Arabs (and some ordinary people, too) remembered a thousand years or more of history. In South Africa the Afrikaners in the long struggles against the English and the Bantu peoples from the 1870's developed a deep consciousness of their "chosen" role in history.[170]

For the most part among the newer nations the history had to be studied anew or for the first time—in order to find common origins (mythical or actual) and inspire national feeling. The new universities, nearly all supported by national funds, had history departments that stressed the history of the nation and the area of which it was a part. In the primary and secondary schools, old and new, students were taught more about "their country" and less about the histories of their former rulers. National-minded citizens and historians formed historical societies and published historical journals and books. Bookstores featured historical works, displaying them prominently on the "front tables." [171] For many of the new nations a common history of their peoples was hard to find, for the ethnic, tribal, and religious differences were enormous, but still national histories, whether mythical or not, were in the making just as they had long been in Europe.

Nationalists were determined to make nations out of peoples. National governments, in spite of the great linguistic diversities, generally gave official blessing to one language as the national and promoted its use: the Turkish a modernized Turkish; the Chinese a modernized, vernacular Chinese; the Tanzanian the Swahili; the white South African the Afrikaner.[172] Every government adopted a national anthem, as India did the "Bande Mataram" ("Hail to Thee, My Mother").[173] Every nation officially established a national holiday (or holidays); usually this commemorated the date of independence, in the case of India, August 15, 1947. On this day the leaders especially tried to inculcate patriotism. National officials everywhere were aware of the value of symbols and heroes in making patriots, of the amuletic effect of national flags and postage stamps, of national slogans—like Kenyatta's *"Harambee"* ("Let us all pull together") —and appealing, often mystical national ceremonies. When Mwalimu Julius Nyerere was inaugurated as President of Tanzania in October, 1965, he took an oath as father and defender of the nation, received the accouterments of a warrior, and then mixed earth from the state houses in Dar es Salaam and Zanzibar in a bowl to symbolize the indissolubility of the union of Tanganyika and Zanzibar. Nationalists sometimes had difficulty in finding heroes and martyrs, but they found them, if not in a nonexistent earlier national history, then, as was true of Nkrumah and Sukarno, in themselves. In China, Mao's first published (1917) article was filled with references to the "heroes, martyrs, and warriors of old." [174] In the chapel of Kings College (Budo) in Uganda there is a plaque "To the glory of God and in grateful memory of the Buganda martyrs. . . ." As Mustapha Kemal had done in Turkey in the 1920's, nationalist officials everywhere erected statues and monuments and asked their peoples to celebrate before and around them. As in the West, so in Asia and Africa they strove (I paraphrase and quote words of Nehru) to give an anthropomorphic form to their country. India, for example, became *"Bharat Mata,* Mother India, a beautiful lady, very old but ever youthful in appearance, sad-eyed and forlorn, cruelly treated by aliens and outsiders, and calling upon her children to protect her." [175]

Evidence of the growing nationalism across Asia and up and down Africa is superabundant. But how pervasive, strong, viable was the sentiment? That there were great differences in its intensity and spread is obvious. Yet there is no way at present of determining just how nationalist most of the various peoples and the millions of individuals were.[176] That the Japanese had generally become nationally conscious and loyal before 1939 is clear, but after the defeat of 1945 some of them, torn by doubt and later by ideological dissension, did not know who they were or where their interests lay.[177] In either of the Congos how many of the millions of individuals among the many tribes were much aware of their nationhood, let alone were nationalists? "Some" is probably the answer to the first part of the question, and "few" to the second. That in much of Africa and Asia by 1970 most individuals knew they had been affected by activities of their nation-state is fairly evident. But how loyal to this state were they and, equally important, did they feel themselves part of a nation and so identify themselves?

They did increasingly participate in some way in national activities, through voting, through political parties or voluntary associations, by payment of taxes, by being in the army and attending school. Larger numbers, such as Kenyan university students[178] in the 1960's, did learn to identify themselves as members of a nation, but in much of Africa tribal identification, like that of the Ibos in Nigeria, still took precedence.[179]

From the early 1930's more Chinese began to feel they belonged to China as they increasingly participated in the so-called mass movement against the Japanese and in support of the Chinese Communist struggle against the Kuomintang government of Chiang Kai-shek.[180] Nevertheless, we do not know just how nationalist the Chinese "masses" really were (or are). Jews in Israel, pressed on all sides by Arabs, have felt their "Jewishness" deeply and have proved their loyalty to Israel. But in spite of the fervent exhortations of the late Nasser and other leaders and the threat that Israel poses, Arabs still have difficulty in deciding where their interests lie, and apparently many, even in Egypt, have been indifferent except when actual fighting occurred.

It has been said again and again that Asian and African nation-states were established before nations came into being. As one authority, Rupert Emerson, remarked, Africa was "a continent rich in nationalism [among leaders] but poor in nations," and this was true as well of Asia.[181] While the nationalism of leaders was intense, many ordinary people scarcely comprehended it. At the beginning of the 1970's, Mali, the two Congos, Togoland, Ceylon, Burma, Iraq, and the Sudan were all nation-states, but did their peoples constitute nations, and how many, aside from some of their leaders, shared nationalist sentiment to a significant degree? As late as 1947 an important Nigerian nationalist who knew some Italian history, Obafemi Awolowo, declared, "Nigeria is not a nation. It is a mere geographical expression." [182] Even in 1964 Julius Nyerere, no mean African authority, believed that "nations in any real sense of the word do not at present exist in Africa. . . . None of our nations is made up of people bound together by a single language or a heritage common to them but not to the people of a neighboring nation. Each exists because its boundaries were historical and administrative conveniences of the colonial powers." [183]

There was no historical reason for the Congo except that it had once been a Belgian colony—it was the creation of surveyors, map makers, and Leopold II's mad desire for profit. The Congolese had "independence thrust" [184] upon them before they had a chance to form a nation if they had so desired. There was nationalist sentiment in Indonesia (particularly Java), but that vast and populous archipelago of over 112 million people speaking twenty or more languages is spread over three thousand islands, and the peoples are little united by history and culture or by anything except dislike of the remembered Dutch occupation.[185] If the Congo and Indonesia are not typical, they are not unique. The very fact that nationalist leaders had to make so many vehement appeals for support reveals the weakness of the sentiment among many peoples.

Family, tribe, clan retained the loyalty of many Asians and Africans even when they began to think in national terms. A huge country like India has many peoples, provinces, languages—500 million quite diverse people, nine official provinces (more actually), three hundred-plus languages, several (at least eleven) major religions, dozens of so-called races, and hundreds of castes. It is indeed a living "museum of cults and customs, creeds and cultures, faiths and tongues, racial types and social systems." [186] And millions of Indians, often poverty-stricken and ignorant, either give their loyalty to entities and groups lesser than India or, destitute, hungry, and sick, are indifferent. Small and poor countries—Zambia and Mali and Ceylon—have fewer diversities, but the people have little to unify them and few of them are ardent nationalists.

For the most part the peoples of Asia and Africa, while they have produced geniuses, philosophers and poets and warriors of justified renown, are still poor and uneducated, and they have trouble comprehending what goes on nationally outside their own immediate communities. Between them and their leaders, their elites, there is a great gap.[187] In spite of the rapid growth of the mass media—especially the number of transistor radios[188]—they are but slowly realizing that they are supposed to become national patriots, eager to defend and help their nation. Peoples, though contemporary prophets may proclaim the opposite, do not change rapidly

—that is, in this case, change their habits and values and allegiances in a hurry—and if they do, their temporary enthusiasms have a high and fast mortality rate.

To repeat, when peoples obtained independence and established new states, expectancy ran high. But the new governments could not and did not meet the expectancies as they encountered almost insoluble political and economic problems.[189] The governments, because their countries were poor and undeveloped, lacked capital for economic development. The number of trained and experienced civil servants was always too low. New administrative agencies and procedures had to be established, and the mistakes were many. The governments had to attempt to do the almost impossible while they carried on the ordinary activities of any government. Of course, they often failed. Hence, disappointments were almost as great as the expectancies had been.

The new national rulers, elected or self-selected, democratic or authoritarian, had to make unhappy compromises between the promising ideals of the independence movements and the hard realities of the immediate needs and conflicting interests. As might have been expected but was not, many of the new officials were (or seemed to be) corrupted by their new power. Indeed, as might have been expected but was not, they often sought the perquisites of power, appointed their friends and supporters to coveted positions, acted harshly against the enemies of their regimes, and sought (as did Nkrumah) personal material gain. While the new states continued to exist, organized military groups or cliques (sometimes only *they were* organized) overthrew governments and established dictatorships (similar to but not exactly like those of South America). Whether this did or did not happen, one-party governments came to be the rule. Moreover, in many of the new states bitter ideological struggles split the peoples as moderate elements contested with radical, as religious groups fought each other.

All this and much more brought disillusion and disappointment, and at the very time the foreign enemy—the imperial white western power—had been eliminated, and the fear and hate that unified colonial peoples had diminished. No wonder, then, that doubts arose concerning the viability of the new states and the depth of nationalist feeling among their peoples. Nationalism everywhere, west and east, has always depended in no small part on foreign threats—animosity as well as hope motivated every people. And now this cementing bond was weakened. It is possible, of course, that some Asian and African countries will discover new national enemies and become aggressive and expansionist, as did Japan before 1945. So far, at least, despite the case of the Israeli Arab wars, this has not generally occurred. If the example of the larger western countries is followed, it doubtless will.

Yet all the new states survived, fragile and often shaken as many of them were. When its much acclaimed national leader, Nkrumah, was overthrown in a coup, Ghana was badly hurt and in danger; however, under its new government—with less known officials—it continued not only to exist but also to carry on its nationalizing activities. Nigeria was torn by bitter civil war beginning in 1967 and the attempted creation of a new tribal nation-state, Biafra. But, recovering with remarkable swiftness, Nigeria bounced back and, displaying self-confidence, seemed again to be a stable nation-state if not yet a unified nation. India, in spite of dire poverty and wide political and cultural diversities, still remained a nation-state after more than twenty years of turmoil and dissension.[190] Not even the world-wide struggle for power among the giants of the earth, the Soviet Union, the United States, and, later, China, slowed the rise of nationalism. Rather, it intensified the nationalism of the new states that, trying to be neutral, were fighting to survive and develop.

Why the nationalisms of Asia and Africa persisted unabated is not as yet clear. Because of the historic struggles for independence and the depth of national feeling they aroused? Because nations and nationalism were still the dominant forms of political organization and sentiment in the West, and the Asian and African peoples had no choice if they wanted to be "free?" Because the nation-state was the largest political unit that could be understood by enough people? Because officials of the new governments and special interest groups within the states wished to maintain themselves in power? Or was it possibly because mass communications enabled national governments to reach and control the varied peoples within the states? Possibly because, as in Europe, the growing urbanism, with its dominant and large capital cities, fostered common feeling?[191]

Certain it was that each people continued to desire the improvement of its conditions and its position in relation to other peoples. Nations and nationalism in Asia and Africa, as in the West, offered, or seemed to offer, hope and relief from fear. Beyond nationalism, one expectancy, at least for the present, could well be more nationalism.[192]

XI

Some Myths—Metaphysical and Physical—About Nations and Nationalism

> . . . it is not Truth but Opinion that can travel the World without a Pass-port. For were it otherwise, and were there not as many internal forms of the mind as there are external figures of men, there were then some possibility to persuade by the mouth of one Advocate—even Equity alone . . . there being nothing wherein nature so much triumpheth as in dissimilitude. From whence it cometh, that there [is] found so great diversity of Opinions; so strong a contrariety of inclinations; so many natural and unnatural, wise and foolish, manly and childish, affections and passions in mortal men.—SIR WALTER RALEGH

Scholars[1] have devoted much attention to historical myths in recent years, and with reason, for myths have much motivated men in all they do and think. By myth here is meant an ill-founded belief held uncritically by a people (or an individual) to explain what otherwise is or seems to be inexplicable or unclear. Psychologically a myth can be wish fulfillment (Freud), an expression of an unconscious dream of a people (Jung), or, more simply, an invented, irrational story to explain what is mysterious in order to provide assurance.[2]

Because myths are beliefs that cannot be substantially verified by evidence, they are generally regarded as partly or completely false and therefore lacking in reality. But it cannot be denied that when people believe them their belief has reality, or that people act, even base their lives, upon them, especially in times of crisis.[3] Mussolini clearly saw the immense significance of myth when, just before his "march on Rome" in 1922, he shouted,

We have created our myth. The myth is a faith, it is a passion. It is not necessary that it be a reality. It is a reality by the fact that it is a good, a hope, a faith, that it is courage. Our myth is the Nation, our myth is the greatness of the Nation! And to this myth, to this grandeur, that we wish to translate into a complete reality, we subordinate all the rest.[4]

In this and the next chapter I wish to point up some of the myths of the nationalist sentiment, for in its origin and development they have immense significance.[5] In doing this I shall occasionally repeat data I have mentioned earlier.

Some Supernatural Myths: God, Nature, and Destiny

A widespread, though not universal, belief of patriots has been that a supernatural force—God or gods—created nations, chose one (their own), and gave it a mission. If the evidence has been scanty, the faith has been fervent. People everywhere seek reasons for their ways of life. Many modern men, like most medieval western Christians, have been certain that a Divine Being determined man's fate, and modern patriots that this Being divided men into nations and chose or blessed their own nation.

In the increasingly secular and skeptical twentieth century, supernatural myths may have lost some of their magic, but they have, no matter how primitive they may seem today, played an enormous role in nationalism. A nation (France) came into being because a dove from Heaven anointed a founder (Clovis) with holy oil, or was saved because one of its martyrs (Jeanne d'Arc) heard "divine voices." A nation (Japan) was founded by a sun-goddess, Amaterasu, who had her August Grandson thrust through "the many-piled clouds of Heaven" down to Kyushu, bringing with him "the sacred Three Treasures, the jewel, the sword, and the mirror, and founding the divine dynasty of emperors." [6]

While the divinities differed, the ideas of divine founding were similar. Early in the eighteenth century the clever author of the *Idea of a Patriot King*, Viscount Bolingbroke, thought it clear that God had created groups of mankind "very differently." [7] A half century later the German philosopher-reformers Herder and Fichte maintained that God had created nations according to His divine plan. For Fichte, enthusiastic and influential convert to nationalism that he was, the nation was the true manifestation of divinity: "Only when each people, left to itself, develops and forms itself in accordance with its own peculiar quality, and only when in every people each individual develops himself in accordance with that common quality . . . does the manifestation of divinity appear . . .

as it ought to be." [8] In America about the same time John Quincy Adams (1767–1848) wrote to his famed father, "The whole continent of North America appears to be destined by *Divine Providence* to be peopled by *one* nation [his own, of course]." [9] A generation or so later Mazzini, who so grieved over his beloved but disunited Italy, thought the nation "the God-appointed instrument of the human race," and told his fellow Italians that God had given them their country, thus providing them with their means of action.[10]

God, then, in creating the different peoples, really created the nations as means and end for men.[11] The myth was carried to logical extremes later, and not only in western nations. In 1907 Sri Aurobindo Ghosh told his fellow Indians that nationalism was a religion that had "come from God," and that they were "merely instruments of God for the work of the Almighty." [12]

Long before Ghosh, Moses told the Israelites they were a "holy people unto the Lord thy God" chosen "above all the nations that are on earth." [13] Other, later peoples also believed God had chosen them. This was particularly true of Christian peoples, and even more so of English and American Puritans, who believed they had a special "calling." But the idea, paradoxically, occurred not only to Englishmen and Americans but also to Russians, Afrikaners, Japanese, and Indians.[14] During the middle of the seventeenth century Cromwell thought Englishmen "had a stamp upon them from God," [15] and not a few of his countrymen at his time and much later, including the great imperialist-financier Cecil Rhodes, agreed with him. In the United States from at least the 1840's, and the Mexican War, publicists proclaimed the "manifest destiny" of their nation.[16] Around 1900 and the time of the Spanish-American War a famed orator from Indiana, Senator Albert Beveridge, won loud acclaim and much support when he declared God had "marked the American people as his chosen nation to finally lead in the regeneration of the world"—the "doing of His inscrutable Work." [17] In Russia during the latter part of the nineteenth century the great novelist Dostoyevsky (1821–81), who was also a Russian patriot, fervently preached Russia's mission to be the "bearer of the idea of Christ." [18] In South Africa during the latter part of the nineteenth century, the Afrikaners (Boers), who were close students of the Bible, felt a deep sense of being chosen—called, like the Israelites had been from Egypt, to enter a Promised Land where they were predestined to live as masters among natives predestined to be their "hewers of wood and drawers of water." [19] In Japan in the early twentieth century a civilian employee of the Army General Staff, Okawa Shumei, along with other

Japanese nationalists, was convinced that "Heaven" had "decided on Japan as its choice for the champion of the East" against the West. "Has not," he asked, "this been the purpose of our three thousand long years of preparation? . . . a truly grand and magnificent mission." [20] And in India about the same time the violent Vinayak Sāvarkar was dreaming of a time when Hindus would be able to "dictate terms to the whole world." [21]

For such prophecies of grandeur there was, of course, no proof, since there was nothing but rhetoric to support them. The will of God in this respect was indeed "inscrutable." Yet the myth was all the more firmly believed, and it still was as the twentieth century entered its last third, for American statesmen and chaplains were still talking of, say, the American mission in Asia, and Russian and Chinese Communist ideologists and politicians of the inexorable economic movement, the messiah of the dialectic, that would conquer the world.

From the seventeenth century nature began to supplant God as explanation of all inexplicable things. Advanced eighteenth-century *philosophes* could not attribute an "anthropomorphic quality" [22] to the nation, but it became for them the product of nature. Often cosmopolitan in outlook, they usually did not stress the nation and national feeling in their writings, but, like Locke and Voltaire, they did, as pointed out earlier, conceive of men as grouped in commonwealths (nations) composed of propertied stockholders engaged in joint national enterprises. Postulating laws of nature, they generally projected backward to the beginning of human history a social contract that could be thought of, in their present, as a national constitution and a natural development of men in nations. The nation thus became the natural group and devotion to it, incipient from the beginning, desirable and good.

This was most evident in the writings of the romantic Jean Jacques Rousseau. At some imagined time in the past a man gave his liberty and power to the natural association (the nation?) and thenceforth was governed (or should be) by the general (the national?) will,[23] through a common (national?) government to which he owed devotion (was patriotic?) and obedience (patriotic duty?). Good, natural men, shaped by wholesome education of their emotions, expressed a "constant, unalterable and pure" general will, in substance an inviolate national will. While Rousseau would perhaps have preferred a city-state like his revered homeland, Geneva, he gave primacy to the community, and this in the eighteenth century was becoming the nation of citizens.

Rousseau apparently was not content to let nature act unaided; his faith was not that great. He advised the king of Poland to emulate Moses and Lycurgus, who excited love of country among Jews and Spartans,[24] and to educate his subjects to love their country and reacquire their "natural repugnance" to strangers. To most of the eighteenth-century *philosophes* not the realities but the revelations of nature held a place comparable to the revealed teachings of their religious predecessors. They argued well and at length; there was no proof, however, other than the proof faith affords, that nature intended any form of social grouping. But that, of course, did not matter: they had the certainty of their natural emotion or reason.

To the sober Scottish rationalist, Adam Smith, the state or sovereignty into which men were born and educated and which protected them was "by nature most strongly recommended" to them. Because it contained "all the objects" of their kindest affections—their children, parents, friends— and provided for safety and property, it was indeed "by nature, therefore endeared" to them. As mentioned earlier, Smith, like some other thinkers of his time, believed that that wisdom, which contrived human affections as well as nature, directed the attention of all men to a "particular portion," and for the author of *The Wealth of Nations,* as well as an increasing number of people of his and later times, that portion was the nation.[25]

If by wisdom Smith meant, as he may have, simply that it was natural for men to love familiar surroundings and company, then there was much sense to his argument. But no natural laws, no outside physical or inner psychological forces so dictated. The idea persisted, won adherents. To the propagandists and politicians of the early French Revolution (Carnot), to German patriots (Fichte and Görres) fighting the French under Napoleon, *la loi naturelle* and *Naturtrieb* became basic philosophic justifications for national patriotism.[26] In the United States since 1776 and 1787, the fundamental documents of independence and nationhood appeal to natural law as fundamental justification for the nation. And everywhere people believe it's just natural for men to live in nations and "unnatural" for anyone to be "unpatriotic" or disloyal. In the limited sense that nearly all modern peoples have established nations and are loyal to them, the institution and sentiment are universal, but that hardly proves them natural.[27] There is no more proof of the natural origin of nations than there is that Germans are descended from Mannus, the son of the god Tuisco who was born from the Earth, or that the Franks were the progeny of Francion by Hector, or that the sons of Oduduwa who created the earth created the Yoruba states and were the progenitors of all the Yoruba people.

Nationalists for whom God and nature were not sufficient have often believed in mystical forces. Usually these explain the nation by the national spirit, which is like saying, as an American historian remarked, that corn grows because of the corn spirit. Herder, with the fertile imagination of a romantic, saw nations as an end product of the eternal *Volkgeist*.[28] The well-known founder of Danish folk schools, the patriotic Bishop Grundtvig, accounted for the unbreakable fellowship of a nation by the "hidden but active life-force" he called *Folkaanden* (national spirit).[29]

The appeal of mystical force ran deep. For the British orator Edmund Burke the nation was a divinely inspired union of the past, the present, and the unborn generations, a historical, organic personality embodying the "moral essences" derived from the experience and wisdom of the ages.[30] Though Georg Wilhelm Friedrich Hegel, German philosopher of the absolute idea, was not in the strict sense a nationalist, he proclaimed that a people was imbued with a peculiar and special purpose and that the state, the final "embodiment of dialectic evolution," resulted from the historical experience and genius of a people.[31] As has been mentioned before, to a distinguished philosopher-patriot in France, Ernest Renan, the nation was "a soul, a spiritual principle" arising not only out of common "memories, sacrifices, glories, afflictions and regrets," but also out of the historically determined will to live together and carry out the heritage. The nation was two things that were really one, the legacy of ancestors and a common will: "To have done great things together, to wish to do more of them, here is the essential condition to be a people." So strongly did Renan believe ancestors made "us what we are" that he thought the "cult of ancestors the most legitimate of all cults." While the skeptical critical scholar did not mention the divine inspiration for nations, he put historical mysticism in its place.[32] Auguste Maurice Barrès, one of the last important French reactionary royalists, carried the cult of ancestral dead to the extreme. What he reiterated in his numerous emotional novels and essays was this: national feeling was a sentiment (or sensibility) arising out of the soil and the relationship of the living to the dead, of whom the living were only a prolongation. The purpose of all history, all thought, all effort was to create the nation and nationalism, the French nation and devotion to it.[33] Probably no nationalist has ever gone further than this in affirmation without substance. And yet, and yet, it was, like the other metaphysical myths, deeply believed and hence became very much a reality of nationalism.

For passionate nationalists their nation became, in Edmund Burke's eloquent words, "an idea of continuity, which extends in time, as well as space," [34] a mystical being (both beloved mother and revered father) who represented all the generations and, as Aurobindo Ghosh of India cried, stood for pride in the past, pain in the present, and passion for the future.[35] These nationalists thought of their nation as a collective soul, a mystical spirit. They thought of it as a living organism, like an individual man, which felt, thought, remembered, hoped.[36] That it might be but a historically evolved and evolving group composed of mortal individuals who for a time shared common traditions, interests, and hopes was not enough for them. They believed it to be an entity, beyond and above petty men. And at their most mystical they believed it bestowed immortality. Barrès wanted "to collaborate in something that" survived him, and he chose, like a later great soldier, De Gaulle, the cult of France.[37] Rudyard Kipling asked as World War I began, "Who dies if England lives?" [38] and Englishmen did die that England might live. *Pro patria mori.*

That a nation was not an organism, an immortal being or soul, but a historically evolving community composed of individuals made no difference to mystical nationalists. They had their faith and they believed it.

Physical Myths: Geography and Race

Beliefs about nations and nationalism are often woven out of both fact and fantasy, hard evidence and imaginative emotion. That physical environmental conditions—the climate and the land—affect the nature and shape of human groupings is easily observable. The question is, how? The answers vary, and many of them are at best conjectural.

It has often been stated that geography determined the varieties of human development, but this is obviously overstatement. There now seems to be agreement that physical conditions permit and set limits for certain kinds of development, or, at most, that "the *environment is a determiner of the extent and kind of change taking place in a particular* [human] *characteristic.*" [39] In spite of much study and more conjecture, however, it is not at all clear just how the physical environment has influenced the rise of nations or the differentiations among them.

That the ties between environments and peoples are close has been well recognized at least from ancient Greek and Roman times, and certainly early modern observers noted them. In the early fourteenth century John of Paris, a Dominican monk who opposed the Roman pope for the French King Philip the Fair, advocated a French state because of differences in climate and character.[40] At the beginning of the eighteenth century Louis XIV's Bishop Bossuet deduced from the Scriptures that "human society requires men to love the land which they occupy together, regarding it as a mother and nurse, attaching themselves to it and finding in it a bond of union." [41] A little later Montesquieu stressed the effect of environment on the formation of the "spirit of the laws" of each nation, and Rousseau, less exhortatively vague than usual, declared that the political order of Europe was the result in part of physical nature as he urged the setting of natural national boundaries.[42] Rousseau's contemporary romantic in the Germanies, Herder, thought the environment, especially the climate, mainly responsible for the branching out of nationalities from the common stem of humanity.[43] For Johann Fichte, who a little later, in opposition to Napoleon, became an intense German nationalist, "certain parts of the earth's surface, together with their inhabitants," were "visibly destined by nature to form political entities." [44]

In mid-nineteenth-century England, Henry Thomas Buckle (1821–62), who modestly proposed to write the history and evolve the laws of civilization, tried to demonstrate scientifically how climate, food, and soil rather than race "originated" the "large and conspicuous differences between nations." [45] The coming "scientists" of geography were impressed. When "scientific methods" began to be applied to geography toward the end of the nineteenth century and later, such scholars as Friedrich Ratzel, Ellen Semple, Jean Brunhes, and Ellsworth Huntington[46] attempted to show specific ways in which the physical environment conditioned men and societies. While their studies were not specifically concerned with the origins of nations, their geographic interpretation of history lent weight to the geographic explanation of nations. Nations began and differed, it was argued, because of the differing nature of the land, the climate, the resources, and natural obstacles.

It cannot be doubted that these have influenced men and the ways in which they have grouped themselves. Further, it cannot be doubted that men tend to love their "native lands," the localities in which they were born and matured—which they became familiar with and comfortable in. They, as Shakespeare did England, may even regard them as other Edens, demiparadises, blessed plots, or, as do some Indonesians their Indonesia, a "pearl," "a beautiful green carpet." [47] As Walter Scott sang, few men have souls so dead that they have never thought, "This is my own, my native land." And many have sung in their national anthems of their great and beloved lands, their "rocks and rills" and "woods and templed hills," or, as do Brazilians, of "their giant land eternally lying in a splendid cradle." [48]

Lands and climates do differ. Certainly people are affected by them. It takes no unusual insight to perceive that a temperate climate and a rich soil enable not only greater economic productivity but also a greater flowering of the arts than an arctic climate and an infertile soil, where the dwellers must constantly fight the elements in order to eat and keep from freezing. Certainly a tropical climate permits easier acquisition of food and brings a higher incidence of certain diseases than does a temperate one. Living habits at high altitudes, even in the days of controlled inside temperatures, must be simpler than those at or near sea level. Social life on desert sands or arctic wastes has to be, even today, nomadic as a group searches for sustenance. In lush jungle, life can be easily sedentary but hardly urban-industrial. A river (the Rhine or the Vistula), a channel (the English), a mountain range (the Alps or the Andes), an ocean (any) *may* divide peoples, make communication between them difficult. Where transportation and communication are easiest, peoples have usually congregated, built Londons or Parises, and therefore had greater chances to unify.

All this and much more can hardly be challenged. But there is no proved connection between the origin and rise of nations *and* the physical environment. Modern nations and nationalism first appeared in temperate zones, in lands with comparatively rich soils and resources, and usually (not always) within territories where natural obstacles were few. But the relationships are tenuous, and those who have seen direct connections commit the old logical error of *post hoc, ergo propter hoc*. Nations and nationalism by the last third of the twentieth century have appeared in every climate (except at the poles), in rich and poor lands, and in territories cut by major "natural" barriers. What precise influence geography has had on the formation of nations is not and cannot be determined with the instruments of research at hand.

All of the large and some of the small nations today possess a variety of soils and climates. In the Soviet Union, the United States, and China the range of climates and physical environments is extreme but not dissimilar, and all three have most of the possible variations. The climates of many nations—France and Germany, Italy and Spain, Britain and Japan —do not widely differ. Weather maps, like maps of the world's resources, little resemble those that mark political boundaries. Nations that, like the United States and France, have had what are called natural national boundaries have pushed out beyond them, and such boundaries have never been permanent or even long lasting. The historically sacred "natural boundaries" of France—the Rhine, the Alps, the Pyrenees, and the Atlantic Ocean—were established not by nature but by Louis XIV and his predecessors and successors—powerful cardinals like Richelieu and "organizers of victory" like Carnot—and once the national boundaries were more or less reached, France went far overseas to Africa and Asia. It is true that the island kingdoms of Britain and Japan were protected by the waters around them, but both have been invaded or occupied, the British islands often in medieval times and the Japanese in 1945; and neither Britain from early modern times nor Japan from 1895 was contained within its islands by water.[49] Water floats both men and goods. Many so-called natural obstacles—the Rockies and the Urals, the Mississippi, the Nile, and the Volga—do not divide; some (the Pyrenees and Himalayas) more or less do. In point of fact, bodies of water—the Mediterranean, for example—while hindrances to armies, have long provided the easiest and cheapest intercommunication. At least since Hannibal and certainly since Napoleon the Alps have not been insurmountable. And in the twentieth century, when most African and Asian nations were forming, airplanes leveled nearly all the mountainous obstacles so that these could only in retrospect be called barriers.

It seems quite understandable that patriots love their native land, the locality of their birth and childhood. Except in small nations, however, they cannot intimately know the whole land of their nation, even in the days of auto and jet travel, and hence, except in imagination, they cannot love the whole land that is called the national. That bit of soil on which they were born, their true *patrie*, may be forever theirs, but can the whole land occupied by the men they call their countrymen? Actually, individuals can know only a fragment. And these fragments, as in the case of the highlands of Kenya or the lake region of England, may be much unlike the rest of the country. Or they may be more like some bit of foreign territory: the American Rockies resemble the European Alps more than they do the Mississippi basin, and the areas around most of the great cities of the world look much alike—in both the slums of the poor and the suburbia of the well-to-do.

It is possible that men have some instinctive desire for land of their own, an inherent feeling about what is exclusively theirs. This could be the "territorial imperative" that a recent popular writer, Robert Ardrey, has so vehemently put forward as an explanation of nations.[50] Or it could be that old agrarian conceptions of private property—called the "agrarian myth" by Francis Delaisi[51]—have been transferred to the political boundaries of the nation. For the "territorial imperative" vehemence is scant foundation. Why the nation rather than some other territorial grouping? The agrarian myth seems more plausible, but it assumes a transfer for which

322

there is no concrete evidence. In any case, why national loyalty rather than loyalty to city, empire, or just the place of birth and maturation?

Exactly when "race" became an explanation of nationality is not clear.[52] It is certain, however, that this was in modern times, for race did not become a significant classification of men until the eighteenth century. And from the earliest attempts to classify, authors used the words nation and race loosely and interchangeably—therefore confusingly. From the second half of the nineteenth century race became a convenient catchall explanation for diversities in human characteristics as well as for the alleged superiority or inferiority of particular human groups. During the eighteenth century such scientists as Linnaeus, Buffon, Dauberton, and Blumenbach did studies that made the term race more than a vague way of naming any group, by using it as a classification based on physical characteristics—skin pigmentation and skull shape.[53] During the nineteenth century the term began to be associated with not only physical qualities but also mental and spiritual character. In the United States and in much of the western world, later and vociferously in South Africa, and still later and as vociferously in·Nazi Germany, it came to be a widely held dogma that, in the words of an American, "the deepest thing about any man—except his humanity itself—is his race."[54] In Nazi Germany, indeed, race was exalted before humanity. There thus arose insistence upon common racial stock as *a* or *the* basis for nationality and nationhood.[55]

Early-nineteenth-century German nationalists—Arndt, Jahn, Görres, Fichte, and Friedrich Schlegel—were not violent racists, but their views pointed toward racial interpretations of history and nations. In the words of Arndt, they claimed, quite unfactually, that the Germans had not been "bastardized by a foreign people."[56] The racialist arguments varied during the century. Michelet, poet-historian of France, believed that "all the races of the world," the Gaels, the Iberians, the Semites, and all the others, had contributed something vital to France.[57] In England a most influential historian, Bishop Stubbs (1825–1901), traced England to "the blood in our veins that came from German ancestors."[58] And in the United States such historians as John Fiske and J. K. Hosmer but echoed German historians like Barthold Niebuhr and Theodor Mommsen in their insistence that race played a major role in history.[59]

Racial interpretations of history expanded enormously after Count Gobineau (1816–62), who had read American authors on the "inferiority" of Negroes, published his famous *Essai sur l'inégalité des races humaines* in 1854 and Charles Darwin his *On the Origins of Species by Means of*

Natural Selection in 1859. After the appearance of these prestigious volumes that profoundly affected all serious thought about men and their groupings, nationalists felt bound to discuss and defend the alleged racial composition of nations in order to demonstrate their own nation's fitness and superiority in the competitive struggle of evolution.

Houston Stewart Chamberlain, an Englishman who was more German than the Germans, carried racial thinking to the extreme in 1899 in the ringing rhetoric and factual emptiness of his *Foundations of the Nineteenth Century*. For him—and for his many important followers, including Kaiser William II of Germany—all of modern civilization since the year 1200 was the creation of "Teutonic blood." [60] "At the fall of the Roman empire in the place of the nations of former history that had disappeared there now sprang up a race of men, the Germanic peoples, just as creative and individualistic (and consequently with the natural inclination for forming States) as the Hellenes and Romans. . . ." The universal divine monarchy therefore fell before "the naturally inevitable formation of nations demanded by the natural instinct [*sic*] of the German people. . . ." [61]

Race thus became one of the stock explanations and justifications of nationhood. Noted publicists, scholars, and patriots in many nations proclaimed its importance. To convey the notion of common blood the belligerent German historian Heinrich von Treitschke declared the word "nationality" had to be used.[62] A French psychologist of renown who was a student of mobs, Gustave Le Bon (1841–1931), detected behind the character of every nation "the unchangeable soul of race weaving . . . its own destiny." [63] Sir Arthur Keith (1866–1955), an eminently respectable English anthropologist, discovered somehow that the feeling of nationality arose out of "tribal instinct," fostered in "nature's cradles" among early men. Nature had, he divined, separated "mankind into herds and tribes and kept them isolated and pure for an endless period . . . by real and most effective barriers in the human heart." [64] According to a temporarily popular English-American psychologist, William McDougall (1871–1938), nations in part arose out of innate moral and intellectual capacities that were racial in character.[65] A major German historian who was no narrow racist, Friedrich Meinecke (1862–1954), nevertheless maintained that there had to be a "natural nucleus which remained through blood intermixture" as the basis of a nation.[66]

Adolf Hitler and the German Nazis dogmatically announced that race, naturally the "Nordic race," had been and was the creator of all that was admirable, including the German nation, while the "Jewish race" personified all that was cunningly evil.[67] But racialist doctrines were not, of course, restricted to the Nazis; they simply carried these doctrines to their most absurd extremes. In the United States nearly all white southerners and most northerners as well were long sure of the superiority of whites and the inferiority of blacks, and therefore of the necessity of white supremacy in the nation. At the beginning of the twentieth century not a few Americans agreed with the Republican senator from Indiana, Albert Beveridge, in his worship of the "blue-eyed flaxen-haired Anglo-Saxon fighters" [68] in the Philippines during the war (1898) with Spain, and with David Starr Jordan, president of Stanford University, "that the blood of a nation" determined "its history." Many Americans, including members of the D.A.R. and two popular writers of the 1920's, Madison Grant and Lothrop Stoddard, were desperately afraid that "lesser" races, if they were admitted to the United States and intermixed with the Anglo-Saxons, would destroy their nation. In South Africa the Afrikaners were just as afraid of the Negroes and just as certain that they, the Afrikaners, were a superior "blood community." [69] Usually color became a kind of sliding scale to measure the quality of an individual or group, the darker the pigmentation the more inferior. During the 1950's and 1960's, some blacks in the United States, France, and Africa, believing "black is beautiful," began, in reaction to white supremacy, to hold racialist doctrines and use them to promote black nations and nationalism.[70]

Whether they are termed blood, instinct, or race, explanation of nationality by inborn qualities has little or no foundation. No one knows (or few can agree on) just what a race is, or if race denotes anything more than classification of men according to one or more physical characteristics.[71] Much has been written on race, and much that is based on nothing more than prejudice and nonsense. What the English historian Buckle wrote over a hundred years ago still seems true: "Inherent natural differences [among nations] may or may not exist but most assuredly have never been proven." [72] A careful student, therefore, finds it almost impossible to draw any conclusions other than that in "averages" the physical characteristics of human groups vary slightly from each other.[73] It is observable that the social characteristics of groups also vary in "averages," but this does not, except by an imaginative leap, indicate any relationship between race and nationality.

In historical time, races, whatever they are, have ceaselessly mixed, and (with such possible exceptions as the Somali) all modern nationalities are probably about as heterogeneous as Daniel Defoe declared Englishmen were. Biologically, all European populations are mixtures of two or more of what have been called races, of Nordics, Baltics, Alpines, Dinarics, Armenoids, Mediterraneans, Atlanto-Mediterraneans, Orientals, Iran-Afghans, East Africans, and likely a good many others.[74] In Asia and Africa the mixtures are at least as great and in some areas, as in parts of India, greater. In modern times throughout the world the boundary lines of nationalities, cultures, and languages so overlap those of the so-called races that even an explanation by racial nuclei seems devoid of sense. Peoples have much and are much mixed. Probably, as the anthropologist Ralph Linton once remarked, only a race with women too hideous to attract men of other tribes and men too cowardly to steal women of other tribes could be "pure." [75] None of whom we have any record has been so unfortunate. In all historical time, every variety of man has sooner or later wandered about, crossed with other varieties, become heterogeneous in physical composition.

As *individuals* of races, tribes, nations, and groups of every kind have crossed, their genes have mixed (*not* blended) with those of individuals of other groups. A result has been that there are as many combinations and recombinations of genes as there are men and possible combinations of men, and these now mount into astronomical numbers.[76] Individuals within the races so vary that, indeed, any generalization about race, except perhaps one based on "averages" of physical characteristics, seems questionable. As an informed geneticist, William Boyd, concisely put it, "since so many variable gene and chromosome structures exist" and form a large variety of combinations, individuals "classified as belonging to one race in so far as some gene, say F, is concerned . . . belong to a different race in regard to gene G, and a still different race in regard to gene H." [77]

We know that in Europe skulls can be divided into broadheads (brachycephalic) and longheads (dolichocephalic). This tells us that some Europeans possess broader, some longer heads[78]—and that is all. We know that throughout the world individuals have different blood types, but how these are related to their other characteristics, let alone their national feeling, is unknown. Measurements of skulls and classifica tions of blood types tell us little about men except about their skulls and blood types. No exclusive racial characteristics that clearly divide peoples can be established, and none that are clearly connected with the formation of nations. Peoples of all so-called races have now formed nations, and all of these are composed of much mixed peoples.

If the relation between race and mental and social characteristics cannot be determined, then race cannot be said to be basic in nationality. Other empirical evidence confirms this negative generalization. Race, in fact, appears to have "nothing to do with modern political nationalities" in Europe. "Northern Germany is prevailingly Nordic, southern Germany Alpine. Northern Italy is Alpine, the rest . . . Mediterranean. All three are definitely represented in France." [79] In our present state of knowledge, in spite of much conjecture, we know in fact little or nothing that is certain about *racial* mental and social characteristics. Further, we cannot disentangle genetic from environmental and cultural factors in the development of individuals, let alone nations. [80]

The reality of the racial myth nonetheless persists—in the minds of nationalists.

XII

Some Cultural Myths, Economic, Political, Linguistic, and Historical

Nations and national feeling appear to be shaped not by nature but by nurture, by everything human and peculiar to times and places.[1] Some cultural explanations oversimplify, however. Among these, as has already been pointed out, is the Marxist that the national state is just one stage of political organization in the historical and dialectic evolution of the world toward communism—the stage of bourgeois capitalism when, as Stalin had it, the bourgeoisie of each nationality became nationalist as it competed in the market with and sought victory over bourgeoisies of other nationalities.[2] Marxism, of course, does not have a copyright on the economic explanation of the national state. Seventeenth- and eighteenth-century theorists and activists like John Locke, the abbé Sieyès, and Alexander Hamilton, thinking the nation-state a kind of joint enterprise, expected dividends in the form of civil rights, security of property, and opportunity to profit.[3] Both the proletarian and the bourgeois interpretations won adherents throughout the world, and with reason, for economic explanations seem substantially to represent human experience. But these interpretations, based on class interests, are much too simple; men of different classes have formed nations and have become loyal to them for many reasons. In Europe it was not the bourgeoisie but the dynasties that created the bases of modern nations; and in Europe not only the bourgeoisie but also many aristocrats, and later the ordinary people, proletariat and peasant, became nationalist. In Africa and Asia, where old peoples are becoming nationalist and new nations are building, the middle classes—the bourgeoisie—have been small and weak, and the new nation-states can hardly be said to be composed of or dominated by the middle class or classes. There may be, as Christians and others have thought, *one* divine key to heaven. The economic key to history is only one key to human history, only one key to unlock the mysteries of nations and nationalism.

As economic factors have been overemphasized, so have the political. That power-seeking monarchs were instrumental in building the early nations, that power-seeking politicians played a like role in the new nations, and that war and colonial rebellion deepened national feeling are so obvious as to be truisms. The search for power on the part of men, kingly or bourgeois, led directly and indirectly to the establishment and strengthening of the national power structures—that is, to nation-states. Wars between these states and colonial revolts against them, with in both cases the accompanying propaganda, taught Europeans, Americans, Asians, and Africans to seek security within and glorify their own nation, and at the same time to fear and hate other nations. But the emphasis on power and war has, on occasion, been pushed beyond the limits of fact and reason.

For the ardently nationalist German historian Heinrich von Treitschke, the state (and he meant the Prussian nation-state) was "the people legally united," a unity "inherently necessary," the result of the "political capacity innate in man." This unity, a collective being, was "capable of willing" and thus of exercising power. Through the exercise of the state's power, the way was cleared for the creation of the nation and the national character. "All historical study" had, therefore, to "return finally to consider the State, for there can be no will without a being capable of willing." [4] What exactly this abstract conception of the state means is as difficult to ascertain as it is to determine what Hegel, upon whom Treitschke leaned, meant by the state being the "power of reason realizing itself as will." In point of fact, the power of the Prussian state (or more precisely of its leaders) was a, if not the, catalytic agent in the creation of modern Germany. But the state is not a mystical abstraction or force above and beyond the societies and individuals who constitute it, except in the fanciful minds that so will it. The state is whatever historical processes, and the individuals (or elites, if you will) who constitute it, make it. It has no being of its own, can create nothing of its own. As an instrument of elites, it has in modern times, as pointed out earlier, been used to build nations; these nations could not have been built, however, had not economic and social institutions and forces, had not individuals been working in the same direction. Treitschke had many followers (or like believers), and not only in Germany, but he carried the realities of state power to extremes that can only be described as mythical.

The same was true of his thesis that war created the nation. "Again and again," he cried, "it has been proved that it is war which turns a people into a nation." [5] That war helped create and certainly accentuated national consciousness, loyalty, and hate is clear. The well-known nineteenth-century French leader and historian, François Guizot (1787–1874), was close to a verifiable diagnosis of national feeling when he concluded that consciousness of national unity arose out of "enmity and war." [6] Wars of nations indeed became Armageddons in which good patriots fought good patriots and many died for their nations. But, again, war is only one of the reasons for nationalism.

After Darwin's great book on *The Origin of Species,* influential publicists (especially in Britain and the United States) applied the idea of struggle for existence to human societies (Social Darwinism) and saw the nations as arising, surviving, or falling in this struggle.[7] An English financial journalist, Walter Bagehot, who was much read on both sides of the Atlantic, fully developed the idea in his *Physics and Politics* published in 1869. Prehistory, he declared, bound men together into groups through "coarse, harsh custom." Out of these first "hereditary co-operative" groups, those who had "the most binding and invigorating customs," the "best customs," conquered—while the others perished. Thus the living nations sprang into existence, developed through, and evolved out of struggle.[8] A reputable English scientist, Karl Pearson, summed up the doctrine with unscientific finality: nature had, he judged, decreed the struggle for survival in groups, and the national group was the only one able to cope with conditions.[9] In the view of an American military adventurer, Homer Lea, nations, like individuals, were subject to the evolutionary law of competition, arising when they became "militarily strong and falling when they were militarily weak." [10] A most vigorous American president, Theodore Roosevelt (1858–1919), believed and preached the doctrine and made it a basis of his foreign policy: ". . . just as in private life," he said, "so in national life as the ages go by we shall find the permanent national types will . . . tend to become those in which, though the intellect stands high, character stands higher; in which rugged strength and courage, rugged capacity to resist wrongful aggression by others will go hand in hand with a lofty scorn of doing wrong to others." The Roman and later the Dutch empire fell, T.R. was sure, because both became opulent, soft, and weak.[11] Social Darwinism thus seemed to explain the rise and fall of nations and to justify the strongest devotion to one nation and hostility to other nations. For some patriots it still does.

The ideas of "struggle for existence" and "survival of the fittest" provide, like Marxist dialectic materialism, fertile hypotheses; but an opposite hypothesis, that men are gregarious and seek to co-operate,[12] and there-fore form nations, possesses as much and as little validity. Actually, "strug-gle" and "survival" have been used as slogans to bulwark nationalist beliefs. The reasoning has been somewhat as follows: (1) nations, like in-dividuals, naturally differ (this is obvious) in physical and mental traits; (2) some are naturally fitter (this is doubtful) and there is struggle; (3) those races and nations that are naturally fittest win in the struggle, and are therefore superior (a *non sequitur*). But nations are not individuals. In-dividuals are born, they think and act as individuals, they proliferate, they die. Nations develop slowly. They do not create other nations. They are *composed* of individuals who all are different. The members of a nation are not related to each other as are the parts of a biological individual. A nation has no central brain (cerebral cortex), no power of reflection; it is not an organic, cognitive being. Italy cannot think, though individual Ita-lians can. If a nation declines, it declines slowly, not just because it lacks "rugged strength and courage" but for many reasons. And even if a nation were like an individual, no one knows what fittest means in relation to nations, or if struggle is more important than co-operation.

Who are the fittest individuals? The giants who play American foot-ball? Or the pale, bespectacled physicists in the atomic laboratories? Which nation is *the* fittest: little Switzerland; little Sweden; or the colossi, the Soviet Union and the United States? And maybe the only way any of them will survive is by co-operation. In point of fact we only *know* today that the survivors, small and large, have thus far survived.

Struggle among men has been a major reason for nation building, and as nations have struggled with each other nationalism has spread and deepened. The French nation rose in part out of the French and English struggles of the fourteenth and fifteenth centuries, and the French Revolu-tionary wars from 1792 aroused national feeling in France and throughout much of Europe as well. Yet the French nation (or any nation) is not only the result of struggle but also of language and literature, of custom and tradition and history and much else. Struggle sharpens national feeling. It fully explains neither why nations begin nor why common national feeling develops. An unproved hypothesis if believed remains a myth, but in this case, to be sure, the believed myth has had a profound effect—in sharpen-ing nationalism.

That language is a basic element in nationalism can only be affirmed.[13] But language has been only one element and not always a decisive one. In the present "countries of the world less than seventy per cent of the populations speak the same language." [14] Unity and difference in language do not clearly unite or separate nations, old or new. Two (or three) languages are spoken and "native" in Belgium, four in Switzerland, and dozens in Nigeria and India, while Portuguese, Spanish, and English are spoken in two or more nations on both sides of the Atlantic and in parts of Africa and Asia.

Nor do language lines correspond with those of race (whatever it is) or even with those of cultures. Within Germany (and it is not unique), "where there is uniformity in language" there is "marked diversity" in the physical characteristics of the people, and in the "non-German part of central Europe where there is marked diversity in language," an approach to uniformity in some physical characteristics.[15] Again, peoples of different so-called races may speak the same language, like the blacks and whites of the United States, may, legally at least, be members of the same nation, but, in some cases, may think of themselves as different nationalities. Further, languages of the same basic stock, say the Aryan, are spoken by peoples of quite different cultures as widely separated by geography as those of India, England, and the United States.

Nationalists generally think of their language as the "native" tongue of their people and in some respect or other as superior. Again fact needs to be separated from fantasy. In modern nations—the United States, for one—that have been peopled largely by immigrants and their offspring, there is, for a large proportion of the people, no common *historical* language. The ancestors of those presently alive spoke German, Swedish, Polish, Italian, Yiddish, or one of a dozen or more other languages, including Chinese. In most of the new nations of Asia and Africa there is not really a common native (though there may be an official) language—unless the English and French of the former colonial rulers can be considered native. And what is true of the new nations was once true of the older. Many of the ancestors of the people who now "natively" use French once spoke Latin or one of the varieties of Celtic or Teutonic tongues.

It may well be that, as has often been argued, one or another developed language is better for this or that purpose than another developed language—that English is best for novelists, German for scientists, French for diplomatists, and Hindi for mystical philosophers. It may be that French is more precise, German more discursive, English simpler, Italian more delicate, Russian warmer, and Arabic more "angelic." [16] But *if* these descriptions were accurate, they would still not prove any one language superior to any other. The fact is, we do not know and cannot know.

Languages are always changing, growing, and even dying, never stable, never the same as they were or will be. French, perhaps the most refined and fixed language at the present, has never ceased expanding and contracting since the time in the Middle Ages that it became recognizable as French and later, in the fourteenth century, the language (rather than Latin) of the government.[17] What are now known as the "native" languages were, even in Europe, rather late in arising, are now native in the sense that they became, for various reasons, national, and, without doubt, will be different a hundred years from now.

Conquerors and governments—in Europe, the Americas, Asia, and Africa—have often more or less *forced* the "official" languages on people. If one goes back far enough, no present European languages were spoken by the ancestors of Europeans; in recent times Swahili was not the language of most of the people of Kenya, Uganda, and Tanzania, and it still is not, though it may so become by governmental fiat and action, just as, in part, French became the language of many people in France who once spoke other languages—Breton, for instance.

Languages are native in the sense that an individual is born within a group using a language, acquires this language, and uses it habitually in early childhood.[18] As he learns the speech of his family and neighborhood, he learns to think this language his. He can communicate with others who use the same language, while at the same time he has trouble understanding those who babble in "strange" tongues. He feels loyal to the group using his "mother" tongue, is uncomfortable with and perhaps distrustful of those who do not. He can communicate and therefore have common ideas, show common feelings with those he understands and who understand him. Other people and their ideas and feelings seem "foreign." In these ways language plays a major role in the development of national consciousness, but it plays only one role.

Just as language, so historical experience, as related by historians and popularizers, plays a major part in the development of nationalism. History itself is not, as has sometimes been said, a cause of nationalism; it is simply the past time during which events and circumstances occurred that led to nationalism. One essential question is *what* in history brought nations and national feeling into being, and another is how groups of individuals acquired the belief that they each had different common histories. Two answers are: through their own remembered experience (as in folklore) and through their popular patriotic writers and historians.

These writers and historians have, of course, embellished *their* histories of *their* countries with glorious legends of heroes and great deeds. These are well known, easily recognizable. They have also contributed to two other kinds of myths that are not so easily detected: they have made it seem (1) as if all or most individuals within a nation really have a common past; and (2) that this common or national past originated much earlier than it actually did.

As the English philosopher John Stuart Mill (1806–73) believed, possibly the strongest of all forces making for nationality has been "identity of political antecedents; possession of a national history, and consequent community of recollections; collective pride and humiliation, pleasure and regret, connected with the same incidents in the past." [19] But the question then arises of *what* in history brought the common consciousness of the common past. One answer is the projection of a specious past, of a continuity among a people that does not really exist except in their minds—or those of their historians. In hard fact, many individuals in contemporary nations, particularly in new ones (Ghana or Ceylon), but also in older ones (the United States) or in still older ones (England and France), can scarcely be said to have a *common* past with many of their countrymen. The ancestors of a majority of Americans did not participate in the winning of American independence in 1776–83, nor did a large proportion in the tragic American Civil War or the winning of the West. Their ancestors were in Ireland, Germany, Italy, Poland, Norway, and in many other European countries, or in Africa and Asia. And what is true of the peoples of the United States is true of those of Canada and Brazil. It is particularly true in other ways of the peoples of most Asian and African countries, whose ancestors may not have been members of any nation but of tribes and clans who lived in the area or migrated (as Bantu peoples did) to the area where the nation *now* exists. Even in old France many of the peoples were not primarily Frenchmen before, say, 1789, but Bretons and Provençals. Before the French Revolutionary and Napoleonic wars, indeed, few inhabitants of, say, Germany thought of themselves as Germans but, rather, as Prussians, Bavarians, Hanoverians, or Saxons. For European peoples a common history, if it much precedes the eighteenth century, for many of the peoples of Asia and Africa a common history if it precedes the twentieth century, is partly fictional. It is real in the sense that people may believe in it; it is in fact compounded of fact and myth. If the ancestors of a contemporary national people did live chiefly in the same country, most of them were illiterate peasants, conscious of little beyond their religion and their village and their daily life, and hardly at all of their nationality. Even most Englishmen do not really have King Arthur's court in common, though they may share the legend.

Patriots and historians, catering to "the vanity of mankind," have been able to divine common histories long before the peoples themselves could have been aware of them, and have thereby given the sanction of age to nationhood and national feeling. As a distinguished American historian, J. Franklin Jameson, remarked, one of the chief tasks of modern historians has been "to clear away those legends of fabulous antiquity, with which each nation . . . invested the story of its antiquity." [20]

Early national histories in Europe saw their nations beginning far back in a mythical past. Just as British history was traced back to giant Albion and Brutus of Troy or to Brut, grandson of Aeneas, so Russian was traced to the "time before the destruction of Troy when the Enety, a Slavic tribe, came from Asia to settle on the shores of the Adriatic." [21]

Later historians in many nations, while generally more sophisticated, have made assertions that go far beyond the evidence. The nationalistic Treitschke gazed into his German crystal ball to see two strong forces *always* at work: "the tendency of every state to amalgamate its population in speech and manners into a single mould," and "the impulse of every vigorous nationality to construct a state of its own." [22] As mentioned earlier, the reputable nineteenth-century historians Augustin Thierry and J. R. Green believed they could date the beginning of their nations, France and England, in 888 and 449, dates when no people then living were conscious of their nationality.[23] A serious twentieth-century Jewish student, Bernard Joseph, seeking the nature of nationality, intuitively perceived it to be "always in process of formation and development." [24] An otherwise critical French intellectual of the 1920's, Julien Benda, perceived medieval Frenchmen then "willing" their nation into existence.[25] Serious historians today would scarcely be so bold as were Thierry and Green in their dating, and certainly they would be skeptical of forces always at work. But the legends live on, at least in the popular mind.

The legends are indeed fabulous. A Martin O'Brennan believed Celtic was spoken in the Garden of Eden,[26] and Greeks, at any rate since Byron, have connected their modern nation with the ancient Greece of Athens and Sparta. The Turks have been pictured by Turkish historians as the creators of the world's first great civilization, the inventors of the first written language of literary value.[27] The Japanese myth of the founding of Japan by Amaterasu, goddess of the sun, has been mentioned, as has the belief of the Indian patriot, Bal Gangadhar Tilak, that his "Aryan" forefathers were "not merely among the first people to attain a high level of civilization" but had "planted the seed of civilization in the world." [28] For an Arab, Sami Shawkat, who was director-general of education of Iraq and a belligerent nationalist in the 1930's, the history of the "illustrious Arab nation" extended over thousands of years, back to the high civilization of Hammurabi at a time when the peoples of Europe were still savages living in forests and swamps.[29]

Ernest Renan, the wise French philosopher, once reportedly said, "To forget and—I will venture to say—to get one's history wrong are essential factors in the making of a nation." [30] Historians are obliged to seek the earliest evidence concerning any group they are studying, and to recount whatever deeds, glorious or otherwise, did occur. But they are guilty of anachronism when they trace a modern nation or nationality back to a time when the nation or nationality had not yet taken form.[31] In the fifteenth century the symbolic heroine of France, Jeanne d'Arc, fought not for France but to restore her rightful king and stop the fighting so that Christians could unite against the infidels. When the Japanese learned they were Japanese may be impossible exactly to determine, but for many of them it was probably not until the last third of the nineteenth century. There was a Ghana before the present Ghana, but between the two, the old and the present, the only connection is the name. To ascribe a common national history or common national feeling to a people before they are a nation is not only inaccurate; it may also be dangerous. For, as Paul Valéry observed, "false memories" did indeed turn "races into daydreamers and drunkards. . . ." [32]

It is not only false memories but mistaken images as well that mislead people. For a long time now it has been assumed that the peoples of nations have developed peculiar or unique national characters, and this supposition has been a commonplace of politicians, patriots, and a good many other individuals. That a people, especially of an older nation, have had common experiences, or experiences they believe they have had in common, is obvious. That, *in very general terms*, each people, if at all established as a people, have at any one time some common traits, customs, values and that these somehow differentiate them from other peoples is undeniable. It is also undeniable that nationalists like to believe and do believe that their own nation has different and somehow superior characteristics. And it is a fact that popularizers, social scientists, and historians have been deeply interested.

The number of recent books and articles on national character, some superficial, some scholarly, mounts into the hundreds. And highly conflicting commentaries of one kind or another have been coming out since at least the sixteenth century, when Erasmus in praising folly noted that apparently nature had implanted self-love not only in individuals but also in various peoples—the English claiming "good looks, music and the best eating [*sic*]," the French "all politeness," the Italians "*belles lettres* and eloquence," and——.[33]

In recent years the number of popular books has *multiplied,* those by Luigi Barzini on the Italians, François Nourrissier on the French, and Anthony Glyn on the British being only illustrative.[34] And reputable social psychologists, anthropologists, and historians have devoted much energy and time and many words to the subject.[35]

The whole subject, of course, is not only filled with nationalist overtones but is slippery and ambiguous.[36] What observers see changes with the observers, the time, and the place. As Claude Lévi-Strauss, a great anthropologist, remarked, it may well be that a description of national character tells us more about the observer than the nation described. Observers think of many different kinds and varieties of characteristics—attitudes, views, opinions, values, customs, behavioral patterns. Recent students have put forward varying vague definitions of what they are studying: "distinctive configurations of traits and behaviors" (Martindale); "enduring personality characteristics and unique life styles found among populations of particular nation states" (De Vos); "relatively enduring personality characteristics and patterns that are modal among the adult members of the society" (Inkeles). Not only is there confusion as to what traits and behaviors constitute character, however; empirically derived data is also lacking, in spite of the many studies. Further, if traits and behaviors exist "modally" on a national scale, they also change. In the sixteenth century some Englishmen, say Henry VIII, may have enjoyed "the best eating," and some have since his time, but "gourmetism" scarcely seems a characteristic of many poor Englishmen in early modern history, nor is it a characteristic of most Englishmen today. Some Frenchmen have, without doubt, been polite, and some are today, but hardly Parisian waiters or taxicab drivers. Some Italians have excelled in belles-lettres, especially during the Renaissance, and some do today, but neither then nor now has this excellence been characteristic of most Italians. Actually, it has been impossible, thus far, to establish patterns that are modal or distinctive for so many differing individuals as have lived or live in England or any other nation.

In Diderot's famous *Encyclopédie* Frenchmen were characterized as "frivolous" and Englishmen as "wicked." [37] Similar descriptions of national character continue to be fabricated. But certainly few, if any, present commentators on national character would think of Frenchmen as being especially "frivolous" or Englishmen as being peculiarly "wicked," whatever the patterns, models, or averages they selected. And for good reasons! Such characterizations chiefly reveal the prejudices of those who fabricate them.

All generalizations, even the most intelligent ones, such as David Potter's *People of Plenty*, a learned and careful analysis of American character, are no more than tentative unproved hypotheses.[38] If they have validity, it is only for a particular moment. If they contain some validity for the people of a whole national group, they probably do not really describe the characteristics of more than a minority or perhaps of only a few individuals at a particular time. Nations are composed of individuals who act and think as *individuals* and who change.

The nonsense that has been written about national character remains nonsense though the prose is poetic. A student of nationality once claimed that the Russian is "morose and melancholy as the steppes of the country," while the Italian is "passionate and excitable" because he is "warmed by the sun." [39] Many Russians, especially those at recent international conferences, seem "morose," and a small part of the Soviet Union is "steppes." Many Italians are "excitable" and the sun shines warmly in parts of Italy. Communists (like crocodiles?) have laughed, and the sun shines in vast parts of the U.S.S.R., even in Moscow. Leonardo da Vinci and Benedetto Croce and a good many Italians were calm and dispassionate at times, and hence they were not Italians. Poetic intuition may connect steppes and sun with gloom and passion—only evidence is missing.

During World Wars I and II the Germans (including the Rhenish peoples?) were supposed to have had a disciplined military character— exactly the opposite of that they were supposed to have had during the Napoleonic era. The French after World War I were thought to be logical, cultivated, and pacifist. Was this their character during the French Revolutionary and Napoleonic wars? The Chinese, being Oriental, have been thought to be mysterious and fond of Oriental despotism. During World War II the Japanese, according to American commentators (even such a serious scholar as Ruth Benedict), were supposed to be authoritarian and submissive because of childhood training.[40] Very likely some Chinese are mysterious (to westerners especially), and some certainly (like westerners) have succumbed to despotism. During World War II some Japanese certainly exhibited authoritarianism and many a willingness to obey—like the peoples in all the countries that were at war.

All this is only to say that there are Germans, Frenchmen, Chinese, and Japanese who fit national stereotypes and some who do not. What is German character, that of Goethe or of Hitler? What is French cultivation, that of Voltaire or of Pétain? Why are the Chinese so mysterious—because of language, their "slant eyes," or western ignorance—and did the twentieth-century Chinese scholar Hu Shih succumb to despotism? Have most of the Japanese been as authoritarian as Tojo was, or have they always been as "compulsive" as many were during World War II? Stereotypes are significant because they are believed—even by the people who are being stereotyped—but they do not well fit most of the individuals of the nations to which they are applied.

In the *present state of study* it is impossible to arrive at meaningful averages or models because individual traits are so many, so various, so varying in intensity, and so changing that they defy measurement—at any rate with present instruments. Hypotheses remain hypotheses until evidence supports them. And if believed, without substantiating evidence, they are myths.

Stereotypes of national character have emerged—probably with reason. Behind them there must be real similarities and differences. But all we can say *now* is that little is known that will permit more than imaginative guesses. For racialists and nationalists to emphasize these is understandable. For scholars to go beyond the scholarly and, with the present lack of evidence, indulge in generalities only contributes to myths that are dangerous because they lead to national enmities with little reason behind them.

Some national peoples—depending on the time and place and observer—are supposed to be warlike in character—the Germans, the Japanese, the Russians, the Americans. Over the course of modern history, however, there is no proof that the citizens of one nation are more warlike than the citizens of other countries—the English have been engaged in war as often as any people, and no one thinks of them as particularly warlike. Individuals in each nation have been peaceful and warlike, sometimes more so in one nation, sometimes more in another.[41] The enemy has always been aggressive and warlike; one's own people have always been civilized and peaceful. The national character of any people is in point of fact "so complex, so contradictory and so largely determined by intangibles that most anything can be read into it." [42] But as David Hume, that skeptical eighteenth-century Scottish philosopher, wrote, "The vulgar are apt to carry all national characters to extremes; and having once established it as a principle that any people are knavish, or cowardly, or ignorant, they will admit of no exception, but comprehend every individual under the same censure." [43]

Oliver Goldsmith's comment to patriotic Englishmen of the eighteenth century could be relevant for any present student of national character. He had heard it said "that the Dutch were a parcel of avaricious wretches; that the French were a set of flattering sycophants; that the Germans were drunken sots and beastly gluttons; and the Spaniards proud, haughty and surly tyrants; but that in bravery, generosity, clemency, and in every other virtue, the English excelled all the other world." Goldsmith's reply was, "For my own part I should have not ventured to talk in such a peremptory strain, unless I had made the tour of Europe, and examined the manners of these several nations with great care and accuracy: that perhaps, a more impartial judge would not scruple to affirm that the Dutch were more frugal and industrious, the French more temperate and polite, the Germans more hardy and patient of labour and fatigue, and the Spaniards more staid and sedate, than the English; who, though undoubtedly brave and generous, were at the same time rash, headstrong and impetuous. . . ." [44]

If and when instruments for determining national characteristics are developed, scholars will have to tour not only Europe but the world. They *may* then find that men in every nation are basically more like men in other nations than they are different; that is, that individuals in and of different nations have a good many characteristics in common. This would perhaps not be so strange, for men are of one species—*homo*—and inhabit, thus far, one small planet—earth. Though, to be sure, men *much* differ as individuals and though, to be sure, their cultures (varieties) *much* differ, they are also much alike, and their *human* likenesses are possibly much more significant than their *national* differences.

Men are multicellular mammals and vertebrates; their pulse rates average around 72 and their bodily temperatures around 98.6 degrees Fahrenheit. They vary in height and weight, but most of them are from about four feet ten inches to six feet two inches tall and weigh from about 90 to 180 pounds[45]—small differences when the height and weight of other animals are considered. All men are not of one blood, as St. Paul said, but all have blood, and the same few O, A, B, and AB types are found among individuals in all the nations. All men are not alike, but they have the same basic chemical properties in their bodies in all nations. All men are not equal in intelligence, but a few are geniuses and more are morons in all nations, and most men in every nation are somewhere in between.[46] As long as there are males and females, reproduction between all national varieties is possible and even likely. The act of procreation is, though positions may differ, everywhere the same, and the Japanese spermatozoa can impregnate an American egg, the Chinese a French. The females of *homo* all carry their young about nine months. Unlike other animals, the desire of adults (especially males) for sexual activity is normally constant. The adult male, if healthy, is capable of starting reproduction at any time and the adult female (between the ages of about thirteen and forty-five) around twelve times a year.

The environments of which men are a part vary. Yet men live almost everywhere on the earth, except at the poles and on the highest mountains and driest wastes of sand. It is not the heat and the cold and the hills and the valleys that divide them: "Nature begins and ends everywhere and nowhere." [47] In spite of his bad astronomy, the seventeenth-century Czech Bishop Comenius (1592–1670) was in principle right when he wrote, "The same sky covers us, the same sun and all the stars revolve about us, and light us in turn." [48]

Oftentimes it is the differences among men that are most interesting, especially to historians (and I am one). But these differences, though real, should not hide similarities in human behavior.

Among the somatic preconditions for this behavior are, as J. N. Spuler has said, "accommodative vision, bipedal locomotion, manipulation, carnivorous-omnivorous diet, cortical control of sexual behavior, vocal communication, and expansion of the association areas in the cerebral cortex." [49] All men have, to greater or lesser extent, developed these and have them in common—and much more.

Within their cultures, as they have confronted their needs for food and shelter, preservation and creativity, they have evolved similar practices and institutions. In every culture the following practices have been found: "age-grading, athletic sports, bodily adornment, [the making of a] calendar, cleanliness training, community organization, cooking, cooperative labor, cosmology, courtship . . . , religious ritual, residence rules, sexual restrictions, soul concepts, status differentiation, surgery, toolmaking, trade, visiting, weaving and weather control." [50] The list could easily be extended to marriage and funeral practices and much more.

What, according to Ndabaningi Sithole, the Rhodesian leader, Africans finally observed about white men, all men might observe about each other:

When the African saw that the white female became pregnant like his own wife, that both the white male and white female fought, that sometimes white males fought over a white female, that sometimes an angry-with-wife white male refused to eat when he was offered food by his wife, that both the white male and white female wrinkled and stooped with age, that white people also died, he was reminded of the experiences he had in his own domestic life, and gradually he began to see through the myth.[51]

All this, of course, does not prove that men are alike—because they are *individuals,* the ways they think and act do differ. But the ceremony of marriage is almost universal among men, though there may be plural husbands or wives, and some societies are exogamous and some endogamous, and some are conjugal and some are consanguine. And so it is with all of men's biological and cultural traits and customs.

As Gordon Allport, a perceptive social psychologist, has written, "Man alone has the capacity to vary his biological needs and to add to these countless psychogenic needs reflecting in part his culture (no other creature has a culture), and in part his own style of life (no other creature worries about his life-style)." And Allport adds, "Man [and man only] talks, laughs, feels bored, develops a culture, prays, has a foreknowledge of death, studies theology, and strives for improvement of personality." [52]

Only men have a history of which they are conscious—though it is also true that commonly they do not learn much from it and, when they do, they often remember the myths more than the realities. Man is, in the words of a great zoologist, George Gaylord Simpson, "unique in peculiar and extraordinary ways"—the "most self-conscious of organisms," the only one with "true language," the only one who can "store knowledge beyond individual capacity," and at the same time the "most adaptable of all organisms." [53]

Men are, as the Christian Bible tells us, a little lower than angels— and probably a little higher than the devil. They might, to the proverbial invader from Mars arriving in a space machine, be scarcely distinguishable from each other. But if the invader attempted to peer more deeply into their natures and their acts he might find, in the reported words of Abdala the Saracen, that, regardless of their nation, "there is nothing more wonderful than man," [54] or, in the phrase of Pope Innocent III, "nothing more miserable."

Nearly all men in the short run try. All men in the long run do die. And this has nothing to do with national characteristics but everything to do with their common human and mortal nature.

XIII

Nationalism—Past, Present, and Prospects: A Summary and Conclusion*

Nature hath plac't us in the world free and unbound, wee emprison ourselves into certaine streights.—MONTAIGNE

I am convinced that the interests of the human race are better served by giving every man a particular fatherland than by trying to inflame his passions for the whole of humanity.—TOCQUEVILLE

. . . the local spirit . . . disappearing every day . . . man's own power will uproot him from the earth . . . to the idea of the universal fatherhood. . . .—MICHELET

Men and nations still fight for land and resources, for principles and pride, but the skies are full of satellites riding high above drawn lines. No one is dominant over his own destiny; no one can really control territory anymore.—FRANK K. KELLY (1970)

Why Nationalism Persists

"A human society," a contemporary sociologist, T. H. Marshall, has observed, "can make a square meal out of a stew of paradox without getting indigestion—at least for quite a long time."

With some indigestion peoples in recent times have subsisted largely on a diet of nationalism, whatever the dangers of its mixtures. They have

---

* In this chapter the author intends no further scholarly analysis but, rather, summarizes his own reflections as he wrote this book. Hence there are no notes.

done so because nations and nationalism met (or were the result of) some of their basic needs and satisfied some of their deeply felt desires. For western peoples for nearly two centuries (in some ways four centuries) the political organizations, the economic and social institutions, the historical experiences, the ideologies, the technologies, the ways of living have channeled, organized, gathered up their needs and desires into national frameworks, made their nations—and their devotion to them—their primary means of attaining such security and liberties as they could and at the same time a primary way of obtaining a sense of achieving, serving, and belonging. Other forms of political, economic, or social groups and loyalties might have done as well, or better, but during the centuries just past (and to the present) nations and nationalism have become the major, dominant ways western peoples did find answers to their needs and desires. People lived in and within nations. They found significance within them. They, reasonably or unreasonably, were devoted to them. In general they had, by the last third of the twentieth century, forgotten older ways, the feudal and dynastic, and only occasionally did they imagine other, more encompassing ways—international organization or a universal religion—to be possible. That because of nationalism they have spent their blood and treasure in war and could destroy themselves—indeed, all humanity; that with nationalism they have at times been oppressed and repressed; that with internationalism they might be able to live more peaceful, freer, and fuller lives; all this has made little difference. They either did not perceive the possibilities or they believed that internationalism would be less satisfactory, more dangerous, or impossible.

There have been (and are) substantial reasons for devotion to the nation. Through their nation and national state people obtained, or thought they did, real and often concrete benefits: (1) some kind of law and order—life did not always have to be "nasty, brutish, and short"; (2) usually a certain, though often low, level of living—a certain basic social security; (3) a variety of liberties, often limited indeed, to pursue their own interests—at a minimum, the opportunity or obligation to participate in communal activities, and sometimes those individual liberties of speech and opinion that are called civil; (4) the chance to engage in some kind of socially approved service to their fellows that, taking them outside their own lives, was exciting—in military service if no other way; and (5) some kind of protection against outsiders, that is, foreigners—though this was often illusory. Further, the national societies into which the people were born and about which they had no choice gave them or enabled them to have (1) their languages, literatures, lores, and customs—the ways they could adjust to life, understand and perhaps even enjoy life; (2) a sense of identity coupled with a means of distinction—a feeling that they were different, perhaps even superior; (3) a means of overcoming loneliness and frustration—if no more than relief from feelings of personal inadequacy; (4) an instrument to realize their personal interests—in prestige or profit or both; and (5) hope that the future, at least for their children, would be better—however problematical this was.

Early in Europe the Christian religion and churches, and elsewhere in the rest of the world other religions and churches, allowed people to gain much the same ends. In Europe village and feudal state and city communities and empires, and in Asia and Africa tribe and clan, village and empire have also often done so. In modern times, on six continents and many islands, it has been people's nations and nation-states that have done so. In modern times where else could they have turned? In modern times no other forms of political and social organization and loyalties have been so deeply rooted or offered as much. No international organization or universal church has really offered viable alternatives. When in Asia and Africa other forms, like federation, seemed possible as older ways of life were disintegrating, the leaders turned instead to western patterns and from their own cloth cut out their own national garments.

Why is this so? In a sense this whole book is an attempt at an answer. No answer can be full or definitive. But, in brief, this book has argued that the nation and nationalism developed because the governments (early the dynastic, later the democratic or the authoritarian) increasingly penetrated the lives of people, because people increasingly participated in the national affairs and identified themselves and their political and cultural interests with those of their respective nations, that out of the penetration, participation, and identification there came to be a kind of consensus within each nation, that once this was established nationalism fed upon itself and grew, and that the national states, once established, encouraged and imposed nationalism, educating and persuading the already loyal to be more patriotic by many means and coercing the reluctant by law and by force.

From roughly the thirteenth century, French and English dynasties built monarchical states by centralizing and expanding royal government within their lands, and by acquiring new lands and peoples and gradually establishing control over them. As a basis of its power each dynasty depended not only on its own resources but also on a small group of followers who had or were acquiring a common language and culture and who could, hence, communicate with each other with some facility, and could perceive and develop common interests.

France and England were not in early modern times the most important states, even in Europe. Nor was Europe, then, the world leader; more important centers of political power and culture were in Asia and the Middle East—the Chinese and Arabic. But during the coming several centuries western European political states and culture were to become dominant and to offer models of nations and nationalism that were to be diversely followed elsewhere. Other European peoples, or, more accurately, elite groups within them, sought to become nations and establish independent nation-states, especially during the nineteenth century. They largely succeeded in doing so. In Asia and Africa leaders with their peoples did likewise during the late nineteenth and the twentieth centuries, especially after World War II. By the 1960's nearly all peoples, or leaders within them, had established more or less independent nation-states, even though their nations and nationalism were sometimes no more than embryo. In each of these states, old and new, nationalizing processes similar to those in Europe earlier continued, as the governments controlled and unified or tried to control and unify their peoples, penetrated their lives and their thinking by imposition of taxes, control of information, and in a thousand other ways—by establishing schools to make "good" citizens; by building post offices, highways, airports to facilitate communication; by providing protection and assistance to business, to farmers, and to urban workers through tariffs, immigration regulations, or outright subsidies; by offering some kind of minimum social security at least to loyal citizens; and by offering protection against foreign threats through diplomacy and ultimately armed force. So multifold and pervasive were the activities of the national governments, both old and new, that few individuals could avoid becoming nationally conscious to some degree. And as many became aware of what they obtained and could gain from their national governments, more looked to these governments for their welfare and happiness, became devoted to their nations, that is, became nationalists. But their nationalism was not just the result of efforts of national governments.

Around the end of the eighteenth century, with the American and French Revolutions, more and more people, first in western countries and then, gradually, nearly everywhere, began to take some part in national affairs. As they did so, they came to think of these affairs as their own. This particularly began to occur during the French Revolution, when hope

of liberty and happiness ran high, and during the Revolutionary and Napoleonic wars, when so many were directly affected by violence and
bloodshed. During the nineteenth century western peoples increasingly
participated in what now became the common, the national affairs because these were *their* affairs, and concerned *their* security, *their* liberty,
and *their* happiness. In the twentieth century, not only in Europe and the
Americas but also in Asia and Africa more and more people participated
in some manner in these affairs—by voting, through political parties, in
mass ceremonies and celebrations, and through employment in governmental service and enlistment and conscription in armed services. This
participation did not always mean that people had more power, that democracy was triumphing. Dictators in authoritarian states, as has been
pointed out, could give their people the *feeling* that they were participating, as did Hitler the Germans. But the more people did participate or felt
they were participating, the more likely they were to become national
patriots. Many of them now had a genuine stake (or believed they did) in
the survival and prosperity of their nation, if not in its expansion. Each
people, it came to be believed, had the right of self-determination, and
this "right" became a principle—often (as in Vietnam) violated, to be
sure—of international morality; in addition, within each nation the people
of that nation, and of that nation only, had a right to determine how it
should be governed and how it should develop.

As national governments responded to the demands of their citizens,
the governments shaped these demands to suit the "national" interests. To
enlarge these interests, to gain prestige, profits and power not only for
their citizens but also for the state itself, the larger nation-states now expanded beyond their borders, competed for empire. This led to new conflicts, national conflicts stemming from national ambitions which now became imperial. There had always been wars, between cities, feudal lords,
monarchs. But now the affairs of the cities, the lords, and the kings became the people's, that is, national, wars. War and threats of war perpetually threatened nations, their survival, and their hope of an expanding
future.

The nations and the national states from their beginning were never
equal, and always between them there were rivalry, envy, jealousy. Now
imperial rivalries, such as those before 1914, sharpened national fears and
hence nationalism. National enemies became ever more the national enemies as nationalist pressures and propaganda, inspired and produced by
the major governments, by military and patriotic organizations (the Pan-
German League and the Royal Empire Society), and by individuals (Sen-

ator Beveridge in the United States and Jules Ferry in France), aroused patriotic emotion for their own nations and distrust of others. Fear, rooted in the actualities of the anarchistic international situation, made each nation-state, small or large, determined to defend itself by increasing its armed forces, by persuading its people to be patriotic or forcing them to acquiesce and therefore give tacit approval. Ambition, accentuated by fear, made already large nations do the same and expand as well. But the great nations did not expand in a vacuum; always what each did was measured in terms of what the others were doing. Thus no other nation— Germany or England before 1914, the United States or Russia after 1945— could be allowed to be too successful in expansion, for if it were, it might dominate or conquer or "impose its way of life" on others, including one's own. Fear and ambition led to more fear and greater ambition, to greater national military preparations, and——. Nationalism begat nationalism.

In the West, as the national political states were being established, they built upon the various already existing cultures, cultures shared in common by small groups that formed the nuclei of what were becoming the nations. Basic though not necessary was a common language (or languages) in which individuals within the groups could communicate. With a common language there could and did develop a vernacular or national literature, and this literature itself became a vehicle of national consciousness. Generally, too, there arose, if not already present, a common dominant religion (Lutheranism in Germany), a real or imagined distinct art, and common customs of diet (wine in France), sports (baseball in the United States), and even dress (at least for the benefit of foreign tourists).

Within the new states of the developing world, the same kind and degree of cultural unity often did not exist when these states were established, for the boundaries of these new states had usually been arbitrarily set by the old colonial powers and within them were peoples (tribes) of quite different cultures. In the long run, however, the new national governments may be as successful as the older ones were in molding congeries of people into nations.

When weighed and balanced, the nation-states and nationalism have provided much that modern men have wanted. The validity of this generalization probably would not require further substantiation if the attacks on nationalism, often justified by fact and morality, were not so frequent and so strong, and if realization of the age-old dream of peace was not, in an atomic-missile age, so imperative. At the risk of some repetition, additional discussion of the reasons for the persistence of nationalism is desirable.

In modern cultures, individuals—not all and not all in the same fashion—have sought security, identity, status, prestige, excitement, and joy. While pursuing these goals they seem, generally, to have needed (1) to hope for a life better than they have had, (2) to be devoted to some idea or entity larger than their individual selves, and (3) to dislike or hate whatever they think threatening or an obstacle—or at any rate they have evinced hope, devotion, and hate. Detailed examination of why they have sought these ends, had these needs is beyond the scope of this book. Probably the desires and needs have been common among most men at most times and places. Probably biological drives are behind them. Certainly the specific ways men have tried to satisfy them at particular times have been shaped by the general nature of their cultures, the forms and levels of their economic life, the state and development of their technologies, the character and patterns of all their social relationships. Here it is enough to say that (1) modern men have had these desires and these needs, and nations and nationalism have offered answers to their questions and solutions for their problems; and (2) this has been increasingly true as their societies have been in transition from the rural agrarian, in which religion and church supplied basic answers, to the urban industrial, in which the answers have been basically secular and governmental. This is to say no more than that, like all human institutions, nations grew out of the desires and needs of particular men at particular times in history, and that now, as the diverse cultures of the world are coming to be similar, nations and nation-states are becoming, paradoxically, the universal ways men, though still diverse and disunited, principally organize their lives and their hopes. And that, this being true, men give their chief loyalties to their nations, become nationalists.

Men do not always put their security first, but they do fear insecurity, whether it be physical or mental. They do dread violence that might harm them and their families. They do fear foreigners with their "strange" ideas, outsiders who could conceivably conquer them, oppress them, impose upon them unwanted ways of life. They do dread loneliness when it brings uncertainty, a feeling of weakness, and emotional discomfort. Perhaps, as the most perceptive of contemporary anthropologists, Claude Lévi-Strauss, remarked, "The one real calamity, the one fatal flaw which can afflict a group of men and prevent them from fulfillment is to be alone." But, above all, they fear death, especially if this means that at the end of their physical lives they will have no significance of any kind.

The nation and its state provided order within the land, assurance (imagined if not actual) against bodily harm, against loss of livelihood (property, too, in capitalist countries), and against the always threatening war of man against man, the Hobbesian anarchy that ever lurks behind the veneer of human politics. The nation and its state gave protection (however illusory) against the "barbarian" abroad, who was all the more dangerous because he was little known, even mysterious—"You can never tell what he will do." The nation and citizenship in it gave a man the feeling that he was not alone, that he belonged to a group that cared, that he was not wholly dependent upon his own feeble forces. And membership in an ongoing group, the nation, which had roots in the past and promise of a future, gave some men hope of immortality at times when they might doubt the existence of a supernatural heaven. While all men die, they want to live forever, and they evolve schemes to perpetuate themselves through their groups.

A nation's passport was not just a document permitting entrance into another country. It gave its holder the feeling of security—because he was a citizen of his nation, his fellow nationals would support him and he had *the* government behind him. The passport also identified him: he was an American, a Frenchman, an Indian, a man with (or so he believed) a distinct personality, a character of his own. As long as there have been records to reveal their questions, individuals have been asking who they are, wanting to be distinct, to be known for themselves, and, as part of the same quest, to be identified with someone—their contemporaries, their ancestors (parents), their descendants (children). In this way they could get a certain sense not only of security (belonging) but also of self-esteem and pride. They, their ancestors and themselves, as members of a group—family, tribe, nation—have done thus and so, have so suffered or so triumphed. Hence they were distinct *and* they belonged to an identifiable group; they *were* somebody. Generally, too, they wanted to believe they were in some way superior, and establishment of identity gave them a basis for invidious comparisons—as the English humanitarian Clutton Brooks put it, patriotism was "pooled self-esteem." At minimum, in modern times, national identity gave them a name—Frenchman, Persian, Japanese—and it allowed them to think of ideas, customs, life styles as theirs. Perhaps as important, other peoples so identified them, and so gave them identity: Sam Jones, United States; Jacques Boulanger, France; Sadao Hasegawa, Japan.

This identification was not equally shared, ostensibly or otherwise, by all members of any group. But nationalism satisfactorily answered, for increasing numbers of people, the ever asked vital question, "What or who am I?" Children learned to identify themselves from the age of six or so with their nations. They were so taught and their nation became *"their* country." Both as children and adults, western and then other peoples increasingly identified themselves by their national languages, customs, ways of initiation into adulthood, kinds of courtship, varieties of clothing and diets, heroes, villains, and symbols. As Sir Lewis Namier, the brilliant Polish-English historian, said, "To every man, as to Brutus, the native land" became "his life-giving Mother and the State raised upon the land his law-giving Father. . . ." And, with deepening intensity, modern men identified with that mother, that father, and therefore thought they knew *who* they were. When all else failed them, that flag, that motherland, that fatherland were "still there." In times of crisis, when values were both sharply challenged and swiftly moving, they could, in the metaphor of psychoanalysis, return to the security of the mother's womb and find the guidance of the father figure, or, in less imaginative rhetoric, a rock or a harbor in a storm.

There may be no natural basis for the desire for status, but nonetheless it seems to be (or to have become) almost universal. The ways it can be won, of course, vary with the society. In modern nations men generally achieve it by their wealth, their political power, and their social position, sometimes by their social contributions, their knowledge, their creativity in the arts. And always status is achieved in relation to other people. Now, most men, as individuals, cannot or do not acquire much status. But nearly all men can acquire it vicariously if they are part of a group (in the modern world a nation) that has some kind of distinction, and nearly all nations do, or so claim—in virtue, if not in world power. This was especially true when even ordinary men, in the nineteenth- and twentieth-century democracies and dictatorships, participated (or believed they did) in larger and larger numbers in the affairs of their governments, and came to believe that government was not only for them but by them as well.

There is no intention here to evaluate whatever it is a nation is or should be proud of, whether wealth, productivity, physical size, or its science and its arts, but only to say that members of nations covet prestige and find their own enhanced by the figure their nation cuts in the world. On the old British Empire the sun never set; the United States is the richest nation in the world; France is the most civilized; the Chinese and Cuban revolutions point the way for all mankind; white Anglo-Saxon nations are superior; black (African) is beautiful. Other distinctions may not be so grandiose, but the superlative is the same: the Swiss make the best chocolate; the French have the most (246?) varieties of cheese; the Germans (or the Danes) brew the best beer; the Costa Ricans grow the best coffee; the Argentineans have the best steaks and the Japanese the best green tea.

Especially in the Christian nations influenced by Calvinism (the United States and England), but in others as well (Japan), status has also been gained by "doing one's duty" and having a calling, doing God's or the emperor's will. This has meant that individuals could work for their nation and, like Woodrow Wilson, gain great acclaim, for to do one's duty meant serving in the armed forces, in the diplomatic corps, and in public office, defending and building the nation, and carrying the blessings and burdens of its God-chosen people to the whole world, in particular caring for "lesser breeds," the "benighted heathen," the "barbarians outside" who were not so fortunate as to have a supernatural blessing bestowed upon them.

Good patriots found excitement and joy both in disliking or hating other peoples and countries and in liking or loving their own countrymen and country. And in both the hating and the loving, their views and their actions were socially approved and praised. Men, it is commonly observed, like the familiar and the usual. It is also obvious that they at times become "sick" of the routine, the tedium and the trivia of their daily lives. Now nationalism offered those bored with their wives and families, or their jobs and their neighborhoods, opportunity to participate alongside their countrymen in celebrations and ceremonies, in national service and in war—to sweat and give their blood, to work, to shout, to wave flags, to fight. Not everyone rushed to serve even in times of national disasters, of hurricanes and earthquakes, or of revolutions and wars. Not everyone loved parades, martial band music, marching in unison, or firing a gun. But for many the activity, the music, the marching, the firing provided welcome thrills—or relief. Not many enjoyed killing (though some individuals did), but national service in peace or in war took men out of their homes, aroused their emotions, brought public praise. In war, individuals could find vent for pent-up emotions of many kinds; killing enemies was legal, and could bring acclaim for bravery besides. Most men undoubtedly hated war, yet it was probably the most exciting activity—game, in contemporary social science jargon—in which they ever engaged. And if they hated it while engaging in it, they later, as old soldiers, enjoyed reminiscing about their "strange" experiences, their buddies, and their often alleged and sometimes actual deeds of heroism. Small boys, their sons, enjoyed their stories, too, and played at war games. From the eighteenth century wars have been between nations, and vivid martial experiences of excitement and joy have been associated with nationalism. And this has been true for succeeding generations—from the old soldiers of Napoleon who marched with him to Egypt, to Italy, or to Russia, to the veterans of World War II who marched, sailed, or flew in, around, and above Europe, North Africa, and the islands of the Pacific.

In each war hope has run high for peace and justice, a victorious peace, of course, and the justice of the victor, but nevertheless peace and justice. One of the most remarkable characteristics of modern men has been their belief in the possibility of a better world, the belief in progress. This progress, they have generally expected, would come within and through their nations. Progress has meant many things, and different things to different men, among them pursuit of the "life, liberty, and happiness" of the American Declaration of Independence; among them the thousand years of rule by a superior "race," the Hitlerian dream; among them, and perhaps the most urgent hope, the creation of an independent nation-state, a Germany, an Italy, a Poland, an Israel, a Ghana, an India.

Whatever the dream of progress has meant, its realization has nearly always, in modern times, been associated with nations—a higher standard of living for Argentineans, Kenyans, or Mexicans, more liberties for French-Canadians, Czechs, or Iranians, more happiness for Swedes, Australians, or Frenchmen. In recent years, for probably the majority of the people in the world, progress has first of all meant less oppression by foreigners, less oppression of, say, Algerians, Tanzanians, and Ukrainians by Frenchmen, Englishmen, and Russians. But in these cases relief from oppression has also meant, or so it has been believed, opportunities for richer, fuller, freer (however these three adjectives are defined) lives within their nations.

For nations have been the groups through which and in which modern men have channeled their efforts and their hopes for better lives than they have had. That the national efforts have not been without result there is much evidence, though the progress has been uneven and often illusory, and the utopias, the gardens of plenty and peace, always recede further into the future. National governments and agencies now care for the most vital needs of people and now hold out hope that these may be progressively met. National constitutions and laws and courts provide for such civil liberties as people now possess, and if these liberties are ever to be extended it will be the national governments that extend them—or so it is believed. Whether men have become happier because of the actions and the pronouncements of their national governments one cannot say. But the national way, *their way,* has become the chief way comprehensible to modern men. And it has been *the* way, often the *only* way, to get things done, for the contemporary way to get things done is to appeal to national pride and fear—"The Russians have it and we Americans don't, therefore. . . ."

Whether pride in one's own country or fear of another is the more effective in getting things done, no documents or psychological studies tell us. Probably both are always present in ambivalent balance. In any case, out of the pride and fear arise mistrust, aversion, hate. As individuals search for security, identity, status, excitement, and as they hope for a better life, they meet obstacles, encounter difficulties, suffer defeats. They ask why. The reasons may be in themselves, in their own society, or in their own environment, but an obvious and easy answer is the outsider, the barbarian foreigner who has interfered or threatens to interfere. That outsiders have interfered is beyond doubt—the Yankees in Latin America, the English, French, Germans, and now the Americans in Asia and Africa, the Germans in France, the English in Greece, the Russians in Poland, and——.

In their fear and uncertainty, adults, like children, turn to the mother —in this case usually called the fatherland—to find security, and they detest other fatherlands that threaten the mother and hence them. Those individuals who are frustrated or have had traumatic experiences—defined in Freudian terms as the "emotional shock of an expressively painful stimulus"—tend to blame "others" easily and quickly; and most individuals, the normal and the abnormal, especially in wartime but also in their "normal" pursuits, are sometimes frustrated and the victims of traumatic experience, and find comfort, perhaps pleasure, in release of pent-up emotion in anger and hate. They must blame someone for their troubles, find some scapegoat, some devil, and who is more obvious than the strange and unfathomable foreigner? As the social psychologist Gordon Allport observed, a prejudiced person tries to find an "island of institutional safety and security. The nation is the island he selects . . . a positive anchorage . . . his country right or wrong." But, as Allport did not observe, everyone is prone, especially in crises, to be prejudiced, to turn to an island of safety, and in the modern world to his nation.

The Greeks of ancient times hated other Greeks and the Persians as well; medieval Christians hated Mohammedans. In the modern world communists hate capitalists, whites look down on and mistrust blacks, and blacks, with reason, sometimes hate whites. All the modern, and a number of the ancient and medieval, "hates" are still with us, but nationalist hate has become the most violent and widespread as peoples have searched for someone to blame—scapegoats, villains, demons. Perhaps nationalist hate is the modern version of the age-old belief in demons, and we can add a new dimension to old theories of demonology. The number of "ethnophaulisms," many having to do with nationality, is legion: gook, slant-eyed bastard, Uncle Shylock, hun, wop, frog. The number of favorable epithets applied to other nationalities is few and usually limited to soldiers of a country allied in war: the World War I American characterization of the British soldier as Tommy. Not all individuals hate, and many do not feel or express hate much of the time. Still, given the nature of men as it has been shaped by modern cultures, men do blame "others" for the misfortunes or failures that beset them, and since in the modern world the "others" are organized in nations, it is other nations that they distrust and hate.

Nations, then, grew out of men's vital needs, and nationalism can and does contain their treasured personal and historical dreams and deeply felt fears. No wonder, therefore, that many of them have found in their nation the larger entity to which they could be devoted. Here but seven reasons for the persistence of nationalism have been discussed. Other reasons and other ways of classifying reasons will occur to anyone. Three others of a different variety need mention. Since the time of the German sociologist Max Weber, it has become commonly believed that leaders often possess peculiar qualities (charisma)—the gift of grace if not of God—that set them apart and endow them, in the eyes of their followers, with supernatural, superhuman, or at least exceptional powers, and that these qualities enable them to set styles, trigger action, dominate people. From the eighteenth century more and more of the famed leaders who possessed charisma have been national patriots who preached nationalist doctrines: political leaders and men of action of otherwise widely different views, like Barère, Kossuth, Cecil Rhodes, Theodore Roosevelt, Mussolini, Gandhi, and Nkrumah; and men of prophecy, like Fichte, Mazzini, Charles Péguy and al-Afghānī. Whether such men became leaders because they were nationalists or nationalists because they were leaders (probably both) makes little difference. They gained and retained prominence and positions of power by appealing to the hopes and fears of followers and of potential followers. Thus they deepened and spread national consciousness and loyalty. When they said "unto" their peoples, "You shall do your patriotic duty for your country and the greater safety and glory of us all," their peoples usually and eventually listened and often believed and acted as they were told. In times of trouble, in war, they believed and acted all the more—even unto death. And it was not just the ordinary people who became patriots but also many of their cultural leaders—historians, novelists, musicians, and poets, the gifted individuals who, on occasion, may have had as much influence as the men of action: the Michelets and Treitschkes, the Dostoyevskys and Paderewskis, the Kiplings and the Senghors. And the message these intellectuals and these artists generally preached was the same: "Go thou and be good patriots." Julien Benda, a French critic, once spoke of the "treason of the intellectuals" (*clercs*), but in modern times most intellectuals thought the appellation patriot praiseworthy.

A man could be, of course, a patriot in many different fashions. As has been said, nationalism could easily marry many different causes, and once the marriage was consummated divorce was difficult. During the revolutionary years from 1789 to 1794 French patriotism was associated primarily with hope and revolutionary reform, during the Napoleonic era of 1799 –1815 with victory and conquest, and after the defeat of 1870 and down to 1918 with loss and revenge.

Just as these sentiments lived on and gave content to French nationalism, so did similar "modernizing" sentiments elsewhere. If a people wanted to improve their economic well-being, and in modern times few peoples have not, the instrument was their nation-state. If businessmen wanted markets, domestic or foreign, they asked for support of their businesses at home through tariffs or subsidies and support of their businesses abroad by diplomacy or force, and in both cases they could and did use the appeal of patriotism. If workers and farmers desired higher incomes, they demanded the elimination of foreign competition by tariffs and limitations on immigration and trade, and when they did they were defending the nation's standard of living and this, too, was praiseworthy.

Once nationalism came into being, it persisted because it was established and approved, and as it persisted it strengthened itself. Once people were conditioned and committed to nationalist views, their mental reflexes were tuned, or so it appeared, to receive nationalist impulses and to exclude whatever outside waves seemed irrelevant to their national interests. Patriots preached patriotism and demanded equal fervor from others. Fathers (and mothers too) taught their children to be patriotic, and the schools taught their pupils patriotism. Such problems as, in our times, those of overpopulation, pollution of the water and the air, and proliferation of atomic missiles were first of all considered to be not international but national problems. Solutions that were not national were unpatriotic and impractical, and therefore wrongheaded and pernicious. For dealing with major human problems, national institutions appeared to be the only institutions that were both effective *and* acceptable. Proposals for federations of somewhat related peoples (as in East Africa) and the various and several "pan" movements (in Europe, South America, and Africa) all foundered on the rock of nationalism. Nationalism thus tenaciously perpetuated itself just as other established and accepted ideas have. Perhaps the law of inertia applies to men and societies just as it does to physical forces.

By the twentieth century the nation and nationalism were the largest community and idea within the comprehension of most men. It is true that for some, especially in parts of Asia and Africa, the nation and nationalism were still too large and abstract. It is likewise true that a few men everywhere were able to think in larger concepts, but they *were* few and were often despised as wild-eyed dreamers, or, worse, as betrayers of the national interest and honor, as "traitors."

Most of men's needs and emotional drives have been and could be satisfied in varying degrees through groups other than the nation and through loyalties other than nationalism. Always, for example, their families and their local communities have given men some security and identity, and historically they have found these in churches and religions, in tribes and clans, in city-states and empires, in feudal relationships, and in dynastic, monarchical states. For a few men who were anarchists, there has seemed to be no real need of a larger entity than self and little devotion except perhaps to the vague idea of humanity. For a minority of youth today, if not yesterday, few of the old groupings have much meaning, though they may be devoted to whatever is the current fashion—rebellion, drugs, or something else.

From ancient times a serious few have given their devotion to communities and ideas larger than nations and nationalism, to all mankind or to churches and religions—the Christian and Islamic—that purport to be universal. The second-century statement of the Roman Stoic Marcus Aurelius has been echoed ever since: "My nature is rational and social, and my city and country, so far as I am Antoninus is Rome, but so far as I am a man, it is the world." For the Christian apostle Paul (d. 67?), all power came from God; God "made of one blood all the nations of men for to dwell on the face of the earth." Christians, when they have followed the teachings of their savior, Jesus of Nazareth, have believed in the brotherhood of all men.

Even such ardent nationalists as the Czech historian Palacký and the Italian idealist Mazzini have, on occasion, put humanity above nation, seeing their nation as the step toward the unity of mankind. Palacký deeply loved his nation but "always," he said, he esteemed "more highly the good of mankind." For Mazzini nationality was the group through which men could truly work for the eventual benefit of all men: "Country and family are like two steps of a ladder without which you could not climb any higher but upon which it is forbidden you to stay your feet."

But if in the past the needs and drives of men can be and have been satisfied by other groups and loyalties, then why nations and nationalism in modern times?

Conjuncture of Circumstances

To this fundamental question there are no completely satisfactory answers and certainly no definitive ones. We simply do not know enough about human nature, the nature of individuals or of individuals in groups. Historians, anthropologists, sociologists, social psychologists, psychoanalysts, and political scientists have not as yet done the studies that could fully explain the "why"; and the behaviorists, so preoccupied with method, have not, with rare exceptions, seriously gotten much beyond discussion of how to approach the question.

One not unsatisfactory explanation, in the present state of knowledge, is "conjuncture" of forces and ideas, a concept that French historians have found useful. While this explanation leaves much to be explained, is too complicated, and cannot be demonstrated quantitatively, it warrants examination as a hypothesis. A broad concept, it attempts to take account of the myriad and moving influences that interact and crisscross in the development of institutions and ways of living. It at least reveals an awareness of the vast complexity of human experience that confronts the historian.

By conjuncture here is meant those continuing junctures of political, economic, social, and cultural forces and ideas during the last seven, and more especially during the last two, centuries that have resulted in nations and nationalism. Feudalism, the great French historian Marc Bloch tells us, arose out of the interplay of the evolving political, social, and economic forces and ideas—the total culture—of the Middle Ages. So it was, it has been argued in these pages, with nationalism. Further brief conjecture about the nature of the mutual and continuous interplay of these forces and ideas in the development of nationalism may be helpful.

As transportation and communication slowly improved and as gunpowder made castle walls less impregnable, the feudal-manorial basis of medieval society was undermined, and great lords were able to extend their jurisdiction and territories. From late medieval times in France and

England powerful dynasties began to accumulate territories and peoples, to unify them and centralize government over them. They—in France the Capetians, the Valois, and the Bourbons, in England the Normans, the Plantagenets, the Tudors—did not know they were creating nations or building nation-states. They were mainly interested in keeping and increasing their personal and family fortunes and power, which they thought included the fortunes of their subjects. They were, they believed, divinely chosen to rule over lands and subjects, and their subjects obeyed them because their religion so taught. Whether God had chosen them or not, they ruled and increased their power and prestige, when and if they could, by creating and controlling armies and courts, by appointing royal officials, by keeping records, by collecting taxes, by rejecting outside interference (as from the papacy), by, in sum, establishing sovereignty over the people within their lands. And as this was happening, the Roman Catholic church, under the impact of increasing secularism, was slowly losing both its authority over men's minds and the universality of its appeal.

In both France and England there were traditions of monarchical rule going back to Roman days, and the boundaries of the territories the kings eventually came to rule or claim had been vaguely set by the ancient Roman imperial administration—something like the way, much later, the traditions of rule and the territorial boundaries of many developing African and Asian states were established by the major modern imperialist nations, France and Britain.

At the height of their power the English and French monarchs—during the reigns of, say, Elizabeth (1558–1603) and Louis XIV (1643–1715) —had clearly and firmly constructed royal central governments, dynastic states with all the machinery, the loyal armed forces and royal civil servants, needed to make their rule effective and felt throughout their realms —which *later*, when more people began to participate through parliaments and assemblies, became the modern nations of France and England.

At the time these families of rulers began to build their states, their subjects neither constituted distinct nationalities nor were they citizens. But both in France and England a small nucleus of the subjects did possess or come to have common ways of seeing and doing things, a common kernel of culture of which they slowly became aware. They could speak and understand each other in what to us today is recognizable French and English; and within each nucleus there came the vague beginnings and then, through the circulation of information and ideas, the flowering of common lore and literature, and hence consciousness of a common past, of common interests, of common hopes for the future, and, during the same time, consciousness of differences from others (Frenchmen from Englishmen, Englishmen from Frenchmen). The nuclei, based on the central cities of Paris and London, grew larger, and the cultures came to be called the national. As the language of the upper classes in the Ile de France spread among more and more of the subjects of the French monarchy, and the language of the lower classes around London was spoken and understood by more and more subjects of the English kings, so more people became nationally conscious. The invention or introduction of movable type in printing, which enabled easy and inexpensive publication of books, made it possible for more people to read and use the vernacular languages and encouraged their standardization *within* separate groups throughout Europe and eventually the world. Printing, as it facilitated communication among a people, was thus an instrument in arousing national consciousness.

In both France and England there was often danger that neither royal power nor common interests would hold subjects together, that the kingdoms might break, be split into smaller states. Indeed, the several civil wars and rebellions in each country reveal the centrifugal forces that again and again threatened the unity of the kingdoms. But over hundreds of years the English and French royal dynasties, supported by their armies and officials and by powerful special interest groups, were able not only to keep their peoples and territories intact but also to acquire more, and to push their rule deeper into the consciousness and lives of their subjects. These subjects generally were faithful and devoted, at least until 1640 (England), 1776 (the English-American colonies), and 1789 (France), and when the rebellions did come they tended to transform the dynastic states into national. As time went on, the kings had to identify their interests with those of the nation, that is, the growing number of people of the upper and middle classes who were literate and aware of their common interests. If they did not do so, they were, as in France, later overthrown by their peoples.

By the end of the eighteenth century changes were under way in Europe and the Americas that finally determined that the nation would become the major group into which peoples organized, and that nationalism would become the most pervasive group sentiment and for many people the supreme loyalty. These changes took place in all aspects of life, the economic and political, the social and cultural. No one change was isolated, for each affected the others and all affected each in complex and multiple interactions. Nor, for the same reason, is it possible to say which was the most important.

From the fifteenth century in western Europe the continuing productivity of land and labor, the inflow of wealth from the New World and from the older worlds of Asia and Africa, and technological inventions (as in artillery) and improvements (as in roads) enabled immense accumulations of capital. This wealth the dynastic states tapped as they created and equipped armies and navies, bridged rivers and built roads (the magnificent military roads running out of Paris), as they assisted business and trade, and as they fostered in many ways their own dynastic interests—interests that would later become the national. As the armed forces became larger, the demand for uniforms (and wool), naval supplies, artillery, and muskets increased enormously, and so did, necessarily, the sums collected by governments in taxes, especially in wartime but also during the constant preparations for war, for wars were frequent and always in the offing.

As business and trade prospered, whether because of government protection and aid or because of individual entrepreneurship, the kingdoms became richer; the governments could then govern more, the royal courts (symbolized by Versailles) could become more magnificent and consume more, and the monarchs could, or so they thought, become more powerful than their rivals within and without their kingdoms. With variations, that is what happened in France and England. With variations, Colbert, Louis XIV's astute finance minister, knew it for the French kingdom in the seventeenth century and Adam Smith, the astute English economist, knew it for all nations, and particularly for England in the eighteenth century. In any case, more and more of the subjects were affected, directly or indirectly, by their governments, and more and more became dependent, through employment or otherwise, on these governments. More and more subjects, then, were affected by and seemed to benefit from their royal governments; and this was true not only of members of the middle classes but also of the aristocracies and, to a much lesser extent, even of some members of the lower classes. National consciousness deepened and spread.

In much of Europe during the nineteenth century, while monarchies were toppling and republics were being established, the same processes continued. The invention and improvement of weapons—the percussion cap, the breech-loading rifle, the machine gun, heavier artillery—in the competitive race for armament accentuated governmental needs for funds, and therefore for national taxes. Troops had to be equipped and re-equipped, or else the nation was threatened. From the 1870's, when armies became larger and conscription customary, the demands of the national military machines multiplied. In England and the United States, where conscription was not introduced until World War I, the construction of new steel navies required great national expenditure. In civilian life technology likewise accentuated the centripetal forces behind nation building. Construction of hard-surfaced roads in eighteenth-century Britain and France accelerated the movement toward unity. The eighteenth-century invention of the steam engine led in the nineteenth century to the construction of railroads that, as in the Italies and the United States, tied larger and larger numbers of people together—still chiefly those people within boundaries already established by the dynastic states and tradition, though in the case of the United States by rebellion. The building of canals, the invention of the steamboat, and the increased use of water transportation on rivers and lakes as well as along seacoasts in the early nineteenth century had similar effects. So also did the invention of the telegraph (1830's) and later of the telephone (1870's). And so did improvements in the keeping of the records with which the burgeoning bureaucracies were so much concerned, for each record made possible a longer memory of each national concern.

These and other technological advances further facilitated communication among people but chiefly, again, among people (particularly their leaders) who already had, for political and cultural reasons, some consciousness of common interests. They also increased demands for central governmental services over wider areas and more people, thus making possible more penetration by the now national governments into the consciousness of people. Many of the technological advances enabled the rulers of the states, whether monarchical or republican, to extend the influence of the government further and to govern more effectively. Now a French government in Paris could send troops to any part of the country not in a few days or weeks but in a few hours, and it could communicate with any of the growing number of its officials anywhere in the country within minutes. The troops, armed with rifles and artillery, could generally bring order, national order, to any locality quickly, while the local officials —mayors, sheriffs, judges—with the power and resources of the central government behind them, could and did constantly exert nationalizing influences.

As these technologically based changes were occurring, they were accompanied by political changes of equal import. Probably the cause-and-effect relationships were reciprocal, though they are indeed difficult to trace and, like the old chicken-and-egg conundrum, will doubtless never be resolved. From the French Revolutionary period, individuals in greater and greater numbers participated or hoped to participate in government. As more and more of them were affected by decisions of their central governments and as more and more of them became literate and informed, more of them, in their own interest, became concerned with what were coming to be called the national interests. The abbé Sieyès in 1789 was a prophet when he wrote *Qu'est-ce que le tiers-état,* answered "everything," and demanded for it a decisive voice in the French government. The nation thus was becoming first the propertied people and then all the people who resided within the old king's and now the national boundaries. These people demanded rights and services, and sometimes they got them —got them, not from their churches or from lords or princes, but from the national, *their* governments. In the revolutions of 1789, 1830, 1848, and 1870, in the many minor revolutions and during the comparatively quiet periods in between, the demands were principally (1) for rights, like the right to vote in national elections, and (2), where an independent nation-state did not exist, as in Poland, for self-determination.

What had happened early in the development of nationhood and nationalism in France and England also happened, usually somewhat later, and of course with variations, in other western European lands, as in the Germanies and Italies. What happened in western Europe happened, again with variations, in the rest of Europe and in North America, in the lands and among the nascent nationalities of the Austro-Hungarian Empire and the Balkan Peninsula, and in Latin America. For historians (including this one) the differences are often more interesting than the similarities. But here it is the main course that is being followed, the conjuncture of circumstances that formed nations and nationalism.

By the beginning of the twentieth century almost everything men attempted to do in the western world was within their nations, and much was for their nations. Their own dominant political views, economic interests, and cultural affinities were national and were contained in and circumscribed by nationalism. As facilities for communication improved, the people within each nation communicated with each other more, became more and more conscious of their common and distinct interests, more and more devoted to their own nation, and more and more distrustful of other nations. Just as had been and was still largely true of the newspapers, the radio and later the television networks were national, appealed to audiences within nations, broadcast chiefly national news, and sold national advertising and national products; and, unlike most newspapers in western nations, these new and more immediate means of communication were either owned or closely controlled by national governments. There were, except in rare times of revolution, few broadcasts that could be called either unpatriotic or antinational. TV did not so much carry the world into people's sitting rooms as it carried national-minded people in their sitting rooms to the world, and these people still judged what they saw in light of what they were and where they were. As one result, their nationalist emotions could be instantly inflamed.

What was true of the media was also true of transportation. The major airlines (BEA or Air France) were national, though it might be that they (like Braniff) were called international. The new highways, the autobahns and expressways, were usually subsidized by national governments and, if they carried international traffic, this traffic and the expressway usually stopped at the customs barrier at the national border. There were no truly international highways or airports. When education was finally provided for the children of the lower economic classes, it was usually free, public, compulsory, *and* national. Instruction was nearly always, and quite naturally so, in the only language the children understood, and a major purpose was to make good citizens, that is, patriots.

While technological, political, and other developments encouraged the formation and strengthening of nations and national feeling, individuals found new opportunities to achieve their self-interests within their nations. Nationalism, as Stalin observed, enabled members of the bourgeoisie to obtain control over home markets and to obtain foreign markets for their goods and thus to make profits. Businessmen in all nations, not just Cecil Rhodes in Africa in the 1890's or Charles Wilson of General Motors in the 1950's, identified their interests with the national and the national with their own, and used their national governments when they could in their quest for profits. But Stalin's theory, as has been said, made too little explain too much. Politicians waved the flag to win popularity, to obtain votes, and to win and retain office. Seekers of government jobs could not obtain them unless they were loyal, and for some of them (in security and intelligence agencies) their jobs were to ferret out the disloyal. Eventually, in western nations, most individuals of every class, acting alone or with a group, sought satisfaction of their self-interests in and through their nation. How could a farmer increase his income? Through national crop controls and subsidies. How could the sciences and arts be fostered, and incidentally benefit scientists and artists? Through national academies and foundations, and subsidies. How could a poor man be helped? By national provision of jobs and welfare payments. How could a minority group, say the blacks in the United States, obtain justice and equality? By national legislation and nationally sponsored and subsidized action in which they participated.

Up to this point only the junctures of circumstances producing nationalism in western countries have been discussed. The circumstances were not quite the same for developing countries, but there was much that was similar, as chapters IX and X have revealed. Western imperialist nations established the borders and the framework of administration for many of the nascent nations, just as had royal dynasties in European nations when they were nascent. In some, probably the majority of the nations, there were cultural groups, kernels, that were dominant or could become so. Japan is a case, Somali another, and Uganda could be one. The same technological developments in railroads or in the media, much telescoped, now affected the new nations as they had and still do the older. The new national governments were trying to shape nations and create national loyalty just as did and do western governments, and they were creating national institutions (armies, courts, welfare agencies, and schools), building roads, railroads, harbors, and airports, and establishing and controlling the means of communication. Among the ordinary people of the new nations there was, perhaps, as much or as little desire to participate in national affairs as there had been in the early nineteenth century among peasants of the Balkan Peninsula, and probably at least as much will and determination among the educated as there had been in much of Europe or in the Americas a century ago, though perhaps not as much as in Europe and the Americas today. In the new countries, in any case, some individuals could satisfy their personal ambitions for financial profit and wealth or political office and status through their nations and through appeals to patriotism. It was true that the developing nations were not as industrialized and urbanized as most of the older nations, that they were much poorer (in capital and in productivity), and that their middle classes were smaller and less influential. It was also true that skin color played a larger role than it did in western nations—South Africa and the United States, for different reasons, possibly excepted. But, in general, the same forces and circumstances were creating nationalism in Asia and Africa as had created it in the developed nations. One further circumstance made it all the more likely that Asian and African peoples would be or become nationalist. They had models—France, Britain, Germany, and, more recently, the United States and Russia—to observe and follow, just as did Japan during the latter half of the nineteenth century when it entered the then modern world of nations and nationalism.

Why Not Internationalism?

Though no explanation of the appeal and persistence of nationalism can be full or definitive, some of the reasons are clear. Nationalism arises out of the vital interests of people and reflects these interests. It originates in the centers of their nerves, it appeals to and pleasurably inflames their emotions, it contains their best hopes, and it soothes their fears. It has become the way to obtain benefits, overcome obstacles, be protected against outrageous fortune. Throughout the world by the last half of the twentieth century combinations of technological, economic, political, and cultural circumstances had made it likely (if not certain) that peoples would be organized in nations, think and act within the circumscribed environments of nations, and be devoted to these nations. Within the immediately foreseeable future probably the same combinations of circumstances would shape (if not determine) how men organized their group life. But this was not certain.

It was possible that different junctures of circumstances, different combinations of both old and new forces, might push men toward larger and more inclusive groupings, toward internationalism, toward some kind of world order. And if man is to survive, this might be imperative.

If men are to organize themselves internationally, what are the combinations of circumstances that could make this possible?

To describe the technological changes that have made internationalism possible is to describe what seems to contemporary men to be the familiar and commonplace. During the past century steam, petroleum, electricity, and finally atomic energy have facilitated, speeded, and extended communication over wider and wider areas and among more and more people, made interchange of information and knowledge swifter, less expensive, and easier. More people, spread over larger territories, could discover and develop common interests and try to solve common problems together—if they so desired. This has, in fact, happened, even without instantaneous visual communication, in the large area and among the diverse peoples of the United States, and in varying extent in other nations, as in Russia. After 1945, in the developed areas of the world, people could hear and see the news as, or almost as, it happened—if they listened or looked. In 1969 a man's first step on the moon was seen on TV screens in most parts of the world—except for South Africa, where TV was then banned, and mainland China for ideological reasons, as well as the poorer regions of the world where TV has not yet been introduced. So swift was communication that men might now see their own destruction coming in a nuclear war. Hopes and fears could be, if they are not as yet, universalized in seconds. The earth, and even outer space, conceivably, could become a "global village," yet the earth still remains divided among about 140 "sovereign," unequal, and fearful nation-states.

Communication has no consequences unless people can *understand* the communication. Illiteracy was still high in many parts of the world, but it was true that more and more people were learning to read and write and, if many still could not, these might listen via transistor radio or see images on a screen—provided they had access to radio or television. Of course, many in developed and undeveloped areas did not understand what they read, heard, or saw, and, of course, some everywhere did not care. Of course, too, what was communicated might or might not be relevant to internationalism, though it generally was, if at all serious, to nationalism. Nonetheless, by the last half of the twentieth century, because of advances in technology and thought, it was possible for men to realize that as men they had common needs and problems, and that they might meet these needs and solve these problems more satisfactorily through international rather than national institutions and actions. Whether or not the technological and other changes will further push them in international directions as they have in nationalist no one can as yet know, but the possibility is there.

The same discoveries and uses of power sources that brought swifter communication advanced industrialization. Industrialization increased the demand for raw materials scattered about the world and for world markets. It also enabled accumulations of the capital and skills required for world ventures. The search for profit, though often cloaked in patriotism, ignored national boundaries. Great multinational banks and corporations, as in the United States, and great state enterprises, as in Russia, engaged in international enterprises, and business became international as well as national. Some businesses, indeed, were becoming part of an emerging world economy that was more than just "linked national economies." While the international sound was, on occasion, greater than the activity, it was becoming profitable for private and public businesses to "go international."

As industrialization proceeded, so did urbanization. Though cities dissolved older family and tribal relationships and fostered the national, they also—now Tokyo and Nairobi as well as London and Paris—became cosmopolitan, with their tourists, their multilingual porters, and their international business offices (IBM and Philips). National governments, to bolster the international urban economies on which the national now in degree depended, found it desirable to contribute to the International Bank for Reconstruction and Development, to give or receive international loans, to stabilize currencies by international agreements, and, in western Europe, to establish the Common Market. After nearly two centuries of intermittent bitter wars, the French and Germans have found economic ways to reconcile their differences. It may be possible for other peoples to do so.

Some political developments pointed toward internationalism as well. At the end of each of the twentieth century's two world wars, when the horrors of war were fresh, the victor nations formed first a League of Nations and then a United Nations and several other international agencies, including the International Court of Justice, the World Health Organization (WHO), and the United Nations Educational, Scientific and Cultural Organization (UNESCO). These international organizations could not act unless member nations approved, and they little touched, as do national governments, the vital concerns of individuals. Sovereignty remained national. But they did have small funds and some prestige, and they did have an undeterminable yet significant influence on public opinion. Though none of the agencies inspired much loyalty beyond their own officers and employees and a few world-spirited citizens, these organizations of nation-states collaborated on many international projects that at least leaders thought important. If the organizations were not effective in preventing war, the most crucial of all problems facing men, they were a step toward international organizations that would have the actual power to enforce decisions and to affect the lives of individuals. They did receive considerable support from informed individuals among the elites throughout the world, and one day the internationalism of these elites might become stronger than their nationalism. In a rough way, the international organizations and their officers probably had about as much influence on the people of nations as western monarchs had over most of their feudal vassals in the late Middle Ages. This was not much but it was, perhaps, a beginning. Again circumstances, in this case the political, pointed toward internationalism. The views of influential intellectuals as well as the nature of the problems of twentieth-century living pointed toward further movement in the same direction.

Scientists and humanists have long exchanged information and ideas. Neither physics nor plagues nor truth nor beauty recognizes national borders. All the great scientific discoveries, in electronics, in nuclear energy, in medicine, have resulted from the work of scientists of many nationalities, and some scientists and statesmen have recognized this and collaborated in international undertakings. The great novels, poems, histories, paintings, and symphonies created throughout the world are known and admired by the educated in many lands, and most symphony orchestras are composed of musicians of many nationalities who play the symphonies of composers of many nationalities under the direction of a conductor very likely from a nation not their own.

Ordinary people, when they had the money, increasingly consumed products from "abroad," and everywhere they wanted these products, no matter where they were produced. Frenchmen drank Coca-Cola, even if it was American; and Americans, if affluent, drank Beaujolais, perhaps because it had the prestige of being a French wine. Americans drove Volkswagens made by the bitter enemy of 1941–45 and Toyotas made by the "cheap" labor of another former bitter enemy, Japan. In some way or in some part, much that most people used or were the victims of came from "abroad." The rifles and machine guns and tear gas came from Czechoslovakia and China, or France and the United States. When an Egyptian villager getting power from a Russian-financed dam turned on his electric bulb, he likely did not know it but he was benefiting from the inventiveness of, among others, a Scot, an Italian, a Frenchman, a German, and an American. When Japanese died at Hiroshima they were the target of a bomb conceived by, among others, Bohr (Danish), Einstein (German-Jewish), Fermi (Italian), and Urey (American). When people around the world could avoid or be treated for smallpox, yellow fever, or bubonic plague, the reason was that scientists from many lands had co-operated to find preventives or cures.

There can be no doubt that more people, especially educated people, were becoming more aware of the products and ways of life of people other than those of their own nationality. When they went to school they sometimes learned that foreigners were not so strange and different or so much to be feared as their parents had thought. Through foreign travel—and more and more people went "abroad"—they could learn (some did) that foreigners were people and that foreign ways could be enjoyed. Yet it was true that education basically remained nationalist, and foreign travel often but confirmed nationalist prejudices—some Parisian waiters *are* rude and some Tokyo taxi drivers *are* reckless.

The one common problem big and shocking enough to change national into international patriots was the possibility, after 1945, of nuclear war. This new circumstance could be decisive. Hiroshima and Nagasaki did not fully awaken human consciousness to the likelihood of the annihilation that national nuclear war would bring. But once again, as with the feudal order and gunpowder, the effects of technological change had made old political arrangements, in this case national sovereignty, obsolete. While few national patriots comprehended this, more possibly will— that is, if they are concerned about the survival of any human life.

Someday, it may be, individuals will become conscious of the fact that they owe whatever they have largely to others, and others of other nationalities, and that neither inventiveness, productiveness, nor consumer demand can be nationally confined. But consciousness of the dependency of each man on everyman and loyalty of each man to everyman will not come easily or quickly. The long-heralded progress to internationalism is still heralded, not accomplished. People change, though usually with glacierlike slowness.

The brutal fact is that the predominant myths and ways of action of most people are still those of the conjuncture of circumstances that produced nationalism.

Technological inventions and improvements are primarily used by people in nations for national purposes. The jet planes and the atomic-powered missiles are national, the TV and the satellites are national, the American astronauts, though they came in "peace for all mankind," carried the *American* flag to the moon.

Industry is still chiefly national and the corporations, public and private, are, with few exceptions, still nationally controlled and operated. Economic production is still *primarily* organized along national lines and so are all economic activities. Trade remains primarily between nations or between individuals within nations. Deficits and surpluses are thought of in the context of national balances of trade. Productivity is measured as the GNP, the gross national product. Workers are organized in national unions, and the socialist internationals, where they still exist, are of little consequence. The workers of the world have not united. Even the communists, Russian, Chinese, Yugoslavian, have gone national.

International political organizations are composed of representatives of nation-states. Because each nation-state is sovereign, it can refuse to support any measure, prevent it from being put into effect within its own territory. On all important issues, the big nations can by veto prevent any action. In almost everything the international organizations do they must function (if they do act) through the sovereign nation-states, and they seldom touch the *individuals* on the fundamental matters of life, liberty, and income that concern them most. The organizations cannot tax or conscript individuals, or order them to do anything, nor do they really, except in times of great natural catastrophes, help individuals in any way these individuals can see or feel. Nor do these organizations have the power greatly to influence people's views through schools or any medium of communication.

In the most awful of all human misfortunes, international war, the organizations remain almost powerless; they cannot prevent such wars or stop them once they start. Further, they offer but few individuals the opportunity to satisfy their self-interests, and but few individuals, as individuals, participate in international work or give any loyalty, except in lip service, to organizations that do. If that government is most viable, as the *Federalist* advocates of the American Constitution believed, that most appeals to the self-interests of the governed, then the present international organizations are moribund, or, perhaps more precisely, still in their infancy.

There is little consciousness on the part of many people (or by some of their historians) of any kind of common human past except that experienced by their nation. The triumphs and the tragedies of men they know are chiefly those of men of their own nations. Men do have a common past on the small planet called the earth. The great inventions—fire, the wheel, the steam engine, and atomic fission and fusion—that now affect all men were the result of many men's efforts over millennia. But the remembered experience, that is, history, is mainly that of their nations.

There is little consciousness, as yet, of common world interests. Professors and plumbers are Americans or Russians before they are professors and plumbers. And so it is with all the professions and crafts in all nations. Studies show that physicians in one nation are more like physicians in other nations than they are like most of their fellow nationals, yet medicine, in spite of the international nature of materia medica, remains largely national. The people of each nation, with rare exceptions, think of their own nation first. Every intelligent person rationally questions the phrase "my country, right or wrong," but much of the time he acts emotionally and supports it whether wrong or right, whether other men benefit or suffer.

There is little consciousness of common world hopes, or it may be more accurate to say that few people hope to achieve freer, happier, more secure lives through international action and organization. People do want peace, but peace with national honor and victory. They nearly always think "other" nations responsible for breaches of peace: the Americans the Russians and Chinese; the Russians the Americans and Chinese; and the Chinese——. Since there is no rival planet, there is no planetary rival to unite the earth's people in order that Earth might surpass it. People define freedom differently, yet they do want it. But the Universal Declaration of Human Rights of 1948, though a step toward internationalism, has remained a declaration without universality or force. Freedoms, if they were enjoyed at all, still were established and guaranteed by national governments. People want happiness; few seek it outside their nations. Where else could *most* of them now do so?

There have been and are few, if any, truly international charismatic leaders, worshiped heroes, or gripping symbols. Most of the famed modern leaders—Napoleon and De Gaulle, Wellington and Churchill, Washington and Lincoln, Senghor and Kenyatta—have won whatever international renown they have as great leaders of nations. There are no truly international Jeanne d'Arcs, Thomas Jeffersons, Simón Bolívars, or Gandhis, no truly international Babe Ruths or Jean-Claude Killys. The international wars between nations have produced national heroes, the international Olympic Games national heroes. For a short time at the end of World War I, Woodrow Wilson, partly because he symbolized the dream of world peace, but also partly because he preached national self-determination, might have become a world leader and hero. It is possible that Dag Hammarskjöld might have achieved this stature had he not been prematurely killed. Two of the greatest men of contemporary times, a scientist and a humanitarian—Albert Einstein and Albert Schweitzer—almost did, and a few movie stars—Charlie Chaplin, for one—have come close. Perhaps moon astronauts or future space explorers could so become. But no earthling has yet really become an international hero or leader for all men, European and American, Asian and African, men of all ideologies, races, and nations, not even the great founders of the world religions, Confucius, Jesus, and Muhammad.

Nor are there any symbols standing for international unity that are universally known, none at least that tie people together as national symbols have united those within nations. In the present world of nations every child knows his country's flag, but how many adults or children can identify the United Nations flag, let alone identify themselves with the organization for which it stands? The dove and the olive branch, it is true, represent peace, but not any international body for which they stand and to which the world's people are devoted. The American eagle arouses the loyalty of Americans. The bundle of rods with projecting ax blade stood for authority in Mussolini's Italy. No such symbols now really stir international loyalty or authority, nor have they ever done so. The romantic and even spiritual appeal that nationalism has offered internationalism still lacks.

Never in the past and not at present has there been an international power that directly affected individuals as the nation-states now do. Only scattered and rare idealists dare hope to create such a power. At present peoples and their elites, national patriots nearly all, would not submit to international authority on any vital issue or give their ultimate loyalty to a state above their own.

And yet? And yet?

Human organization has evolved, from family to clan and tribe, from city-state to feudal principality and dynastic state to nation. Is there a kind of uneven progression in human affairs from the small to the large, and, if so, could international world organization be next?

Among peoples everywhere there is awareness of the nuclear threat, and among a considerable number great fear. This common fear could unite enough men to make effective international action possible, for the alternative is elimination of the species in nuclear holocausts. Other dangers could unite men as well—the dangers of pollution, plague, and over-population.

Many of the peoples of the world, not only in the new nations but also in the old, are expectant. Their common expectancies could lead them to submerge their national differences in hope of realizing the old dream of life, liberty, and happiness.

If men wish to survive, prosper, and be happy, well, then, what is to be done?

History does not teach lessons valid for all times and places. It can only afford to "feeling, thinking, acting men" (Henri Marrou) an abundance of facts and ideas on which to base their judgments. No historian, as historian, can or should be a prophet, and history is not a crystal ball.

A new messiah is perhaps too much to hope for—and likely he would be a general. And the workers of the world have not united to form a classless world society, nor are they likely to do so as the communist nation-states compete. The best and last hope for men's survival is probably some kind of international world community. The question then comes to be: how facilitate *that* conjuncture of circumstances that will produce *that* community?

If the history of nationalism contains meaning for the future, men will move beyond their present nationalism to internationalism only when this internationalism offers more security and hope than nationalism does at present. And if new international groupings, whatever they are, are to become established, they will have to (1) penetrate the consciousnesses of *individuals*—at least those of elites; (2) encourage *individuals* to participate in the larger group's affairs—thus afford them a sense of belonging; and (3) enable *individuals* to relate their interests to those of the international community and thereby give them a sense of significance and identification. Otherwise, they will not be or feel secure or dare to hope. Otherwise, they will not give their loyalty.

Technological bases for new international groupings now exist—jet planes and spaceships, electronic and satellite communication, nuclear energy. These, plus the bomb, have made the present 140 national boundaries and flags obsolete. When any people, say Asians (not just Parisians), catch influenza, all the peoples of the world are exposed. The technology is ready to treat world disease—war—and to foster world health—peace.

It is now possible through schooling, travel, and the media to educate great numbers of people to know something not just about their nations but about the world. This means that they could be informed on, take an interest in, and help in the solution of world (*their*) problems—too big bombs, too many babies, too many artificial chemicals and gases in the water and air. This means, too, that they could find community in common hopes for life, liberty, and happiness.

It is, then, possible, with the techniques, experience, and knowledge available, to establish international organizations that have authority and can enforce decisions, really touch individuals, penetrate their consciousnesses, and inspire loyalty. It is now clear that individuals of different nationalities can function together in such organizations (the Common Market) and that the demands of special interests, like those of business and farming, can be satisfied in communities larger than nations. Peoples have had and can have many loyalties. To be loyal to their local community and nation need not prevent a higher loyalty to an international community.

All the faces of nationalism attracted people because of what they offered or seemed to offer. Internationalism could attract people in decisive numbers if the new realities and old myths were recognized for what they are. The barriers to international community are high but not insurmountable. People could learn, and some have, that old myths that nationally divide them and threaten to destroy them do not correspond with the new realities.

The question then is: is there time? The optimist will answer "yes," the pessimist "no." There is no way of knowing who is right.

But there is a chance. A chance that, as Raymond Aron has written, the peoples of "the nations will gradually surmount their prejudices and their egoism . . . and science will give humanity, grown conscious of itself, the possibility of administering the available resources of the world rationally. . . ." When and if that time arrives, though people may still live in small and distinct families and cultural communities, just as they often do now within nations, they will have to give their supreme loyalty to the international community that represents the interests not of nation-states but of humanity.

Notes

A Bibliographical Essay

Index

Notes

Chapter I

1. This consensus is all the more important because the scholars came from different nations, held different philosophic values, and often disagreed, as scholars always do, on emphases and details.
2. Only a description of some length, of the kind attempted by Carlton Hayes, Hans Kohn, and this author, can contain enough information and analysis to reveal the complexities of nationalism and the difficulties in interpreting it.
3. *Essays on Nationalism,* New York, 1926, p. 6.
4. *The Historical Evolution of Modern Nationalism,* New York, 1931, p. 6.
5. Royal Institute of International Affairs, *Nationalism: A Report by a Study Group of Members of the Institute,* London, 1939, pp. xvi–xx, 249 ff.
6. *The Idea of Nationalism: A Study of Its Origins and Background,* New York, 1944, pp. 10, 16.
7. *The Meaning of Nationalism,* New Brunswick (N.J.), 1954, pp. 196–97. The short definitions of a similar nature that could be cited, of course, are many. Snyder, pp. 74 ff., includes many of them. See also Boyd C. Shafer, *Nationalism: Myth and Reality,* New York, 1955, pp. 241–45, for other attempts up to 1954; and for other books that describe nationalism up to 1967, his *Nationalism: Interpretations and Interpreters,* 3rd ed., Washington, D.C., 1966.
8. *Nigeria: Background to Nationalism,* Berkeley, 1965, p. 425.
9. *Nationalism in Iran,* Pittsburgh, 1967, p. 3. Emerson does not directly define nationalism but speaks of the nation as "the largest community which, when the chips are down, effectively commands men's loyalty . . . ," and he defines a nation as "a community of people who feel they belong together in the double sense that they share deeply significant elements of a common heritage and that they have a common destiny for the future." *From Empire to Nation,* Cambridge (Mass.), 1960, pp. 95–96.
10. *Nationalismus,* Hamburg, 1964, vol. II, p. 149. A famous Russo-American sociologist Pitirim Sorokin, in "sociologese" defined "nation," and by implication "nationalism," as "a multibonded (multifunctional), solidary, semiclosed sociocultural group . . . made up of individuals (1) who are citizens of the same state, (2) who have a common or similar language

379

and a set of cultural values both resulting from a common past history
. . . , and (3) who occupy a common area regarded as their territory.
. . ." "The Essential Characteristics of the Russian Nation in the Twentieth Century," in Don Martindale, ed., *National Character in the Perspective of the Social Sciences, Annals of the American Academy of Political
and Social Science*, vol. 370, 1967, pp. 101–02.

11. *Le Nationalisme français 1871–1914*, Paris, 1966, p. 9.

12. Nor is it possible to agree with the definition of Elie Kedourie, *Nationalism*, London, 1960, p. 9, that "nationalism is a doctrine invented in Europe
at the beginning of the nineteenth century" that "pretends to supply a
criterion for the determination of the unit of population proper to enjoy a
government exclusively its own, for the legitimate exercise of power in
the state, and for the right organization of a society of states," though,
with exceptions noted, there is some validity in this definition.

13. See pages 336–40.

14. The present author has also been criticized for allowing morality to influence his judgments of nationalism. Lemberg, *Nationalismus*, vol. I, p. 14.

15. *Expectant Peoples: Nationalism and Development*, New York, 1963,
pp. 19–20. But I must also add that Silvert, apparently, has not read
deeply on the history of western nationalism.

16. New York, 1967, p. 6. A number of recent students of nationalism,
especially political scientists and sociologists, are more interested in
national policy than in what nationalism is. See the works, cited elsewhere,
of Bendix, Kautzky, Lipset, Rustow, as examples. And for some scholars
method and typology seem of greater importance; for examples see the
works of Karl Deutsch, Eugen Lemberg, and Konstantin Symmons-
Symonolewicz, cited elsewhere.

17. See pages 156–58.

18. In Caroline Ware, K. M. Pannikar, and J. M. Romein, *History of
Mankind: The Twentieth Century*, vol. VI, London, 1966, p. 54,
Modrzhinskaya debates the nature of nationalism, though he comes to
the standard Marxist view—"nationalism is a constituent element of
bourgeois ideology." But N. P. Ananchenko, *Voprosy Istorii*, 1967, no. 3,
p. 222, says definitions of nations have been too limited, have failed to
comprehend "the multiform and constantly developing essence of a nation."
There are other relevant articles in the *Voprosy Istorii* of recent years; I
have read only those that have been translated or abstracted.

19. *Lectures on the Philosophy of History*, tr. by Sibree, rev. ed., New York,
1900, pp. 53, 77: "Each particular National genius is to be treated as only
one Individual in the process of Universal History," and "A Nation is
moral and vigorous when young, then after overcoming its contradictions
attains full reality, and is less active; then it gets old and enjoys what it
was able to attain." Charles Cole commented on "The Heavy Hand of
Hegel," in Edward Mead Earle, ed., *Nationalism and Internationalism,
Essays Inscribed to Carlton J. H. Hayes*, New York, 1950, pp. 65–78.

20. For further discussion see pages 201–05.

21. And in degree occurs among all primates and most animals.

22. Quoted in Albert Hourani, *Arabic Thought in the Liberal Age, 1798–1939,* London, 1962, p. 23.
23. *La Politique tirée des propres paroles de l'écriture sainte,* liv. I, art. II, prop. 3.
24. In his pamphlet *De la convocation de la prochaine tenue des états-généraux,* 1789, p. 20. Another pamphlet, *Catéchisme national,* 1789, p. 10, succinctly defined the nation: "Une nation est une société d'hommes libres qui vivent sous un même chef, ou plusieurs chefs qu'ils se sont données volontairement, pour ne faire qu'une seul et même corps dont l'âme sont les loix par lesquelles ils prétendent être gouvernés."
25. Quoted by F. Baldensperger, *La Révolution française,* vol. XLIX, 1905, pp. 263–64. See also Girardet, ed., *Le Nationalisme français,* p. 7. One is always able to find the use of a word before the "earliest." The earliest use of the word nationalism was perhaps by Herder.
26. Robert Scalapino's remark about Asian nationalism could have wider application: "Nationalism, if defined as a sense of or prior commitment to the nation-state, is largely confined to the urban, better educated classes." "Nationalism in Asia: Reality and Myth," *Orbis,* vol. X, 1967, pp. 1176–84. But in the twentieth century in the West, farmers and urban workers often made this commitment.
27. Cf. R. E. Lane, "Tense Citizen and the Casual Patriot: Role Confusion in American Politics," *Journal of Politics,* vol. 27, 1965, pp. 735–60.
28. *The Colonial Reckoning: The End of Imperial Rule in Africa in the Light of British Experience,* New York, 1962, p. 26.
29. Part of this conceptional scheme is taken from Robert E. Ward and Dankwart A. Rustow, eds., *Political Modernization in Japan and Turkey,* Princeton, 1964, pp. 458–59, where three of the terms, integration, penetration, and participation, are used to give "structure" to the study. For a clear description of a similar "structure," see Stein Rokkan, "Models and Methods in the Comparative Study of Nation-building," *Acta Sociologica,* vol. 12, 1969, pp. 64–66.
30. Karl Deutsch assigns first importance to communication in the development of nationalism. *Nationalism and Social Communication: An Inquiry into the Foundations of Nationality,* 2nd ed., Cambridge (Mass.), 1966 (1st ed., 1953), esp. pp. 170 ff.
31. Byron K. Marshall, *Capitalism and Nationalism in Prewar Japan: The Ideology of the Business Elite, 1868–1941,* Stanford (Calif.), 1967, p. 1. Individuals, argued Erving Goffman, *The Presentation of Self in Everyday Life,* New York, 1959, play a role on a team, and this could apply to patriots who play a role on the national team.
32. See Guido Zernatto, "Nation: The History of a Word," *Review of Politics,* vol. VI, 1944, pp. 351 ff. *Natio* originally meant a group of men belonging together because of similarity of birth, but the contemporary word nation is similar in that most people of a nationality are usually born within the wide confines of the territory of the actual or desired political state. Nationality may be acquired quite apart from place of birth, by naturalization, treaty, conquest, or perhaps just the will of the

individual, as in Macedonia. A member of a nation may not belong to the same state or be born in the same territory as his fellow nationals; further, as was true of the Jews until recently, he may not have a state to which he may aspire or belong; finally, a state, like Switzerland, may contain several culturally different peoples who juridically, nevertheless, are one nationality and who possess a national consciousness.

33. See page 110. Over the world the words used as equivalents for nation, nationalism, and kindred words are never exact equivalents. In Russian the word *natsiya* refers to a nation having a common language, territory, culture, but the word *narod*, which also refers to a nation, literally means people or folk, and the word *narodnost* means nationality in this sense. The words *naradnii patriotizm* express patriotism to the Soviet Union, but *natsional'nii patriotizm* pertains to patriotism of any one of the peoples of the Soviet Union. *Natsionalizm* is defined by Communist dictionaries as "a reactionary, bourgeois ideology" (but see pages 5–6). All these words except *narod* are borrowed from western languages. My information comes chiefly from Professor A. Guss of Macalester College. In the Middle East the Arabs, Iranians, and Turks may use quite similar words but give them differing meanings. The Arabic for nationality is *qawm* (peoplehood), and for nationalism *qawmiyya,* which denotes loyalty to the whole Arab nation, while *wataniyya* is the feeling of loyalty to the specific fatherland, and *watan* (*vatan* in Turkish) the place of birth (Syria, for instance). But in Iran the Persian word *mihan* is increasingly used instead of *watan.* The Arab word for nation, *umma,* has kept its original meaning: the community of believers in Allah, that is, the whole community of Islam irrespective of national or ethnic origin. Non-Arabic-speaking peoples like the Persians and Turks use the word *millet* (*millat* in Arabic, though not much used by Arabs) to denote nation but also in the sense of a religious group. This information comes principally from Professor Yahya Armajani of Macalester College. See also Sylvia Haim, ed., *Arab Nationalism,* Berkeley, 1962, pp. 39–40, and her "Islam and the Theory of Arab Nationalism," in Walter Z. Laqueur, ed., *The Middle East in Transition: Studies in Contemporary History,* New York, 1958, pp. 288 ff.; and Bernard Lewis, "The Impact of the French Revolution on Turkey," *Cahiers d'histoire mondiale,* vol. I, 1953, pp. 107–08.

34. First usages are never certain, but see the standard historical dictionaries (Oxford, Littré, Larousse); Zernatto, "Nation"; Gustave Dupont-Ferrier, "Le Sens des mots 'Patria' et 'Patrie' en France au moyen âge et jusqu'au début du XVIIᵉ siècle," *Revue Historique,* 1940, p. 89; and Bertier de Sauvigny, "Liberalism, Nationalism and Socialism: The Birth of Three Words," *Review of Politics,* vol. 32, 1970, pp. 155–60.

35. The idea of natural boundaries was present in Renaissance Italy. See Felix Gilbert, *Machiavelli and Guicciardini: Politics and History in Sixteenth Century Florence,* Princeton, 1965, p. 255. But until the French Revolution feudal practices prevented exact demarcations of boundaries, and to the present they are often contested.

36. "The Spirit of Whiggism," 1836, reprinted in *Whigs and Whiggism, Political Writings of Benjamin Disraeli*, London, 1913, p. 343.
37. *Della Nazionalità come fondamento de diritto delle Genti*, reprinted in *Saggi sulla nazionalità*, no. 3, Sestante, 1944, p. 39. Francis Lieber's 1868 definition of a nation was somewhat similar. *Fragments of Political Science on Nationalism and Internationalism*, New York, 1868, pp. 7–8.
38. Renan's famous discourse, "Qu'est-ce qu'une nation?" first given at the Sorbonne, is in his *Discours et conférences*, 2nd ed., Paris, 1887. Renan's definition was close to that of Fustel de Coulanges in his debate with Mommsen in 1870 over Alsace-Lorraine, and G. P. Gooch, following Renan, in 1920 thought the nation an "organism, a spiritual entity." *Nationalism*, London, 1920, p. 6.
39. Or even if they thought of it as a "collective personality," they would say this personality reflected the consciousness of individual members, as did Don Luigi Sturzo, *Nationalism and Internationalism*, New York, 1946, p. 17. Sturzo added, ". . . the consciousness of the single members who understood the aim for whose attainment they have gotten together to cooperate, or who understand that aim in a different way and dissent therefrom, so that in the end there comes about that maximum and that minimum of consent and of reciprocal influence which create action."
40. Quoted in Haim, ed., *Arab Nationalism*, p. 228. Haim includes, pp. 120–127, other definitions, for example that of 1941, by Abdullah al-Alayili, which is restricted to Arab nationalism.
41. The earliest definition known to me that includes race is that of Friedrich Schlegel of 1804–06, but there must be earlier examples. See Walter Langsam, *The Napoleonic Wars and German Nationalism in Austria*, New York, 1930, pp. 357–58. The Nazi German definitions of the 1930's stressed *Volk* or race. Even the scholarly definition of the great German historian Friedrich Meinecke placed emphasis on the "naturhaften Kern, der durch Blutverwandschaft enstanden ist." *Weltbürgertum und Nationalstaat*, Munich, 1928, p. 1.
42. Often even good students have used the words nation and nationality interchangeably. Thus René Johannet, *Le Principe des nationalités*, new ed., Paris, 1923, pp. 404–05, following Durkheim, defined *nationalité* as the idea of a "collective personality." But sometimes moral distinctions are introduced, as by Martin Buber, the influential Viennese Jewish philosopher: "Being a people is simply like having eyes in one's head which are capable of seeing; being a nationality is like having learned to perceive their function and to understand their purpose; nationalism is like having diseased eyes and hence being constantly preoccupied with the fact of having eyes." See Salo W. Baron, *Modern Nationalism and Religion*, New York, 1947, p. 3.
43. But the distinctions that must be made are many. The Scots and Welsh are nationalities, yet belong to the United Kingdom. Nationalities are always in process not only of becoming but also apparently of disappear-

ing. Do the American Indians constitute a nationality? A few years ago the answer would have been in the negative, but today? Four hundred years ago Burgundians could have been considered a nationality; today they are Frenchmen.

44. This author, were he writing in French instead of English, would carefully distinguish between national patriotism and nationalism, make the distinction that a great Dutch historian, Johan Huizinga, made: national patriotism is the "will to maintain and defend what is one's own and cherished," and nationalism "the powerful desire to dominate, the urge to have one's own nation assert itself. . . ." *Men and Ideas,* New York, 1959, p. 97.

45. "Jingoism" comes from a British song in agitation against Russia in 1877 after the Russian-Turkish war. See chapter VI. Chauvinism, which has somewhat the same connotation in English but means superpatriotism, probably comes from the name of a soldier of Napoleon, Nicolas Chauvin; it is also the name of a character in Cogniard's satire, *La Cocarde tricolor* (1831), who sang, "I am French, I am Chauvin, I beat down the Bedouin."

46. See Thomas Hodgkin, "A Note on the Language of African Nationalism," *St. Anthony's Papers,* vol. 10, 1961, pp. 22–40, for a first-rate discussion.

Chapter II

1. Generally we must reason from analogy with modern "primitive" peoples. But E. Westermarck, *The Origin and Development of Moral Ideas,* 2nd ed., 1912, vol. II, pp. 167 ff., believed patriotism widespread among early uncultured peoples and detected elements of it among the lowest "savages." James Harvey Robinson agreed. "What Is National Spirit," *The Century Magazine,* vol. XCIII, 1916, pp. 57–64. F. E. Williams, *Orokaia Society,* London, 1930, pp. 156, 325, showed this tribe had, like a nation, a common territory, distinctive customs and dialect, and common enemies, and so have most tribes. Fred Voget, "Acculturation at Caughnawaga," *American Anthropologist,* vol. LIII, 1952, pp. 220–31, described the feeling of separateness, of "being a chosen people," among the people of one American tribe; and Claude Lévi-Strauss does the same for a Brazilian people, the Mbaya, to whom the God gave the function of "oppressing and exploiting all other tribes." *Tristes tropiques,* New York, 1968, p. 164. Anthropologists and historians in recent years have debated the nature of the tribe at length. The word itself began to be generally used, in the modern senses, by Europeans in the nineteenth century to apply to primitive non-European groups or communities that had a chief and claimed common descent. As Philip Curtin points out, some modern African tribes, like the Ashanti, meet certain criteria, e.g., a common language, usually applied to nations. "Nationalism in Africa, 1945–1965," *Review of Politics,* vol. 28, 1966, pp. 143–53.

2. Herodotus, Rawlinson tr., bk. VIII, chap. 144. It is not difficult to find evidence of earlier group enmities. Homer, *Iliad,* Chapman tr., bk. 12,

lines 254–55: "One augury is giv'n / To order all men, best of all: Fight for thy Country's right."

3. A. H. Chroust, "Treason and Patriotism in Ancient Greece," *Journal of the History of Ideas*, vol. 15, 1954, pp. 280–88. Whether there was nationalism among ancient European peoples has been disputed. Cf. Theodore Haarhoff, *The Stranger at the Gate: Aspects of Exclusiveness and Cooperation in Ancient Greece and Rome* . . . , Oxford, 1948; M. T. Walek-Czernecki, "Le rôle de la nationalité dans l'histoire de l'Antiquité," *Bulletin of the International Committee of Historical Sciences*, vol. II, pt. II, 1929, pp. 303–20; Moses Hadas, "Aspects of Nationalist Survival under Hellenistic and Roman Imperialism," *Journal of the History of Ideas*, vol. XI, 1950, pp. 131–39; and M. Rostovtzeff, *A History of the Ancient World*, 2nd ed., Oxford, 1930, vol. I, pp. 229–37.

4. *Dialogues of Plato*, Jowett tr., New York, 1937, vol. I, p. 435.

5. Ernst H. Kantorowicz, "*Pro Patria Mori* in Medieval Political Thought," *American Historical Review*, vol. LVI, 1951, p. 474. M. L. Gordon shows how slaves eagerly sought and accepted citizenship in Rome. "The Nationality of Slaves under the Early Roman Empire," in M. T. Finley, ed., *Slavery in Classical Antiquity*, Cambridge (Eng.), 1960, pp. 110–11.

6. *De Officiis* (On Duty), I, XVII, 57.

7. Deuteronomy 7:6.

8. Yahya Armajani, *Middle East Past and Present*, Englewood Cliffs (N.J.), 1970, pp. 54–55.

9. William H. Tarn, *Hellenistic Civilization*, London, 1930, p. 73.

10. *Meditations*, VI, 44.

11. But serious students do differ as to the time in the medieval period. For the view here see A. F. Pollard, *Factors in Modern History*, London, 1926, chap. I; Edward P. Cheyney, *The Dawn of a New Era, 1250–1453*, New York, 1936, p. 337; and Halvdan Koht, "The Dawn of Nationalism in Europe," *American Historical Review*, vol. LII, 1947, p. 271. But H. A. L. Fisher, *The Common Weal*, Oxford, 1924, p. 195, believed nationalism "the product of historic forces which have only fully worked themselves out in Western Europe in our own day," while Ernesto Sestan, *Stato e Nazione nell'alto Medioevo: Ricerche sulle origini nazionali in Francia, Germania*, Naples, 1952, shows nascent nations but not nationalism as early as the eighth century; and Gaines Post sees nationalism in the twelfth and thirteenth centuries in "Two Notes on Nationalism in the Middle Ages," *Traditio*, vol. IX, 1953. Part of the difficulty is semantic. Nascent nations do not mean the presence of nationalism, and Apostolos Vacalopoulos, *Origins of the Greek Nation: The Byzantine Period, 1204–1461*, pp. xxii–iii, finds "new Hellenism" appearing at that time. See pages 334–36.

12. J. Franklin Jameson, "The Development of Modern European Historiography," *Atlantic Monthly*, vol. LXVI, 1890, p. 325. In 1758 a Dr. J. G. Zimmerman (native of Zurich) remarked, "The vanity of mankind has ever filled the immense vacuity beyond the authentic memorials of the

origin of every nation with fabulous history. . . ." *Essay on National Pride* (originally *Vom Nationalstolze,* 1758), New York, 1799.

13. J. W. Thompson, *A History of Historical Writing,* New York, 1942, vol. I, pp. 492, 626. A good many of the legends of early England were apparently started by Geoffrey of Monmouth.

14. Hajo Holborn, *Ulrich von Hutton and the German Reformation,* tr. by Roland Bainton, New Haven, 1937, p. 77.

15. For other French examples see René Johannet, *Le Principe des nationalités,* Paris, 1918, pp. 27–28. See also G. Monod, *Du rôle d'opposition des races et des nationalités dans la dissolution de l'Empire Carolingien,* Annuaire de l'Ecole pratique des hautes études,* Paris, 1896.

16. *A Short History of the English People,* New York, n.d., p. 7. A popularized version of the Anglo-Saxon early origins of Britain was Grant Allen's *Anglo-Saxon Britain,* London, 1884.

17. Stanley Wolpert, *Tilak and Gokhale: Revolution and Reform in the Making of Modern India,* Berkeley, 1962, pp. 63–65.

18. Richard Storry, *A History of Japan,* London, 1960, pp. 25–26.

19. Robert Rotberg, *A Political History of Tropical Africa,* New York, 1965, p. 357.

20. But cf. Guido Kisch, "Nationalism and Race in Medieval Law," *Seminar, an Extraordinary Number of the Jurist,* vol. I, Washington, D.C., 1943, p. 58.

21. But "In the tenth century a Lombard bishop, indignant at the claims . . . of the Byzantines to Apulea, wrote 'that this region belongs to the kingdom of Italy is proved by the speech of its inhabitants.' " Marc Bloch, *Feudal Society,* tr. by L. A. Manyon, Chicago, 1960, p. 435.

22. Hans Kohn, *The Idea of Nationalism: A Study of Its Origins and Background,* New York, 1944, p. 94; Bloch, *Feudal Society,* p. 436.

23. *Chanson,* Leon Gautier tr.; and Johannet, *Le Principe,* pp. 38–39.

24. Joseph Strayer, "The Laicization of French and English Society in the Thirteenth Century," *Speculum,* vol. XV, 1940, pp. 77–78.

25. Bloch, *Feudal Society,* p. 432.

26. The modern use of the word state as a body politic possibly first occurred in Italy in the early sixteenth century; it was not so used in England until 1635. George Sabine, "State," *Encyclopedia of Social Sciences,* vol. XIV, pp. 328 ff. But development of the state in England and France, of course, happened earlier. See Joseph Strayer, *Medieval Origins of the Modern State,* Princeton, 1970, p. 57.

27. Clear concepts of political entities were slow in developing because of hierarchical and conflicting feudal entities and the idea of a universal Christian *sacerdotium.* L. D. K. Kristof, "The Nature of Frontiers and Boundaries," *Annals,* Association of American Geographers, September 1959, pp. 569–82; and his "The State-Idea, the National Idea and the Image of the Fatherland," *Orbis,* vol. XI, 1967, pp. 238–55. It is rather commonly believed that the rise of nationalism could have come only after the Renaissance, Reformation, and Enlightenment, and the conse-

quent diminution of church influence. Gunnar Myrdal [et al.], *Asian Drama*, New York, 1968, vol. II, pp. 2109–10, repeats this generalization. But the question is more complex.

28. Suggestive is the argument of R. H. Lowie, *The Origin of the State*, New York, 1927, pp. 116–17, that administrative ability and war in addition to kinship and territorial association contributed to the origin of the state. He believed, "A coercive force . . . whether vested in a person or a group seems the short cut to intensifying and bringing into consciousness the incipient feeling of neighborliness that has been found a universal trait of human society. Once established and sanctified, the sentiment may well flourish, without compulsion, glorified as loyalty to a sovereign being or to a national flag."

29. Johannet, *Le Principe*, p. 382.

30. Kantorowicz, *"Pro Patria,"* p. 477.

31. The pertinent, somewhat dated volumes of Ernest Lavisse, ed., *Histoire de France* and Halphen and Sagnac, eds., *Peuples et civilisations,* are still basic. A useful survey is Régine Perroud, *La Formation de la France*, Paris, 1966 (rev. ed. of *L'Unité française*, 1949). Albert Sorel cogently argued that the "politics of the Capetians, considered by their consequences and tradition, had two principal objects: internally to build a homogeneous and coherent nation; externally to assure the best frontiers, the independence of the nation and the power of the state." *L'Europe et la Révolution française*, Paris 1946, vol. I, p. 189. But he was using hindsight, as I am.

32. These points are made in Derwent Whittlesey, *Environmental Foundations of European History*, New York, 1949, p. 83.

33. Control of nearly all western France was disputed by English rulers until the sixteenth century.

34. Where many nationalist historians err is in assuming that the historical development that came was inevitable, that the nations which did evolve were the only ones that could. It is quite conceivable that Burgundy, Provence, Wales, Scotland, Bavaria, Prussia, and other early states could have developed into and remained separate nations.

35. Contemporary political scientists and sociologists often treat nation building as if it happened only in our own time—how unhistorical and naïve.

36. Subsequently, the monarchy lost and won these lands several times. Definite dates for the acquisition of these and other territories can scarcely be established. Rulers and their lawyers began to try to establish "precise frontiers" rather than spheres of influence in the thirteenth century. Strayer, "The Laicization of French and English Society," p. 81. But they were seldom successful.

37. John had stolen the betrothed of one of Philip's vassals.

38. The significance of these territorial acquisitions for the modern nation is nowhere shown more clearly than in the thirteenth-century change in the royal title from *Rex Francorum* to *Rex Franciae*, a fact which indicated that, unlike the Roman practice, the state was beginning to be

associated with a definite territory. Kantorowicz, *"Pro Patria,"* p. 487 n.

39. Myron Gilmore has a good chapter on "Dynastic Consolidation" in his *The World of Humanism, 1453–1517,* New York, 1952.

40. Strayer, "The Laicization," p. 84, says that the governments of France and Britain had as early as 1300 begun "to see that nationalism could be useful to them," and that the "concentration of political authority . . . encouraged the growth of nationalism by decreasing the differences between provinces and increasing the differences between countries."

41. Edouard Fournier, *L'Esprit dans l'histoire,* Paris, 1867, p. 266 fn., says Elizabeth of England may have used the words "the State, it is I," but I have not been able to verify this.

42. In Spain the monarchy, though old and established, was less successful in unifying the country, and left it until quite recent times "a congeries of separate states, differing from one another in race, in traditions, in language, and in government. . . ." Roger B. Merriman, *The Rise of the Spanish Empire in the Old World and the New,* New York, 1918, vol. II, p. 74. But cf. Gifford Price, "The Incipient Sentiment of Nationality in Medieval Castile," *Speculum,* vol. XII, 1937, pp. 351–58.

43. The pertinent chapters of the *Cambridge Medieval History* and the *New Cambridge Modern History* (as well as the old) provide good detailed analyses of the growth of monarchical power in England, but there is a wealth of studies. For a detailed account of thirteenth-century England there is the classic work of F. M. Powicke, *King Henry III and the Lord Edward: The Community of the Realm in the Thirteenth Century,* 2 vols., Oxford, 1947.

44. The first systematic study of English law was made by Ranulf de Glanvil (d. 1190) during the last decade of Henry II's reign in his *Tractatus de legibus et consuetudinibus regni Angliae.* Bracton wrote his more important work, comprising nearly two thousand cases, a work that became a cornerstone of English law, in the 1250's.

45. Bloch, *Feudal Society,* p. 430.

46. G. M. Trevelyan, *History of England,* New York, 1926, pp. 140–41.

47. According to Esmé Wingfield-Stratford, *The History of English Patriotism,* London, 1913, vol. I, pp. 57–58, Edward I was perhaps the first great English patriot king. But in his own patriotism Wingfield-Stratford saw the English brand arising much earlier than would the cautious student.

48. Henry V (1413–22) had started the navy but it had since been neglected. Conyers Read's comment on Henry VIII is pertinent: "In short, by the beginning of the year 1537 Henry had established his kingdom, established his church, established his line." *The Tudors,* New York, 1936, p. 83.

49. During the thirteenth century the French kings gradually gained the power to impose a tax *pro defensione regni* that went beyond the old feudal aids. "In other words, by the end of the thirteenth century the national monarchy of France was strong enough and sufficiently advanced to proclaim itself as *patria* and to impose taxes, including church taxes, *ad defensionem natalis patriae.*" Kantorowicz, *"Pro Patria,"* p. 479. Joseph R. Strayer, "Consent to Taxation under Philip the Fair," in Strayer

and Charles H. Taylor, *Studies in Early French Taxation*, Cambridge (Mass.), 1939.

50. In 1439 the Estates-General gave the monarchy, on its demand, the sole right to levy troops and collect certain taxes (*tailles* and *aides*) for military purposes. Charles VII (1422–61), it may be said, established France's first royal standing army. See the doctoral dissertation of Paul Solon, Brown University, 1970, "Charles VII and the Compagnies d'Ordonnance."

51. Pierre Dubois in his *De Recuperatione Terrae Sanctae* (1305–07) went so far as to assert, "It would be expedient for the whole world to be subject to the realm of the French." G. G. Coulton, "Nationalism in the Middle Ages," *Cambridge Historical Journal*, vol. V, 1935, p. 36.

52. John Wolf, *Louis XIV*, New York, 1968, pp. 383–99.

53. Wolf, *Louis XIV*, pp. 371, 379, 462.

54. Wolf, *Louis XIV*, p. 372. As V. L. Tapié, in Roland Mousnier et al., *Comment les Français voyaient la France au XVIIᵉ siècle*, *Bulletin de la Société d'Etude du XVIIᵉ Siècle*, nos. 25–26, Paris, 1955, pp. 45–46, points out, it followed from the king's divine right that the king should be obeyed and the subjects owed the prince the same services as they owed the *patrie*.

55. In the sixteenth century diplomatic relations were still not conducted on a national level. See Felix Gilbert, "The Concept of Nationalism in Machiavelli's *Prince*," in William E. Peery, ed., *Studies in the Renaissance*, vol. I, 1954, p. 46; see also Garrett Mattingly, *Renaissance Diplomacy*, Boston, 1955, pp. 152–53.

56. The clergy was not taxed, but gave a "free gift" to the state.

57. *The Seventeenth Century*, Oxford, 1950, pp. 125, 140, 219.

58. *History of Germany in the Nineteenth Century*, tr. by Eden and Cedar Paul, New York, 1915, vol. I, p. 46.

59. Louis' conception of his role is clear: "In my person alone resides the sovereign power. . . . All public order emanates from me. My people and I are one, and the rights and interests of the nation, which some dare to make a body separate from the monarch, are necessarily united with mine, and rest in my hands alone." Henri Martin, *Histoire de France*, Paris, 1865, vol. XVI, p. 253.

60. J. A. Williamson, "England and the Sea," in Ernest Barker, ed., *The Character of England*, London, 1947, p. 509.

61. *Principall Navigations* . . . , London, 1927, vol. I, p. 19.

62. Charles W. Cole, *Colbert and a Century of French Mercantilism*, New York, 1939, vol. I, p. 25, believed, "Mercantilism represented the economic counterpart of *étatism*. In practice it sought to bring all phases of economic life under royal control." Robert Livingston Schuyler, on the other hand, thought mercantilism was the "economic phase of nationalism." *Political Science Quarterly*, vol. 37, 1922, p. 445. Perhaps it was both.

63. But travel was still slow. In seventeenth-century France, to go from Paris to Lyons, less than 250 miles by air, took eleven days.

64. Eli Hecksher, *Mercantilism*, tr. by Schapiro, London, 1935, vol. I. pp. 22–23.

65. See page 332. Hector Munro Chadwick, *The Nationalities of Europe and the Growth of National Ideologies*, Cambridge (Eng.), 1945, pp. 69–70, argues that "the linguistic map of western and west central Europe had assumed more or less its present form" by the end of the sixth century but that great changes continued much longer in the north, east, and southeast. Much, however, depends upon the interpretation of what is a distinct and developed language.

66. The discussion in Cheyney, *The Dawn of a New Era*, pp. 247 ff., is an introduction. As V. H. Galbraith has pointed out in the case of fourteenth-century England, however, the growth of a vernacular is not necessarily connected with national feeling and any contrived relation could be anachronistic. "Nationality and Language in Medieval England," *Transactions of the Royal Historical Society*, vol. XXIII, 1941, pp. 113–28.

67. Catalan began to replace Latin in Catalonian documents in the thirteenth century. J. L. and C. L. Schneidman, "Factors in the Emergence of Catalan Nationalism during the Thirteeenth Century," *Historian*, vol. 27, 1965, pp. 331–32. The first imperial (Holy Roman Empire) law in German as well as Latin appeared in 1235. Kisch, "Nationalism and Race," *Seminar*, p. 61. But many languages that would be the bases of later national languages were developing, Bulgarian from the ninth century, for example. Marin Pundeff, "Les Racines du nationalisme bulgare," *Revue des Etudes Slaves*, vol. 46, 1967, p. 137. Classical Chinese, of course, developed much earlier, Arabic not later than the time of the Koran in the seventh century, and Persian from at least the tenth century and the poetry of Ferdosi.

68. Dante denied even to Tuscan the honor of "illustrious Italian vulgar tongue" in his *De Vulgare Eloquentia*.

69. The "Sequence de Sainte Eulalie," a formless rhapsody of the ninth century, is possibly the first literary effort in recognizable French.

70. Villehardouin's work has been called "the first work of importance and sustained dignity in the French tongue. . . ." See Thompson, *A History of Historical Writing*, vol. I, p. 322. The earliest known history in French, however, was the *Histoire des Engles* written about the mid-twelfth century by the Norman Geoffrey Gaimar. Charles Haskins, *The Normans in European History*, Boston, 1915, pp. 183–84. The Latin text of the famous *Grand Chronique de France* or *Grands Chroniques de St. Denis*, which more or less officially recorded the events of the French monarchy from 1247, terminated in 1340.

71. The time of the first translation of the Bible into the vernacular is significant because so much life centered upon religion. On Wyclif see H. B. Workman, *John Wyclif, a Study of the English Medieval Church*, 2 vols., Oxford, 1926.

72. Quoted in Trevelyan, *History of England*, p. 235 n.

73. Trevissa's observation is a modification of a like earlier one in Ranulf Higden, *Polychronicon*, ed. by Churchill Babington and Joseph R. Lumby,

9 vols., London, 1865–86, Rolls series no. 41. *Piers Plowman,* XV, 1, 368, notes the change from learning in French to learning in English eight years earlier.

74. Royal Institute of International Affairs, *Nationalism: A Report by a Study Group of Members of the Institute,* London, 1939, p. 14; Froissart, *Chronicles,* ed. by Kervynde de Lettenhove, Brussels, 1867–77, vol. II, p. 236.

75. In *Deux dialogues du nouveau langage français italianizé* (1578) and *La Précellence du langage français* (1579).

76. The King James version was based in part on William Tyndale's translation, 1525–36.

77. His *Epistle concerning the Excellence of the English Tongue* is in William Camden's *Remaines Concerning Britaine* (his notebooks), published first in 1605.

78. Quoted in Ferdinand Brunot, *Histoire de la langue française,* Paris, 1937, vol. VI, pt. II, by Alex François, p. 870.

79. Madame de Sévigné, speaking of Breton peasants at the time of troubles of 1675, wrote, "Ils sont six ou sept mille, dont le plus habile n'entend pas un mot de française. . . . Dès que nos pauvres bas-bretons voient les soldats, ils se jettent à genoux et disent; Mea culpa, c'est le seul mot de français qu'ils sachent." Quoted in Tapié, *Comment les Français,* p. 40.

80. The development of language loyalties in France and Britain was more or less paralleled, usually but not always, later in most European and some other countries. Examples that could be cited are almost as many as peoples and languages. Two illustrations will suffice here. As early as the eleventh century an Arab philologist, al-Tha'ālibī (d. 1038), wrote, "Whoever loves the Prophet loves the Arabs, and whoever loves the Arabs loves the Arabic language in which the best of books was revealed . . . believes the Arabs are the best of peoples . . . and that Arabic is the best of languages." Quoted in Bernard Lewis, *The Middle East and the West,* Bloomington (Ind.), 1964, p. 86. In 1663 one Georg Schottelius published a book extolling German for its "antiquity, purity, power . . . excellence." Kohn, *The Idea,* p. 339.

81. Sorel, *L'Europe et la Révolution française,* vol. I, p. 210; see also Walter Sulzbach, *National Consciousness,* Washington, D.C., 1943, pp. 12–13. The statement was first attributed to Henry IV by Pierre Mathieu in his *Histoire de Henri IV,* published in Paris in 1631.

82. See the informed discussion in Otto Jespersen, *Mankind, Nation and Individual from a Linguistic Point of View,* Oslo, 1925. But the relationship of language and nation is complicated, as E. Haugen demonstrated in "Dialect, Language, Nation," *American Anthropologist,* vol. 68, 1966, pp. 922–35.

83. W. H. V. Reade, "Political Theory to c. 1300," *Cambridge Medieval History,* vol. VI, New York, 1929, p. 633, held "the irregular boundary between the medieval and the modern is crossed as soon as the conception of Christendom, embodied for Dante in the Roman Empire, gives way to the belief that the largest autonomous community should be the territorial

or national state." This was also the view of Mandell Creighton in the *Cambridge Modern History*, vol. I, p. 2.

84. See Koppel S. Pinson, *Pietism as a Factor in the Rise of German Nationalism*, New York, 1934.

85. Salo W. Baron, *Modern Nationalism and Religion*, New York, 1947, p. 11; Marcel Handelsman, "Le rôle de la nationalité dans l'histoire de Moyen Age," *Bulletin of the International Committee of Historical Sciences*, vol. II, pt. II, 1929, pp. 244–45, stressed the role of exterior forces in the formation of nationality.

86. Nevertheless, though a direct connection cannot be shown, it is possible that love of one's nation or fellow nationals is an outgrowth of Christian charity, as Tolomeo of Lucca in his continuation of Aquinas' *De regimine principum* directly states: "Love of the fatherland is founded in the root of charity which puts, not one's own things before those common, but the common things before one's own. . . ." Kantorowicz, *"Pro Patria,"* p. 488.

87. *Protestantism and Progress: A Historical Study of the Relation of Protestantism to the Modern World*, tr. by W. Montgomery, London, 1912, p. 127.

88. As did Marsiglio of Padua earlier in the *Defensor Pacis* (1324), and Machiavelli in the *Prince* in Luther's time.

89. What Ernest Barker wrote of English Protestantism seems valid for much early Protestantism: "There is what I should call *Étatism*, as well as nationalism in our English Reformation, and in the beginnings there is more *Étatism* than nationalism, though there was always some nationalism there. In other words the English Church began as a State Church rather than a national Church; but in the course of time the position was gradually changed and inverted. I should say that it became a national Church . . . in 1660." "The Reformation and Nationality," *Modern Churchman*, vol. XXII, 1932, p. 340.

90. In the Arab world the states were religious, and not until secularism became strong in the twentieth century did the various Arab nationalisms of consequence arise.

91. F. J. C. Hearnshaw, ed., *The Social and Political Ideas of Some Great Medieval Thinkers*, London, 1923, pp. 216 ff.

92. Quoted in Baron, *Modern Nationalism*, p. 11.

93. This was not, of course, an isolated case. The Old Testament, as H. G. Wells remarked, is something of a nationalist history. *The Anatomy of Frustration*, London, 1936, pp. 181–82. The relationship between Puritanism and national feeling in the United States is demonstrated by Alan Heimert, *Religion and the American Mind: From the Great Awakening to the Revolution*, Cambridge (Mass.), 1966; and Ernest L. Tuveson, *Redeemer Nation: The Idea of America's Millennial Role*, Chicago, 1968.

94. *The Letters and Speeches of Oliver Cromwell, with Elucidations by Thomas Carlyle*, ed. by S. C. Lomas, London, 1904, vol. II, pp. 404 ff. Hans Kohn sums up the relation of Puritanism to nationalism in his *The Idea*, pp. 165 ff., and his previously published article, "Genesis and

Character of English Nationalism," *Journal of the History of Ideas*, vol. I, 1940, pp. 84–89. See also Ernest Barker, *Cromwell and the English People*, Cambridge (Eng.), 1937, pp. 24, 82, 104. A detailed study is George Lanyi, "Oliver Cromwell and His Age, a Study in Nationalism," Ph.D. dissertation, Harvard, 1949, typescript.

95. Probably religious and nationalist motivations were often indissolubly mixed. The Hussites went to war in 1420 "to liberate the truth of the Law of God and the Saints and to protect the faithful believers of the Church, and the Czech and Slavonic language." Kohn, *The Idea*, p. 111.

96. Tr. by R. F. Jones and G. H. Turnbull, Chicago, 1922, p. 136. See also Hans Kohn, *Prelude to Nation-States: The French and German Experience, 1789–1815*, Princeton, 1967, p. 243.

97. Charles Maurras, the French nationalist, was not as wrong as usual when he wrote, "L'humanité avait alors pour garantie la chrétienté. Depuis que la Réforme a coupé en deux notre Europe, la chrétienté n'existe plus. Où est le genre humain, pour chaque homme? Dans sa patrie." Quoted in Johannet, *Le Principe*, p. 72.

98. This was particularly true of enthusiastic religious groups in the seventeenth and eighteenth centuries. For examples, see Pinson, *Pietism*. In the services of the Catholic church Latin continued to be chiefly used until the third quarter of the twentieth century.

99. Claus Petri translated the Old and New Testaments into Swedish in 1540–41. Christiern Petersen published the first Danish Bible in 1543. There was a Finnish translation of the New Testament in 1548. The *Statenbybil*, published in 1626-37, was instrumental in making the dialect of Holland accepted in the northern Lowlands. All dates are approximate, but the Bible, or parts of it, appears to have been translated into English in 1388, German 1521–31, Polish 1553, Welsh 1588, Latvian 1687.

100. George C. Powers showed some was present at the Council of Constance, but, as at medieval universities, the word nation was not used in the same sense as it is today. *Nationalism at the Council of Constance (1414–1418)*, Washington, D.C., 1927. See also Louise Loomis, "Nationality at the Council of Constance," *American Historical Review*, vol. XLIV, 1939, pp. 508–27, where it is pointed out that the "nations" showed "touchy conceit," "unscrupulous assertiveness" at the council.

101. Wolf, *Louis XIV*, p. 379, comments, "Letters, minutes, orders, decrees, patents, grants, the registers of household officials, and the correspondence of secretaries of state all show the same pattern; the growing impact of the royal government upon the kingdom is reflected in an ever-increasing flow of paper. What could be cared for in 1661 by a secretary with an assistant and a few clerks required a small army of copyists, clerks, secretaries, and bureaucrats." And it might be added here that the multiplication of papers became geometrical by the twentieth century and required vastly increased national bureaucracies.

102. Jean Pange, Comte de, *Le Roi très chrétien*, Paris, 1949, p. 439. Dorothy Kirkland, an able student, giving other specific illustrations for France, concluded, "Articulate patriotism must be sought in vain before the

fifteenth century, although certain aspects of the national sentiment can be seen here and there, stronger at one time than another, present in one place and absent in the next, but on the whole gaining ground. . . ." "The Growth of the National Sentiment in France before the 15th Century," *History*, vol. XXIII, 1938, p. 24. Even in sixteenth- and early seventeenth-century England, "my country" generally meant "my county." See Lawrence Stone, "The English Revolution," in Robert Forster and Jack P. Greene, *Preconditions of Revolution in Early Modern Europe*, Baltimore, 1970, p. 71.

103. As Bloch, *Feudal Society*, p. 432, remarked, "As a reaction against romantic historiography, it has been the fashion . . . to deny that the early centuries of the Middle Ages had any group consciousness at all, either national or racial. This is to forget that in the crude and naive form of antagonism to the stranger, the 'outsider' (*horsin*), such sentiments did not require a very great refinement of mind. We know today that they manifested themselves in the period of the Germanic invasions with much more strength than Fustel de Coulanges, for example, believed."

104. *Matthew Paris's English History from the Year 1234 to 1273*, tr. by Giles, London, 1854, vol. I, p. 312, vol. III, p. 84. For original see the Luard (Rolls series) edition of the *Chronica Majorca*, vol. V, p. 450. His descriptions of the Tatars remind one of present-day western attitudes toward the Russians.

105. Quoted in Coulton, "Nationalism in the Middle Ages," p. 19. A little earlier Guibert de Nogent (1053–1124) in his *Gesta Dei per Francos* refuted the German Archdeacon of Mainz, who thought the French weak and cowardly, with "If the French had not by their strength and courage opposed a barrier to the Turks, not all you Germans, whose name is not even known in the East, would have been of use." Thompson, *A History of Historical Writing*, vol. I, p. 233. For other illustrations, particularly between East and West, see E. N. Johnson, "American Medievalists and Today," *Speculum*, vol. XXVIII, 1953, pp. 849–50.

106. Quoted in Thompson, *History*, vol. I, p. 516.

107. The poem, a part of the *Grand Testament*, is translated in D. B. Wyndham Lewis, *François Villon: A Documentary Survey*, New York, 1928, pp. 295–96.

108. Kantorowicz, *"Pro Patria,"* pp. 482–91. Kantorowicz's remarks referring to the mid-thirteenth century are, "Once the *corpus mysticum* had been identified with the *corpus morale et politicum* of the people and has become synonymous with nation and 'fatherland,' death *pro patria* . . . regains its former nobility." But Kantorowicz, I believe, here gave too much weight to isolated cases.

109. Kantorowicz, *"Pro Patria,"* pp. 482–91.

110. Petrarch, *Sonnets and Songs*, tr. by Anna Maria Armi, New York, 1946, pp. 203, 209.

111. Quoted in Wingfield-Stratford, *The History of English Patriotism*, vol. I, p. 72.

112. Quoted in H. F. Stewart and Paul Desjardins, eds., *French Patriotism in the Nineteenth Century (1814–1833)*, Cambridge (Eng.), 1923, introd.
113. Quoted in Johannet, *Le Principe*, p. 37.
114. *The Prince*, tr. by W. K. Marriott, Everyman's ed., p. 213. Several of the best-known Italian poets of the period expressed deep feeling for Italy which Vincent Ilardi called *"Italianita." " 'Italianita'* Among Some Italian Intellectuals in the Early Sixteenth Century," *Traditio*, vol. XII, 1956, pp. 339–67. During the sixteenth, seventeenth, and early eighteenth centuries, Muzio, Boccalini, and Muratori as well as a few others spoke of the glories of Italy and in some cases pleaded for national sovereignty. Emiliana Noether, *Seeds of Italian Nationalism, 1700–1815*, New York, 1951, passim. See Gilbert, "The Concept of Nationalism," pp. 41–42, for additional evidence of Italian national feeling in the early sixteenth century.
115. Though he liked Italy, he thoroughly disliked Frenchmen and ridiculed Spaniards. But see Cumberland Clark, *Shakespeare and National Character*, London, 1928; and R. V. Lindabury, *A Study of Patriotism in the Elizabethan Drama*, Princeton, 1931. A little earlier, one of the fathers of the English church, Thomas Becon, was declaring that men ought to love their native country more than "parents, kinsfolk, friends." "Our parents only gave us this gross, rude and mortal body. Our country doth not only receive and joyfully sustenate it, but also most opulently adorn and garnish both that and the mind with most goodly and godly virtues." Quoted in "The Policy of War," Wingfield-Stratford, *The History of English Patriotism*, vol. I, pp. 144–45.
116. Marquess of Halifax (George Savile), "The Character of a Trimmer," *Complete Works of George Savile*, ed. by Walter Raleigh, Oxford, 1912, p. 97. "The Character of a Trimmer" was first published in 1688.
117. Tr. by H. H. Hudson, Princeton, 1941, pp. 71–72.
118. Trevelyan, *History of England*, p. 233. An English physician, Andrew Borde, in his *Fyrst Boke of the Introduction of Knowledge*, characterized most of the peoples of Europe in a way that made them inferior to the English—they did not speak English. Julian Huxley and A. C. Haddon, *We Europeans*, Oxford, 1940, pp. 44–45.
119. Kohn, *The Idea*, pp. 139–46. Wimpheling wrote, "Of no art can we Germans be more proud than of the art of printing which has made us the intellectual bearers of the doctrines of Christianity, of all divine and earthly sciences, and thus the benefactors of the human race."
120. Holborn, *Ulrich von Hutten*, p. 42.
121. J. Malye, "Leibniz, theoricien du nationalisme allemand," *L'Acropole*, vol. I, 1920, pp. 442–58. H. J. C. Grimmelshausen in his *Simplicissimus* (1669) sought "to bring forth a German hero who needs no soldiers and still shall reform the whole world. . . . Then I will banish completely the Greek language and have only German spoken. . . ." Quoted in Pinson, *Pietism*, p. 162.
122. Frederick L. Nussbaum, *The Triumph of Science and Reason, 1660–1685*, New York, 1953, pp. 13–14; and see note 78.

123. The details come from diverse primary and secondary sources, including writings of the historians mentioned and Thompson, *A History of Historical Writing.*
124. Charles Haskins, *Renaissance of the Twelfth Century,* Cambridge (Mass.), 1928, p. 275.
125. That the last chapter of Bede's (673–735) much earlier *Ecclesiastical History* is titled in translation "Of the Present Stage of the English Nation" should not be overlooked. But for several centuries after Bede little history that is relevant here was written.
126. Geoffrey probably started the legend that the Trojan wanderer Brutus established Britain. He also worked at the Arthurian legend.
127. Paraphrase of quotation in Johannet, *Le Principe,* pp. 31–32.
128. Thompson, *History,* vol. I, p. 608.
129. Johannet, *Le Principe,* pp. 50 ff. On Du Tillet see also Donald Kelley, "Jean du Tillet, Archivist and Antiquary," *Journal of Modern History,* vol. 38, 1966, pp. 350–52.
130. Whether Guicciardini or Machiavelli should be called Italian or Florentine historians is debatable. But see Felix Gilbert, *Machiavelli and Guicciardini: Politics and History in Sixteenth Century Florence,* Princeton, 1965.
131. For Asian and especially African peoples, "national" histories do not appear until the late nineteenth and early twentieth century, but history was written much earlier in China and Persia, for example.
132. Of course, a great number of other sixteenth-century historians could be mentioned. At the time he died (1508), the German humanist Konrad Celtis was planning a *Germania illustrata,* probably in imitation of Flavio Biondo's *Roma illustrata.*
133. Halvdan Koht, *Driving Forces in History,* Cambridge (Mass.), 1964, pp. 167–68; and Erica Simon, *Réveil national et culture populaire en Scandinavie: La Genèse de la Højskole Nordique (1844–1878),* Paris, 1960, p. 6.
134. Vincent Trumpa, "Simonas Daukantas, Historian and Pioneer of Lithuanian National Rebirth," *Lituanus,* vol. II, 1965, p. 6.
135. Noether, *Seeds of Italian Nationalism,* pp. 65–77; and L. Salvatorelli, "L'Historiographie italienne au XVIIIᵉ siècle," *Cahiers d'histoire mondiale,* vol. VII–2, 1963, pp. 321–40. Muratori dedicated his work to Italy, his "mother."
136. Kantorowicz, *"Pro Patria,"* p. 475.
137. E. Littré, *Dictionnaire de la langue française,* "patrie." Alphonse Aulard thought *patrie* was first used in 1539 in the *Songe de Scipion traduit nouvellement du Latin en Français.* See his *Le patriotisme français de la Renaissance à la Révolution,* Paris, 1916, p. 14; and Jean Lestocquoy, *Histoire du patriotisme en France des origines à nos jours,* Paris, 1968, pp. 17–40, for the various meanings given *la patrie.*
138. Quoted in Martin Buber, "The Beginning of the National Idea," *Review of Religion,* vol. X, 1946, p. 254.
139. *Caractères,* ed. Nelson, Paris, 1954, p. 315.
140. But, as Tapié, *Comment les Français,* p. 56, says at the end of the reign

of Louis XIV, "l'ancienne France patriciale et terrienne modifiait insensiblement son propre visage. Une nation de citoyens commençait à poindre parmi ces peuples des sujets et les liens qui les rassemblaient en feraient glisser l'expression du royaume à la patrie."

Chapter III

1. There is no way to prove this assertion beyond doubt. But later research does not seem to contradict the statement of a social psychologist, Hadley Cantril, of over twenty years ago: "People are not gangsters or law-abiding citizens, Fascists or Communists, agnostics or believers, good or bad because of innate dispositions. . . . People's actions take the direction they do because a certain set of conditions have provided status, meaning satisfaction. . . ." "Don't Blame It on Human Nature," *New York Times Magazine,* July 6, 1947. Cantril's *The Psychology of Social Movements,* New York, 1941, treats the whole question. See T. W. Adorno et al., *The Authoritarian Personality,* New York, 1950, for experimental evidence upon related subjects. For a later sociological view see T. H. Marshall, *Class, Citizenship, and Social Development,* New York, 1965. A highly opinionated and popular contrary view is Robert Ardrey, *The Territorial Imperative: A Personal Inquiry into the Animal Origins of Property and Nations,* New York, 1966.

2. The books are too many to cite, but see Hans Kohn, *Prelude to Nation-States: The French and German Experience, 1789–1815,* Princeton, 1967, esp. pp. 144–202, as well as his *The Idea of Nationalism: A Study of Its Origins and Background,* New York, 1944; Emiliana Noether, *Seeds of Italian Nationalism, 1700–1815,* New York, 1951; and Hans Rogger, *National Consciousness in Eighteenth-Century Russia,* Cambridge (Mass.), 1960.

3. Among the numerous studies bearing upon this theme are: Louis Hartz, ed., *The Founding of New Societies,* New York, 1964, esp. chap. IV; Seymour Lipset, *The First New Nation,* New York, 1963; Karl Deutsch and William Foltz, eds., *Nation-Building,* New York, 1963, esp. chap. IV by Richard L. Merritt; Max Savelle, *Seeds of Liberty,* New York, 1948, as well as his "Nationalism and Other Loyalties in the American Revolution," *American Historical Review,* vol. LXVII, 1962, pp. 901–23; and Richard B. Morris, *The Emerging Nations and the American Revolution,* New York, 1970, chap. I.

4. There are many editions of *L'Esprit des lois.* A late edition of his works is *Oeuvres complètes,* ed. by Andre Masson, 3 vols., Paris, 1950–55. An old but useful biography is Albert Sorel, *Montesquieu,* Chicago, 1888. Later research is summed up in R. Shackleton, *Montesquieu: A Critical Biography,* London, 1961.

5. He wrote this to the Duc de Chevreuse, August 4, 1710, *Oeuvres complètes . . . ,* Paris, 1850, vol. VII, p. 321. See also H. F. Stewart and Paul Desjardins, eds., *French Patriotism in the Nineteenth Century (1814–1833),* Cambridge (Eng.), 1923, p. xvi.

6. *L'amour de la patrie: 19e Mercuriale prononcée à la Saint Martin*, 1715, in Stewart and Desjardins, eds., *French Patriotism*, p. xxi. Probably Alphonse Aulard made too much of this panegyric in his *Le Patriotisme français de la Renaissance à la Révolution*, Paris, 1916.

7. Tr. by Nugent, New York, 1900, vol. I, p. 34, and the *avertissement* in some French editions.

8. Quoted in René Johannet, *Le Principe des nationalités*, new ed., Paris, 1923, p. 78.

9. Frances Acomb, *Anglophobia in France, 1763–1789: An Essay in the History of Constitutionalism and Nationalism*, Durham (N.C.), 1950, p. 54.

10. Alfred Cobban, *A History of Modern France*, Baltimore, 1961, vol. I, p. 127; R. Bickart, *Les Parlements et la notion de souveraineté nationale*, Paris, 1932, p. 28; Robert Palmer, "The National Idea in France before the Revolution," *Journal of the History of Ideas*, vol. I, 1940, p. 104.

11. Bolingbroke's works have been published many times. I have used here the London, 1775, edition of T. Davies. These essays are paged together in this edition in vol. I.

12. Pp. 148–49.

13. P. 191. Cf. Carlton Hayes, *The Historical Evolution of Modern Nationalism*, New York, 1931, pp. 17–21; and Kohn, *The Idea*, pp. 212–15.

14. *The Life, Unpublished Letters and Philosophical Regimen of Anthony, Earl of Shaftesbury*, ed. by B. Rand, 1900, pp. 103, 105, and *Characteristicks*, 1732, vol. I, p. 106, vol. II, p. 143; Friedrich O. Hertz, *Nationality in History and Politics: A Study of the Psychology and Sociology of National Sentiment and Character*, London, 1944, p. 313. Similar ideas were expressed by Shaftesbury's contemporary, Francis Hutcheson, in *An Inquiry Into the Original of Our Ideas of Virtue or Moral Good* (1725).

15. Palmer, "The National Idea," pp. 98–99; and Daniel Mornet, *Les Origines intellectuelles de la Révolution française, 1715–1787*, 4th ed., Paris, 1947, pp. 263–64, which gives other examples. Part of Coyer's work was included in the *Encyclopédie's* article on the "Patrie."

16. The anonymous author was a Dr. (medical) J. G. Zimmerman from Zurich, later (from 1768) personal physician to His Britannic Majesty at Hanover. There were several German editions. I have used the 1768 4th ed. and the English translation of Samuel Wilcocke, published as the *Essay on National Pride* in New York in 1799. There was also a French translation by Mercier and another, poor English translation, *Strictures on National Pride*, Philadelphia, 1778. Zimmerman wanted to restrain "excessive" national pride, criticized the "fabulous" myths of antiquity of national origin, declared that in many cases love of country was little more than "love of an ass for his manger," but believed in pride and wanted to excite children with stories of famous men and national exploits. See discussion in Harold Lasswell, *World Politics and Personal Insecurity*, New York, 1935, pp. 40–41; and his "Two Forgotten Studies in Political Psychology," *American Political Science Review*, vol. 19, 1925, pp. 707–12.

17. Robert R. Ergang, *Herder and the Foundations of German Nationalism*,

New York, 1931, p. 43; Koppel S. Pinson, *Pietism as a Factor in the Rise of German Nationalism,* New York, 1934, p. 183.

18. Mornet, *Les Origines,* p. 264.

19. Palmer, "The National Idea," p. 108.

20. For examples of other patriotic writings in France, see Mornet, *Origines,* pp. 260–66.

21. Ferdinand Brunot, *Histoire de la langue française,* Paris, 1930, vol. VI, pt. 1, p. 137. Turgot spoke of the state as "un assemblage d'hommes réunis sous un seul gouvernement" and a nation as an "assemblage d'hommes qui parlent une même langue maternelle." The 1694 dictionary of the French Academy defined the nation as "tous les habitans d'un mesme Estat, d'un mesme pays, qui vivent sous mesmes loix et usent le mesme langage." Cf. Turgot's definition in his letter to Dupont de Nemours, February 20, 1766, *Oeuvres,* ed. by Schelle, Paris, 1914, vol. II, pp. 513–14.

22. *Correspondance littéraire,* ed. by Tourneux, vol. II, December 15, 1754, p. 445.

23. Brunot, *Histoire,* vol. VI, pt. 1, pp. 135–36, and vol. IV, p. 580. As the standard historical dictionaries show, the phrases "good patriot" and "bad patriot" were beginning to be used in France and Britain in the seventeenth century, but general usage in France came swiftly after 1750–60. For a detailed examination see Gustave Dupont-Ferrier, "Le Sens des mots 'Patria' et 'Patrie' en France au moyen age et jusqu'au début du XVIIᵉ siècle," *Revue Historique,* 1940. pp. 89–104.

24. Brunot, *Histoire,* vol. VI, pt. 1, 133 ff. In the *Encyclopédie* the phrase was modified to *"le despotisme oriental."* The Baron d'Holbach added, *"Le patriotisme* véritable ne peut se trouver que dans les pays où les citoyens libres, et gouvernés par des loix équitable, se trouvent heureux, sont bien amis, cherchent à mériter l'estime et l'affection de leurs concitoyens." *Ethocratie ou le Gouvernement fondé sur la Morale,* Amsterdam, 1776, p. 288.

25. C. E. Vaughan, ed., *The Political Writings of Jean-Jacques Rousseau,* Cambridge (Eng.), 1915, vol. II, pp. 427, 492, 512.

26. Signed by the hack writer Chevalier de J[acourt], the article varied somewhat in different editions and included part of the essay by Coyer.

27. But as Mornet, *Les Origines,* p. 263, remarked, "Au XVIIᵉ siècle . . . il y avait, avec religion, le religion du roi. Vers 1760, on commence à perdre la religion de la royauté. . . . Puis, on commence à comprendre que le roi n'est pas la France. . . ."

28. See page 91.

29. Leon Duguit, *Law in the Modern State,* tr. by Frida and Harold Laski, New York, 1919, p. 11, put it: "The king was a person, a subject of right, the holder of sovereign power; like him, the nation will be a person, the subject of right, the holder of sovereign power." See also Brunot, *Histoire,* vol. IX, p. 636.

30. *Contrat social,* bk. I, chaps. 5–6; and Paul Léon, "La notion de la souveraineté dans la doctrine de Rousseau," *Archives de philosophie du droit et de sociologie juridique,* 1938, p. 269: "Il [Rousseau] monopolisait tout

le dynamisme du droit au profit d'une seule communauté nationale."

31. Boyd C. Shafer, "Bourgeois Nationalism in the Pamphlets on the Eve of the French Revolution," *Journal of Modern History*, vol. X, 1938, pp. 31–50.

32. See page 9.

33. In the third edition of the pamphlet, pp. 9, 57, 61, 64, 89.

34. Quoted in Aulard, *Le Patriotisme*, fn. 6.

35. This discussion is largely based on the author's own reading of cahiers but draws heavily also on the intensive analysis of two solid books by Beatrice Hyslop, *French Nationalism in 1789 according to the General Cahiers*, New York, 1934; and *A Guide to the General Cahiers of 1789*, New York, 1936.

36. Hyslop, *French Nationalism*, p. 101.

37. Brunot's words, *Histoire*, vol. IX, p. 636, are eloquent: the nation "s'était incarnée. C'est un nom propre, le nom d'une personne, multiple et une, de la France souveraine, longtemps confondue avec son Roi, qui s'en dégage désormais pour entrer bientôt en discussion, puis en conflict et en lutte ouverte avec lui." And Michelet, later, was not only poetic when he wrote, "La Révolution française, matérialiste en apparence dans sa division départmentale qui nomme les contrées par les fleuves, n'en efface pas moins les nationalités des provinces qui jusque-la, perpétuaient les fatalités locales au nom de la liberté. . . ." *Introduction à l'histoire universelle*, ed. définitif, Paris, n.d., p. 460.

38. Johannet, *Le Principe*, p. 85, made clear the intimate relationship between internal right and external sovereignty in discussing the Rights of Man and Citizens of the French Constitution of 1791: "Ce sont ceux où il est proclamé que la souveraineté réside dans la nation et que la loi est l'espression de la volonté générale. Il s'ensuit que la volonté générale, seule détentrice de la loi, a compétence pour définir sa souveraineté."

39. See his almost classic report "sur la réunion au territoire de la République de la ci-devant principauté de Monaco," *Archives Parlementaires*, vol. 58, February 14, 1793, pp. 546–51.

40. Brunot, *Histoire*, vol. IX, p. 663.

41. See the perceptive discussion in Alexis de Tocqueville, *The State of Society in France* . . . , tr. by Reeve, London, 1888, pp. 92–93.

42. *Oeuvres*, vol. IV, p. 579; Brunot, *Histoire*, vol. VI, p. 140; and see page 97.

43. As early as 1758 the popular writer abbé Mably wrote on *Des Droits et des devoirs du citoyen*, though his essay was not published until 1789. See vol. XI of *Collection complète des oeuvres de l'abbé Mably*, Paris, 1794–95. An author named Saige published in 1775 (Bachaumot) the pamphlet that appeared again in 1788 as *Catéchisme de Citoyen, ou Elément du droit public français.* . . .

44. *Democracy in America*, tr. by Reeve, ed. by Bowen and Bradley, New York, 1945, pp. 242 ff. He added, "The most powerful, and perhaps the only means of interesting men in the welfare of their country . . . is to make

them partakers in the government . . . civic zeal seems to me to be inseparable from the exercise of political rights."

45. The best recent authority on the French Revolution, Georges Lefebvre, perhaps exaggerated in declaring that the National Assembly "accomplished the juridical unity of the nation" in a few hours on the night of August 4, 1789, when it wiped out the feudal regime, the domination of the aristocracy, and started financial, legal, and ecclesiastical reform. *Quatre-Vingt-Neuf,* Paris, 1939, p. 189. The exaggeration, however, is chiefly one of time.

46. According to Brunot, *Histoire,* vol. VI, p. 140, "Dans l'usage, en France, au nom de citoyen s'attachait de plus en plus l'idée de certains droits, mais surtout de certains devoirs envers la collectivité." The *Encyclopédie* defined a citizen as a "membre d'une société libre de plusieurs familles, qui partage les droits de cette société et qui jouit de ses franchises."

47. Mirabeau remarked in 1782, "When the *patrie* is nothing, a man owes it nothing, because duties are mutual." Palmer, "The National Idea," p. 108.

48. In 1776 the Parlement of Paris still maintained that France was a monarchy "composed of several distinct estates," and it defined their duties in the old feudal fashion: "The clergy is to fulfill all the functions relative to instruction and worship. The nobles consecrate their blood to the defense of the State, and assist the sovereign with their advice. The lowest class of the nation, which cannot render to the King services so distinguished, acquits itself toward him by its tributes, its industry, and bodily service." Quoted in Charles D. Hazen, *The French Revolution,* New York, 1932, vol. I, pp. 128–29.

49. As Lefebvre, *Quatre-Vingt-Neuf,* pp. 41–42, put it, "L'aristocratie a engagé la lutte contre l'absolutisme au nom de la nation, mais avec la ferme volonté de ne pas se confondre avec elle."

50. Vaughan, ed., *Political Writings,* vol. I, p. 453. *Oeuvres Complètes,* 1826 ed., vol. VI, pp. 241–42. His views were echoed by a good many writers, including the conservative Coleridge later in *The Friend* and *Table Talk.*

51. Among those who proposed plans for international peace were the abbé de Saint Pierre, *Projet de paix perpetuelle,* which Rousseau condensed and published in 1761; and Kant, *Zum ewigen Frieden* (1795). A good history of eighteenth-century cosmopolitanism is needed. Albert Mathiez's last published essay is a good introduction, "Pacifisme et nationalisme au dix-huitième siècle," *Annales historiques de la Révolution française,* vol. XIII, 1936, pp. 1–17; a brief treatment is Elizabeth Souleyman, *The Vision of Peace in 17th–18th Century France,* New York, 1941; and John Stevens examined the death of the idea in "Anacharsis Cloots and French Cosmopolitanism," Ph.D. dissertation, Arkansas, 1954, typescript.

52. Sorel, *Montesquieu,* p. 52.

53. Vaughan, ed., *Political Writings,* vol. I, pp. 251–52.

54. Brunot, *Histoire,* vol. IX, p. 663.

55. Brunot, *Histoire*, vol. VI, pt. 1, p. 135. A valuable survey is Halvdan Koht's "L'esprit national et l'idée de la souveraineté du peuple," *Bulletin of the International Committee of Historical Sciences*, vol. II, pt. II, 1929, pp. 217–24.

56. *Oeuvres complètes de Voltaire*, 1785, vol. XLII, pp. 263–64.

57. *Système de la nature*, London, 1770, p. 261. D'Holbach, an atheist, went on, "Religion orders him [the citizen] to obey, without murmuring, the tyrants who oppress his country, to serve them against it, to merit their favors by enslaving their fellow citizens. . . ."

58. In H. W. Schneider, ed., *Adam Smith's Moral and Political Philosophy*, New York, 1948, pp. 240–42. The book was first published in 1759. For further discussion see page 105.

59. Herder's views are not easily followed or always clear, but see especially the *Ideen zur Philosophie der Geschichte der Menschheit*, in *Sämmtliche Werke*, ed. by Bernard Sulphan et al., Berlin, 1877–1913, vol. VIII; Kohn, *The Idea*, pp. 427–41; Carlton Hayes, "Contributions of Herder to the Doctrine of Nationalism," *American Historical Review*, vol. XXXII, July 1927, pp. 719–36; Ergang, *Herder*, which is the best study of Herder's nationalism; and F. M. Barnard, *Herder's Social and Political Thought: From Enlightenment to Nationalism*, Oxford, 1965.

60. *Reflections on the Revolution in France* (1790), in *Works*, Bohn ed., London, 1861, vol. II, p. 359, passim. Some of the ideas are in his *Reform of Representation in the House of Commons*, in *Works*, vol. VI, pp. 146 ff. For further discussion of Burke's views see pages 122, 318.

61. Cf. Hertz, *Nationality*, p. 364; and Kohn, *Prelude*, pp. 190–92, esp. on Adam Müller.

62. From "Annus Mirabilis" (1667), *Dryden's Poetical Works*, Oxford ed., London, 1948, p. 36. Similar statements of belief in the civilizing mission of particular nations become more and more frequent from the seventeenth century.

63. Karl Marx, *Capital*, Everyman's ed., vol. II, p. 848; Lenin, *Selected Works*, vol. IV, London, 1936, "On the Right of Nations to Self-Determination," and his *Critical Remarks on the National Question*, Moscow, 1951; Stalin, *Marxism and the National and Colonial Question*, New York, n.d. A further "official" development of the Stalin "line" is M. D. Kammari, *The Development by J. V. Stalin of the Marxist-Leninist Theory of the National Question*, Moscow, 1951. Among the numerous commentaries are: Richard Pipes, *The Formation of the Soviet Union: Communism and Nationalism 1917–1923*, Cambridge (Mass.), 1954; Alfred D. Low, *Lenin and the Question of Nationality*, New York, 1958; and the socialist-oriented Horace B. Davis, *Nationalism and Socialism: Marxist and Labor Theories of Nationalism to 1917*, New York, 1967. And see pages 328–29.

64. Cf. J. B. Condliffe, *The Commerce of Nations*, New York, 1950, p. 29; and W. R. Scott, *The Constitution and Finance of English, Scottish and Irish Joint-Stock Companies to 1720*, Cambridge (Eng.), 1912, vol. I, pp. 440–41.

65. Carlton Hayes, *Essays on Nationalism,* New York, 1926, p. 163, applies this same reasoning to the "masses in every national state."

66. On the importance to be given cultural factors in the rise of nationalism in western nations I differ from Hans Kohn, who stresses political factors. To give primacy to either politics or culture is to argue whether the chicken comes before the egg. In any case, politics is part of culture.

67. On the Russian intellectuals see Rogger, *National Consciousness.*

68. The influence of cities, of urbanism, on nationalism has yet to be studied in detail. Certainly in 1789 the urban populations were more nationally conscious than the rural, and during the eighteenth century cities were rapidly growing, their influence mounting. For an example, see Hyslop, *French Nationalism,* pp. 215–16. Bernard Grosperrin describes the influence of Paris in *L'influence française et le sentiment national français en Franche-Comté, Cahiers d'Études Comtoises,* no. 11, Paris, Les Belles Lettres, 1967.

69. Sanche de Gramont's popular *The French, Portrait of a People,* New York, 1969, pp. 44–64, contains interesting comments on the "sheer centripetal force of Paris" in French history.

70. How bad were some roads? In 1698 Burgundy had a bronze statue of Louis XIV sent from Auxerre to Dijon, a distance of seventy-five miles as the crow flies. It was stuck in the mud and not delivered for twenty-one years. But the main roads out of Paris were good.

71. The great age of statistics had not yet arrived; all figures are approximate.

72. Brunot, *Histoire,* vol. VII, p. 3.

73. That this was realized at the time Carnot's 1792 observation reveals: "The need for communication . . . includes all other needs, because where it is easy to travel, education spreads, industry expands. . . . The lack of communication results in adjoining districts being strangers to each other . . . preserves particularism, and indifference to the general affairs of the Republic. . . . The Republic will never be one, indivisible and prosperous until all come to the aid of each." Quoted in Huntley Dupre, *Lazare Carnot, Republican Patriot,* Oxford (Ohio), 1940, pp. 61–62.

74. Karl W. Deutsch imaginatively develops some theories (not always clear) about communication as a basis for nationalism in *Nationalism and Social Communication: An Inquiry into the Foundations of Nationality,* 2nd ed., Cambridge (Mass.), 1966.

75. Ira O. Wade, *The Clandestine Organization and Diffusion of Philosophic Ideas in France from 1700 to 1750,* Princeton, 1938, p. 262.

76. Of the 1751–65 edition of the *Encyclopédie* six thousand sets (including the Geneva reprint) were printed and sold, and there were six editions. The original set sold at 980 livres. Letter of Arthur Wilson, the biographer of Diderot, to author, April 2, 1969.

77. Daniel Mornet, *Eighteenth Century French Thought,* tr. by Lawrence Levin, New York, 1929, pp. 264 ff.; and *Les Origines,* pp. 477 ff.

78. *Correspondance littéraire,* vol. VII, September 15, 1767, p. 420.

79. Quoted in Roland Mousnier, Ernest Labrousse, and Marc Bouloiseau, *Le XVIIIᵉ siècle,* Paris, 1953, p. 223.

80. See Ergang, *Herder*, pp. 24 ff., for the current *Gallomania*.
81. Acomb, *Anglophobia*, p. 65. For other evidence revealing the French feeling of superiority toward Britain see Minnie Miller's article in *Modern Philology*, vol. 34, 1937, pp. 365–76.
82. Acomb, *Anglophobia*, pp. 56 ff.; Mousnier, Labrousse, and Bouloiseau, *Le XVIIIe siècle*, p. 224.
83. *Correspondance inédite, 1789, 1790, 1791*, ed. by Henri Carré, Paris, 1932, letter to his wife, June 28, 1789, p. 78.
84. Robert Redslob, a keen student, saw the origins of the "principe des nationalités" in "le mouvement d'emancipation qui, depuis les temps de la Renaissance, agite les peuples, leur inspire la conscience d'eux-mêmes et la résolution de prendre en main les rênes de leurs destinées." *Le Principe des nationalités; leur origines, les fondements psychologiques, les forces adverses, les solutions possibles*, Paris, 1930, p. 1.

Chapter IV

1. *Quatre-Vingt-Neuf*, Paris, 1939, p. 23.
2. Ferdinand Brunot, *Histoire de la langue française*, Paris, 1927, vol. IX, p. 638.
3. What is said here does not apply necessarily to Great Britain, from 1707 composed of England, Scotland, and Wales, and from 1800 Ireland (though only Northern Ireland today). The Scots, Welsh, Irish have different histories and cultures, have manifested national sentiment in different ways.
4. See especially Burke's *Reflections on the Revolution in France* (many editions); there are many commentaries. See page 122.
5. Hans Kohn, "Genesis and Character of English Nationalism," *Journal of the History of Ideas*, vol. I, 1940, pp. 69–94.
6. Quoted in R. K. Webb, *Modern England from the Eighteenth Century to the Present*, New York, 1968, p. 14. I have drawn, of course, on two indispensable volumes on eighteenth-century England, Sir Lewis Namier, *England in the Age of the American Revolution*, London, 1930; and *The Structure of Politics at the Accession of George III*, 2nd ed., London, 1957.
7. Hans Kohn, *The Idea of Nationalism: A Study of Its Origins and Background*, New York, 1944, pp. 382–85.
8. Koppel S. Pinson, *Pietism as a Factor in the Rise of German Nationalism*, New York, 1934, pp. 183–85; Kohn, *The Idea*, pp. 374 ff.
9. See Emiliana Noether, *Seeds of Italian Nationalism, 1700–1815*, New York, 1951; and Gaudens Megaro, *Vittorio Alfieri, Forerunner of Italian Nationalism*, New York, 1930.
10. The word "real" is taken from Hans Rogger, *National Consciousness in Eighteenth-Century Russia*, Cambridge (Mass.), 1960, p. 1; on Poland see the substantial article of Jerzy Szacki, "L'Evolution du concept de 'Nation' en Pologne à la fin du XVIIIe et au début du XIXe siècle," *Cahiers d'histoire mondiale*, vol. IX, 1965, pp. 59–79.
11. Luis Monguio, "Nationalism and Social Discontent as Reflected in

Spanish-American Literature," *Annals of the American Academy of Political and Social Science,* vol. 334, 1961, p. 64.

12. That this was true does not need to be labored as much as I have. Still, it may be worth noting that in the eighteenth century Frederick II of Prussia preferred to use French, that high officers in most armies as well as many troops were "foreign," and that most men of all classes were chiefly occupied with their own interests—Mozart in 1789 was in Leipzig becoming acquainted with Bach's vocal compositions, Louis XVI went hunting on July 14, 1789, and on that day many Parisians were more interested (or finding pleasure) in destroying a symbol of the old regime (the Bastille) than they were in national affairs.

13. *Oeuvres complètes de J. J. Rousseau,* Baudoin, 2nd ed., Paris, 1826, vol. VI, pp. 240–41. Complaining of the then prevalent cosmopolitanism, he advised, "Donnez une autre pente aux passions des Polonois, vous donnerez à leurs âmes une physionomie nationale qui les distinguera des autre peuples, qui les empêchera de se fondre, de se plaire, de s'allier avec eux; une vigueur qui remplacera le jeu abusif des vains préceptes, qui leur fera faire par gôut et par passion ce qu'on ne fait jamais assez bien quand on ne le fait que par devoir ou par intérêt" (pp. 241–42). Rousseau claimed that men were dehumanized by cosmopolitanism. See Alexandre Choulguine, "Les origines de l'esprit national moderne et Jean-Jacques Rousseau," *Annales de la Société Jean-Jacques Rousseau,* vol. XXVI, 1937, pp. 9–283, for development of Rousseau's thought.

14. Noether, *Seeds of Italian Nationalism,* p. 93.

15. *The Federalist,* rev. ed., New York, 1901, no. 16, p. 83, written by Hamilton.

16. Alphonse Aulard, *Le Patriotisme français de la Renaissance à la Révolution,* Paris, 1916, p. 111; Frances Acomb, *Anglophobia in France, 1763–1789: An Essay in the History of Constitutionalism and Nationalism,* Durham (N.C.), 1950, p. 114. The account of Hans Kohn, *Prelude to Nation-States: The French and German Experience, 1789–1815,* Princeton, 1967, pp. 7–116, demonstrates this.

17. For 1789 see the superb study of Georges Lefebvre, *La grande peur de 1789,* Paris, 1932; for 1793 see Richard Cobb, "Quelques aspects de la mentalité révolutionnaire," *Revue d'histoire moderne et contemporaine,* vol. VI, 1959, pp. 81–120. Just as there was *"grande peur"* so there was always *"grand espérance."*

18. Both quotations are from J. M. Thompson, *The French Revolution,* New York, 1945, pp. 14, 17.

19. *Quatre-Vingt-Neuf,* p. 112.

20. As Jacques Godechot, *La Prise de la Bastille,* Paris, 1965, pp. 332–33, says, "L'insurrection du 14 juillet est en effet une insurrection vraiment nationale. . . . L'insurrection parisienne marque en quelque sorte le sommet de l'insurrection nationale. C'est donc à bon droit que les trois couleurs adoptées par les insurgés parisiens comme signe de ralliement du 14 juillet sont devenues l'emblème national, que l'anniversaire de cette insurrection a été choisi pour le jour de la fête nationale."

21. John Hall Stewart, ed., *A Documentary Survey of the French Revolution*, New York, 1951, pp. 106–110, for the text.
22. The provision of the Constitution of 1791 defining French citizenship did not mention property, but another provision limited active citizenship —the right to vote—to those men at least twenty-five years old who paid direct taxes equal to three days' labor, who were not servants, who were on the roll of the National Guard, and who took the civic oath to be faithful to "the nation, the law, and the King." In 1791, according to a census, over 4,200,000 male adults were active citizens and about 3 million were "passive." Of the active citizens in 1791 only about 700,000 cast ballots.
23. Until 1792 executive power was constitutionally delegated to the king, who also was considered to represent the nation.
24. The documents are handily available in Stewart, ed., *A Documentary Survey;* and usually in the newspaper *Moniteur universelle;* in the *Archives Parlementaires*, vols. 1–82; or in Jean Duvergier, ed., *Collection complète des lois, décrets, ordonnances . . .* , Paris, 1834–1906, vols. 1–12.
25. See pages 36–37.
26. C. E. Vaughan, ed., *The Political Writings of Jean-Jacques Rousseau*, Cambridge (Eng.), 1915, vol. II, pp. 128, 350, 428, and elsewhere. Once nations had a civic religion, said Rousseau, any violation of the law would be an impiety.
27. Albert Mathiez, *Les Origines des cultes révolutionnaires (1789–1792)*, Paris, 1904, p. 31.
28. Stewart, ed., *A Documentary Survey*, p. 513.
29. Pinson. *Pietism*, p. 91; and see page 35.
30. The idea and the practice were not new. American revolutionary armies were composed in the main of citizens. In 1781 a Joseph Servan (or one Guibert) published a book called *Soldat Citoyen*. Of course, both the idea and the practice were as ancient as the Greeks and Romans, but then, little is entirely new except to those who know little history. On the French army see Richard Cobb, *Les Armées révolutionnaires, instrument de la Terreur dans les départements*, 2 vols., Paris, 1961–63.
31. The French National Assembly established the National Guard on August 10, 1789, out of the bourgeois guards that sprang into existence in July, and Lafayette became the head. Lafayette visited the United States in 1824 and the states' militia began to be called the National Guard.
32. *Moniteur universelle*, August 25, 1793, p. 1008. On Barère see Leo Gershoy, *Bertrand Barère: A Reluctant Terrorist*, New York, 1962, esp. pp. 176–78.
33. *Moniteur*, June 3, 1794, pp. 1038–39.
34. The quoted words are Robespierre's, from James Eagan, *Maximilien Robespierre, Nationalist Dictator*, New York, 1938, p. 185. Robespierre thought "bearing arms has a natural attraction for all men," and (Eagan, p. 188) he believed the French army "not only the terror of tyrants" but the "glory of the nation and humanity. Marching to victory, our soldiers cry, 'Long live the Republic'; it is their cry as they fall beneath the sword

of the enemy. Their last words are hymns of liberty; their final signs are vows for the fatherland." Politicians probably do often believe their own rhetoric.

35. The British army had some able professional officers, but its common soldiers were often the dregs of English society.

36. August Neithardt von Gneisenau, German general and patriot, discovered the importance and superiority of patriotic troops when he joined the British forces in North America in 1782, and he helped transform the Prussian army after its defeats in 1806. See page 125, and Kohn, *The Idea*, p. 379. In their published doctoral dissertations, students of Carlton Hayes, such as Ergang, Langsam, Pundt, and Engelbrecht,. well described, though perhaps overemphasized, the patriotism of the Germans of this period. See also Eugene Anderson, *Nationalism and the Cultural Crisis in Prussia, 1806–1815*, New York, 1939.

37. See Herder, *Ideen zur Philosophie der Geschichte der Menschheit*, in *Sämmtliche Werke*, ed. by Bernard Sulphan et al., vol. XIII, p. 350, for his well-known analogy.

38. This is a paraphrase of a 1790 letter from Limoges to Bishop Grégoire of the National Assembly in Brunot, *Histoire*, vol. IX, pt. I, p. 10. On the desire for and development of French the volumes of Brunot, particularly pt. I of vol. VII and pts. I and II of vol. IX, are exhaustive and indispensable. Germans, Herder and Fichte especially, made much of the last argument, but it was held quite generally. On the drive to eliminate dialects, patois, and the insistence on the use of French, see Cobb, "Quelques aspects," pp. 325–26.

39. Quoted in Brunot, *Histoire*, vol. VII, pt. I, p. 91. A like view was the abbé Coyer's in his *Plan d'éducation* (1785): "Du Latin. Qu'apprend on en sixième? Du Latin. En cinquième? Du Latin. En quatrième? Du Latin. En troisième? Du Latin. En seconde? Du Latin. Nulle connaissance de la Nature, des Arts, des Sciences utiles. Point de choses, mais des mots; et encore quels mots? Pas même la langue nationale, rien de ce qui convient le plus à l'homme."

40. Kohn, *The Idea*, contains much information on language usages. For other information in this paragraph see also the volumes of Barnard, Chaconas, Chadwick, Megaro, and Pinson cited elsewhere.

41. On Noah Webster see Harry Warfel, *Noah Webster, Schoolmaster to America*, New York, 1936. In Italy many patriots, like Galeani-Napione, a Piedmontese noble, were demanding a national language to be used by all inhabitants of the nation. Noether, *Seeds*, pp. 127–29. Alfieri left *Mémoires*, Paris, 1862, which, with self-pity, depict his struggles.

42. Josep Dobrovský, at a meeting of the Czech Society of Sciences in 1791, in the presence of Emperor Leopold II, enthusiastically emphasized the right to use the Czech language. Francis S. Wagner, "Széchenyi and the Nationality Problem in the Habsburg Empire," *Journal of Central European Affairs*, vol. XX, 1960, p. 290. Emperor Joseph II had ordered the use of German instead of Latin in all official transactions in 1784, and this aroused much opposition in the Empire.

43. Radu R. Florescu, "The Uniate Church: Catalyst of Rumanian National Consciousness," *Slavonic and East European Review*, vol. 45, 1967, p. 337.

44. For additional illustrations for Hungary, see George Barany, *Stephen Széchenyi and the Awakening of Hungarian Nationalism, 1791–1841*, Princeton, 1969, pp. 31–32, passim. On Lomonosov, see Rogger, *National Consciousness*, pp. 100–03. The examples from many lands that could be cited are many.

45. Or, as Brunot, *Histoire*, vol. IX, p. 421, had it, "La langue elle-même, sans être sous l'autorité de l'Etat, a gagné à la Révolution de devenir chose d'Etat." See also his fine summary of the relation between the spread of the French language and patriotism, pp. 407–08.

46. *Moniteur*, January 28, 1794, pp. 519–20. The earlier National Assembly had sent out its laws and decrees in "tous les idiomes."

47. Quoted in Brunot, *Histoire*, vol. IX, p. 8.

48. *Moniteur*, January 28, 1794, pp. 519–20.

49. Mirabeau's plea for "perfectly intelligible laws" in French was only half realized. The laws were written in French but the gothic style was not buried with the remains of feudalism as he recommended. *Courrier de Provence*, vol. CXII, 1790.

50. In Brunot, *Histoire*, vol. IX, p. 412.

51. *The Spirit of Laws*, tr. by Nugent, New York, 1900, bk. IV, par. 5, p. 34. Montesquieu thought parental example the best teacher, but in the preface to his great study he declared that he would think himself the happiest of mortals if he succeeded in giving "new reasons to every man to love his prince, his country, his laws. . . ."

52. Brunot, *Histoire*, vol. VII, pp. 141–42. Dupont de Nemours actually wrote what Turgot here suggested. About the same time President Rolland, a director of secondary education, also was looking for a plan of education able to bring "cette révolution . . . faire renaître l'amour de la patrie."

53. *Considérations sur le gouvernement de Pologne et sur sa réformation projettée en Avril 1772* is in vol. VI and the *Lettre à d'Alembert* is in vol. II of *Oeuvres complètes de J. J. Rousseau*, 1826 ed.

54. *Oeuvres*, vol. VI, p. 256.

55. *Oeuvres*, vol. II, pp. 190–91, 205–07.

56. Ibid., p. 28. Rousseau was not satisfied that education alone would make patriots. He prescribed an oath for the Corsicans that reminds of oaths exacted of citizens in the twentieth century: "Au nom de Dieu tout-puissant et sur les saints Évangiles, par un serment sacré et irrevocable, j'unis de corps, de biens, de volonté et de toute ma puissance, à la nation corse. . . . Je jure de vivre et mourir pour elle, d'observer toutes ses lois et d'obéir à ses chefs et magistrats. . . . Vivent á jamais la liberté, la justice et le République des Corses. Amen." But, of course, there were religious and feudal oaths long before the eighteenth century.

57. Barère quoted Rousseau at length in his successful proposal for an *Ecole de Mars. Moniteur*, June 3, 1794, pp. 1038–39.

58. Stewart, ed., *A Documentary Survey*, p. 232.

59. For discussion see Carlton Hayes, *The Historical Evolution of Modern Nationalism*, New York, 1931, p. 62.

60. *Oeuvres*, vol. II, pp. 28, 205–07.

61. Stewart, ed., *A Documentary Survey*, p. 232.

62. Boyd C. Shafer, "When Patriotism Became Popular," *Historian*, vol. V, 1943, pp. 77–96, treats the whole 1790 federation movement. Herder called the celebration a "divine and sacred festival," and his views were widely shared in western Europe.

63. The plan for the *Fête* is in the *Moniteur*, June 7, 1794, pp. 653–54, and Robespierre's speech on pp. 683–84. When Robespierre burned the statues of Atheism, Vice, and Folly, the smoke blackened the statue of Wisdom and some Parisians laughed. But patriotism was no laughing matter in 1794. See the impassioned speech of Billaud-Varenne of April 20, 1794: "Take hold of man from his birth. . . . Let every heroic deed have its trophy, let every generous sentiment be celebrated in frequent public festivals." See Kohn, *Prelude*, pp. 84–85.

64. An outdated but handy summary is Edward H. Reisner, *Nationalism and Education Since 1789: A Social and Political History of Modern Education*, New York, 1922. On educational attempts to inculcate patriotism, see pages 195–99.

65. On the United States see Warfel, *Noah Webster,* pp. 56–60, 88, 93–94; Allen O. Hansen, *Liberalism and American Education in the Eighteenth Century*, New York, 1926, pp. 48 ff., where nine plans for an American national educational system from 1785 to 1900 are described; Charles Cole, "Jeremy Belknap: Pioneer Nationalist," *New England Quarterly*, vol. X, 1937, pp. 743–51; and Russel Nye, *This Almost Chosen People: Essays in the History of American Ideas*, East Lansing (Mich.), 1966.

66. Rogger, *National Consciousness*, pp. 216, 221.

67. Rogger, *National Consciousness*, p. 249. See also Richard Pipes, *Karamzin's Memoir on Ancient and Modern Russia*, Cambridge (Mass.), 1959.

68. Kohn, *The Idea*, p. 544; Kohn, pp. 329–576, gives many examples of early patriotic histories; on Paisi, see also Marin Pundeff, "Les Racines du nationalisme bulgare," *Revue des Etudes Slaves*, vol. 46, 1967, pp. 127–38.

69. Florescu, "The Uniate Church," pp. 334–35; J. C. Campbell, French Influence and the Rise of Roumanian Nationalism," Ph.D. dissertation, Harvard, 1940, typescript, pp. 15–21. For other Balkan illustrations see Albert B. Lord, "Nationalism and the Muses in Balkan Slavic Literature in the Modern Period" in C. and B. Jelavich, eds., *The Balkans in Transition: Essays in the Development of Balkan Life and Politics in the Eighteenth Century*, Berkeley, 1963. For the early awakening in Italy see Noether, *Seeds,* esp. pp. 63–86. The revolutionaries in France, as benefits revolutionaries, wrote little history as such though they drew lessons from it. It is worth noting that the French revolutionary assemblies did not appoint official historiographers as did many kings and lesser rulers, but in 1794 the Committee of Public Safety asked historians to depict "the great

epochs of the regeneration of Frenchmen . . . and infuse with republican morality writings designed for public instruction." Gershoy, *Bertrand Barère*, p. 234.

70. Carlton Hayes, "Contributions of Herder to the Doctrine of Nationalism," *American Historical Review*, vol. XXXII, July 1927, p. 728.

71. This is a paraphrase of Oscar Falnes, *National Romanticism in Norway*, New York, 1933, p. 250. See also Hans Kohn, "Romanticism and the Rise of German Nationalism," *Review of Politics*, vol. 12, 1950, pp. 452–53; and Rogger, *National Consciousness*, pp. 126–185. The works on folklore are numerous and voluminous, but no one as yet has done a much needed special study of the intricate relationship between the "discovery" of folklore and the rise of nationalism.

72. These demands for national cultures are admirably summarized in Kohn, *The Idea* and *Prelude*. On the use of the French theater to inculcate patriotism see J. A. Rivoire, *Le Patriotisme dans le théâtre sérieux de la Révolution, 1789–1799*, Paris, 1950. There were many demands for national academies, societies, theaters, and some were established, especially in western Europe. Not unrepresentative is Mozart's plea for support of German opera: "Were there but one good patriot in charge. . . . But then, perhaps, the German national theater would actually begin to flower, and of course that would be an everlasting blot on Germany, if we Germans were seriously to begin to think as Germans, to act as Germans, to speak German, and Heaven help us, to sing in German." Emily Anderson, ed., *The Letters of Mozart and His Family*, London, 1938, vol. III, p. 1325–28.

73. Gershoy, *Bertrand Barère*, pp. 232–36.

74. The remarks of T. H. Marshall, *Class, Citizenship, and Social Development*, New York, 1965, p. 101, are to the point: "Citizenship requires a . . . direct sense of community membership based on loyalty to a civilization which is a common possession. It is a loyalty of free men endowed with rights and protected by a common law. Its growth is stimulated both by the struggle to win those rights and their enjoyment when won. We see this clearly in the eighteenth century, which saw the birth, not only of modern civil rights, but also of modern national consciousness. . . . And with it came a patriotic nationalism. . . ."

75. In his Farewell Address, Washington saw the "most commanding motives" for the Union in the economic advantages of trade and commerce between the North and South, the East and West. *Messages and Papers*, ed. by Richardson, vol. I, pp. 213 ff. This argument becomes common in the nineteenth century.

76. Later, by the Fourteenth and Fifteenth Amendments (1868, 1870), no state was to deprive any person of life, liberty, or property without "due process of law." These amendments were supposed to assure rights to the newly emancipated Negro citizens, though in practice they did not do so, and the Fourteenth Amendment was used to give national protection to corporate property.

77. Everyman's ed., vol. I, bk. 4, chap. 2, p. 408. About the same time David

Hume, no narrow patriot, made a nationalist argument for *laissez faire* when he prayed for "the flourishing commerce of Germany, Spain, Italy and even France itself"—for he was certain "that Great Britain and all other nations would flourish more" were this policy adopted. "Of the Jealousy of Trade," *Essays, Moral, Political and Literary*, ed. by T. H. Green and T. H. Grose, London, 1898, p. 348. See also Eli Hecksher, *Mercantilism*, tr. by Shapiro, London, 1935, vol. II, p. 14.

78. "Report on Manufactures," to House of Representatives, December 5, 1791, *The Works of Alexander Hamilton*, ed. by Henry Cabot Lodge, vol. IV, p. 135.

79. Fichte's *The Closed Commercial State* (1800) pointedly asked for national intervention in economic affairs for the welfare of the citizen. The classic argument of List came forty years later. In mid-eighteenth-century Italy the abbé Genovesi lectured at Naples on the elimination of economic and political divisions in order to increase Italian prosperity. Noether, *Seeds*, pp. 89 ff.

80. The Bank of England was established in 1694 but it was not nationalized until 1946.

81. For peoples just outside the border it was sometimes economically advantageous to ask for annexation. Avignon silk manufacturers, for example, desired union with France in 1790–91 to avoid the tariff.

82. *Moniteur*, May 13, 1794, pp. 949–52. For earlier French monarchical, local, and other assistance to the poor and sick, see Shelby McCloy, *Governmental Assistance in Eighteenth-Century France*, Durham (N.C.), 1946.

83. Cobb, *"Quelques aspects,"* p. 335, is quite right when he says, "The [ordinary] revolutionary [of '93] was . . . fond of honors, sashes, and gold braid as they were to compensate him for his years of obscurity and unimportance." And so have ardent patriots usually been, obscure or famous.

84. For a discussion see Cobb, "Quelques aspects," p. 323.

85. George Rudé, *The Crowd in the French Revolution*, Oxford, 1959, p. 179. Rudé once more effectively destroys the old and crudely romantic distortions of Carlyle and the high-sounding psychological generalizations of Le Bon about the revolutionary mobs. Those who have witnessed twentieth-century violence might not think the vindictive Defarges of Dickens' *Tale of Two Cities* so "abnormal."

86. Parties in the modern sense had not yet developed, but the Jacobin Society was close and for a while in '93–'94 almost the single controlling party. For the governmental publications sent to the provinces, see P. Caron, "Les Publications officieuses du Ministère de l'Intérieur en 1793 et 1794," *Revue d'histoire moderne et contemporaine*, vol. XIV, 1910, pp. 5–43.

87. *Archives Parlementaires*, vol. 8, p. 211. Grégoire's view was like that of Adam Smith, *The Theory of Moral Sentiments*, in H. W. Schneider, ed., *Adam Smith's Moral and Political Philosophy*, New York, 1948, pp. 240–41: "The patriot who lays down his life for the safety, or even the vainglory of this [his] society, appears to act, with the most exact propriety. . . .

The traitor . . . who . . . fancies he can promote his own little interest by betraying to the public enemy that of his native country . . . appears to be of all villains the most detestable."

88. *Arch. Parl.*, vol. 55, p. 79.

89. Quoted in Alfred Cobban, *Aspects of the French Revolution*, New York, 1968, p. 171.

90. Quoted in A. Kuscinski, *Dictionnaire des Conventionnels*, Paris, 1916, vol. I, p. 145. Another representative on mission, Marc-Antoine Baudot, going to the north at the same time, declared, "I forewarn the society [Jacobin] that in changing climate I shall not change my revolutionary ardor and I shall do in the North as I have done in the South. I shall make patriots, or they will die or I shall."

91. Cobb, "Quelques aspects," p. 316.

92. Brunot, *Histoire*, vol. IX, pp. 664–65, notes the whole family of words built in the 1790's around the word patriot: *archi-patriote, ultra-patriote, lèse-patrie, patriotiser, patriotcide*, and the like. But later, during the Directory (1795–99), overusage and association with radicalism discredited the word, though not love of *patrie*.

93. Quoted in Albert Sorel, *L'Europe et la Révolution française*, Paris, 1946, vol. I, p. 419 fn.

94. F. X. Joliclerc, *Volontaire aux armées de la Révolution: ses lettres 1793–1796*, ed. by Etienne Joliclerc, Paris, 1905, letter of December 13, 1793, pp. 141–43.

95. Quoted in Kohn, *Prelude*, pp. 310–11.

96. *Discours et rapports de Robespierre*, ed. by C. Vellay, Paris, 1908, p. 391.

97. H. F. Stewart and Paul Desjardins, eds., *French Patriotism in the Nineteenth Century (1814–1833)*, Cambridge (Eng.), 1923, p. 51. The even more stilted words of Roland (de La Platière), Girondist minister, could be quoted. P. B. J. Buchez and P. C. Roux, eds., *Histoire parlementaire de la Révolution française*, Paris, 1834–38, vol. XV, p. 42; and see page 133.

98. Of course, enmities were old. See Acomb, *Anglophobia*. But now in war they were deeper and more often expressed.

99. Quoted in René Johannet, *Le Principe des nationalités*, new ed., Paris, 1923, pp. 18–19. For xenophobia in 1793–94 see Cobb, "Quelques aspects," 324–34.

100. See F. Baldensperger, *La Révolution française*, vol. XLIX, 1905, pp. 263–64. But Charles Schmidt, *La Révolution française*, vol. XLVI, 1904, notes that in 1813 a journalist, one Becker, defending himself against Napoleon for having formed a secret league of Germans, defined nationalism without reference to foreign country: "cet attachement à la nation, qu'on pourrait appeler *Nationalisme*, s'accordant parfaitement avec le patriotisme voué à l'état dont on est citoyen. . . ."

101. Hans Kohn, like a good many recent historians, dates the nationalist quickening in the Germanies somewhat later, 1807–08. "The Eve of German Nationalism," *Journal of the History of Ideas*, vol. XII, 1951, pp. 256–84, and his *Prelude*.

Chapter V

1. The best way, naturally, to understand Schiller's influential romanticism is to read his plays and histories, especially his *Don Carlos*. Hans Kohn succinctly describes Schiller's cosmopolitanism in *The Idea of Nationalism: A Study of Its Origins and Background*, New York, 1944, pp. 403–13.
2. During the eighteenth century not only Kant but the abbé Saint-Pierre, Rousseau, and others dreamed of perpetual peace.
3. See particularly the *Conversations of Goethe with Eckermann 1830*, London, 1850. About the same time the English utilitarian Jeremy Bentham wrote, "The more we become enlightened, the more benevolent shall we become; because we shall see that the interests of men coincide upon more points than they oppose each other." *Works*, ed. by John Bowring, Edinburgh, 1842, vol. I, p. 562.
4. *Oeuvres complètes*, 1826 ed., vol. VI, pp. 291–92.
5. Quoted in Robert R. Ergang, *Herder and the Foundations of German Nationalism*, New York, 1931, p. 96.
6. The *Addresses* were translated by R. F. Jones and G. H. Turnbull, Chicago, 1922. And see Hans Kohn, *Prelude to Nation-States: The French and German Experience, 1789–1815*, Princeton, 1967, pp. 229–46.
7. Frederick Page, ed., *An Anthology of Patriotic Prose*, London, 1915, pp. 130–31. Like views were expressed in 1809 by the cleric Sydney Smith, who held, "Our sphere of thought has hardly any limits, our sphere of action hardly any extent . . . if we contract a distaste for the good we can do, because it is not equal to the good we can conceive, we only sacrifice deeds to words, and rule our lives by the maxims of the most idle and ostentatious sentiment."
8. In the introduction to the *History of the Russian State*, written during the Napoleonic wars, eight volumes published by 1816. See Royal Institute of International Affairs, *Nationalism: A Report by a Study Group of Members of the Institute*, London, 1939, p. 67; and Richard Pipes, *Karamzin's Memoir on Ancient and Modern Russia*, Cambridge (Mass.), 1959.
9. Albert Mathiez, *Les Origines des cultes révolutionnaires (1789–1792)*, Paris, 1904, p. 27.
10. Albert Sorel, *L'Europe et la Révolution française*, Paris, 1946, vol. I, p. 419. See also François Delaisi, *Political Myths and Economic Realities*, New York, 1927, pp. 149–50.
11. Among the many accounts see Stephen G. Chaconas, *Adamantios Korais: A Study in Greek Nationalism*, New York, 1942; and Aristotle J. Manessis, "L'Activité et les projets politiques d'un patriote grec dans les Balkans vers la fin du XVIIIᵉ siècle," *Balkan Studies*, vol. 3, 1962, pp. 75–118. The enthusiasts, it might be noted, were *not* predominantly young but middle-aged.
12. See Gaudens Megaro, *Vittorio Alfieri, Forerunner of Italian Nationalism*, New York, 1930.
13. Title VI of the Constitution of 1791 contained the following formal re-

nunciation: "The French nation renounces the undertaking of any war with a view to making conquests, and it will never use its forces against the liberty of any people." John Hall Stewart, ed., *A Documentary Survey of the French Revolution*, New York, 1951, p. 260.

14. After the frightening summer of 1792 French governments actively propagandized abroad, Condorcet, for example, writing pamphlets addressed to Spaniards, Germans, Dutch, and Swiss. See Beatrice Hyslop, "French Jacobin Nationalism and Spain," in Edward Mead Earle, ed., *Nationalism and Internationalism, Essays Inscribed to Carlton J. H. Hayes,* New York, 1950, pp. 204–22.

15. Quoted in J. M. Thompson, *The French Revolution*, New York, 1945, p. 278.

16. Stewart, ed., *A Documentary Survey* pp. 307–11.

17. Stewart, ed., *A Documentary Survey*, p. 381, and the *Archives Parlementaires*, vol. 53, pp. 474 ff. But cf. Sorel, *L'Europe et la Révolution française,* vol. III, p. 129.

18. See the remarks of the Girondist journalist Jean-Louis Carra, *Moniteur universelle,* November 20, 1792, p. 516.

19. Stewart, ed., *A Documentary Survey*, p. 383; Sorel, *L'Europe*, vol. III, pp. 177–78.

20. As the National Convention stated in its proclamation to Savoy, October 6, 1792, *Arch. Parl.*, vol. 52, p. 472.

21. Quoted in René Johannet, *Le Principe des nationalités*, new ed., Paris, 1923, p. 114. The italics are added.

22. Sorel, *L'Europe*, vol. III, p. 152. A geographer named Philippe Buache made the idea of river basins a basic concept of national territory in a book published in 1753. Johannet, *Le Principe*, p. 93. But cf. Gaston Zeller, *Les Temps modernes*, vol. II, *De Louis XIV à 1789*, Paris, 1955, who says that Louis XIV and Louis XV were simply after territory.

23. Herder also believed in it as an expression of "national individuality," a "necessary and natural division of the human race." F. M. Barnard, *Herder's Social and Political Thought: From Enlightenment to Nationalism,* Oxford, 1965, p. 99. R. Randle, "From National Self-Determination to National Self-Development," *Journal of the History of Ideas*, vol. 31, 1970, pp. 49–68, well describes the ideas behind the principle.

24. *Arch. Parl.*, vol. 58, pp. 546–51.

25. George Rudé, *Revolutionary Europe, 1783–1815*, New York, 1964, p. 218.

26. As Max Beloff, *The Age of Absolutism*, London, 1960, p. 18, remarked, "French conscription and the British income-tax, the two great weapons of the modern state were both creations of the 1790's."

27. John Gazley, "Arthur Young, British Patriot," in Earle, ed., *Nationalism and Internationalism*, pp. 170–72. See also Crane Brinton, *A Decade of Revolution, 1789–1799*, New York, 1934, pp. 167–74; and for excerpts from the sources, Alfred Cobban, ed., *The Debate on the French Revolution,* London, 1950.

28. *Reflections . . . ,* in *Works*, Bohn ed., London, 1861, vol. 7, pp. 306, 359, 368. For a short discussion see Friedrich Hertz, *Nationality in History and*

Politics: A Study of the Psychology and Sociology of National Sentiment and Character, London, 1944, pp. 325–29. The studies of Burke are numerous. Carl Cone's two-volume biography, *Burke and the Nature of Politics,* New York, 1957–64, is thorough; and Alfred Cobban's *Edmund Burke and the Revolt Against the 18th Century,* New York, 1929, is incisive.

29. The word is Hans Kohn's, *Prelude,* p. 105.

30. As De Gaulle believed a century and a half later, Napoleon was defeated not on the military level but because he found before him "nations called Spain, Austria, Prussia, Russia." André Malraux, "Une présence humaine et généreuse," *Nouvelle frontière,* January 5, 1964.

31. Sorel, *L'Europe,* vol. VII, pp. 403–04, concisely demonstrated this: "Holland had to be taken in order to secure Belgium, Germany to be . . . dominated for the retention of the left bank of the Rhine, Naples to be subjected, Rome to be annexed so that Piedmont, Lombardy, and Venetia might be kept; the conquest of Spain was dictated by the need to have forces free to deal with Austria . . . ; the annihilation of Prussia . . . necessary for the securing of one of the empire's flanks, the enslavement of Austria for that of the other."

32. Adam Smith in 1772, for example, asked that Britain "expand her colonial empire seizing the islands from the Falklands to the Philippines" to gain control of the Pacific. Gazley, "Arthur Young, British Patriot," in Earle, ed., *Nationalism and Internationalism,* pp. 150–51. By 1815 Britain had taken overseas possessions of France, Spain and Holland.

33. We know little about the thinking of German peasants and workers; the evidence available does not indicate that many became patriots.

34. The best and latest biographical and descriptive sketches of the nationalist leaders of the German uprising are in Kohn, *Prelude,* pp. 119–301. Among the other studies I have used are those by Eugene Anderson, Hannah Arendt, F. M. Barnard, H. C. Engelbrecht, Jerry Dawson, Lucien Levy-Bruhl, Georg Iggers, Friedrich Meinecke, Koppel Pinson, Alfred Pundt, H. S. Reiss, William O. Shanahan, and Louis Snyder (*German Nationalism*); Fichte's *Addresses* (*Reden*) *to the German Nation* (1808), available in translation, is the usual introduction to the wordy sources.

35. Anderson developed his imaginative hypothesis well in *Nationalism and the Cultural Crisis in Prussia, 1806–1815,* New York, 1939, chap. 1, but cf. T. W. Adorno et al., *The Authoritarian Personality,* New York, 1950. Perhaps, in any case, we ought to pay more attention to personal experiences. Schleiermacher was humiliated by French soldiers when they occupied Halle; they took his watch, his money, and all but two shirts, and forced him to billet three Frenchmen. Jerry Dawson, "The Evolution of Friedrich Schleiermacher as a Nationalist," Ph.D. dissertation, Texas, 1964, typescript, pp. 96–97, 106. But one should not overlook cases such as that of the poor and lame Serbian patriot Karadzić; see Duncan Wilson, *The Life and Times of Vuk Stefanović Karadzić 1787–1864,* Oxford, 1970, pp. 350 and passim.

36. Quoted from *Geist der Zeit* by Alfred Pundt, *Arndt and the Nationalist*

Awakening in Germany, New York, 1935, p. 80. Similar sentiments were expressed by Jahn, Friedrich Schlegel (in Austria), and many others.

37. This is substantially the view of Hans Kohn, *Prelude*, p. 254.

38. Louis Snyder, *German Nationalism: The Tragedy of a People*, Harrisburg (Pa.), 1952, p. 28.

39. Quoted in Anderson, *Nationalism and the Cultural Crisis*, p. 183.

40. In a letter of 1811 to Hardenberg. Kohn, *Prelude*, p. 216.

41. On the military reforms see William O. Shanahan, *Prussian Military Reforms, 1786–1813*, New York, 1945; Guy Stanton Ford, "Boyen's Military Law," *American Historical Review*, vol. XX, 1914–15, pp. 528–38; and the paper of Paul Paret, "Nationalism and the Sense of Military Obligation," AHA paper, typescript, New York, 1966, as well as the studies of Friedrich Meinecke and Gerhard Ritter.

42. Koppel S. Pinson, *Pietism as a Factor in the Rise of German Nationalism*, New York, 1934, p. 201.

43. *Addresses*, tr. by Jones and Turnbull, pp. 140–41.

44. See Arndt's *Der Rhein, Teutschlands Strom, ober nicht Teutschlands Grenze* (1813).

45. Definitions of "race," however vague, were not the same then as now, but German racialism was incipient.

46. Quoted in Walter Langsam, *The Napoleonic Wars and German Nationalism in Austria*, New York, 1930, pp. 67–68.

47. I here quote and paraphrase Schleiermacher and Arndt. See Pinson, *Pietism*, p. 193, and Pundt, *Arndt*, p. 80.

48. Kant attempted a description of German character that was not much different, and so have Germans and others since.

49. Even in dress, a Caroline Pichler wrote, "to break away from foreign dictates." Langsam, *Napoleonic Wars*, p. 184.

50. This is a common nationalist argument, but in the case of German it seems, and not only to Frenchmen, more than usually dubious.

51. Edward Thaden, "The Beginnings of Romantic Nationalism in Russia," *American Slavic and East European Review*, vol. 13, 1954, pp. 509–10; and his *Conservative Nationalism in Nineteenth-Century Russia*, Seattle, 1964; and see chapter IV, note 67.

52. The studies are numerous. Among those I have used are Kohn, *The Idea*, esp. pp. 527–76; the several papers and essays in two volumes of the *Austrian History Yearbook*, vol. III, pts. I and II, 1967, and in Peter Sugar and Ivo Lederer, eds., *Nationalism in Eastern Europe*, Seattle, 1969, on the arising nationalisms in the old Hapsburg monarchy and in eastern Europe; Carl Buck, "Language and the Sentiment of Nationality," *American Political Science Review*, vol. X, 1916, pp. 44–69; Hector Munro Chadwick, *The Nationalities of Europe and the Growth of National Ideologies*, Cambridge (Eng.), 1945; G. F. Cushing, "The Birth of a Nationalist Literature in Hungary," *Slavonic and East European Review*, vol. 38, 1960, pp. 459–75; Dimitrije Djordjević, *Révolutions nationales des peuples Balkaniques, 1804–1914*, Belgrade, 1965; Keith Hitchins, *The Rumanian National Movement in Transylvania, 1789–1849*, Cambridge (Mass.),

1969; Manessis, "L'Activité et les projets politiques d'un patriote grec [Rhigas]"; Jack Stukas, *Awakening Lithuania: A Study in the Rise of Modern Lithuania*, Madison (N.J.), 1966; Andreas Elviken, "Genesis of Norwegian Nationalism," *Journal of Modern History*, vol. III, 1931, pp. 365–91; and Erica Simon, *Réveil national et culture populaire en Scandinavie: La Genèse de la Højskole Nordique (1844–1878)*, Paris, 1960.

53. Two articles incorporating recent research are Edward J. Goodman, "Spanish Nationalism in the Struggle Against Napoleon," *Review of Politics*, vol. XX, 1958, pp. 330–46; and Richard Herr, "Good, Evil, and Spain's Rising Against Napoleon," in Richard Herr and Harold T. Parker, eds., *Ideas in History: Essays Presented to Louis Gottschalk by His Former Students*, Durham (N.C.), 1965.

54. Among the studies I have found useful are Arthur Whitaker, *Nationalism in Latin America, Past and Present*, Gainesville (Fla.), 1962, and Arthur Whitaker, ed., *Latin America and the Enlightenment*, 2nd ed., Ithaca (N.Y.), 1961; Gerhard Masur, *Nationalism in Latin America: Diversity and Unity*, New York, 1966; Leopoldo Zea, *The Latin-American Mind*, tr. by Abbott and Dunham, Norman (Okla.), 1963; Frederick Turner, *The Dynamic of Mexican Nationalism*, Chapel Hill (N.C.), 1968—the best single volume; and Luis Monguio, "Nationalism and Social Discontent as reflected in Spanish-American Literature," *Annals of the American Academy of Political and Social Science*, vol. 334, 1961, pp. 63–73. On the independence movements see the bibliographical article, Robert A. Humphreys, "The Historiography of the Spanish American Revolutions," *Hispanic American Historical Review*, vol. 36, 1956, pp. 81–83.

55. See pages 67 and 142.

56. But as early as 1765 Christopher Gadsen said, "There ought to be no New England man, no New Yorkers . . . but all of us Americans," and Patrick Henry in 1774, "The distinctions between Virginians, Pennsylvanians, New Yorkers, and New Englanders are no more. I am not a Virginian but an American." These views were not universal, however, and still are not. Cf. Russel Nye, *This Almost Chosen People: Essays in the History of American Ideas*, East Lansing (Mich.), 1966, p. 54; and Robert Meade, *Patrick Henry, Patriot in the Making*, Philadelphia, 1957, vol. I, p. 325.

57. Kohn, *The Idea*, p. 283.

58. Stanley Elkins and Eric McKitrick, "The Founding Fathers, Young Men of the Revolution," *Political Science Quarterly*, vol. LXXVI, 1961, p. 208.

59. H. S. Commager, ed., *Documents of American History*, New York, 1938, p. 170. Richard B. Morris' solid *The Emerging Nations and the American Revolution*, New York, 1970, surveys relevant American ideas of the revolutionary era.

60. On Hamilton and Webster see Nye, *This Almost Chosen People*, pp. 63–64. The quoted words of Morris are from his letter to John Jay, July 10, 1784, in Henry Cabot Lodge, "Gouverneur Morris," *Historical and Political Essays*, Boston, 1898, p. 83.

61. See George Dangerfield, *The Awakening of American Nationalism*,

1815–1828, New York, 1965, p. 4, and his whole excellent book. The phrase "hopes and fears" is from *The Federalist*, no. 16.

62. On the religious aspect of the nationalism see two excellent recent volumes: Alan Heimert, *Religion and the American Mind: From the Great Awakening to the Revolution,* Cambridge (Mass.), 1966; and Ernest L. Tuveson, *Redeemer Nation: The Idea of America's Millennial Role,* Chicago, 1968; and an older volume, Edward Humphrey, *Nationalism and Religion in America, 1774–1789,* Boston, 1924. On nature's role see Ralph N. Miller, "American Nationalism as a Theory of Nature," *William and Mary Quarterly,* vol. XI, 1955, pp. 74–95. On the larger subject of destiny cf. Albert K. Weinberg, *Manifest Destiny: A Study of Nationalist Expansionism in American History,* Baltimore, 1935; and Frederick Merk, *Manifest Destiny and Mission in American History: A Reinterpretation,* New York, 1963.

63. See Earl Bradsher, "The Rise of Nationalism in American Literature," in Nathaniel Caffee and Thomas A. Kirby, eds., *Studies for William Alexander Read,* Baton Rouge (La.), 1940, pp. 269–87; James Coberly, "The Growth of Nationalism in American Literature, 1800–1815," Ph.D. dissertation, George Washington University, 1949, typescript; Charles Cole, "The Beginnings of Literary Nationalism in America, 1775–1800," Ph.D. dissertation, George Washington University, 1939, typescript; and John McCloskey, "The Campaign of Periodicals After the War of 1812 for National American Literature," *PMLA,* vol. L, 1935, pp. 262–73.

64. The prophecies were many. For examples see Henry Nash Smith, *Virgin Land: The American West as Symbol and Myth,* Cambridge (Mass.), 1950.

65. See his letter of 1816 to John Adams, in C. F. Adams, ed., *Works,* Boston, 1850–56, vol. X, p. 223.

66. Quoted in Lillian Miller, *Patrons and Patriotism: The Encouragement of the Fine Arts in the United States, 1790–1860,* Chicago, 1966.

67. This is the version of the toast in the *Niles Weekly Register,* April 20, 1816.

68. Carlton Hayes, himself a Catholic, stresses this in his *Nationalism: A Religion,* New York, 1960.

69. *Archives Parlementaires,* vol. 78, November 5, 1793, pp. 373–75. See also A. Aulard, *Le Culte de la raison et le culte de l'Être Suprême,* Paris, 1892, p. 35.

70. Pinson, *Pietism,* p. 184.

71. Thompson, *The French Revolution,* p. 258.

72. Pinson, p. 98.

73. Quoted in Carlton Hayes, *The Historical Evolution of Modern Nationalism,* New York, 1931, p. 68.

74. P. B. J. Buchez and P. C. Roux, eds., *Histoire parlementaire de la Révolution française,* Paris, 1834–38, vol. XV, p. 42.

75. *Histoire de la langue française,* Paris, 1927, vol. IX, pt. I, p. 625.

76. On July 9, 1789, after the priest Grégoire spoke in the National Assembly of the crime of *"lèse-Majesté Nationale,"* the Assembly established a

special court for it at Orleans. Brunot, *Histoire*, vol. IX, pt. I, p. 637. Very soon the term "nationomicide" was also invented.

77. Fichte gave the ultimate justification for this conformity when he declared, "What spirit has an undisputed right to summon and to order everyone concerned, whether he himself be willing or not, and to compel anyone who resists, to risk everything including his life? Not the spirit of the peaceful citizen's love for the constitution and the laws, but the devouring flame of higher patriotism, which embraces the nation as the vesture of the eternal, for which the noble-minded man joyfully sacrifices himself, and the ignoble man, who only exists for the sake of the other, must likewise sacrifice himself." *Addresses*, tr. by Jones and Turnbull, pp. 140–41.

78. *Arch. Parl.*, vol. 55, speech of Thuriot, p. 79.

79. *L'Ami des Patriotes ou le défenseur de constitution*, vol. II, p. 89, cited in Brunot, *Histoire*, vol. IX, p. 635 n.

80. Mathiez, *Les Origines des cultes révolutionnaires*, p. 31.

81. *Moniteur universelle*, August 25, 1793, p. 1008. He was arguing for the *levée en masse*.

82. Boyd C. Shafer, "When Patriotism Became Popular," *Historian*, vol. V, 1943, pp. 77–96. And see page 101.

83. Brunot, *Histoire*, vol. IX, pp. 664–66. The comment of the contemporary newspaper *Journal des clubs ou sociétés patriotes* is pertinent here: "Mon énergumène monte sur l'impériale, harangue le peuple, fait sonner les mots d'accaparement, de sang du peuple . . . et surtout de patriotisme. Les têtes se tournent. . . . Aujourd'hui c'est tout dire: le patriotisme! Soyez mauvais fils, mauvais père, mauvais mari, mauvais ami, mauvais citoyen aux yeux de la loi; soyez sans foi, sans honneur, sans vertus, sans talents; soyez sans état, banqueroutier, flétri; si vous avez du patriotisme . . . vous êtes le type et le prototype des bons citoyens." In Sigismond Lacroix, *Actes de la Commune de Paris*, Paris, 1906–, 2nd series, vol. II, p. 582.

84. A convenient compendium of patriotic songs is Martin Shaw and Henry Coleman, eds., *National Anthems of the World*, 2nd rev. ed., London, 1963.

85. Quoted in Brunot, *Histoire*, vol. IX, p. 73.

86. John Adams, as early as July 3, 1776, thought Independence Day ought to be solemnized with "pomp and parade, with shows, sports, guns, bells, bonfires, and illuminations, from one end of the continent to the other, from this day forward, forever more." Boston made the Fourth a holiday in 1783 and this later became the general custom. See Merle Curti, *The Roots of American Loyalty*, New York, 1946, pp. 136–37. The first celebration of July 14 was at the *Fête de la Fédération*, July, 1790.

87. A John Arbuthnot invented John Bull in 1712 to represent the doggedness of the Whigs in the war against France. The term Uncle Sam, which may have been derisively used by opponents of the War of 1812, could derive from the letters "U.S." on uniforms or from Samuel Wilson, inspector of army supplies at Troy, New York, whom workingmen called Uncle Sam.

88. See Boyd C. Shafer, "When Patriotism Became Popular," *passim*. The oath taken in France in 1790 to the Nation, the Law, and the King may have originated in Rousseau's suggested oath for Corsicans. See C. E. Vaughan, ed., *The Political Writings of Jean-Jacques Rousseau*, Cambridge (Eng.), 1915, vol. II, p. 350.

89. See Carlton Hayes, *France: A Nation of Patriots*, New York, 1930, p. 12.

Chapter VI

1. As Crane Brinton observed, nationalism became "one of the *working forms* the new doctrines of popular sovereignty, progress, the perfectibility of man took in the world of reality." *Ideas and Men*, New York, 1950, p. 419.

2. Cf. the informed discussion in Guido de Ruggiero, *The History of European Liberalism*, tr. by R. G. Collingwood, London, 1927, esp. pp. 414–15.

3. *Mémoire adressé au Roi en juillet 1814*, Brussels, 1814. See Carlton Hayes, *France: A Nation of Patriots*, New York, 1930, p. 12; Huntley Dupre, *Lazare Carnot, Republican Patriot*, Oxford (Ohio), 1940, pp. 272–73, and his article, "Carnot's Nationalism," *South Atlantic Quarterly*, vol. XXXVIII, 1938, pp. 291–306.

4. Quoted in Carlton Hayes, *The Historical Evolution of Modern Nationalism*, New York, 1931, p. 115.

5. See, among the many studies, Sean O'Faolain's eloquent *King of the Beggars*, London, 1938. A short account can be found in William Langer, *Political and Social Upheaval, 1832–1852*, New York, 1969, pp. 239–45. For various aspects of Irish nationalism Lawrence McCaffrey's *The Irish Question, 1800–1922*, Lexington (Ky.), 1968, is excellent.

6. C. H. Van Tyne, *The War of Independence: American Phase*, Boston, 1929, p. 271. But a later authority on the Revolution, John Alden, believes many of the ingredients of nationalism were present and there was much loyalty to the causes of independence and liberty: "a man might not be willing to die for New Hampshire or North Carolina; but for America the answer was often 'yes.' " Letter to author, June 20, 1968.

7. In the novelist Conrad Richter's great trilogy, *The Awakening Land*, New York, 1956, there is almost no mention of national affairs or interests, and Richter has perhaps come closer to the historical realities of the hinterland than have historians who wrote from the documents of the government in Washington.

8. For a brilliant analysis see George Dangerfield, *The Awakening of American Nationalism, 1815–1828*, New York, 1965.

9. Editorial in the *Berliner Politisches Wochenblatt*, quoted in Langer, *Political and Social Upheaval*, p. 258. But the historian Ranke was not, as Langer says, the editor of this paper. For Ranke's similar views see Georg Iggers, *The German Conception of History: The National Tradition of Historical Thought from Herder to the Present*, Middletown (Conn.), 1968, pp. 78–80.

10. See John A. Rath, "The 'Carbonari': Their Origins, Initiation Rites, and Aims," *American Historical Review*, vol. 69, 1964, pp. 353–70.

11. The literature on Metternich and the restoration is enormous and need not be listed here. But see Hannah Straus's slight *The Attitude of the Congress of Vienna Toward Nationalism in Germany, Italy, and Poland*, New York, 1929; and Ernest L. Woodward's brilliant *Three Studies in European Conservatism: Metternich; Guizot; the Catholic Church in the Nineteenth Century*, London, 1929. While Metternich's memoirs are unreliable and dull, they reveal not only how little he, the leading statesman of Europe from 1815 to 1848, understood nationalism but also how little nationalist many European leaders then were.

12. As Hans Kohn observed, "So strong was the influence of ideas that while the new nationalism in western Europe corresponded to changing social, economic, and political realities, it spread to central and eastern Europe long before a corresponding social and economic transformation." *The Idea of Nationalism: A Study of Its Origins and Background*, New York, 1944, p. 457. The significant and in many ways peculiar experience of Poland is discussed by Jerzy Szacki, "L'Evolution du concept de 'Nation' en Pologne à la fin du XVIIIᵉ et au début du XIXᵉ siècle," *Cahiers d'histoire mondiale*, vol. IX, 1965, pp. 59–79.

13. Joseph de Maistre argued in 1797 that the French Revolutionary constitutions, made for man, were fit for none because there were only particular men. *Considérations sur la France*, in *Oeuvres complètes*, vol. I, Paris, 1924, p. 74.

14. Adapted and corrected from Dankwart Rustow, *A World of Nations, Problems of Political Modernizaton*, Washington, D.C., 1967, p. 292. Only some of many qualifications and exceptions to dates are noted, and "independence" is a relative term.

15. On the relation of liberalism and nationalism see note 1; Max Boehm, *Das eigenstände Volk: Volkstheoretische Grundlagen der Ethnopolitik und Geisteswissenschaften*, Göttingen, 1932; and H. L. Featherstone, *A Century of Nationalism*, London, 1939; but nationalism combined with conservatism, though of a different variety, was as strong or stronger in the Germanies and central and eastern Europe. See Walter M. Simon, "Variations in Nationalism During the Great Reform Period," *American Historical Review*, vol. LIX, 1954, pp. 305–21.

16. Few, if any, gave up any territory willingly or peacefully.

17. C. W. Crawley, *The Question of Greek Independence*, Cambridge (Eng.), 1930, p. 10, argued that nationalism had less to do with the struggle for Greek independence than did "a sense of injustice, a growing measure of prosperity and power, combined with religious zeal. . . ." But, of course, these are ingredients of nationalism.

18. J. L. Comstock, *History of the Greek Revolution*, New York, 1828, p. 143 n.

19. The fervent Mazzinian oath of Young Italy (1831) reveals the same feelings of shame, oppression, and hope. J. H. Rose, *Nationality in Modern History*, New York, 1916, pp. 81–82.

20. Georges Weill, *L'Europe du XIXe siècle et l'idée de nationalité,* Paris, 1938, is still a good survey.

21. Belgium contained two "nationalities," Flemings and Walloons.

22. See pages 200–05.

23. See Robert C. Binkley, *Realism and Nationalism 1852–1871,* New York, 1935, pp. 157–63 and ff.; Robert A. Kann, *The Multinational Empire: Nationalism and National Reform in the Hapsburg Monarchy, 1848–1918,* 2 vols., New York, 1950, for possibilities in the old Empire; and the idealistic Denis de Rougemont, *The Idea of Europe,* New York, 1966, pp. 270–92.

24. The best recent works in English are by D. Mack Smith, esp. his *Cavour and Garibaldi 1860: A Study in Political Conflict,* Cambridge (Eng.), 1954, and his *Italy, a Modern History,* Ann Arbor (Mich.), 1959; Charles F. Delzell, ed., *The Unification of Italy, 1859–1861,* New York, 1965, lists recent work; and Bolton King, *A History of Italian Unity,* 2 vols., London, 1898, is a good old standard account.

25. Once more the literature is too vast to cite. A good recent treatment that lists relevant studies is Otto Pflanze, *Bismarck and the Development of Germany: The Period of German Unification,* Princeton, 1963; an older standard work is Erich Brandenberg, *Die Reichsgründung,* 2 vols., Leipzig, 1923.

26. He went so far, for strategic reasons, as to include the doubtfully German Alsace-Lorraine, and thus provided France with a nationalist cause for a half century.

27. This could be part of the reason that Germany and Italy became so aggressive under Hitler and Mussolini. And Germany, because of big-power and ideological conflict, is again divided.

28. See the imaginative thesis of C. N. Degler, "One Among Many," *Virginia Quarterly Review,* vol. 39, 1963, pp. 289–306, which suggests that the American Civil War was one manifestation of nation building, just as were the wars and revolutions of the mid-nineteenth century in Europe.

29. In addition to the works cited in chapter V, note 52, see R. W. Seton-Watson, *The Rise of Nationality in the Balkans,* London, 1917; and the new volume edited by Peter Sugar and Ivo Lederer, eds., *Nationalism in Eastern Europe,* Seattle, 1969.

30. But, of course, six counties in the northeast were still under Britain, and it was not until 1949 that Eire became a republic and left the British Commonwealth.

31. Of the several general historical treatments of heroes, none are outstanding, but see Sidney Hook, *The Hero in History,* New York, 1942; and Eric Bentley, *A Century of Hero Worship,* Philadelphia, 1944. Otto Rank, a psychoanalyst, thought it possible that national heroes "replaced the real father by a more distinguished one." *The Myth of the Birth of the Hero,* tr. by Robins and Jelliffe, New York, 1952, p. 67.

32. All over Europe heroes and villains were "resurrected." For the Irish *the* villain was Cromwell; see R. J. Loftus, *Nationalism in Modern Irish Poetry,*

Madison (Wis.), 1964, pp. 25–27. In France Jeanne d'Arc did not become a heroic symbol until the nineteenth century and she was not sainted until 1920; see Gilbert Gadoffre, "French National Images and the Problem of National Stereotypes," *International Social Science Bulletin*, vol. III, 1951, p. 550. But see Hans Kohn, *Nationalism and Liberty: The Swiss Example*, London, 1956.

33. Switzerland may be the only exception. Of course, the intensity of feeling varied as did the action to "regain" people or territory.

34. Or, as Sir W. Ivor Jennings once remarked, "On the surface [self-determination] seemed reasonable: let the people decide. It was in fact ridiculous because the people cannot decide until somebody decides who are the people." *The Approach to Self-Government*, Cambridge (Eng.), 1956, p. 56. For a dated but good discussion see C. A. Macartney, *National States and National Minorities*, London, 1934, pp. 209–20. See pages 57, 66.

35. Sidney B. Fay, *The Origins of the World War*, New York, 1930, vol. II, p. 133. Vladimir Dedijer, *The Road to Sarajevo*, New York 1966, pp. 257–60 and 319, shows how the young assassins were inspired by the deed of Milos Obilić.

36. For his complete argument see "The Principle of Nationality and Its Applications," in *Essays and Addresses in War Time*, New York, 1918, pp. 141–75. He was, of course, following John Stuart Mill, *Considerations on Representative Government*, 1861, chap. XVI. The argument of the idealists of the wartime years was concisely put by Theodore Ruyssen, *The Principle of Nationality*, International Conciliation Pamphlet No. 109, December, 1916. But cf. Lewis Namier, *Basic Factors in Nineteenth Century European History*, London, 1952, pp. 1–2.

37. And his words were echoed a generation later by the promise of the Atlantic Charter (1941) of Churchill and Roosevelt, "the right of all people to choose the form of government under which they will live."

38. Linguistic determination of nationality, though often advocated, was, of course, impossible and impractical; forty to fifty languages were spoken in Europe and no exact boundaries could be set to clearly demarcate the peoples who spoke different languages. Hector Munro Chadwick, *The Nationalities of Europe and the Growth of National Ideologies*, Cambridge (Eng.), 1945.

39. Race and nationality were often considered to be the same. But Disraeli thought nationality a "newfangled sentimental principle" and race, blood, "the key to history." See his novel *Endymion*.

40. Their books respectively were *Races of Man* (1846); *Essai sur l'inégalité des races humaines* (1854); and *Types of Mankind* (1854) and *The Indigenous Races of the Earth* (1857). There are hundreds of books on race, many of them trash. Among the more scholarly, impartial books consulted were Jacques Barzun, *Race: A Study in Superstition*, rev. ed., New York, 1965; Philip Curtin, *The Image of Africa: British Ideas and Action, 1780–1850*, Madison (Wis.), 1964; Thomas F. Gossett, *Race: The History*

of an Idea in America, Dallas, 1964; and William Stanton, *The Leopard's Spots: Scientific Attitudes Toward Race in America, 1815–1859,* Chicago, 1960.

41. *The Inequality of the Human Races,* tr. by Adrian Collins, New York, 1915, pp. 205–10.

42. See pages 323–27. Bagehot's *Physics and Politics* was published in 1875; Chamberlain's *The Foundations of the Nineteenth Century* in 1899 (Eng. tr. 1911). Beveridge's views are best found in his papers in the Manuscript Division of the Library of Congress; his most famous speech, that of January 9, 1900, which might be titled "God, the United States, and the Philippines," is in *Cong. Record,* 56 Cong., 1st Sess., p. 711.

43. Contrary to Frederick Merk, *Manifest Destiny and Mission in American History: A Reinterpretation,* New York, 1963, the mission (reinforced by Puritan doctrine) idea may be of greater importance in the United States than the idea of a model. The interpretation of Albert K. Weinberg, *Manifest Destiny: A Study of Nationalist Expansionism in American History,* Baltimore, 1935, seems closer to the evidence. But cf. the solid books of Julius Pratt, *Expansionists of 1812,* New York, 1925; *Expansionists of 1898,* Baltimore, 1936; and his later writings; and the thinner "realist" arguments of Norman Graebner, ed., *Ideas and Diplomacy,* New York, 1964.

44. Are Canada and Switzerland and a few other small nations exceptions? See pages 314–15.

45. *Life and Writings,* London, 1891, vol. III, p. 33. As a contemporary scholar, Ladis Kristof, says, "The justification of a state's existence is [often] in terms of precisely such a destiny and mission," but I cannot agree with his generalization that it is "a semiconscious tendency rooted in the collective psychology of national traditions and ambitions." "The State-Idea, the National Idea and the Image of the Fatherland," *Orbis,* vol. XI, 1967, p. 239.

46. A spirited introduction is Hans Kohn, *Prophets and Peoples: Studies in Nineteenth Century Nationalism,* New York, 1946.

47. *The Last Will and Testament of Cecil Rhodes,* London, 1902, p. 48.

48. Rose, *Nationality in Modern History,* pp. 163–66; and Andreas Dorpalen, *Heinrich von Treitschke,* New Haven, 1957, p. 210. Roberto Michels described many of the myths in *Der Patriotismus: Prolegomena zu zeiner soziologischen Analyse,* Munich, 1929. Geibel, the poet, saw Germany's calling in its "Macht und Freiheit, Recht und Litte" and thought German ways "Einmal doch die Welt genesen."

49. Langer, *Political and Social Upheaval,* pp. 268–69; Robert E. MacMaster, *Danilevsky: A Russian Totalitarian Philosopher,* Cambridge (Mass.), 1967, p. 273. See also Nicholas V. Riasanovsky, *Nicholas I and Official Nationality in Russia, 1825–1855,* Berkeley, 1959, pp. 124–25; and Edward Thaden, *Conservative Nationalism in Nineteenth-Century Russia,* Seattle, 1964, pp. 83–85. For Dostoyevsky in *The Possessed,* God was the "synthetic personality of whole people," and a people who did not believe truth to be found "in itself alone" ceased to be a nation.

50. Deuteronomy 14: 2. Examples of the modern messianic prophets could be multiplied. See pages 314–15. For the poet Mickiewicz "the Poles were a chosen people, crucified, as Christ had been, in the cause of human freedom" and called to "open the way to a new federation of nations." Langer, *Political and Social Upheaval*, p. 248. See also Olga Scherer-Virski, "Mickiewicz et Towianski: Libération nationale ou assomption mystique," *Etudes Slaves et Est-Européennes*, vol. 11, 1966, pp. 21–22.

51. Interpretations of Darwin are many and diverse, but Social Darwinists departed far from Darwin. In Darwin's world "man and all other living things" evolved "in accordance with entirely natural, material processes," in part randomly and in part by adaptive relationships. The process did not guarantee "any given lineage of populations." "On the contrary, it usually leads to eventual extinction and a repeopling of the world by the newly divergent offspring. . . ." George Gaylord Simpson, "The World into Which Darwin Led Us," *Science*, vol. 131, 1960, p. 973.

52. The quoted phrase is from Binkley, *Realism and Nationalism*, p. 30. On Social Darwinism Richard Hofstadter's *Social Darwinism in American Thought, 1860–1915*, Philadelphia, 1945 (little change in later edition), is still a good introduction.

53. Fiske, Harvard professor, historian, popular lecturer, grandiloquently summed up the belief with special predictions for the United States in his *The Destiny of Mankind Viewed in Light of His Origin*, Boston, 1884.

54. This is close to the assertion of Homer Lea, *The Valour of Ignorance*, New York, 1909, pp. 8 ff.

55. *Physics and Politics, or Thoughts on the Application of the Principles of "Natural Selection" and ."Inheritance" to Political Society*, New York, 1948, p. 46.

56. See page 330.

57. *Capital*, Everyman's ed., vol. II, p. 848. Among the many commentaries from differing viewpoints see John Maynard, *The Russian Peasant and Other Studies*, London, 1942; Richard Pipes, *The Formation of the Soviet Union: Communism and Nationalism 1917–1923*, Cambridge (Mass.), 1954; Frederick C. Barghoorn, *Soviet Russian Nationalism*, New York, 1956; Alfred D. Low, *Lenin and the Question of Nationality*, New York, 1958; Horace B. Davis, *Nationalism and Socialism: Marxist and Labor Theories of Nationalism to 1917*, New York, 1967 (pro-Marxist); B. D. Wolfe, "Nationalism and Internationalism in Marx and Engels," *American Slavic and East European Review*, vol. 17, 1965, pp. 403–17; R. V. Vystkin and S. L. Tikhvinsky, "Some Questions of Historical Science in the Chinese Peoples Republic," *Voprosy Istorii*, October 1963, in *Current Digest of the Soviet Press*, vol. 16, 1964, pp. 3–10; R. Rosdolsky, "Worker and Fatherland: A Note on a Passage in the Communist Manifesto," *Science and Society*, vol. 29, 1965, pp. 330–37 (pro-Marxist); and N. A. Martin, "Marxism, Nationalism, and Russia," *Journal of the History of Ideas*, vol. 29, 1968, pp. 231–52.

58. *Marxism and the National and Colonial Question*, New York, n.d., pp.

13–15. For further elaboration of the Stalin line see M. D. Kammari, *The Development by J. V. Stalin of the Marxist-Leninist Theory of the National Question*, Moscow, 1951; and for a critical recent analysis, Martin, "Marxism, Nationalism, and Russia."

59. Ithaca (N.Y.), 1968, p. 32. Theodore Hamerow in his *The Social Foundations of German Unification, 1858–1871*, Princeton, 1969, makes a strong case that it was merchants, bankers, manufacturers, professional men, not aristocrats or members of the lower classes, who were national-minded in the Germanies. John Gagliardo argues that German writers made much of the peasant in order to protect property. *From Pariah to Patriot* . . . , *1740–1840,* Lexington (Ky.), 1969.

60. See pages 328–29.

61. Among the versions of this thesis were those of the radical Christian philosopher-novelist Count Leo Tolstoy (1828–1910) of Russia and the radical, iconoclastic economist Thorstein Veblen of the United States. "Patriotism," declared Tolstoy, "in its simplest, clearest, and most in-dubitable signification is nothing else but a means of obtaining for rulers their ambitious and covetous desires. . . ." "Patriotism and Peace," *Complete Works*, Crowell ed., New York, 1898–99, vol. 21, pp. 44–45. For Veblen patriotism was the way "masters, rulers, authorities . . . magnates, notables, kings and mandarins" obtained prestige at the expense of others like them. *An Inquiry into the Nature of Peace* . . . , New York, 1919, pp. 57 ff.

62. See chapters XI and XII.

63. Informative discussions of this generalization, particularly for France, are in Raoul Girardet, ed., *Le Nationalisme français 1871–1914*, Paris, 1966, pp. 20–23; and Guy Michelat and Jean-Pierre Thomas, *Dimensions du nationalisme: Enquête par questionnaire 1962*, Paris, 1966, pp. viii–ix.

64. See, for example, Riasanovsky, *Nicholas I and Official Nationality*, pp. 73–74, 78, 124–25; Hans Rogger, "Nationalism and the State: A Russian Dilemma," *Comparative Studies in Society and History*, vol. IV, 1962, pp. 263–74; and Kristof, "The State-Idea, the National Idea and the Image of the Fatherland," pp. 244–49.

65. It is impossible once again to set an exact date for the expansion of national governmental activities, but Britain created the Metropolitan Police in 1829, appointed the first factory inspectors and emigration officers in 1833, assumed a share of responsibility for elementary educa-tion the same year, set up the Poor Law Commission in 1834, and instituted prison inspection in 1835. F. H. Hinsley, "Introduction," *New Cambridge Modern History*, vol. XI, p. 18 n.

66. When Lloyd George brought in his then huge budget of 1909 and greatly increased taxes to pay for expanded governmental military and social service activities he said, "A tax has got to come from some pocket, and the only question is whether it won't do more good in the national purse than in the pocket of the individual. . . ." *Independent,* vol. 67, December 16, 1909, p. 1346. His question was answered by national governments everywhere in the same way.

67. Sir John Wheeler-Bennett, *A Wreath to Clio*, London, 1967, p. 154.
68. The following table for selected and at present "democratic" countries is instructive. A similar table for authoritarian countries could be equally instructive.

	Year of First Constitution		Year of Current Constitution (always with changes)
United States	1787		1787
United Kingdom	1688?	(unwritten)	1832?
Canada	1867		1867
Norway	1814		1814
Sweden	1720		1809
Netherlands	1795		1815
West Germany	1848		1949
France	1791		1958
Switzerland	1798		1874
Japan	1889		1946
Mexico	1814		1917

This table is adapted from Rustow, *World of Nations*, p. 290.

69. Historians and social scientists (including behaviorists) have not as yet been able to develop instruments, quantitative or other, to measure exactly cause-and-effect relationships in most human affairs. Historians, and the writer is one, usually favor pluralistic explanations because they are useful and because they are closer to the realities of human conduct.
70. Frederick Turner, *The Dynamic of Mexican Nationalism*, Chapel Hill (N.C.), 1968, pp. 157–62.
71. An opinion of an American sociologist, William Graham Sumner, expressed in his famed *Folkways* in 1907, was extreme but relevant here: "For modern man patriotism has become one of the first duties and one of the noblest sentiments. It is what he owes to the state for what the state does for him, and the state is, for the modern man, a cluster of civic institutions from which he draws security and conditions of welfare." New York, 1959, p. 15.
72. This was precisely the argument of a Wilhem Schulz in 1832 who wrote *German Unity through the Representation of the People*, one chapter of which is titled, "The Necessity of the Representation of the People in Germany as a Means of Preserving Internal Peace and as a Protection against Foreign Countries." Thomas R. Hinton, *Liberalism, Nationalism, and German Intellectuals*, London, 1951, pp. 127–28.
73. During the bourgeois monarchy, 1830–48, about one adult male in thirty could vote. Most adult Frenchmen could vote under the Second Empire, 1851–70, but the vote meant only acquiescence to Napoleon's wishes.
74. John Hawgood, *Modern Constitutions Since 1787*, New York, 1939, is a convenient introduction to the laws on the suffrage.
75. In the United Kingdom and United States around seventeen per cent, France about twenty-nine per cent. In Australia and New Zealand, in which

women had the vote, the percentage had risen to over sixty. For the best guesses see Rustow, *World of Nations,* p. 290.

76. "Reconstruction," in *Collected Works,* New York, 1890, vol. VI, pp. 211–14.

77. Hayes, *France: A Nation of Patriots,* pp. 30–31.

78. For further discussion see page 101.

79. The attack of Julien Benda on intellectuals is unsurpassed for its biting irony. *La Trahison des clercs,* Paris, 1927. But intellectuals did not, of course, conceive of themselves as traitors to high humane ideals when they professed patriotism; rather they thought of themselves as proponents of the highest ideals of civilization. When, for example, French geographers of the 1870's and 1880's ardently advocated French colonial expansion, they equated French interests with the good of humanity. See Henri Brunschwig, *Mythes et réalités de l'impérialisme colonial français, 1871–1914,* Paris, 1960, pp. 23–28.

80. There are many American studies, from the popular work of Walter Millis, *The Martial Spirit,* New York, 1931, to the more scholarly Pratt, *Expansionists of 1898;* a little-known study of "grass roots" reaction is Peter Mikelson, "Nationalism in Minnesota during the Spanish-American War," *Minnesota History,* vol. 41, 1968, pp. 1–12, which is part of his undergraduate honors thesis. The Spanish side is not as well known, but the quick defeat did shock Spanish leaders. On the opposition to the war in the United States see Robert L. Beisner, *Twelve Against Empire: The Anti-Imperialists 1898–1900,* New York, 1968. But the anti-imperialists chiefly argued from nationalist grounds.

81. Alsace had become a French province 1680–97 and Lorraine 1735–66.

82. It has often been stated that Bismarck was not motivated by the issue of nationality because he once said he wanted only the fortresses of Metz and Strasbourg. But why did he want them? To protect what? Probably the Prussian state and Junker class, but did he and other Germans equate the interests of Prussia, Germans, and Germany? Treitschke wrote that the provinces were German by "right of the sword," and he meant by the right of the superiority of the German nation. Cf. Rose, *Nationality in Modern History,* pp. 130–32.

83. This is the thesis of Herbert Tint, *The Decline of French Patriotism, 1870–1940,* London, 1964. But the motivations of French nationalism were broader, as is demonstrated by the remarks of Girardet in his documentary volume, *Le Nationalisme français;* and by David Sumler, "Domestic Influences on the Nationalist Revival in France, 1909–1914," *French Historical Studies,* vol. VI, 1970, pp. 517–537.

84. Barrès' trilogy, *Le Roman de l'énergie nationale,* beginning with *Les Déracinés,* widely read and admired, inspired not a few young Frenchmen. Most of the scholarly studies done have been on the rightist nationalism and not enough on the liberal and radical, but see Claude Digeon, "Origines et signification du nationalisme littéraire en France (1870–1914)," *Revue des travaux de l'Académie des Sciences Morales et Politiques,* vol. 115, 1962, pp. 144–56; Pierre Nora, "Ernest Lavisse: son

rôle dans la formation du sentiment national," *Revue historique*, vol. 228, 1962, pp. 73–106; and three books, William Curt Buthman, *The Rise of Integral Nationalism in France, with Special Reference* . . . [to] *Charles Maurras*, New York, 1939; Girardet, ed., *Le Nationalisme français* (important excerpts from major nationalist speeches and writings); and Eugen Weber, *The Nationalist Revival in France, 1905–1914*, Berkeley, 1959. The first four chapters of Weber's *Action française: Royalism and Reaction in Twentieth Century France*, Stanford (Calif.), 1962, survey royalist views down to 1918.

85. This general point is made by E. H. Carr, *The Twenty Years Crisis 1919–39*, London, 1946, p. 144, and more specifically by H. Gollwitzer, "Esquisse d'une histoire générale des idées politiques au XIXe siècle et plus particulièrement du nationalisme et de l'impérialisme," *Cahiers d'histoire mondiale*, vol. IV, 1957, pp. 109–19. Aldous Huxley, *Themes and Variations*, London, 1950, p. 5, obviously exaggerated when he wrote, "Every oppressed nationality . . . within two or three generations, sometimes within a single generation . . . becomes, if circumstances are propitious, an imperialist aggressor . . . ," but his point is well taken.

86. Expansion began, of course, long before 1870, and other nations—Spain, Portugal, and Belgium—were imperialist.

87. The quoted words are from J. M. Robertson, *Patriotism and Empire*, London, 1900, p. 138.

88. The classic statement is J. A. Hobson's *Imperialism, a Study*, London, 1902, and several later editions; in the later editions Hobson himself modified his economic determinism. The sharpest assertion of the last is V. I. Lenin, *Imperialism, the Highest Stage of Capitalism*, New York, 1939 (many other editions). In this section I have relied heavily on the old and informative Parker T. Moon, *Imperialism and World Politics*, New York, 1926; Raymond F. Betts, *Europe Overseas: Phases of Imperialism*, New York, 1968 (introductory but balanced); Grover Clark, *A Place in the Sun*, New York, 1936; D. K. Fieldhouse, *The Colonial Empires: A Comparative Survey from the Eighteenth Century*, New York, 1967 (most substantial recent survey); Richard Koebner and Helmut Schmidt, *Imperialism: The Story and Significance of a Political Word, 1840–1960*, Cambridge (Eng.), 1964; George H. Nadel and Perry Curtis, eds., *Imperialism and Colonialism*, New York, 1964; Ronald Robinson and John Gallagher, with Alice Denny, *Africa and the Victorians*, New York, 1961; Bernard Semmel, *Imperialism and Social Reform, English Social-Imperial Thought 1895–1914*, Cambridge (Mass.), 1960; and the truly ground-breaking book of Eugene Staley, *War and the Private Investor* . . . , New York, 1935.

89. Betts, *Europe Overseas*, p. 49.

90. The phrase is that of the British imperialist statesman, Lord Curzon. Margery Perham, *The Colonial Reckoning: The End of Imperial Rule in Africa in the Light of British Experience*, New York, 1962, p. 137. Or one could quote Hilaire Belloc's couplet, "Whatever happens we have got / The Maxim gun and they have not."

91. Herbert Feis, with much evidence, succinctly summed up the view that private investment was "a servant of national purposes." *Europe the World's Banker, 1870–1914,* New Haven, 1930, pp. 465–66.

92. As in Africa. See Robinson and Gallagher, *Africa and the Victorians,* pp. 463–64.

93. Rhodes was at once "financier and politician, capitalist and statesman, profit-seeker and visionary empire builder." Staley, *War and the Private Investor,* p. 195.

94. Quoted in J. L. Talmon, *The Unique and the Universal: Some Historical Reflections,* New York, 1966, p. 39. A most blatant propagandist for this view was the Scotsman John Adam Cramb (1862–1913), professor of history at London and lecturer to the military, for whom empires were "successive reincarnations of Divine ideas." See his *Germany and England,* London, 1913.

95. Quoted in D. K. Fieldhouse, "The New Imperialism: The Hobson-Lenin Thesis Revised," in Nadel and Curtis, eds., *Imperialism and Colonialism,* p. 94.

96. Quoted in Klaus Schröter, "Chauvinism and Its Tradition: German Writers and the Outbreak of the First World War," *The Germanic Review,* vol. XLIII, 1968, pp. 125–26.

97. The quotation is from a Ferry speech in 1885. Charles Seignobos, *L'Evolution de la 3ᵉ République,* Paris, 1921, p. 113. Ferry might have been willing to give up Alsace-Lorraine and co-operate with Bismarck if France could expand overseas. On Delcassé see Brunschwig, *Mythes et réalités,* p. 179. On Maurras and the "French peace" see his *Kiel et Tanger,* and the discussion in Buthman, *Integral Nationalism,* p. 326.

98. Fay, *Origins of the World War,* vol. I, pp. 242, 288–89. Maurice Barrès, *Scènes et doctrines du nationalisme,* thought the French surrender of Fashoda to the English (1898) a "cruel betrayal of national honor," and he cried, "We cannot succeed overseas without increasing French prestige, and we cannot fail there without greatly lessening our prestige." Quoted in Hayes, *The Historical Evolution of Modern Nationalism,* p. 201. In the United States Preside ᵗ Theodore Roosevelt talked much about "honor." In light of what happened, "national honor" seems an empty, even hypocritical term, but men then believed in it as some still do believe.

99. House of Commons, March 1, 1848, *Hansard,* vol. XCVII (third series), cols. 113–20. See Georg Schwarzenberger, *Power Politics . . . ,* London, 1941, pp. 99–100.

100. There is no one general study of diplomats before 1914 comparable to Gordon Craig and Felix Gilbert, eds., *The Diplomats, 1919–1939,* Princeton, (N.J.), but there are many special studies, and there is no reason to believe those before 1914 differed much from those after.

101. Grey's *Twenty-five Years, 1892–1916,* London, 1926, tells one of the most pathetic stories in diplomatic history, for he realized the consequences of international anarchy and his own failure.

102. The "classic" accounts are those of Albertini, Fay, Langer, and Schmitt,

but see also the later and corrective Fritz Fischer, *Germany's War Aims in the First World War*, New York, 1967 (German edition, 1961) on German war aims.

103. The quoted words are those of Sir Eyre Crowe, a key British Foreign Office expert. Memorandum, January 1, 1907, *British Documents on the Origins of the War*, vol. III, London, 1928, p. 403; for discussion see Schwarzenberger, *Power Politics*, pp. 117–18. Crowe's was a standard explanation. The same idea was repeated everywhere, including German schoolbooks. See Walter Langsam, "Nationalism and History in Prussian Elementary Schools under William II," in Edward Mead Earle, ed., *Nationalism and Internationalism, Essays Inscribed to Carlton J. H. Hayes*, New York, 1950, p. 225.

104. Fay, *Origins of the World War*, vol. I, p. 35.

105. As well as, of course, on its economic productivity and the patriotism of its citizens.

106. The argument over who started the race is pointless, for all nations, large and small, engaged in it and which nation did what first cannot be determined.

107. Quoted in Carlton Hayes, *A Generation of Materialism*, New York, 1941, p. 239.

108. Among the papers of a leading "big navy" advocate in the United States, Admiral Alfred Mahan, is a photostat of an editorial in the *Scientific American*, December 9, 1911: "To place the conclusion concretely and succinctly the question of command of the sea is one of annual increase of the navy. The question is not 'naval' in the restricted sense of the word. It is one of national policy, national security, and national obligation." This accurately expressed the view of Mahan and other influential Americans including Theodore Roosevelt. Mahan Papers, Manuscript Division, Library of Congress, AC5932 add. 4 vol. 2.

109. Estimates drawn from Quincy Wright, *A Study of War*, Chicago, 1942, vol. I, pp. 670–71. See also M. E. Howard, "The Armed Forces," *New Cambridge Modern History*, vol. XI, pp. 204–42; and Admiral G. J. H. Miles and Field Marshal Earl Wavell, "Armed Forces and the Art of War," ibid., vol. XII, pp. 236–76.

110. *Twenty-five Years*, pp. 89–90.

111. A. J. P. Taylor, *Rumours of Wars*, London, 1951, describes some of them in a series of disconnected essays on diplomatic history from the mid-nineteenth century to 1950.

112. But Richard Cobden's *The Three Princes* (1862) demonstrates how English fear of French invasion from 1848 then excited English national feeling.

113. I here quite closely follow the fine study by I. F. Clarke, *Voices Prophesying War, 1763–1984*, London, 1966.

114. I paraphrase Clarke, *Voices*, p. 32, who was describing only the reactions of Englishmen.

115. He was Queen Alexandra's favorite novelist. When the articles were published as a book, Lord Roberts, a leading militarist who desperately

wanted conscription, wrote a laudatory introduction. Roberts had helped Le Queux with his research and been in on the negotiations with Harmsworth.

116. Clarke, *Voices*, p. 148.

117. Harmsworth, Hearst, and Pulitzer have all been the subjects of biographies of varying quality. How the news was made and controlled has often been described, though the relationships between nationalism and the press are yet to be fully studied. A now little remembered path-making study is E. Malcolm Carroll, *French Public Opinion and Foreign Affairs, 1870–1914*, New York, 1931.

118. Nietzsche's mordant comment is relevant. "Whenever in our time a war breaks out, there also breaks out, and especially among the most noble members of the people, a secret desire: they throw themselves with delight against the new dangers of death, because in the sacrifice for fatherland they believe they have found at last the permission they have been seeking. . . . War is for them a short-cut to suicide. It enables them to commit suicide with a good conscience." Quoted in Frederick Schuman, *The Commonwealth of Man*, New York, 1952, pp. 228–29.

119. In 1910 Sir Norman Angell in his influential book, *The Great Illusion*, observed, "A sedentary, urbanized people find the spectacle of war even more attractive than the spectacle of football. Indeed our Press treats it as a sort of glorified football match." But this was before 1914–18.

120. The quoted phrases are from Bernhardi's *Germany and the Next War*, tr. by Allen H. Powles, London, 1914 (originally published, 1912). Similar views were expressed by, among others, Wordsworth, Tennyson, Karl Pearson, Lord Elton, and John Cramb in Britain; Karl von Clausewitz, Heinrich von Treitschke, and Heinrich Class in Germany; Ernest Renan and Maurice Barrès in France; Feodor Dostoyevsky in Russia; and Admirals Luce and Mahan, as well as Theodore Roosevelt, in the United States. See pages 352–53.

121. Memorial Day Speech, Mt. Vernon, Indiana, 1892(?), Manuscript Division, Library of Congress, AC9648 carton 297. Beveridge called the Spanish-American War of 1898 a "national blessing" that God had given to his "chosen people." Letter to John Temple Graves, July 13, 1898, Library of Congress, AC9204 container 266.

122. See the essay "Pathological Nationalism," *In the Margin of History*, London, 1939.

123. Cf. Arno Mayer, "Post War Nationalisms, 1918–1919," *Past and Present*, no. 34, 1966, pp. 114–26.

124. As H. Lauterpacht wrote in 1933, "The sovereign State does not acknowledge a central executive authority above itself; it does not recognize a legislature above itself; it owes no obedience to a judge above itself." *The Function of Law in the International Community*, Oxford, 1933, p. 166.

125. *La Trahison des clercs*, p. 40.

126. Quoted in E. Hanbury Hankin, *Nationalism and the Communal Mind*, London, 1937, p. 129.

Chapter VII

1. I can here but touch upon these important topics. Fundamental historical studies on the relation of transportation and communication to nationalism have not yet been done, perhaps because exact causal relationships are difficult to ascertain.

2. Quoted in George Barany, *Stephen Széchenyi and the Awakening of Hungarian Nationalism, 1791–1841*, Princeton, 1969, p. 268.

3. Quoted in Theodore Hamerow, *Restoration, Revolution, Reaction: Economics and Politics in Germany, 1815–1871*, Princeton, 1958, pp. 254–255.

4. A Belgian economist, Emile de Laveleye (1822–92), made sense when he wrote, "In regions where half animal men are living, let us establish schools, let us construct a railway, and tolerate a printing-press. Twenty years later national feeling will be born. After two generations it will explode if you try to suppress it. In this manner the national question is born out of the very nature of civilization." Quoted in Oszkár Jászi, *The Dissolution of the Habsburg Monarchy*, Chicago, 1929, p. 251.

5. For a good short survey see L. Girard, "Transport," *Cambridge Economic History of Europe*, vol. VI, pt. 1, Cambridge (Eng.), 1965, pp. 212–73; also Herbert Heaton, "Economic Change and Growth," *New Cambridge Modern History, The Zenith of European Power: 1830–1870*, vol. X, pp. 22–48. For the United States see Bureau of Census, *Historical Statistics of the United States: Colonial Times to 1957*, Washington, D.C., 1961. The telegraph statistics are equally enlightening. In 1870 Western Union (the chief company) in the United States had about 4,000 offices and transmitted over 9 million messages; in 1912 it had over 25,000 offices and transmitted over 109 million messages.

6. Girard, "Transport," p. 254.

7. See, for example, Howard Robinson, *The British Post Office*, Princeton, 1948; and Arthur E. Summerfield, *U.S. Mail . . .* , as told to Charles Hurd, New York, 1960.

8. See, for example, John Roach, "Education and the Press," *New Cambridge Modern History, The Zenith of European Power*, vol. X, pp. 120–133.

9. See the introductory essays of F. H. Hinsley and David Thomson to vols. XI and XII of the *New Cambridge Modern History;* and *Historical Statistics of the United States;* as well as *Cambridge Economic History of Europe*, vol. VI, 2 pts., esp. the long essay by David Landes in vol. I, pt. I, revised and published separately as *The Unbound Prometheus*, Cambridge (Eng.), 1969.

10. *The Psychology of Jingoism*, London, 1901, p. 8.

11. But the generalization must not be carried too far. In Australia "the early nationalist outlook grew faster in the bush than in the colonial capitals." Russel Ward, "Social Roots of Australian Nationalism," *Australian Journal of Politics and History*, vol. I, 1956, p. 189. Something, of course, depends on how nationalism is defined. If in terms of opposition to a ruling power,

like that of American colonists to England, then American colonial frontiersmen were nationalists even though they generally paid little attention to their own national government when it was established.

12. See W. O. Henderson, *The Zollverein,* 2nd ed., Cambridge (Eng.), 1959; Frederick Artz, *Reaction and Revolution, 1814–1832,* New York, 1934, pp. 236–37; and P. W. L. Ashley, *Modern Tariff History,* London, 1904, p. 14.

13. Did nationalism promote economic development or economic development nationalism? The answer is both, though Walt Rostow credits "reactive nationalism" with the crucial role in his *Stages of Economic Growth,* Cambridge (Mass.), 1960; and Ernest Gellner, *Thought and Change,* Chicago, 1964, believed the need for growth generated nationalism.

14. But, as Lionel Robbins declared, the English classical economists, whose theory was behind the policy of free trade, seldom went "beyond the test of national advantage as a criterion of policy. . . . It was the consumption [and, I should add, the production as well] of the national economy which they regarded as the end of economic activity." *The Theory of Economic Policy in English Classical Political Economy,* London, 1961. p. 9.

15. See the germinal essay, in which the term "psychic income" is used, of Albert Breton, "The Economics of Nationalism," *Journal of Political Economy,"* vol. LXXII, 1964, pp. 376–86.

16. Or was it economic interests that were to be defended? Near the end of the nineteenth century (the later Marshal) Ferdinand Foch told French military officers at the *Ecole Supérieure de la Guerre,* "If war is still national today, it is for the sake of securing economic benefits and profitable trade agreements." I. F. Clarke, *Voices Prophesying War, 1763–1984,* London, 1966, p. 77.

17. "Der Nationalstaat und die Volkswirtschaftspolitik," in *Gesammelte Politische Schriften,* Munich, 1921.

18. *An Inquiry into the Nature of Peace* . . . , New York, 1919, p. 292.

19. *Socialism National or International,* London, 1942, pp. 57–58.

20. Cf. John A. Moses, "Nationalism and Proletarian Germany—1914," *Australian Journal of Politics and History,* vol. XI, 1965, pp. 57–69, a solid, short interpretation; Carlton Hayes, "Influence of Political Tactics on Socialist Theory in Germany," in Charles Merriam and Harry Elmer Barnes, eds., *A History of Political Theories, Recent Times,* New York, 1924; and William Maehl, "The Triumph of Nationalism in the German Socialist Party on the Eve of the First World War," *Journal of Modern History,* vol. XXIV, 1952.

21. On the French socialists see Harold Weinstein, *Jean Jaurès: A Study of Patriotism in the French Socialist Movement,* New York, 1936; and Harvey Goldberg, *The Life of Jean Jaurès,* Madison (Wis.), 1962. Shepard Clough, *France: A History of National Economics, 1789–1939,* New York, 1939, pp. 222, 453, specifically discusses how Jean Jaurès, the great French socialist, put national interests first. On the British workers see Bernard Semmel, *Imperialism and Social Reform, English Social-Imperial*

Thought 1895–1914, Cambridge (Mass.), 1960, p. 234. Semmel also suggests that in 1914 the proletariats were convinced that the working classes of losing nations would suffer more than those of the victorious.

22. *Manifesto of the Communist Party*, New York, 1938, p. 19. But Marx, it should also be noted, believed the struggle of the proletariat had first to be carried on nationally, that the proletariat must "raise itself to the position of the national class, and must constitute itself the nation."

23. In Czarist Russia and possibly some other nations in 1914, some politicians favored war because it would arouse patriotism and thus prevent social revolution. Sidney B. Fay, *The Origins of the World War*, New York, 1930, vol. II, p. 305.

24. Maurras believed the absence of strikes in the Stinnes, Thyssen, and Krupp industrial companies was owing to the "German national spirit," and for that reason he thought "popular education oriented in the national sense . . . more and more indispensable." William Curt Buthman, *The Rise of Integral Nationalism in France, with Special Reference . . . [to] Charles Maurras*, New York, 1939, p. 328.

25. See Shepard Clough and Charles Cole, *Economic History of Europe*, Boston, 1952, passim, esp. pp. 693–94; and Helen I. Clarke, *Social Legislation*, New York, 1940, pp. 389–93. In the United States the state governments enacted more social legislation than the federal down to the 1930's.

26. See page 239.

27. *Political Myths and Economic Realities*, New York, 1927, p. 217.

28. Two solid older studies are J. T. Delos, *La Nation*, vol. I, *Sociologie de la nation*, Montreal, 1944, esp. pp. 140–53; and Florjan Znaniecki, *Modern Nationalities: A Sociological Study*, Urbana (Ill.), 1952. A major, though not always clear, more recent study is Karl Deutsch, *Nationalism and Social Communication: An Inquiry into the Foundations of Nationality*, New York, 1953; 2nd ed., Cambridge (Mass.), 1966.

29. Among the better-known ones were Margaret Mead (who apparently is willing to comment on any subject), Geoffrey Gorer, Ruth Benedict, Weston La Barre, and Erik Erikson; they gave to infant discipline the importance earlier writers sometimes gave to race and geography. Margaret Mead summarized part of the argument in "The Study of National Character," in Daniel Lerner et al., eds., *The Policy Sciences . . .* , Stanford (Calif.), 1951, pp. 70–85. There are many adverse critiques. See page 337.

30. Gerald Pearson, "Some Early Factors in the Formation of Personalities," *American Journal of Orthopsychiatry*, vol. I, 1931, p. 290. See also H. Meltzer, "Hostility and Tolerance in Children's Nationality and Race Attitudes," ibid., vol. XI, 1941, pp. 662–76.

31. J. Piaget and Anne-Marie Weil, "The Development in Children of the Idea of the Homeland and of Relations with Other Countries," *International Social Science Bulletin*, vol. III, 1951, p. 561; and Piaget's *Judgment and Reasoning in the Child*, London, 1928, pp. 119–34. Jerome Bruner gives a glowing estimate of Piaget's work in the *New York Times Book Review*, February 11, 1968, p. 6. Robert Hess and Judith Torney,

in their *The Development of Political Attitudes in Children,* Chicago, 1967, devote a few pages to children's "growth of attachment to the nation," but chiefly repeat what a few elementary school children said and do not show the origin or growth of the attachment. A number of other students have done research on related questions with more conclusive results. See, for example, A. F. Davies, "The Child's Discovery of Nationality," *Australian and New Zealand Journal of Sociology,* vol. 4, 1968, pp. 107–25, which admirably sums up several studies; Eugene Hartley, Max Rosenbaum, and Shepard Schwartz, "Children's Use of Ethnic Frames of Reference . . . ," *Journal of Psychology,* vol. 26, 1948, pp. 367–86; E. L. Horowitz, "Some Aspects of Development of Patriotism in Children," *Sociometry,* vol. III, 1940, pp. 329–41; Gustav Jahoda, "Development of Scottish Children's Ideas and Attitudes About Other Countries," *Journal of Social Psychology,* vol. 58, 1962, pp. 91–108; Edwin D. Lawson, "Development of Patriotism in Children—A Second Look," *Journal of Psychology,* vol. 55, 1963, pp. 279–86; and Wallace Lambert and Otto Klineberg, "A Pilot Study of the Origin and Development of National Stereotypes," *International Social Science Journal,* vol. 11, 1959, pp. 221–38. The last shows a steady development in consciousness of nationality from the age of six to fourteen among Canadian, English, Belgian, and Dutch children. But see their conclusions in *Children's Views of Foreign Peoples,* New York, 1967, pp. 199–228.

32. Paraphrased from a Clemenceau speech in 1907, quoted in Alexandre Choulguine, "Les Origines de l'esprit national moderne et Jean-Jacques Rousseau," *Annales de la Société Jean-Jacques Rousseau,* vol. XXVI, 1937, p. 27.

33. What is "traditionally learned and internalized in infancy and early childhood tends to be most resistant to change." Edward Bruner, "Cultural Transmission and Cultural Change," *Journal of Anthropology,* vol. XII, 1956, pp. 191–97. See also Floyd Allport, "The Psychology of Nationalism," *Harper's Magazine,* vol. CLV, 1927, p. 294. Bertram Schaffner used this thesis in *Fatherland: A Study of Authoritarianism in the German Family,* New York, 1945.

34. Hugh Miller, a well-known Scot, "first became thoroughly a Scot" when he was about ten (1812 or 1813) as he read Blind Harry's "Wallace" and "was intoxicated with the fiery narratives of the blind minstrel . . . ." H. J. Hanham, *Scottish Nationalism,* Cambridge (Mass.), 1969, pp. 64–65. This kind of experience was not infrequent. When a well-known American historian, Roy Nichols, was a young child in the early twentieth century, he read two picture books in his home called *Noble Lives and Brave Deeds* and *The History of the United States Told in One Syllable Words.* "In one was a representation of Joan of Arc clad in armor with blood running from an arrow wound in her leg. The other depicted brown Indians, Redcoats of the Revolution, and blue-uniformed Union soldiers and the guns of the *Constitution* and the *Guerrière* spitting scarlet fire." *A Pilgrim's Progress,* New York, 1968, p. 6.

35. On education and nationalism during the nineteenth and early twentieth

centuries there are many studies. Among those used here are Walter Langsam, "Nationalism and History in the Prussian Elementary Schools under William II," in Edward Mead Earle, ed., *Nationalism and Internationalism, Essays Inscribed to Carlton J. H. Hayes*, New York, 1950; Charles Merriam, *The Making of Citizens*, Chicago, 1931 (the best summary of early research); Ruth Miller, "Nationalism in Elementary Schoolbooks Used in the United States from 1776 to 1885" (a good Ph.D. dissertation), Columbia University, 1952, typescript; Bessie Pierce, *Civic Attitudes in American School Textbooks*, Chicago, 1930 (the single best study); Edward H. Reisner, *Nationalism and Education Since 1789: A Social and Political History of Modern Education*, New York, 1922 (a good survey); Jonathan Scott, *Patriots in the Making: What America Can Learn from France and Germany*, New York, 1916 (in Scott's title the word "should" should have been used instead of "can," but the book contains valuable information); and Mark Starr, *Lies and Hate in Education*, London, 1929. Later studies are cited in chapter VIII, note 46.

36. The ardent German nationalist Professor Treitschke was a student of the ardent German nationalist Arndt and a teacher of the ardent German nationalists Tirpitz and Heinrich Class.

37. Two good introductory surveys of education in the nineteenth century that pay little attention to its "civic" aspects are Roach, "Education and the Press," pp. 104-21; and A. Victor Murray, "Education," *New Cambridge Modern History, Material Problems and World-Wide Problems: 1870-98*, vol. XI, pp. 177-203.

38. Speech, "La Loi sur la liberté d'enseignement supérieur," in *Discours et opinions de Jules Ferry*, ed. by Paul Robiquet, Paris, 1895, vol. III, p. 66. For discussion of Ferry and education see Evelyn Acomb, *The French Laic Laws (1879-1889)*, New York, 1941.

39. See John Wuorinen, "Scandinavia and National Consciousness," in Earle, ed., *Nationalism and Internationalism*, pp. 469-70; and Erica Simon, *Réveil national et culture populaire en Scandinavie: La Genèse de la Højskole Nordique (1844-1878)*, Paris, 1960, p. xxi, passim.

40. Langsam, "Nationalism and History," p. 242. Earlier in the Russia of Nicholas I the stress was on "official nationality," on "orthodoxy, autocracy, and nationality." Nicholas V. Riasanovsky, *Nicholas I and Official Nationality in Russia, 1825-1855*, Berkeley, 1959, p. 74.

41. Speech at De Paw [sic] College, 1903, printed, in Beveridge Papers, Manuscript Division, Library of Congress.

42. Quoted in Arthur Whitaker, *Nationalism in Latin America, Past and Present*, Gainesville (Fla.), 1962, p. 41, from Rojas' *La restauracion nacionalista*. On the beginnings of similar views in Cuba and Mexico see Leopoldo Zea, *The Latin-American Mind*, tr. by Abbott and Dunham, Norman (Okla.), 1963, p. 111; and Frederick Turner, *The Dynamic of Mexican Nationalism*, Chapel Hill, (N.C.), 1968, p. 93.

43. In 1883 Paul Bert, patriotic Minister of Education under Gambetta in France, wrote a book called *De l'éducation civique*.

44. *Political and Literary Essays*, London, 1916, p. 156.

45. *The American Mind: An Interpretation of American Thought and Character Since the 1880's*, New Haven, 1950, pp. 38–39.

46. Miller, "Nationalism in Elementary Schoolbooks," pp. 394, 401; Pierce, *Civic Attitudes*, pp. 125–29.

47. Quoted in Jean Lestocquoy, *Histoire du patriotisme en France des origines à nos jours*, Paris, 1968, p. 2. For excerpts from French elementary textbooks see Raoul Girardet, ed., *Le Nationalisme français 1871–1914*, Paris, 1966, pp. 70–84.

48. Reisner, *Nationalism and Education*, pp. 88–90. The sad story of the "Last Lesson" in French in Alsace in 1871 is too well known to repeat.

49. From Gabriel Compayré, *Eléments d'instruction morale et civique*, 112 editions before World War I; see Scott, *Patriots in the Making*, p. 31.

50. In Chicago in 1900 the Board of Education, on the initiative of John T. Keating, president of the Ancient Order of Hiberians, threw out a book that spoke of England as the "mother country" because "the United States is the only country." Beveridge Papers, Manuscript Division, Library of Congress. The story was in the *Chicago Times Herald*, Jan. 5, 1900. Twenty-seven years later a Chicago mayor, Bill Thompson, won national acclaim from many and some adverse comment from intellectuals by "twisting the Lion's tail" and waging war against George III (king, 1760–1820).

51. Scott, *Patriots in the Making*, p. 41, quoting Aulard and Bayet, *Morale et instruction civique*, pt. I, p. 51.

52. The magazine *Youth's Companion* originated this pledge in 1892 as part of a publicity campaign. It was first publicly given during a National Public School celebration, October 21, 1892, at the opening of the Columbian Exposition (world's fair) in Chicago and then, according to a letter of publisher R. P. Joy of *Youth's Companion* to Professor Edward Mead Earle, June 29, 1925 (copy in my possession), was repeated by 12 million schoolchildren. There is dispute over the authorship, but the pledge was likely written by a Francis Bellamy in the *Youth's Companion* office in two hours. *Youth's Companion*, vol. LXV, 1892, carries self-congratulatory stories May 19, p. 256; August 12, p. 412; September 8, pp. 446–47; and November 17, p. 608. Cf. Harold Helfer, "How the Pledge of Allegiance Came to be Written," *American Legion Magazine*, vol. LIX, 1955, pp. 14–15, 68–70. More modestly in Britain it was claimed that only 500,000 children participated in Empire Day in 1928. Starr, *Lies and Hate in Education*, p. 67. The legal aspects of the pledge are thoroughly examined by David Manwaring, *Render unto Caesar, the Flag Salute Controversy*, Chicago, 1962.

53. There were, of course, variations. School attendance was low in rural Spain and for black children in the United States, especially in the South.

54. *Historical Statistics of the United States*, pp. 207, 214. The rate of growth of school attendance increased much faster than the population and hence the percentage of children in school increased.

55. Thomas N. Brown, "Nationalism and the Irish Peasant," *Review of Politics*, vol. XV, 1953, p. 420.

56. Lucy M. Salmon, "Study of History Below the Secondary School," app. II of "The Study of History in the Schools," *Annual Report of the American Historical Association*, Washington, D.C., 1898, p. 512 n., but see Charles Langlois and Charles Seignobos, *Introduction to the Study of History*, tr. by G. G. Perry, London, p. 331 n., whom Miss Salmon cited but who argued for objectivity.

57. *Civic Attitudes*, pp. 125–29. An observation of H. G. Wells, the British novelist and internationalist, seems supported by the facts: "We have all been so taught and trained to patriotic attitudes . . . [at] home, at school, in book, drama, in the common idioms of thought, that it is only by a considerable intellectual effort that any of us can liberate ourselves. . . . " *The Common Sense of World Peace*, London, 1929, p. 29.

58. See pages 334–35.

59. A fine analysis (little known in the United States) of historical scholarship in the nineteenth century is to be found in George Gusdorf, *Introduction aux sciences humaines*, Paris, 1960, pp. 408–24.

60. *English Historical Review*, vol. I, no. I, 1886, pp. 9–10. Acton, the first editor of the *EHR*, was writing its prospectus.

61. As a few Italian and French historians had earlier.

62. The final report of the committee is in the Admiral Mahan Papers, Manuscript Division, Library of Congress, AC5932 box 6, and a printed copy in box 18. The committee recommended the establishment of the Commission on National Historical Publications, finally created in the 1930's but not really active until the 1950's.

63. To his own question "Must History Stay Nationalist?" an informed English historian, David Thomson, has recently given a reluctant affirmative, because the methods, concepts, and styles of studying history are rooted in the community's culture and because the national community is the "most intense and self-conscious in the modern world." *Encounter*, vol. XXX, 1968, pp. 22–28.

64. Ernst Posner has done as yet unpublished work on the national archival establishments of many nations.

65. President Harry Truman told this author that he learned his history from Ridpath.

66. Louis Halphen, *L'Histoire en France depuis cent ans*, Paris, 1914, is still a good account. Bainville's concise *History of France*, published in 1924, went through three hundred editions, but likely Michelet's much earlier multivolumed republican *History of France* was the most popular.

67. On his tombstone is the epitaph: "He made it the high purpose of a life/ Which nearly spanned a century/To trace the origin of his country/To show her part in the advancement of man/And from the rare resources/ Of his genius, his learning, and his labor/To ennoble the story of her birth."

68. I have drawn upon many historiographical volumes, including those of Thompson and Gooch on European history and those of Higham, Kraus, and Wish in American history, as well as my own reading of the historians. See the short bibliographies in Boyd C. Shafer et al., *Historical Study in*

the West, New York, 1968, pp. 27–29, 71, 170–71, 225–228. An old but good survey of nationalist historians is H. Morse Stephens, "Nationality and History," *American Historical Review,* vol. XXI, 1916, pp. 225–36, which refers to his own earlier 1887 essay.

69. The German historians were quite self-conscious and left many accounts of their work and activities that I have only sampled. There is a thoughtful chapter in Louis Snyder, *German Nationalism: The Tragedy of a People,* Harrisburg (Pa.), 1952. On Treitschke see Andreas Dorpalen's excellent *Heinrich von Treitschke,* New Haven, 1957. A good recent introduction to the whole subject of German nineteenth-century historiography is Georg Iggers, *The German Conception of History: The National Tradition of Historical Thought from Herder to the Present,* Middletown (Conn.), 1968, but Iggers does not pay much attention to nationalism as such. A recent brief account is Wolfgang Mommsen, "Historical Study in Western Germany," in Shafer et al., *Historical Study in the West,* pp. 75–128.

70. G. P. Gooch, *History and Historians in the Nineteenth Century,* Boston, 1959, pp. 400–07; and J. P. T. Bury, "Nationalities and Nationalism," *New Cambridge Modern History,* vol. X, p. 225.

71. It would be possible to make a long list of the historians who helped awaken nationalist consciousness, such as Palacký, who wrote a *History of the Czech Nation* in five volumes (1836–67) and has been called the "Father of the [Czech] Nation." For other examples see Peter Sugar and Ivo Lederer, eds., *Nationalism in Eastern Europe,* Seattle, 1969, passim; the first chapters of the volumes of John A. Armstrong and John S. Reshetar on Ukrainian nationalism; and Vincent Trumpa, "Simonas Daukantas, Historian and Pioneer of Lithuanian National Rebirth," *Lituanus,* vol. II, 1965, pp. 5–17.

72. On the influence of these in the Germanies see R. Hinton Thomas, *Liberalism, Nationalism and the German Intellectuals* (*1822–1847*). . . , Cambridge (Eng.), 1951, pp. 13 ff.

73. On those, for example, in the United States, see Walter Whitehill, *Independent Historical Societies* . . . , Boston, 1962; and David Van Tassel, *Recording America's Past* . . . *1607–1884,* Chicago, 1960.

74. Monod was summing up his "Du progrès des études historiques en France depuis le XVIᵉ siècle," p. 38, the first article in the *Revue Historique* and its prospectus.

75. *Lettres sur l'histoire de France pour servir d'introduction à l'étude de cette histoire,* 5th ed., Paris, 1836, preface, p. 14.

76. As a German contemporary historian, Dietrich Schäfer, observed, "In him [Treitschke] German youth saw the embodiment of its ideals; he was the inspired and inspiring prophet of German unity, his clear and firm political opinions being its infallible guide. His lectures were by far the best attended." *Mein Leben,* Berlin, 1926, pp. 63–64.

77. Ramsey Muir, *Nationalism and Internationalism: The Culmination of Modern History,* London, 1917, pp. 43, 48. The motto of Jonas Basanávicus, peasant-born editor of the Lithuanian *Ausra* (*Awakening,* 1883–

1886), was *Homines historiarum ignari semper sunt pueri* ("A people who do not know their history always remain children").

78. Brown, "Nationalism and the Irish Peasant," p. 435. Sir Charles Gavan Duffy in 1881 claimed, "Irishmen had [before] learned the history of Ireland from a source [English] where it was deliberately falsified." *Young Ireland, A Fragment of Irish History, 1840–1850*, New York, 1881, p. 155.

79. Fustel de Coulanges, himself a French patriot, believed the most significant cause of error in historical study was patriotism. History he thought a science and patriotism a virtue, and the two should not be confused.

80. At the risk of repetition, it must again be said that the variations were many. Americans may have felt the need for history all the more because their history as a nation began only in 1776, or at least this was the view of the well-known George Templeton Strong in his *Diary*, ed. by Allan Nevins and Milton Thomas, New York, 1952, vol. II, pp. 196–97. The Slovaks had little history of their own and their "awakening" was late, while Hungarian nationalists mystically looked back to Hungary's medieval greatness.

81. Quoted in E. Malcolm Carroll, *French Public Opinion and Foreign Affairs, 1870–1914*, New York, 1931, p. 253.

82. Who in 1913 dared examine the motives of the "founders" of the Constitution in *An Economic Interpretation of the Constitution of the United States*.

83. Committee on Textbooks, New England History Teachers' Association, *Publications*, no. 3, report of October 15, 1898, p. 5; and quoted in Frederick Allis, "The Handling of Controversial Material in High School Textbooks in American History," *Massachusetts Historical Society, Proceedings*, vol. 72, 1957–60, pp. 325–26.

84. See Chapter VI, note 31. See also Dixon Wecter, *The Hero in America . . .* , New York, 1941. Thomas Carlyle, of course, led the way. But see the articles by Otto Klineberg and Gilbert Gadoffre on national stereotypes, *International Social Science Bulletin*, vol. III, 1951, pp. 505–14, 579–87.

85. *Regards sur le monde actuel*, Paris, 1931, p. 63.

86. "Nationality and History," p. 236.

87. Joshua Fishman et al., *Language Loyalty in the United States: The Maintenance and Perpetuation of Non-English Mother Tongues by American Ethnic and Religious Groups*, The Hague, 1966, introduction.

88. Otto Jespersen, *Mankind, Nation and Individual from a Linguistic Point of View*, Oslo, 1925, p. 23.

89. Three old basic studies are Carl D. Buck, "Language and the Sentiment of Nationality," *American Political Science Review*, vol. X, 1916, pp. 44–69; Karl Deutsch, "The Trend of European Nationalism—The Language Aspect," *American Political Science Review*, vol. XXXVI, 1942, pp. 533–41; and Stanley Rundle, *Language as a Social and Economic Factor in Europe*, London, 1946.

90. Generally there has been the "greatest uniformity where markedly centralized government." Jespersen, *Mankind*, p. 59.

91. Quoted by Barany, *Stephen Széchenyi*, p. 297. The original is in italics.

92. Quoted in Harry Warfel, *Noah Webster, Schoolmaster to America*, New York, 1936, pp. 59–60. See also Howard Mumford Jones, *O Strange New World. American Culture: The Formative Years*, New York, 1964, pp. 322–23.

93. Ivo Lederer, "Nationalism and the Yugoslavs," in Sugar and Lederer, eds., *Nationalism in Eastern Europe*, pp. 414–15; and Hans Kohn, *The Idea of Nationalism: A Study of Its Origins and Background*, New York, 1944, pp. 550–51.

94. Jan Havránek, "The Nationality Problem in the Habsburg Empire: The Czechs," mimeographed paper, conference at University of Indiana, April 1966, p. 17, later published in the *Austrian Yearbook*.

95. Andreas Elviken, "Genesis of Norwegian Nationalism," *Journal of Modern History*, vol. III, 1931, pp. 389–90. See also Oscar Falnes, *National Romanticism in Norway*, New York, 1933, chaps. XII–XVI.

96. The accounts are too numerous to list but see, for example, R. J. Loftus, *Nationalism in Modern Irish Poetry*, Madison (Wis.), 1964; Desmond Williams, ed., *The Irish Struggle, 1916–1926*, Toronto, 1966; Reginald Coupland, *Welsh and Scottish Nationalism*, London, 1954; Owen Dudley Edwards et al., *Celtic Nationalism*, New York, 1968; John H. Wuorinen, *Nationalism in Modern Finland*, New York, 1931; Alfred E. Senn, *The Emergence of Modern Lithuania*, New York, 1959; and Stavro Skendi, *The Albanian National Awakening*, Princeton, 1967.

97. For graphic examples see Walter Kolarz, *Myths and Realities in Eastern Europe*, London, 1946, pp. 16 ff.

98. See Fishman et al., *Language Loyalty*, front pages, quoting E. R. Leach, *Political Systems of Highland Burma*.

99. Brian O'Cuiv, "Education and Language," in Williams, ed., *The Irish Struggle*, pp. 158–59. In 1891 only eight out of every thousand Irishmen could not speak English and eighty-five per cent could not speak Irish.

100. Trumpa, "Simonas Daukantas," p. 15.

101. Senn, *The Emergence of Modern Lithuania*, p. 7.

102. C. Grant Robertson, *Bismarck*, New York, 1919, p. 16.

103. Quoted in Artz, *Reaction and Revolution*, p. 107. There is an English translation of his poems by G. L. Bickersteth, 1923. For other Italian examples see Edmund G. Gardner, *The National Idea in Italian Literature*, Manchester (Eng.), 1921.

104. Simon, *Réveil national*, pp. 148–51. According to H. J. Hanham, Sir Walter Scott created a "new vision of Scotland, the Scotland of the modern tourist industry, Scottish story, Scottish dress, Scottish castles, Scottish scenery. . . ." *Scottish Nationalism*, p. 70.

105. Zea, *The Latin-American Mind*, p. 99. An early champion of national literature in Mexico was Ignacio M. Altamirano, who "consciously developed national sentiment on the scenes he chose to depict." Turner, *The Dynamic of Mexican Nationalism*, pp. 258–59.

106. See the discussion in Earl L. Bradsher, "The Rise of Nationalism in Ameri-

can Literature," in Nathaniel Caffee and Thomas A. Kirby, eds., *Studies for William Alexander Read*, Baton Rouge (La.), 1940, p. 274.

107. For the beginning of the agitation see Charles Cole, "The Beginnings of Literary Nationalism in America, 1775–1800," Ph.D. dissertation, George Washington University, 1939, typescript; James Coberly, "The Growth of Nationalism in American Literature, 1800–1815," Ph.D. dissertation, George Washington University, 1949, typescript; and Robert Bolwell, "Concerning the Study of Nationalism in American Literature," *American Literature*, vol. X, 1939, pp. 405–16.

108. In a letter to Edward Dowden, 1872, in Bliss Perry, *Walt Whitman, His Life and Work*, Boston, 1906, pp. 200–01. The whole of *Democratic Vistas* is an appeal for a great American democratic culture.

109. Donald Davie, "The Young Yeats," in Conor Cruise O'Brien, ed., *The Shaping of Modern Ireland*, Toronto, 1960, p. 145.

110. Loftus, *Nationalism in Modern Irish Poetry*, p. 6.

111. Quoted in Senn, *The Emergence of Modern Lithuania*, p. 7.

112. A thorough analysis of children's literature and nationalism is much needed. J. C. Crandall, "Patriotism and Humanitarian Reform in Children's Literature, 1825–1860," *American Quarterly*, vol. XXI, 1969, pp. 3–22, reveals how children's literature reinforced the "established" national order but stresses the second subject in his title more than the first. See also Helen Martin, "Nationalism in Children's Literature," *Library Quarterly*, vol. VI, 1936, pp. 405–16, which is only an introduction to the subject.

113. Among the many surveys and anthologies of patriotic writings are John Drinkwater, *Patriotism in Literature*, London, 1924; Gardner, *The National Idea in Italian Literature;* Girardet, ed., *Le Nationalisme français;* Ch. Lenient, *La poésie patriotique en France au moyen âge. La poésie patriotique en France, XVIe et XVIIe siècles. La poésie patriotique en France dans les temps modernes*, 3 vols., Paris, 1891–94; Frederick Page, ed., *An Anthology of Patriotic Prose*, London, 1915; David and Ruth Stevens, eds., *American Patriotic Prose and Verse*, Chicago, 1918; H. F. Stewart and Paul Desjardins, eds., *French Patriotism in the Nineteenth Century (1814–1833)*, Cambridge (Eng.), 1923; and Esmé Wingfield-Stratford, *The History of English Patriotism*, 2 vols., London, 1913.

114. Examples are many and can be drawn from the history of any western country. Széchenyi proposed the *Magyar Tudós Társaság* (the Hungarian Academy of Sciences, formed in 1827) "to promote sciences and arts in the language of the country . . . to strengthen the national spirit." Francis S. Wagner, "Széchenyi and the Nationality Problem in the Habsburg Empire," *Journal of Central European Affairs*, vol. XX, 1960, pp. 293–94. In 1867 Slovaks founded the *Slovenská Matica* to foster the development, culture, and material welfare of the nation. Václav Beneš, "The Slovaks in the Habsburg Empire," mimeographed paper, conference at University of Indiana, April 1966, p. 42. From 1839 there were occasional national meetings of Italian scientists and finally in 1907 a *Società*

Italiana per il progresso della scienze. Thomas, *Liberalism, Nationalism and the German Intellectuals*, p. 44.

115. Stanley B. Kimball, *Czech Nationalism: A Study of the National Theater Movement, 1845–1883,* Urbana (Ill.), 1964, p. ix, passim. See also Havránek, "The Nationality Problem in the Habsburg Empire," for other similar illustrations of rising Czech national consciousness.

116. Kimball, *Czech Nationalism*, pp. 80 ff.

117. See Bishop Fan S. Noli, *Beethoven and the French Revolution*, New York, 1947.

118. Wagner wrote, "We shall befruit [*sic*] a fresh young Germany. . . . We shall do things *Germanly* and grandly. . . ." *Richard Wagner's Prose Works,* tr. by William Ellis, London, 1892–99, vol. IV, p. 140. Sydney Finkelstein remarked that Wagner "had to an extraordinary degree the national faculty for duping himself with his own words. . . ." *Composer and Nation: Folk Heritage of Music,* New York, 1960, p. 139.

119. Quoted in *Minneapolis Symphony Program*, March 18, 1966, p. 638.

120. See the two perceptive articles by Gerald Larner, "Degrees of Patriotism" and "Disillusion," *Manchester Guardian Weekly,* March 19 and 26, 1964.

121. Among the studies touching on music and nationalism on which I have drawn are Jacques Barzun, *Berlioz and the Romantic Century,* vol. I, Boston, 1950, and *Darwin, Marx, Wagner, Critique of a Heritage,* Boston, 1941; Coupland, *Welsh and Scottish Nationalism* (for the Welsh *Eisteddfod*), pp. 344 ff.; Alfred Einstein, *Music in the Romantic Era,* New York, 1947; Carl Engel, *An Introduction to the Study of National Music,* London, 1866 (earliest study known to me); Richard Gorer, "Music and Nationalism," *Music Review,* August 1963, pp. 218–22; Paul Lang, *Music in Western Civilization,* New York, 1941; and Ralph Vaughan, *National Music,* New York, 1935.

122. See pages 135–36.

123. A convenient compendium is Martin Shaw and Henry Coleman, eds., *National Anthems of the World,* 2nd rev. ed., London, 1963.

124. A serious scholarly study of national holidays is much needed; most of the studies are either patriotic tracts or superficial. There are a couple of good essays on American patriotic holidays in Trevor Dupuy, ed., *Holidays,* New York, 1965; and a good critical essay on the Australian, K. S. Inglis, "Australia Day," *Historical Studies,* vol. 13, 1967, pp. 20–41. For the first celebration (1790) of July 14 in France see Boyd C. Shafer, "When Patriotism Became Popular," *Historian,* vol. V, 1943, pp. 77–96.

125. In the United States the President and the Congress designate holidays only for the District of Columbia and for federal employees, the states having jurisdiction over holidays. Pennsylvania, the first state to do so, made July 4 a legal holiday in 1783, though the day may have been celebrated in Charleston in 1778 and was in Boston in 1783. Other patriotic federal legal holidays are Washington's Birthday (February 22), Memorial or Decoration Day (May 30), and Veterans' Day (November 11).

126. For the Serbs before the War of 1914 the date of the Turkish defeat of the Serbs, June 28, 1389, was a day of national mourning.

127. David Holbrook, DAR, *Journal of Proceedings of the First National Patriotic Instructors' Institute*, in Minnesota Historical Society library.

128. Hanham, *Scottish Nationalism*, p. 70.

129. For an imaginative article on African and on dress in general see Ali Mazrui, "The Robes of Rebellion: Sex, Dress, and Politics in Africa," *Encounter*, vol. XXXIV, 1970, pp. 19–30.

130. Eugen Weber, "Pierre de Coubertin and the Introduction of Organized Sports in France," AHA paper, typescript, Washington, D.C., December, 1969. De Coubertin was responsible for the revival of the Olympic games held in Athens, 1896. On the Olympic games of 1936 see Richard D. Mandell, *The Nazi Olympics*, New York, 1971.

131. Among interesting studies of later stereotypes are George Coelho, *Changing Images of America: A Study of Indian Students' Perceptions*, Glencoe (Ill.), 1958; Gilbert Gadoffre, "French National Images and the Problem of National Stereotypes," *International Social Science Bulletin*, vol. III, 1951, p. 584; and A. N. J. den Hollander, "As Others See Us: A Preliminary Inquiry into Group Images," *Synthese*, vol. VI, 1948, pp. 214–37.

132. Said Paul Deschanel, president of the French Chamber of Deputies, and his was a typical eulogy of a national flag, "This flag carries in its folds, with the genius of France and the destiny of the Republic, fifteen centuries of heroism, power and glory. . . ." Quoted in Georges Goyau, *L'Idée de patrie et l'humanitarisme: Essai d'histoire française, 1866–1901*, Paris, 1913, p. xi. Generally, accounts of the flags are patriotic exhortations. One that is better history than most is Milo Quaife, *The Flag of the United States*, New York, 1942.

133. *Essays and Treatises*, vol. I, London, 1770, p. 251.

134. The quoted words are from the fine paper of Morton Grodzins, "The Basis of National Loyalty," *Bulletin of Atomic Scientists*, vol. VII, 1951, p. 360. See also Harold Guetzkow, *Multiple Loyalties*, Princeton, 1955, p. 29; and John H. Schaar, *Loyalty in America*, Berkeley, 1957.

135. All membership figures of these organizations are suspect. But see, with its excellent notes, John A. Rath, "The 'Carbonari': Their Origins, Initiation Rites, and Aims," *American Historical Review*, vol. 69, 1964, p. 370; and Artz, *Reaction and Revolution*, p. 281.

136. The materials on Young Ireland would fill a small library. But see William Langer, *Political and Social Upheaval, 1832–1852*, New York, 1969, pp. 239–45; Sir Charles Gavan Duffy (a participant), *Young Ireland;* and the several fine studies of Irish nationalism by Thomas Brown, especially, "Nationalism and the Irish Peasant."

137. Rath, "The 'Carbonari.' "

138. J. L. Comstock, *History of the Greek Revolution*, New York, 1828, p. 143 n.

139. Quoted in J. H. Rose, *Nationality in Modern History*, New York, 1916, pp. 81–82. The oaths of later nationalist organizations to throw off foreign

rule, such as that of the Serbian Union or Death ("The Black Hand"), of which Princip, the assassin of the Austrian Archduke Francis Ferdinand, was a member, were as fervent; the initiates of the Serbian society swore, "before God, by the blood of my ancestors, on my honor and on my life . . . to be faithful to . . . this organization and . . . be ready to make any sacrifice for it." Joachim Remak, *Sarajevo*, New York, 1959, p. 59.

140. Among the many serious studies see Ernst Curtius, *Maurice Barrès und die geistigen Grundlagen des französischen Nationalismus*, Bonn, 1921; Charles Le Bâtonnier Chenu, *La Ligue des patriotes*, Paris, 1916; Carlton Hayes, *France: A Nation of Patriots*, New York, 1930; Pierre Nora, "Les deux apogées de l'Action Française," *Annales: Economies, Sociétés, Civilisations*, vol. XIX, 1964, pp. 127–41; Eugen Weber, *Action Française: Royalism and Reaction in Twentieth Century France*, Stanford (Calif.), 1962; Avaline Folsom, *The Royal Empire Society: Formative Years*, London, 1933; R. W. Tims, *Germanizing the Prussian Poles, the H-K-T Society of the Eastern Marches, 1894–1914*, New York, 1941; Mildred S. Wertheimer, *The Pan-German League 1890–1914*, New York, 1924; Wallace Davies, *Patriotism on Parade: The Story of Veterans' and Hereditary Organizations in America, 1783–1900*, Cambridge (Mass.), 1956; Mary Dearing, *Veterans in Politics: The Story of the G.A.R.*, Baton Rouge (La.), 1952; Rodney G. Minott, *Peerless Patriots: The Organized Veterans and the Spirit of Americanism*, Washington, D.C., 1963; and Bessie Pierce, *Citizens' Organizations and the Civic Training of Youth*, New York, 1933.

141. The occupations of members of the Pan-German League in 1901 were:

Academics	5,899
Businessmen	5,288
Liberal professions, teachers, artists, officials	4,022
Industrial and land workers	2,859
Farmers	444
Miscellaneous	1,284

Wertheimer, *Pan-German League*, pp. 65, 73. In the *Action Française* the proportion of nobles—one-fifth—among the leaders was high. Weber, *Action Française*, p. 267.

142. On the German see Wertheimer, *Pan-German League*, pp. 237–39; on those in the United States, Davies, *Patriotism on Parade*.

143. Proud accounts by the organization are to be found in *U.S. Senate Documents*, as *Senate Document 164*, 55 Cong. 3rd Sess., 1899; in the *American Monthly Magazine* beginning in 1892; and in Mary S. Lockwood and W. H. Regan (Emily Lee Sherwood), *Story of the Records*, Washington, D.C., 1906.

144. From their original constitution and publicity literature.

145. This analysis in part comes from the English sociologist, Ernest Gellner, in his volume *Thought and Change*, p. 157. Gellner, p. 152, observed, "Men do not in general become nationalists from sentiment or sentimentality, atavistic or not, well-based or myth-founded: they become nationalist through genuine, objective, practical necessity."

146. But this did not mean they liked their government. See Laurence Wylie, *Village in the Vauclause*, 2nd ed., Cambridge (Mass.), 1964, pp. 206–12; and E. F. Durbin and John Bowlby, *Personal Aggressiveness and War*, New York, 1939, pp. 37–39.

147. As an economist, E. B. Ayal, put it, nationalism provided the "most comprehensive and down-to-earth answer to the question, what, or who, am I?" "Nationalist Ideology and Economic Development," *Human Organization*, vol. 25, 1966, p. 232.

148. A. A. Roback, *Dictionary of International Slurs (Ethnophaulisms)*, Cambridge (Mass.), 1944, lists several thousand national and ethnic slurs. Roback, p. 11, remarked that if he were asked why he collected slurs rather than compliments, he would reply, "There are practically none of the latter." See also Eric Partridge, *Words! Words! Words!*, London, 1933, especially the chapter "Offensive Nationality."

149. Quoted in Hans Kohn, *Prelude to Nation-States: The French and German Experience, 1789–1815*, Princeton, 1967, p. 261.

150. Page, ed., *An Anthology of Patriotic Prose*, p. 158. But much study is needed. For some insights see Grodzins, "The Basis of National Loyalty," p. 357; Guetzkow, *Multiple Loyalties*, pp. 20–21; and Daniel Katz, "The Psychology of Nationalism," in *Fields of Psychology*, ed. by J. P. Guilford, New York, 1940, p. 164.

151. See pages 314–16.

152. This was true in degree even, say, of Germans, whose "essential aspiration," as Golo Mann said, may have been to secure "a national free state or constitutional state in one form or another." See Geoffrey Barraclough, "German Unification," *Historical Studies*, vol. IV, 1963, p. 71.

153. *Political Messianism, the Romantic Phase*, New York, 1961, pp. 513–14, passim.

154. Viscount James Bryce, "The Principle of Nationality and Its Applications," in *Essays and Addresses in War Time*, New York, 1918, p. 141.

155. As Claude Digeon, a French scholar, remarked, writers and scholars systematized this belief, "réclament la fin de l'asservissement de leur peuple, combattent des institutions socials archaïques et promettent un avenir lumineux à la future communauté nationale," but Digeon believed that French nationalism after 1870 was basically pessimistic and reactionary. "Origines et signification du nationalisme littéraire en France (1870–1914)," *Revue des travaux de l'Académie des Sciences Morales et Politiques*, vol. 115, 1962, p. 150.

156. The nationalist poets expressed this most vividly. Paul Déroulède sang, "Mon premier frère est le frère français."

157. Mazzini's writings all exude this personal involvement, this realization of personal aims in national ideals. This is especially shown in *Mazzini's Letters*, tr. by Jervis, London, 1930; and in the animated essay on Mazzini by Hans Kohn in his *Prophets and Peoples: Studies in Nineteenth Century Nationalism*, New York, 1946.

158. See the discussion in Barany, *Stephen Széchenyi*, pp. 203–13.

159. In the monthly journal *Time*, quoted in Louis Snyder, ed., *The Dynamics*

of Nationalism: Readings in Its Meaning and Development, Princeton, 1964, p. 210.

160. As Lord Bryce remarked, of no people has hope been more characteristic than the Americans. *The American Commonwealth*, New York, 1924, vol. II, p. 290. For general discussion see A. A. Ekirch, Jr., *The Idea of Progress in America, 1815–1860*, New York, 1944; and Boyd C. Shafer, "The American Heritage of Hope," *Mississippi Valley Historical Review*, vol. XXXVII, 1950, pp. 427–51. The last two list significant sources.

161. See, of course, David Potter, *People of Plenty: Economic Abundance and the American Character*, Chicago, 1954. But Potter probably overdoes this theme.

162. A theme often repeated, but see Jedidiah Morse, *American Geography* (1789); and Russel Nye's comment in *This Almost Chosen People: Essays in the History of American Ideas*, East Lansing (Mich.), 1966, p. 166.

163. Samuel G. Goodrich, *Lights and Shadows of American History*, Boston, 1844, p. 14. Goodrich as the prolific and popular "Peter Parley" wrote, with assistants, over one hundred children's tales.

164. On the messianic quality see Will Herberg, *Protestant-Catholic-Jew*, 2nd ed., New York, 1960, p. 292; on the Edenic myth, Charles Sanford, *The Quest for Paradise: Europe and the American Moral Imagination*, Urbana (Ill.), 1961, p. 266.

165. But it must be understood that not only Americans believed in a national utopia.

166. Sebastian de Grazia's *The Political Community: A Study of Anomie*, Chicago, 1948, though it took an extreme view, was a path-making study of the role of anxiety in politics. But the basic study is still Harold Lasswell, *World Politics and Personal Insecurity*, New York, 1935. See also Drs. (sic) Auke Th. Alkema, "Nationalism—A Short Survey," Cambridge (Mass.), Harvard Business School study, EA-R, 368, 1964 (mimeo), p. 11; Girardet, ed., *Le Nationalisme français*, pp. 27–29; and Hans Morgenthau, *Politics Among Nations: The Struggle for Power and Peace*, New York, 1949.

167. There has been some ·psychological research on the role of anxiety in creating desire for affiliation, but the results are inconclusive and contradictory. See, for example, Stanley Schacter, *The Psychology of Affiliation: Experimental Studies in the Sources of Gregariousness*, Stanford (Calif.), 1959; and I. Sarnoff and P. G. Zimbardo, "Anxiety, Fear, and Social Affiliation," *Journal of Abnormal and Social Psychology*, vol. 62, 1961, pp. 356–63.

168. After the pogroms in Russia in the early 1880's, a university student in Kiev addressed weeping Jews gathered in a synagogue: "We are your brothers, we are Jews like you, we regret and repent that we considered ourselves Russians and not Jews until now. The events of the past weeks . . . have shown us how tragically we were mistaken. Yes, we are Jews." Ben Halpern, *The Idea of the Jewish State*, Cambridge (Mass.), 1961, p. 62.

169. The French nationalist leader Gambetta was of Italian descent, the Hungarian Kossuth of Slovak, the Irish Parnell of English, the Polish Lelewel of German, the German Hitler of Austrian—and the number of such cases could be extended. See Walter Sulzbach, *National Consciousness*, Washington, D.C., 1943, pp. 106–17. Jews and Germans were among the most patriotic Hungarians after World War I. Rustem Vambery, "Nationalism in Hungary," *Annals of the American Academy of Political and Social Science*, vol. 232, 1944, p. 82. But a few dozen among the hundreds of cases does not prove a hypothesis.

170. *The History of Freedom and Other Essays*, London, 1922, p. 286.

171. "But it was from life in America that [Irish-American nationalism] derived its most distinctive attitudes: a pervasive sense of inferiority, intense longing for acceptance and respectability, and an acute sensitivity." Thomas Brown, "The Origins and Character of Irish American Nationalism," *Review of Politics*, vol. XVIII, 1956, p. 23.

172. *Mazzini's Letters*, p. 123. K. R. Minogue was "tempted to generalize the idea of exile, and regard modern nationalism as a recourse of those who feel spiritually exiled from their communities, the outsiders, the alienated, the excluded." *Nationalism*, New York, 1967, p. 24. But this is too far-fetched; too many nationalists seem well adjusted.

173. The psychological studies do not tell us much about the general or specific relevance to nationalism, but see Erving Goffman, *Stigma: Notes on the Management of Spoiled Identity*, New York, 1963; and B. Wright, *Physical Disability: A Psychological Approach*, New York, 1960.

174. Karl W. Deutsch and Norbert Wiener, "The Lonely Nationalism of Rudyard Kipling," *Yale Review*, vol. LII, 1963, pp. 499–517.

175. Jack Stukas, *Awakening Lithuania: A Study on the Rise of Modern Lithuanian Nationalism*, Madison (N.J.), 1966, p. 92.

176. Barany, *Stephen Széchenyi*, pp. 37 ff., 65–66, 74, 178.

177. The controversial writing on Wagner is voluminous, but see Frank Josserand, "Richard Wagner and German Nationalism," *Southwestern Social Science Quarterly*, vol. XLIII, 1962, pp. 223–34.

178. E. Victor Wolfenstein in *The Revolutionary Personality, Lenin, Trotsky, Gandhi*, Princeton, 1967, argues that these three revolutionaries became revolutionaries because of unsatisfactory relationships with their fathers, but then was Gandhi's revolutionary personality the result of his identification with his mother and his own "feminine" personality? A great many young men, including Hitler, had unsatisfactory relationships with their fathers, including some who were and some who were not revolutionaries or nationalists, and some nationalists had satisfactory relationships.

179. Vladimir Dedijer, *The Road to Sarajevo*, New York, 1966.

180. "Single critical or traumatic events in a person's life normally do not exercise major influence upon the development of personality." Bernard Berelson and Gary Steiner, eds., *Human Behavior: An Inventory of Scientific Findings*, New York, 1964, pp. 74–75. T. W. Adorno et al. argued in 1950 that there were no certain relationships between mental states and

the authoritarian personality. *The Authoritarian Personality*, New York, 1950, pp. 891–970.

181. Paul Rosenblatt, "Origins and Effects of Group Ethnocentrism and Nationalism," *Journal of Conflict Resolution*, vol. 8 (2), 1964, pp. 131–146.

182. And see page 300.

183. "The Abolitionists and Psychology," *Journal of Negro History*, vol. XLVII, 1962, pp. 183–91.

184. Quoted in Robert Soucy, "Barrès and Fascism," *French Historical Studies*, vol. V, 1967, p. 97. Camus, however, added, "But our task is not to unleash them on the world; it is to fight them in ourselves and in others."

185. See the provocative analysis of Charles Hanley, "A Psychoanalysis of Nationalist Sentiment," in Peter Russell, ed., *Nationalism in Canada*, New York, 1966.

Chapter VIII

1. Cf. Ernest Barker, who believed that after the French Revolution it was "the nation" that made "the State, and not the State the nation." *National Character and the Factors in Its Formation*, London, 1927, p. 124. Barker was not alone in this opinion, but it is too simple a hypothesis because it does not cover the facts. See page 329.

2. C. A. Macartney, *National States and National Minorities*, London, 1934, p. 102.

3. Gerhard Masur, *Prophets of Yesterday*, New York, 1961, p. 202. See Arthur Mitzman, *The Iron Cage: An Historical Interpretation of Max Weber*, New York, 1970, pp. 50–51, passim, for the development of Weber's ideas.

4. Among the many studies see Stanley G. Payne, *Falange: A History of Spanish Fascism*, Stanford (Calif.), 1961. Payne, "Spanish Nationalism in the Twentieth Century," *Review of Politics*, vol. 26, 1964, pp. 403–22, argues that nationalism was a device for Franco's supporters to gain power. But, of course, the nationalism was not any the less a reality.

5. See the major, exhaustive and exhausting two volumes of Kurt P. Tauber, *Beyond Eagle and Swastika: German Nationalism since 1945*, Middletown (Conn.), 1967. In the 1960's German writers were much concerned with *Deutschtum* and its future. See Christian Graf von Krokow, *Nationalismus als deutsches Problem*, Munich, 1970, which lists some of the more serious books.

6. E. H. Carr, *Nationalism and After*, London, 1945, p. 18. From the mid-1930's the Soviet government vigorously promoted patriotism in the schools, the textbooks, the theater, and all the media. Among the studies see Mark Krug and Ida Paper, "History, Soviet Style," *Social Education*, vol. 28, 1964, pp. 73–80; and Spencer E. Roberts, *Soviet Historical Drama: Its Role in the Development of a National Mythology*, The Hague, 1965. On some of the larger issues of Soviet nationalism and the minorities see Adam Ulam, *Expansion and Coexistence, the History of Soviet Foreign Policy, 1917–67*, New York, 1968, pp. 69, 74, 719 and passim.

7. This is a paraphrase of a Hungarian diplomat's supposed observation, *Minneapolis Tribune,* editorial, April 25, 1965.
8. But cf. Victor Alba, *Nationalists Without Nations: The Oligarchy Versus the People in Latin America,* New York, 1968, who maintains that the Latin American oligarchies have used nationalism to keep themselves in power and the people do not feel they belong; and Maryea Gerassi, *Argentine Nationalism of the Right: The History of an Ideological Development, 1930–1946,* New York, 1965, which stresses the "anti" nature of the rightist nationalism. Charles Ameringer well develops the thesis that nationalism in Latin America was arising from World War I, the Mexican Revolution, and the beginnings (1924) of the *Aprista* movement. "The State of Nationalism . . . ," in Jan Prybyla, ed., *Communism and Nationalism,* Pennsylvania State University, 1968, mimeo.
9. Among the many general books touching on recent western nationalism on which I have drawn are Eugen Lemberg, *Nationalismus,* 2 vols., Hamburg, 1964; Guy Michelat and Jean-Pierre Thomas, *Dimensions du nationalisme: Enquête par questionnaire 1962,* Paris, 1966; K. R. Minogue, *Nationalism,* New York, 1967; Louis Snyder, *The New Nationalism,* Ithaca (N.Y.), 1968; Barbara Ward, *Nationalism and Ideology,* New York, 1966; and Arthur Whitaker, *Nationalism in Latin America, Past and Present,* Gainesville (Fla.), 1962.
10. Press Conference, September 5, 1950, quoted in Snyder, *The New Nationalism,* p. 182.
11. Guido de Ruggiero, *The History of European Liberalism,* tr. by R. G. Collingwood, London, 1927, pp. 414–15.
12. Cf. Ruggiero, *The History,* pp. 410–11, and see page 328.
13. The sense of belonging was probably stronger in Germany than in Italy.
14. *The Federalist,* no. 16. A few years earlier at Valley Forge, George Washington argued that a "great and lasting war can never be supported by" patriotism "alone . . . must be aided by a prospect of Interest or some reward." But this is exactly the point here—patriotism and interest became, more often than not, identical.
15. When Thorstein Veblen over forty years ago argued that the chief material use of nationalism was to assist those engaged in foreign trade, he took much too limited a view. *An Inquiry into the Nature of Peace . . . ,* New York, 1919, pp. 75, 184.
16. Andreas Dorpalen, *Heinrich von Treitschke,* New Haven, 1957, pp. 223–224; and Louis Snyder, *German Nationalism: The Tragedy of a People,* Harrisburg (Pa.), 1952, p. 144.
17. *Cohens* v. *Virginia,* 6 Wheaton 1820, 413–14; the decision is discussed by Albert Beveridge, *Life of John Marshall,* Boston, 1916–19, vol. IV, pp. 353–56.
18. *My Battle,* abridged ed., tr. by Dugdale, Boston, 1933, pp. 247–48.
19. It is obvious but still must be pointed out that authoritarian governments had different ideologies and exercised their power in different fashions. "Italian Fascism . . . groped toward a pragmatic reconciliation of socialist and nationalist aspirations; German National Socialism talked of

socialism only to submerge it beneath nationalism." Payne, *Falange*, p. 1. And the Russian Communist national state never gave up the aspiration to unite the proletariats of the world.

20. *Mein Kampf*, Boston, 1943, p. 439.

21. From *The Doctrine of Fascism*, Florence, 1938, in Louis Snyder, ed., *The Dynamics of Nationalism: Readings in Its Meaning and Development*, Princeton, 1964, p. 198.

22. Massimo Salvadori, "Nationalism in Modern Italy: 1915 and After," *Orbis*, vol. X, 1967, p. 1170.

23. Bruce M. Russett et al., eds., *World Handbook of Political and Social Indicators*, New Haven, 1964, p. 60.

24. The percentages were naturally higher in communist nations, where the governments owned and operated most enterprises, but no comparable statistics are available. In wartime, of course, all national governments expended much larger proportions of the national incomes.

25. This book supplied the title and quite likely many of the ideas of Theodore Roosevelt's "New Nationalism."

26. The arguments were old and were made in the eighteenth century by Adam Smith and Alexander Hamilton, among others.

27. Government employment in communist and capitalist nations is, of course, not strictly comparable and neither is such employment in any two nations. In France schoolteachers are employees of the national government, in the United States of local governments—though in some cases with federal subsidies.

28. The size of the armed forces of Germany (and Japan, too) was severely limited by the victors of 1945.

29. See tables in Russett et al., *World Handbook*, pp. 71–78.

30. In 1945 the armed forces of the U.S. totaled over 12 million and included the majority of men of military age, 18 to 35. Military service, with its indoctrination programs, usually increased national feeling. Robert Gage, "Patriotism as a Function of the Degree of Military Training," *Journal of Social Psychology*, vol. 64, 1964, pp. 101–11.

31. In the late 1920's Carlton Hayes, a great authority on nationalism, seemed shocked that "at least one of every twenty French citizens" was "a state functionary, a state bureaucrat." *France: A Nation of Patriots*, New York, 1930, pp. 30–31.

32. For a cogent discussion see Gunnar Myrdal, *Beyond the Welfare State*, New Haven, 1960. C. E. Black, *The Dynamics of Modernization: A Study in Comparative History*, New York, 1966, argued that nationalism is a way to modernization in undeveloped countries. This is true, and it is also true that modernization leads to nationalism.

33. See Frank Blackaby, "History's Greatest Dead End," *Saturday Review*, March 14, 1970, p. 20.

34. See chapter VI, note 99. In 1936 Sir Arthur Salter, *World Trade and Its Future*, Philadelphia, 1936, p. 39, showed how every official concerned with foreign trade was imprisoned by national interest. And in 1950, an

American confidant of President Franklin Roosevelt, Robert Sherwood, remarked of World War II diplomats, "It was always safest for those who wrote reports to take an aggressively chauvinistic line toward all foreigners." *Roosevelt and Hopkins,* New York, 1950, p. 796. Nor was it different in 1960 or 1970. W. Rostow, who advised President Lyndon Johnson, believed, "We are a nation like any other, and in the end we will fight for our vital interests." Marvin Kalb and Elie Abel, *Roots of Involvement: The United States in Asia, 1784–1971,* New York, 1971, p. 119.

35. The discussions are many but see the relevant remarks of Julius Braunthal in *The Paradox of Nationalism, an Epilogue to the Nuremberg Trials: Commonsense Reflections on the Atomic Age,* London, 1947, pp. 72–92.

36. For illustration see L. B. Namier's chapter "Pathological Nationalism," *In the Margin of History,* London, 1939.

37. *Nationalism and Internationalism,* New York, 1946, p. 16.

38. Dugdale tr., 1933, p. 10.

39. Eric Hoffer, *The True Believer, Thoughts on the Nature of Mass Movements,* New York, 1951, p. 24, was not wrong when he asserted some people become loyal because they "crave to dissolve their spoiled, meaningless selves in some soul-stirring spectacular communal undertaking."

40. On the various ways Americans identify themselves with their nation Harold Guetzkow has a brilliant essay, *Multiple Loyalties,* Princeton, 1955. But see the somewhat questionable statistics for four Latin American countries in K. H. Silvert, "National Values, Development, and Leaders and Followers," *Revue internationale des sciences sociales,* no. 4, 1963. Other quantitative studies are even more questionable. Harold Isaacs keenly analyzes the "identity" problem in "Nationalism Revisited: Group Identity and Change," *Survey: a Journal of Soviet and East European Studies,* no. 68, 1968, pp. 76–98.

41. But cf. Roy Grinker and John Spiegel, *Men Under Stress,* Philadelphia, 1945, pp. 40–44, who report the obvious: not all Americans "have been able to develop a range of identification large enough to include the nation and thus to develop strong feelings of loyalty and obligation."

42. Dankwart Rustow, *A World of Nations, Problems of Political Modernization,* Washington, D.C., 1967, p. 290. In voting, what was true of the major democratic nations was generally true of nearly all. The number of voters in Brazil, for example, doubled from 1930 to 1955 when nearly 9 million went to the polls. Bradford E. Burns, *Nationalism in Brazil: A Historical Survey,* New York, 1968, pp. 131–32. On June 14, 1970, about 150 million Soviet citizens voted for members of the Supreme Soviet (parliament), though they had no choice of candidates. *Minneapolis Tribune,* June 15, 1970, p. 3.

43. During the crises of the Vietnam war and the student revolt of early 1970, home flag sales mounted—in Minneapolis, Minnesota, they went up as much as thirty per cent. *Minneapolis Tribune,* June 17, 1970, p. 1.

44. An Ohio bank advertised "red, white, and blue service," a Minnesota supermarket chain "all American prices"; home decorators in Indiana used

the colors of the flag for furniture and "even in the kitchen canister and pottery departments." The taste is questionable, but the list could be amplified with dozens of examples.

45. An assiduous search (by Marie Thourson Jones and the author) of the recent literature (some fifty articles and books) on the "mass media" and their effect on opinion revealed that the media chiefly reinforced rather than changed opinions, that people chiefly saw or listened to programs that did not offend. But see Karl Deutsch, *Nationalism and Social Communication: An Inquiry into the Foundations of Nationality*, 2nd ed., Cambridge (Mass.), 1966; Kurt Lang and Gladys Engel, *Politics and Television*, Chicago, 1968; and some articles in Bernard Berelson and Morris Janowitz, eds., *Reader in Public Opinion and Communication*, 2nd ed., New York, 1966. That the mass media deepened awareness of national problems is obvious, but the many studies do not tell us how much. For other evidence, see chapter X, note 188.

46. Cecilia H. Bason described German indoctrination in the 1930's with some approval. *Study of the Homeland and Civilization in the Elementary Schools of Germany*, New York, 1937. A. V. Shestakov, in *A Short History of the USSR*, Moscow, 1938, a communist textbook that won a prize in the U.S.S.R., ended his introduction, "We love our country. . . . Those who know history . . . are better able to fight the enemies of our country. . . ." Harold J. Noah et al., in 1962, declared American textbooks constructed "wholly improbable stereotypes of say, patriotic, unselfish Founding Fathers or god-like superstatesmen . . . ," and conducted discussion of the Cold War "in terms of good guys and bad guys." "History in High School Textbooks: A Note," *School Review*, vol. 70, 1962, p. 432. There are many studies of nationalism in education, including the articles of Mark Krug in *School Review*, vol. 69, 1961, pp. 461–81, and *Social Education*, vol. 28, 1964, pp. 73–80; and Ray Allen Billington et al., *The Historian's Contribution to Anglo-American Misunderstanding*, New York, 1966, which demonstrates the nationalist misunderstandings occurring even among the friendliest nations.

47. A June, 1970, count of corporations listed on the New York Stock Exchange showed that the names of thirty began with "American," twenty-five with "National," and twelve with "United States."

48. See, for example, the popular (!) book by Geoffrey Gorer, *Death, Grief, and Mourning in Contemporary Britain*, New York, 1965.

49. Christine Alix, *Le Saint-Siège et les nationalismes en Europe 1870–1960*, Paris, 1962, p. 32, passim.

50. See pages 216, 338–40.

51. In *Mein Kampf*, 1943 ed., p. 427, Hitler declared, "The crown of the folkish state's entire work of education and training must be to burn the racial sense and racial feeling into the instinct and the intellect . . . an ultimate realization of the necessity and essence of blood purity. . . ." The commentaries are endless. For exemplification of the doctrine, see Alfred Rosenberg, *Der Mythus des 20 Jahrhunderts* (1930); for a descrip-

tion, Peter Pulzer, *The Rise of Political Anti-Semitism in Germany and Austria,* New York, 1964.

52. The expositions and the commentaries are again voluminous. A black student of mine, Barbara Phillips, has helped in compiling a bibliography of interpretive studies. John Bracey, Jr., August Meier, and Elliott Rudwick have edited a valuable collection of source materials and a selected bibliography, *Black Nationalism in America,* Indianapolis, 1969. Among the many studies I have found helpful are August Meier, *Negro Thought in America, 1880–1915: Racial Ideologies in the Age of Booker T. Washington,* Ann Arbor (Mich.), 1963; A. J. Gregor, "Black Nationalism: A Preliminary Analysis of Negro Radicalism," *Science and Society,* vol. 27, 1963, pp. 415–32; E. U. Essien-Udom, *Black Nationalism: A Search for an Identity in America,* Chicago, 1962; and Theodore Draper's summing up of recent writing, "The Father [Dr. Martin Robinson Dulany] of American Black Nationalism," *New York Review of Books,* March 12, 1970, pp. 33–41. Draper's own book, *Rediscovery of Black Nationalism,* New York, 1970, in spite of minor criticisms, is an able interpretation.

53. Manning Nash, "Economic Nationalism in Mexico," in Harry G. Johnson, ed., *Economic Nationalism in the Old and New States,* Chicago, 1967, p. 167.

54. Once more the literature is voluminous, my own bibliography consisting of over two hundred items. For a superficial analysis and partial bibliography see the article in the *International Encyclopedia of the Social Sciences.* Recent and controversial views and opinions can be sampled in Don Martindale, *Community, Character and Civilization,* Glencoe (Ill.), 1963; and Walter P. Metzger, "Generalizations About National Character: An Analytical Essay," in Louis Gottschalk, ed., *Generalization in the Writing of History,* Chicago, 1963. (Metzger, incidentally, misinterpreted the views of this author.) For other studies and sources, see pages 337–40 and chapter XII, note 35.

55. For various illustrations see Walter Laqueur, *Young Germany: A History of the German Youth Movement,* New York, 1962; Payne, *Falange;* Kurt Tauber, "Nationalism and Social Restoration: Fraternities in Postwar Germany," *Political Science Quarterly,* vol. LXXVII, 1963, pp. 66–85, and his *Beyond Eagle and Swastika;* and Arthur Whitaker and David Jordan, *Nationalism in Contemporary Latin America,* New York, 1966, pp. 63–64. A new analytical synthesis of the relation of "youth and nationalism" is much needed.

56. Even among the most nationalist peoples, such as the Germans of a generation ago. See Christopher Sykes, *Troubled Loyalty* (Adam von Trott zu Solz), London, 1969. On the dissident Germans among the Nazis see Harold C. Deutsch, *The Conspiracy Against Hitler in the Twilight War,* Minneapolis, 1968; Hans Rothfels, *The German Opposition to Hitler,* New York, 1962; and Terence Prittie, *Germans Against Hitler,* Boston, 1964. But see Guetzkow, *Multiple Loyalties,* for illustrations of how different loyalties reinforce each other.

57. For striking illustrations see Nathan Glazer and Daniel Patrick Moynihan, *Beyond the Melting Pot: The Negroes, Puerto Ricans, Jews and Irish of New York City,* Cambridge (Mass.), 1963; and Joshua Fishman et al., *Language Loyalty in the United States: The Maintenance and Perpetuation of Non-English Mother Tongues by American Ethnic and Religious Groups,* The Hague, 1966. Russians are patriotic, but within the Soviet Union there are nearly two hundred ethnic groups and over one hundred large groups, the members of which, except perhaps for officials, seldom think of themselves as of Soviet nationality. See Pitirim Sorokin, "The Essential Characteristics of the Russian Nation in the Twentieth Century," in Don Martindale, ed., *National Character in the Perspective of the Social Sciences, Annals of the American Academy of Political and Social Science,* vol. 370, 1967; and Richard Pipes, "The Forces of Nationalism," *Problems of Communism,* vol. XIII, 1964.

58. R. E. Lane's study, "Tense Citizen and the Casual Patriot: Role Confusion in American Politics," *Journal of Politics,* vol. 27, 1965, pp. 735–60, is based on too meager a sample, but it does show how casual the patriotism of some American workingmen has been.

59. John Gallagher and R. Robinson, "The Imperialism of Free Trade," in George H. Nadel and Perry Curtis, eds., *Imperialism and Colonialism,* New York, 1964, p. 101.

60. The hopes of many familiar individuals could be cited. For those of one not so well known, see Michel Karpovich, "Vladimir Soloviev on Nationalism," *Review of Politics,* vol. VIII, 1946, pp. 182–91.

61. Everyman's ed., chap. 5, esp. pp. 54–55; and *Letters,* tr. by Jervis, London, 1930, p. 175.

62. See the encyclical letter of Pope Pius XI, *Mit brennender Sorge,* March 14, 1937, as well as the encyclicals of John XXIII. Among the books on high Catholic doctrine are Alix, *Le Saint-Siège;* Sturzo, *Nationalism and Internationalism;* and Maurice Vaussard, *Enquête sur le nationalisme,* Paris, 1924.

63. Raymond Aron, *Peace and War,* New York, 1967, pp. 296–97. But cf. the study of R. Weissberg, "Nationalism, Integration, and French and German Elites," *International Organization,* vol. 23, 1969, pp. 337–47, which concludes, on the basis of an analysis of the views of a limited number of the elites, that "there is probably a little bit of integrationism in every nationalist and a little bit of nationalism in every integrationist."

64. Albert Guerard, "The Quick and the Dead," *Chap Book,* College English Association, 1951. Joseph de Maistre remarked (see chapter VI, note 13), "I have seen . . . Frenchmen, Italians, and Russians; I even know, thanks to Montesquieu, that one may be a Persian; but as for *Man,* I declare that I have never met him in my life. . . ." And a prominent contemporary philosopher, Eliseo Vivas, in 1966 echoed de Maistre: "The sophisticated man is above feelings of loyalty for so artificial a symbol as the flag . . . so fortuitous a relationship as country of birth; the foci of his loyalty are humanity, mankind. . . . But these abstractions stand for nothing concrete; they merely serve to cover a man's inability to love." From *The*

Intercollegiate Review, quoted in *Minneapolis Tribune,* January 25, 1966.

65. The fear arising from the threat was widespread, evidenced even in the hinterland of the American Midwest, where the author lives. See the inspired plea for world patriotism by the homespun Minnesota philosopher Jim Kimball, *Minneapolis Tribune,* May 17, 1970.

66. See pages 131 ff. The germinal study on contemporary nationalism and religion was that of Carlton Hayes in his *Essays on Nationalism,* New York, 1926, pp. 93–125. See also his final summing up, *Nationalism: A Religion,* New York, 1960; and for interesting ideas, Salo W. Baron, *Modern Nationalism and Religion,* New York, 1947; Dorothy Dohen, *Nationalism and American Catholicism,* New York, 1967; Will Herberg, *Protestant-Catholic-Jew,* 2nd ed., New York, 1960; and Martin E. Marty, *Varieties of Unbelief,* New York, 1964.

67. J. L. Talmon likely went too far, but he was not entirely wrong when he wrote, "With the rejection of the Church, and of transcendental justice, the State remained the sole source and sanction of morality." *The Origins of Totalitarian Democracy,* New York, 1960, p. 4.

68. *The Man Without a Country* was first published anonymously in the *Atlantic Monthly* in 1863 and had many printings.

69. J. Loewenberg, ed., *Hegel: Selections,* New York, 1929, p. 445.

70. Theodore Roosevelt, "True Americanism," *American Ideals and Other Essays,* New York, 1897, pp. 15–34; and Maurice Barrès, *Scènes et doctrines du nationalisme,* Paris, n.d., p. 814, passim. "Le nationalisme," wrote Barrès, "c'est de résoudre chaque question par rapport à la France."

71. *Le Peuple,* Paris, 1946, p. 267.

72. Charles Maurras first used the phrase "integral nationalism" in an article in *Le Soleil,* March 2, 1900. William Curt Buthman, *The Rise of Integral Nationalism in France, with Special Reference . . . [to] Charles Maurras,* New York, 1939, p. 110. On Maurras and other "integral" and right-wing nationalists see also Edward R. Tannenbaum, *The Action Française: Die-Hard Reactionaries in Twentieth Century France,* New York, 1962; the thorough study of Eugen Weber, *Action Française: Royalism and Reaction in Twentieth Century France,* Stanford (Calif.), 1962; and Robert Soucy, "Barrès and Fascism," *French Historical Studies,* vol. V, 1967, pp. 67–97.

73. Theodore Sorenson, *Kennedy,* New York, 1965, p. 241.

74. Quoted in Jonathan Scott, *Patriots in the Making: What America Can Learn from France and Germany,* New York, 1916, p. 31, from Gabriel Compayré, *Eléments d'instruction morale et civique.*

75. Buthman, *Integral Nationalism,* p. 29.

76. David and Ruth Stevens, eds., *American Patriotic Prose and Verse,* Chicago, 1918, pp. 63–64.

77. Letter to Jules Claretie, *Lettres de Gambetta,* ed. by D. Halévy, no. 224, 1874, quoted in Herbert Tint, *The Decline of French Patriotism, 1870–1940,* London, 1964, p. 22.

78. See his *The Undying Spirit of France;* and Buthman, *Integral Nationalism,* p. 86.

79. Quoted in Ernst H. Kantorowicz, *"Pro Patria Mori* in Medieval Political Thought," *American Historical Review*, vol. LVI, 1951, p. 472.
80. The quoted words are those of Erich Fromm, *Escape from Freedom*, New York, 1941, p. 177, though he was using them in a somewhat different context.
81. This is, of course, a paraphrase of Diderot's "Posterity is for the philosopher what the other world is for the religious man."
82. The quoted words are from J. G. Frazer, *Totemism and Exogamy*, London, 1910, pp. 91 ff. Frazer's interpretations were, as is well known, roundly attacked by Alexander Goldweiser and others, but do not seem irrelevant here.
83. Edmund Stillman and William Pfaff thus explain western man's proclivity to war. *The Politics of Hysteria*, New York, 1965.
84. This was especially true among peoples who believed themselves oppressed by foreign powers, such as those of the so-called satellite countries of the U.S.S.R. In Romania in 1970, where the Communist party's nationalism had won it "massive support," a journalist explaining why said, "Our nationalism is normal." Jonathan Steele, *Manchester Guardian Weekly*, July 18, 1970, p. 6.

Chapter IX

1. Speech at Lucknow, in William L. Holland, ed., *Asian Nationalism and the West*, New York, 1953, pp. 353–54.
2. The number 140 is, of course, arbitrary. There were two Germanies, two Koreas, and two Vietnams. And were Nauro (pop. est. 6,000), Monaco (pop. 23,000), and some other small political entities nations, states, or what? As of September, 1969, 126 nations or states were members of the U.N., but not the Germanies and a few other nations and states. Further, a few peoples, like the Ibo, who have aspired to nationhood have not achieved it, and some African states can hardly be called nation-states.
3. My debt in this and the following chapter to pioneer scholars in the fields of Asian and African nationalism should be obvious: to, among others, George Antonius, Yahya Armajani, G. Balandier, Delmar Brown, Chow Tse-tsung, James Coleman, Philip Curtin, Rupert Emerson, John Fairbank, Sylvia Haim, John Halstead, Charles Heimsath, Thomas Hodgkin, David Kimble, Joseph Levenson, Masao Maruyama, Ali Mazrui, George Shepperson, Immanuel Wallerstein, and Henry Wilson. I should also like to express my gratitude to numerous students and scholars in Japan and East Africa, and, in particular, to my student Okete (James) Shiroya of Kenya, who now teaches at Makerere University (Uganda), for much information, for correcting false impressions arising out of my ignorance, and for offering hypotheses that modified my own.
4. Though Hans Kohn argued, "The comparative study of nationalism will not reveal any fundamental differences between . . . nationalism in the western and non-western worlds. . . . On the whole, the 'new' nations show trends and problems similar to those shown by the 'new' nations

of central Europe in the nineteenth century and of east-central Europe in the early twentieth century." Article on "Nationalism," *International Encyclopedia of the Social Sciences*, vol. XI, p. 69.

5. And to this author, who is not an expert on either Asia or Africa, who sees pitfalls and may, probably will, stumble into them.

6. Definitions of tribe, largely the conceptions of Europeans, also varied during the nineteenth and twentieth centuries. For cogent remarks see Philip D. Curtin, "Nationalism in Africa, 1945–1965," *Review of Politics*, vol. 28, 1966, pp. 143–53, a revised version of an A.H.A. paper of 1964; P. Mercier, "On the Meaning of 'Tribalism' in Black Africa," in Pierre L. van den Berghe, ed., *Africa: Social Problems of Change and Conflict*, San Francisco, 1965, pp. 483–501; J. B. Webster, "Tribalism, Nationalism and Patriotism in Nineteenth and Twentieth-Century Africa," Makerere University, 1970, mimeo, who argues, as do some other Africanists, that many of the so-called tribes (like the Asante) were really nations and that hence nationalism was not new in Africa; W. J. Argyle, "European Nationalism and African Tradition," in P. H. Gulliver, ed., *Tradition and Transition*, London, 1969, pp. 41–57; and the useful "Note on Concepts and Terms" in James Coleman, *Nigeria: Background to Nationalism*, Berkeley, 1965, appendix, pp. 420–27.

7. The inverse is true of the Afrikaner nationalism, which is based on the "superiority" of a white minority; and, in addition, Afrikaners have no fatherland they can "in honesty call [their] own." William Henry Vatcher, Jr., *White Laager: The Rise of Afrikaner Nationalism*, New York, 1965, p. ix.

8. Chong-sik Lee, *The Politics of Korean Nationalism*, Berkeley, 1965, pp. 19–20.

9. In Sylvia Haim, ed., *Arab Nationalism*, Berkeley, 1962, p. 228. The variations on this variation are several, but basically similar. See, for example, Munif Al-Razzāz, *The Evolution of the Meaning of Nationalism*, tr. by Abu-Lughod, New York, 1963, pp. 6–9; Bernard Lewis, *The Arabs in History*, London, 1950, pp. 9–10; Hans E. Tütsch, "Arab Unity and Arab Dissensions," in Walter Z. Laqueur, ed., *The Middle East in Transition: Studies in Contemporary History*, New York, 1958, pp. 12–32, and his *Facets of Arab Nationalism*, Detroit, 1965, p. 32. The more or less official view was expressed in the *Digest of Major Arab Issues*, New York, 1959, which declared that "the deciding factor" was whether a person had "*the spirit of the Arab community.*"

10. The literature is enormous. Possibly the best source is the writings of Herzl. An informed, fairly objective treatment is Ben Halpern's *The Idea of the Jewish State*, Cambridge (Mass.), 1961. It might be added that until recently the Jews of modern times not only had no land but no common language.

11. Thomas Hodgkin has a superb short essay on the meaning of African terms: "A Note on the Language of African Nationalism," *St. Anthony's Papers*, vol. 10, 1961, pp. 22–40. For another informed discussion see David Kimble, *A Political History of Ghana, 1850–1928*, Oxford, 1963,

pp. 554–62. The great African poet, statesman, and nationalist L. S. Senghor carefully and well distinguished between the African *patries* and the nation in a speech in 1959 at Dakar: "La Patrie, c'est l'héritage que nous ont transmis nos ancêtres: une terre, un sang, une langue . . . des moeurs, des coutumes, un folklore, un art. . . . La Nation, si elle rassemble les patries, c'est pour transcender . . . la Nation fait, de provinces différentes . . . un seul pays pour un seul peuple, animé d'une même foi et tendu vers un même but." In Pierre Bonnafé, ed., *Nationalismes africaines,* Paris, 1962, mimeo, pp. 15–16.

12. Chow Tse-tsung, *The May Fourth Movement,* Cambridge (Mass.), 1960, is a path-making, first-rate book.

13. Among the many accounts see Stuart R. Schram, *Mao Tse-tung,* London, 1967. The latter part of the Ch'ing period (1644–1912) "was one of transition from *t'ien-hsia* to *kuochia,* empire and world to nation. Chinese nationalism involved a scaling up from a collection of provinces, a scaling down from the world." Joseph Levenson, "The Province, the Nation, and the World," in Albert Feuerwerker et al., eds., *Approaches to Modern Chinese History,* Berkeley, 1967, p. 287.

14. Delmer Brown's *Nationalism in Japan,* Berkeley, 1955, is a basic work, but see the provocative Weberian interpretations of Masao Maruyama, *Thought and Behaviour in Modern Japanese Politics,* ed. by Ivan Morris, London, 1963. The remarks here are in part drawn from the lucid book of Robert E. Ward and Dankwart A. Rustow, eds., *Political Modernization in Japan and Turkey,* Princeton, 1964, p. 438.

15. See, for example, A. A. Mazrui and G. F. Engholm, "Rousseau and Intellectualized Populism in Africa," *Review of Politics,* vol. 30, 1968, pp. 19–32.

16. Hodgkin, "A Note on the Language," pp. 27 ff., 40. See also Niyazi Berkes, *The Development of Secularism in Turkey,* Montreal, 1964, p. 194, who argues, using Turkey as his example, "Ideas begin to mean something only when certain sociological conditions come into existence."

17. In Ssu-yü Teng, John K. Fairbank, et al., *China's Response to the West: A Documentary Survey, 1839–1923,* Cambridge (Mass.), 1965, p. 221. See Joseph R. Levenson's imaginative and difficult *Liang Ch'i-ch'ao and the Mind of Modern China,* 2nd rev. ed., Berkeley, 1967.

18. *African Nationalism,* 2nd ed., London, 1968, p. 57.

19. Yahya Armajani, *Middle East Past and Present,* Englewood Cliffs (N.J.), 1970, p. 252; and Richard W. Cottam, *Nationalism in Iran,* Pittsburgh, 1964, pp. 25–27.

20. As pointed out in chapter I, note 12, Elie Kedourie began his book entitled *Nationalism,* New York, 1960: "Nationalism is a doctrine invented in Europe at the beginning of the nineteenth century."

21. Some relevant documents and observations are in Wm. Theodore de Bary et al., *Sources of Indian Tradition,* New York, 1958, pp. 602–738. Among the plethora of controversial writings it is impossible to choose, but see the short survey of R. C. Majumdar, "The Growth of Nationalism in India," *Indo-Asian Culture,* vol. 10, 1961, pp. 96–113. There is agreement

that there was no nationalism in India at the beginning of the nineteenth century but little consensus on time otherwise. Controversy over origins is a mark of nationalist writing, which always pridefully seeks "firsts."

22. The quotation is from J. Jacobs, "The Damascus Affair and the Jews of America," *Publications of the American Jewish Historical Society*, 1902, p. 120. J. P. T. Bury, "Nationalities and Nationalism," *New Cambridge Modern History*, vol. X, p. 224, briefly discusses the affair, thirteen Jews charged with the ritual murder of a Capuchin friar.

23. Again the writings are too numerous to cite, but see *The Diaries of Theodor Herzl*, ed. and tr. by Marvin Lowenthal, New York, 1962, especially for the period from June, 1895; and Ludwig Lewisohn, *Theodor Herzl, a Portrait for This Age*, Cleveland, 1955. Herzl wrote his *Judenstaat* in 1895. Almost certainly a critic will note that I did not mention Moses Hess, *Rome and Jerusalem: A Study in Jewish Nationalism*, a book written in 1862 and published in translation (by Meyer Waxman), New York, 1943, and so I do mention it now.

24. Teng and Fairbank, *China's Response*, p. 35. For later developments see, among other studies, John Israel, *Student Nationalism in China, 1927–1937*, Stanford (Calif.), 1966, a good doctoral dissertation; and Chow, *May Fourth Movement*.

25. Haim, ed., *Arab Nationalism*, p. 3. Cf. George Antonius, *The Arab Awakening: The Story of the Arab National Movement*, Philadelphia, 1939, who thought the awakening came earlier. For a balanced view see Hazem Zaki Nuseibeh, *The Ideas of Arab Nationalism*, Ithaca (N.Y.), 1956.

26. The Turkish, for example, from about 1908, the Moroccan from the early 1930's. Bernard Lewis, *The Emergence of Modern Turkey*, London, 1961; and John P. Halstead's thorough *Rebirth of a Nation: The Origins and Rise of Moroccan Nationalism, 1912–1944*, Cambridge (Mass.), 1967.

27. Relevant well-edited documents are in Henry S. Wilson, ed., *Origins of West Africa Nationalism*, London, 1969. Among the many studies see Hollis R. Lynch's good biography of *Edward Wilmot Blyden, Pan-Negro Patriot, 1832–1912*, London, 1967.

28. Kimble, *Ghana*, p. 554.

29. Richard B. Morris, *The Emerging Nations and the American Revolution*, New York, 1970, competently surveys the far-reaching effect of the American. As far as I know, there is no comparable (even by Godechot) single study of the world effects of the French, but the subject is much discussed. There is no way to decide whether the effect of the French was greater than that of the American (lately a much debated question in the United States); but Asians and Africans read French authors more than American, and France was a world power and an empire before the United States. I did not find that Seymour Lipset's *The First New Nation*, New York, 1963, contributed much that was new or different beyond excited value judgments based on hypotheses of Max Weber.

30. Quoted in K. R. Minogue, *Nationalism*, New York, 1967. According to C. F. Andrews, a Turkish consul of long experience observed that even "the most ignorant peasants" in the interior of India tingled with the

news; and, Andrews added, throughout Asia "the sleep of centuries was finally broken." See J. F. C. Fuller, *India in Revolt*, London, 1931, p. 91.

31. But Nehru was skeptical also of the Communist program. Frank Moraes, *Jawaharlal Nehru*, Bombay, 1956, p. 108; Nehru, *Toward Freedom: The Autobiography of Jawaharlal Nehru*, New York, 1941, p. 229. See also S. N. Mukherjee, ed., "The Movement for National Freedom in India," *St. Anthony's Papers*, vol. 18, London, 1966, pp. 81, 89, 97.

32. As Ndabaningi Sithole, *African Nationalism*, 1st ed., Capetown, 1959, pp. 155–56, observed, "The emergent African nationalism . . . represents the degree to which the white man's magic spell, which at the beginning of the nineteenth century, had been cast on the African, is wearing off." Sithole, pp. 56–60, also demonstrates how, on the other hand, the U.N. provisions for developing self-government were taken seriously in Africa.

33. Adapted and revised from Dankwart Rustow, *A World of Nations, Problems of Political Modernization*, Washington, D.C., 1967, pp. 292–93. It can and has been said that in Asia and Africa nationalism arose without nations.

34. Or in Africa it may happen that retribalization will become more significant. See Ali Mazrui, "Violent Contiguity and the Politics of Retribalization in Africa," *Journal of International Affairs*, vol. 23, 1969, pp. 89–105.

Chapter X

1. Answers are many and diverse. Differing intelligent summaries may be sampled in James Coleman, *Nigeria: Background to Nationalism*, Berkeley, 1965, p. 410; the papers of Paramount Chief Anthony Enahoro and Rayford Logan, both in American Society of African Culture, *Pan-Africanism Reconsidered*, Berkeley, 1962, pp. 67–74, 37–52; Rupert Emerson, *From Empire to Nation*, Cambridge (Mass.), 1960, pp. 3–21, 378–396; D. K. Fieldhouse, *The Colonial Empires: A Comparative Survey from the Eighteenth Century*, New York, 1967, pp. 284–85 (on India); Joseph Kennedy, *Asian Nationalism in the Twentieth Century*, London, 1968, pp. 79 ff.; J. Lonsdale, "Emergence of African Nations: A Historiographical Analysis," *African Affairs*, vol. 67, 1968, pp. 11–28; V. D. Mahajan, *The Nationalist Movement in India and Its Leaders*, New Delhi, 1962, pp. 1–6; and Robert Rotberg, "The Rise of African Nationalism: The Case of East and Central Africa," *World Politics*, vol. XV, 1962, pp. 78–90. But, of course, every commentator has his own hypotheses or convictions. I found Ndabaningi Sithole's *African Nationalism*, 2nd ed., London, 1968, most convincing.

2. See the first-rate doctoral dissertation of Joseph R. Levenson, *Liang Ch'i-ch'ao and the Mind of Modern China*, 2nd rev. ed., Berkeley, 1967, pp. 110, 159. A solid, little-known study is Maurice Neufeld, *Italy: School for Awakening Countries*, Ithaca (N.Y.), 1961. The diffusion of ideas from Europe will possibly be the subject of a separate essay by the present author.

3. Among the newer general serious works that I have used are Henri Brunschwig, *Mythes et réalités de l'impérialisme colonial français, 1871–1914*, Paris, 1960; Fieldhouse, *The Colonial Empires;* L. H. Gann and Peter Duignan, *Burden of Empire: An Appraisal of Western Colonialism in Africa South of the Sahara*, New York, 1967; Richard Koebner and Helmut Schmidt, *Imperialism: The Story and Significance of a Political Word, 1840–1960*, Cambridge (Eng.), 1964; and George H. Nadel and Perry Curtis, eds., *Imperialism and Colonialism*, New York, 1964.

4. Britain's determination to expand and defend its empire and trade to and in Asia and Africa, to keep open the route to India, is the clearest example. But Britain was not unique. In 1925, at a time of crisis, Premier Paul Painlevé of France declared, "We must either defend [keep and control] Morocco . . . or else abandon North Africa. . . . It would be the end of our colonial empire, the end of our economic independence, which is impossible without the colonies, the end of the prestige and influence of France in the world." Quoted in John P. Halstead, *Rebirth of a Nation: The Origins and Rise of Moroccan Nationalism, 1912–1944*, Cambridge (Mass.), 1968, p. 47.

5. David Kimble, *A Political History of Ghana, 1850–1928*, Oxford, 1963, p. 557.

6. The examples could be multiplied. See, for example, almost any work on Indian nationalism, such as Karan Singh, *Prophet of Indian Nationalism: A Study of the Political Thought of Sri Aurobindo Ghosh, 1893–1910*, London, 1963, pp. 62–63.

7. Carl G. Rosberg and John Nottingham, *The Myth of Mau Mau: Nationalism in Kenya*, Nairobi, 1966, passim. See also Tom Mboya's discussion and reaction in *Kenya Faces the Future*, New York, 1959.

8. René Lemarchand, *Political Awakening in the Belgian Congo*, Berkeley, 1964, p. 34, passim. A typical belief was that of Jules Renkin (in 1908), who was to become Belgian Minister of Colonies: "The Congo will constitute for Belgium an excellent colony; . . . its ivory, rubber, and mineral deposits . . . will provide an inexhaustible source of riches."

9. Jamal Mohammad Ahmed, *The Intellectual Origins of Egyptian Nationalism*, New York, 1960, pp. 67–68; and Christina Harris, *Nationalism and Revolution in Egypt: The Role of the Muslim Brotherhood*, The Hague, 1964, pp. 34–35. Fourteen foreign communities in Egypt enjoyed varying judicial, police, and fiscal immunities.

10. Ahmed, *Intellectual Origins*, pp. 74–75. But Gorst in many ways simply shared the views of a far greater colonial administrator, Lord Cromer, that the Egyptian was inferior. Ahmed, pp. 66, 71–72.

11. The Englishman was Douglas Sladen. See Charles D. Cremeans, *The Arabs and the World: Nasser's Arab Nationalist Policy*, New York, 1963, p. 50. The sources are full of similar contemptuous remarks.

12. Boris Gussmann, *Out in the Mid-Day Sun*, New York, 1963, p. 17.

13. Sir Harry (Henry) Johnston, an outstanding British African official, wrote: "A gentle insistence that the native should contribute his fair share to the revenue of the country by paying his hut-tax, is all that is neces-

sary on our part to secure his taking that share of life's labour which no human being should evade." Quoted in Robert I. Rotberg, *The Rise of Nationalism in Central Africa: The Making of Malawi and Zambia, 1873–1964,* Cambridge (Mass.), 1965, pp. 39 ff.

14. For these six points see, in particular, Kathleen Gough, "Indian Nationalism and Ethnic Freedom," in David Bidney, ed., *The Concept of Freedom in Anthropology,* The Hague, 1963, pp. 181–82; and on different points in different countries, Coleman, *Nigeria,* pp. 44–45, passim; Halstead, *Rebirth of a Nation,* pp. 114–15; George McT. Kahin, *Nationalism and Revolution in Indonesia,* Ithaca (N.Y.), 1952, pp. 37 ff.; Kimble, *Ghana,* pp. 556–57; and Bisheshwar Prasad, *Changing Modes of Indian National Movement[s],* New Delhi, 1966, pp. 24–25.

15. Roland Oliver and Anthony Atmore, *Africa Since 1800,* Cambridge (Eng.), 1967. For informed discussions see Henri Brunschwig, *L'Avènement de l'Afrique noire du XIXᵉ siècle à nos jours, Paris 1963,* last chapter and passim; John Halstead, "A Comparative Historical Study of Colonial Nationalism in Egypt and Morocco," *African Historical Studies,* vol. II, 1969, pp. 85–100; and Immanuel Wallerstein, *Africa, the Politics of Independence,* New York, 1961, pp. 65–67.

16. *An Arab Tells His Story: A Study in Loyalties,* London, 1946, p. 165, quoted in Cremeans, *The Arabs and the World,* p. 55.

17. For three illustrations see Philip D. Curtin, "Nationalism in Africa, 1945–1965," *Review of Politics,* vol. 28, 1966, p. 150, John Israel, *Student Nationalism in China, 1927–1937,* Stanford (Calif.), 1966, p. 184; and Hazem Zaki Nuseibeh, *The Ideas of Arab Nationalism,* Ithaca (N.Y.), 1956, pp. 42–43 fn.

18. New York, 1941, p. 74.

19. This is a paraphrase of Gussmann, *Out in the Mid-Day Sun,* p. 101.

20. Kahin, *Nationalism and Revolution in Indonesia,* pp. 19–30.

21. Thomas Hodgkin, *Nationalism in Colonial Africa,* London, 1956, pp. 120–121.

22. In the Congo, Belgians held nearly all the civil service jobs. In 1887 in India the British, who were few in numbers, held twenty-nine per cent of the government appointments, at salaries of seventy-five rupees and over a month, and most of the highest-paying and responsible positions, and, while the percentage declined during the years before independence, they still held most of the highest positions. See, for example, Anil Seal, *The Emergence of Indian Nationalism: Competition and Collaboration in the Later Nineteenth Century,* London, 1968, pp. 357–61.

23. In Nigeria in 1949, six firms handled sixty-six per cent of Nigeria's imports and nearly seventy per cent of its exports. The "annual profits and royalties of alien firms exceeded annual expenditures on education . . . the mining royalties paid to one firm over a ten-year period equaled nearly one-sixth of the total Nigerian budget." Coleman, *Nigeria,* pp. 80–81, 89.

24. See, for example, Rosberg and Nottingham, *Myth of Mau Mau,* p. 352, passim. As Sir Henry Johnston reported in *British Central Africa,* London

1897, they sometimes gave a few pounds' worth of inferior trade goods: a British evangelist obtained 26,537 acres for 1,750 yards of calico. See Rotberg, *The Rise of Nationalism in Central Africa,* pp. 30–31. Or, as in eastern Asia, they broke up communal ownership and forced individual ownership. Giorgio Borsa, "Nationalism and the Beginning of Modernization in Eastern Asia," *Il Politico,* vol. 29, 1964, p. 323.

25. Statistics of the 1950's show that life expectancy and infant mortality in Sweden were 71 to 75 and 13.6; in Senegal, 37 and 92.9; in Tanganyika, 35 to 40 and 190. See the *United Nations Demographic Yearbooks.*

26. For a cogent discussion see E. B. Ayal, "Nationalist Ideology and Economic Development," *Human Organization,* vol. 25, 1966, pp. 230–39. See also C. E. Black, *The Dynamics of Modernization: A Study in Comparative History,* New York, 1966; and for comparison with Europe, W. W. Rostow, *The Stages of Economic Growth,* Cambridge (Mass.), 1960. For comparable European experience see chapters VI and VII, and p. 242.

27. Touré, *Expérience guinéene et unité africaine,* Paris, n.d., p. 6; see Claude Waulthier, *L'Afrique des Africains: inventaire de la négritude,* Paris, 1964, p. 139. For Quezon, see Theodore Friend, *Between Two Empires: The Ordeal of the Philippines, 1929–1946,* New Haven, 1965, p. 40.

28. This is close to the observation of an English sociologist, Ernest Gellner, *Thought and Change,* Chicago, 1964, p. 172. For a supporting commentary see the germinal article of Albert Breton, "The Economics of Nationalism," *Journal of Political Economy,* vol. LXXII, 1964, pp. 376–86.

29. *An Eye for the Dragon: Southeast Asia Observed, 1954–1970,* New York, 1970, p. 31.

30. *Ghana: Autobiography,* London, 1957, pp. 162–63. Professor Yahya Armajani has brought to my attention the words of a Persian school song, "A hundred dead in freedom is better than one living in servitude."

31. Coleman, *Nigeria,* p. 41.

32. *West African Studies,* 2nd ed., London, 1899, pp. 326–27.

33. *Facing Mount Kenya, the Tribal Life of the Kikuyu,* London, 1953, pp. 47–49.

34. From Tewfik el Hakim, *Maze of Justice,* London, 1947, pp. 20–21, quoted in Harris, *Nationalism and Revolution in Egypt,* p. 108.

35. Of course, the list of slights, insults, and humiliations could be multiplied many times. These are only illustrations and by no means the worst. For vivid examples see Halstead, *Rebirth of a Nation,* pp. 61–62; and the less scholarly but eloquent Gussmann, *Out in the Mid-Day Sun,* passim. It may be added that Africans who came from or went to the United States, for instance Edward Blyden, Azikiwe of Nigeria, and Nkrumah of Ghana, were especially offended by the insults they suffered there, and the memories rankled.

36. W. R. Crocker, *Self-Government for the Colonies,* London, 1949, p. vi, argued that the "essence of the colonial grievance was not economic [but] political." There is no way of proving this, but it could be true.

37. At the time, 1960, of his trial for the burning of his pass, the South African leader Albert Luthuli, who won the Nobel Prize that year, wrote

but could not make the following statement to the court: "It cannot be easy for you, sir, to understand the very deep hatred all Africans feel for a pass. . . . Can anyone who has not gone through it possibly imagine what has happened when they read in the Press of a routine police announcement [of] a pass raid . . . ? The fear of a loud, rude bang on the door in the middle of the night, the bitter humiliation of an undignified search, the shame of husband and wife being huddled [*sic*] out of bed in front of their children by the police and taken off to a police cell." *Let My People Go*, New York, 1962, p. 244.

38. The Rowlat Bill of 1918 provided that in political cases judges could conduct trials without juries and authorities could intern persons suspected of disloyalty without trial. Milton Meyer, *India and Pakistan and the Border Lands*, Totowa (N.J.), 1960, p. 147. In times of crisis "natives" were often arbitrarily arrested and jailed and sometimes ill-treated without legal process of any kind.

39. *African Nationalism*, 2nd ed., chap. XIV.

40. Richard W. Cottam, *Nationalism in Iran*, Pittsburgh, 1964, pp. 158–242.

41. See in particular Chow Tse-tsung, *The May Fourth Movement*, Cambridge (Mass.), 1960, pp. 20–22.

42. Coleman, *Nigeria*, p. 97.

43. Margery Perham, *The Colonial Reckoning: The End of Imperial Rule in Africa in the Light of British Experience*, New York, 1962, p. 36. Colin Turnbull, an anthropologist, dramatically demonstrated Africans' anguish in the biographical sketches of his *The Lonely African*, New York, 1962, as he foresaw possibilities for the development of national feeling through the tribal structures.

44. J. L. and B. Hammond, *The Age of the Chartists, 1832–1854*, London, 1930, p. 16, describing the early modernization and industrialization of England, spoke of the "changes that destroy the life of custom . . . bring into men's minds the dreaded questions which have been sleeping beneath the surface of habit." But, as Victor Ferkiss, *Africa's Search for Unity*, New York, 1966, p. 116, said of urban Africans, perhaps the uprooted peoples were simply "confused rather than anomic or rootless." See the essays of varying quality in Clifford Geertz, ed., *Old Societies and New States: The Quest for Modernity in Asia and Africa*, New York, 1963, for sociological discussion of the disintegrating tensions and integrating forces.

45. Examples are manifold. See Friend, *Between Two Empires*, pp. 37–39; Gussmann, *Out in the Mid-Day Sun*, pp. 17–19; and Rosberg and Nottingham, *Myth of Mau Mau*, p. 353.

46. Tibor Mende, *South-East Asia Between Two Worlds*, London, 1955, p. 292.

47. Quoted in Robert Rotberg, "The Federation Movement in British East and Central Africa, 1889–1953," *Journal of Commonwealth Political Studies*, vol. II, 1964, p. 153.

48. Among the studies see Edward Feit, *South Africa, the Dynamics of the African National Congress*, London, 1962; Edwin S. Munger, *Afrikaner*

and African Nationalism: South African Parallels and Parameters, London, 1967—an informed, solid book in spite of the subtitle; F. A. van Jaarsveld, *The Awakening of Afrikaner Nationalism, 1868–1881*, Cape Town, 1961; William Henry Vatcher, Jr., *White Laager: The Rise of South Afrikaner Nationalism*, New York, 1965; and, of course, the basic historical volumes of C. W. De Kiewiet and the novels and writings of Alan Paton and Nadine Gordimer.

49. And, in spite of popular belief to the contrary, predominantly white Muslim Arabs were also prejudiced against blacks. See Bernard Lewis' learned essay, "Race and Colour in Islam," *Encounter*, vol. XXXV, 1970, pp. 18–36.

50. Hollis R. Lynch, *Edward Wilmot Blyden, Pan-Negro Patriot, 1832–1912*, London, 1967; and Henry S. Wilson, ed.; *Origins of West African Nationalism*, London, 1969, pp. 35–39, passim.

51. *Ghana: Autobiography*, pp. 42–43. Incidents of this kind are innumerable and many times described. Delve at random in John Bracey, Jr., August Meier, and Elliott Rudwick, eds., *Black Nationalism in America*, Indianapolis, 1969; and in Robert I. Rotberg and Ali A. Mazrui, eds., *Protest and Power in Black Africa*, New York, 1970.

52. In James Duffy and Robert Manners, eds., *Africa Speaks*, Princeton, 1961, pp. 90–91.

53. For documents of Blyden see Wilson, ed., *Origins of West African Nationalism*, pp. 239–62; and Colin Legum, *Pan-Africanism: A Short Political Guide*, London, 1962, pp. 263–65; and for discussion Lynch, *Edward Wilmot Blyden*, pp. 29–30, 61–62; and Robert July, "Nineteenth Century *Négritude*: Edward W. Blyden," *Journal of African History*, vol. V, 1964, pp. 73–86. On Aggrey, see Kimble, *Ghana*, p. 548; and Coleman, *Nigeria*, p. 223.

54. The literature on *Négritude* is vast. The writings of Diop, Césaire, and Senghor should, naturally, be read, as well as the excellent studies of, among others, Abiola Irele, "*Négritude*—Literature and Ideology," *Journal of Modern African Studies*, vol. 3, 1965, pp. 499–527; Lilyan Kesteloot, *Les Ecrivains noirs de la langue française: naissance d'une littérature*, 2nd ed., Brussels, 1965; and Waulthier, *L'Afrique des Africains*.

55. Wm. Theodore de Bary et al., *Sources of Indian Tradition*, New York, 1958, pp. 878 ff. Other, less violent Indian prophets held similar views; see Karan Singh, *Prophet of Indian Nationalism*, p. 80.

56. Wm. Theodore de Bary et al., *Sources of Chinese Tradition*, New York, 1960, p. 847. The idea that China was superior, a world order in itself, was old and deeply rooted. See, for example, John K. Fairbank, ed., *The Chinese World Order: Traditional China's Foreign Relations*, Cambridge (Mass.), 1968, esp. the essays by Wang Gungwu and Benjamin I. Schwartz, pp. 34–62, 276–88, and Joseph Levenson, "The Past and Future of Nationalism in China," *Survey; a Journal of Soviet and East European Studies*, No. 67, 1968, pp. 29, 40.

57. Robert Bellah, "Japan's Cultural Identity: Some Reflections on the Work of Watsuyi Tetsurō," *Journal of Asian Studies*, vol. XXIV, 1965, p. 585;

see also Ryusaku Tsunoda et al., eds., *Sources of the Japanese Tradition*, New York, 1958, p. 796. Individuals among many peoples, including the Arabs and the Turks, have had the idea of world mission, of course.

58. From *African Nationalism*, 1st ed., quoted in Rupert Emerson and Martin Kilson, eds., *The Political Awakening in Africa*, Englewood Cliffs (N.J.), 1965, p. 91.

59. Until the fall of 1969 this author would have given race and color the greatest weight in explaining at least African nationalism. But then, after conversations with Japanese, Chinese, Kenyan, Ugandan, and Tanzanian scholars and students in their own lands, as well as with western students of Africa in Africa, color appeared to him to be less important—except, as Professor Ali Mazrui, Makerere University, remarked, when talking about the situation in the Portuguese colonies and South Africa. Asian and African protests, always tinged by the color question, very likely were more basically directed against political domination and economic exploitation than racial discrimination. But there is no way of divorcing the latter from domination and exploitation. I am especially indebted to my student, Dr. Okete (James) Shiroya of Makerere University, for a memorandum and for conversations on the subject.

60. Halstead, *Rebirth of a Nation,* p. 102.

61. Coleman, *Nigeria,* pp. 120–26.

62. Coleman, p. 120.

63. Halstead, *Rebirth of a Nation,* pp. 72, 180–82, and passim; J. Abun-Nasr, "The Salafiyya Movement in Morocco: The Religious Bases of the Moroccan Nationalist Movement (1963)," in Immanuel Wallerstein, ed., *Social Change: The Colonial Situation,* New York, 1966, p. 500.

64. See R. P. Beaver, "Nationalism and Missions," *Church History,* vol. 26, 1957, pp. 22–23. Among the many commentaries on the Indian reaction see K. M. Sardar, *Asia and Western Dominance,* London, 1953.

65. Sylvia Haim, "Islam and the Theory of Arab Nationalism," in Walter Z. Laqueur, ed., *The Middle East in Transition: Studies in Contemporary History,* New York, 1958, pp. 306–07; and Bernard Lewis, *The Middle East and the West,* Bloomington (Ind.), 1964, p. 71.

66. These are but two examples. George Antonius, *The Arab Awakening: The Story of the Arab National Movement,* Philadelphia, 1939, pp. 41 ff.; Claude Welch, Jr., *Dream of Unity: Pan-Africanism and Political Unification in West Africa,* Ithaca (N.Y.), 1966, pp. 43, 47 ff.

67. The epic of Chilembwe is superbly described in George Shepperson and Thomas Price, *Independent African: John Chilembwe and the Origins, Setting and Significance of the Nyasaland Native Rising of 1915,* Edinburgh, 1958. For a sympathetic later view see Robert Rotberg, "Psychological Stress and the Question of Identity: Chilembwe's Revolt Reconsidered," in Rotberg and Mazrui, eds., *Protest and Power,* pp. 337–76.

68. *African Nationalism,* 2nd ed., pp. 85–86.

69. The connection seems tenuous. It is true that a Simon Kimbangu of the Congo claimed to be Christ and was tortured by the Belgians, and that a few Africans identified themselves with the Jews and white men with

Egyptians in their oppression of the Jews. But see Efriam Anderson, *Messianic Popular Movements in Lower Congo*, Uppsala, 1958; G. Balandier, "Messianism and Nationalism in Black Africa," in Pierre L. van den Berghe, ed., *Africa: Social Problems of Change and Conflict*, San Francisco, 1965, pp. 443–60 (reprint of an earlier article); Crawford Young, *Politics in the Congo, Decolonization and Independence*, Princeton, 1965, p. 284; Vittorio Lanternari, *The Religions of the Oppressed: A Study of Modern Messianic Cults*, tr. by L. Sergio, New York, 1963.

70. R. C. Majumdar, "The Growth of Nationalism in India," *Indo-Asian Culture*, vol. 10, 1961, pp. 107–08; Seal, *Emergence of Indian Nationalism*, p. 249; and Halstead, *Rebirth of a Nation*, pp. 119–20, 134.

71. Vartan Gregorian, "Mahmud Tarzi and Saraj-ol-Akhbar: Ideology of Nationalism and Modernization in Afghanistan, " *Middle East Journal*, vol. XXI, 1967, p. 360.

72. Majumdar, "The Growth of Nationalism in India," pp. 108–09.

73. I. M. Lewis, *The Modern History of Somaliland from Nation to State*, New York, 1964, p. 16.

74. *Ideas of Arab Nationalism*, p. 31. See also Hans E. Tütsch, *Facets of Arab Nationalism*, Detroit, 1965, p. 60; and Zeine N. Zeine, *Arab-Turkish Relations and the Emergence of Arab Nationalism*, Beirut, 1958, pp. 118–22.

75. See note 48; and Lewis, *The Middle East and the West*, p. 91.

76. Irele, "*Négritude*," p. 338.

77. Roland Oliver, "Crisis in Central Africa; Too Cheaty, Too Thefty: The Seeds of Nationalism in Nyasaland," *20th Century*, vol. 165, 1959, p. 362. And see Shepperson and Price, *Independent African*.

78. Italics mine. See, for example, Akinsola Akiwowo, "The Place of Mojola Agbebi in African Nationalist Movements: 1890–1917," *Phylon*, vol. XXVI, 1965, pp. 132–33.

79. *Daily Service* (Nigeria), July 2, 1945, quoted in Coleman, *Nigeria*, p. 107. For a similar opinion see Nkrumah's *Ghana: Autobiography*, pp. 22–23.

80. Tsunoda et al., eds., *Source of the Japanese Tradition*, pp. 785–90; Masao Maruyama, *Thought and Behaviour in Modern Japanese Politics*, ed. by Ivan Morris, London, 1963, pp. 14–20; Delmer Brown, *Nationalism in Japan*, Berkeley, 1955, p. 229; and P. C. Holton, *Modern Japan and Shinto Nationalism*, Chicago, 1947, p. 16.

81. Bary et al., *Sources of Indian Tradition*, pp. 728–29; Karan Singh, *Prophet of Indian Nationalism*, pp. 74–76.

82. In William L. Holland, ed., *Asian Nationalism and the West*, New York, 1953, pp. 13–14.

83. In Rosberg and Nottingham, *Myth of Mau Mau*, p. 246. For another see Ali Mazrui, "The Robes of Rebellion: Sex, Dress, and Politics in Africa," *Encounter*, vol. XXXIV, 1970, pp. 27–28.

84. This is a paraphrase of Johnston, *British Central Africa*, pp. 183–84.

85. See the observations of Théodore Monod quoted in Brunschwig, *L'Avènement de l'Afrique noire*, p. 199.

86. Quoted in Kimble, *Ghana*, p. 520.
87. *Let My People Go*, p. 31. Examples of the puzzlement of Africans and Asians about their identity are manifold, and the search still goes on, nowhere more so than in post-World War II and defeated Japan, where this author in the fall of 1969 was asked again and again, "Are we western or Asian or——?"
88. Stanley Wolpert, *Tilak and Gokhale: Revolution and Reform in the Making of Modern India*, Berkeley, 1962, imaginatively discusses how the thought of these two different and differing nationalists developed.
89. Wolpert, *Tilak and Gokhale*, pp. 13 ff., 296–97; and M. N. Das, *India Under Morley and Minto: Politics Behind Revolution, Repression and Reforms*, London, 1964, p. 96.
90. Levenson, *Liang Ch'i-ch'ao*, pp. 2, 112 ff.
91. Harold Z. Schriffen, *Sun Yat-sen and the Origins of the Chinese Revolution*, Berkeley, 1968, passim.
92. Stuart R. Schram, *Mao Tse-tung*, London, 1967; and in particular his "What Makes Mao a Maoist," *New York Times Magazine*, March 8, 1970, pp. 57 ff. For similar information and views see Robert Jay Lifton, *Thought Reform and the Psychology of Totalism: A Study of Brainwashing in China*, New York, 1961, pp. 374–75; and Borsa, "Nationalism and the Beginning of Modernization," pp. 326, 333. A classic statement is that of Han Su-yin, *A Many Splendored Thing*, Boston, 1952.
93. Maruyama, *Thought and Behaviour*, pp. 140–41. In Sōseki's *Since Then*, Daisuke and his sister-in-law converse about their father's success, and Saisuke remarks, "Yes, if one can make as much money as Father has by serving the nation, I wouldn't mind serving it myself." But in Japan the issue was never clearly resolved. The radical nationalist Kita Ikki believed Japan should "determine the particular configuration of its modern society" and argued against westernization. George M. Wilson, *Radical Nationalist in Japan: Kita Ikki . . .* , Cambridge (Mass.), 1969, p. 172.
94. G. E. von Grunebaum, *Modern Islam: The Search for Cultural Identity*, Berkeley, 1962, pp. 220–24. Somewhat similar tensions occurred in Iran and Turkey; see Cottam, *Nationalism in Iran;* and Robert E. Ward and Dankwart A. Rustow, eds., *Political Modernization in Japan and Turkey*, Princeton, 1964.
95. Abun-Nasr, "The Salafiyya Movement," pp. 489–90.
96. Still, the Buganda, for example, were often admonished not to lose their traditions. See the reasoned and informed article of Lloyd A. Fallers, "Ideology and Culture in Uganda Nationalism," *American Anthropologist*, vol. 63, 1961, pp. 678–83.
97. See the intelligent comments of J. F. A. Ajayi in "The Place of African History and Culture in the Process of Nation-Building in Africa South of the Sahara," *Journal of Negro Education*, vol. XXX, 1961, pp. 206–09. For the view that emphasis should be on the native roots of the emerging nationalisms see J. Lonsdale, "Emergence of African Nations: A Historiographical Analysis," *African Affairs*, vol. 67, 1968, p. 16.

98. Nairobi, 1966.
99. Halstead, *Rebirth of a Nation*, p. 87.
100. As Ali Mazrui remarked, one aspiration of Africans might be called "dignitarianism." "On the Concept 'We Are All Africans,'" *American Political Science Review*, vol. LVII, 1963, p. 96.
101. Albert Hourani speaks of three new classes in the Arab world: the middle class, the intelligentsia, and the urban proletariat. *Arabic Thought in the Liberal Age, 1798–1939*, London, 1962, pp. 349 ff. But class interpretations, while much argued, tend to be blunt instruments. See the discussion of varying views on the role of classes in Ghana by Jon Kraus, "On the Politics of Nationalism and Social Change in Ghana," *Journal of Modern African Studies*, vol. 7, 1969, pp. 107–30.
102. As Khosrow Mostofi remarked, an "amazing aspect of [the nationalizing] process is the fact that often the paradise on earth, one's country, is no paradise at all. In fact, in most cases the actual conditions of life are so miserable that hell would be a more appropriate name than paradise." *Aspects of Nationalism: A Sociology of Colonial Revolt*, 2nd ed., Salt Lake City, 1964, p. 42.
103. In 1963 Sithole spoke in Tanganyika with representatives of sixty-five countries present: "In Zimbalwe we are engaged in a bitter struggle to destroy the government of the white settlers, by the white settlers, for the white settlers, so that it is replaced by the government of the people, by the people, for the people," and "deafening cheers went up." *African Nationalism*, 2nd ed., p. 35. Lincoln's clarion phrase rang around the world all through the twentieth century up to 1970, and it's still ringing.
104. What Fayez Sayegh wrote of the Arab national movement can be applied to others: "As it came into its own [it] was animated by three kindred urges, for emancipation from foreign domination, for socio-economic development, and for political unification. The corresponding ideas of independence, progress and unity jointly became the principal components of the total concept of Arab nationalism." *Arab Unity, Hope and Fulfillment*, New York, 1958, pp. 5–9. For some peoples, of course, unlike the Arabs, there was little about which to unify except opposition to foreign rule and a faint hope for socioeconomic progress.
105. Mazrui makes this point for Africans in "On the Concept 'We Are All Africans,'" pp. 89–91.
106. As Coleman states, when nationalists became more hopeful of victory, their grievances multiplied and became more intolerable. *Nigeria*, p. 317.
107. Charles H. Heimsath, *Indian Nationalism and Hindu Social Reform*, Princeton, 1964, p. 136; and Haim, "Islam and the Theory of Arab Nationalism," p. 284. The phraseology differs but similar statements are many and become more numerous. At the end of the nineteenth century Swami Vivekananda of India, who defended Hindu values, was preaching, "My ideal is growth, expansion, development on national lines." Bimanbehari Majumdar, *Militant Nationalism in India and Its Socioreligious Background, 1897–1917*, Calcutta, 1966, pp. 18 ff. Later this kind of statement would be commonplace.

471

108. Herbert Spiro, in his otherwise slight book, *Politics in Africa*, Englewood Cliffs (N.J.), 1962, pp. 15 ff., effectively makes this point.

109. Article in the *New York Colonization Journal*, August 1954, quoted in Lynch, *Edward Wilmot Blyden*, pp. 19–20.

110. Quoted in Rotberg, *The Rise of Nationalism in Central Africa*, p. 86.

111. Quoted in Louis Snyder, *The New Nationalism*, Ithaca (N.Y.), 1968, p. 165.

112. Quoted in B. Oetomo, "Some Remarks on Modern Indonesian Historiography," in D. C. E. Hall, ed., *Historians of South East Asia*, London, 1961, pp. 73–84.

113. For lucid analyses see the essays of Thomas Hodgkin and Kathleen Gough in Bidney, ed., *The Concept of Freedom in Anthropology*. To my surprise, however, I have found little emphasis on what the West calls civil liberties.

114. A. A. Mazrui and G. F. Engholm, "Rousseau and Intellectualized Populism in Africa," *Review of Politics*, vol. 30, 1968, pp. 23–25.

115. Jean Guiart, "Forerunners of Melanesian Nationalism," *Oceania*, vol. XXII, 1951, pp. 81–90.

116. See the warnings in the *La Voix du peuple* (Donala), Jan. 1, 1960, quoted in Victor T. Le Vine, "The Trauma of Independence in French-Speaking Africa," *Journal of Developing Areas*, vol. 2, 1968, pp. 216–17.

117. Heimsath, *Indian Nationalism*, p. 338.

118. Robert Rotberg, *A Political History of Tropical Africa*, New York, 1965, p. 349.

119. See, for example, the histories of Indian nationalism, especially their pages on the Indian National Congress; and Nicola Ziadeh, *Origins of Nationalism in Tunisia*, Beirut, 1962, pp. 103 ff.; and Halstead, *Rebirth of a Nation*, pp. 211 ff. Ziadeh shows the great influence of the anonymous detailed nationalist plan, *La Tunisie martyr*, of 1920. See also Dwight L. Ling, *Tunisia from Protectorate to Republic*, Bloomington (Ind.), 1967, p. 115, for the effect of this bible of the resistance movement on the young Habib Bourguiba, who became the first president of Tunisia.

120. Brunschwig, *L'Avènement de l'Afrique noire*, pp. 202–03.

121. *The Diaries of Theodor Herzl*, ed. and tr. by Marvin Lowenthal, New York, 1962, pp. 30–31, 45–47, 58; and Ludwig Lewisohn, *Theodor Herzl, a Portrait for This Age*, Cleveland, 1955, p. 303.

122. When, for example, the Ottoman revolution of the Young Turks in 1908 appeared to have succeeded, "Macedonia seemed to have become Utopia." Henceforth, cried Enver Bay, "We are all brothers. There are no longer Bulgars, Greeks, Roumans, [sic] Jews, Musselmans; under the same blue sky we are all equal. . . ." See William Miller, *The Ottoman Empire and Its Successor*, Cambridge (Mass.), p. 476; and Ernest E. Ramsaur, Jr., *The Young Turks: Prelude to the Revolution of 1908*, Princeton, 1957, p. 137. This kind of rhetoric seems universal in nationalist revolts, but it remains rhetoric.

123. Quoted in Wolpert, *Tilak and Gokhale*, pp. 10–11.

124. The testimonies are many and voluminous. See, for example, the diary of Moses Leib Lilienbaum (1843–1910) in Arthur Hertzberg, ed., *The Zionist Idea: A Historical Analysis and Reader*, New York, 1966, pp. 168 ff. Andrew Sarvis, an honors student of mine, contributed to my understanding of Jewish nationalism.

125. Harris, *Nationalism and Revolution in Egypt*, p. 74; and Ahmed, *Intellectual Origins of Egyptian Nationalism*, pp. 62 ff. That the facts and figures of most incidents are controversial and uncertain, and rumor and allegation rife, needs only to be mentioned.

126. See note 67, this chapter.

127. Ziadeh, *Origins of Nationalism in Tunisia*, pp. 83–84; and Ling, *Tunisia from Protectorate to Republic*, pp. 108–09.

128. Vidya Mahajan, *The Nationalist Movement in India and Its Leaders*, pp. 29–35; and Meyer, *India and Pakistan*, p. 147.

129. Nehru's *Toward Freedom*, New York, 1941, recounts his reactions to this and other violent repressions. See also D. Mackenzie Brown, [ed.], *The Nationalist Movement: Indian Political Thought from Renade to Bhave*, Berkeley, 1961, pp. 131–32, 144–151; and Frank Moraes, *Jawaharlal Nehru*, Bombay, 1956, p. 199.

130. Israel, *Student Nationalism in China*, p. 4.

131. The accounts are so numerous that they defy citation. But for illustrations see Rosberg and Nottingham, *Myth of Mau Mau;* Jacques Goutor, *Algeria and France, 1830–1963*, Muncie (Ind.), 1965; and the several books on Vietnam of Bernard Fall. Before nationalism fully appeared there were many "primary" resistance movements. See T. O. Ranger, "Connexions Between Primary Resistance Movements and Modern Mass Nationalism in East and Central Africa," *Journal of African History*, vol. 9, 1968, pp. 437–53, 631–41.

132. Rotberg, *Political History of Tropical Africa*, p. 367. Yatuta Chiseza, later minister of home affairs in Malawi, threatened, "We mean to embarrass . . . the Nyasaland Government . . . about our demands. This is the only way. Negotiations won't do . . . we mean to create disturbances . . . even if it means every person in the country dies."

133. I have collected information, insufficient to be sure, on about fifty leaders. Someone should do a thorough study.

134. See the sympathetic biography, Austin Coates, *Rizal: Philippine Nationalist and Patriot*, New York, 1968. Again, the patriot Manuel Roxas was born eight months after Spanish guards shot his father, and Carlos Romulo when he was three saw a beloved neighbor hanged by Americans in the village square. Friend, *Between Two Empires*, pp. 45–46.

135. And so did violent repression within a country by native rulers. Mao's second wife, whom he loved, was beheaded by the Kuomintang, and one brother and his sister-in-law were executed.

136. See *The Diaries of Theodor Herzl*, pp. 4–8, 56, for graphic illustration.

137. *The Dual Mandate in British Tropical Africa*, London, 1922, p. 618.

138. The literature is full and overflowing. For one example see the thirty-odd essays in Rotberg and Mazrui, eds., *Protest and Power*.

139. Where the ideas of "passive resistance" and civil disobedience (Thoreau?) first arose in modern times is uncertain, but see Prasad, *Changing Modes of Indian National Movement[s]*, pp. 74–75.
140. *African Nationalism*, 2nd ed., pp. 160, 166.
141. R. Randle, "From National Self-Determination to National Self-Development," *Journal of the History of Ideas*, vol. 31, 1970, p. 50.
142. See pages 157–58. For developing peoples, as Immanuel Wallerstein said, "There were two quite separate lessons symbolized by the Russian Revolution. . . . One was a way of analyzing the world. The other was a way of changing it—by organized, militant, mass action." *Africa, the Politics of Independence*—an informed, helpful book.
143. Maruyama, *Thought and Behaviour*, p. 143.
144. Kita Ikki, for one; see Wilson, *Radical Nationalist in Japan*, passim.
145. See page 233. I. Potekin developed the Marxist views of the Stalin period, arguing that "nations are the product of capitalist development." "The Formation of Nations in Africa," in Wallerstein, ed., *Social Change*, pp. 561, 570. But Marxist-Leninists thought it their duty to assist any people to throw off the imperialist yoke, participate in and correctly lead "all the democratic movements and especially the national movement for independence." Comintern statement, 1933, quoted in John P. Haithcox, "Nationalism and Communism," *Journal of Asian Studies*, vol. XXIV, 1965, pp. 472–73.
146. Irele, "*Négritude*," p. 340.
147. *Quotations from Chairman Mao Tse-tung*, Peking, 1966, pp. 175–76.
148. Immanuel Wallerstein, *Africa: The Politics of Unity; An Analysis of a Contemporary Social Movement*, New York, 1967, pp. 14–15.
149. In the Arab world the Ba'thist leader Michel 'Aflaq declared, "Our Socialism is nationalist," saying, "Socialism must be suited to our nation. . . . We want socialism to serve our nationalist cause. . . ." Hisham Sharabi, *Nationalism and Revolution in the Arab World*, Princeton, 1966, p. 111.
150. Cf. Legum, *Pan-Africanism*, p. 22, who thinks the African idea originated with the missionary Joseph Booth (b. 1857). The term Pan-Africanism may have first been used in 1900 by the Trinidad lawyer Henry Sylvester Williams at the London conference. Hollis Lynch, "Pan-Negro Nationalism in the New World Before 1862," *Boston University Papers on Africa*, vol. II, 1966, p. 149.
151. Nikki R. Keddie, *An Islamic Response to Imperialism: Political and Religious Writing of . . . "al-Afghānī,"* Berkeley, 1968.
152. The delegates included W. E. B. Du Bois from the United States, who was to play a leading role for a generation or more. See C. G. Contee, "Emergence of Du Bois as an African Nationalist," *Journal of Negro History*, vol. 54, 1969, passim. An American historian, Rayford Logan, depicts his own experience in "Historical Aspects of Pan-Africanism: A Personal Chronicle," *African Forum*, vol. I, 1965, pp. 90–104.
153. This congress got attention in the then popular *Picture Post* of England. See Dennis Johnson, "Dead But Not Forgotten," *Manchester Guardian Weekly*, October 31, 1970, p. 11.

154. The studies are numerous and of varying value. Among them are American Society of African Culture, *Pan-Africanism Reconsidered* (papers by specialists), Berkeley, 1962; R. Emerson, "Pan-Africanism," *International Organization*, vol. 16, 1962, pp. 275–90; Ferkiss, *Africa's Search for Unity;* Joseph Nye, Jr., *Pan-Africanism and East African Integration*, Cambridge (Mass.), 1965; Legum, *Pan-Africanism;* Immanuel Wallerstein, *Africa: The Politics of Unity;* Welch, *Dream of Unity*. See also the accounts of such participants as Nkrumah and George Padmore.

155. Quoted in Ali Mazrui, *Towards a Pax Africana: A Study of Ideology and Ambition*, Chicago, 1967, p. 48; and his "On the Concept 'We Are All Africans,'" pp. 88–97.

156. Yahya Armajani, *Middle East Past and Present*, Englewood Cliffs (N.J.), 1970, pp. 343–44. Once more the literature is voluminous, particularly since Pan-Arabism (or Arab nationalism) and Pan-Islamism, both important, are in many ways related. I have learned, by way of illustration, from Sylvia Haim, ed., *Arab Nationalism*, Berkeley, 1962, an anthology of source materials; A. H. Hourani, *Syria and Lebanon*, London, 1946; Dwight Lee, "The Origins of Pan-Islamism," *American Historical Review*, vol. 47, 1942, pp. 278–87; John Major, "The Search for Arab Unity," *International Affairs*, vol. 39, 1963, pp. 551–63; and H. Siegman, "Arab Unity and Disunity," *Middle East Journal*, vol. XVI, 1962, pp. 48–59. The last quarterly has had articles on the topic almost every issue since it was established.

157. Nasser's views are best found in his *The Philosophy of Revolution* and *Egypt's Liberation*. See also Richard Frye, ed., *Islam and the West*, The Hague, 1957, pp. 18–19 (particularly the essay by G. E. von Grunebaum).

158. I have drawn particularly on the papers by specialists in Thomas M. Franck, ed., *Why Federations Fail: An Inquiry into the Requisites for Successful Federation*, New York, 1968; Welch, *Dream of Unity;* and the fine article of Ajayi, "The Place of African History and Culture in the Process of Nation-Building in Africa South of the Sahara."

159. This was true of communist and socialist leaders and of humanists like Senghor. On the latter see Irele, "*Négritude*," p. 520. Of course, the Bandung Conference of 1955 symbolically indicated the need and desire for co-operation between Asian and African peoples, but the conference had little effect.

160. *Africa, the Politics of Independence*, p. 86.

161. Part of the document is in Tsunoda, et al., eds., *Sources of the Japanese Tradition*, pp. 785–94; see also Brown, *Nationalism in Japan*, pp. 207–08; and on the economic side Byron K. Marshall, *Capitalism and Nationalism in Prewar Japan: The Ideology of the Business Elite, 1868–1941*, Stanford (Calif.), 1967.

162. Richard Robinson, *The First Turkish Republic*, Cambridge (Mass.), 1963, pp. 84–85; Niyazi Berkes, *The Development of Secularism in Turkey*, Montreal, 1964, p. 470, passim; Lord Kinross, *Ataturk: A Biography of Mustafa Kemal, Father of Modern Turkey*, New York, 1965, passim; and

the solid quantitative article by F. W. Frey, "Socialization to National Identification Among Turkish Peasants," *Journal of Politics*, vol. 30, 1968, pp. 934–57.

163. The newspapers of Asia and Africa, often at government command, daily reported all the activities and urged further nationalization. On October 20, 1969, for example, Kenyatta proclaimed "Economic *Uhuru* Next" as he told a "mammoth rally" the biggest task facing his government was "to transfer the country's economy from foreign to citizen hands." *East African Standard*, Nairobi, October 21, 1969, p. 1.

164. Kinross, *Ataturk*, pp. 412–15; Cremeans, *The Arabs and the World*, pp. 47–48; *Manchester Guardian Weekly*, October 24, 1970, p. 11. The whole subject is treated in high humor and with other illustrations by Mazrui, "The Robes of Rebellion: Sex, Dress, and Politics in Africa."

165. David Gordon provides an informed discussion of the different uses of history in *Self-Determination and History in The Third World*, Princeton (N.J.), 1971. For examples see Kimble, *Ghana*, pp. xv, 521–26; R. C. Majumdar, "Nationalist Historians," in C. H. Philips, ed., *Historians of India, Pakistan and Ceylon*, London, 1961, pp. 416–28; Johannes Voight, "Nationalist Interpretations of Arthásāstra in Indian Historical Thought," in S. N. Mukherjee, ed., "The Movement for National Freedom in India," *St. Anthony's Papers*, vol. 18, London, 1966; and Wallerstein, *Africa, the Politics of Independence*, pp. 125–29. On the other hand, there was almost no Indonesian study of Indonesian history during the first half of the twentieth century. See Oetomo, "Some Remarks on Modern Indonesian Historiography."

166. Quoted in Nuseibeh, *Ideas of Arab Nationalism*, p. 78.

167. In Majumdar, "Nationalist Historians," p. 428.

168. See Maurice Neufeld, *Poor Countries and Authoritarian Rule*, Ithaca (N.Y.), 1965, p. 24. The same kinds of appeals to history were made in many lands. See, for example, Gregorian, "Mahmud Tarzi," pp. 361–62.

169. *Présence Africaine*, in Brunschwig, *L'Avènement de l'Afrique noire*, p. 201.

170. L. M. Thompson, "Afrikaner Nationalist Historiography and the Policy of Apartheid," *Journal of African History*, vol. V, 1962, is a first-rate short study.

171. This paragraph is based on observations in East Africa in 1969 and on many talks with scholars and students.

172. Language was and is a major problem of the new states, and much has been written on the subject. Nigeria by one count has 248 languages. But see the twenty-nine essays in Joshua Freeman, Charles Freeman, and Jyotirinda Das Gupta, *Language Problems of Developing Nations*, New York, 1968.

173. A convenient compilation is Martin Shaw and Henry Coleman, eds., *National Anthems of the World*, 2nd rev. ed., London, 1963. I have read and tried to analyze over one hundred anthems, but someone should do the linguistic analysis of which I am not capable.

174. Schram, "What Makes Mao a Maoist," p. 37.

175. *Toward Freedom*, p. 274. For African examples see Wallerstein, *Africa, the Politics of Independence*, pp. 98–100, 122.

176. Karl Deutsch discusses some of the problems of knowing in his path-making study, *Nationalism and Social Communication: An Inquiry into the Foundations of Nationality*, 2nd ed., Cambridge (Mass.), 1966, but he did not present enough empirical data, probably because these data are just becoming available in studies such as the article of Frey, "Socialization to National Identification Among Turkish Peasants."

177. See note 87. For an interesting study of the identity crisis of Japanese students who have studied in the United States, see John Bennett, Herbert Passin, and Robert McKnight, *In Search of Identity*, Minneapolis, 1958. It is likely, nevertheless, that right-wing nationalism is growing again in Japan; at least, this is the impression one gets from the press and in conversations with Japanese scholars.

178. In the early 1960's, students attending the University College at Nairobi, when asked on standard forms who they were, generally gave the name of their tribe; by 1969 many were answering "Kenyan."

179. A Luo student in substance told me in November, 1969, after a beer party, "We [I paraphrase] talk about Kenya but I'm a Luo and we're going to kill all those damned Kikuyus" (the dominant tribe). He could have been serious.

180. Chalmers Johnson, *Peasant Nationalism and Communist Power: The Emergence of Revolutionary China 1937–1945*, Stanford (Calif.), 1962, p. 3. Donald Gillin, in his review of this book, stated that he believed Chinese peasants supported the Chinese Communists before the Japanese invasion of 1937. *Journal of Asian Studies*, February 1964, pp. 269–289.

181. Foreword to Saadia Touval, *Somali Nationalism*, Cambridge (Mass.), 1963, p. v. As Mostafa Rejai remarked, nationalism in Asia and Africa "apparently does not require [as it had in the West] a great deal of social and cultural integration." "Periodization of Nationalism," *Social Science*, vol. 44, 1969, p. 23. But this may be only a matter of time.

182. Coleman, *Nigeria*, p. 320.

183. *The Student*, vol. VIII, no. 1, 1964, p. 4.

184. Lemarchand, *Political Awakening in the Belgian Congo*, p. 51.

185. Herbert Luethy, "Indonesia Confronted," *Encounter*, vol. XXV, 1965, pp. 80–81.

186. D. K. Hingorani, "The Role of Languages in the Development of National Consciousness in India," *PMLA*, vol. LXXII, 1957, pp. 32–37. For a recent, intelligent view see Robert R. R. Brooks, "Can India Make It?" *Saturday Review*, August 9, 1969, pp. 12–16.

187. How great the gap has been between the charismatic leaders and the ordinary people is demonstrated by Jean Lacouture's fine *The Demigods: Charismatic Leadership in the Third World*, tr. by Patricia Wolf, New York, 1970.

188. With a student, Marie Thourson Jones, I have searched (see chapter VIII, note 45) through much of the recent literature—books and articles—on

mass communication in Asia and Africa and found much excited commentary but few serious studies showing how the press, the radio, and TV (where it exists) make people nationalists. The one solid quantitative study to prove, on the basis of data, that exposure to mass media is positively related to national identification is Frey, "Socialization to National Identification Among Turkish Peasants," esp. pp. 951 ff. Three important, perceptive articles are Ibrahim Abn-Lughod, "The Mass Media and Egyptian Village Life," *Social Forces*, vol. 42, 1963, pp. 97–104; Paul J. Deutschmann, "The Mass Media in an Underdeveloped Village," *Journalism Quarterly*, vol. 41, 1963, pp. 27–35; and Daniel Lerner, "International Cooperation and Communication in National Development," in Daniel Lerner and Wilbur Schramm, *Communication and Change in the Developing Countries*, Honolulu, 1967, pp. 103–25.

189. For examples see Le Vine, "The Trauma of Independence in French-Speaking Africa."

190. See the remarkable series of articles on Ghana, Nigeria, and India in the *Christian Science Monitor*, August 20 and September 20, 1969, and October 17, 1970.

191. There is much conjecture on the influence of urbanism but little hard evidence. This will be a fruitful field for further investigation.

192. S. Kajaratman, "Beyond Nationalism, More Nationalism," *Solidarity*, vol. LV, 1969, pp. 42–47.

Chapter XI

1. And so has Senator William Fulbright with his two recent books on "myths and realities" in American foreign policy. The first use of "myth and reality" known to me was in the title of Francis Delaisi's sharp *Political Myths and Economic Realities* in 1927. Walter Kolarz's provocative *Myths and Realities in Eastern Europe* was published in London in 1946, though I did not know the book until 1968. The date of my own *Nationalism: Myth and Reality* was 1955. Since that time the phrase has been used dozens of times in titles of books and articles.

2. Or, as C. M. Bowra wrote in his book on *Primitive Song*, New York, 1963, pp. 217–18, "A myth is a story whose primary purpose is not to entertain but to enlighten primitive man on matters which perplex him and cannot be made intelligible, as they can to us by analysis or abstraction. . . ." But I would think the definition applicable not only to primitive but also to modern man.

3. Ernst Cassirer, *The Myth of the State*, New Haven (Conn.), 1946, pp. 278–79.

4. Quoted in Herman Finer, *Mussolini's Italy*, New York, 1935, p. 218.

5. I am swiftly going over ground once trodden in my previous book, *Nationalism: Myth and Reality*. I can add to what I said but subtract very little.

6. Versions of all the myths vary, but in substantial form they are long-lived. The Japanese myth was commemorated the most recent time in Tokyo in

1940. On the founding of the Japanese see Richard Storry, *A History of Japan*, London, 1960, pp. 25–26; and Delmer Brown, *Nationalism in Japan*, Berkeley, 1955, pp. 15–17. The basic documents of the eighth century, *Kojiki and Nihonga*, are in part in Ryusaku Tsunoda et al., eds., *Sources of the Japanese Tradition*, New York, 1958, pp. 15–35. And see page 264.

7. See Carlton Hayes, "Philosopher Turned Patriot," in James Shotwell, *Essays in Intellectual History*, New York, 1929, p. 29.

8. *Addresses to the German Nation*, tr. by R. F. Jones and G. H. Turnbull, Chicago, 1922, p. 232. I have changed the translation slightly to conform to English usage.

9. From Samuel Flagg Bemis, *John Quincy Adams and the Foundations of American Foreign Policy*, New York, 1949, p. 182.

10. This is the constant theme of his *Duties of Man*. And see his letter to Melegari, October 2, 1833, in Bolton King, ed., *Mazzini's Letters*, tr. by Jervis, London, 1930, p. 3.

11. A variation on the theme was the British nationalist J. A. Cramb's faith that empires (the British) were successive reincarnations of the divine idea. *The Origins and Destiny of Imperial Britain and Nineteenth Century Europe*, New York, 1915, pp. 230–31.

12. In Wm. Theodore de Bary et al., *Sources of Indian Tradition*, New York, 1958, pp. 728–29. And see pages 256–57.

13. Deuteronomy 14:2. "The historic, eschatological myth of the Exile and Redemption of the Jews, cultivated by successive generations in every country . . . and binding them in a self-conscious union of fate and destiny, was a major theme in the culture and education of all Jews." Ben Halpern, *The Idea of the Jewish State*, Cambridge (Mass.), 1961, p. 5.

14. I have not found much evidence of the myth in smaller older nations, like Switzerland or Sweden, or among most small new nations. But probably this is only because my search was limited. The subject cries for a major comparative study.

15. *The Letters and Speeches of Oliver Cromwell, with Elucidations by Thomas Carlyle*, ed. by S. C. Lomas, London, 1904, vol. II, pp. 404 ff.; and George Lanyi, "Oliver Cromwell and His Age, a Study in Nationalism," Ph.D. dissertation, Harvard, 1949, typescript. Milton held a similar view. On Rhodes, see *The Last Will and Testament of Cecil Rhodes*, London, 1902, p. 98. The testimonies of Englishmen on the "destiny" are too numerous to list.

16. The solid studies are several and include Frederick Merk, *Manifest Destiny and Mission in American History: A Reinterpretation*, New York, 1963; Julius Pratt, *Expansionists of 1812*, New York, 1925, and his *Expansionists of 1898*, Baltimore, 1936; and Albert K. Weinberg, *Manifest Destiny: A Study of Nationalist Expansionism in American History*, Baltimore, 1935. A convenient old compendium of the rhetoric is Frederick Saunders, ed., *Addresses . . . Delivered in the Several States of the Union, July 4, 1876–1883 . . . 1892–1893*, New York, 1893.

17. The writings and speeches of Beveridge that I have perused are collected in his papers in the Manuscript Division of the Library of Congress.

18. Edward Thaden, *Conservative Nationalism in Nineteenth-Century Russia,* Seattle, 1964, pp. 83–85. Dostoyevsky has an eloquent passage in *The Possessed* (1871–72); see chapter VI, note 49. See also Robert E. Mac-Master, *Danilevsky: A Russian Totalitarian Philosopher,* Cambridge (Mass.), 1967.

19. William Henry Vatcher, Jr., *White Laager: The Rise of South Afrikaner Nationalism,* New York, 1965, pp. 35, 223.

20. Tsunoda et al., eds., *Sources of the Japanese Tradition,* p. 796.

21. See chapter X, note 55.

22. A fine American historian, Robert Binkley, made a similar remark about nineteenth-century intellectuals. *Realism and Nationalism 1852–1871,* New York, 1935, p. 304. But, as Nehru remarked, it is "curious" that patriots still "cannot resist the tendency to give an anthropomorphic form to a country." Probably, as Nehru also said, "Such is the force of habit and early associations." *Toward Freedom: The Autobiography of Jawaharlal Nehru,* New York, 1941, p. 274.

23. *The Social Contract,* New York, 1946, p. 17. Alexandre Choulguine wrote a detailed study, "Les Origines de l'esprit national moderne et Jean-Jacques Rousseau," *Annales de la Société Jean-Jacques Rousseau,* vol. XXVI, 1937, pp. 9–283.

24. *Considérations sur le gouvernement de Pologne . . . ,* in *Oeuvres complètes,* 1826 ed., vol. VI, pp. 229–376. And see pages 88–89.

25. See page 72.

26. On Carnot see René Johannet, *Le Principe des nationalités,* Paris, 1918, pp. 97–98; for Fichte, the *Addresses to the German Nation.* For Görres it was "reiner Naturtrieb, dass ein Volk, also scharf und deutlich im seine natürlichen Grenzen eingeschlossen, aus der Zerstreung in die Einheit sich zu sammeln sucht." Lord Acton, "Nationality," in *Essays on Freedom and Power,* Boston, 1948, p. 178.

27. But analogies *from* nature continued to be drawn. Moses Hess, an early Jewish nationalist, like Herder and Mazzini compared differentiation in men to that in plants and animals: "The life of man in society begins with a primal differentiation of folk types, which at first, plantlike, existed side by side; then, animal-like, fought each other . . . but which will finally . . . live together in friendship and *each for the other,* without surrendering their particular and typical identities." *Rome and Jerusalem,* in Arthur Hertzberg, ed., *The Zionist Idea: A Historical Analysis and Reader,* New York, 1966, pp. 129–130.

28. Robert R. Ergang, *Herder and the Foundations of German Nationalism,* New York, 1931, pp. 85–86.

29. Peter Manniche, *Denmark, a Social Laboratory,* New York, 1939, pp. 87–89. The best study is Erica Simon, *Réveil national et culture populaire en Scandinavie: La Genèse de la Højskole Nordique (1844–1878),* Paris, 1960.

30. See page 85.
31. Hegel seems profound, but he may only be obscure in his *Philosophy of Right* and *Philosophy of History*. There are many commentaries, but on this subject I have found Charles Cole, "The Heavy Hand of Hegel," in Edward Mead Earle, ed., *Nationalism and Internationalism, Essays Inscribed to Carlton J. H. Hayes*, New York, 1950, pp. 65–78, most relevant.
32. The quoted remarks are from his "Qu'est-ce qu'une nation?" and the preface to his *Pages françaises*, Paris, 1921, pp. 4–5, 68–69, 72. The organism theory has been held by patriots in many nations, especially by fascists like Rocco of Italy—see Howard Marraro, *Nationalism in Italian Education*, New York, 1927, p. 2. A most forceful expression of it is Mussolini's article on fascism in the edition of *Enciclopedia Italiana* of his time.
33. The principal ideas are in *Scènes et doctrines du nationalisme*, Paris, n.d., particularly pp. 10–13, 84–96. Barrès and Charles Maurras, who held somewhat similar views, are discussed in scholarly fashion by Eugen Weber, *Action Française: Royalism and Reaction in Twentieth Century France*, Stanford (Calif.), 1962; and in William Curt Buthman's doctoral dissertation, *The Rise of Integral Nationalism in France, with Special Reference . . .* [to] *Charles Maurras*, New York, 1939. See also chapter VIII, note 72.
34. A. B. C. Cobban, "Edmund Burke and the Origins of the Theory of Nationality," *Cambridge Historical Journal*, vol. II, 1926–28, p. 36.
35. K. R. Minogue, *Nationalism*, New York, 1967, p. 99.
36. For an example, Italy, see Massimo Salvadori, "Nationalism in Modern Italy: 1915 and After," *Orbis*, vol. X, 1967, p. 1160.
37. Robert Soucy, "Barrès and Fascism," *French Historical Studies*, vol. V, 1967, p. 75; G. van den Berghe, "Contemporary Nationalism in the Western World," *Daedalus*, vol. 95, 1966, pp. 834–35.
38. In "For All We Have and Are."
39. Benjamin Bloom, *Stability and Change in Human Characteristics*, New York, 1964, p. 209.
40. Salo W. Baron, *Modern Nationalism and Religion*, New York, 1947, p. 12.
41. *La Politique tirée des propres paroles de l'écriture sainte*, in *Oeuvres complètes de Bossuet*, ed. by Abbé Migne, vol. XI, liv. I, art. II, prop. 3, p. 486. Two centuries later Lord Acton, a great English Catholic historian, approvingly quoted Bossuet in his essay "Nationality," in *Essays on Freedom and Power*, p. 190.
42. In his comment on the abbé Saint-Pierre's *Project for a Treaty of Perpetual Peace*.
43. Ergang, *Herder*, p. 89.
44. Quoted in H. S. Reiss, *The Political Thought of the German Romantics, 1793–1815*, Oxford, 1955, p. 94.
45. *History of Civilization in England*, 2nd ed., New York, 1883, p. 29 (first published in 1859–61).
46. Among their influential books were, respectively, *Anthropogeographie*,

2 vols., Stuttgart, 1882–91; *Influences of Geographic Environment,* New York, 1911; *Human Geography,* New York, 1920; and *Civilization and Climate,* 3rd ed., New Haven, 1924.

47. Among answers to 355 newspaper questionnaires in Indonesia in 1957. Guy Pauker, "Indonesian Images of Their National Self," *Public Opinion Quarterly,* vol. 22, 1958, p. 313.

48. Gerhard Masur remarked that Brazilians might more accurately speak of a "great land in search of a people." *Nationalism in Latin America: Diversity and Unity,* New York, 1966, p. 45. And many parts of the United States do not have rocks, rills, woods, or hills, though most do have supermarkets and filling stations that have all but blotted out the land.

49. But as Robert E. Ward and Dankwart A. Rustow remarked, "During the early modernizing period, there was never any serious doubt as to where [Japan's] major boundaries lay. They were naturally defined by the sea." *Political Modernization in Japan and Turkey,* Princeton, 1964, p. 448.

50. *The Territorial Imperative: A Personal Inquiry into the Animal Origins of Property and Nations,* New York, 1966.

51. *Political Myths and Economic Realities,* pp. 152–53.

52. Florjan Znaniecki briefly and well described the "myth of common descent and racial unity" in *Modern Nationalities: A Sociological Study,* Urbana (Ill.), 1952, pp. 89–93. A solid recent work on the history of racial ideas in one country is Thomas F. Gossett, *Race: The History of an Idea in America,* Dallas, 1964; an older and now revised work on racial myths in Europe is Jacques Barzun, *Race: A Study in Superstition,* rev. ed., New York, 1965, originally published in 1937; an able study of the American myths is William Stanton, *The Leopard's Spots: Scientific Attitudes Toward Race in America, 1815–1859,* Chicago, 1960; and of the myths in four societies, Pierre van den Berghe, *Race and Racism: A Comparative Perspective,* New York, 1967.

53. Perhaps Johann F. Blumenbach's *De generis humani varietate,* Göttingen, 1775, was the first "scientific" study; he measured skulls and divided mankind into five races by color. But Linneaus' *Systeme naturae* (1739) was earlier, and in 1684 François Bernier divided people into four groups by facial lineaments and bodily conformation. Gossett, *Race,* pp. 32–33.

54. E. G. Murphy, *The Basis of Ascendancy,* New York, 1909, pp. 88–90.

55. A most fanatical racist before the Nazis, Houston Stewart Chamberlain, believed the "Teutonic race" responsible for all modern civilization and at the same time that the nation created the conditions for the formation of race. *The Foundations of the Nineteenth Century,* tr. by Lees, London, 1913, vol. I, p. 292. This kind of thinking is exemplified in the writings of Americans such as H. F. Osborn and Madison Grant.

56. Hannah Arendt, "Race-Thinking Before Racism," *Review of Politics,* vol. VI, 1944, p. 49. Herder had a contrary view, that all men were of one race. Ergang, *Herder,* p. 89. On Schlegel see Walter Langsam, *The Napoleonic Wars and German Nationalism in Austria,* New York, 1930, pp. 65–66.

57. *Histoire de France,* Paris, 1869, vol. I, pp. 105–09. A common view in

France, from the Comte de Boulainvilliers (1658–1722), to the Thierrys, Comte de Montlosier, and then Gobineau, was that France was composed of two races.

58. *Lectures on Early English History,* London, 1906, pp. 3–75.

59. The literature is too vast to cite. This author, if time permits, may do a full study on the relation of "race" and nationalism, but someone else should do it very soon.

60. No words were more misused or loosely used than "Teutonic," "Aryan," "Nordic," "Caucasian."

61. *Foundations,* vol. I, p. xv; vol. II, pp. 149, 187.

62. *Politics,* tr. by Dugdale and De Bille, London, 1916, p. 271.

63. *The Psychology of Peoples,* London, 1899, pp. 19–20. Le Bon frequently used such terms as "national soul."

64. *Nationality and Race,* London, 1919, p. 33; see also his *The Place of Prejudice in Modern Civilization,* New York, 1931.

65. *The Group Mind,* New York, 1928, p. 283; see also his *National Welfare and Decay,* London, 1921. The voices of patriots such as those just mentioned were not isolated, but it is hardly of much use to cite the many books, for instance those of the noted American geographer Ellsworth Huntington.

66. *Weltbürgertum und Nationalstaat,* Munich, 1928, p. 1. There is now a translation by Robert Kimber, *Cosmopolitanism and the National State,* Princeton, 1970. See chapter I, note 41.

67. This is the chief message of *Mein Kampf,* but the Nazi doctrine is most completely developed in Alfred Rosenberg, *Der Mythus des 20 Jahrhunderts,* Munich, 1930.

68. See Beveridge's three articles in the *Saturday Evening Post,* vol. 172, 1900, pp. 834 ff., 881 ff., 1018 ff. For Jordan see his speech reported in the *Indianapolis Sentinel,* March 12, 1900, p. 8.

69. F. A. van Jaarsveld, *The Awakening of Afrikaner Nationalism, 1868–1881,* Cape Town, 1961, p. 3, passim.

70. A striking example is Cheikh Anta Diop's *Nations nègres et culture,* Paris, 1954, in which he tried to prove the ancient inhabitants of Egypt were black.

71. Of the hundreds of definitions of race, that of Melville Herskovits, *Man and His Works: The Science of Cultural Anthropology,* New York, 1949, p. 133, seems closest to what can be said with certainty: "A race is a principal division of mankind marked by physical characteristics which breed true." But I'm not certain about the "breed true." Cf. the books and articles of Carleton S. Coon, as, for example, his *The Origin of Races,* New York, 1962.

72. *History of Civilization,* World Classics ed., vol. I, p. 30 n.

73. G. M. Morant's conclusion of thirty years ago is still sound: "The differences in body characters which distinguish the races of Europe are only small differences between the *averages* for the groups." *The Races of Central Europe: A Footnote to History,* London, 1939, pp. 51, 142. For views of outstanding anthropologists and geneticists, see the UNESCO

booklet, *The Race Concept, Results of an Inquiry,* Paris, 1952. Recent research has modified these views very little. But see the much discussed study of Arthur R. Jensen in the *Harvard Educational Review,* Winter 1969, which purports to show differences in some kinds of intelligence between peoples.

74. The old, well-known classification of A. L. Kroeber is used here. *Anthropology: Race, Language, Culture, Psychology, Prehistory,* rev. ed., New York, 1948, p. 144.

75. *The Study of Man,* New York, 1936, pp. 34–35.

76. Though "differential reproduction" means "the consistent production of more offspring, on the average, by individuals with certain genetic characteristics than by those without those particular characteristics." George Gaylord Simpson, "The World into Which Darwin Led Us," in Jesse Jennings et al., eds., *Readings in Anthropology,* New York, 1966, pp. 11–12.

77. *Genetics and the Races of Men,* Boston, 1950, p. 202.

78. H. J. Fleure, *The Peoples of Europe,* London, 1925, p. 42.

79. Morant, *The Races,* p. 150.

80. As a report of the National Academy of Sciences in the United States cautiously states, "The problem of disentangling hereditary environmental factors for complex intellectual and emotional traits where many genes may participate . . . where it is not certain what is being measured and where subtle environmental factors are involved is extremely difficult. It is unrealistic to expect much progress unless new methods appear." Quoted in *Saturday Review,* May 17, 1969, p. 67. This statement is very close to that of Julian Huxley in *Man Stands Alone,* New York, 1941, pp. 111–12.

Chapter XII

1. While Alexander Alland, a recent authority, stresses "biological mechanisms," he says "man is, behaviorally, the most flexible of all animals. Humans are born with a largely uncoded behavioral potential, the capacity to learn language and culture." *Evolution and Human Behavior,* New York, 1967, p. 219.

2. For fuller explanation see pages 156–58.

3. One exposition of this view is in Boyd C. Shafer, "Bourgeois Nationalism in the Pamphlets on the Eve of the French Revolution," *Journal of Modern History,* vol. X, 1938, pp. 31–50. It must be added that I am no longer so certain about the use of the adjective "bourgeois."

4. *Politics,* tr. by Dugdale and De Bille, London, 1916, vol. I, pp. 3–18, 54–55, 77. Of course, Treitschke's view of history was restricted—to Prussia, and he was inaccurate about Prussia. See pages 203–04.

5. *Politics,* vol. I, p. 51.

6. *History of European Civilization,* tr. by W. Hazlitt, Bohn ed., 1846, London, vol. I, p. 138.

7. See page 156. A major and important study of scientific findings after

Darwin is C. D. Darlington, *The Evolution of Man and Society*, New York, 1969.

8. *Physics and Politics*, New York, 1881, pp. 17, 81–111.

9. *National Life from the Standpoint of Science*, London, 1901, pp. 19, 34, and passim. See page 156.

10. *The Valour of Ignorance*, New York, 1909.

11. *Biological Analogies in History*, New York, 1910, pp. 25–26, 34, 38.

12. This is an argument of the anthropologist Ashley Montagu, for instance. See his *On Being Human*, New York, 1951.

13. Still the best basic book on the development of national languages is Otto Jespersen, *Mankind, Nation and Individual from a Linguistic Point of View*, Oslo, 1925. Carlton Hayes, a great authority and my teacher, believed that I did not stress language sufficiently in my earlier volume, *Nationalism: Myth and Reality*. I do not know what he would have thought with the proliferation of new nations, few of which had one common "native" language. In a recent study Ronald Inglehart and Margaret Woodward argue, on the basis of evidence, "that political separatism is not inherent in the existence of linguistic pluralism," that the centrifugal force is dependent on "the level of economic and political development" and "the degree to which social mobility is blocked because of membership in a given language group." "Language Conflicts and Political Community," *Comparative Studies in Society and History*, vol. X, October 1967, p. 28.

14. Dankwart Rustow, "Nation," *International Encyclopedia of the Social Sciences*, vol. XI, p. 11.

15. Stanley Rundle, *Language as a Social and Economic Factor in Europe*, London, 1946, pp. 46–47; and Geoffrey M. Morant, *The Races of Central Europe: A Footnote to History*, London, 1939, pp. 132–43.

16. See pages 97 ff. For hundreds of years patriots have believed their own language better. More than one Englishman has agreed with R. Carew, in Camden's *Remaines concerning Britain* (1614), 6th imp., London, 1657, p. 43, who maintained that English, though it borrowed from other tongues, had all the beauties and none of the ugliness of the others. In the eighteenth century M. V. Lomonosov found in Russian "the majesty of Spanish, the vivacity of French, the firmness of German, the delicacy of Italian, the richness and concise imagery of Greek and Latin . . ." and concluded Russian most suitable for the "most subtle philosophical speculations. . . ." Hans Rogger, *National Consciousness in Eighteenth-Century Russia*, Cambridge (Mass.), 1960, p. 103. Examples could be multiplied down to the present among speakers of many languages.

17. Ferdinand Brunot's multivolumed *Histoire de la langue française*, Paris, 1905–53, is a record of change and growth as it also reveals how uncommon French was for many "Frenchmen" down to the eighteenth century. See also C. T. Onion, "The English Language," in Ernest Barker, ed., *The Character of England*, London, 1947; or any of the great historical dictionaries: Littré, Larousse, or the Oxford.

18. To Jespersen, "the language of a nation" was no more than "the set of habits by which members of the nation are accustomed to communicate with one another." *Mankind*, p. 23.
19. *Representative Government*, in *Utilitarianism, Liberty, Representative Government*, Everyman's ed., p. 360.
20. "The Development of Modern European Historiography," *Atlantic Monthly*, vol. LXVI, 1890, p. 325. One direct assault on the nationalist sentiments of historians is E. H. Dance, *History the Betrayer: A Study in Bias*, 2nd ed., London, 1964.
21. For these illustrations see J. W. Thompson, *A History of Historical Writing*, New York, 1942, vol. I, pp. 492, 626; and Rogger, *National Consciousness*, p. 216. But historians and patriots of many countries apparently believed or at least propagated similar myths. And they have not stopped doing so. See the absurd Nazi-inspired Kurt Pastenaci, *Das viertausendjahrige Reich der Deutschen*, Berlin, 1940.
22. *Politics*, vol. I, p. 272.
23. See pages 200 ff.
24. *Nationality: Its Nature and Problems*, London, 1929, p. 313.
25. *Esquisse d'une histoire des Français dans leur volonté d'être une nation*, Paris, 1932.
26. Thomas Brown, *Irish-American Nationalism 1870–1890*, Philadelphia, 1966, p. 30. Douglas Hyde in 1892 thought the modern Celts—that is, Irishmen—were the remnant of the race that "established itself in Greece and burned infant Rome." R. J. Loftus, *Nationalism in Modern Irish Poetry*, (Wis.), 1964, p. 6.
27. Richard Robinson, *The First Turkish Republic*, Cambridge (Mass.), 1963, p. 85; and for other "half-truths," Bernard Lewis, *The Emergence of Modern Turkey*, London, 1961, p. 353. Mustapha Kemal (Atatürk) wanted Turks to believe their true history began twelve thousand years before Jesus Christ; see the excerpt from Tekin Alp, *Le Kémalisme* (Paris, 1937), in Elie Kedourie, ed., *Nationalism in Asia and Africa*, New York, 1970, pp. 207–24.
28. See pages 307–08.
29. Sylvia Haim, "Islam and the Theory of Arab Nationalism" in Walter Z. Laqueur, ed., *The Middle East in Transition: Studies in Contemporary History*, New York, 1958, pp. 280–81. See also G. E. von Grunebaum, *Modern Islam: The Search for Cultural Identity*, Berkeley, 1962, pp. 242–243. But Choudhary Rahmat Ali claimed that Pakistan was "the birthplace of human culture and civilization" in his *Pakistan, the Father of the Pak Nation* (Cambridge, Eng., 1947), in Kedourie, ed., *Nationalism in Asia and Africa*, pp. 245–49.
30. From "What Is a Nation," in Alfred Zimmern, ed., *Modern Political Doctrines*, 1939, p. 190.
31. As Arnold Toynbee wrote many years ago, "It is impossible to argue *a priori* from the presence of one or even several . . . factors [like language] to the existence of a nationality; they may have been there for

ages and kindled no response." *Nationality and the War,* London, 1915, p. 14.

32. *Regards sur le monde actuel,* Paris, 1931, p. 63; and see page 205.

33. *Praise of Folly,* tr. by H. H. Hudson, Princeton, 1941, pp. 71–72. Montaigne a little later in his *Essays* wrote of the "Antarctic" people, "I find nothing barbarous and savage in this nation . . . except that everyone calls barbarism that which is not his own usage." In one's own country, "one finds always the perfect religion, the perfect government, the most perfected and accomplished usage in all things." Everyman's ed., vol. I, p. 219.

34. Respectively, *The Italians,* New York, 1964—a sophisticated analysis; *The French,* tr. by A. Foulke, New York, 1968; *The British,* New York, 1970. The abundance of books of this kind precludes listing except in my own bibliography. But among those of the past seventy-five years, see the works by Grant Allen, Jules d'Auriac, Ernest Barker, J. E. C. Bodley, Gustave Le Bon, Emile Boutmy, Denis Brogan (it's intelligent), Edward Bulwer (it's charming), Michael Demiashkevich, Abbé Dimmet, Alfred Fouillée, Sanche de Gramont, Nyozeken Hasegawa, William McDougall, Salvador Madariaga, Jean-François Revel, Andre Siegfried (informed), and Watsuyi Tetsurō.

35. See pages 51–52. Recent work with bibliographies is summed up in Don Martindale, ed., *National Character in the Perspective of the Social Sciences, Annals of the American Academy of Political and Social Science,* vol. 370, 1967—but only a few of the essays in this volume, such as those of Sorokin and Virtenan, are worth reading. George De Vos, "National Character," *International Encyclopedia of the Social Sciences,* vol. XI, pp. 14–19, in social science jargonese unconsciously reveals how little is known. Thomas Hartshorne, *The Distorted Image: Changing Conceptions of the American Character Since Turner,* Cleveland, 1968, comments intelligently on the lack of rigor in most studies. Otto Klineberg, "A Science of National Character," *Journal of Social Psychology,* vol. XIX, 1944, pp. 147–62, was a path-making study. Other studies of the 1940's, such as those by Ruth Benedict, Margaret Mead, Geoffrey Gorer, and others, have been rightly criticized, but we must remember there was a war going on.

36. Early attacks that *might* have led to the dismissal of the whole subject include Hamilton Fyfe, "The Illusion of National Character," *Political Quarterly,* vol. IX, 1938; Max Nordau, *The Interpretation of History,* tr. by Hamilton, London, 1910, pp. 130 ff.; and Adam de Hegedus, *Patriotism or Peace,* New York, 1947. Peter Stearns concludes in a recent study of "National Character and European Labor," AHA paper 1969, typescript, that "the national framework [for character] causes more trouble than it's worth." Sir John Seeley's comment may be relevant: "No explanation is so vague, so cheap, and so difficult to verify." Thomas Peardon, "Sir John Seeley, Pragmatic Historian in a Nationalist Age," in Edward Mead Earle, ed., *Nationalism and Internationalism: Essays Inscribed to Carlton J. H. Hayes,* New York, 1950, p. 291.

37. See page 80; and Aria Kemilainen, *Nationalism: Problems Concerning the Word, the Concept and Classification,* Jyäskyla, 1964, pp. 62–68.

38. The studies of stereotypes are so numerous and generally so superficial that they need not be cited, but see the pioneer work of William Buchanan and Hadley Cantril, *How Nations See Each Other,* Urbana (Ill.), 1953, a UNESCO study; and the two unusually sharp analyses, Harold Isaacs, *Scratches on Our Minds,* New York, 1958, and Wallace Lambert and Otto Klineberg, "A Pilot Study of the Origin and Development of National Stereotypes," *International Social Science Bulletin,* vol. 11, 1959, pp. 221–238.

39. Bernard Joseph, *Nationality: Its Nature and Problems,* p. 86.

40. Cf., for example, D. G. Haring, "Japanese National Character: Cultural Anthropology, Psychoanalysis, and History," *Yale Review,* March 1953, pp. 375–92; and the various essays in Bernard Silberman, ed., *Japanese Character and Culture,* Tucson, 1963.

41. See Julius Braunthal, *The Paradox of Nationalism, an Epilogue to the Nuremberg Trials: Commonsense Reflections on the Atomic Age,* London, 1946, pp. 45–47.

42. Peter Drucker, *The End of Economic Man,* New York, 1939, pp. 113–14.

43. "Of National Characters," in *Essays and Treatises . . . ,* London, 1770, vol. I.

44. In Frederick Page, ed., *An Anthology of Patriotic Prose,* London, 1915, pp. 198–201.

45. According to Alfred Kroeber, *Anthropology: Race, Language, Culture, Psychology, Prehistory,* rev. ed., New York, 1948, pp. 126–27, no race averages less than four feet ten inches and none more than five feet ten inches, while the majority of populations do not deviate more than two inches from the general average of five feet five inches. It is true that peoples in developed nations, because of adequate diets and medical care, seem to be getting taller and heavier.

46. Much has been made of differences in intelligence, and they are real *among* individuals. But, as Thomas Hobbes wrote in his *Leviathan* (1651), "Nature hath made men so equal, in the faculties of the body and mind" that "yet when all is reckoned together the difference between man and man is not so considerable as that one man can thereupon claim to himself any benefit to which another may not pretend. . . ." Blackwell reprint of 1651 ed., pp. 81–82.

47. Walter Sulzbach, *National Consciousness,* Washington, D.C., 1943, p. 52.

48. Quoted in Julian Huxley and A. C. Haddon, *We Europeans,* Oxford, 1940, p. 3. Symmachus, a Roman official of the fourth century, arguing that no one religion had exclusive claim to truth, wrote, "We look upon the same stars, the heaven is common to us all, the same world surrounds us. . . ." Quoted in Roland Bainton, *Early Christianity,* Princeton, 1960, pp. 70–71.

49. For discussion see Alland, *Evolution and Human Behavior,* pp. 160–62.

50. G. P. Murdock, "The Common Denominator of Cultures," in R. Linton, ed., *The Science of Man in the World Crisis,* New York, 1945, pp. 128–33. See also Melville Herskovits, *Man and His Works: The Science of Cultural*

Anthropology, New York, 1949, pp. 231–34; and B. Malinowski, *A Scientific Theory of Culture and Other Essays,* Chapel Hill (N.C.), 1944, p. 92.

51. *African Nationalism,* 2nd ed., London, 1968, p. 160.
52. *Becoming: Basic Considerations for a Psychology of Personality,* New Haven (Conn.), 1955, p. 22.
53. "The World into Which Darwin Has Led Us," *Science,* vol. 131, 1960, p. 973.
54. Pico della Mirandola, "Oration on the Dignity of Man," in Ernst Cassirer et al., eds., *The Renaissance Philosophy of Man,* Chicago, 1948, pp. 219, 223. Strangely enough, St. Augustine, in the *City of God,* believed we "can distinguish the common human nature, from that which is peculiar, and therefore wonderful."

A Bibliographical Essay

All through the writing of this book I have debated with myself the kind of bibliography that ought to be appended. Should I list (as I did in *National-ism: Myth and Reality*, 1955, with around four hundred titles) the now roughly three thousand books and articles I have consulted, or should I write a short bibliographical essay (as in the American Historical Association pamphlet, *Nationalism: Interpretations and Interpreters*, 3rd ed., 1966)? For two reasons I decided on the second alternative: (1) Karl Deutsch and Richard Merritt have just compiled a bibliography, *Nationalism and National Development: An Interdisciplinary Bibliography* (MIT Press, 1970), which covers a selected list of studies mostly in English on nationalism and other subjects from 1935 to 1966, and which, though spotty, goes far beyond the bibliographies of Koppel Pinson (1935) and Deutsch (1956); (2) the notes in this volume are rather full and another lengthy listing would be superfluous. But I should note one danger in my choice. Though the citations are numerous, they do not indicate all the works seen and read or, certainly, all that I would deem it essential to include in a formal bibliography.

Since nationalism is part of all modern history, one ought to have read all the documents and studies of modern history. Of course, no one could. I have read and used documents and studies on nationalism in some of the western languages and in translation many of those originally written or spoken in other languages.

The real stuff of history is in the primary sources, in this case in the writings of the nationalists and in the documents created by nationalists and their governments, their societies, their organizations. I have, as the notes indicate, read a not inconsiderable number of the writings (and speeches) of nationalists: (1) those of the West including, for example, Alfieri (Italy), Bagehot (England), Barère (France), Barrès (France), Beveridge (United States), H. S. Chamberlain (England or Germany), Dostoyevsky (Russia), Fichte (Germany), Mazzini (Italy), Michelet (France), Mussolini (Italy), Theodore Roosevelt (United States), and Treitschke (Germany); (2) those of Asia and Africa, including Awolowo (Nigeria), Blyden (Liberia and Sierra Leone), Gökalp (Turkey), Herzl (before Israel), Kaunda (Zambia), Kenyatta (Kenya), Liu Shao-chi (China), Luthuli (South Africa), Mboya (Kenya), Nasser (Egypt and Arab), Nehru (India), Nkrumah (Ghana), Nyerere (Tanzania), Senghor (Senegal), Sithole (Rhodesia), and Sun Yat-sen (China).

Fortunately, many of the writings and documents in languages I do not read have been translated and published in edited collections and anthologies, including those by Wm. Theodore de Bary and Ryusaku Tsunoda et al., of Chinese, Indian, and Japanese sources; Sylvia Haim, ed., *Arab Nationalism*, Berkeley, 1962; Hans Kohn and Wallace Sokolsky, eds., *African Nationalism in the Twentieth Century*, Princeton, 1965; Louis Snyder, ed., *The Dynamics of Nationalism*, Princeton, 1964; and Henry S. Wilson, ed., *Origins of West African Nationalism*, London, 1969.

In the course of my studies I have worked (as any serious student should) in the Library of Congress, the Bibliothèque Nationale, the British Museum, the Institute of Historical Research (London), the Archives Nationales, the Archives of the United States, the Widener Library, the New York Public Library, the university libraries of Columbia and Chicago, of Cornell and Wisconsin, of Minnesota and Missouri, of Arkansas and Arizona, and several others, as well as borrowed books and obtained copies of articles from dozens of others. I have also visited libraries and archives, though *not* done systematic work in them, in several other countries. I have much benefited from the library of the small college, Macalester, where I teach and which now has a fair collection of materials on nationalism. I must add that I have also much profited from conversations with scholars and students in sixteen western, four Asian, and three African nations.

I have, naturally, dug deeper into certain subjects and periods than others —into the rise of national patriotism in France from 1788 to 1794, for example, and into American thought from 1865. In the course of these "diggings," I have read such ephemeral publications as pamphlets and newspapers, the records of patriotic organizations, novels and essays, and the writings of scholars of several other disciplines.

To predecessors and colleagues about the world I owe more than I can express.

It is perhaps invidious to single out individuals, some of whom I have had the privilege of knowing and some of whom I unfortunately have known only through their works. I owe most to my teacher, Carlton J. H. Hayes, who pioneered in the field, to the learned scholar Hans Kohn, to René Johannet who wrote one of the best early books, to Karl Deutsch and his bibliographies and his studies of communication, to Louis Snyder who has published so much of value, to Arthur Whitaker who has deepened our knowledge of Latin America; and to Yahya Armajani for his Persian wisdom, to Delmer Brown whose book introduced me to Japanese nationalism, to Rupert Emerson for his pioneering work on Asian and African nationalism, to Sylvia Haim for her essays and edited works on Arab nationalism, to John Halstead for his insights on Moroccan nationalism, to Thomas Hodgkin for his brilliant writings on African nationalism, to Masao Maruyama for his incisive Weberian analyses of Japanese nationalism; to Ndabaningi Sithole for his superb *African Nationalism;* and, of course, to a great many others.

But this is getting to be a list of people from whom I have gained the little (no fault of theirs) I know. What are the studies that a student might find it desirable to know? Here is a sampling (mostly books) of those from which I have drawn; its omissions specialists will quickly note—I am not happy about them myself, but the citations in the text should in part compensate. In general, systematic research stopped in early 1971, and but few studies after this time are listed.

General Treatments, Western

Almond, Gabriel, and Verba, Sidney, *The Civic Culture*, Princeton, Princeton U. Press, 1963, a remarkable behaviorist study based on over five thousand interviews in five western nations.

Braunthal, Julius, *The Paradox of Nationalism: An Epilogue to the Nuremberg Trials*, London, St. Botolph, 1946, which did indeed have *Common-sense Reflections on the Atomic Age* (the subtitle), though he wrote in 1946.

Delaisi, Francis, *Political Myths and Economic Realities*, New York, Viking, 1927, a keen and imaginative critique that revealed the contradictions— yes, a germinal book.

Deutsch, Karl, *Nationalism and Social Communication: An Inquiry into the Foundations of Nationality*, 2nd ed., Cambridge, MIT Press, 1966, a path-making study that led to others, though the social science terminology sometimes interferes with understanding.

Hayes, Carlton J. H., *Essays on Nationalism*, New York, Macmillan, 1926; *The Historical Evolution of Modern Nationalism*, New York, Richard Smith, 1931; and *Nationalism: A Religion*, New York, Macmillan, 1960. These three books sum up his great work; the last is really a tribute to the dozens of students who, stimulated by him, made significant contributions.

Hertz, Friedrich O., *Nationality in History and Politics: A Study of the Psychology and Sociology of National Sentiment and Character*, London, Clarendon Press, 1944, a solid older survey that still bears reading.

Issacs, Harold, "Nationalism Revisited, Group Identity and Political Change," *Survey; a Journal of Soviet and East European Studies*, October, 1968, pp. 76–98, sharply analyzes the processes in several groups.

Johannet, René, *Le Principe des nationalités*, new ed., Paris, Nouvelle Librairie Nationale, 1923, one of the earliest systematic surveys that opened up the study.

Kohn, Hans, *The Idea of Nationalism: A Study of Its Origins and Background*, New York, Macmillan, 1944; and *Prelude to Nation-States: The French and German Experience, 1789–1815*, Princeton, Van Nostrand, 1967, the two major works of this prolific and learned scholar. All students of nationalism must know his contributions. He proceeded chiefly by analyses of the ideas of major nationalist thinkers.

Lemberg, Eugen, *Nationalismus*, 2 vols., Hamburg, Rowohlt, 1964, vol. I, *Psychologie und Geschichte*, vol. II, *Soziologie und Politische Pädagogik* which seeks a systematic and theoretical structure.

Minogue, K. R., *Nationalism*, New York, Basic Books, 1967, a short objective yet critical survey.

Renan, Ernest, "Qu'est-ce qu'une nation?" in *Discours et conférences*, 2nd ed.,

Paris, Calmann-Levy, 1887, pp. 277–310, and reprinted often, in part (as in Snyder, ed., *Dynamics of Nationalism*) as a classic statement.

Royal Institute of International Affairs, *Nationalism: A Report by a Study Group of Members of the Institute,* London, Oxford U. Press, 1939, a basic description and analysis.

Shafer, Boyd C., *Nationalism: Myth and Reality,* New York, Harcourt, Brace and World, 1955, a precursor of this book; and *Nationalism: Interpretations and Interpreters,* 3rd ed., Washington, D.C., Service Center for Teachers of History, American Historical Association, 1966, a bibliographic introduction.

Smith, Anthony D., *Theories of Nationalism,* London, Duckworth, 1971, an intelligent sociological attempt at theory relating nationalism to modernism.

Snyder, Louis, ed., *The Dynamics of Nationalism: Readings in Its Meaning and Development,* Princeton, Van Nostrand, 1964, useful sources and commentary; *The Meaning of Nationalism,* New Brunswick, Rutgers U. Press, 1954, descriptive definitions from different disciplines; *The New Nationalism,* Ithaca, Cornell U. Press, 1968, a comprehensive but uneven survey of recent nationalism, including that of Asia and Africa.

Talmon, J. L., *The Origins of Totalitarian Democracy,* New York, Praeger, 1960 (originally 1952); and *Political Messianism, the Romantic Phase,* New York, Praeger, 1961, two books that brilliantly illuminate aspects of nationalism in the nineteenth and twentieth centuries.

Ward, Barbara, *Nationalism and Ideology,* New York, Norton, 1966, eleven superb lectures with a sense of humanity and hope.

Znaniecki, Florjan, *Modern Nationalities: A Sociological Study,* Urbana, U. of Illinois Press, 1952, a substantial sociological survey mercifully without jargon.

WESTERN AND CENTRAL EUROPE AND BRITAIN

Acomb, Frances D., *Anglophobia in France, 1763–1789: An Essay in the History of Constitutionalism and Nationalism,* Durham, Duke U. Press, 1950, based on extensive research that shows the rise of national feeling out of enmity for England.

Anderson, Eugene N., *Nationalism and the Cultural Crisis in Prussia, 1806–1815,* New York, Farrar & Rinehart, 1939, an imaginative, serious examination with attention to psychology.

Barker, Ernest, ed., *The Character of England,* London, Clarendon Press, 1947, serious but laudatory essays.

Barzini, Luigi, "Risorgimento: Historical Reflections on the Making of Italy," *Encounter,* vol. XXXVII, 1971, pp. 29–38, a cool reappraisal, showing the "intricate confluence of many currents."

Buthman, William Curt, *The Rise of Integral Nationalism in France, with Special Reference . . . [to] Charles Maurras,* New York, Columbia U. Press, 1939, a good doctoral dissertation (Hayes) made into a good book.

Coupland, Reginald, *Welsh and Scottish Nationalism,* London, Collins, 1954, learned, sympathetic, and path-breaking.

Digeon, Claude, "Origines et signification du nationalisme littéraire en France (1870–1914)," *Revue des travaux de l'Académie des Sciences et Politiques,* vol. 115, 1962, pp. 144–56, an acute short paper on the origins of rightist patriotism.

Dorpalen, Andreas, *Heinrich von Treitschke,* New Haven, Yale U. Press, 1957, a well-documented, objective biography.

Edwards, Owen Dudley, et al., *Celtic Nationalism,* New York, Barnes & Noble, 1968, thoughtful and informed essays on Ireland, Wales, and Scotland.

Ergang, Robert R., *Herder and the Foundations of German Nationalism,* New York, Columbia U. Press, 1931, a first-class doctoral dissertation (Hayes) that made a fine book.

Girardet, Raoul, ed., *Le Nationalisme français 1871–1914,* Paris, Colin, 1966, excerpts from nationalist writings with a fine introduction.

Hanham, H. J., *Scottish Nationalism,* Cambridge, Harvard U. Press, 1969, a well-written scholarly account by a first-class historian.

Hayes, Carlton, J. H., *France: A Nation of Patriots,* New York, Columbia U. Press, 1930, dated, good, still worth perusal.

Hyslop, Beatrice, *French Nationalism in 1789 According to the General Cahiers,* New York, Columbia U. Press, 1934, a major investigation done as dissertation (Hayes).

Kantorowicz, Ernst H., "*Pro Patria Mori* in Medieval Political Thought," *American Historical Review,* vol. LVI, 1951, pp. 472–92, brilliant, imaginative, germinal.

McCaffrey, Lawrence J., *The Irish Question, 1800–1922,* Lexington, U. of Kentucky Press, 1968, a solid short book stressing the hope and dignity nationalism offered.

Megaro, Gaudens, *Vittorio Alfieri, Forerunner of Italian Nationalism,* New York, Columbia U. Press, 1930, a doctoral dissertation (again under Hayes) that shows the origins in Italy in reaction to the French dominance.

Meinecke, Friedrich, *Cosmopolitanism and the National State,* Princeton, Princeton U. Press, 1970, tr. by Kimber of *Weltbürgertum und Nationalstaat: Studien zur Genesis des deutschen Nationalstaates,* Munich, 1928, the important work of one of Germany's best twentieth-century historians, profound but not always clear.

Michelat, Guy, and Thomas, Jean-Pierre, *Dimensions du nationalisme: Enquête par questionnaire 1962,* Paris, Colin, 1966, a study of the attitudes of 223 students at the time of the Algerian crisis revealing the relation to other political attitudes.

Noether, Emiliana, *Seeds of Italian Nationalism, 1700–1815,* New York, Columbia U. Press, 1951, a good dissertation revealing origins earlier than the French Revolution.

Payne, Stanley G., "Spanish Nationalism in the Twentieth Century," *Review of Politics,* vol. 26, 1964, pp. 403–22, describing Franco's victory as more a conservative than a nationalist triumph, and his "Catalan and Basque Nationalism," *Journal of Contemporary History,* vol. VI, 1971, pp. 15–51, which keenly surveys these regional nationalisms.

Pinson, Koppel S., *Pietism as a Factor in the Rise of German Nationalism,* New

York, Columbia U. Press, 1934 (Octagon, 1968), a doctoral dissertation (Hayes) that delved imaginatively and on the basis of evidence into a previously neglected aspect.

Simon, Erica, *Réveil national et culture populaire en Scandinavie: La Genèse de la Højskole Nordique (1844–1878)*, Paris, Presses Universitaires, 1960, based on extensive research over years, first-class.

Stewart, H. F., and Desjardins, Paul, eds., *French Patriotism in the Nineteenth Century (1814–1833)*, Cambridge, Cambridge U. Press, 1923, a valuable collection of excerpts from sources.

Strayer, Joseph, *On the Medieval Origins of the Modern State*, Princeton, Princeton U. Press, 1970, lectures summing up years of research chiefly on France and England.

Tauber, Kurt P., *Beyond Eagle and Swastika: German Nationalism Since 1945*, 2 vols., Middletown, Wesleyan U. Press, 1967, huge, detailed, not so much on nationalism as on neo-Nazi and rightist acts and ideas to about 1963.

Tint, Herbert, *The Decline of French Patriotism, 1870–1940*, London, Weidenfeld and Nicolson, 1964, equating patriotism with *revanche*.

Weber, Eugen, *Action Française: Royalism and Reaction in Twentieth Century France*, Stanford, Stanford U. Press, 1962, a major treatment of a royalist and nationalist movement.

Zernatto, Guido, "Nation: The History of a Word," *Review of Politics*, vol. VI, 1944, pp. 351–66, a careful, informed history of the word in western Europe.

EASTERN AND SOUTHEASTERN EUROPE

Armstrong, John A., *Ukrainian Nationalism*, 2nd ed., New York, Columbia U. Press, 1963, a substantial survey.

Austrian Yearbook, vol. III, 1967, *The Nationality Problem in the Hapsburg Monarchy in the Nineteenth Century* . . . : pt. I, *Centripetal Forces, Nationalism as a Disintegrating Force, the Ruling Nationalities;* pt. II, *The National Minorities,* eighteen papers with comments from a conference of specialists from the "new" nations of the old monarchy and from the United States held at the University of Indiana in 1966. Some of the papers are invaluable.

Barany, George, *Stephen Széchenyi and the Awakening of Hungarian Nationalism, 1791–1841*, Princeton, Princeton U. Press, 1968, a fine, thorough biography based on firsthand research.

Barghoorn, Frederick C., *Soviet Russian Nationalism*, New York, Oxford U. Press, 1956, scholarly though not always objective, maintaining Soviet (Russia) is most highly centralized nation-state in world.

Chaconas, Stephen G., *Adamantios Korais: A Study in Greek Nationalism*, New York, Columbia U. Press, 1942, one of the few competent studies on Greek nationalism, originally a doctoral dissertation (Hayes).

Jászi, Oszkár, *The Dissolution of the Habsburg Monarchy*, Chicago, U. of Chicago Press, 1929, dated, but a pioneer work, stresses Hungary.

Jelavich, Charles, *Tsarist Russia and Balkan Nationalism*, Berkeley, U. of California Press, 1958, scholarly, careful, useful.

Kann, Robert A., *The Multinational Empire: Nationalism and National Reform in the Hapsburg Monarchy, 1848–1918*, 2 vols., New York, Columbia U. Press, 1950 (Octagon, 1964), thorough, full of information, and sometimes dull.

Kolarz, Walter, *Myths and Realities in Eastern Europe*, London, Lindsay Drummond, 1946, by an author who, with intimate knowledge, examines the myths and makes a case for federation.

MacMaster, Robert E., *Danilevsky: A Russian Totalitarian Philosopher*, Cambridge, Harvard U. Press, 1967, a scholarly biography of this man who was more totalitarian than either pan-Slavist or nationalist.

Petrovich, Michael B., *The Emergence of Russian Panslavism 1856–1870*, New York, Columbia U. Press, 1956, a well-written, thoughtful, and critical study.

Pipes, Richard, *The Formation of the Soviet Union: Communism and Nationalism 1917–1923*, Cambridge, Harvard U. Press, 1954, a learned discussion of the nationalities problem that led to Pipes' significant later writings.

Pundeff, Marin, "Les Racines du nationalisme bulgare," *Revue des Etudes Slaves*, vol. 46, 1967, pp. 127–38, short but knowledgeable, though it may see antecedents as more nationalist than they were.

Reshetar, John S., *The Ukrainian Revolution 1917–1920: A Study in Nationalism*, Princeton U. Press, 1952, with essential documentation showing the rise and failure of the Ukrainian.

Riasanovsky, Nicholas V., *Nicholas I and Official Nationality in Russia, 1825–1855*, Berkeley, U. of California Press, 1959, a fine analysis of the reactionary policies of orthodoxy and the rise of radical nationalism.

Rogger, Hans, *National Consciousness in Eighteenth-Century Russia*, Cambridge, Harvard U. Press, 1960, which shows with able scholarship the dawning realization of consciousness of being Russian.

Schapiro, Leonard B., *Rationalism and Nationalism in Russian Nineteenth-Century Political Thought*, New Haven, Yale U. Press, 1967, six lectures sharply developing the twin themes.

Scherer-Virski, Olga, "Mickiewicz et Towianski: Libération nationale ou assomption mystique," *Etudes Slaves et Est-Européennes*, vol. 11, 1966, pp. 19–34, vividly depicting the romantic influences that made Mickiewicz a nationalist.

Senn, Alfred E., *The Emergence of Modern Lithuania*, New York, Columbia U. Press, 1959, with a first chapter that supplies background for Lithuanian nationalism.

Seton-Watson, R. W., *The Rise of Nationality in the Balkans*, London, Constable, 1917, (reprinted 1966) an early (World War I) informed work that is still useful.

Sugar, Peter, and Lederer, Ivo, eds., *Nationalism in Eastern Europe*, Seattle, U. of Washington Press, 1969, varying in quality, nine essays (none on Russia) by specialists that provide valuable information.

Szacki, Jerzy, "L'Evolution du concept de 'Nation' en Pologne à la fin du

XVIIIe et au début du XIXe siècle," *Cahiers d'histoire mondiale*, vol. IX, 1965, pp. 59–79, an orderly, documented re-examination of the ideas of the intellectuals.

Thaden, Edward, *Conservative Nationalism in Nineteenth-Century Russia*, Seattle, U. of Washington Press, 1964, good for use of Russian intellectual sources but sometimes misleading on European.

Wuorinen, John H., *Nationalism in Modern Finland*, New York, Columbia U. Press, 1931, again a dissertation under Hayes and a solid little book.

UNITED STATES

Curti, Merle, *The Roots of American Loyalty*, New York, Columbia U. Press, 1946, a short preliminary inquiry by a man who knows American thought.

Dangerfield, George, *The Awakening of American Nationalism, 1815–1828*, New York, Harper, 1965, a beautifully written book that delves deep, though the "awakening" came earlier.

Heimert, Alan, *Religion and the American Mind: From the Great Awakening to the Revolution*, Cambridge, Harvard U. Press, 1966. See under religion.

Kohn, Hans, *American Nationalism, an Interpretative Essay*, New York, Macmillan, 1957, more on American ideas and character than on nationalism.

Morris, Richard B., *The Emerging Nations and the American Revolution*, New York, Harper, 1970, a good survey of the American influence that possibly overemphasizes it.

Noble, David, *Historians Against History*, Minneapolis, U. of Minnesota Press, 1965, which argues well that at least six prominent American historians oversimplify in saying Americans were different and somehow escaped the evils and complexities others encountered.

Nye, Russel, *This Almost Chosen People: Essays in the History of American Ideas*, East Lansing, Michigan State U. Press, 1966, an informed survey based on wide reading.

Potter, David, *People of Plenty: Economic Abundance and the American Character*, Chicago, U. of Chicago Press, 1954, thoughtful lectures arguing that abundance more than the frontier shaped American character.

Pratt, Julius, *Expansionists of 1898*, Baltimore, Johns Hopkins U. Press, 1936, along with his similar volume on 1812, one of the best examinations of nationalism in American foreign policy.

Savelle, Max, "Nationalism and Other Loyalties in the American Revolution," *American Historical Review*, vol. LXVII, 1962, pp. 901–23, demonstrating how the war years were years of gestation.

Smith, Henry Nash, *Virgin Land: The American West as Symbol and Myth*, Cambridge, Harvard U. Press, 1950 (Vintage, 1957), a wonderful book combining imagination and knowledge in examination of the impact of the West on literature.

Weinberg, Albert K., *Manifest Destiny: A Study of Nationalist Expansionism in American History*, Baltimore, Johns Hopkins U. Press, 1935 (Quadrangle, 1963), a first-rate examination of a major manifestation, however mythical, of American national ambition.

LATIN AMERICA

Alba, Victor, *Nationalists Without Nations: The Oligarchy Versus the People in Latin America,* New York, Praeger, 1968, which maintains all Latin American countries except Mexico (on which he has another book) are not nations because their people have no awareness of belonging.

Bailey, Samuel L., ed., *Nationalism in Latin America,* New York, Knopf, 1971, a useful little volume of documents and commentaries.

Burr, Robert N., "Latin America's Nationalistic Revolutions," *Annals of the American Academy of Political and Social Science,* vol. 334, 1961, an objective, quick survey along with essays by others, such as K. H. Silvert, in this volume of the *AAAPSS* with the same title.

Gerassi, Maryea, *Argentine Nationalism of the Right: The History of an Ideological Development, 1930–1946,* New York, Columbia U. Press, 1965, a dissertation on the nationalist authoritarian movement.

Glauert, E. T., "Ricardo Rojas and the Emergence of Argentine Cultural Nationalism," *Hispanic American Historical Review,* vol. 43, 1963, pp. 1–13, a competent sketch.

Halperin, Ernst, *Nationalism and Communism in Chile,* Cambridge, MIT Press, 1965, more on communism than nationalism, but a sophisticated book.

Humphreys, Robert A., "The Historiography of the Spanish American Revolutions," *Hispanic American Historical Review,* vol. 36, 1956, pp. 81–93, an indispensable short guide.

Masur, Gerhard, *Nationalism in Latin America: Diversity and Unity,* New York, Macmillan, 1966, a general survey.

Turner, Frederick, *The Dynamic of Mexican Nationalism,* Chapel Hill, U. of North Carolina Press, 1968, an able analysis, based on research and interviews, that seeks every possible evidence of nationalism and may overemphasize.

Whitaker, Arthur, *Nationalism in Latin America, Past and Present,* Gainesville, U. of Florida Press, 1962, slender volume of three lectures, with a short useful bibliography, that sums up a lifetime of research and much that is now known.

Zea, Leopoldo, *The Latin-American Mind,* tr. by Abbott and Dunham, Norman, U. of Oklahoma Press, 1963, covering the postindependence period and the influence of romanticism and positivism as Hispano-Americans act out the "colonial script of oppression" under native dictators.

And see the symposia in the following section for other essays.

Africa and Asia

General and Symposia (including some essays on Latin American and other western countries)

Bendix, Reinhard, *Nation-Building and Citizenship: Studies of Our Changing Social Order,* New York, Wiley, 1964, largely essays previously published which, the author says, illustrate the comparative method and Weberian analysis, and cover three continents.

Deutsch, Karl W., and Foltz, William J., eds., *Nation-Building*, New York, Atherton, 1963, eight papers covering the subject about the world.

Emerson, Rupert, *From Empire to Nation: The Rise to Self-Assertion of Asian and African Peoples*, Cambridge, Harvard U. Press, 1960, the germinal survey that led to so many studies, and a work of objective scholarship.

Geertz, Clifford, ed., *Old Societies and New States: The Quest for Modernity in Asia and Africa*, New York, Free Press of Glencoe, 1963, essays on a high level of sociological abstraction that are not always clear, but the essay by Shils is especially informative.

Kautzky, John H., ed., *Political Change in Underdeveloped Countries: Nationalism and Communism*, New York, Wiley, 1962, thirteen essays from the viewpoints of social scientists.

Kedourie, Elie, ed., *Nationalism in Asia and Africa*, New York, World, 1970, well-chosen excerpts from speeches and writings of leaders, with a long introductory essay by the editor, who argues, as he did in his volume on *Nationalism* (New York and London, Humanities Press, 1960), that nationalism is a "European invention," and that "imperialism" was not so much economic as the result of aristocratic traditions.

Sigmund, Paul E., Jr., ed., *The Ideologies of the Developing Nations*, New York, Praeger, 1963, excerpts from the writings of leaders.

Silvert, K. H., ed., *Expectant Peoples: Nationalism and Development*, New York, Random House, 1963, a dozen essays of uneven value, some of which lack historical perspective.

MIDDLE EAST AND NORTH AFRICA

Ahmed, Jamal Mohammed, *The Intellectual Origins of Egyptian Nationalism*, New York, Oxford U. Press, 1960, an excellent historical summary.

Al-Razzāz, Munif, *The Evolution of the Meaning of Nationalism*, tr. by Abu-Lughod, New York, Doubleday, 1963, really speeches about Arab nationalism and for democratic socialism.

Antonius, George, *The Arab Awakening: The Story of the Arab National Movement*, Philadelphia, Lippincott, 1939 (Putnam, 1965), a brilliant pathmaking book, marred by some prejudice at end.

Berkes, Niyazi, *The Development of Secularism in Turkey*, Montreal, McGill U. Press, 1964, a knowledgeable book that argues the state had to promote change.

Cottam, Richard W., *Nationalism in Iran*, Pittsburgh, U. of Pittsburgh Press, 1964, solid, thoughtful description of the impact on political behavior.

Finkelstein, Louis, ed., *The Jews: Their History, Culture and Religion*, 2 vols., New York, Harper, 1949, a standard account.

Frey, F. W., "Socialization to National Identification Among Turkish Peasants," *Journal of Politics*, vol. 30, 1968, pp. 934–65, a major investigation based on interviews with 6,500 peasants, and the important results well stated.

Gökalp, Ziya, *Turkish Nationalism and Western Civilization: Selected Essays*, ed. and tr. by Berkes, New York, Columbia U. Press, 1959, writings of an ardent early Turkish nationalist (see Heyd vol. below).

Grunebaum, G. E. von, *Modern Islam: The Search for Cultural Identity*, Berkeley, U. of California Press, 1962, one of the many informed writings of this authority, who is sympathetic but critical.

Haim, Sylvia, ed., *Arab Nationalism*, Berkeley, U. of California Press, 1962, twenty essays by Arabs on nationalism plus an essay by the editor, who has herself made significant scholarly contributions.

Halpern, Ben, *The Idea of the Jewish State*, Cambridge, Harvard U. Press, 1961, a well-documented account of the beginnings to the realization, but involved and repetitive.

Halstead, John P., *Rebirth of a Nation: The Origins and Rise of Moroccan Nationalism, 1912–1944*, Cambridge, Harvard U. Press, 1967, the result of firsthand investigation, a substantial contribution.

Hertzberg, Arthur, ed., *The Zionist Idea: A Historical Analysis and Reader*, New York, Harper, 1966, anthology of writings of thirty-seven Zionist leaders.

Herzl, Theodor, *The Diaries of Theodor Herzl*, ed. and tr. by Marvin Lowenthal, New York, Grosset and Dunlap, 1962, a most important source on the formative ideas from 1895 to 1904.

Heyd, Uriel, *Foundations of Turkish Nationalism*, London, Harvill Press, 1950, the life and times of Gökalp.

Hourani, Albert, *Arabic Thought in the Liberal Age, 1798–1939*, London, Oxford U. Press, 1962, based on lectures, a readable, authoritative account.

Keddie, Nikki R., *An Islamic Response to Imperialism: Political and Religious Writings of Sayyed Jamāl al Dīn "al-Afghānī,"* Berkeley, U. of California Press, 1968, a good beginning study of this Islamic charismatic leader that will lead to a bigger book.

Laqueur, Walter Z., ed., *The Middle East in Transition: Studies in Contemporary History*, New York, Praeger, 1958, thirty-three essays now worth reading as histories of opinion then.

Lewis, Bernard, *The Arabs in History*, London, Hutchinson, 1950; *The Emergence of Modern Turkey*, London, Oxford U. Press, 1961; and *The Middle East and the West*, Bloomington, U. of Indiana Press, 1964, three books by a learned scholar who knows the significant questions and how to express his deep knowledge.

Nuseibeh, Hazem Zaki, *The Ideas of Arab Nationalism*, Ithaca, Cornell U. Press, 1956, well summarizes the ideas and goes beyond Antonius.

Ramsaur, Ernest E., Jr., *The Young Turks: Prelude to the Revolution of 1908*, Princeton, Princeton U. Press, 1957, substantial research that reveals the sources of the nationalist revolt.

Tütsch, Hans E., *Facets of Arab Nationalism*, Detroit, Wayne State U. Press, 1965, a popular account by a Swiss journalist that is soundly based on knowledge of the area.

Ward, Robert E., and Rustow, Dankwart A., eds., *Political Modernization in Japan and Turkey*, Princeton, Princeton U. Press, 1964, skillful papers within a common framework to account for relative success in modernization.

Zeine, Zeine N., *The Emergence of Arab Nationalism: With a Background Study of Arab-Turkish Relations in the Near East*, Beirut, Khayats, 1966, mostly on diplomacy but a relevant conclusion.

AFRICA

(Chiefly south of the Sahara)

Berghe, Pierre L. van den, ed., *Africa: Social Problems of Change and Conflict*, San Francisco, Chandler, 1965, collection of previously published articles some of which, like those by Balandier and Mercier, are worth reading in the original.

Bonnafé, Pierre, *Le Nationalisme africain: Aperçus sur sa naissance et son développement*, Paris, Fondation Nationale des Sciences Politiques, 1964, only sixty mimeographed pages but full of insights. Bonnafé has a well-chosen selection of writings and sources in his *Nationalismes africaines*, 1962.

Brunschwig, Henri, *L'Avènement de l'Afrique noire du XIXe siècle à nos jours*, Paris, Colin, 1963, an informed, scholarly study that clarifies important issues.

Carter, G. M., *Independence for Africa*, New York, Praeger, 1960, which reads now like a primary source because it's outdated by events, but is still worth looking at.

Cary, Joyce, *The Case for African Freedom and Other Writings on Africa*, Austin, U. of Texas Press, 1962, early 1950's writings that, along with the novels of Paton (*Cry, the Beloved Country*, 1948) and the more recent novels of Nadine Gordimer (*A Guest of Honour*, 1970), are all worth reading as the reaction of sensitive whites in Africa—but likely Mary Kingsley, that wonderfully strange Victorian Englishwoman (*West African Studies*, 3rd ed., New York, Barnes & Noble, 1964; 2nd ed. 1899) who traveled and pried into so much of Africa, is as great.

Coleman, James, *Nigeria: Background to Nationalism*, Berkeley, U. of California Press, 1965, a first-rate work based on thorough research about which one can use the cliché a mine of information.

Curtin, Philip D., "Nationalism in Africa, 1945–1965," *Review of Politics*, vol. 28, 1966, pp. 143–53, a paper that takes a fresh look on the basis of deep knowledge of African history.

Gussmann, Boris, *Out in the Mid-Day Sun*, New York, Oxford U. Press, 1963, badly edited, full of sharp and wonderful humane comments, a book that should have had more notice than it did.

Hailey, Lord William, *An African Survey: A Study of Problems Arising in Africa South of the Sahara*, rev. ed., London, Oxford U. Press, 1957, huge, standard work of reference.

Hodgkin, Thomas, *Nationalism in Colonial Africa*, London, Muller, 1956—probably will be called a classic because its author knows Africa and can think and write.

Irele, Abiola, "Négritude or Black Cultural Nationalism," *Journal of Modern African Studies*, vol. 3, October 1965, first of two fine articles.

Jaarsveld, F. A. van, *The Awakening of Afrikaner Nationalism, 1868–1881*, Cape Town, Human & Rousseau, 1961, which argues that this nationalism arose as a reaction to the "Imperial Factor" and speaks of the Afrikaner as a "blood group."

Kaunda, Kenneth, *Zambia Shall Be Free*, New York, Praeger, 1963, the first prime minister makes the case.

Kenyatta, Jomo, *Facing Mount Kenya, the Tribal Life of the Kikuyu*, London, Secker & Warburg, 1953 (originally 1938), an anthropological study that becomes a fundamental human document of nationalism in Africa.

Kesteloot, Lilyan, *Les Ecrivains noirs de la langue française: naissance d'une littérature*, 2nd ed., Brussels, Université Libre, 1965, a substantial doctoral dissertation that perhaps for the first time covers the literature.

Lemarchand, René, *Political Awakening in the Belgian Congo*, Berkeley, U. of California Press, 1964, which unravels some of the tangled skeins skillfully; one of the rare good accounts of the Congo.

Lonsdale, J., "Emergence of African Nations: A Historiographical Analysis," *African Affairs*, vol. 67, 1968, pp. 11–28, an indispensable guide, since it maintains African development was not just a result of European stimuli.

Mazrui, Ali, *Towards a Pax Africana: A Study of Ideology and Ambition*, Chicago, U. of Chicago Press, 1967, one of the studies of a professor at Makerere University that are imaginative, different, and exciting.

Munger, Edwin S., *Afrikaner and African Nationalism: South African Parallels and Parameters*, London, Oxford U. Press, 1967, an intelligent survey in spite of the subtitle.

Nkrumah, Kwame, *Ghana: Autobiography*, London, Nelson, 1957, a vain human document revealing the drive for fame and Ghanian freedom.

Nyerere, Julius K., *Freedom and Unity*, Dar es Salaam, Oxford U. Press, 1966, an honest leader's and socialist's speeches and writings as he speaks for Tanzania.

Perham, Margery, *The Colonial Reckoning: The End of Imperial Rule in Africa in the Light of British Experience*, New York, Knopf, 1962, BBC lectures of a wise scholar who regretted what was happening but saw it clearly.

Rosberg, Carl G., and Nottingham, John, *The Myth of Mau Mau: Nationalism in Kenya*, New York, Praeger, 1966, by two authors who know Kenya, have dug into the records, comment intelligently as they write the political history of Kenya from 1888.

Rotberg, Robert I., *The Rise of Nationalism in Central Africa: The Making of Malawi and Zambia, 1873–1964*, Cambridge, Harvard U. Press, 1965, a survey based on firsthand research by an author who is prolific.

Rotberg, Robert I., and Mazrui, Ali A., eds., *Protest and Power in Black Africa*, New York, Oxford U. Press, 1970, thirty-five essays by specialists covering about every conceivable aspect of the protests that brought national consciousness.

Shepperson, George, and Price, Thomas, *Independent African: John Chilembwe and the Origins, Setting and Significance of the Nyasaland Native Rising of 1915*, Edinburgh, University Press, 1958, the tragic story based on thorough knowledge and told with keen insight into the motivations behind the African protest.

Sithole, Ndabaningi, *African Nationalism*, 2nd ed., London, Oxford U. Press, 1968, a powerful volume by an outstanding leader who understands both Africans and nationalism.

Thompson, L. M., "Afrikaner Nationalist Historiography and the Policy of Apartheid," *Journal of African History*, vol. V, 1962, pp. 125–41, a good paper that is a necessary preliminary for further study.

Touval, Saadia, *Somali Nationalism*, Cambridge, Harvard U. Press, 1963, a short but competent account showing the deep historical roots.

Turnbull, Colin, *The Lonely African*, New York, Simon and Schuster, 1962, biographical sketches of an anthropologist that vividly reveal the loneliness.

Wallerstein, Immanuel, *Africa, the Politics of Independence*, New York, Vintage, 1961, and *Africa: The Politics of Unity; An Analysis of a Contemporary Social Movement*, New York, Random House, 1967, two of the books of this able Africanist that are excellent on the politics.

Waulthier, Claude, *L'Afrique des Africains: inventaire de la négritude*, Paris, Editions du Seuil, 1964, a knowledgeable journalist intelligently discussing the ideas.

ASIA

Bary, Wm. Theodore de, et al., *Sources of Chinese Tradition*, New York, Columbia U. Press, 1960, a fine collection of historical sources, especially valuable for nationalism in the later period.

Bary, Wm. Theodore de, et al., *Sources of Indian Tradition*, New York, Columbia U. Press, 1958, the same comment as above.

Brown, Delmer, *Nationalism in Japan*, Berkeley, U. of California Press, 1955, a basic book, objective, fair, based on extensive research.

Chow Tse-tsung, *The May Fourth Movement*, Cambridge, Harvard U. Press, 1959, a big important study of this germinal movement from which so much of importance developed.

Fairbank, John K., ed., *The Chinese World Order: Traditional China's Foreign Relations*, Cambridge, Harvard U. Press, 1968, fourteen important essays by specialists.

Francis, John de, *Nationalism and Language Reform in China*, Princeton, Princeton U. Press, 1950, over twenty years old but still useful as a basic western study.

Friend, Theodore, *Between Two Empires: The Ordeal of the Philippines, 1929–1946*, New Haven, Yale U. Press, 1965, understanding based on research —this book is a contribution.

Heimsath, Charles H., *Indian Nationalism and Hindu Social Reform*, Princeton, Princeton U. Press, 1964, showing the intimate relation between reform and nationalism; chapters VI and XII particularly valuable.

Holland, William L., ed., *Asian Nationalism and the West*, New York, Macmillan, 1953, the papers of a symposium that opened many doors to the study in southern and southeastern Asia.

Johnson, Chalmers, *Peasant Nationalism and Communist Power: The Emergence of Revolutionary China 1937–1945*, Stanford, Stanford U. Press, 1962, a major study of the resistance against Japan, though not too knowledgeable or important on the nationalist aspect.

Kahin, George McT., *Nationalism and Revolution in Indonesia*, Ithaca, Cornell U. Press, 1952, dated but one of the few solid works on Indonesia; could be supplemented by Herbert Luethy, "Indonesia Confronted," *Encounter*, vols. XXV–XXVI, 1965–66, pp. 80–89, 75–83.

Kennedy, Joseph, *Asian Nationalism in the Twentieth Century*, London, Macmillan, 1968, a competent survey.

Lee, Chong-sik, *The Politics of Korean Nationalism*, Berkeley, U. of California Press, 1965, dull but the best description.

Levenson, Joseph R., *Liang Ch'i-ch'ao and the Mind of Modern China*, 2nd rev. ed., Berkeley, U. of California Press, 1967 (2nd ed., 1959), a brilliant, profound, sometimes obscure study of a major nationalist.

Liu Shao-chi, *Internationalism and Nationalism*, Peking, 1952, a Marxist-Leninist-Stalinist interpretation and a valuable source.

Majumdar, R. C., "The Growth of Nationalism in India," *Indo-Asian Culture*, vol. 10, 1961, pp. 96–113, a general survey, but there are many other views and studies.

Marshall, Byron K., *Capitalism and Nationalism in Prewar Japan: The Ideology of the Business Elite, 1868–1941*, Stanford, Stanford U. Press, 1967, a revised doctoral dissertation that ably attempts to show the relationship.

Maruyama, Masao, *Thought and Behaviour in Modern Japanese Politics*, ed. by Ivan Morris, London, Oxford U. Press, 1963, a collection of the articles of this sharp Japanese scholar influenced by Marx and Weber.

Morris, I. I., *Nationalism and the Right Wing in Japan, a Study of Postwar Trends*, New York, Oxford U. Press, 1960, repetitious but argues well that the postwar nationalism was, by contrast, inward-looking.

Myrdal, Gunnar, [et al.], *Asian Drama: An Inquiry into the Poverty of Nations*, 3 vols., New York, Pantheon, 1968, a monumental work, some parts of which are relevant and perspicacious, but it attempts too much and is hardly dramatic.

Schram, Stuart R., *Mao Tse-tung*, London, Penguin, 1966, not everyone agrees, but a first-rate biographical study that reveals the nationalist side of this great Chinese Communist leader.

Schriffen, Harold Z., *Sun Yat-sen and the Origins of the Chinese Revolution*, Berkeley, U. of California Press, 1968, the best study, I think, of this relatively moderate Chinese nationalist leader.

Seal, Anil, *The Emergence of Indian Nationalism: Competition and Collaboration in the Later Nineteenth Century*, London, Cambridge U. Press, 1968, concentrating on Bengal, Bombay, and Madras nationalist movements.

Singh, Karan, *Prophet of Indian Nationalism: A Study of the Political Thought of Sri Aurobindo Ghosh, 1893–1910*, London, Allen & Unwin, 1963, an intelligent, sympathetic treatment, with a foreword by Nehru.

505

Storry, Richard, *The Double Patriots: A Study of Japanese Nationalism,* New York, Houghton Mifflin, 1957, some insights not found elsewhere.

Sun Yat-sen, *The Principle of Nationalism,* tr. by Price, abridged, Taipei, Chinese Cultural Service, 1953, from lectures in Canton, 1924, a principal source but Sun's original notes were destroyed.

Teng, Ssu-yü; Fairbank, John K., et al., *China's Response to the West: A Documentary Survey, 1839–1923,* Cambridge, Harvard U. Press, 1954, excerpts of important sources.

Tsunoda, Ryusaku, et al., eds., *Sources of the Japanese Tradition,* New York, Columbia U. Press, 1958, like the other *Tradition* volumes cited, of great value for western students.

Ward, Robert E., and Rustow, Dankwart A. eds., *Political Modernization in Japan and Turkey,* see under Middle East.

Wolpert, Stanley, *Tilak and Gokhale: Revolution and Reform in the Making of Modern India,* Berkeley, U. of California Press, 1962, first-rate, imaginative analysis of the forces of tradition and modernism exemplified by these two men.

Some Special Subjects

(Only studies related to nationalism are noted)

RACE

Barzun, Jacques, *Race: A Study in Superstition,* rev. ed., New York, Harper, 1965 (1st ed., 1937), a critical study covering what is known.

Benedict, Ruth, *Race: Science and Politics,* New York, Viking, 1940, an outstanding anthropologist's critical examination—partly in response to Hitler's racial myths.

Boas, Franz, *Anthropology and Modern Life,* 2nd ed., New York, Norton, 1932, so germinal that it cannot be omitted.

Gossett, Thomas F., *Race: The History of an Idea in America,* Dallas, Southern Methodist U. Press, 1963, an excellent study that succeeds in its purpose to show the cruelty and absurdity of racism.

Lévi-Strauss, Claude, *Race and History,* Paris, UNESCO, 1958, a pamphlet by a great anthropologist.

Morant, Geoffrey M., *The Races of Central Europe: A Footnote to History,* London, Allen & Unwin, 1939, dated but still usable.

Myrdal, Gunnar, et al., *An American Dilemma,* with a postscript by Arnold Rose, New York, McGraw-Hill, 1964 (originally 1944), a classic study of the Negro in a white nation that supplied the starting point of many studies.

Stanton, William, *The Leopard's Spots: Scientific Attitudes Toward Race in America, 1815–1859,* Chicago, U. of Chicago Press, 1960, the views of American "scientists" ably described.

UNESCO, *The Race Concept, Results of an Inquiry,* Paris, 1952, in which the experts agree that mankind is one and race a group of the species.

RELIGION

(Both the relation to nationalism and nationalism as a religion)

Alix, Christine, *Le Saint-Siège et les nationalismes en Europe 1870–1960*, Paris, Sirey, 1962, a prize-winning doctoral dissertation that objectively carries out the promise of the title.

Baron, Salo W., *Modern Nationalism and Religion*, New York, Harper, 1947, a profound Jewish scholar's reflections.

Cecil, Lord Hugh, *Nationalism and Catholicism*, London, Macmillan, 1919, a prominent "high Anglican" and internationalist pleading for one Christian body.

Hayes, Carlton J. H., *Nationalism: A Religion*, New York, Macmillan, 1960. See under general.

Heimert, Alan, *Religion and the American Mind: From the Great Awakening to the Revolution*, Cambridge, Harvard U. Press, 1966, a big and important book on the theme that colonial Calvinists promoted a democratic and nationalist ideology.

Herberg, Will, *Protestant-Catholic-Jew*, Garden City (N.Y.), Doubleday, 1955, a sociological essay and plea for common understanding.

Lanternari, Vittorio, *The Religions of the Oppressed: A Study of Modern Messianic Cults*, tr. by L. Sergio, New York, Knopf, 1963, of peripheral interest here but an imaginative book that affords insights.

Mannoni, O., *Prospero and Caliban: The Psychology of Colonization*, tr. by Powesland, 2nd ed., New York, Praeger, 1964 (originally 1950), depicting (especially in Madagascar) the corrosive effect of colonialism on the security of ancestor-worshiping peoples.

Marty, Martin E., *Varieties of Unbelief*, New York, Holt, Rinehart, & Winston, 1964, provocative lectures partly devoted (pp. 163–72) to nationalism.

Tuveson, Ernest Lee, *Redeemer Nation: The Idea of America's Millennial Role*, Chicago, U. of Chicago Press, 1968, a rigorous examination of the American Protestant belief that the millennium would come in the United States and that it would save the world.

HISTORY, LANGUAGE, AND THE ARTS

Barnard, F. M., *Herder's Social and Political Thought: From Enlightenment to Nationalism*, Oxford, Clarendon Press, 1965, valuable work partly on Herder's theory of community, which was so influential.

Brunot, Ferdinand, *Histoire de la langue française*, 21 vols., Paris, Colin, 1905–1953, a monumental work of erudition and patriotism; vols. IV–IX particularly relevant.

Cushing, G. F., "The Birth of a Nationalist Literature in Hungary," *Slavonic and East European Review*, vol. 38, 1960, pp. 459–75, a good essay.

Dance, E. H., *History the Betrayer: A Study in Bias*, London, Hutchinson, 1960, attacking texts that are biased and too European centered.

Fishman, Joshua, et al., *Language Loyalty in the United States: The Maintenance and Perpetuation of Non-English Mother Tongues by American*

Ethnic and Religious Groups, The Hague, Mouton, 1966, a big work that sheds light on the tenacity of languages.

Francis, John de, *Nationalism and Language Reform in China,* see under Asia.

Jespersen, Otto, *Mankind, Nation and Individual from a Linguistic Point of View,* Oslo, Aschehoug, 1925, a classic work by a great and humane scholar.

Kimball, Stanley B., *Czech Nationalism: A Study of the National Theater Movement, 1845–1883,* Urbana, U. of Illinois, 1964, which well describes the long struggle of Czechs for their own theater.

Lawerys, J. A., *History Textbooks and International Understanding,* Paris, UNESCO, 1953, pleading for elimination of obvious biases.

Miller, Lillian, *Patrons and Patriotism: The Encouragement of the Fine Arts in the United States, 1790–1860,* Chicago, U. of Chicago Press, 1966, with a good chapter on art and nationality.

Nora, Pierre, "Ernest Lavisse: son rôle dans la formation du sentiment national," *Revue historique,* vol. 228, 1962, pp. 73–106, a balanced account of how a major historian formed national sentiment.

Roberts, Spencer E., *Soviet Historical Drama: Its Role in the Development of a National Mythology,* The Hague, Nihoff, 1965, learned, lucid because of its use of concrete examples.

Rundle, Stanley, *Language as a Social and Economic Factor in Europe,* London, Faber & Faber, 1946, still a good study.

Schapiro, Leonard B., *Rationalism and Nationalism in Russian Nineteenth-Century Political Thought,* see under Eastern and Southeastern Europe.

Thomson, David, "Must History Stay Nationalist?" *Encounter,* vol. XXX, 1968, pp. 22–28, a good historian reluctantly answering "yes."

Walworth, Arthur, *School Histories at War,* Cambridge, Harvard U. Press, 1938, an early and critical study.

CHILDREN AND EDUCATION

Davies, A. F., "The Child's Discovery of Nationality," *Australian and New Zealand Journal of Sociology,* vol. 4, 1968, pp. 107–25, which in expert fashion sums up many studies that otherwise might be included here.

Lambert, Wallace E., and Klineberg, Otto, *Children's Views of Foreign Peoples. A Cross-National Study,* New York, Appleton-Century-Crofts, 1967, a major sampling of children in eleven countries that further develops and refines the findings of Piaget.

Lawson, Edwin D., "Development of Patriotism in Children—A Second Look," *Journal of Psychology,* vol. 55, 1963, pp. 279–86—intelligently does what the title indicates.

Piaget, J., and Weil, Anne-Marie, "The Development in Children of the Idea of the Homeland and of Relations with Other Countries," *International Social Science Bulletin,* vol. III, 1951, pp. 561–78, developed out of Piaget's now classic studies in Switzerland that are in part summed up in *Judgment and Reasoning in the Child,* London, Paterson, Littlefield & Adam, 1959.

Pierce, Bessie, *Civic Attitudes in American School Textbooks*, Chicago, U. of Chicago Press, 1930, and *Citizens' Organizations and the Civic Training of Youth*, New York, Scribner, 1933, pioneer works of merit that led to many other studies.

Reisner, Edward H., *Nationalism and Education Since 1789: A Social and Political History of Modern Education*, New York, Macmillan, 1922, dated, but no one has recently done the thorough work Reisner did.

PATRIOTIC ORGANIZATIONS

Davies, Wallace, *Patriotism on Parade: The Story of Veterans' and Hereditary Organizations in America, 1783–1900*, Cambridge, Harvard U. Press, 1955, based on original research and objective.

Folsom, Avaline, *The Royal Empire Society: Formative Years*, London, Allen & Unwin, 1933, a good description.

Minott, Rodney G., *Peerless Patriots: The Organized Veterans and the Spirit of Americanism*, Washington, D.C., Public Affairs Press, 1963, a good, short doctoral dissertation covering the period from about 1898.

Nora, Pierre, "Les deux apogées de l'Action Française," *Annales: Economies, Sociétés, Civilisations*, vol. XIX, 1964, pp. 122–41, a short account of the November, 1918, and autumn, 1940, heights of this reactionary organization.

Payne, Stanley G., *Falange: A History of Spanish Fascism*, Stanford, Stanford U. Press, 1961, more than a history of a patriotic organization, but I list it here.

Weber, Eugen, *Action Française*, see under Western and Central Europe and Britain.

Wertheimer, Mildred S., *The Pan-German League, 1890–1914*, New York, Columbia U. Press, 1924, one more of the good dissertations at Columbia during the Hayes period.

STEREOTYPES

Buchanan, William, and Cantril, Hadley, *How Nations See Each Other*, Urbana, U. of Illinois Press, 1953, a UNESCO study by expert students.

Düyker, H. C. J., and Frÿda, N. H., *National Character and National Stereotypes: A Trend Report . . .* , Amsterdam, North Holland Publishing Co., 1960, excellent on method but does not go much beyond.

Gadoffre, Gilbert, "French National Images and the Problem of National Stereotypes," *International Social Science Bulletin*, vol. III, 1951, pp. 579–87, one of a series of perceptive papers growing out of a 1949 conference concerned with images.

Green, Martin B., *A Mirror for Anglo-Saxons: A Discovery of America, a Rediscovery of England*, New York, Harper, 1960, sparkling literary study of symbols.

Isaacs, Harold, *Scratches on Our Minds*, New York, Day, 1958, based largely on intensive interviews, an analysis of American images of India and China.

Klineberg, Otto. "The Scientific Study of National Stereotypes," *International Social Science Bulletin,* vol. III, 1951, pp. 505–14, a pioneer study, summarizing work and with a good bibliography to that date.

Lambert, Wallace, and Klineberg, Otto, "A Pilot Study of the Origin and Development of National Stereotypes," *International Social Science Journal,* vol. 11, 1959, pp. 221–38, revealing steady increase in children's consciousness of nationality.

Reigrotski, E., and Anderson, N., "National Stereotypes and Foreign Contacts," *Public Opinion Quarterly,* vol. 23, 1959–60, pp. 515–28, which examines stereotypes of Germans and French.

NATIONAL CHARACTER

Fyfe, Hamilton, "The Illusion of National Character," *Political Quarterly,* vol. IX, 1938, pp. 254–70, an early critical study that demolished myths.

Hartshorne, Thomas, *The Distorted Image: Changing Conceptions of the American Character Since Turner,* Cleveland, Case-Western Reserve U. Press, 1968, shows with evidence that the word "caricature" might well be substituted for "character" in many of the writings.

Klineberg, Otto, "A Science of National Character," *Journal of Social Psychology,* vol. XIX, 1944, pp. 147–62, a fine social psychologist intelligently summed up a quarter century ago about all that is known.

Martindale, Don, ed., *National Character in Perspective of the Social Sciences, Annals of the American Academy,* vol. 370, 1967, contains uneven essays, two or three of which are ably done, but is representative of recent work.

Metzger, Walter P., "Generalizations About National Character: An Analytical Essay," in Gottschalk, Louis, ed., *Generalization in the Writing of History,* Chicago, U. of Chicago Press, 1963, attempts with only partial success to use model concepts.

IMPERIALISM AND WAR

Aron, Raymond, *Peace and War,* New York, Doubleday, 1967, a profound and wise book, nearly as long as Tolstoy's *War and Peace,* which does not see nationalism as a special cause of war.

Betts, Raymond F., *Europe Overseas: Phases of Imperialism,* New York, Basic Books, 1968, an introductory survey with a good short bibliography.

Bramson, Leon, and Goethals, George, eds., *War: Studies from Psychology, Sociology, Anthropology,* New York, Basic Books, 1964, a reader compiled from famous writings with a good selective bibliography.

Brunschwig, Henri, *Mythes et réalités de l'impérialisme colonial français, 1871–1914,* Paris, Colin, 1960, a quick, insightful survey that particularly sheds light on influence of geographers.

Clarke, I. F., *Voices Prophesying War, 1763–1984,* London, Oxford U. Press, 1966, vivid, scholarly account breaking new ground.

Fieldhouse, D. K., *The Colonial Empires: A Comparative Survey from the Eighteenth Century*, New York, Delacorte Press, 1967, a solid general survey.

Gann, L. H., and Duignan, Peter, *Burden of Empire: An Appraisal of Western Colonialism in Africa South of the Sahara*, New York, Praeger, 1967, balanced conservative treatment of imperial rule stressing the transformations imperialism brought.

Gollwitzer, H., "Esquisse d'une histoire générale des idées politiques au XIXᵉ siècle et plus particulièrement du nationalisme et de l'impérialisme," *Cahiers d'histoire mondiale*, vol. IV, 1957, pp. 83–120, a sketch revealing the intimate connection between nationalism and imperialism.

Hobson, J. A., *Imperialism, a Study*, London, Allen & Unwin, 1954 (many eds., first published 1902), a classic of economic interpretation that has been rightly attacked (see Kedourie, under Africa and Asia) but is still the book from which others take off.

Koebner, Richard, and Schmidt, Helmut, *Imperialism: The Story and Significance of a Political Word, 1840–1960*, Cambridge, Cambridge U. Press, 1964, an important work showing not only the development of the idea but revealing the contradictions between nationalism and imperialism.

Lenin, V. I., *Imperialism, the Highest Stage of Capitalism*, new rev. tr., New York, International Publishers, 1939 (many eds., first published 1917), setting the standard communist interpretation.

Nadel, George H., and Curtis, Perry, eds., *Imperialism and Colonialism*, New York, Macmillan, 1964, twelve essays by authorities.

Perham, Margery, *The Colonial Reckoning*, see under Africa.

Robinson, Ronald, and Gallagher, John, with Alice Denny, *Africa and the Victorians*, New York, St. Martin's 1961, revealing the many motivations behind British imperialism.

Sorel, Albert, *L'Europe et la Révolution française*, 8 vols., Paris, Plon, 1946, a classic diplomatic history that depicts the deep roots of French revolutionary policy.

Wright, Quincy, *A Study of War*, 2 vols., Chicago, U. of Chicago Press, 1942, a major and careful analysis.

FEDERALISM AND INTERNATIONALISM

(Since 1950 only)

Carter, Gwendolen, ed., *National Unity and Regionalism in Eight African States . . .* , Ithaca, Cornell U. Press, 1966, seven authors discussing the interplay of demands for national unity and supranational regionalism.

Deutsch, Karl, *Nationalism and Its Alternatives*, New York, Knopf, 1969, an expert on nationalism looking about intelligently as he proposes more behavioristic analysis and something like an international income tax.

Franck, Thomas M., ed., *Why Federations Fail: An Inquiry into the Requisites for Successful Federation*, New York, New York U. Press, 1968, five uneven but useful essays.

Haas, Ernest B., *Beyond the Nation-State: Functionalism and International*

Organization, Stanford, Stanford U. Press, 1964, an attempt to use functional analysis to enable prediction.

Kindleberger, Charles, *The International Corporation,* Cambridge, MIT Press, 1970, which reveals how economic, unlike political, organization is becoming international.

Myrdal, Gunnar, *Beyond the Welfare State,* New Haven, Yale U. Press, 1960, an eloquent plea for a world welfare state.

Padelford, N. J., and Goodrich, L. M., eds., *The United Nations in the Balance: Accomplishments and Prospects,* New York, Praeger, 1965, a sober summing up to the mid-sixties—and the outlook is now still sober.

Pearson, Lester, *Democracy in World Politics,* Princeton, Princeton U. Press, 1955, a Canadian statesman realistically and idealistically facing the issues.

Schuman, Frederick, *The Commonwealth of Man,* New York, Knopf, 1952, hard thinking about "man's search" for unity.

Turner, Louis, *Invisible Empires,* New York, Harcourt Brace Jovanovich, 1971, a popular discussion of the thrust of western multinational corporations toward a world economy.

Walters, F. P., *A History of the League of Nations,* 2 vols., London, Oxford U. Press, 1952, a standard factual account of problems, accomplishments, failures by a former official.

Ward, Barbara, *Nationalism and Ideology,* see under General Treatment.

Welch, Claude E., Jr., *Dream of Unity: Pan-Africanism and Political Unification in West Africa,* Ithaca, Cornell U. Press, 1966, partly based on field research about reasons for failure.

Many times as I was working at this book during the last seven years I have wanted more solid information than I have had on which to base my own hypotheses and conclusions—a common complaint of scholars. Several times in the text I have indicated studies needed. But so much needs to be done—so much hard evidence accumulated, so much reflection by reflective minds! Just about every topic connected with nationalism might be mentioned. Here are a few that need immediate attention in order to push ahead:

(1) Solid factual studies (like Frey's on Turkish peasants) that really reveal the effects of the media—and fewer evangelistic claims. (2) Analyses of the effect of popular literature, novels, almanacs, comic strips (Steve Canyon), even pornography (love and revolution). (3) Comparative linguistic studies of words and phrases used by patriots, in national anthems, oaths, speeches. (4) Analyses of leaders, their class, physical characteristics, psychological experiences—how they differ from "other" people if they do—and fewer attempts to explain the inexplicable by the inexplicable word charisma (though Jean Lacouture has written a perceptive study, *The Demigods: Charismatic Leadership in the Third World,* New York, Knopf, 1970). (5) Investigations of the relationship of urbanism to nationalism, and an end to empty assertions on the subject. (6) More studies of how people really identify themselves, and fewer that pose the methodological problems and then stop. (7) More attempts to *define* national character and *then* to pursue systematic analyses, with, let us pray, an end to popular patriotic self-examinations and to "scholarly" jargonese that

obscures. (8) Further studies of what people gain, for example the "psychic income" Albert Breton talks about in his "The Economics of Nationalism," *Journal of Political Economy,* vol. LXXII, 1964, pp. 376–86. (9) This last combined with studies of the effect of economic conditions on the kinds and intensities of national feeling. (10) A comparative study of how modern loyalties differ (if they do) from those of ancient and medieval times in Europe, from those of tribalism in Africa—probably, since no one person knows enough, this calls for co-operative work. (11) Quantitative comparisons of age groupings and nationalism—is youth more or less nationalist than . . . , and let's not generalize until we have evidence. (12) Comparative studies of people's beliefs in mission and destiny (like Richard Pipes' "Russia's Mission, America's Destiny," *Encounter,* vol. XXXV, October 1970, pp. 3–11). (13) Good, thorough histories of Polish and American nationalism—all we have are scattered studies, some good, but all quite limited. (14) Some imaginative and daring work (plans and ideas) on internationalism beyond the idealistic pleas and the dull descriptions of the League of Nations and the United Nations—after the enthusiastic burst of books and speeches following World War II little has been added.

A list of needed studies, like this list of books and articles, could go on forever. What we really need are all the basic studies that would enable a genius (as Marc Bloch did on feudalism) to bring the political, economic, social, and cultural experience of men to bear upon nationalism. We can, of course, only work toward that time, and by that time, if it ever comes, the world may be so different that only historians will be interested.

Index

Index

Index

Mommsen, Theodor, 323
Monod, Gabriel, 203
Montaigne, Michel, 343
Montesquieu, Baron Charles, 58, 60, 70, 76, 77, 79, 99, 109, 295, 320
Monumenta Germaniae Historica (Pertz), 148, 200
More, Sir Thomas, 42
Morocco, 169, 177; education in, 288; religion in, 289; Berbers of, 289; Salifiyya of, 290, 294; socialism in, 303
Morris, Gouverneur, 130
Moser, Friedrich Karl von, 61, 86, 132
Moses, 24, 315, 316
Mozambique, 272
Muhammad, 372
Munch, Peter, 202
Muratori, Ludovico, 54
Murray, Sir James, 208
Music, patriotism and, 207, 213–14, 248, 255, 308, 320
Muslims, nationalism and, 251, 263, 289, 302–3. *See also* Islam
Mussolini, Benito, 6, 150, 231, 235, 236, 237, 245, 313–14, 355
Mussorgski, Modest, 213

Namier, Sir Lewis, 181, 351
Nantes, rebellion in, 108
Naples, 89
Napoleon I, 94, 95, 96, 100, 101, 113, 114, 115, 117, 119, 122–23, 124, 128, 140, 141, 142, 222, 317, 372
Napoleon III, 149, 165, 191
Nariño, Antonio, 128
Nassau, 150
Nasser, Gamal Ab-del, 6, 304, 309
Nassington, William, 41
National Alliance for the Increase of the French Population, 218
National Archives, 201
National Consciousness (Zurayq), 307
Nationalism, 11, 13, 56; myths and realities of, *xiii, xiv,* 3, 4, 7, 17, 21, 27, 52, 72, 92, 116, 158, 225, 230, 301, 313–42, 370, 374; definitions of, 3–8, 16–17, 22, 265; beginnings and spread of, 8–9, 10, 11, 23–26, 48–57, 102–3, 111, 116, 139, 144–45, 148–149, 158, 163, 167, 175, 331, 345, 348; and hostility to foreign nations

and peoples, 8, 10, 18–19, 21, 23, 49, 79–80, 81, 111, 123, 156, 166, 173, 176, 181, 192, 195, 196, 197, 198, 201, 204, 205, 219, 221, 245, 248, 265, 266, 311, 317, 329, 330, 333, 344, 348, 349, 350, 352, 354–55, 363, 369, 371; loyalties contained in, 8, 18, 249–50, 258–59; dynastic, 9, 17, 29, 33, 47, 73, 75, 132, 143, 328, 358–59; in wartime, 10, 11, 19, 48, 71, 81, 88, 113, 116–17, 139, 162, 164, 229, 230, 231, 235–36, 245, 251, 260, 329, 330, 347, 355; race and color and, 10–11, 18, 154–56, 231, 232, 263, 286, 288, 303, 365; in peacetime, 11, 12, 19, 48, 71, 164, 230, 251; degrees of, 12–13; basic attributes of, 17–21; self-determination and, 18, 57, 58, 66, 118–20, 124, 150, 152, 153, 268, 269, 272, 302, 347, 363; development of modern, 56–58, 64, 66, 68, 71–82, 84–89, 107, 131, 139–40, 144, 150; class basis of, 76, 156–58, 188, 192, 328; hate and, 107, 110, 349, 354–55; as a religion, 114, 131–33, 134–35, 136, 216, 224, 254–59, 291–92, 315; Social Darwinism and, 156, 330–31; glorification of war and, 180–81, 352–53; exiles and, 225–26, 247; insecurity and, 226–28; nuclear weapons and, 232, 244, 252, 260, 348, 369–70, 373, 374; provincialism and, 250, 252, 258, 322–23, 357; conjuncture of circumstances and, 358–66, 370. *See also* Communication and transportation; Cultures; Government; Imperialism; Language; Nations and Nation-states; Patriotism; Religion; individual countries
Nationalism: Myth and Reality (Shafer), *xiv*
Nationalism and American Catholicism (Dohen), 5
Nations and Nation-states, 14–16, 28–29, 56; consciousness of, 4, 12, 28–29, 39, 40, 52, 83, 90, 183, 186, 187, 193, 194, 202, 203, 206, 209, 217, 229, 240, 245, 247, 261, 266, 305, 307, 330, 346, 348, 355, 360, 361, 371; development of, 7, 9, 11, 25–26, 29–30, 32, 34, 56–63, 66, 68,

Index